Social Statistics

An Introduction Using SPSS® for Windows®

SECOND EDITION

J. Richard Kendrick, Jr.
State University of New York College at Cortland

PEARSON

Boston • New York • San Francisco
Mexico City • Montreal • Toronto • London • Madrid • Munich • Paris
Hong Kong • Singapore • Tokyo • Cape Town • Sydney

Senior Editor: Jeff Lasser
Development Editor: Shannon Morrow
Editorial Assistant: Sara Owen
Senior Editorial-Production Administrator: Beth Houston
Editorial-Production Service: Walsh & Associates, Inc.
Senior Marketing Manager: Krista Groshong
Composition and Prepress Buyer: Linda Cox
Manufacturing Buyer: JoAnne Sweeney
Cover Administrator: Joel Gendron
Electronic Composition: Publishers' Design and Production Services, Inc.

Between the time Website information is gathered and then published, it is not
unusual for some sites to have closed. Also, the transcription of URLs can result in
typographical errors. The publisher would appreciate notification where these errors
occur so that they may be corrected in subsequent editions.

Library of Congress Cataloging-in-Publication Data

Kendrick, J. Richard.
   Social statistics: an introduction using SPSS for Windows / J. Richard Kendrick.—
2nd ed.
     p. cm.
   An instructor's manual and data disk are available to supplement the text.
   Includes index
   ISBN 0-205-39508-2
   1. SPSS for Windows.   2. Social sciences—Statistical methods.   I. Title.

HA32.K46 2005
300'.285'555—dc22

2004044291

Printed in the United States of America

10 9 8 7 6 5 CRS 12 11 10 09

Contents

Preface

As you begin looking over this text, you are probably wondering why someone would undertake to write yet another statistics book. I have asked myself this question often, but the answer is simple. I have been teaching an Introduction to Statistics course to sociology undergraduates for over thirteen years, and I am always looking for—but not often finding—ways to help students master course material they approach with a great deal of trepidation. Many are fearful of the mathematical content and uncertain about their ability to do the computer work that is a part of the course. On the other hand, most students have at least an inkling that the skills learned *might* be useful in their daily lives and careers, if only they knew how to apply them and make sense of the results.

With these considerations in mind, I thought that the ideal statistics text for reaching the students in my classes would meet four goals:

- Make the mathematical content clear and accessible.
- Build confidence in the manual computations of statistics and the computer skills for performing the same functions.
- Help students understand how to apply statistics.
- Develop skills for the interpretation of statistics.

At the same time, the book would not sacrifice conceptual understanding—there would be as much "why" as "how to." Does this text "walk the walk"? I think it does, by incorporating a number of unique features.

INTERACTIVE PEDAGOGY

The text includes built-in opportunities for students to test their conceptual understanding and practice the mathematical skills as they are introduced. In addition, I show students how to evaluate their own work and I try to clear up common misconceptions.

- Concepts and computations are introduced in manageable segments. Each segment is followed by relevant examples to work in "Skills Practices" sections. Students can check their answers against the answers to the "Skills Practices" found at the end of each chapter.

■ The answers to the "Skills Practices" are followed by additional problem sets, and the answers to the odd-numbered problems in these additional practice sets are included at the back of the text.

■ Students are shown how to evaluate their work in the "Checking Your Work" sections.

■ I try to anticipate the ways students often get stuck or confused—and offer tips about how to get unstuck—in the "Avoiding Common Pitfalls" sections.

STRONGER INTEGRATION OF SPSS

The text integrates learning statistical concepts with learning about the General Social Survey (GSS) and an up-to-date version of the Statistical Product and Service Solutions (SPSS) computer software program for the analysis of quantitative data. Explanations of statistical concepts are followed by examples students use to perform the SPSS functions with several subsets of variables from the 2002 General Social Survey.

■ There are many opportunities to practice the computational skills for statistics, both manually and using the computer. The book integrates manual computations with instructions for using SPSS to do statistical computations.

■ The text shows students how to set up data in SPSS. Most texts assume the existence of databases. These databases are helpful for showing students how to apply and interpret statistics, but students should also know how the data got there to begin with.

■ There is greater consistency in this text between manual computations of statistics and SPSS computations. Whereas some texts already attempt to integrate manual and computer computations, their formulas for manual computations are not always consistent with the formulas SPSS uses for the same statistic. As a result, these texts don't take advantage of the ability to create practice problems using SPSS.

■ SPSS basics are highlighted in each chapter as clearly delineated "SPSS Guides." Advanced SPSS features are covered in an appendix, "Bells and Whistles," so students can learn some of the ins and outs of the program.

INCREASED EMPHASIS ON THE APPLICATION AND INTERPRETATION OF STATISTICS

I find that most students can do the relatively simple mathematics and execute the computer commands necessary for the computation of introductory statistics. Students experience more difficulty with explaining what their results mean. As a result, I give more attention to the interpretation and analysis of statistics.

■ There are a number of "News to Use" sections—examples of research from newspapers, magazines, and the Internet. These sections demonstrate how statistics are used in everyday life and, at the same time, provide models for the analysis and interpretation of data. The models are then applied to relevant variables extracted from the General Social Survey for 2002.

- Each chapter is oriented to a question or set of questions that the statistics help answer.
- Examples show students how statistics are interpreted. They are followed by opportunities for students to practice their own analytical skills.
- A codebook for one of the GSS datasets is included as an appendix so students can better understand the data they will be interpreting.

INSTRUCTOR'S MANUAL AND DATA DISK

Along with the text, students and instructors receive a data disk containing three subsets of the 2002 GSS variables. An Instructor's Manual is also available that contains answers to the even-numbered problems at the end of each chapter, shows instructors how to create practice problems with answers using SPSS, explains how to download GSS data from the Internet, and provides a test bank for instructors.

CHANGES FOR THE SECOND EDITION

Although the goals of this text and its pedagogies remain essentially unchanged from the first edition to the second, I have made several revisions in response to the concerns of those who have used and reviewed the text.

First, the text is now based in SPSS Student Version 11.0. Students may purchase the text with the SPSS Student Version and three subsets of data drawn from the 2002 General Social Survey. The data sets have been created to fit the Student Version of SPSS. Students will find it easier to do the SPSS work associated with the text, because they will be able to complete the SPSS exercises at their own computers (if their computers meet the technical requirements of SPSS Student Version 11.0).

Second, SPSS skills are now grouped together and placed at the end of each chapter. I have not skimped on my explanations of SPSS skills. Rather, the SPSS skills now have their own section so that faculty who teach a social statistics course with a lab component will find it easier to identify the lab work that is incorporated into each chapter.

Third, the order of the chapters has been reorganized so that the introduction to inferential statistics occurs earlier in the text and so that inferential statistics follow their descriptive counterparts. For example, the chapters that begin to explain how inferences are made using sample statistics as point estimates, "An Introduction to Making Inferences" and "Making Inferences for Single Variables," follow the chapters on measures of central tendency and dispersion. The chapter "Making Inferences for Associations between Categorical Variables: Chi-Square" follows the chapters on contingency table analysis and measures of association for contingency tables.

Finally, the text has been updated in a number of ways. It uses the most recent Student Version of SPSS (11.0 as of the writing of the second edition) and the 2002 General Social Survey. The "News to Use" items, and the General Social Survey variables that correspond to them, have been made more current. Examples that may be of greater interest to students have been incorporated. One of the General Social Survey datasets (GSS subset B) consists almost entirely of numerical-level variables, thus affording instructors more variety in their illustrations of statistics involving numerical variables. The three subsets are thematically oriented—subset A is oriented to issues of civic engagement, subset B to issues concerning television and Internet usage, and subset C is oriented to sexual attitudes and behaviors.

I hope you will find that these changes make the text easier and more interesting for you to use, and I welcome your comments on them. I can be contacted at kendrickr@cortland.edu.

ACKNOWLEDGMENTS

The composition of any text is a daunting task. This text would not have been possible without the support of the many people who helped out along the way. First and foremost, I would never have undertaken to write this text or prepare a second edition were it not for the support and vision of Serina Beauparlant, Senior Editor at Mayfield Publishing. I am grateful for the opportunity that Jeff Lasser, Acquiring Editor at Allyn and Bacon, provided for me to publish a second edition. I appreciate the guidance of Shannon Morrow, Development Editor at Allyn and Bacon, in the preparation of the second edition. I would also like to thank the following people for their help.

- The reviewers of the first edition: Peter Brandon, University of Massachusetts; John R. Dugan, Central Washington University; Susan Eve, University of North Texas; Marilyn Fernandez, Santa Clara University; Lisa M. Frehill, New Mexico State University; A. Leigh Ingram, University of Colorado at Denver; Max Kashefi, Eastern Illinois University; Debra S. Kelley, Longwood College; Rhoda Estep Macdonald, California State University at Stanislaus; Randall MacIntosh, California State University at Sacramento; David Mitchell, University of North Carolina at Greensboro; Melanie Moore, University of North Colorado; Pam Rosenberg, Gettysburg College; Robert Tillman, St. John's University; John Tinker, California State University at Fresno; and Roger Wojtkiewicz, Louisiana State University, whose detailed attention to the manuscript improved it in countless ways. The reviewers of the second edition:

  Joseph Bankenau, Wayne State College

  Walter Carroll, Bridgewater State College

  Jill E. Fuller, University of North Carolina, Greensboro

  Ahmed Khalili, Slippery Rock University

  Charles Parker, Wayne State College

  I am also appreciative of the input offered by reviewers from the University of Hartford, University of Wyoming, Southern Illinois University, University of Houston–Downtown, Hampton University, Southern Carolina University, and University of Tennessee–Chattanooga.

- Although I benefited from their many ideas and suggestions, ultimately I am the one responsible for the text and any errors—sins of commission or omission.

- SUNY Cortland—in particular, Craig Little and Jamie Dangler, Department Chairs for Sociology–Anthropology.

- The staff at Allyn and Bacon, including Beth Houston, Production Editor; Krista Groshong, Marketing Manager; as well as Linda Cox, JoAnne Sweeney, and Joel Gendron. Thanks for your hard work and dedication to this project.

- Kathy Whittier, of Walsh & Associates, Inc., who was the copyeditor and handled the "nuts and bolts" of production, and Mark Bergeron, of Publishers' Design and Production Services, Inc., who designed the second edition. Thank you for your many contributions that enhanced the second edition.

- Gilda Votra, Betsy Zaharis, Matthew Burdick, Josh Prior, and the work–study students in the Sociology–Anthropology Department at SUNY Cortland who stepped in to provide secretarial assistance at critical moments.

- My students, especially those who gave this text its trial run in the Spring semester of 1999.

- Alma Krause, Ed Richter, and Chris Osiecki, who made several helpful suggestions.

- My family—my wife, Marcia, and my children, Ben, Hope, and Tim—who encouraged me and, most important, simply made time for me to get it done. This book is dedicated to them.

## CHAPTER 1

Getting Started: Fundamentals of Research Design

INTRODUCTION

There is no getting around statistics. **Statistics**—numbers that help us find patterns in data, such as averages and medians—are in use nearly every day on TV and in magazines and newspapers, including the sports pages. For example, if you log on to *USA Today* online at <http://www.usatoday.com> you will be treated to "USA Today Snapshots®," like the one in Figure 1.1.[1]

Most of us are entertained by illustrations like this one, because we already know enough about statistics to understand them. We also probably take this knowledge for granted. ∎

---

[1]*USA Today Snapshots* can be found at <http://www.usatoday.com>. The Internet addresses cited in footnotes are for documenting the sources of information you see in the text. What is available on the Internet changes rapidly, and the information you see here may no longer be available online.

It is because you already know something about statistics that you can interpret charts like the one in Figure 1.1. The better we are at understanding statistics, the better we will be at assessing what is going on in the world around us. What do the numbers mean that we see in use every day? How have they been generated? Should we change our behavior on the basis of the statistics we are reading or hearing about, or are they suspect?

There are almost always stories in the news debating the interpretations and applications of research to social policy. (You will find two examples in the section entitled "News to Use: Statistics in the 'Real' World.") The first article examines the impact of raising the price of cigarettes on teenage smoking. Although this seems to be a popular approach, some research suggests there has not been a significant reduction in the number of teenagers who start smoking in those states that have raised cigarette prices compared to those that haven't.[2] The second article reports the result of an experiment evaluating various methods of sex education among African American middle school students in Philadelphia. The researchers conclude that students who receive abstinence education engage in more sexual activity than those who receive sex education that includes information about condom use, and, not surprisingly, they are less likely to use birth control. As the article points out, though, we are spending a good deal of our sex education money on abstinence education.[3] Understanding

---

[2]"Disputed Statistics Fuel Politics in Youth Smoking," by Barry Meier, *The New York Times on the Web*, 20 May 1998, <http://www.nytimes.com/yr/mo/day/news/washpol/tobacco-forecasts.htm>.
[3]"Condom Emphasis Works Over Abstinence," Associated Press, *USA Today*, 20 May 1998, <http://www.usatoday.com/life/health/sexualit/lhsex005.htm>.

N E W S *to* **U S E**
Statistics in the "Real" World

Disputed Statistics Fuel Politics in Youth Smoking[4]

BARRY MEIER

It is the mantra of the nation's opponents of smoking: that sweeping changes in the way cigarettes are marketed and sold over the next decade will stop thousands of teenagers each day from starting the habit and spare a million youngsters from untimely deaths. . . .

Social issues often spark unfounded claims cloaked in the reason of science. But the debate over smoking, politically packaged around the emotional subject of the health of children, is charged with hyperbole, some experts say. Politicians and policy makers have tossed out dozens of estimates about the impact of various strategies on youth smoking, figures that turn out to be based on projections rather than fact.

"I think this whole business of trying to prevent kids from smoking being the impetus behind legislation is great politics," said Richard Kluger, the author of *Ashes to Ashes* (Knopf, 1996), a history of the United States' battle over smoking and health. "But it is nonsense in terms of anything that you can put numbers next to."

Everyone in the tobacco debate agrees that reducing youth smoking would have major benefits because nearly all long-term smokers start as teenagers. But few studies have analyzed how steps like price increases and advertising bans affect youth smoking. And those have often produced contradictory results.

Consider the issue of cigarette pricing. In . . . Congressional testimony, Lawrence H. Summers, Deputy Treasury Secretary [in the Clinton administration], cited studies saying that every 10% increase in the price of a pack of cigarettes would produce up to a 7% reduction in the number of children who smoke. Those studies argue that such a drop would occur because children are far more sensitive to price increases than adults.

"The best way to combat youth smoking is to raise the price," Mr. Summers said. But a recent study by researchers at Cornell University came to a far different conclusion, including a finding that the types of studies cited by Mr. Summers may be based on a faulty assumption.

Donald Kenkel, an associate professor of policy analysis and management at Cornell, said earlier studies tried to draw national patterns by correlating youth smoking rates and cigarette prices in various states at a given time.

But in the Cornell study, which looked at youth smoking rates and cigarette prices over a period of years, researchers found that price had little effect. For example, the study found that states that increased tobacco taxes did not have significantly fewer children who started smoking compared with states that raised taxes at a slower rate or not at all.

Mr. Kenkel added that he had no idea how the price increase being considered by Congress—$1.10 per pack or more—would affect smoking rates because the price of cigarettes, now about $2 a pack, has never jumped so much. And he added that there were so few studies on youth smoking rates and price that any estimate was a guess.

"It is very difficult to do good policy analysis when the research basis is as thin and variable as this," Mr. Kenkel said.

Jonathan Gruber, a Treasury Department official, said that the Cornell study had its own methodological flaws and that the earlier findings about prices supported the department's position. He also pointed out that Canada doubled cigarette prices from 1981 to 1991 and saw youth smoking rates fall by half.

---

[4]*The New York Times on the Web*, 20 May 1998, <http://www.nytimes.com>.

Under the tobacco legislation being considered in the United States, cigarette prices would increase by about 50%. And while advocates of the legislation say that the increase would reduce youth smoking by 30% over the next decade, they say that an additional 30% reduction would come through companion measures like advertising restrictions and more penalties for store owners who sold cigarettes to under-age smokers and for youngsters who bought them. . . .

In California, for example, youth smoking began to decline in the early 1990s, soon after the state began one of the most aggressive anti-smoking campaigns in the country. But it has begun to rise again in recent years.

Dr. John Pierce, a professor of cancer prevention at the University of California at San Diego, said he thought that reversal might reflect the ability of cigarette makers to alter their promotional strategies to keep tobacco attractive to teenagers even as regulators try to block them. . . .

Experts agree that unless significant changes are made in areas like price and advertising, youth smoking rates will not decline. But unlike politicians, many of them are unwilling to make predictions. Instead, they say that the passage of tobacco legislation would guarantee only one thing: the start of a vast social experiment whose outcome is by no means clear.

Condom Emphasis Works Over Abstinence[5]
THE ASSOCIATED PRESS

CHICAGO—Safe-sex lessons for children are more effective if condom use instead of abstinence is emphasized, researchers found in a study of inner-city Blacks.

A separate finding underscored the compelling need for the grown-up subject matter: Although the youngsters' average age was just 11, 25% of them said they were no longer virgins.

"We have to begin earlier to give children the kind of information they need to protect themselves," said Princeton University psychologist John B. Jemmott III, the lead author. The study of 659 sixth- and seventh-graders at three inner-city Philadelphia schools sought ways to stem the high rate of sexually transmitted diseases among Black adolescents.

Among 13-to-19-year-olds with AIDS, Blacks represented 57% and Whites just 23% in 1996, federal statistics show, while the gonorrhea rate among 15-to-19-year-olds was about 24 times higher among Blacks than Whites.

The researchers in the Philadelphia study divided the youngsters into three groups, each

receiving 8 hours of health education. One focused on abstinence, one concentrated on condom use, and a control group addressed avoiding nonsexual diseases.

Three months later, 12.5% of the abstinence-group students reported having recent sex, compared with 16.6% among the condom group and 21.5% in the control group.

At 6 months, slightly more of the abstinence-group students were having sex than the condom-group students. By 12 months, 20% of the abstinence group had recent sex, compared with 16.5% of the condom group and 23.1% of the control group.

The abstinence group also reported having engaged in more unprotected sex than the condom group.

"If the goal is reduction of unprotected sexual intercourse, the safer-sex strategy may hold the most promise, particularly with those adolescents who are already sexually experienced," the researchers wrote in Wednesday's *Journal of the American Medical Association*.

Conservative groups such as the Family Research Council have pushed the abstinence approach, and the federal government has mandated that states use $50 million in sex education money for abstinence-only programs.

[5]*USA Today Desktop News*, 20 May 1998, <http://www.usa-today.com/life/health/sexualit/lhsex005/htm>.

But in a JAMA editorial, Emory University psychologist Ralph DiClemente said the findings "indicate a need to reconsider the role of abstinence programs" in safe-sex education.

Gracie Hsu, a Family Research Council policy analyst, said the abstinence program probably would have had more success if the class lasted longer.

FIGURE 1.2
SCANS report "Workplace Competencies."   See the complete SCANS report, "Principles and Recommendations" from *Learning a Living: A Blueprint for High Performance* at <http://wdr.doleta.gov/SCANS/lal/LAL.HTM>.

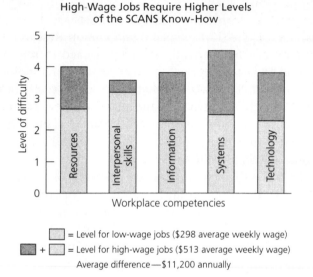

the social policy research on issues like these helps us to make more informed decisions—as citizens and as social science professionals.

Another indication that statistics play an important part in our lives is that it *pays* to understand statistics! The secretary of labor established a commission (called SCANS—Secretary's Commission on Achieving Necessary Skills) to come up with a list of the skills needed to succeed in the job market of the year 2000 and beyond. Their list is grouped into five "Workplace Competencies." One of the competency categories is "Information," which includes the ability to "acquire and evaluate data, organize and maintain files, interpret and communicate, and use computers to process information." The commission estimates that people with superior skills in the five listed areas will make, on average, over $11,000 a year more than people who don't have superior skills in these five areas (see Figure 1.2).

Many organizations are creating specific jobs that use information skills. The *New York Times* reported on a new workplace trend—the development of knowledge managers, "a growing number of employees whose job it is to take the overwhelming mass of information in our lives and make it tangible, accessible and useful."[6]

We can make information "tangible, accessible and useful" by finding the patterns in it—and statistics help us do that. They are invaluable tools, from very simple statistics that simply describe data, like percentages, to more complex

---

[6]"New Breed of Worker Transforms Raw Information Into Knowledge," by Matt Richtel, *The New York Times on the Web,* 15 October 1997, <http://www.nytimes.com>.

ones that assess the accuracy with which we can make generalizations from relatively small numbers of people to much larger groups.

The goal of this text is to teach you how to understand and use these important tools. We begin with a review of the concepts that form the foundation for understanding statistics, starting with how researchers conduct their projects. As the concepts are introduced, they will be illustrated with examples from newspapers, magazines, online news sources, and scholarly journals. You will be doing your own analysis of variables, like the ones in the examples, using sets of data included with this text. The data sets are drawn from the 2002 General Social Survey (GSS) of the National Opinion Research Center (NORC) at the University of Chicago, and they are designed to represent the population of American adults, 18 years of age or older, who are English-speaking and noninstitutionalized. The data sets that you will use each consist of 1,500 cases and about 50 variables drawn from the much larger GSS that consists of nearly 3,000 cases and hundreds of variables. Finally, you will be learning to do your analysis two ways: with pencil, paper, and calculator; and using a software program on a computer, SPSS for Windows.[7]

The text is divided into two sets of statistical skills: skills for computing and interpreting descriptive statistics and skills for computing and interpreting inferential statistics. **Descriptive statistics** are numbers that summarize sets of data. They help us to *describe* patterns in sets of data like the General Social Survey, which is a sample drawn from a larger population. Some statistics simply describe the prevalence of a characteristic (sex, age, race), whereas other statistics describe relationships between characteristics (sex and education, or sex and income). Descriptive statistics don't tell us anything about whether the samples are actually representative of the populations from which they are drawn. **Inferential statistics**, on the other hand, help us to assess whether generalizations, or *inferences,* from samples to populations are appropriate. Inferential statistics let us see whether what we are learning about a sample, like the General Social Survey, is also likely to be true of the larger population from which the sample was drawn.

Let's get started on understanding descriptive and inferential statistics by going over the process of doing research, reviewing some of the fundamental concepts for social research design, and seeing how these concepts are applied in the General Social Survey.

THE PROCESS OF SOCIAL RESEARCH

Some students come to a statistics course after taking a course on research design or research methodology. In these courses you learn that research in the social sciences follows a process, and adherence to the process is what makes the research scientific. Typically, the **research process** involves the following steps.[8]

---

[7]At one time, SPSS stood for "Statistical Package for the Social Sciences." However, SPSS is no longer an acronym because it pertains to both the software package and the company that produces it.
[8]From *Finding Out* (2nd ed., pp. 35–36), by Jane Audrey True, 1989, Belmont, CA: Wadsworth. You will find a description of a process similar to this one in the first few chapters of most textbooks on social science research methods.

1. **Specify research goals**
   - Decide what it is you want to study and come up with a research question to guide your investigation.
2. **Review the literature**
   - Place your question in the context of what is already known—relevant theory and the research to date.
3. **Formulate hypotheses**
   - Come up with one or more hypotheses from which variables of interest are identified.
4. **Measure and record**
   - Decide how to make observations of your variables—for example, using surveys, direct observations, or experiments—and how to record your observations as data.
   - Make systematic observations and collect data.
5. **Analyze the data**
   - Extract patterns from the data you collect.
   - Test hypotheses.
   - Draw conclusions.
6. **Invite scrutiny**
   - Make your research and analysis available to others.
   - Open yourself up for review of the processes you followed, data you collected, and the conclusions you reached.

Let's go through these steps, using as an example a research project I completed examining the impact of service learning on student achievement in an Introduction to Sociology course.[9] Service learning is an approach to teaching in which community service assignments are incorporated into a course. In the Introduction to Sociology course I teach, students have a choice of assignments. Some work with the group on campus doing education and advocacy to reduce hunger and homelessness in Cortland, New York. Others work in day-care centers, serve as teaching assistants in the public schools, or volunteer in an adult literacy program. My *research goal* was to find out whether these service learning assignments improve student achievement compared to a more traditional, classroom-based approach to teaching an Introduction to Sociology course.

Before I decided how to conduct my research project (or even whether it was worth it to do research in this area at all), I had to find out what researchers had already learned about service learning and its effect on student achievement. I began by *reviewing the literature* already published on this topic. I found that little research had been done that attempted to isolate the effects of service learning on college students. The few studies in this area involved students in journalism, psychology, and political science, but not sociology. There was more about the effects of service learning on high school students, but not very much.

---

[9]"Outcomes of Service Learning in an Introduction to Sociology Course," by J. R. Kendrick, Jr., 1996, *Michigan Journal of Community Service Learning, 3,* pp. 72–81.

Reviewing the literature in light of my research goals helped me to *formulate a hypothesis:* Students in service learning courses show higher levels of achievement than students in non–service learning courses. More specifically, I hypothesized that students in the section of my Introduction to Sociology course that included service learning would show higher levels of achievement than students in the section that did not involve service learning.

The question remained: How could I find out whether students in my service learning course do better than students in my non–service learning course? What counts as "achievement," and how can it be measured? I had to come up with a plan for *measuring and recording* data related to the variables of interest in my project. I decided to use the students' grades, along with other measures like course attendance, to measure achievement. In addition, I asked students to respond to a questionnaire designed to measure attitudes in a variety of areas, such as concern for social justice, responsibility for addressing social issues, and ability to make changes in society. However, I couldn't limit my observations to just two variables, the independent variable (type of course: service learning or not) and dependent variable (student achievement). I had to collect some background data on the students in the course, like age, sex, race, high school GPA, and SAT scores. All of the data I collected were entered into an SPSS data file by a student assistant.

The process of *analyzing the data and drawing conclusions* started by simply describing the students in the two sections of my Introduction to Sociology course to establish that the students in the two sections were, for all practical purposes, comparable. Then I began testing my hypothesis. Did students in the service learning course achieve more than students in the non–service learning course? I concluded that students in the service learning course did, in fact, do better than the other group in some areas but not others. Students in the service learning section showed greater growth in the areas of developing a sense of social responsibility and personal efficacy. Even though there wasn't a significant difference in grades between the two courses, the students in the service learning section believed that they had learned more as compared with students in the other section of the course.

Finally, I subjected my results to the *scrutiny of others.* First, I asked colleagues in my college to read my conclusions in a paper I wrote about the project. Then I submitted the paper for publication to a journal. Before publishing the paper, the editor of the journal asked a set of reviewers to critique it. After I revised the paper, the editor agreed to publish it. The act of publishing the paper subjected it to scrutiny by the larger community of scholars interested in service learning in general and service learning as an approach to teaching sociology in particular.

As I started thinking about how to gather data to answer the question of interest to me, I had to decide whom (or what) to study, how the individuals (or other entities of interest) would be selected, what information to collect about each of them, and how to collect it. The next section covers the concepts associated with these tasks—population, sample, hypothesis, variables (including independent, dependent, and control variables)—and ties them to the two articles in "News to Use" and the General Social Survey, the set of data you will be working with throughout the text.

FUNDAMENTALS OF RESEARCH DESIGN

Populations, Elements of Populations, and Units of Analysis

As researchers identify research questions, they think about whom (or what) they must study to answer their questions. Researchers have to collect information (data) about the characteristics of those individuals, groups, organizations, or other units they want to study. A **population** is the set of those elements a researcher wants to know something about. An **element** is a single entity of the population.

The set of elements may be large, as in the population represented by the **General Social Survey (GSS)**, which is designed to represent all English-speaking Americans 18 years old or older who live in households (as opposed to group quarters, like college dormitories or other institutional settings).[10] The set may also be relatively small, as in the population of students in your college or university.

The single elements that make up a set may be individuals, groups, organizations, or institutions, or any other socially organized unit (like a city, state, or nation), formal or informal. Some populations consist of sets of individuals, in which case a single element of the population is an individual. Used this way, the term *population* means about the same as it does generally—to denote a set of individuals. Other populations may consist of sets of cities, states, or nations, of which a single element is a specific city, state, or nation. A researcher interested in crime rates in large cities may study the population (or set) of all large cities in the United States, of which a single element would be a specific large city like Los Angeles, New York, Dallas, or Chicago. A researcher interested in the level of support for public education may study the population of all states in the United States, of which a single element would be a single state like California, New York, Texas, or Illinois. A researcher interested in poverty at the global level could study the population of all nations, of which a single element would be one nation like the United States, Brazil, or Zimbabwe.

> *Avoiding Common Pitfalls: Defining a population*   The meaning of the term *population* is sometimes confusing, because it has a more specific meaning for researchers than it does in general usage. When most people talk about a population, they are referring to a group of individuals who make up a community, state, or nation. When researchers use the term, it can refer to any set of elements about which researchers gather information: individuals, groups, organizations, cities, states, or nations.

Researchers collect information from the elements in a population to discover the patterns in one or more characteristics of the population as a whole. What are those characteristics of the population in which the researcher is inter-

---

[10]*The NORC General Social Survey,* by James A. Davis and Tom W. Smith, 1992, Newbury Park, CA: Sage. You can learn more about the General Social Survey at the Web site <http://www.norc.uchicago.edu/projects/gensoc.asp>.

ested? The answer to this question leads us to the unit of analysis. A **unit of analysis** is the specific entity the researcher wants to know something about. Usually, the elements of a population and the units of analysis are the same. For most questions in the General Social Survey, the unit of analysis is the individual. General Social Survey researchers gather information in face-to-face interviews from individuals about characteristics of the individuals themselves, like sex, race, religion, and the respondent's income. However, there are also questions in the GSS about other units of analysis. For example, there are a number of questions about households, like household income and the number of wage earners in the household. For these variables, the unit of analysis is the household.

Avoiding Common Pitfalls: Units of analysis   Identifying the units of analysis in a study involves separating who is being asked to participate in a survey from what they are being asked about. It is an important point, because researchers often use individuals in a population to gather information about other entities. For example, researchers may ask one person in a household to answer questions *about* the entire household (total income of everyone in the household; number of people in the household). In this case, the household is the unit of analysis. Researchers may also ask a representative of an organization to answer questions *about* the entire organization (total budget, number of employees). In this case, the organization is the unit of analysis. To correctly identify the units of analysis, it is important to distinguish between the entity *from* which a researcher is collecting information and the entity *about* which he or she is collecting information.

Skills Practice 1   Use the two news stories in "News to Use"—"Disputed Statistics Fuel Politics in Youth Smoking" (the Cornell study) and "Condom Emphasis Works Over Abstinence" (the Philadelphia study)—to identify the populations, elements, and the units of analysis of interest to the researchers.

Samples and Sampling Frames

Researchers can rarely study entire populations—they are simply too large. Think about trying to gauge the attitudes of U.S. adults on an issue like abortion. It would be an impossible task to interview everyone in the United States. To deal with this problem, researchers have devised ways to draw samples from populations. A **sample** is a smaller, more manageable set of elements—a subset of a population—selected to represent the population from which it is drawn. To maximize the likelihood that a sample will be representative of a population, researchers draw samples according to the rules of probability. A **probability sample** is one that is selected in such a way that each element in the population has a known likelihood of being drawn into the sample.

Before any sample can be drawn, however, researchers have to come up with a **sampling frame**, or a list of the elements in the population. A population, remember, is the set of elements that researchers want to learn about. In order to sample, researchers have to know which elements, specifically, make up the population. If the elements of a population are individuals, then the researchers need a list of the people in the population. If the elements of a population are states, then they need a list of all of the states in the population. With a frame or list in hand, researchers can draw samples. Some common methods of drawing probability samples include simple random sampling and systematic sampling.

Simple random sampling   **Simple random sampling** is like drawing names out of a hat: listing each element in a sampling frame on separate slips of paper, mixing them up, and then drawing out a certain number of them. This same procedure can be done electronically using computer programs for creating random samples, or it can be done by hand using a random number table. The researcher numbers each element on a list and then uses a random number table to select the elements from the list for the sample.

Systematic sampling with a random start   **Systematic sampling with a random start** is like simple random sampling, except that only the first element is selected using a random number table. After identifying the first participant in the sample that way, the researcher simply selects every *n*th—second, third, fourth, fifth—element after that (depending on how large the population is and how large the sample needs to be).

Multistage sampling processes   Some sampling procedures are more complex in design, involving a number of different steps (or stages—**multistage sampling processes**). Researchers may first *stratify* the frames from which they draw their samples. **Stratification** involves grouping the elements on a list by a characteristic such as ethnicity or sex. Researchers stratify sampling frames to ensure that their samples will be representative of one or more important characteristics in a population. For example, researchers may divide a frame into categories by sex, creating separate lists of males and females. Then they may draw either a simple random sample or a systematic sample from each list. Stratification allows the researchers to make sure their sample includes males and females in proportion to their representation in the entire population.

Another sampling strategy involves **clustering**. Clusters are used when researchers can't come up with a good frame, or list, of the elements in a population. As a result, they create a list of the clusters, or socially organized entities, in which the elements of interest can be found. For example, researchers who want to survey the population of U.S. adults won't be able to find a list of all U.S. adults. However, they can find a frame for all of the geographic units in which U.S. adults can be found, whether the units are rural areas or city blocks. With this frame, they can draw a random sample of clusters, using simple random sampling or systematic sampling. Then they can randomly select individuals within each cluster to respond to their survey.

The General Social Survey is an example of a research project that uses clustering extensively. Beginning in 1994, GSS researchers started taking a probability sample of nearly 3,000 adults every two years to represent the population of noninstitutionalized, English-speaking U.S. adults (at least 18 years old). The sample is selected using a multistage process that involves dividing the United

States into geographic areas or units, sampling from those units to ensure representation of the population by certain characteristics (such as ethnicity), selecting blocks or districts from each geographic unit, selecting households within each block, and then selecting respondents from the households.[11]

Variables

Researchers sample to select the specific elements in a population from which data will be collected—but what does the researcher want to know? If we can answer this question, we are on our way to understanding the concept of variables—those characteristics about which data are collected. A **variable** is any aspect of a unit of analysis that can vary from one unit to the next. If the unit of analysis is an individual, variables can include characteristics like age, sex, race, years of education, and religion.

Researchers who administer the General Social Survey are interested in a large number of variables. They collect quite a bit of information on the demographic or background characteristics of the individuals who are selected for participation. In addition to the variables mentioned, they collect data on variables like marital status, class identification (lower-, working-, middle-, or upper-class), political affiliation (Democrat, Independent, Republican), and political views (liberal, moderate, conservative). They also collect information on the attitudes of GSS respondents toward a variety of issues, like abortion, and GSS researchers ask about behaviors like church attendance and voting. Each GSS includes some special topics about which researchers ask questions. In 2002 these topics included prejudice, quality of working life, and altruism. Appendix E is a guide to some of the GSS variables we will be using in this text.

 Skills Practice 2   Identify the variables discussed in each of the two articles, "Disputed Statistics Fuel Politics in Youth Smoking" (the Cornell study) and "Condom Emphasis Works Over Abstinence" (the Philadelphia study). List the variables (characteristics of each of the units of analysis) that are mentioned in the articles.

Categories, Values, and Data

For each variable, researchers gather data (specific pieces of information about the variables) in categories. If you ever answered a survey, you are familiar with the **categories of a variable**—they are the response categories the researcher asked you to check off. Typically, surveys ask respondents to check off whether they are male or female (categories of the variable *sex*), or they may ask how old you are. The number you give in response forms a category of the variable *age*. Variables must have at least two categories. (If a variable has only one category, there is nothing to vary from one respondent to another. When a characteristic does not vary from one respondent to another, it is called a **constant**.)

---

[11]See Footnote 10.

Sometimes researchers assign numbers to the categories of variables. For example, they may assign the number 1 to everyone who answers "male" in response to a sex variable. Everyone who answers "female" becomes a 2. The numbers that researchers assign to variable categories are called **values**.

The **data** for each variable consist of the specific responses obtained for each question. For example, the data for the variable *sex* are the specific responses given by a set of respondents to the question about sex. The data for the variable *age* are the exact answers given by everyone who answered the question about age. In Appendix E you can see the response categories and values for some of the GSS variables.

At this point, the concepts of population, elements (and units of analysis), samples, and variables and their categories should be sounding familiar. In addition, you should be developing an understanding of how these concepts are related to one another. The diagram in Figure 1.3 shows how these concepts can be applied to the General Social Survey.

Hypotheses

Sometimes researchers gather data about variables simply to describe their respondents. The variables in the GSS can be used for this purpose. What is the proportion of males to females? What percentage of respondents is married? How educated are they? Are they employed? More often, researchers are trying to learn about associations between variables. Do men have more education, on average, than women? Are men more likely to have full-time jobs than women? Who is more likely to be working in the home as opposed to outside of the home?

Usually researchers embark on a research project with one or more guesses or hunches about an association in mind. These guesses or hunches may be based on knowledge of the theory and research already developed in a specific

FIGURE 1.3
Diagram of relationship between population, sample, elements, variables, categories of variables, and values for the 2002 General Social Survey.

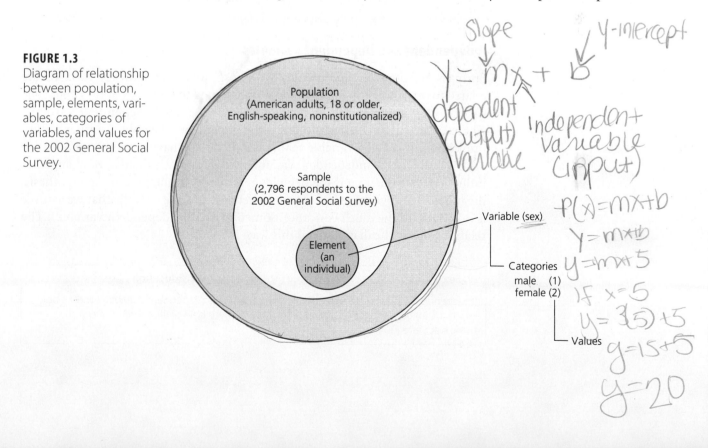

area of study, or they may be based on the personal experiences or observations a researcher has made of some phenomenon. When researchers express these guesses or associations as statements that describe a relationship between at least two variables, they have developed a **hypothesis** about an association. Take the following hypothesis as an example:

Men are more educated, on average, than women.

This statement expresses an association between the variables *sex* (male or female) and *education*. It is also specific about the nature of the association, how the variables are related to one another (men are more educated than women). To assess whether the hypothesis is valid, we could gather data from a group of men and women and ask how many years of education they have completed. Then we could compare how many years of education men have as compared to women.

Hypotheses can go further, though, and express relationships that involve third variables. For example, we may hypothesize that men are more educated than women because they are more likely to have to support themselves than are women. If our hypothesis has merit, we would expect to find proportionately more men than women as the primary breadwinners in their families. We would also expect to see that, among those who are the primary breadwinners, women are no less educated than men. If so, we could conclude that how much education one has achieved has less to do with one's sex and more to do with whether one has to earn one's own living.

 Skills Practice 3   Write possible hypotheses for the Cornell ("Disputed Statistics Fuel Politics in Youth Smoking") and Philadelphia ("Condom Emphasis Works Over Abstinence") studies in "News to Use," one for each study.

Independent and Dependent Variables

From the relationship specified in a hypothesis, we can tell how the variables are related to one another—which variable is assumed to be affecting the other. The variable that is producing or creating the effect is the **independent variable**, whereas the variable being affected is the **dependent variable**. Another way to think about it is that a variable that is assumed to be having an impact on some other variable is the independent variable; the variable assumed to be changed or influenced in some way is the dependent variable. In the preceding hypothesis, the independent variable is sex, male or female. It is the variable that we assume is influencing how much education someone has (the dependent variable). The relationship can be diagrammed this way:

IV: Sex		DV: Education
(Independent Variable—the variable doing the influencing or producing the impact/effect)		(Dependent Variable—the variable being influenced or affected)

Note that I avoided using the word *cause* to describe this relationship. Whereas the variable *sex* is assumed to be having some influence on the variable *education,* we cannot assume that one's sex *causes* one to have (or prevents one from having) a certain level of education. Although we often think of independent–dependent variable relationships in terms of cause and effect, the most we can do is establish an association between two variables. When the characteristic of one variable is found (sex is male), then we tend to find a particular characteristic of a second variable to be present as well (educational achievement is high).

Independent–dependent variable relationships can have a *predictive* quality to them, though. When the characteristic of one variable is present, then we can predict, with varying degrees of accuracy, the presence of a second characteristic. In a later chapter we will be applying techniques for prediction to examine the association between variables like parents' educational levels and their offsprings' educational levels. Do the educational achievements of one's parents allow us to predict the educational achievements of their children?

Sometimes it's hard to figure which variable in a relationship should be the dependent variable and which one should be the independent variable. For some sets of variables, it appears that neither variable is independent or dependent in relation to the other. How can you tell what to do? There are several guidelines you can use to decide how to treat variables:

Logic of the relationship between the variables   There has to be a logical reason to think that the independent variable can influence the dependent variable. Can you think of *how* one variable influences the other? For instance, if we are interested in exploring the relationship between sex and party affiliation, can you think of reasons why one's gender might have an influence on one's political affiliations? One explanation may be that Democrats are perceived to be more likely to support issues of concern to women, like education or childcare. On the other hand, Republicans may be perceived to be more likely to support issues of concern to men, like defense and balancing the federal budget. One way to check yourself is to look at the relationship between two variables in reverse. Does it make any sense to say that one's political affiliation has an effect on one's sex? No, so we are left with treating the variable *sex* as the independent variable.

Time   Independent variables must happen in time before dependent variables. In our example, one's sex is assigned (one's sexual identity develops) before one's party affiliation.

Ascribed vs. achieved characteristics   Ascribed characteristics (characteristics one inherits or over which one has little or no control) are almost always independent variables. Ascribed variables are variables such as *sex, ethnicity,* and *age.* Some variables may be treated as ascribed (or inherited traits) even though they can be changed, such as the socioeconomic status of one's family of origin (the family a person was born into and grew up in) or the religion of one's family of origin.[12] **Achieved characteristics** are often (but not always) treated as dependent variables. Achieved characteristics are those attributes that one develops or

---

[12]Most introductory sociology texts discuss these concepts.

earns as one grows up, "acquired through some combination of choice, effort, and ability" (Ferrante, 1995, p. 303).[13] The attitudes one develops or behaviors one engages in are achieved characteristics, as are the years of education one completes and the socioeconomic status one attains as an adult.

What if neither variable seems to be independent in relation to the other?   Sometimes two variables in a relationship are neither independent nor dependent in relation to the other, although they may be associated with one another. For example, researchers are often interested in the attitudes of those they study. However, one attitude does not necessarily cause or have an effect on another attitude. If one is liberal, for example, one may be pro-choice on the issue of abortion and also more likely to favor affirmative action. However, it doesn't make much sense to say that one's attitude toward abortion causes one to be more or less supportive of affirmative action. These attitudes are associated with one another, though. Among those who are pro-choice, it is more likely that you will find attitudes favorable to affirmative action. Relationships in which the two variables being analyzed are neither independent nor dependent in relation to one another are called **symmetrical** relationships or associations. (The importance of this concept will be clearer when we start looking at statistical measures of association.) In these cases, it usually doesn't matter which variable you treat as independent. Either variable could be the independent variable in a contingency table. However, you may decide to treat one variable as independent in relation to another based on the specific research question you are trying to answer.

 Skills Practice 4   Identify the independent and dependent variables in each of the hypotheses you constructed for Skills Practice 3.

Control Variables

Control variables are any variables (other than the independent or dependent variables) that can have an influence on an independent–dependent variable relationship. For example, when we hypothesized that men are more educated than women *because* they are more likely to have to support themselves, we introduced a control variable—employment status. We speculated that the reason men might have more education than women has more to do with whether they support themselves than with any difference based on gender alone.

As another example, let's use my own research on the effects of service learning on student academic achievement. Can you think of other variables that might affect a student's learning in a course other than the way that the course was taught? You could probably quickly list several. Take ability, for instance. Maybe you broke ability down into more measurable characteristics like a student's high school GPA or SAT scores. These variables could be control vari-

---

[13]*Sociology: A Global Perspective* by Joan Ferrante, 1995, Belmont, CA: Wadsworth.

ables. If you looked at those students with the highest grade point averages, you might expect that they would do well in a course regardless of the specific teaching strategy employed.

Skills Practice 5   Identify control variables for the hypotheses you wrote for Skills Practice 3. What are some of the variables that could influence the relationship between tobacco prices and smoking rates among youth? What are some of the variables that might affect the association between health education and safe-sex practices?

As we explore the General Social Survey, we will be analyzing variables one at a time, associations between variables, and the effects of third variables on relationships between independent and dependent variables. First, however, we have to become familiar with the program we will be using to help with the analysis, SPSS, and we have to become familiar with the set of GSS variables with which we'll be working. Let's begin by having a look at the General Social Survey using SPSS.

USING SPSS

Introducing SPSS for Windows Student Version 11.0

SPSS is a widely available computer software program (SPSS, Inc., says it serves 95% of the Fortune 100 companies) for analyzing quantitative data used by researchers in colleges and universities, public institutions, and private companies.[14] Consequently, it is likely that over the course of your career—whether in an applied setting (like criminal justice, social work, policy analysis, or law) or an academic environment—you will encounter SPSS or a program like it. (There are a variety of other software programs that perform similar functions, such as MicroCase, SAS, and Minitab. The skills you learn doing SPSS are easily transferred to these other programs.)

GETTING FAMILIAR WITH THE PROGRAM

SPSS is a complex program. You will be learning about selected features of the program to gain a fundamental understanding of the software. Throughout the course, you may very well find yourself exploring some features of the program on your own and learning more about it than can be covered in one introductory-level text. You may even learn things about the program your instructor doesn't know.

I will be taking you through each of the functions in the program step by step, using a series of "SPSS Guides."

---

[14]To learn more about SPSS, Inc., the company that markets the software program, visit its Web site at <http://www.spss.com>.

USING SPSS

To start, you can use the SPSS program that is available on your campus. (Your instructor may have to give you directions on how to open the SPSS program on your campus computers.) You may also want to install your SPSS Student Version software program on your computer. (Follow directions that came with your software program.) If you are using your campus computers or if you have installed SPSS on your own computer, computers operating with Windows will display a menu of icons (symbols) when you boot (start) them up. To begin, look for an icon for SPSS for Windows Student Version 11.0 on your computer screen. It will look like the illustration on the left.[15] Then use the SPSS Guide that follows to open your SPSS program.

SPSS GUIDE: OPENING THE SPSS PROGRAM

Use your mouse to place your cursor on the SPSS icon and double-click. You will see a set of windows like the ones here.

1 Click on the ○ (called a radio button) next to Type in data.

2 Then click on OK.

---

[15]If you do not see such an icon, you can also start SPSS from the Start button in the lower left-hand corner of your computer screen. Place your cursor on the Start button and click. A menu will pop up. Look for the word Programs on the menu. Place your cursor on the word Programs and hold the cursor there for a second. Another menu listing all of the programs available on your computer will open. Find the label for the SPSS program that you (or your campus) may be using. Put your cursor on the label and click. The SPSS program should open.

SPSS GUIDE: EXPLORING THE SPSS PROGRAM

The menu

After opening the program, you will be at the SPSS Data Editor window. Notice that within the Data Editor window there are two "views" that you can use to see your data. The first is called Data View. It allows you look at all of the variables and any data that you may have entered for your variables. When SPSS opens, you will normally see the Data View option in the Data Editor window. The second view is called Variable View. You can switch to Variable View by clicking on the "Variable View" tab in the lower left corner of the screen. In Variable View, you can see the characteristics of any variables you may have in a data file—their names, labels, categories, category labels, and so forth. You are probably not seeing very much now because we have not yet opened a data file.

Switch back to Data View by clicking on the Data View tab in the lower left-hand corner of your computer screen. Let's explore the Data View screen a little. (We will learn a lot more about the Variable View screen in Chapter 3).

Begin by looking at the menu items across the top of the screen: File, Edit, View, Data, and so on. Point at the first item, File, and click once. A list of options for each item will open up, like the one shown on the next page. This list is called a pulldown menu. Get used to moving the cursor from menu item to menu item, holding it on each one for a second, to see the options under each one. (We will explore how to use many of these features later in the book.) Place your cursor on File and click again to close the pulldown menu.

USING SPSS

Untitled - SPSS Data Editor

File   Edit   View   Data   Transform   Analyze   Graphs   Utilities   Window   Help

New	▶
Open	▶
Open Database	▶
Read Text Data	
Save	Ctrl+S
Save As...	
Display Data Info...	
Apply Data Dictionary...	
Cache Data...	
Print...	Ctrl+P
Print Preview	
Stop Processor	Ctrl+.
Recently Used Data	▶
Recently Used Files	▶
Exit	

| var | var | var | var | var |

The toolbar

Move your cursor to the next row, a row of icons (symbols) called the *toolbar*. A toolbar provides easy access to many of the most frequently used features of a program. Hold your cursor on each item until a box appears describing the item, starting with the first icon, which looks like a file folder. The words Open File appear when you hold your cursor on the icon. You will see labels for each of the icons as you move your cursor across the toolbar.

Untitled - SPSS Data Editor

File   Edit   View   Data   Transform   Analyze   Graphs   Utilities   Window   Help

1 : Open File

| var | var | var | var | var | var |

SPSS GUIDE: OPENING SPSS DATA FILES

With your SPSS program open, click on the Open File icon on your toolbar. The Open File window appears. You will see a list of data files that come with the SPSS software. You may want to explore them later on. For now, we will assume you are working with a set of data on a CD (compact disc).

To open a data file on your CD, insert your CD into the appropriate slot in the computer. Then click on the down arrow ▼ you see next to the Look in box. A list of options will appear. These are different locations in the computer for retrieving files. Among the options is the drive for your CD. On my computer it looks like this: DVD/CD-RW Drive [D:]. Click on the option for your CD drive.

A list of the files on your CD will appear. The one we will use first is called GSS 2002 subset A (for General Social Survey, 2002). The GSS 2002 subset A is a file of 1,500 cases (respondents) and about 50 variables from the larger General Social Survey sample of nearly 3,000 adults who answered questions about hundreds of variables.

1 Click on GSS 2002 subset A.

2 Click on Open.

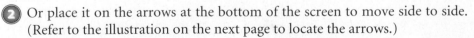

Your data file will appear in the SPSS Data Editor window, illustrated on page 23. This window may look familiar if you have had any experience with spreadsheet programs like Excel, Dbase, or Lotus. Each *row* in the window contains the responses of a single respondent to the variables in the 2002 General Social Survey. Each *column* lists all responses to a single variable. The first variable, *id*, is the identification number of each of the respondents to the GSS.

Having opened a file, let's have a look at some of the variables in our data. Follow the directions in the next SPSS Guide to explore the variables in your file.

SPSS GUIDE: EXPLORING VARIABLES

With your GSS 2002 subset A file open, look at the Data Editor to see the variables that are listed across the columns of the table and the cases that are listed down the side. Not all of the data fit on one screen. You have to use your cursor to *scroll*—move up and down and side to side—to see all of your cases and all of your variables.

1 Place your cursor on the arrows at the side of the screen to scroll up and down.

2 Or place it on the arrows at the bottom of the screen to move side to side. (Refer to the illustration on the next page to locate the arrows.)

	id	wrkstat	hrs1	marital	age	educ	degree	sex	hompop	income98
1	1	1	40	3	25	14	1	2	1	16
2	3	1	40	4	30	13	1	2	2	17
3	5	1	40	3	37	7	0	1	1	18
4	7	5	-1	1	57	16	3	2	2	23
5	8	7	-1	1	71	12	1	2	2	17
6	9	1	40	3	46	14	1	1	2	20
7	11	1	45	1	52	14	1	1	3	21
8	12	1	50	1	48	11	0	1	4	23
9	13	2	30	1	49	18	4	1	5	22
10	14	2	24	3	71	12	1	2	1	13
11	15	7	-1	1	30	12	1	2	2	3
12	20	1	55	5	28	15	1	1	1	15
13	23	1	70	1	33	16	3	1	4	22
14	24	3	-1	1	46	16	1	2	5	22
15	29	2	24	5	23	12	1	2	3	5
16	30	2	6	5	28	9	1	2	4	13
17	31	1	40	3	52	14	2	2	1	20
18	37	1	46	1	26	14	0	2	2	14
19	39	1	35	3	43	14	1	1	2	24
20	42	1	37	4	27	10	0	2	3	9
21	43	1	50	3	60	17	3	2	2	17

With your cursor on the arrow, hold down the left-most click key on your mouse, and you will see the data start to move.

Now look at the SPSS variable names. You will notice that SPSS variable names are no more than 8 characters long, and they look strange because they are shortened versions of much longer variable labels (which we will look at in a minute). These shortened variable names are called **mnemonics.** They are labels designed to jog our memories about what the variables represent. Some of them—like *age* and *sex*—are easy to figure out, and you can probably guess what *marital* stands for (marital status). It's harder to guess what variables like *work-stat, hrs1,* and *hompop* are about. To get more information about each of the variables, simply hold your cursor on a variable name, like *id.* A variable label (a lengthier variable description) will appear to give you an idea of what each variable is about. (See the next illustration.) Refer to the codebook in Appendix E to become more familiar with each of the variables.

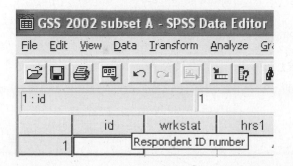

When you get to the variable *degree,* you encounter a commonly used abbreviation in the variable label, *RS,* which stands for *respondent's,* so *degree* is respondent's highest degree earned.

	id	wrkstat	hrs1	marital	age	educ	degree	sex
1	1	1	40	3	25	14	RS highest degree	

Now let's take a look at the General Social Survey variables along with the categories of the variables (called **value labels** in the SPSS program) and their values, using the Variables window. Note that the terms *categories* and *value labels* will be used interchangeably as you use "SPSS Guide: The Variables Window" to tour the SPSS variables, their values, and their value labels.

SPSS GUIDE: THE VARIABLES WINDOW—VARIABLES, VALUES, AND VALUE LABELS

To see a description of each of the GSS variables along with their values and value labels, click on the toolbar Variables icon (the one with the blue question mark on it).

A window called Variables opens up. You will see an alphabetical list of each variable in the GSS 2002 subset A file. Put your cursor on the variable *fund* and click. To the right of the variable, there is a box labeled Variable Information.

You will see the variable name *fund* along with the longer variable label. Following the variable label, you will see the level of measurement listed—ordinal for *fund*—and the value labels for the variable. The value labels represent the categories of the variable—FUNDAMENTALIST, MODERATE, and LIBERAL in this case. You will also see some other categories listed, like NAP, DK, and NA. These are categories for people who did not answer or were not asked this particular question. NAP means the question is not applicable (wasn't asked for one reason or another), DK means the respondent answered "don't know," and NA means no answer. Categories like these—NAP, DK, and NA—are generally treated as **missing values** of the variable, responses that are not meaningful for describing characteristics of the respondents. Missing values are generally excluded from the analysis of a variable's categories.

Click on some of the other variables to see the information about them. As you do so, you will notice that the only value labels some variables have are the ones for the people who didn't respond to the question. Let's look at the variable *age* as an example. The only two categories listed are DK (don't know) and NA (no answer). This doesn't mean that those variables have no categories. What it means is that these variables are being measured at the numerical level, as indicated by the absence of any values or value labels (other than missing values codes). The researcher doesn't need to provide value labels for the categories, because the numerical values for the variable are meaningful. You will learn more about levels of measurement and these kinds of variables in the next chapter.

When you are finished looking at the variables, click on the X—the exit button—in the top right-hand corner of the window to exit.

To see the General Social Survey data, you have to look no further than the SPSS Data Editor window. The Data Editor window is one of several output screens you will learn to use. Others will be introduced as we come to them. Follow the "SPSS Guide: Exploring Data Using Data View" to take a look at the data for each of the variables in your file.

SPSS GUIDE: EXPLORING DATA USING DATA VIEW

Look at the SPSS Data Editor window and read down the column of numbers under each variable. The first variable, *id*, is simply the identification number for each respondent in the survey. Under *age* you see the ages of each GSS respondent: The first respondent is 25 years old, the next respondent is 30 years old, and so on.

GSS 2002 subset A - SPSS Data Editor

File   Edit   View   Data   Transform   Analyze   Graphs   Utilities   Window   Help

1 : id   1

	id	wrkstat	hrs1	marital	age	educ	degree	sex
1	1	1	40	3	25	14	1	2
2	3	1	40	4	30	13	1	2
3	5	1	40	3	37	7	0	1
4	7	5	-1	1	57	16	3	2
5	8	7	-1	1	71	12	1	2
6	9	1	40	3	46	14	1	1

The data under the variable *marital* (respondent's marital status) make a little less sense. What does the piece of data for the first respondent, the value 3, mean? What about the value 4 for the next respondent? There are several ways to find out. To see the value labels for the variable, open up the Variables window (using the Variables toolbar icon—the one with the blue question mark). Then find and click on the variable *marital*. You can quickly see that the value 3 stands for DIVORCED and the value 4 stands for SEPARATED.

Variables

grppol
happy
hompop
hrs1
hrsrelax
id
income98
lotofsay
marital
news
othshelp
partthon
partyid
polviews
pres00
protest

Variable Information:

marital
Label: Marital status
Type: F1
Missing Values: 9
Measurement Level: Nominal

Value Labels:
1 MARRIED
2 WIDOWED
3 DIVORCED
4 SEPARATED
5 NEVER MARRIED
9 NA

Go To   Close   Help

Next, let's look at the Variable View window in SPSS.

SPSS GUIDE: EXPLORING SPSS VARIABLES USING VARIABLE VIEW

In the Data Editor window, it is easy to switch from looking at the data using Data Editor to looking at how the variables are set up using Variable View. Just click on the Variable View tab in the bottom left corner of your screen. You will see a window like the one here.

In Variable View, you can see how each of the variables in the General Social Survey is set up. (We will be using this window a great deal in Chapter 3 when you learn how to create data sets with SPSS.) Starting on the left-hand side of the screen and reading across, it is important at this point to notice a few features of Variable View. (More of them will be explained in Chapter 3).

1 The name of each variable (the 8-character variable mnemonic). For example, the first variable in the file is named *id*.

2 The longer label assigned to each variable. The label for the *id* variable is Respondent ID number. (When you first open Variable View, you may only see a portion of each label.)

3 To see the entire label, place your cursor on the line that separates the Label cell from the Values cell. You will see a bar with two arrows, one pointing left and one pointing right. If you place your cursor on this bar while holding the left-click key down, you can scroll to the right and expand the size of the cell to see the entire variable label.

You should also have a look at the values and labels assigned to the categories of each of the variables. In order to see these values and labels you will need to

1 Place your cursor on one of the cells under the heading "Values." When you do so, notice that the cell becomes highlighted with a black border, and a blue box with three dots in it appears. Try this with the label for the variable *wrkstat*.

2 Click on the blue box. A Value Labels window will open that will allow you to see the values and value labels for each category of a variable. For the variable *wrkstat* you will see values like 0 = "NAP," 1 = "WORKING FULL TIME," and so on.

3 To exit from the window click on the X in the upper right-hand corner of the window.

Now return to Data View by clicking on the Data View tab in the lower left-hand corner of your screen. In the next section I will show you how to exit from the SPSS program when we are finished with our work each day. Use "SPSS Guide: Exiting from the SPSS Program."

SPSS GUIDE: EXITING FROM THE SPSS PROGRAM

There are two options for exiting:

Option 1: Click on the X box in the upper right-hand corner of the screen (as you would to exit from any Windows program); or

Option 2:

1 Click on the menu item File.

2 Then click on Exit.

GSS 2002 subset A - SPSS Data Editor

| File | Edit | View | Data | Transform | Analyze | Graphs |

New	▶
Open	▶
Open Database	▶
Read Text Data	
Save	Ctrl+S
Save As...	
Display Data Info...	
Apply Data Dictionary...	
Cache Data...	
Print...	Ctrl+P
Print Preview	
Stop Processor	Ctrl+.
Recently Used Data	▶
Recently Used Files	▶
Exit	

hrs1
40
40
40
-1
-1
40
45
50
30
24
-1
55

If the window below opens up, click on No. You will go back to your main Windows menu.

SPSS for Windows Student Version

⚠ Save contents of data editor to C:\Documents and Settings\Richard Kendrick\Local Settings\Application Data\Microsoft\CD Burning\GSS 2002 subset A.sav?

| Yes | No | Cancel |

SUMMARY

In this chapter we examined the steps in the research process: specifying research goals, reviewing the research literature, formulating hypotheses, measuring and recording observations, analyzing data, and inviting scrutiny. I illustrated the steps with examples from a research project about the impact of service learning on student achievement in the classroom.

You were introduced to some of the fundamental concepts for research design and the analysis of quantitative data: a population, a sample from the population, elements and units of populations and samples, variables, categories of variables, values of variables, hypotheses, independent and dependent variables, and control variables. These concepts were applied to the set of data you will be using throughout this text, the General Social Survey (GSS) for 2002. The population for the GSS consists of all English-speaking, American, noninstitutionalized adults 18 years old or older. The entire GSS sample is a multistage probability sample of nearly 3,000 adults. The GSS 2002 subset A contains 1,500 cases from the larger sample of nearly 3,000. Variables include many demographic characteristics, like sex, age, race, and education. There are also variables designed to measure attitudes toward various issues, like support for abortion and confidence in government, and variables that measure behaviors, like church attendance and voting.

Before moving on to the next chapter, be sure you can open a data set you will use with this text, a subset of the 2002 GSS variables called GSS 2002 subset A. You should also be able to move around in the file to view the variables and their labels.

In the next chapter you will learn to assess the levels at which variables are being measured, including the GSS variables we will be working with.

KEY CONCEPTS

SPSS	Sampling frame	Data
Statistics	Simple random sampling	Hypothesis
Descriptive statistics	Systematic sampling with a	Independent variable
Inferential statistics	random start	Dependent variable
Research process	Multistage sampling process	Ascribed characteristic
Population	Stratification	Achieved characteristic
Element	Clustering	Symmetrical relationship
General Social Survey (GSS)	Variable	Control variable
Unit of analysis	Categories of a variable	Value label
Sample	Constant	Mnemonics
Probability sample	Values of a variable	Missing values

ANSWERS TO SKILLS PRACTICES

1. The population of the Cornell study consists of states in the United States—those that have raised prices for cigarettes and those that haven't. The elements and the units of analysis are the same—the states. The population of the Philadelphia study consists of sixth and seventh graders in three inner-city schools in Philadelphia, Pennsylvania. The elements and

the units of analysis are individuals, or the sixth and seventh graders about which the researchers are collecting data.

2. Cornell study variables include cigarette prices, smoking rates among children, enforcement of laws against tobacco sales to children, enforcement of laws prohibiting children from buying cigarettes, restrictions on advertising tobacco products to children, investment in health education (like antismoking campaigns). Philadelphia study variables include health education class, sexual activity, safe-sex practices, age, grade in school, sexual experience, school attended.

3. Answers to this Skills Practice may vary. However, they should be along the lines of the following:

Cornell study: States with higher tobacco prices will show lower rates of smoking among children than states with lower tobacco prices; or the higher a state's tobacco prices, the lower the rate of youth smoking.

Philadelphia study: Sex education programs that emphasize abstinence are less effective at preventing teenage pregnancy than programs that include information about safe-sex prac-

tices; or sex education programs that include information on condom use are more likely to result in safe-sex behaviors than sex education programs that emphasize abstinence.

4. Cornell study independent variable: tobacco prices; dependent variable: smoking rates among children or youth. Philadelphia study independent variable: health education class (type of health education to which the study participants were exposed); dependent variable: safe-sex practices.

5. Cornell study control variables (characteristics of states that could affect the association between tobacco price and the smoking rate among children): enforcement of laws against tobacco sales to children, enforcement of laws prohibiting children from buying cigarettes, restrictions on advertising tobacco products to children, investment in health education (like antismoking campaigns), activities by tobacco companies to promote smoking. Philadelphia study control variables (characteristics of middle school students that could affect the association between health education and safe-sex practices): age, grade in school, sexual experience, school attended.

GENERAL EXERCISES

1. In the "Process of Social Research" section of this chapter, I described a research project to evaluate the effects of service learning on students in an Introduction to Sociology course at the college at which I work, the State University of New York College at Cortland.
   a. What is the population for the research project?
   b. What are the elements of the population?
   c. What is the unit of analysis?
   d. Identify the independent and dependent variables in the hypothesis I constructed for the study.
   e. List possible control variables.

2. Read the newspaper article in Box 1.1, then answer the following:
   a. What is the population?

b. What are the elements of the population?
c. What is the unit of analysis of interest to the researcher?
d. Write a hypothesis relevant to the study.
e. Identify the independent and dependent variables in the hypothesis.
f. List control variables.

3. Write a hypothesis for the relationship between sex and volunteering to work for a charitable organization (the *volchrty* variable in Appendix E). Identify the independent and dependent variables in the hypothesis. Suggest a control variable and explain how it could affect the association between the independent and dependent variables.

4. Write a hypothesis for the relationship between voting in the 2000 presidential election

and level of educational achievement (the *degree* variable in Appendix E). Identify the independent and dependent variables in the hypothesis. Suggest a control variable and explain how it could affect the association between the independent and dependent variables.

5. Write a hypothesis for the relationship between age and participation in the activities of a political party (the *grppol* variable in Appendix E). Identify the independent and dependent variables in the hypothesis. Suggest a control variable and explain how it could af-

fect the association between the independent and dependent variables.

6. Look through Appendix E and write three hypotheses for variables you find in the General Social Survey (other than the ones I used in Exercises 3–5).
   a. Identify the independent and dependent variables in each hypothesis.
   b. For each hypothesis, suggest a control variable and explain how it could affect the association between the independent and dependent variables in your hypothesis.

BOX 1.1

Amount of Schooling Affects Earning Potential[16]

ASSOCIATED PRESS

If you are a high school student thinking about college, consider this: Someone with a bachelor's degree earns nearly $1 million more over his or her lifetime than a high school graduate. A Census Bureau survey released Thursday shows a college graduate can expect to earn $2.1 million working full-time between ages 25 and 64, which demographers call a typical work-life period. A master's-degree holder is projected to earn $2.5 million, while someone with a professional degree, such as a doctor or lawyer, could make even more—$4.4 million.

In contrast, a high school graduate can expect to make $1.2 million during the working years, according to the bureau report that tracked the influence of education on lifetime earnings.

Not all students look at college as an investment, "but I'm sure parents do," said Jacqueline King, policy analyst with the American Council Education, a higher education advocacy group. "The challenge is to convince those high school students on the margins that it is really worth their time to go to college."

Kevin Malecek, a graduate student in American politics at American University in Washington, said most of his classmates find higher education to be worth the time and financial commitment.

"They go to every single class, and they are trying to get the most out of their own dollar," he said.

The survey was conducted between March 1998 and March 2000. All estimates are based on 1999 salaries and probably will increase as salaries rise over time, Census Bureau analyst Jennifer Day said.

The estimates do not account for inflation or for differences in the earning potential of various fields of study. For example, people with computer science degrees tend to earn more than those with social work degrees.

---

[16]*USA Today*, 18 July 2002, <http://www.usatoday.com/news/census/2002-07-18-degree-dollars.htm#more>.

BOX 1.1

(Continued)

"It's pretty integral right now that you have a bachelor's degree," said Kaydee Bridges, a senior studying international relations at Georgetown University. "It is an investment and it's a lot of money."

Disparities remained between men and women, especially among older workers with higher degrees. Men with professional degrees may expect to earn almost $2 million more than women with the same level of education.

More men hold better-paying executive positions in corporations, hospitals and law firms, Day said. Also, more women than men leave work to care for children and women often do not return to their jobs full-time after childbirth.

Other highlights:

- Non-Hispanic whites can expect to make slightly more than minorities on all schooling levels except among the most educated. Among people with any type of graduate degree (including doctors and lawyers), Asians and whites are expected to make $3.1 million.
- Americans overall continue to stay in school longer. In 2000, 84% of adults 25 and older had at least a high school degree, and 26% had a bachelor's degree or more, both records.

The survey was conducted separately from the 2000 census. The bureau last released such figures in 1992, though the estimates are not directly comparable because they have not been adjusted for inflation.

In 1992, a high school graduate could expect to make $820,870 at work between 25 and 64. A college graduate could make $1.4 million, while a professional-degree holder could make more than $3 million.

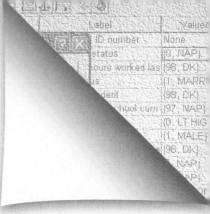

CHAPTER 2

Levels of Measurement

INTRODUCTION

As an instructor, I am always on the lookout for examples of social science research to use in my classes. I received an email announcing the publication of an article, "Short-Term Impacts, Long-Term Opportunities: The Political and Civic Engagement of Young Adults in America."[1] The article led me to the home page for the Center for Information and Research in Civic Learning and Engagement (CIRCLE) at <www.civicyouth.org>. The CIRCLE organization—along with the Center for Democracy and Citizenship, the Partnership for Trust in Government, and the Council for Excellence in Government—sponsored a study of 1,500 young adults to assess their attitudes toward civic engagement in the period following the September 11, 2001, attacks on the World Trade Center in New York City and on the Pentagon. Some excerpts from the survey are included in the "News to Use" section. Read them over now. I will refer to them throughout the next several chapters as the CIRCLE survey. We will use examples from the General Social Survey and the CIRCLE survey to learn to assess the levels at which variables are measured, use that skill to create data sets of our own, and then begin to analyze variables.

Apart from my own personal interest in it, the CIRCLE survey makes an interesting case study for several reasons. First, it illustrates uses of statistics covered in this text. Second, the researchers asked questions that are similar to some of the questions in the GSS. For example, they gathered data about demographic variables for each of the respondents, like sex and age. In addition, they gathered

[1] Lake Snell Perry & Associates and The Tarrance Group, Inc., "Short-Term Impacts, Long-Term Opportunities: The Political and Civic Engagement of Young Adults in America," March 2002, <http://www.civicyouth.org/research/products/National_Youth_Survey_outside.htm>.

data about attitude variables pertinent to the topic of their study—attitudes towards civic engagement and levels of participation in civic activities, like voting and volunteering, topics about which General Social Survey researchers also collected data. Third, and most important for the skills we will be learning in this chapter, it includes information about how the researchers measured their variables. ∎

 N E W S *to* **U S E**
Statistics in the "Real" World

Short-Term Impacts, Long-Term Opportunities: The Political and Civic Engagement of Young Adults in America[2]

LAKE SNELL PERRY & ASSOCIATES

THE TARRANCE GROUP, INC.

Just as President John F. Kennedy's assassination is a critical moment for the baby boomer generation, the terrorist attacks of September

[2]Lake Snell Perry & Associates, with The Tarrance Group, designed and administered this survey, which was conducted by telephone using professional interviewers from January 6 through January 17, 2002. The survey reached a total of 1,500 young people between the ages 15 and 25 nationwide, including 1,200 randomly distributed interviews, and oversamples of 150 African-American and 150 Hispanic young people.

Telephone numbers for the survey were drawn from a random digit dial sample (RDD). The data were weighted by age and race to reflect actual distribution of the national population of young people. The oversamples were weighted into the base sample to reflect the racial distribution of the national population of young people.

In interpreting survey results, all sample surveys are subject to possible sampling error; that is, the results of a survey may differ from those which would be obtained if the entire population were interviewed. The size of the sampling error depends upon both the total number of respondents in the survey and the percentage distribution of responses to a particular question. For example, in Question 13, which all respondents answered, 53% said that generally speaking, you can't be too careful in dealing with people; we can therefore be 95% confident that the true percentage will fall within 2.5% of this percentage, or between 55.5% and 50.5%. . . . The margin of sampling error for subgroups is greater than the margin of error for the entire sample.

11th are likely to be a defining moment for today's young adults. On the heels of September 11th and another momentous national event—the election controversy of 2000—social scientists, political practitioners, and others who have long been concerned with the civic and political engagement of young adults could not help but wonder how recent events would affect the political attitudes and beliefs of young adults. The results of this survey provide some of the answers about the impact of current events, as well as highlight trends and issues in young adults' attitudes towards political and community engagement, and offer recommendations for candidates who want to engage young adults.

Overall, the terrorist attacks and the war appear to have influenced the way young adults *feel*—about the government, their communities, and—in theory—about their own civic and political involvement. Young adults are now more trusting of government and institutions like their older counterparts since 9/11. We also see important upsurges in reported interest in community and issue organization involvement. However, these tragic recent events have not yet impacted young adults' community or political *behavior*. Relative to two, four, and six years ago, levels of voter registration and volunteering are down, and young adults show no change in their likelihood to think of voting as important. Yet, with young adults evaluating their views of government and politics, there is hope that more positive feelings and political actors' and institutions' subsequent actions may cause further shifts in the future. . . .

- **September 11th and the war fuel positive feelings towards political participation and government for significant majorities of young adults.** Seventy percent of young adults say the war on terrorism makes them at least somewhat more likely to participate in politics and voting, including a full third (34%) who say they are now *much* more likely to participate. Similarly, youth say the war has made them more favorable towards government (72% at least somewhat more favorable, including 33% much more favorable). Fewer than ten percent say the war has made them less likely to participate, and just 12% say they feel less favorable towards the government as a result of the war. Asked specifically about the September 11th attacks, two thirds of young adults (67%) say they are at least somewhat more likely to participate in politics and voting (29% much more likely to participate) because of the attacks, and an equal share (69%) say they feel more favorable towards government (30% much more favorable). Just sixteen percent say they feel less favorable towards government as a result of September 11th. . . .
- **Sizable shares of young adults say September 11th has made them more likely to consider pursuing careers in community and issue-focused organizations.** More than half of all young adults (56%) say they would be at least somewhat likely to consider working for a community service organization, and just under half (49%) say they would be at least somewhat likely to work for an organization that focuses on a particular issue; a minority say they are extremely likely or very likely to consider

these careers (30% and 25%, respectively). Interest in these occupations has increased in the wake of the terrorist attacks—a plurality of young adults (44%) say they are *more likely* to work for a community service organization as a result of 9/11, and a significant minority say they are *more likely* to work for an issue-focused organization (36%). . . .
- **Despite their stated intention to participate more vigorously in politics and community life, young adults' civic and political involvement has not increased in recent months.** Voter registration and volunteerism rates are lower in this survey than in previous national surveys.
- **Despite the fact that three quarters of young adults continue to insist that neither registering to vote nor voting itself is difficult, claims of voter registration have declined slightly.** In this study, 66% of 18 to 24 year olds claim to be registered to vote. In 1998 and 2000, surveys conducted for the National Association of Secretaries of State (NASS) and The White House Project Education Fund, respectively, both found that 70% of 18 to 24 year olds said they were registered voters. As in a 1996 study for the John and Teresa Heinz Family Foundation, very few young adults say registering (16%) or voting (15%) is difficult. Rather, young adults abstain from registering and voting for other reasons discussed throughout this report.
- **Reported episodic community volunteerism is down.** Compared with an April 2000 survey conducted for The White House Project Education Fund, the percentage of young adults who volunteer at least once a month has stayed about the same (27% now, 30% in 2000), but episodic volunteering – people who volunteer anywhere from "less often than once a year, but sometimes" to every two or three months – has declined by 7 points (31% now, 38% in 2000). The share who "never" volunteer is up 10 points (37% now, 27% in 2000), and now exceeds the share who volunteer at least once a month.

- **Reports of specific kinds of non-political community involvement—donating to a charity, volunteering with a community organization like a homeless shelter, joining a non-political club or organization—have become less common since the NASS study in 1998.** Comparing the habits of today's 18 to 24 year olds to those of November 1998, self-reported donations of money, clothes and food have dropped 14 points (72% now, 86% in 1998); reports of joining a club or organization that does not deal with politics or government have declined 11 points (46% now, 57% in 1998); volunteering with a homeless shelter or other community organization decreased by 10 points (40% now, 50% in 1998).

The concept, measurement, is fundamental to understanding how to use the statistical tools to which you'll be exposed. Just like the tools in a toolbox, statistics have specific uses. Which statistics are used depends on how variables are measured. In this chapter you will learn to identify the levels of measurement—first distinguishing between categorical and numerical levels of measurement and then, for categorical variables, determining if the level of measurement is nominal or ordinal—and to distinguish between discrete and continuous variables as a first step toward the application of statistics.

CLASSIFYING VARIABLES BY LEVELS OF MEASUREMENT

Levels of measurement refers to the way researchers collect data about variables. To learn about the characteristics of the elements of a population, researchers have to make observations. Although there are many techniques for making observations, researchers who employ quantitative methods often use survey instruments. The survey instrument may be administered through the mail, over the phone, face-to-face, or even on the Internet. As a researcher develops an instrument, decisions have to be made about how to collect data and what data to collect—the specific pieces of information about each characteristic or variable of interest.

 Skills Practice 1 What are the variables of interest to the researchers in the excerpts from the CIRCLE study in the "News to Use" section? Make a list of the variables mentioned in the article.

Data for a single variable, such as *age,* can be gathered in a variety of ways. Data about age can be collected in categories. You may have been asked to respond to a survey question that asked you to circle (or check off) an age category (as opposed to writing down your age or your birthday). The question may have looked like this:

Which of the following categories includes your age?

____ 18–20	____ 30–34	____ 45–49	____ 60–64
____ 21–24	____ 35–39	____ 50–54	____ 65–70
____ 25–29	____ 40–44	____ 55–59	

On the other hand, researchers for the General Social Survey ask this question: "What is your date of birth?" The answer is then converted to the actual age of the respondent.

Researchers decide how to gather data based on what they want to know, how likely people are to respond, and how researchers want to use the data. For some projects, researchers need to know the exact ages of their respondents. For other projects, age categories are sufficient. There are variables, like income, to which people are more likely to respond if the data are being collected in categories. People are less likely to answer if they are asked to write down their annual income to the nearest dollar. Finally, how the data will be used by researchers in their analysis influences how the data are collected. As we will see later, some statistics require us to use data that have been gathered as numbers (a respondent's exact age) rather than categories.

The different ways of gathering data can be classified into levels. Let's begin by understanding the differences between categorical and numerical levels of measurement. In my experience, this is one of the easiest distinctions to make. When you can tell the difference between categorical and numerical variables, it is much easier to make the other distinctions necessary to apply statistics correctly.

The Differences between Categorical and Numerical Variables

To decide whether variables are categorical or numerical, you have to look at how the researcher is collecting the data about the variables. Just about any given variable can be measured at more than one level. For example, the variable *age* as measured by the question, "which of the following age categories includes your age," is categorical. The same variable, *age*, in the General Social Survey is numerical, because the data are gathered as a date from which a respondent's age is computed. How can we tell which is which?

Categorical variables   **Categorical variables** are those variables for which data are gathered in response categories that have been set up or predetermined by the researcher. Examples of variables for which data are often collected at the categorical level are illustrated in Box 2.1.

If you have had a course that has covered survey construction, you may have been exposed to the ideas that categories of variables have to be exhaustive and mutually exclusive. When we say that categories of a variable are **exhaustive**, we mean that the categories of a variable must cover all possible answers for the variable. For example, a variable asking about political affiliation has to cover all possible affiliations. This does not mean that a researcher has to think of every conceivable political affiliation a respondent might have (unless you need answers that precise). One solution is to create categories for the answers you think

BOX **2.1**

Examples of Categorical Variables

Demographic variables

The following are examples from the General Social Survey:

Sex—male and female
Race—Black, White, American Indian, Asiatic/Oriental, Other/Mixed
Marital status—married, widowed, divorced, separated, never married

Attitude variables

Data are almost always gathered in categories, like these examples adapted from the CIRCLE survey:

- How important is voting to you personally?

  1 Extremely important
  2 Very important
  3 Somewhat important
  4 A little important
  5 Not important at all

- Thinking about problems you see in your community, how much difference do you believe YOU can personally make in working to solve problems you see?

  1 A great deal of difference
  2 Some difference
  3 A little difference
  4 Almost no difference
  5 No difference at all

Behaviors

Data are often collected in categories, as in this question adapted from the CIRCLE survey:

- Some people find time to volunteer with community organizations and groups, while many do not. How often do you personally participate in volunteer activities with an organization or community group?

  1 More than once a week
  2 About once a week
  3 A couple of times a month
  4 About once a month
  5 Every two or three months
  6 At least once a year
  7 Less often than once a year, but sometimes
  8 Never

will be most commonly given—Democrat, Republican, and Independent (in the United States). But what if someone is a member of the Green Party? Or the Libertarian Party? You can cover all of these bases by adding the category *Other,* and you can cover the possibility that a respondent has no political affiliation at all by adding the category *None.*

The idea that categories have to be **mutually exclusive** means that answer categories should not overlap. It should be clear to respondents that their answer to a variable belongs in one and only one category of the variable. Sometimes we see examples of categories that are NOT mutually exclusive when someone sets up the categories of a variable like age this way: 18–25, 25–35, 35–45, and so on. To which category would a 25-year-old respond? Or a 35-year old? This does not mean that respondents won't have difficulty choosing which one category best matches the attitude, behavior, or other characteristic being measured. However, it does mean that a single characteristic of a respondent should not belong to more than one category of a variable.

Numerical (or scale) variables   Numerical variables (also called *scale* variables in the SPSS program) are those variables for which data are gathered as numbers with no attempt by the researcher to precategorize the answers (Box 2.2).

BOX 2.2

Examples of Numerical Variables

The following two questions from the GSS illustrate how variables can be measured numerically.

1. How long have you worked in your present job for your current employer?

2. After an average workday, about how many hours do you have to relax or pursue activities that you enjoy?

There are two types of numerical variables: **ratio** and **interval** variables. Although you should be aware of the differences between the two, for statistical purposes all numerical (scale) variables—whether ratio or interval—are usually treated the same way.

Ratio variables   Ratio-level measures are first and foremost numerical, but the numbers being gathered have some unique characteristics.

- Any response of zero collected at the ratio level means the absence of the characteristic being measured. For example, if you entered a zero in answer to the question "How many brothers and sisters do you have?" we could assume that you don't have any.
- The distances between each of the units on a ratio scale of measurement are the same. Take *income,* for example. When the variable is measured numerically, there is the same "distance" between someone who earns $10,000 a year and someone who earns $11,000 a year—$1,000—as there is between someone who earns $20,000 a year and someone who earns $21,000.
- As a consequence, the distances between each of the units on a ratio scale are proportional. The proportionality of distance allows us to make meaningful comparisons among units on the scale. Someone who has $10,000 in the bank has twice as much as someone who has $5,000.

For the measurement of a variable to be considered ratio, both of these characteristics must be present: Zero must be meaningful and represent the absence of the characteristic being measured, the distance between each unit on the scale must be the same or constant so that the distances between each of the units are proportional.

Interval variables   Interval-level measures are also numerical, but they do not share the characteristics of ratio-level measures. For one thing, interval-level scales either do not use zero, or, if they do, zero doesn't mean the absence of the characteristic. In the social sciences, the interval-level measure most of us have read about is the IQ scale. It is designed to measure levels of intelligence, but the scale has no true zero. In the natural sciences, the thermometer is an example of an interval-level measure. Zero is on the thermometer, but it doesn't mean absence of the characteristic (temperature). The zero indicates a certain level of the characteristic. On the Celsius thermometer, zero is the freezing point of water. By way of contrast, the Kelvin thermometer measures temperature on a ratio scale. Zero on the Kelvin thermometer represents the absence of heat.

Second, the distances between units of measurement on an interval scale are not proportional. Consequently, we can't make statements like, "someone who scores 120 on an IQ scale is 20% more intelligent than someone who scores 100," or "someone who scores 50 is half as intelligent as someone who scores 100." It isn't twice as hot at 100 degrees as at 50 degrees, and it isn't half as cold at 10 degrees as it is at 20 degrees.

Avoiding Common Pitfalls: Categorical and numerical variables   There are several ways of getting confused about making the distinction between categorical and numerical variables.

Categorical data can be gathered as numbers   We often see categorical data gathered using numbers, because researchers attach numbers to categories (variable values) to help with data entry and analysis. For example, an attitude variable may be gathered by asking respondents to enter a number from a scale like this one:

1 = Always wrong
2 = Almost always wrong
3 = Wrong only sometimes
4 = Not wrong at all

In this case, even though a number is being collected as the response, it has no meaning apart from the word category it represents, and it is simply a shorthand representation of a word category. Consequently, data collected this way are categorical, not numerical.

Data that could be collected numerically are often collected categorically   A fairly common example is how researchers gather data about the variable *income*. Rather than asking people how much money they make (and collect data about income at the numerical level), researchers often set up response categories for the variable. Here's one way to measure income in categories.

(continued)

Avoiding Common Pitfalls: (continued)

Total annual household income

Under $30,000

$30,000–49,999

$50,000–74,999

$75,000–99,999

$100,000–124,999

$125,000 or more

Even though variables like income could be measured at the numerical-ratio level, we have to pay attention to how the researcher is actually gathering the data to determine the level of measurement.

Categories can be numbers The previous example about income illustrates another common pitfall—the categories themselves can be numbers. When you have categories as numbers, how do you tell the difference between categorical-level and numerical-level variables? Look to see whether the numbers have been grouped into intervals or ranges of values, as in the previous example. If they have, then you are dealing with categorical-level measures. If not, then you are probably looking at a variable that is being measured numerically.

Numerical variables can look categorical Some numerical variables have only a few categories, so researchers list them all when they collect data about the variable. Think about the research involving sex education among middle school students summarized in Chapter 1. The students involved were in grades 6 and 7, so the ages of the participants were probably limited to only a few possibilities. Consequently, researchers *could* gather age in categories, like this:

How old are you? (Circle one)   10   11   12   13   14

However, the categories cover the entire range of possibilities for the variable. Consequently, there is no difference between the question asked this way and the question asked as simply, "How old are you?"

Categorical Variables: The Differences between Nominal and Ordinal Variables

Learning how to tell the difference between categorical and numerical level variables is half the battle. The other half is learning to distinguish between types of categorical variables—**nominal** and **ordinal.**

Nominal variables Nominal variables are those being measured in such a way that the categories simply indicate differences among respondents, with no hierarchy or rank order implied in those differences. One very common example of a nominal-level variable is *sex*, when it is measured in the categories of male and female. Male and female are categories of difference, with no rank order or hierarchy inherent in the categories. Another common example is the variable *race*, sometimes measured this way:

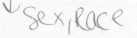

White non-Hispanic	Native American
Latino	Asian/Pacific Islander
African American	Other race

The categories are categories of difference, not rank.

Ordinal variables   Ordinally measured variables, by comparison, have categories in which there is some inherent rank, hierarchy, or order to the categories. By hierarchy or rank it is not implied that individuals who respond in one category are necessarily better than (or higher than) individuals who respond in another category. Instead, hierarchy or rank means that the categories enable us to arrange individuals along some dimension or in some order. These dimensions

---

Avoiding Common Pitfalls: Dichotomous variables

Dichotomous variables   Students are sometimes confused about how to handle **dichotomous variables**, variables with only two categories. Dichotomous variables can be nominal, like

Sex: male or female
Race: White or non-White
Religion: Christian or non-Christian

They may also be ordinal, such as

Attitude: agree or disagree
Behavior: yes or no

What's the difference between nominal and ordinal dichotomies? The same as the difference between any other nominal- and ordinal-level variables. In nominal dichotomies there is no inherent rank or order to the categories of the variable. In ordinal dichotomies the categories of the dichotomy can be ranked or ordered. For example, when people are asked to agree or disagree with a particular statement, they are ranking the extent of their support for the statement. People who agree support the statement more than those who disagree. If people are asked to respond "yes" or "no" to a particular behavior, we can conclude that people who respond "yes" engage in the behavior more frequently than those who say "no."

As you move on in the study of statistics, you will find that dichotomous variables may be treated differently from nondichotomous variables. You will also be exposed to a particular type of dichotomous variable called a **dummy variable**. Dummy variables are special kinds of dichotomies with their own properties. Generally, a dummy variable has two categories: one to indicate the absence of a characteristic and the other to indicate its presence. For example, *sex* could be constructed as a dummy variable by treating one category as the absence of a characteristic (not male) and the other as its presence (male).

Although it is beyond the scope of the skills introduced in this chapter, you should be aware that sometimes nominal dichotomies are treated as ordinal- or numerical-level variables, and ordinal dichotomies and dummy variables are sometimes treated as though they are numerical. At this point it is sufficient to make the nominal/ordinal distinction and to recognize when nominal and ordinal variables are also dichotomies.

may be ones in which individuals in one category express stronger or weaker feelings toward something or feel more or less favorable toward it. Likewise, categories can measure how often something happens or someone does something; how long someone has been doing something; or how much of something (like money) someone has.

Some examples of categories that have this quality of rank or order to them include these two sets of commonly used answer scales for measuring attitudes:

Very important	Always wrong
Somewhat important	Almost always wrong
Not too important	Wrong only sometimes
Not at all important	Not wrong at all

In addition, the categories of variables—like *total annual household income,* which I described in the Avoiding Common Pitfalls section on pages 42–43—are ordinal, because they have an inherent rank or order to them.

The Hierarchy of Measurement

In addition to correctly classifying variables according to their level of measurement, we should understand that there is a **hierarchy** to the levels. Numerical variables are treated as the highest level of measurement, followed by variables that are categorical and ordinal. Variables that are categorical and nominal are at the bottom of the hierarchy. Figure 2.1 is a diagram of the relationship among the levels of measurement.

Statistics that are appropriate for the lowest level of measurement, nominal variables, can also be applied to variables at the higher levels—ordinal and numerical. Statistics appropriate for ordinal variables can be applied to numerical variables. However, statistics appropriate for numerical variables can be applied only to that level and not to ordinal and nominal variables. Consequently, there are many tools for the analysis of numerical-level variables, somewhat fewer tools available for ordinal variables, and even fewer for nominal variables.

FIGURE 2.1
The hierarchy of levels of measurement.

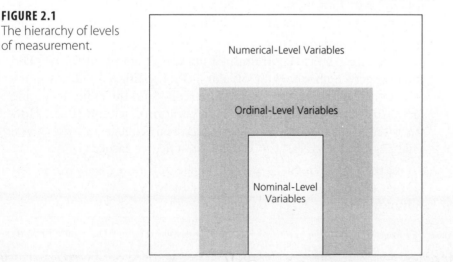

Skills Practice 2 Classify the following General Social Survey variables. First decide whether they are categorical or numerical. Then, decide whether the categorical variables are nominal or ordinal.

A. MARITAL STATUS: Are you currently married, widowed, divorced, separated, or have you never been married?

1 Married   4 Separated
2 Widowed   5 Never married
3 Divorced

B. SUBJECTIVE CLASS IDENTIFICATION: If you were asked to use one of four names for your social class, which would you say you belong in: the lower class, the working class, the middle class, or the upper class?

1 Lower class   3 Middle class
2 Working class   4 Upper class

C. DOES RESPONDENT OR SPOUSE BELONG TO UNION: Do you (or your spouse) belong to a labor union? (Who belongs?)

1 Respondent belongs   3 Respondent and spouse belong
2 Spouse belongs   4 Neither belongs

D. LABOR FORCE STATUS: Last week were you working full-time, part-time, going to school, keeping house, or what?

1 Working full-time   5 Retired
2 Working part-time   6 In school
3 Temporarily not working   7 Keeping house
4 Unemployed, laid off   8 Other

E. R.'S RELIGIOUS PREFERENCE: What is your religious preference? Is it Protestant, Catholic, Jewish, some other religion, or no religion?

1 Protestant   4 None
2 Catholic   5 Other
3 Jewish

F. WEEKS R. WORKED LAST YEAR: Now I'd like to ask you about last year. In 2001 how many weeks did you work either full-time or part-time not counting work around the house—including paid vacations and sick leave? _____

G. R.'S HIGHEST DEGREE: If finished ninth through twelfth grade: Did you ever get a high school diploma or a GED certificate? Did you complete one or more years of college for credit—not including schooling such as business college, technical or vocational school? If yes: How many years did you complete? Do you have any college degrees? (If yes, what degree or degrees?) Circle the highest degree earned.

0 Less than high school   3 Bachelor
1 High school   4 Graduate
2 Junior college

(continued)

> **Skills Practice 2**   *(continued)*
>
> H.   NUMBER OF HOURS R. WORKED LAST WEEK: If working full- or part-time, how many hours did you work last week, at all jobs? _____
>
> I.   NUMBER OF HOURS SPOUSE WORKED LAST WEEK: If working full- or part-time, how many hours did your spouse work last week, at all jobs? _____
>
> J.   THINK OF SELF AS LIBERAL OR CONSERVATIVE: We hear a lot of talk these days about liberals and conservatives. I'm going to show you a 7-point scale on which the political views that people might hold are arranged from extremely liberal—point 1—to extremely conservative—point 7. Where would you place yourself on this scale?
>
> | | |
> |---|---|
> | 1 Extremely liberal | 5 Slightly conservative |
> | 2 Liberal | 6 Conservative |
> | 3 Slightly liberal | 7 Extremely conservative |
> | 4 Moderate | |

CLASSIFYING VARIABLES AS DISCRETE OR CONTINUOUS

In addition to classifying the measurement of variables as categorical (and nominal or ordinal) or numerical, we should be able to determine whether the variables being measured are discrete or continuous. Knowing whether variables are continuous or discrete, like the assessment of levels of measurement, helps us apply statistics correctly. Unlike making the categorical–numerical distinction, whether variables are discrete or continuous has less to do with how researchers are gathering data about the variables than it does with the nature of the characteristic being measured. Different statistical tools may be used depending on the nature of the variables being analyzed.

Discrete Variables

Variables or characteristics that are **discrete** can be counted. In addition, they are countable in discrete quantities, or quantities that cannot be reduced to ever smaller units or numbers. For example, if you are asking people about how many brothers and sisters they have, you are measuring a discrete variable. People come in discrete quantities—units of 1. We do not report having $1\frac{1}{2}$ brothers or sisters. Income is another discrete variable. If you ask someone exactly how much they earn before taxes each week, they will not report anything less than dollars and cents.

Continuous Variables

Continuous variables, on the other hand, are variables for which the characteristic being measured is infinitely reducible. For example, variables that have a time dimension—like age, length of time spent doing something, number of

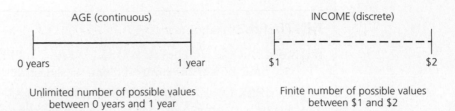

Unlimited number of possible values
between 0 years and 1 year

Finite number of possible values
between $1 and $2

years involved in some activity—are continuous, because time is infinitely reducible, to years, hours, minutes, seconds, fractions of seconds. (However, if you are asked about your age or how many years you have been involved in some activity, like getting an education or working in a particular job, you respond with the nearest year and you don't reduce the variable to its most precise measurement.)

Variables that measure attitudes are also continuous, because attitudes come in an infinite array of perspectives (even though it is more convenient to treat attitudes as if they do not). Whereas you may be asked if you think something is always wrong, almost always wrong, wrong only sometimes, or not wrong at all, your actual attitude may fall at a given category or anywhere in between—between always wrong and almost always wrong, for instance. You usually check off the attitude *closest* to the one that represents your point of view. If you have ever been involved with doing a survey of attitudes, this phenomenon is readily apparent. Invariably, at least a few respondents will refuse to check off one of the appropriate boxes, choosing instead to indicate that their attitude falls somewhere in between the boxes. They will resist treating a continuous variable as if it were discrete!

You can get a sense of the continuous nature of many characteristics by looking at the different approaches to measuring them. Compare, for example, the way that researchers for the General Social Survey ask about race (in three categories: White, Black, and Other) with the way other researchers may subdivide the categories of a similar variable (using six categories: White, Latino, African American, Native American, Asian/Pacific Islander, Other). Do you think the categories of a variable like race are infinitely reducible?

Figure 2.2 summarizes the important difference between continuous and discrete variables. Between any two response categories of a continuous variable, there are an unlimited or infinite number of other possible responses. For example, between the ages 0 and 1, there are an unlimited number of other possible ages, although we don't tend to think in those terms. Between any two response categories of a discrete variable, there are either no other possibilities (between one child and two children) or the possibilities are limited (finite)—between $1 and $2 there *are* other possibilities, but not more than 99 of them.

 Skills Practice 3   Classify variables F through J in Skills Practice 2 as either continuous or discrete.

Avoiding Common Pitfalls: Discrete and continuous variables

Discrete variables can be turned into continuous variables   Sometimes, researchers take variables that are, by nature, discrete and turn them into variables that are continuous. For example, researchers may ask how much money you earned last year, a discrete variable; or they may ask how much money you earned, on average, for the last three years, a continuous variable. The amount you earned last year is discrete because your earnings for a single year is a number that is not infinitely reducible. Then why are earnings averaged over a three-year period continuous? Because an average can be carried out to an unlimited number of decimal places. If someone earns $100,000 over a three-year period, the average ($100,000 ÷ 3) equals $33,333.3333.

Continuous variables can be treated as if they are discrete   Researchers often treat continuous variables as if they are discrete. For example, when asked about our age, we don't write 21 years 6 months 5 days 3 hours 18 minutes and 7.12359 seconds. Instead, we round off to our last birthday. Similarly, when someone asks us what time it is, it is common to round it off to the nearest hour and minute. Even variables like attitudes, which are by nature continuous, are often treated as if they are discrete. We either agree or disagree, nothing in between.

One way to determine whether a variable is truly discrete or is simply being treated as if it is discrete is to ask yourself, "Are there an infinite number of other possible categories between any two given categories of this variable?" If you have two attitude categories, Agree and Disagree, are there an infinite variety of other possible attitudes between those two answer categories? The answer is yes. What about the income categories $1,000 and $2,000? The answer is no. Although there are a number of other possible categories, the number is not infinite. The smallest possible category between the two would be increments of a penny. Thus you could have categories $1,000.01, $1,000.02, $1,000.03, and so on between $1,000 and $2,000, but you couldn't have anything smaller than that (such as $1,000.001 or $1,000.0001).

SUMMARY

We began this chapter by learning to distinguish between categorical and numerical variables. Generally speaking, categorical variables are those for which researchers gather data in predetermined categories. Numerical variables are those for which researchers gather data as numbers. Categorical variables can be further subdivided into two levels: nominal and ordinal. Nominal variables are those for which there is no rank or order among the categories—the categories indicate difference, nothing more. Ordinal variables are those for which the categories have a rank or order.

We learned that many variables (age and level of education are examples) can be measured in different ways, depending on what researchers want to know and how they want to analyze the variables. Consequently, classifying a variable's level of measurement requires us to look at the way a researcher gathers information about it.

On the other hand, deciding whether variables are continuous (have infinitely divisible categories) or discrete (do not have infinitely divisible categories) requires us to think about the nature of the variable itself. If we are measuring numbers of people, we are dealing with a discrete variable—something that cannot be subdivided past a unit of one. If we are measuring age, we are dealing with a continuous variable—something that can be infinitely subdivided.

In the next chapter, you will learn how to organize data once they have been collected by setting up data files in SPSS, and you will be applying the concept of levels of measurement as you create an SPSS data file.

KEY CONCEPTS

Levels of measurement
Categorical variable
Exhaustive categories
Mutually exclusive categories
Numerical (scale) variable

Ratio variable
Interval variable
Nominal variable
Ordinal variable
Dichotomous variable

Dummy variable
Hierarchy of measurement
Discrete variable
Continuous variable

ANSWERS TO SKILLS PRACTICES

1. The variables in the survey include age, trust in government, interest in becoming involved in community issues, voter registration (were respondents registered to vote or not), attitudes toward (importance of) voting, feelings about political participation, feelings about government, likelihood of participating in politics, likelihood of voting, likelihood of pursing careers in community organizations, likelihood of pursuing careers in issue-focused organizations, volunteering in one's community, donating to a charity, and joining a nonpolitical club or organization.

2. For categorical vs. numerical (scale) variables: categorical variables are A–E, G, and J; numerical variables are F, H, and I. For nominal vs. ordinal variables: nominal variables are A, C, D, and E; ordinal variables are B, G, and J.

3. Variables F–J are all continuous.

GENERAL EXERCISES

1. Here is a set of variables with their categories adapted from the CIRCLE survey of 18-to-25-year-olds.[3] Classify each of the variables as categorical or numerical. Then decide whether the categorical variables are nominal or ordinal.

[3]Lake Snell Perry & Associates and The Tarrance Group, Inc., "Short-Term Impacts, Long-Term Opportunities: The Political and Civic Engagement of Young Adults in America," March 2002, <http://www.civicyouth.org/research/products/National_Youth_Survey_outside3.htm>.

A. How often do you attend church or other place of worship?
   More than once a week
   Once a week
   Once or twice a month
   Several times a year
   Almost never
B. Are you . . .
   Married
   Unmarried with partner
   Single

Separated or divorced

Widowed

C. What is the highest level of schooling you expect to complete?

11th grade or less

High school degree or equivalent

A non-college post–high school degree (e.g., technical school)

Some college

An associate's degree (2-year college)

A bachelor's degree (4-year college)

A post-graduate degree

D. From what you remember while you were growing up, would you say that your parents voted . . .

Every election

Most elections

Only in important elections

Rarely

Not at all

E. In what month and year were you born?

_____

F. Do you agree or disagree that the government addresses the needs and concerns of young people like you?

Strongly agree

Not so strongly agree

Not so strongly disagree

Strongly disagree

G. How many paid jobs do you have? _____

H. How many children do you have? _____

I. Generally speaking, do you consider yourself as a Republican, Democrat, an Independent, or something else?

Republican

Independent

Democrat

Other

J. When you were growing up, did either of your parents take you with them when they went to vote?

Yes

No

2. Classify the variables below as continuous or discrete.

A. If you are working full- or part-time, how many hours did you work last week at all jobs?

B. How many people live in your household?

C. Do you agree or disagree that the government addresses the needs and concerns of young people like you?

Strongly agree

Not so strongly agree

Not so strongly disagree

Strongly disagree

D. Do you consider yourself to be

Extremely liberal

Liberal

Somewhat liberal

Moderate

Somewhat conservative

Conservative

Extremely conservative

E. What was your total income for the last calendar year before taxes?

3. Classify variables A, C, F, and H in General Exercise 1 as continuous or discrete.

4. Classify each of the variables in Appendix E as categorical (and nominal or ordinal) or numerical. (Some of them will be familiar from Skills Practice 2.)

5. Find a survey—perhaps one you received in the mail or found in a newspaper or magazine. You may even come across one online if you are an Internet surfer. Classify the variables in the survey: Are they categorical or numerical? If categorical, are they nominal or ordinal? Which variables are continuous and which are discrete?

SPSS EXERCISES

1. Check your work for General Exercise 4 using the SPSS program. (Use the SPSS Guides in Chapter 1 to open the program and the Variables window. In the Variables window, you can see the level of measurement for each of the variables in the GSS 2002 subset A file.)

CHAPTER 3

Creating an SPSS Data File

INTRODUCTION

As you begin working with the General Social Survey, you may wonder how all these data were set up in the computer in the first place. Also, although there are many sets of data like the General Social Survey—already formatted for SPSS and waiting to be analyzed—it is very likely you will be asked at some point in your career to do research that will require you to create your own data set.

In this chapter you will learn how to set up a data file in SPSS using a small set of responses randomly selected from the GSS. You will be working with many of the same variables with which you became familiar in Chapters 1 and 2—variables similar to those used in the GSS and the Center for Information and Research in Civic Learning and Engagement study—along with some new ones. To demonstrate the process of creating a data set, let's assume that you have collected data from 20 people using the survey instrument in Box 3.1, and now you want to get it ready for analysis.

The process of setting up data in SPSS has five steps:

STEP 1. Prepare the survey questions to be defined in the SPSS program.
STEP 2. Use SPSS to set up, or define, each of the variables in the survey.
STEP 3. Enter the data.
STEP 4. Check the data to be sure it has been entered accurately.
STEP 5. Save the data file. ∎

BOX 3.1

Survey of Ten Questions Adapted from the General Social Survey

1. What is your age as of your last birthday? _____
   Check here if you don't know or you're not sure. _____

2. Are you
   _____ Male   _____ Female

3. Are you currently
   _____ Married   _____ Separated
   _____ Widowed   _____ Never married
   _____ Divorced

4. Generally speaking, do you usually think of yourself as a Republican,
   Democrat, Independent, or what?
   _____ Strong Democrat
   _____ Not very strong Democrat
   _____ Independent, close to Democrat
   _____ Independent
   _____ Independent, close to Republican
   _____ Not very strong Republican
   _____ Strong Republican
   _____ Other party

5. People should be willing to help others who are less fortunate.
   _____ Strongly agree
   _____ Agree
   _____ Neither agree nor disagree
   _____ Disagree
   _____ Strongly disagree

6. During the past twelve months how often have you done volunteer work for
   a charity?
   _____ Not at all in the past year
   _____ Once in the past year
   _____ At least two or three times in the past year
   _____ Once a month
   _____ Once a week
   _____ More than once a week

7. Over the past five years have you participated in a marathon or walkathon to
   raise money for a cause?
   _____ No
   _____ Yes

(continued)

BOX 3.1

Survey of Ten Questions Adapted from the General Social Survey
(continued)

8. People sometimes belong to different kinds of groups or associations. Have you participated in the activities of a political party, club, or association in the past twelve months?

_____ I do not belong to such a group

_____ I belong to such a group but never participate

_____ I have participated once or twice

_____ I have participated more than twice

9. In 2000, you remember that Gore ran for President on the Democratic ticket against Bush for the Republicans. Do you remember for sure whether you voted in that election?

_____ Voted

_____ Did not vote

_____ Ineligible to vote

10. Generally speaking, would you say that most people can be trusted, or that you can't be too careful in life?

_____ Can't be too careful

_____ It depends

_____ Most people can be trusted

PREPARING THE SURVEY QUESTIONS

We will begin the process of setting up our data by deciding how to treat the variables in our survey. The first thing we must be sure to do is to create an identification number for each respondent from whom we collect data.

Creating a Respondent ID Number

As questionnaires are completed or survey forms are returned, it is customary to assign each respondent an identification number. This identification number can be very useful if you need to go back and check to be sure the responses from a particular survey form have been entered accurately. Also, this number is usually used as a code for filing surveys once the data have been entered from them. Add the number to the top left corner of the survey form. Treat it like any other variable. Name it, label it, and specify its level of measurement. (It is a nominal-level variable because the identification number is simply a substitute for naming each respondent.)

The next step is to give each variable a name.

Naming the Variables

Each variable has to be named, and we have to decide what to name it. Remember each **variable name** is a mnemonic, which means that it is an abbreviated version of the lengthier variable label. The name we assign to a variable should remind us of what it stands for. Box 3.2 gives a few rules to follow for assigning names to make them compatible with the SPSS program.

BOX 3.2

Rules for Naming Variables—Making Up SPSS Mnemonics

- Variable names can be only 8 characters long.
- There can be no spaces in the name.
- The name has to start with a letter or the symbol @, but the rest of the characters can be letters or numbers or some combination of the two.
- The characters _.@#$ can be used, which might be tempting if the program gives us any trouble!

If you make a mistake, SPSS will let you know. If you try to put in a name longer than 8 characters, SPSS will accept only the first 8 characters entered. If you try to start with a number, SPSS will tell you about your mistake when you try to enter the variable name.

 Skills Practice 1   Give each of the variables in Box 3.1 an 8-character name. Write the name next to the variable it describes. There is no right or wrong answer as long as the name means something to you and it conforms to the rules listed in Box 3.2. If you get stuck, see how similar variables are named in the General Social Survey (using the codebook in Appendix E).

Specifying Levels of Measurement

SPSS will want to know how the variables are being measured. How the variables are measured affects the process of assigning values to variable categories (the next step), so it's important to get this right.

 Skills Practice 2   Classify each variable in Box 3.1 as categorical or numerical (scale). If the variable is categorical, classify it as nominal or ordinal. Write the level of measurement next to each variable.

Coding the Variable Categories

Coding **variable categories** involves assigning **category values,** or numbers, to the categories of each of the variables. For numerical (scale) variables this task is easy, because the responses to numerical variables are meaningful and can be entered as they were written by the respondent. The only problem you might encounter is how to treat missing values.[1] For categorical variables, the variable categories have to be turned into numbers, and, as with numerical variables, you have to decide how to treat any missing data.

Start the process by taking the variables in Box 3.1 one at a time, beginning with the first (and the easiest), the respondent's age. This variable is a numerical variable; no codes are necessary except for missing value codes. In the next section we will discuss how researchers deal with missing data and assign codes to keep track of it.

Move on to the second variable, the respondent's sex. There is a little more for us to do with this one. Begin by assigning values (numbers) to the meaningful variable categories, those categories that are responses to the question being asked. (Disregard, for the time being, any categories that are not responsive to the question, like Don't Know.) The simplest way to do that is to number the categories consecutively, starting with the first one. The categories for the variable *sex* would be numbered as follows:

1 male
2 female

Skills Practice 3   Assign category values to the rest of the variables in Box 3.1. Write your category values next to the categories of each of the variables.

Assigning Missing Values

The term **missing values** is a little misleading, because the values themselves aren't missing. What *is* missing is a respondent's answer to a particular question. The missing values are the category codes or numbers assigned to keep track of the missing answers. Specifying missing values is important, because we are deciding which values of our variables will be regarded as meaningful and which ones we are going to treat, in effect, as a failure to respond (regardless of the reason). Treating a response as missing excludes it from any statistical analysis we might do with the variable.

There are several reasons why data could be missing. Sometimes, respondents are not asked a question. Some respondents may simply overlook one or more questions. Others refuse to answer certain questions. Although missing data

---

[1]You may recall from Chapter 1 that missing values are those categories of response that are not meaningful answers to a question. They are assigned when individuals simply don't answer a question (skip over it, perhaps), say they don't know, refuse to answer, or aren't asked a particular question for one reason or another.

are usually excluded from the statistical analysis of the responses to variables, it is important to keep track of them. Researchers need to be sure that there aren't a lot of missing data as a result of respondents' overlooking or refusing to answer their questions, and they need to be sure that there isn't any *systematic* overlooking of or refusal to answer certain questions. To make sure this isn't happening, researchers need to be able to see how many data are missing. If there are a lot of missing data, they have to examine the characteristics of those who don't answer the questions and compare them with those who do. If those who don't answer are different in important ways (for example, male vs. female, young vs. old, high income vs. low income), then the ability to generalize from the results of a survey can be affected by missing data and researchers have to point that out.

Missing values categories are only sometimes listed as response categories on survey forms. For example, a researcher might list Refuse to Answer or Don't Know as one of the response options for a question and then treat everyone who chose that option as "missing" for that variable. However, sometimes people skip over a question entirely and give no answer, or they give an answer that has nothing to do with the question. Think about how you would code these nonresponses. Box 3.3 is a list of the guidelines to use for assigning values to missing data.

BOX 3.3

Guidelines for Assigning Missing Values

- Use numbers that aren't already category values and cannot be category values. Generally, use no more digits for the missing value than there are digits in the category values. If your category values are all single-digit values, then use a single-digit missing value code. If your category values can take up to three digits, then use a 3-digit missing value code. For example, if you are assigning a missing value to the variable *sex*, which can be assigned the value categories 1 and 2, you can use 9 as the missing value code. However, if you are assigning a missing value to the variable *age*, use 99 or 999.

- Be as consistent as possible. The numbers 9, 99, 999, 9999, and so on, are often used as missing values because they usually (but not always) fall outside the range of all possible values for variables. In the General Social Survey, you will also see negative 1 (–1) and zero (0) used as missing values along with variations of 8 (like 8, 98, and 998). Decide in advance which response categories will be used for which kinds of missing data. The GSS uses –1 or 0 whenever a question isn't applicable to a particular respondent, 8 (or a variation) for respondents who don't know the answer to a particular question, and 9 (or a variation) for respondents who don't answer a question. We will follow these practices and use 9, 99, or 999 whenever an answer is missing (simply skipped over), and use 8, 98, or 998 for all "don't know" answers.

 Skills Practice 4   Assign missing values to each of the variables in Box 3.1. Write your missing values next to their respective variables.

At this point, you should have a name for each variable, the level of measurement for each variable, and a numbering scheme for the categories of each variable, including missing values. Compare what you have with Box 3.4. The variable labels, levels of measurement, category values, and missing values are in a different typeface. With this information in hand, we can start to create our data set in SPSS.

BOX 3.4

Survey of Ten Questions Adapted from the General Social Survey with Coding Instructions

ID NUMBER =   *ID*
                                                                                 CATEGORICAL-NOMINAL

1. What is your age as of your last birthday? _____   *AGE*
    98 Check here if you don't know or you're not sure. _____   *NUMERICAL*
                                                                                 NO ANSWER = 99

2. Are you

    1 _____ Male   *2* _____ Female   *SEX*
                                                                                 CATEGORICAL NOMINAL
                                                                                 NO ANSWER = 9

3. Are you currently

    1 _____ Married   *4* _____ Separated   *MARITAL*
    2 _____ Widowed   *5* _____ Never married   *CATEGORICAL-NOMINAL*
    3 _____ Divorced   *NO ANSWER = 9*

4. Generally speaking, do you usually think of yourself as a Republican, Democrat, Independent, or what?

    1 _____ Strong Democrat   *PARTYID*
    2 _____ Not very strong Democrat   *CATEGORICAL-NOMINAL*
    3 _____ Independent, close to Democrat   *NO ANSWER = 9*
    4 _____ Independent
    5 _____ Independent, close to Republican
    6 _____ Not very strong Republican
    7 _____ Strong Republican
    8 _____ Other party

5. People should be willing to help others who are less fortunate.

    1 _____ Strongly agree   *OTHSHELP*
    2 _____ Agree   *CATEGORICAL-ORDINAL*
    3 _____ Neither agree nor disagree   *NO ANSWER = 9*
    4 _____ Disagree
    5 _____ Strongly disagree

6. During the past twelve months how often have you done volunteer work for a charity?

    1 _____ Not at all in the past year   *VOLCHRTY*
    2 _____ Once in the past year   *CATEGORICAL-ORDINAL*
    3 _____ At least two or three times in the past year   *NO ANSWER = 9*
    4 _____ Once a month
    5 _____ Once a week
    6 _____ More than once a week   *(continued)*

Survey of Ten Questions Adapted from the General Social Survey with Coding Instructions
(continued)

7. Over the past five years have you participated in a marathon or walkathon to raise money for a cause?

1 _____ No

2 _____ Yes

PARTTHON
CATEGORICAL-ORDINAL
NO ANSWER = 9

8. People sometimes belong to different kinds of groups or associations. Have you participated in the activities of a political party, club, or association in the past twelve months?

1 _____ I do not belong to such a group

2 _____ I belong to such a group but never participate

3 _____ I have participated once or twice

4 _____ I have participated more than twice

GRPPOL
CATEGORICAL-ORDINAL
NO ANSWER = 9

9. In 2000, you remember that Gore ran for President on the Democratic ticket against Bush for the Republicans. Do you remember for sure whether you voted in that election?

1 _____ Voted

2 _____ Did not vote

3 _____ Ineligible to vote

VOTE00
CATEGORICAL-NOMINAL
NO ANSWER = 9

10. Generally speaking, would you say that most people can be trusted, or that you can't be too careful in life?

1 _____ Can't be too careful

2 _____ It depends

3 _____ Most people can be trusted

TRUST
CATEGORICAL-ORDINAL
NO ANSWER = 9

USING SPSS

Setting Up (Defining) Data in the SPSS Program

Defining and Naming Variables

The first step for setting up data in SPSS is telling the program about the variables. The process, called defining variables, has six steps:

Step 1. Name each variable.

Step 2. Specify variable type, column width, and decimals.

Step 3. Assign labels to each variable.

Step 4. Create values and value labels for each category of a variable.

Step 5. Designate missing values.

Step 6. Format the columns for each variable.

Step 7. Identify the level of measurement of each variable.

All seven steps are completed in one window, the Variable View window. As you go through the process, have your survey with the variable names, levels of measurement, and category and missing value codes (Box 3.4) in front of you.

Start by opening the SPSS program and moving to the SPSS Data Editor screen. (Use the SPSS Guide in Chapter 1, "Opening the SPSS Program," if you need help.) The Data Editor is ready to receive data, but before it can make sense of any numbers you might give it, you have to tell it something about the data. Use the SPSS Guide, "Defining Variables in SPSS," to open the Variable View window and begin the process of naming your variables.

SPSS GUIDE: DEFINING VARIABLES IN SPSS

To start, put your cursor on the Variable View tab in the bottom left-hand corner of your screen and click to display the Variable View window. Everything you need to do to define your variables is in this window.

Step 1: Name the variable

Type in the name of your first variable, *age* (directly from your answer to Skills Practice 1), in the cell under Name. As you begin to type, the default variable name, VAR0001, will be replaced by your new variable name. When you're done, use the tab key, the enter key, or the right cursor key to move to the next cell, the one labeled Type.

Step 2: Define variable type, column width, and decimals

This feature tells SPSS about the format of the variables.

The choice Numeric appears in the Type cell, which means that Numeric is the **default position** or default setting—the choice that SPSS will make in the absence of any other directions or instructions from you. The default positions can usually be changed and often have to be changed. You can see more options if you put your cursor on the box with the three dots on it and click. The Define Variable Type window will open.

Even though you will see a lot of options here, there are really only two choices. SPSS variables are formatted as numeric variables (or some variation thereof) or string variables. In SPSS, **numeric variables** are any variables that will be entered as numbers. **String variables** are any variables that will be entered as letters, like someone's name or initials. It is important to note that in SPSS numeric variables are not the same as numerical- (or scale-) level variables. All of the variables we are working with are numeric variables, but only some are numerical (scale). Most of the choices you see—such as Comma, Dot, Scientific Notation, and so on—are options for formatting numeric variables. For example, if you want commas to appear in your numbers, you can select the Comma option, and if you want dollar signs to appear, use the Dollar option.

① Select one of the Variable Type choices by clicking on the circle next to it. If you forget what the options mean, remember that a very helpful feature of SPSS allows you to place your cursor on almost any of the choices you see on the screen and click your right-most click key to make a brief explanation of the choice appear. Try it: Put your cursor on the choice Numeric and right-click. A box will open:

> A variable whose values are numbers. Values are displayed in standard numeric format, using the decimal delimiter specified in the Regional Setting control panel. The Data Editor accepts numeric values in standard format; or in scientific notation.

To close the box, click again with the left click key.

② Check the variable Width. To change the width, put your cursor in the box next to Width, click, and type in the desired width. The default setting is 8. This means that you can enter up to 8 digits (or characters) for the variable.

3 Check Decimal Places. Unless the data contain decimals, change the decimal place setting to zero. Put your cursor in the box next to Decimal Places, click, and type in 0. The default position is 2 decimals, but usually we don't need any. Your Define Variable Type window should look like the one below.

4 Click on OK to close the Variable Type window. In Variable View, use your tab key or right cursor key to move to the cell under Label.

Step 3: Create variable labels

This feature allows us to assign variable and value labels to describe our variables to the SPSS program. We can give our variables labels (phrases that explain what each variable means), and we can tell SPSS what each of the values and value labels (categories) of the variable will be. Begin by entering a longer description of the variable in the Label cell. The **variable label** is a descriptive phrase, usually only a few words long, that captures the essence of what the variable is about. There is no right or wrong answer for making up variable labels—use whatever will help you make sense of your data. Variable labels can have up to 20 characters (although SPSS will not always display labels that long), and you can use spaces, numbers, or other symbols in your label. When we create variable labels in SPSS, we will follow the practice of capitalizing the first word of our variable labels and then using lowercase letters for the rest of the label. The reason we are doing this is so that the labels will appear distinct from the variable names. SPSS capitalizes variable names, so we will make our labels mostly lowercase. For the variable *age,* let's type in "Respondent's age" in the Label cell to see how this works.

Now use your Tab key or your right cursor key to move over to the cell under the column headed Value.

Step 4: Create values and value labels for each variable

For each categorical variable in our set of data we have to specify the values and create **value labels**. For each numerical variable, we have to at least specify the values and the labels for those categories that we are going to treat as missing data. To create the values and value labels for a variable, click on the cell under the Values heading and then click on the box with the three dots in it to open the Value Labels window. We are ready to begin entering our values and value labels.

The values and value labels come directly from your survey form. Because the variable *age* is numerical, there are only two categories: one for "don't know" and one for those who didn't answer the question. Both are missing values categories. (When you are working with categorical variables, nominal or ordinal, there will be more values and value labels to enter.)

1. Click on the box next to Value and type in the first value, 98, for the category Don't Know.

2. Hit the tab key to move to the Value Label box and type in the category label, Don't Know, that goes with the value.

3. Click on Add (or use the Alt-A keys) to create your first value and value label.

Your Value Labels window should look like this:

Value Labels [?][X]

┌─ Value Labels ──────────────────────────┐   ┌──────┐
│ Value: [   ]   │   │ OK │
│ Value Label: [   ] │   └──────┘
│   │   ┌──────┐
│ [Add]   ┌─────────────────────────────┐ │   │Cancel│
│   │ 98 = "Don't Know"   │ │   └──────┘
│ [Change] │   │ │   ┌──────┐
│   │   │ │   │ Help │
│ [Remove] │   │ │   └──────┘
│   └─────────────────────────────┘ │
└───┘

Repeat Steps 1 through 3 for the next category of the variable *age*—No Answer. Add the value, 99, and value label, No Answer. Then, click on Add. The Define Labels window should now look like this:

Value Labels [?][X]

┌─ Value Labels ──────────────────────────┐   ┌──────┐
│ Value: [   ]   │   │ OK │
│ Value Label: [   ] │   └──────┘
│   │   ┌──────┐
│ [Add]   ┌─────────────────────────────┐ │   │Cancel│
│   │ 98 = "Don't Know"   │ │   └──────┘
│ [Change] │ 99 = "No Answer"   │ │   ┌──────┐
│   │   │ │   │ Help │
│ [Remove] │   │ │   └──────┘
│   └─────────────────────────────┘ │
└───┘

Review your values and labels and correct any mistakes. If you find an error, click on the value and its label in the window to highlight it. Click on Remove to delete the incorrect value and value label. Type in your corrected value and label, using the Value and Value Label boxes. Then click on Add. When you are satisfied with your values and labels, click on OK. You will go back to the Variable View window. Use your tab or right arrow key to move to the cell under Missing.

Step 5: Define missing values

The missing values feature allows us to tell SPSS which values are to be disregarded as meaningful values of a variable. Values designated as missing are not included in the statistical calculations that SPSS runs. Click on the cell under the heading Missing. Then click on the box with the three dots in it to open the Missing Values window. You will see three options for specifying missing values.

Untitled - SPSS Data Editor

File   Edit   View   Data   Transform   Analyze   Graphs   Utilities   Window   Help

	Name	Type	Width	Decimals	Label	Values	Missing	C
1	age	Numeric	8	0	Respondent's age	{98, Don't Kno	None ...	8
2								
3								
4								
5								
6								
7								
8								
9								
10								
11								
12								

Missing Values [?] [X]

- ● No missing values
- ○ Discrete missing values
  [ ] [ ] [ ]
- ○ Range plus one optional discrete missing value
  Low: [ ]   High: [ ]
  Discrete value: [ ]

OK
Cancel
Help

The default setting is No missing values. However, the variable *age* has the missing values of 98 and 99, so we have to pick another option. In most cases, the Discrete missing values option allows us enough room to list each of our missing values.

Missing Values [?] [X]

- ○ No missing values
- ① ● Discrete missing values
  ② [98] ③ [99] [ ]
- ④ OK
- Cancel
- Help

We follow these steps to define our missing values:

① Click on Discrete missing values.

② Type the first missing value, 98, in the first box.

③ Tab over to the second box and type in the second missing value, 99.

④ When you're finished, click on OK to return to the Variable View window. At the Variable View window, use your tab key or right cursor key to move to the cell under Columns.

Step 6: Define column format alignment

With the column format feature we can tell the SPSS program how we want each column to look. Usually, the column format is set automatically, depending on the type of variable we have (numeric or string) and the width we specified under Type. Sometimes we need to correct one or more of the column format settings.

Generally, the default settings will be acceptable. However, if you changed the variable width in the Type box, make sure the change also appears in the Column Width box. For numeric variables, the values will be right-justified (aligned with the right margin of each column in which they're displayed) when you type them in; for string variables, the words you type in will be left-justified (aligned with the left margin). There is usually no need to change this setting, but if you should need to change it all you have to do is place your cursor on the cell under Width and enter a different number—just start typing the new number. If you make a mistake, use the backspace key. You can also use the arrow keys on the right-hand side of the cell to increase or decrease the column width.

Now let's have a look at column alignment. Use your tab key or right cursor key to move to the cell under the heading Align and click on it.

Just click on the arrow on the right-hand side of the cell. You will see some choices for aligning the numbers or text in a cell at the left, right, or center. Just place your cursor on the choice you want to make and click.

Use your tab key or right cursor key to move to the cell under Measure.

Step 7: Specify level of measurement

SPSS allows us to tell the program at what level each of our variables is being measured. Click on the cell under the heading Measure. Then click on the arrow key in the right-hand side of the cell. Choose the Measurement level from the list of options. The Scale (numerical) level is the default value. The variable *age* is numerical, so we don't need to change the level of measurement.

We are finished defining our first variable, *age*. Go back to Data View by clicking on the tab in the lower left-hand corner of your screen. The name of your variable appears in the Data Editor window.

To check the variable and its definition, click on the Variable (blue question mark) icon on the toolbar. You will have only one variable on your list at this point.

Variables

Variable Information:

age
Label: Respondent's age
Type: F8
Missing Values: 98, 99
Measurement Level: Scale

Value Labels:
98 Don't Know
99 No Answer

Go To   Close   Help

Make sure everything is OK. After checking your variable, click on Close. If you need to correct errors, return to the Variable View window by clicking on the tab in the bottom left-hand corner of your screen.

At this point, you now have one variable set up and ready to receive data. You could enter the ages of each of the respondents to your survey. However, researchers usually don't begin entering data until all of their variables are set up, so let's finish defining our variables. We will try another example, this time with a categorical variable, *sex*.

Another Example: Categorical Variables

Let's run through one more example, using the second variable in our survey (Box 3.4), *sex*. Look at how you numbered the categories of the variable, assigned missing values, and specified the level of measurement. Start by opening the Variable View window by clicking on the Variable View tab in the bottom left-hand corner of your screen.

Step 1. Name the variable

In the second cell under Name, enter a variable name: *sex*. Then move to the second cell under Type.

Untitled - SPSS Data Editor

File   Edit   View   Data   Transform   Analyze   Graphs

	Name	Type	Width	D
1	age	Numeric	8	0
2	sex			
3				

Variable Type

- ( ) Numeric
- ( ) Comma
- ( ) Dot
- ( ) Scientific notation
- ( ) Date
- ( ) Dollar
- ( ) Custom currency
- ( ) String

Width: 8
Decimal Places: 0

[OK] [Cancel] [Help]

Step 2. Define variable type

The default settings, Numeric and Width, are correct and don't need to be changed. The values of this variable have no decimal places, so set Decimal Places to zero (delete the 2 and replace it with a 0). Click on OK.

Value Labels

Value Labels
Value:
Value Label:

[Add] [Change] [Remove]

```
1 = "Male"
2 = "Female"
9 = "No Answer"
```

[OK] [Cancel] [Help]

Step 3. Create variable labels

Type your variable label, Respondent's Sex, in the second cell under Label. Then tab over to the second cell under Values.

Step 4. Create values and value labels

Enter the values and value labels for each category of the variable, *sex*. Type in a value, then hit the tab key. Type in the value label that corresponds to the value. Click on Add. Don't forget to enter a value for the Missing Values category. Click on OK when you're done. Tab over to the second cell under Missing.

Missing Values

- ( ) No missing values
- (•) Discrete missing values

  [9] [ ] [ ]

- ( ) Range plus one optional discrete missing value

  Low: [ ]   High: [ ]

  Discrete value: [ ]

[OK] [Cancel] [Help]

Step 5. Define missing values

Open the Missing Values window. Specify the discrete missing value, 9, for the variable *sex*. Then click on OK.

Step 6. Define column format and set alignment

Tab over to the cells under Columns and Align. As is usually the case, the default settings are fine. Tab over to Measure.

Step 7. Specify level of measurement

Click on the appropriate level of measurement. The variable *sex* is nominal.

Columns	Align	Measure
8	Right	Scale
8	Right	Nominal ▼

USING SPSS

To conclude the process, return to the Data View window. The variable *sex* will now appear in your SPSS Data Editor, and you can check it using the Variables icon.

Variables ⊠

Variable Information:

age
grppol
id
marital
othshelp
partthon
partyid
sex
trust
volchrty
vote00

sex
Label: Respondent's sex
Type: F8
Missing Values: 9
Measurement Level: Nominal

Value Labels:
1 Male
2 Female
9 No Answer

Go To   Close   Help

Skills Practice 5   Define the rest of the variables in Box 3.4. Check your work using the Variables icon (the one with the blue question mark). Compare what you have with the answers at the end of the chapter. If you need to fix anything, just double-click on the variable name in the Data Editor window to return to the Define Variable window.

Adding the ID Variable

To complete the process of setting up your data file, let's add the respondent identification variable. You will treat this just like the addition of any other variable to your file. But if you want to put the identification variable at the beginning of the file, as I do, you will have to make room for it. So you will have to insert a new variable. To do so, follow these directions for inserting a new variable into an SPSS data set.

SPSS GUIDE: INSERTING A VARIABLE

Return to the Variable View window, then put your cursor on the cell with number 1 in it (the cell to the left of your variable name, *age*) and click. You will notice that the entire row becomes highlighted in black. Now click on the Insert Variable icon on the toolbar (the one that looks like a grid with a little red heart on the top of it).

Untitled - SPSS Data Editor

File   Edit   View   Data   Transform   Analyze   Graphs   Utilities   Window   Help

	Name	Type	Width	De	Label	Values	N
1	age	Numeric	8	0	Respondent's age	{98, Don't Kno	98, 9
2	sex	Numeric	8	0	Respondent's sex	{1, Male}...	9
3							

(Insert Variable)

You will notice that a new row appears across the top of your file, as you see illustrated below.

Untitled - SPSS Data Editor

File   Edit   View   Data   Transform   Analyze   Graphs   Utilities   Window   Help

	Name	Type	Width	Decimals	Label	Values
1	var00001	Numeric	8	2		None
2	age	Numeric	8	0	Respondent's age	{98, Don't Kn
3	sex	Numeric	8	0	Respondent's sex	{1, Male}...

You have successfully inserted a new variable, but you will have to define it. Just put your cursor in the first cell (the one under the heading Name) and start defining the identification variable. Type in the variable name, *id*. (Don't worry—as you type, the black highlighting will disappear.) Then move across the row and specify the variable type (numeric with no decimal places) and label the variable (let's call it Respondent's id). Identification variables have no values or value labels, not even missing values (because every survey that we use is going to receive an identification number). Finally, specify its level of measurement (nominal, just like a social security number or a student identification number).

Entering and Checking Data

Now we are ready to enter the data. As a practical matter, data are usually entered directly from the survey forms that respondents (or interviewers) fill out. Sometimes data are entered directly into computer programs as people answer. However, to save space and simplify the process of data entry, we will be working with data that a researcher has already transferred from survey forms onto a **code sheet** (Table 3.1). A code sheet lists each of the variables across the top (the columns of the sheet) and each of the responses in the rows. For example, Table 3.1 tells us the first respondent said that she is 48 years old, female (2), married (1), is an Independent, close to Democrat (3), and so on.

Setting your data up on a code sheet eases the transfer from paper to computer, because it matches the format of the SPSS Data Editor. You should note that the Data View window lists the variables across the top of the screen (in columns), and it assumes that the responses of each of your cases (the elements

TABLE 3.1   Code Sheet for Responses to Survey Questions in Box 3.1

ID	AGE	SEX	MARITAL	PARTYID	OTHSHELP	VOLCHRTY	PARTTHON	GRPPOL	VOTE00	TRUST
1	48	2	1	3	2	1	9	1	2	1
2	82	1	1	5	9	9	1	9	1	9
3	62	1	4	5	2	1	9	3	1	3
4	71	2	1	4	2	4	9	1	1	9
5	21	1	5	5	1	2	9	4	2	9
6	58	2	3	1	3	1	9	1	2	9
7	33	2	5	9	2	2	9	1	1	1
8	70	2	2	9	3	1	9	9	1	9
9	72	1	2	3	2	5	9	9	1	2
10	39	2	5	1	1	1	9	1	1	9
11	60	2	2	3	1	1	9	1	2	1
12	31	2	5	3	2	3	9	1	2	2
13	36	2	5	5	2	1	9	1	2	1
14	55	1	3	6	9	9	1	9	1	9
15	63	2	2	9	9	9	1	9	1	9
16	53	1	2	5	1	1	9	4	2	3
17	46	2	3	3	9	9	1	9	1	9
18	46	1	5	1	9	9	2	9	2	9
19	47	2	3	5	9	9	1	9	2	9
20	37	2	3	1	1	1	9	1	1	9

of your sample) will be listed across the rows. To enter data, begin with the first respondent and the first variable on the code sheet (Table 3.1).

SPSS GUIDE: ENTERING DATA

To begin, place your cursor in the first cell of the first variable in the Data View window and click. The cell is highlighted with a black border.

Type in the value of the first respondent to the first variable, *id*—1. The value won't appear in the cell as you type it; it shows up in a box at the top of the screen instead. To make the value appear in the cell, do one of the following:

press the Tab key,

press the right cursor key on the keyboard (the cursor key pointing to the right), or

simply click on the first cell under the next variable, *age.*

Then your screen will look like this:

	id	age	sex	marital	partyid
1	1	.	.	.	.
2					

Continue across the row entering the data for the first respondent. The first several variables will look like these:

	id	age	sex	marital	partyid	othshelp	volchrty
1	1	48	2	1	3	2	1

 Skills Practice 6 Finish entering the data in Table 3.1 in the Data Editor window. *Check your work* against Table 3.1 to make sure all of the data have been entered correctly. If you make a mistake, put your cursor on the cell that contains the error, then replace the wrong value with the correct one. Press the Tab key to enter the correction.

Checking your data is an important part of the process of setting up a data file. You should always verify that the data you entered matches their original source. One way to do that is to check the numbers on the screen against the data source (a survey form or code sheet, for example). Another way to do it is to create a list of the cases with the values entered for each variable. The Statistics ➡ Summary ➡ Case Summaries command path in SPSS allows you to do that. For more information on this procedure, see "Using Case Summaries to Check Data" in Appendix F.

Saving Your Data

Once you are satisfied that your data are just as you want, you can save your data as an SPSS data file. (Actually, you can save your file any time you want to save your work, whether you have finished checking your data or not.) I will assume you will be saving your work on a floppy disk.

SPSS GUIDE: SAVING AN SPSS DATA FILE

With your Data Editor window open, click on the Save File icon (the diskette) on the toolbar.

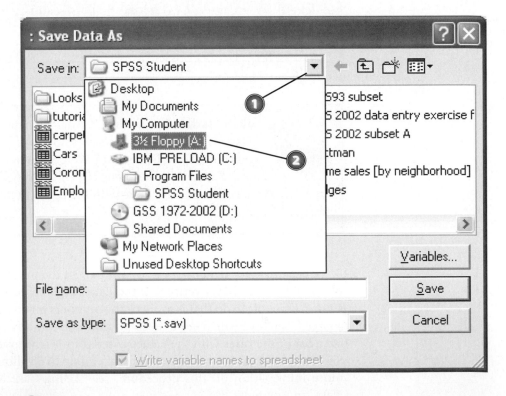

The Save Data As window opens. Next,

1 Click on the down arrow in the box next to Save In.

2 Click on 3½ Floppy [A]:

3 Type in a file name next to the File Name box. You can name a file anything you want, but be sure it's a name that will remind you of what's in the file. Let's use "civic engagement survey" so everyone who is doing this exercise will use the same file name.

4 Click on Save.

: Save Data As

Save in: 3½ Floppy (A:)

Keeping 11 of 11 variables.

File name: civic engagement survey

Save as type: SPSS (*.sav)

Variables...

Save

Cancel

☑ Write variable names to spreadsheet

If you want to be sure you have saved your file, click on the Open File icon.

Untitled - SPSS Data Editor

File   Edit   View   Data   Transform   Analyze   Graphs   Utilities   Window   Help

You should now see a list of all files on your 3½-inch disk, including the file you just created.

Open File

Look in: 3½ Floppy (A:)

civic engagement survey

File name:

Files of type: SPSS (*.sav)

Open

Cancel

Close this window by clicking on the X in the upper right-hand corner of the Open File screen.

SUMMARY

In this chapter you learned how to set up a data file in SPSS. The process assumes that you are entering data from a survey instrument. The first step is to prepare your survey form by defining each of the variables on it and adding an identification variable. This step involves naming each variable, classifying its level of measurement, coding the response categories of the variable (if the variable is a categorical one), deciding how to code missing values, and creating an identification code.

The second step is to set up the variables in the SPSS program by using the Variable View window. The Variable View window is where you can type in a variable name, a variable label, values and value labels, and missing values. You can specify the column format for the variable and its level of measurement.

The third step involves entering your data. Often data are entered directly from the survey forms as they are completed. Sometimes, data are coded for entry (as in Table 3.1).

The fourth step, checking your data, is an extremely important part of the process. Unless you can be confident that you have entered your data accurately, you cannot be confident in the results you obtain.

The fifth step is to save your data file. This step is one of the easiest, involving nothing more than using the Save File As command and naming your data file.

In the next chapter we will begin the process of analyzing data. You will use the GSS 2002 subset A file to produce frequency distributions and describe the respondents to the General Social Survey for 2002.

KEY CONCEPTS

Variable name
Variable category
Category (variable) value
Missing values

Code sheet
Default position
Numeric variable
String variable

Variable label
Value label

ANSWERS TO SKILLS PRACTICES

1. Notice that the variable names are either identical or similar to the ones used in the General Social Survey.

1	*age*	6	*volchrty*
2	*sex*	7	*partthon*
3	*marital*	8	*grppol*
4	*partyid*	9	*vote00*
5	*othshelp*	10	*trust*

2. Type of variable and levels of measurement are as follows:
   1: numerical (scale)
   2 through 4 and 9: categorical and nominal
   5 through 8 and 10: categorical and ordinal

3. Category values for the variables are as follows:

   marital

1	married	4	separated
2	widowed	5	never married
3	divorced		

   partyid

   1   Strong Democrat
   2   Not very strong Democrat
   3   Independent, close to Democrat
   4   Independent
   5   Independent, close to Republican

6   Not very strong Republican
7   Strong Republican
8   Other party

othshelp

1   Strongly agree
2   Agree
3   Neither agree nor disagree
4   Disagree
5   Strongly disagree

volchrty

1   Not at all in the past year
2   Once in the past year
3   At least 2 or 3 times in the past year
4   Once a month
5   Once a week
6   More than once a week

partthon

1   No   2   Yes

crgrppol

1   I do not belong to such a group
2   I belong to such a group but never participate
3   I have participated once or twice
4   I have participated more than twice

vote00

1   Voted
2   Did not vote
3   Ineligible to vote

trust

1   Can't be too careful
2   It depends
3   Most people can be trusted

4. Missing values are as follows:

age

98   Don't know
99   No answer

sex, marital, partyid, othshelp, volchrty, part-thon, grppol, vote00, trust

all have missing values of 9

5. Check each of your new variables using the Variables icon. They should look like these:

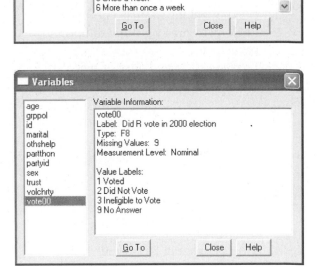

For some variables, like *partyid* and *volchrty*, you need to use the scroll bar on the right-hand side of the Variables window to see all of the categories of the variables. Below, you see only the first six categories of the *partyid* variable (and you will only see the first six categories of the *volchrty* variable), but this should be enough to see whether you are on the right track.

GENERAL EXERCISES

1. Use the variables from the levels of measurement exercise in General Exercise 1 in Chapter 2 to name each variable, specify its level of measurement, and decide on a coding scheme for each variable (including a code for missing data). Be sure to add a variable for an identification code for each respondent.

2. Using the survey you found for General Exercise 5 in Chapter 2, name each variable in the survey and decide on a coding scheme for each variable (including a code for missing data). You should have already specified its level of measurement. Be sure to add a variable to identify each respondent.

SPSS EXERCISES

1. Set up a new SPSS data file in the SPSS Data Editor for the survey you coded in General Exercise 1. Use the Variable View window to name and label each variable and specify variable type, labels, missing values, column format (if necessary), and level of measurement; then save your new data file to your A: drive with the file name "SPSS Exercise Chapter 3."

2. Set up a new SPSS data file in the SPSS Data Editor for the survey you coded in General Exercise 2. Use the Variable View window to name each variable and specify variable type, labels, missing values, column format (if necessary), and level of measurement; then save your new data file to your A: drive.

CHAPTER 4

Analyzing Frequency Distributions

INTRODUCTION

In the "News to Use" section of Chapter 2 I introduced you to a survey designed to examine the political and civic engagement of 15-to-25-year-olds in the aftermath of the events of September 11, 2001. The survey was done under the auspices of the Center for Information and Research in Civic Learning and Engagement (CIRCLE), along with other organizations. Among the findings that you read about in the "News to Use" excerpt were these.

- "Seventy percent of young adults say the war on terrorism makes them at least somewhat more likely to participate in politics and voting."
- "More than half of all young adults (56%) say they would be at least somewhat likely to consider working for a community service organization."
- "In this study, 66% of 18-to-24-year-olds claim to be registered to vote."[1]

What are researchers looking at to come up with these conclusions? The answer is *frequency distributions*. To understand how young people may have responded to the war on terrorism that followed the attacks on the United States of September 11, 2001, researchers conducted telephone surveys and asked young adults to respond to a number of questions. One question was, "Please tell me if the [war on terrorism has] made you more or less likely to participate in pol-

---

[1] Lake Snell Perry & Associates and the Tarrance Group, Inc., "Short-Term Impacts, Long-Term Opportunities: The Political and Civic Engagement of Young Adults in America," March 2002, <http://civicyouth.org/research/products/National_Youth_Survey_outside.htm>, pp. 4–5.

itics and voting." Those who answered more likely or less likely were then asked, "Is that much [more], somewhat more, or less likely?" The answers were recorded (including "it makes no difference" and "don't know"). Then the answers of the respondents were analyzed using frequency distributions like the ones in Table 4.1 on page 85. Take a look at those now.

Similarly, Harvard University did a survey of 1,200 undergraduates in 2003 to assess their level of involvement in volunteer work and political activities. They, too, conducted telephone surveys and recorded the answers of those who responded. The "News to Use" item in this chapter is a summary of what the Harvard University researchers found out. Many of the conclusions you see in the article were arrived at using frequency distributions like the ones in Table 4.2 (see page 86).

As you go through this chapter you will be learning to do what the CIRCLE and Harvard University researchers did—use frequency distributions, very simple yet very powerful tools, to describe respondents to a survey. With frequency distributions, you will be analyzing variables one at a time. This type of analysis is called **univariate** (uni = one; variate = variable) analysis. Let's begin by looking at the characteristics of frequency distributions. ∎

 # N E W S *to* U S E
Statistics in the "Real" World

Campus Kids: The New Swing Voter[2]

JOHN DELLA VOLPE

Working with members of Harvard University's Institute of Politics, Schneiders, Della Volpe, and Schulman conducted 1,201 telephone interviews with college undergraduates from April 22 to April 30, 2003. The objectives of the survey were to track the attitudes of college undergraduates related to politics and public service from earlier [Institute of Politics] studies, and to measure opinions of college undergraduates regarding:

- The 2004 presidential election, their political beliefs and ideology;
- Current events, the War in Iraq and other issues; and

[2] Report for the Harvard University, John F. Kennedy School of Government, Institute of Politics. 21 May 2003. <http://www.iop.harvard.edu/IOP_Executive_Summary_Spr03.pdf>.

- Media habits, sources of news and information.

The margin of sampling error for this survey is ± 2.8% at the 95% confidence level, but is higher for subgroups.

KEY FINDINGS

It is our belief that that this survey breaks significant new ground on a number of fronts and should mark the beginning of a new dialogue between political figures and college students. Specifically, there are five key findings of particular note in the short-term:

1. **Campus Kids, the Political Offspring of "Soccer Moms" and "Office Park Dads," Could be Key Swing Group of 2004**
   From "soccer moms" to "office park dads," each election year a new demographic

group of voters is anointed "kingmaker" by the political media and pundits.

By virtue of three (which we believe are false) assumptions: (1) they don't vote, (2) they're not engaged, and (3) they're all Democrats—college students have always been left out of this equation. Our recent survey indicates that "Campus Kids," the political offspring of "soccer moms" and "office park dads," could be—and should be—one of this election cycle's key voting groups.

False Assumption 1: They Don't Vote— While only 32% of all 18 to 24 year olds voted in the 2000 election for President—our survey indicates that among 18 to 24 year olds who are enrolled in college—close to 3 in 5 (59%) report that they will "definitely be voting" in the 2004 general election for president. An additional 27% report that they "probably will vote," with the rest indicating that their chances of voting are 50-50, or that they would not be voting.

With close to 9.5 million 18 to 24 year olds enrolled in a college or university—the impact students could have on the popular vote nationally and in key states is significant if properly targeted and mobilized by one of the presidential campaigns.

False Assumption 2: They're Not Engaged— Over the course of the last three years of conducting surveys among college undergraduates, it has become clear that college students care about their communities, and since 9/11 and the War in Iraq are becoming more engaged in the political process.

In our Fall 2002, survey students' commitment to community service remained strong (61% volunteered for community service in last year), while the percentage of those who think politics is relevant to their lives has increased, as has the number of students who participated in a political rally or demonstration (from 20% in the Fall of 2002 to 35% this Spring).

Additionally, more than four out of five (85%) students report following current events—with 26% indicating that they follow current events "very closely."

False Assumption 3: They're All Democrats— Although more college students are Democrats than Republicans—the gap between the two major parties is closing and . . . a plurality of students do not consider themselves a member of either party.

2. **Students' Votes are Up for Grabs in '04— Democrats Should Not Count on Them and Republicans Should Not Count Them Out**
While Democratic campaigns might have counted on the votes of large numbers of college students in the past and Republicans might have ignored them—it would be wise for each campaign in '04 to target messages and outreach to this constituency. The pre-election data we have collected indicates that although college students are (1) not as supportive of the President as the nation is as a whole and (2) are not certain that they would vote to re-elect him for another four years—they approve of the job he is doing and believe the country is headed in the right direction.

Taken as a whole the data indicates that college students are currently split in their preferences for president and could fall into either the Democratic or Republican column—depending on which candidate makes a greater effort to reach out to them and speak to the issues that concern them most. . . .

3. **Unlike Previous Generations, College Students Today Say They Lean to the Left on Social Issues but to the Right on Economic Policy**
Another indication that college students today define the "Swing Voter" is their desire to not be placed into any one ideological category.

Overall, 36% (26% very liberal) of students consider themselves liberal thinkers on most political issues; while nearly the same number—32% (25% very conservative)—consider themselves conservatives.

Twenty-nine percent are self-described moderates. . . . [S]tudents are slightly more conservative when it comes to economic issues and more liberal when it comes to social issues (defined by students as education, health care, affirmative action, health care, among others). . . .

4. **Hawks Outnumber Doves 2:1—College Students Supportive of War in Iraq and the New Bush Doctrine**

A likely departure from the days in which "soccer moms" and "office park dads" attended college—today there are more "hawks" on college campuses than "doves."

At the time the survey was taken, support for the War in Iraq outpaced opposition by more than 2:1. Perhaps most strikingly hard-core support (37% strongly support) outnumbered hard-core opposition (14% strongly opposed) by nearly 3:1.

Continuing the hawkish trend on campuses, 59% agree with the change in U.S.

military policy from one in which the U.S. responds to military actions by hostile countries—to one in which the U.S. initiates military action when there is a threat of hostility.

. . .

5. **"Swing Voting" Parents Most Responsible for Shaping Political Beliefs of Campus Kids; TV, Newspapers Major Source of Current Events Information**

Asked for the two things in their lives that are most responsible for shaping their political beliefs—members of their inner circle such as parents (30%), family (17%), friends (14%) and educators (18%) rank at the top of the list—with media/news (15%) following a distant second.

Similar to other Americans, college students get their current events news from traditional sources, such as television (74%) and newspapers (49%). Less than three in ten (29%) report getting information on current events online.

WHAT IS A FREQUENCY DISTRIBUTION?

When researchers first collect data, all they have is a set of **raw data** and **raw scores**—data that have not been processed and scores that have not been summarized in any way. Raw data may consist of a collection of survey forms that people have filled out or a set of questionnaires to which a researcher has gathered responses in face-to-face interviews. These survey forms or questionnaires may be sitting in a stack on the researcher's desk awaiting processing. If the researcher created an SPSS data file as the data came in, the raw data would become raw scores. Raw scores are a list of the responses of each participant in a study to each variable. If you open an SPSS file and look down the columns of each variable, you are looking at raw scores. When there are 1,500 cases, as there are in the GSS 2002 subset A file, having raw scores isn't very useful for seeing patterns in the data. Tools are needed to help sift out the general characteristics from all the specific details.

A very useful tool for seeing patterns in single variables is the frequency distribution. A **frequency distribution** is a summary of the responses to the categories of a variable. In its simplest form, it lists the frequencies of response (number of responses) to each category of a variable—but frequency distributions take many forms. Some display the percentages of response to each category of a variable in addition to (or instead of) the frequencies of response. Frequency distributions in SPSS are even more elaborate, as you will see.

The frequency distribution is such an important tool that you can scarcely pick up a newspaper or magazine without reading the results of frequency distribution analysis. Sometimes you're not even aware that what you're reading is a description of a frequency distribution.

Characteristics of a Frequency Distribution

Frequency distributions can be used for all kinds of variables, numerical and categorical, continuous and discrete. Researchers use them to summarize demographic characteristics—like age, sex, race, marital status, religion, and political identity—and they use them to analyze the attitudes and behaviors of those they study (such as their political affiliation and whether they registered to vote). The specific form a frequency distribution takes can vary. However, the examples in Tables 4.1 and 4.2 illustrate some of the essential features of a frequency distribution.

TABLE 4.1   Frequency Distributions from the Report "Short-Term Impacts, Long-Term Opportunities: The Political and Civic Engagement of Young Adults in America"

Question: Please tell me if the [war on terrorism has] made you more or less likely to participate in politics and voting. If [more likely or less likely] is that much [more likely or unlikely or] somewhat [more likely or less likely]?

	Number of Responses	Percentage
Much more likely	251	34%
Somewhat more likely	270	36
Somewhat less likely	34	5
Much less likely	26	3
Makes no difference	149	20
Don't Know	13	2

Question: Now . . . tell me how likely it is that you would consider [the] occupation [of working for a community service organization]—extremely likely, very likely, somewhat likely, a little likely, or not likely at all.

	Number of Responses	Percentage
Extremely likely	63	8%
Very likely	158	21
Somewhat likely	197	26
A little likely	130	17
Not at all likely	184	25
Don't Know	13	2

Question: Now I want to talk to you about voting. Often things come up and people are not able to register to vote. Would state or local records show that you are currently registered to vote or are you not registered to vote at this time?

	Number of Responses	Percentage
Yes	707	66%
No	326	30
Ineligible	19	2
Don't Know	27	2

TABLE 4.2 Frequency Distributions from the Report "Campus Kids: The New Swing Voter"

Question: When it comes to voting, do you consider yourself to be affiliated with the Democratic Party, the Republican Party, or are you Independent or Unaffiliated with a major party?

	Percentages
Democrat	29%
Republican	26
Independent/Unaffiliated	41
Other	1
Refused [to answer]	3

Question: When it comes to most political issues, do you think of yourself as a liberal, a conservative or a moderate? (If moderate, . . . do you lean liberal or conservative?)

	Percentages
Liberal	26%
Moderate-Liberal	10
Moderate	29
Moderate-Conservative	7
Conservative	25
Don't Know/Refused [to answer]	3

Question: Generally speaking, how closely do you follow the news and current events?

	Percentages
Very closely	26%
Somewhat closely	59
Not very closely	13
Not at all	2

- **They each describe a variable of interest:** The first variable in Table 4.1 might be labeled "participation in politics and voting," whereas the second variable in Table 4.1 might be called "working for a community service organization."
- **They list the categories of a variable:** The categories of the first variable, *participation in politics and voting,* include "much more likely," "somewhat more likely," and so on. The categories of the second variable, *working for a community service organization,* include "extremely likely," "very likely," "somewhat likely," etc.
- **They list the distribution of responses for the categories of the variable:** In Table 4.1, the response frequencies are expressed as numbers of people responding to each category of a variable and as percentages. We can see how many and what percentage of the respondents answered in each of the categories. The frequency distributions in Table 4.2 give us only percentages, but not numbers, of respondents to each category of a variable.

As we will see in the next section, SPSS frequency distributions look a little different from these illustrations. Nevertheless, they share the essential characteristics of these examples while telling us more about the distribution of responses to each of our variables.

Later on in this chapter, you will learn how to produce frequency distributions using SPSS. For now, let's look at some examples of variables in the General Social Survey that are similar to those in the CIRCLE and Harvard surveys. In Figure 4.1, you will see a frequency distribution for the variable *volchrty*, how often respondents to the General Social Survey did volunteer work for a charity in a year's time. A frequency distribution produced by SPSS includes all of the information in our examples in Tables 4.1 and 4.2 plus a lot more. Figure 4.1 explains how to interpret the SPSS frequency distribution, and a description of the most important features of the frequency distribution follows.

Values and frequencies   One of the first distinctions to make is between the values of a variable and the frequencies of response to a particular value and its category. The values and categories of a variable are listed in the first column of the frequency distribution. If we want to know the **frequency of response**—how many respondents answered with a particular value or in a particular category—we have to use the Frequency column. For the variable *volchrty*, we can see that 400 respondents (the frequency) said they did not volunteer at all (the category). The value associated with the category is 1.

Percent and Valid Percent   The Percent and Valid Percent columns are very helpful for finding patterns in data. They allow us to get a sense of where the respondents fall in relation to the categories of a variable, and they standardize the responses to a variable so that we can make comparisons between distributions

FIGURE 4.1
Understanding an SPSS frequency distribution.

SPSS lists meaningful categories of a variable separately from categories that represent missing values. The meaningful response categories—like NOT AT ALL and ONCE IN THE PAST YR—are listed first.

The number of responses to each of the categories of the variables are listed in the Frequency column.

VOLCHRTY R done volunteer work for a charity

		Frequency	Percent	Valid Percent	Cumulative Percent
Valid	1 NOT AT ALL IN PAST YR	400	26.7	54.9	54.9
	2 ONCE IN THE PAST YR	100	6.7	13.7	68.6
	3 AT LEAST 2 OR 3 TIMES IN PAST YR	109	7.3	15.0	83.5
	4 ONCE A MONTH	57	3.8	7.8	91.4
	5 ONCE A WEEK	29	1.9	4.0	95.3
	6 MORE THAN ONCE A WEEK	34	2.3	4.7	100.0
	Total	729	48.6	100.0	
Missing	0 NAP	766	51.1		
	8 DONT KNOW	3	.2		
	9 NO ANSWER	2	.1		
	Total	771	51.4		
Total		1500	100.0		

Missing values categories—like NAP, DON'T KNOW, and NO ANSWER are listed separately.

There are two separate calculations of percentage—one that uses all cases (valid and missing) in its computation of percentage, labeled Percent, and one that includes only valid cases, labeled Valid Percent.

The Cumulative Percent column is a running total of the Valid Percent column.

with different numbers of responses. We will make use of this standardizing feature a little later on as we look at how different groups of respondents respond to the same variable.

For computing **Percent**, SPSS divides the frequency of response to a particular category by the sum of all cases, valid and missing. For example, to find the Percent for the category Not at All in Past Year, divide 400 by 1,500 and multiply your answer by 100. To compute **Valid Percent**, SPSS divides the frequency of response to a particular category by the sum of valid cases only. To find Valid Percent for Not at All in Past Year, divide 400 by 729 (the total number of valid cases) and multiply the result by 100.

Cumulative Percent   The **Cumulative Percent** column uses only valid cases in its computation of cumulative percentage. It uses running total of all responses, and it is computed by adding the number of respondents to a particular category to those of all preceding categories, dividing by the number of valid cases, and multiplying by 100. For example, the cumulative percentage for the Once in the Past Year category is computed by adding the number of people who answered "Once in the Past Year" to those who answered "Not at All": 400 + 100 = 500. To get the cumulative percentage, divide 500 by the number of valid cases (729) and multiply by 100. Round to the first decimal.

Interpreting the Frequency Distribution

What does the frequency distribution for the variable *volchrty* tell us about the General Social Survey respondents? One way to answer this question is to ask yourself, "If I were to carry away one impression from the frequency distribution, what would it be?" You could also put yourself in the position of a newswriter who has to come up with a headline to describe the state of volunteerism among the GSS respondents. What would you write?

To decide how to interpret the data, start by noticing the percentage of respondents who actually answered the question related to the variable. Look down the Percent column until you get to the Total percentage for valid cases. Second, draw out the general characteristics of those who responded, using the Valid Percent and Cumulative Percent columns. For the variable *volchrty,* you could point out that

> the respondents to the 2002 GSS did little or no volunteer work for charities. Of those who responded (valid cases) to the question asking, "during the past 12 months, have you done volunteer work for a charity," the majority (54.9%) said they had not volunteered at all. Another 13.7% said they had volunteered only once. Only 16.5% volunteered at least once a month. Fifteen percent said they volunteered two or three times in the past year.

Heterogeneous and homogeneous distributions   In addition to helping us see the general patterns in data, frequency distributions help us to evaluate the **dispersion** (or distributions) of responses to a variable to determine whether these distributions are **heterogeneous** or **homogeneous**. Heterogeneous distributions are those in which the respondents are fairly evenly distributed, dispersed, or spread out across all of the categories of a variable. In perfectly heterogeneous distributions, each category of a variable has the same number (and percentage)

FIGURE 4.2
Continuum for describing extent to which frequency distributions are homogeneous or heterogeneous.

Respondents are more alike   Respondents are more dissimilar

Very homogeneous   Very heterogeneous

Somewhat homogeneous   Somewhat heterogeneous

of respondents. For example, for the variable *sex,* a perfectly heterogeneous distribution is one in which 50% of the respondents are male and 50% are female. For the variable *class*—a four-category variable in the General Social Survey—a heterogeneous distribution is one in which 25% of the respondents identify themselves as lower class, 25% as working class, 25% as middle class, and 25% as upper class. The more a distribution deviates from an even dispersion of respondents across the categories of a variable, the less heterogeneous it is.

Homogeneous distributions, on the other hand, are those in which the respondents are clustered or grouped into only a few categories of a variable. A perfectly homogeneous distribution is one in which all respondents are in a single category of a variable, as follows.

Sex	*Percentage*	*Class*	*Percentage*
Male	100	Lower	0
Female	0	Working	100
		Middle	0
		Upper	0

We rarely see perfectly heterogeneous or perfectly homogeneous distributions, so we have to describe distributions on a continuum from very heterogeneous to somewhat heterogeneous or fairly heterogeneous on one end to fairly homogeneous or somewhat homogeneous to very homogeneous on the other, depending on how far the distribution deviates from perfectly heterogeneous or homogeneous. Figure 4.2 illustrates this continuum for describing a distribution of responses to a variable.

 Avoiding Common Pitfalls: Homogeneous and heterogeneous distributions   A confusing aspect of frequency distributions is that distributions are most *hetero*geneous when the frequencies and percentages of response are *alike,* because the more alike the frequencies and percentages are, the more dissimilar the respondents are from one another. Conversely, distributions are most *homo*geneous when the frequencies and percentages of response are *dissimilar,* because the more dissimilar the frequencies and percentages of response are from one another, the more alike the respondents are in relation to one another. Compare the frequency distribution for the variable *volchrty* with the one for the variable *partyid* (in Table 4.3). Which distribution is more heterogeneous, and which one is more homogeneous?

The answer: The distribution of responses to the variable *partyid* is more heterogeneous; the distribution of responses to the variable *volchrty* is more homogeneous.

(continued)

Avoiding Common Pitfalls: Homogeneous and heterogeneous distributions (continued)

TABLE 4.3 Frequency Distribution for the GSS 2002 subset A Variable *partyid*.

PARTYID Political party affiliation

		Frequency	Percent	Valid Percent	Cumulative Percent
Valid	0 STRONG DEMOCRAT	214	14.3	14.4	14.4
	1 NOT STR DEMOCRAT	293	19.5	19.8	34.2
	2 IND,NEAR DEM	139	9.3	9.4	43.6
	3 INDEPENDENT	291	19.4	19.6	63.2
	4 IND,NEAR REP	101	6.7	6.8	70.0
	5 NOT STR REPUBLICAN	255	17.0	17.2	87.2
	6 STRONG REPUBLICAN	162	10.8	10.9	98.1
	7 OTHER PARTY	28	1.9	1.9	100.0
	Total	1483	98.9	100.0	
Missing	9 NA	17	1.1		
Total		1500	100.0		

How do we know? Notice that the response frequencies and the percentages (using Valid Percents) for the variable *volchrty* are fairly *dissimilar,* ranging from a high of 54.9% down to 4.0%. This tells us that the respondents are somewhat alike—the distribution is more homogeneous—with over half saying they haven't done any volunteer work over the preceding year. Now look at the frequency distribution for the variable *partyid* (party identification) in Table 4.3.

In this distribution, the response frequencies look more alike (hovering around 200 or 300 respondents in many categories), and the percentages (using Valid Percents) are somewhat alike, too, at around 10 to 20%. One category, Other Party, has very few respondents, with only 1.9% of those who answered the question. Even though the frequencies and the percentages are somewhat alike, what this means is that the respondents are more dissimilar from one another, or more dispersed, across the categories of the variable. They are very heterogeneously distributed across the categories of the variable *political party affiliation.*

Another common pitfall is that it is easy to confuse heterogeneity or homogeneity of a distribution across the categories of a variable with whether the categories of a variable are themselves homogeneously or heterogeneously distributed. For example, think about a demographic variable like *age.* The categories of the variable can vary widely. In the General Social Survey, the categories for the variable *age* range from 18 to 89. The categories of the variable are widely distributed. However, in other populations, the categories may not be as widely distributed. Suppose we survey students in a high school. Chances are the age categories will range from 14 to 18, give or take a couple of years. The categories of the variable *age* in a high school population are not very spread out or dispersed.

When analyzing data, it is worth noting the range of categories for a variable. However, in assessing whether the responses are homogeneously or heterogeneously distributed, look at the dispersion of responses across the categories of the variable. It is possible to have a very homogeneous distribution of responses to an age variable even when the range of ages is 18 to 89, and a very heterogeneous distribution of responses when the range of ages is only 14 to 18. In Chapter 6, you will learn some statistical techniques for assessing whether distributions of responses are homogeneous or heterogeneous.

In the next section, we will begin learning to construct a frequency distribution by hand. This is the first section of several in the text that will show you how to compute statistics with a pencil, paper, and a calculator. Learning to compute statistics manually is useful for several reasons.

- It will improve your understanding of what the statistics mean. If we know how statistics are calculated, our ability to interpret them is enhanced.
- It provides you with a set of simple techniques for organizing and making sense of data, which can be very helpful if you are working with fairly small sets of data or when you don't have immediate access to a computer for processing data.

However, even as we learn how to calculate statistics by hand, we won't be leaving the computer, SPSS, or our GSS variables behind, as you will see in the next section. We will use some of the variables in the GSS to practice the skills for building frequency distributions by hand.

CONSTRUCTING A FREQUENCY DISTRIBUTION BY HAND

Suppose a researcher has collected data from 20 respondents, asking the same kinds of questions that GSS researchers asked. Among the variables for which data have been collected is *volchrty*. Table 4.4 shows the raw scores collected from each of the respondents, which are numbered 1 through 20 to keep track of how many scores have been gathered. Let's construct a frequency distribution to analyze the data by following these steps.

TABLE 4.4   Summary of Responses to the Variable *volchrty*

Case Summaries

	Volunteer work for charity in past year
1	NOT AT ALL IN PAST YR
2	ONCE IN THE PAST YR
3	MORE THAN ONCE A WEEK
4	NOT AT ALL IN PAST YR
5	NOT AT ALL IN PAST YR
6	ONCE A MONTH
7	NOT AT ALL IN PAST YR
8	ONCE A WEEK
9	NOT AT ALL IN PAST YR
10	NOT AT ALL IN PAST YR
11	NOT AT ALL IN PAST YR
12	ONCE A WEEK
13	ONCE IN THE PAST YR
14	NOT AT ALL IN PAST YR
15	AT LEAST 2 OR 3 TIMES IN PAST YR
16	AT LEAST 2 OR 3 TIMES IN PAST YR
17	NOT AT ALL IN PAST YR
18	NOT AT ALL IN PAST YR
19	MORE THAN ONCE A WEEK
20	ONCE A MONTH
Total N	20

Step 1: Listing Each of the Categories of Response

The categories of a variable should be listed in some logical sequence. For ordinal and numerical variables, we will follow the practice of arranging the categories in order from low to high. For an ordinal variable like *volchrty*, your list of categories would look like this:

> *Volunteer work for charity in past year*
>
> Not at all in the past year
>
> Once in past year
>
> 2 or 3 times in past year
>
> Once a month
>
> Once a week
>
> More than once a week

Step 2: Counting the Responses

Count how many responses fall into each of the categories of the variable. You can either cross off each of the responses as you count them, or you might want to make a tick mark next to the categories on your frequency distribution as you count each response. Either way, the result is the frequency of response for each category of the variable. List it next to each of the categories in a column labeled Frequency. Your frequency distribution for the variable *volchrty* should now have two columns: one for the categories of the variable and one for the frequency count for each category, like the frequency distribution in Table 4.5.

Step 3: Totaling the Responses to Find *N*

Find *N*, the number of respondents we have for a particular variable. If we add up the frequencies—sum the frequency column—we can easily see how many people answered the question about the variable *volchrty*.

Expressed as a formula,

Formula 4.1: $N = \Sigma f$

where Σ means "add up (or sum) the following," and *f* stands for frequencies of the categories of a variable.

TABLE 4.5   Step 2, Counting Frequencies for Constructing a Frequency Distribution by Hand

Volunteer work for charity in past year	Frequency
Not at all in past year	10
Once in past year	2
2 or 3 times in past year	2
Once a month	2
Once a week	2
More than once a week	2

TABLE 4.6   Step 3, Finding *N*, for Constructing a Frequency Distribution by Hand

Volunteer work for charity in past year	Frequency
Not at all in past year	10
Once in past year	2
2 or 3 times in past year	2
Once a month	2
Once a week	2
More than once a week	2
	N = 20

EXAMPLE:

To find *N* for the frequency distribution for the table we are constructing, add up the frequencies using Formula 4.1 as follows:

$$N = \Sigma f = 10 + 2 + 2 + 2 + 2 + 2 = 20$$

Enter the result, *N*, in your table in the Frequency column as illustrated in Table 4.6.

CHECKING YOUR WORK

You can make sure you have included all of your scores on the frequency distribution by counting your raw scores and confirming that *N* is the same number.

Step 4: Computing the Percentages of Response

Calculate the percentage of response for each category of your variable, and then total the percentage column. A **percentage** is simply the proportion of respondents in a particular category of a variable multiplied by 100. A **proportion** is computed by dividing the frequency for a given category by the total number of respondents to a variable. The formula for a proportion is

Formula 4.2: Proportion $= \dfrac{f}{N}$

where *f* stands for the frequency for a given category, and *N* is the total number of respondents for a given variable.

To turn the proportion into a percentage, multiply the result by 100. Expressed as a formula,

Formula 4.3:   Category percentage $= \left(\dfrac{f}{N}\right) \times 100$

where *f* stands for the frequency for a given category, and *N* is the total number of respondents for a given variable.

EXAMPLE:

We can find out what percentage of respondents did not volunteer at all by doing the following calculation, using Formula 4.3.

$$\left(\frac{f}{N}\right) \times 100 = \left(\frac{10}{20}\right) \times 100 = .50 \times 100 = 50\%$$

As we compute the category percentage, we enter the result in our frequency distribution under a third column heading, Percent. See Table 4.7 for an illustration.

CHECKING YOUR WORK

You can make sure you have computed the percentages correctly by adding them up. They should total 100%. (If you round the percentages you compute to the nearest whole percent, the total percentage may add up to a little less than or a little more than 100%.)

With the percentages in place, it is easy to see that half (50%) of the respondents did not volunteer at all for a charity in a year's time. Ten percent volunteered only once in the past year, 10% volunteered at least two or three times in the past year, and so on.

Step 5: Calculating the Cumulative Frequencies

Although SPSS does not calculate cumulative frequencies in its frequency distributions, learning to do so is helpful for calculating cumulative percentages. **Cumulative frequencies** are simply the running totals of the frequency column in a frequency distribution table. You find the cumulative frequency, symbolized by *cum f,* for a given category of a variable by adding its frequency to the frequencies of all preceding categories. The cumulative frequency for the first category of a variable is the same as its frequency (because there are no categories ahead of it). For example, the cumulative frequency for the first category of the variable *volchrty,* Not at All in the Past Year, is the same as its frequency, 10. The cumulative frequency for the second category of the variable Once in the Past Year is found by adding its frequency, 2, to the frequency for the preceding cat-

TABLE 4.7 Step 4, Finding Percentages, for Constructing a Frequency Distribution by Hand

Volunteer work for charity in past year	Frequency	Percent
Not at all in past year	10	50.0
Once in past year	2	10.0
2 or 3 times in past year	2	10.0
Once a month	2	10.0
Once a week	2	10.0
More than once a week	2	10.0
	N = 20	100.0

egory Not at All in the Past Year, 10. The cumulative frequency for the category Once in the Past Year is 2 + 10 = 12.

CHECKING YOUR WORK

The cumulative frequency for the last category in a frequency distribution is always the same as N.

Have a look at Table 4.8 to see how the cumulative frequency column should look.

Step 6: Calculating the Cumulative Percentages

Calculate the cumulative percentage for each category of your variable. Cumulative percentages are running totals of the percentages for each category of a variable. They are computed most accurately by adding the frequency for a particular category to the frequencies of all preceding categories, dividing by N, and multiplying by 100.

Expressed as a formula,

Formula 4.4:   Cumulative percentage $= \left(\dfrac{\text{cum} f}{N} \right) \times 100$

where cum f is the sum of the frequency for a given category and the frequencies of all preceding categories, and N is the total number of respondents for a given variable.

EXAMPLE 1:

To find the cumulative percentage for the category Once in the Past Year, divide the cumulative frequency by N (20), and multiply the result by 100. Using Formula 4.4, our computations for the cumulative percentage of the category Once in the Past Year are as follows:

$$\left(\frac{\text{cum} f}{N} \right) \times 100 = \left(\frac{12}{20} \right) \times 100 = .60 \times 100 = 60\%$$

TABLE 4.8   Step 5, Finding Cumulative Frequences, for Constructing a Frequency Distribution by Hand

Volunteer work for charity in past year	Frequency	Percent	Cumulative Frequencies
Not at all in past year	10	50.0	10
Once in past year	2	10.0	12
2 or 3 times in past year	2	10.0	14
Once a month	2	10.0	16
Once a week	2	10.0	18
More than once a week	2	10.0	20
	N = 20	100.0	

Cumulative percentages are entered into a fourth column of the frequency distribution, Cumulative Percent.

EXAMPLE 2:

To compute the cumulative percentage for the category At Least 2 or 3 Times, you first find cum f:

$$\text{cum } f = 2 + 2 + 10 = 14$$

Then apply Formula 4.4:

$$\left(\frac{\text{cum } f}{N}\right) \times 100 = \left(\frac{14}{20}\right) \times 100 = .70 \times 100 = 70\%$$

Now finish the table by finding the cumulative percentage for the remaining categories—Once a Month, Once a Week, and More than Once a Week. Your frequency distribution should look like Table 4.9.

CHECKING YOUR WORK

For the first category, the cumulative percentage will always be the same as the percentage for that category, and the cumulative percentage for the last category will always be at or near 100%. If it isn't, then it is likely there is a mistake, so go back and check your work.

There is another pattern here. The cumulative percentage for each of the categories is the same as the percentage for that category plus the percentages for all preceding categories. Therefore, another way to get cumulative percentages is to add them up using the Percent column. For example, if you add the percentage of respondents who never volunteer to the percentage of respondents who volunteer once a year, you get 60%, the cumulative percentage for the category Once in the Past Year. This is a less accurate way of computing cumulative percentage, but you will come close to the correct answer, and it is another way to check your work.

TABLE 4.9 Step 6, Finding Cumulative Percentages, for Constructing a Frequency Distribution by Hand

Volunteer work for charity in past year	Frequency	Percent	Cumulative Frequencies	Cumulative Percentages
Not at all in past year	10	50.0	10	50
Once in past year	2	10.0	12	60
2 or 3 times in past year	2	10.0	14	70
Once a month	2	10.0	16	80
Once a week	2	10.0	18	90
More than once a week	2	10.0	20	100
	N = 20	100.0		

What does the cumulative percentage tell us? It lets us know the percentage of respondents who fall at or below a particular category. For example, we can tell that 70 percent of the respondents in our survey volunteer very little or not at all (the cumulative percentage at the category At Least 2 or 3 times in the Past Year).

Percentages and percentiles   Another way to interpret percentages and cumulative percentages is by viewing them as response percentiles. A **percentile** is simply the point at or below which a specified percentage of responses fall. You are probably somewhat familiar with this term if you have ever taken a standardized test. Your scores are usually reported along with their corresponding percentiles. If you score a 90 on a reading test, for example, you may also learn that your score was at the 93rd percentile. This means that 93% of the people who took the test scored a 90 or lower. Only 7% of the people who took the test scored higher than 90.

Using Table 4.9, we can use the Percent column to say, as we did earlier, that 50% of the respondents did not volunteer for a charity in the past year—or we can say that the response Not at All falls at the 50th percentile because it includes the first 50% of the respondents. Likewise, we can use the Cumulative Percent column to say that 70% of the respondents have volunteered a little or not at all—or we can say that the category At Least 2 or 3 times a Year falls at the 70th percentile. The category 2 or 3 Times a Year, along with the preceding categories, includes the first 70% of the responses. We will use this concept in Chapters 5 and 6 to find values or categories at specified intervals, or percentiles, of responses.

Before moving on, take a minute to review what you have learned. The steps for constructing a frequency distribution are summarized next. Use these steps as a guide for completing Skills Practice 1.

1. List the categories of the variable.
2. Count the frequencies of response for each category.
3. Add up the frequencies of response to find N.

$$N = \Sigma f$$

4. Calculate the percentages of response for each category:

$$\left(\frac{f}{N}\right) \times 100$$

5. Calculate the cumulative frequencies, cum f, for each category.
6. Calculate the cumulative percentages of response for each category:

$$\left(\frac{\text{cum } f}{N}\right) \times 100$$

Skills Practice 1   Construct a frequency distribution for the randomly selected set of raw scores in the following table gathered in response to the variable *givchrty*—has respondent given to charity in the past year. Notice that this is an ordinal-level variable. As you construct your frequency distribution, arrange the categories of the variable in order, from low to high. After you finish the frequency distribution, write a few sentences describing the respondents.

Case Summaries

	Given to charity in past year
1	ONCE A MONTH
2	AT LEAST 2 OR 3 TIMES IN PAST YR
3	ONCE A MONTH
4	NOT AT ALL IN PAST YR
5	AT LEAST 2 OR 3 TIMES IN PAST YR
6	ONCE A WEEK
7	NOT AT ALL IN PAST YR
8	NOT AT ALL IN PAST YR
9	AT LEAST 2 OR 3 TIMES IN PAST YR
10	NOT AT ALL IN PAST YR
11	AT LEAST 2 OR 3 TIMES IN PAST YR
12	ONCE IN THE PAST YR
13	ONCE A WEEK
14	AT LEAST 2 OR 3 TIMES IN PAST YR
15	ONCE A WEEK
16	AT LEAST 2 OR 3 TIMES IN PAST YR
17	ONCE IN THE PAST YR
18	AT LEAST 2 OR 3 TIMES IN PAST YR
19	ONCE A WEEK
20	MORE THAN ONCE A WEEK
Total N	20

In the next section you will be learning to produce and analyze frequency distributions for variables using SPSS.

Obtaining a Frequency Distribution

USING SPSS TO PRODUCE A FREQUENCY DISTRIBUTION

Frequency distributions are fairly easy to obtain using SPSS. We will begin by obtaining a frequency distribution for one of the variables in the General Social Survey examining the issue of civic engagement among American adults— *volchrty*. Use the "SPSS Guide: Obtaining a Frequency Distribution" to produce a frequency distribution for the variable.

SPSS GUIDE: OBTAINING A FREQUENCY DISTRIBUTION

Open the SPSS program and your GSS 2002 subset A file (see the SPSS Guides in Chapter 1, "Opening the SPSS Program" and "Opening SPSS Data Files," if you need help). Then, click on the Analyze menu item. A list of options will open in a dropdown menu.

Click on Descriptive Statistics. A second list of options appears in another dropdown menu. Click on Frequencies.

A Frequencies window opens. This window is called a **dialog box**. Each statistical procedure you use in SPSS has its own dialog box. These boxes have several features in common:

1 A source variable list of all of the variables in a file; the GSS 2002 subset A variables in this case.

2 A target variable list in which to place the variables you want to use—the box labeled Variable(s).

3 Several command buttons, which cause SPSS to run various functions.

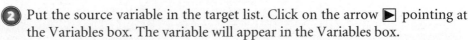

To use these features, the steps are similar from one dialog box to another.

1 Find the source variable you want. (Scroll down to the variable *volchrty*, and click). The variable will be highlighted.

2 Put the source variable in the target list. Click on the arrow ▶ pointing at the Variables box. The variable will appear in the Variables box.

If you make a mistake, click on the variable in the Variable(s) window, then click on the arrow pointing at the list of variables. Your variable moves from the Variable(s) box to the variables list.

3 Click on OK, one of the command buttons, to produce a frequency distribution for the variable *volchrty*.

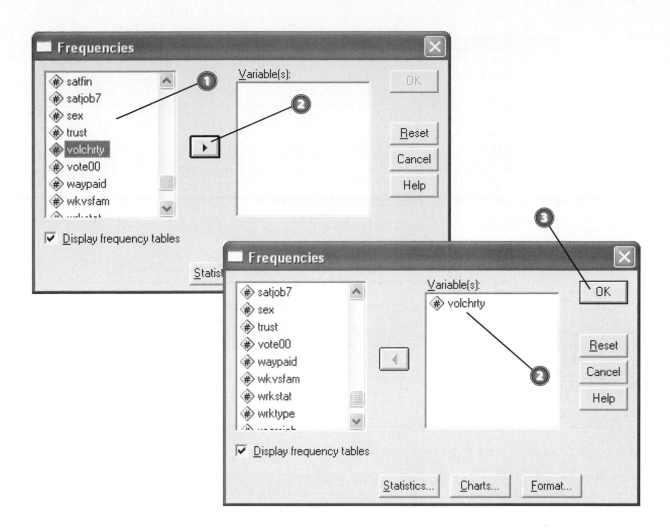

SPSS GUIDE: USING THE OUTPUT WINDOW

Your frequency distribution and a few summary statistics will appear in a separate Output window. As the frequency distribution opens, an Output - SPSS Viewer window appears. This Output window keeps track of your work during each of your SPSS sessions. All of the work you do is temporarily stored in the Output window, and you can go back to it at any time. (When you exit from the SPSS program, your session is ended. The work in your Output window is automatically deleted unless you save it to a specific output file.)

You may also see an Output outline **1**. You can hide this Output outline by putting your cursor on the bar between the outline and the rest of the screen **2**. Hold the left click key down while you move your mouse to the left to close the outline.

Several advanced features of SPSS are available in the Output window. For example, you can learn how to use the outline to move around in the Output window, and you can save output to its own file for later use. The section in Appendix F called "Using the Outline Feature in the Output Window" shows you how to use some of these features. You can switch from the Output window to the SPSS Data Editor window by pointing and clicking on the appropriate buttons at the bottom of the screen, as shown on the next page.

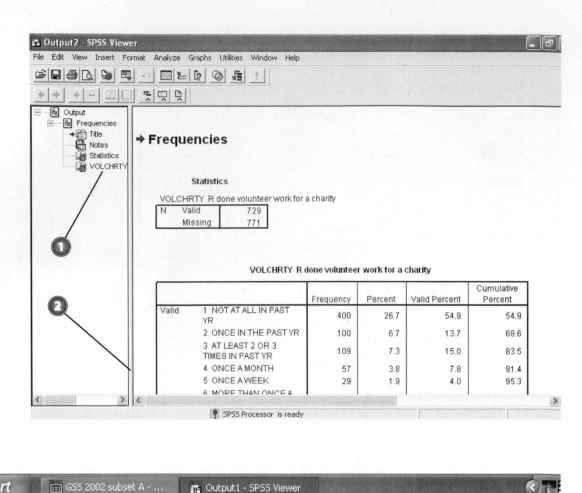

There is a button ❶ for the Data Editor (it has your file name, GSS 2002 subset A, on it), and there is a button ❷ for the Output—SPSS Viewer (it has Output on it). Try clicking on each of the buttons to see what happens.

Another way to move between screens in any Windows program is to use the Alt–Tab key combination on the keyboard. Press the Alt key and hold it down while pressing the Tab key. You will see a box open up on your screen. Continue to hold down the Alt key, and tap the Tab key until the icon for the SPSS Data Editor is highlighted. Then release the Alt and Tab keys. You will go to the Data Editor screen.

UNDERSTANDING THE SPSS OUTPUT FOR A FREQUENCY DISTRIBUTION

The output you get for the variable *volchrty* will look like Table 4.10. You learned how to read the frequency distribution in the second section of this chapter entitled, "What Is a Frequency Distribution?" However, you will notice that, in addition to the frequency distribution, SPSS also produces another small table labeled "Statistics."

TABLE 4.10   Frequency Distribution for the GSS 2002 subset A Variable *volchrty*

Statistics

VOLCHRTY R done volunteer work for a charity

N	Valid	729
	Missing	771

VOLCHRTY R done volunteer work for a charity

		Frequency	Percent	Valid Percent	Cumulative Percent
Valid	1 NOT AT ALL IN PAST YR	400	26.7	54.9	54.9
	2 ONCE IN THE PAST YR	100	6.7	13.7	68.6
	3 AT LEAST 2 OR 3 TIMES IN PAST YR	109	7.3	15.0	83.5
	4 ONCE A MONTH	57	3.8	7.8	91.4
	5 ONCE A WEEK	29	1.9	4.0	95.3
	6 MORE THAN ONCE A WEEK	34	2.3	4.7	100.0
	Total	729	48.6	100.0	
Missing	0 NAP	766	51.1		
	8 DONT KNOW	3	.2		
	9 NO ANSWER	2	.1		
	Total	771	51.4		
Total		1500	100.0		

The Statistics box—the small box at the top of Table 4.10—tells us the number of valid cases there are for a variable. **Valid cases** are the number of meaningful responses to a question. You will also see the number of **missing cases**—the number of cases for which respondents did not know the answer to a question, did not answer a question, or were not asked the question for a variable.

One of the most important pieces of information in the Statistics output is *N*. *N* represents the number of responses we have to a particular variable. *N* can be viewed several ways: as the number of all valid responses we have or as the total number of all responses, both meaningful and missing. In most of its computations, SPSS regards *N* as the number of valid cases. For the variable *volchrty*, there are 729 valid cases, or 729 people who gave a meaningful response to the variable. 771 respondents were not asked, didn't know the answer to, or did not answer the question about volunteer work done for a charity. The number of both valid and missing cases is 1,500 (the 729 valid cases plus the 771 missing, cases).

Now that you have worked with SPSS a little and you know how to open a frequency distribution, I will describe the process of opening a frequency distribution using a command path like this one: Analyze ➥ Descriptive Statistics ➥ Frequencies. Command paths are a shortcut way of reminding you how to access various SPSS functions. A single arrow pointing from one command to another means that you single click on the first command to get to the second. If you see two arrows between commands, it means that you double-click on one command to get to the next. Use this command path to open the Frequencies dialog box so that you can do the next Skills Practice.

Skills Practice 2 Use SPSS to produce and interpret frequency distributions for the following variables: *othshelp*, *givchr*, and *grppol*. When the Frequencies window opens, click on the Reset button to clear your previous work. Then select your first variable for analysis, *othshelp*.

Hints for writing your interpretations of the variables: Start out with a newspaper-style headline—how would you summarize each of the tables? Support your headline using information from the table (as we did when we analyzed the frequency distribution for the variable *volchrty*). Is the distribution of responses homogeneous or heterogeneous?

In addition to assessing the characteristics of all respondents to a survey on a particular variable, it is very useful to be able to construct frequency distributions for subgroups within a survey. For example, we might be interested in seeing if there are differences between males and females in how much they volunteer their time or give to charities. Let's see how you can separate a data file by the categories of a variable for the purpose of comparing the responses of different groups to a particular variable.

Splitting a Data File

The technique for dividing a set of data into groups according to the categories of one of its variables is called *split file*, because you are literally splitting the data file—dividing it up—by the characteristics of the respondents. For example, if you want to know how males and females compare on volunteering for charities, you can split the file by the variable *sex*. Splitting the file divides the data set into two groups: one of male respondents and one of female respondents. Use the SPSS Guide "The Split File Command" to learn the split-file procedure.

SPSS GUIDE: THE SPLIT FILE COMMAND

With the GSS 2002 subset A file open (see the SPSS Guides in Chapter 1, "Opening the SPSS Program" and "Opening SPSS Data Files," if you need help), click on Data from the menu, then click on Split File.

1 When the Split File dialog box opens, click on Compare groups.

2 Scroll down to the variable *sex*. Click on it to highlight it, and then click on the ▶ pointing at the Groups Based on box to select it.

3 Click on OK to return to the SPSS Data Editor window.

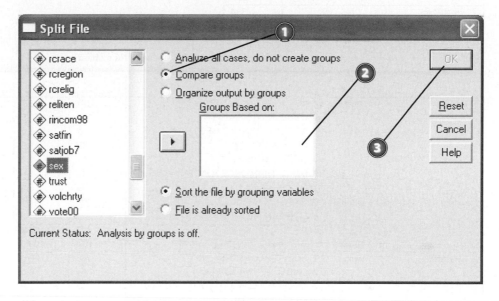

When you return to the SPSS Data Editor, notice that the Split File On message appears in the bottom right corner of the screen.

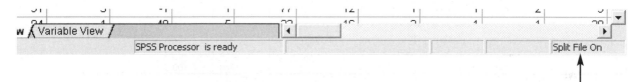

You won't see any "output" just by turning on the Split File. However, notice what happens when you run a frequency distribution. Let's use the variable *volchrty*. Click on Analyze ➥ Descriptive Statistics ➥ Frequencies to open the Frequencies window, and click on Reset to clear any previous work. Select the variable *volchrty*. (Highlight the variable, move it to the Variable(s) box by clicking on the ▶ pointing at the Variable(s) box.) Then click on OK. You will get two frequency distributions—one for male respondents, one for female respondents—like the ones in Table 4.11.

Compare the respondents. Which group—males or females—is more likely to say they have volunteered in the prior year?

To answer this question, focus on the valid percentages because they standardize the responses. Focusing on the frequencies can be misleading. Notice that in Table 4.11 there are more female respondents than male respondents to this variable.

If you pay attention to the larger number of responses to a category of a variable, you can be misled into thinking that one group is more likely than the other to have a particular characteristic simply because there are more respondents in that group as compared to the other. To standardize the responses to a variable,

TABLE 4.11 Frequency Distribution for the Variable *volchrty,* with the GSS 2002 Subset A File Split by *sex*

Statistics

VOLCHRTY R done volunteer work for a charity

1 MALE	N	Valid	345
		Missing	309
2 FEMALE	N	Valid	384
		Missing	462

VOLCHRTY R done volunteer work for a charity

SEX Respondents' sex			Frequency	Percent	Valid Percent	Cumulative Percent
1 MALE	Valid	1 NOT AT ALL IN PAST YR	214	32.7	62.0	62.0
		2 ONCE IN THE PAST YR	49	7.5	14.2	76.2
		3 AT LEAST 2 OR 3 TIMES IN PAST YR	42	6.4	12.2	88.4
		4 ONCE A MONTH	17	2.6	4.9	93.3
		5 ONCE A WEEK	11	1.7	3.2	96.5
		6 MORE THAN ONCE A WEEK	12	1.8	3.5	100.0
		Total	345	52.8	100.0	
	Missing	0 NAP	308	47.1		
		8 DONT KNOW	1	.2		
		Total	309	47.2		
	Total		654	100.0		
2 FEMALE	Valid	1 NOT AT ALL IN PAST YR	186	22.0	48.4	48.4
		2 ONCE IN THE PAST YR	51	6.0	13.3	61.7
		3 AT LEAST 2 OR 3 TIMES IN PAST YR	67	7.9	17.4	79.2
		4 ONCE A MONTH	40	4.7	10.4	89.6
		5 ONCE A WEEK	18	2.1	4.7	94.3
		6 MORE THAN ONCE A WEEK	22	2.6	5.7	100.0
		Total	384	45.4	100.0	
	Missing	0 NAP	458	54.1		
		8 DONT KNOW	2	.2		
		Total	462	54.6		
		9 NO ANSWER	2	.2		
	Total		846	100.0		

look at the percentages of response to the categories of the variable. More specifically, pay attention to the percentage of meaningful (valid) responses. When you use the valid percentages to compare male and female respondents, you should come to conclusions like these:

A larger percentage of males (76.2%) say they either did not volunteer for a charity at all or only did so once in the prior year as compared to females (61.7%). A higher percentage of females said they volunteered two or three times in the past year, once a month, once a week, and more than once a week as compared to males. Overall, females are more likely to say that they volunteered for a charity than are males.

When you are through with your analysis, turn the Split File off by going back to the SPSS Data Editor (using the GSS 2002 subset A button at the bottom of your screen). Use the command path Data ➥ Split File to return to the Split

File window. At the Split File window, click on Reset and OK, in that order. You will return to the SPSS Data Editor, but now there will be no Split File On message in the bottom right corner of the screen.

 Skills Practice 3   Split the file by the variable *sex*. Produce a frequency distribution for the variable *givchrty*, which asks about giving money to charities. (Remember to use the Reset button in the Frequencies window to clear your previous work.) Which group—males or females—is more likely to say that they give money to charity?

Let's turn our attention next to looking at data pictorially—using graphs to display frequency distributions for the purpose of analyzing our variables.

Using Charts and Graphs to Analyze Distributions

To help us analyze distributions of variables, SPSS has a number of options for producing charts and graphs that give us visual representations of frequency distributions like the one in Figure 1.1 at the beginning of this text. Take a look at some of the choices.

SPSS GUIDE: EXPLORING GRAPH OPTIONS

With your GSS 2002 subset A file open, at the SPSS Data Editor click on Graphs in the SPSS menu. A list of options appears. Click on Gallery. A screen opens illustrating the different types of graphs available.

	id	wrkstat	hrs
1	5	1	
2	9	1	
3	11	1	
4	12	1	
5	13	2	
6	20	1	
7	23	1	
8	39	1	
9	48	5	
10	52	5	
11	53	1	
12	55	1	
13	56	1	
14	66	5	

Put the cursor on one of the graphs. The cursor turns into a hand with a pointed finger. Now click. (Try the chart labeled Bar to begin with.)

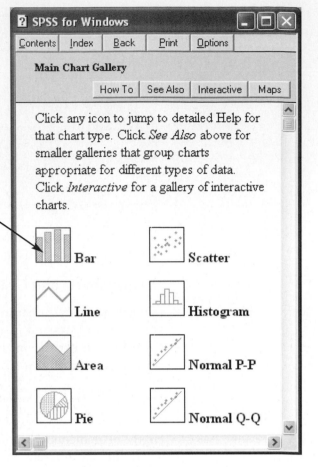

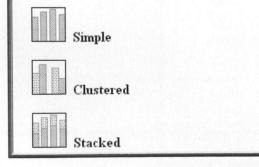

A window with a description of the graph appears. Across the top of the window are several options. Click on How To. Instructions appear for creating the graph you have selected. Look them over. Then click on the X button to exit.

Click on any icon to get detailed Help for any of the other chart types. Click on the X button when you're through.

There are many graphs to choose from, and I'm not going to cover them all, so let's narrow the field down a little by looking at a few of the most commonly used ones for displaying frequency distributions.

Bar Charts and Histograms

Use the command path Graphs ➤ Gallery. Look at the charts labeled Bar and Histogram. You will see that they look very much alike. **Bar charts** and **histograms** are bar graph-type representations of data, with the size of the bar depending on the number or percentage of respondents in a particular category of a variable. The difference between the two is that bar chart bars don't touch each other but histogram bars do. For this reason, bar charts are often used to represent discrete variables, whereas histograms are reserved for continuous variables. However, the features that SPSS includes with each of these options assume that the decision to use a bar chart or histogram will be based on the categorical–numerical distinction. In SPSS, bar charts are set up to handle categorical variables and histograms are for numerical variables. (Refer to Chapter 2 if you need to refresh your memory about levels of measurement.)

Creating a bar chart   Use the SPSS Guide "Creating a Bar Chart" with the categorical variable *volchrty* to produce a bar chart.

SPSS GUIDE: CREATING A BAR CHART

Click on the Graphs menu item. A list of options appears. Then click on Bar.

When the Bar Charts window opens, click on Define.

The Define Simple Bar: Summaries for Groups of Cases dialog box opens. For univariate analysis of frequency distributions, most of the default settings in the Bar Charts window are fine—they describe a simple bar chart with summaries for groups of cases, which means that each bar will represent all of the cases for a particular category of a given variable. There are several settings to change, though.

① Under Bars Represent, click on the radio button next to % of cases.

② Select a variable by highlighting it. Scroll down to *volchrty* and click. Move it to the Category Axis box by clicking on ▶ pointing at Category Axis. The variable appears in the Category Axis box.

③ Turn off the default settings to prevent missing values from appearing in the bar graph. Click on the Options button.

The Options window will open next.

When the Options window opens, click on the box next to Display groups defined by missing values to make the ✔ disappear.

Click on Continue.

When you return to the Define Simple Bar: Summaries for Groups of Cases dialog box, click on OK.

A graph like the one in Figure 4.3 appears in the SPSS Output window.

Interpreting a bar chart The bar chart contains information much like a frequency distribution. The variable label "R done volunteer work for a charity" is displayed across the bottom of the chart, and the categories of the variable (Not at All, Once in the Past Year, and so on) are displayed on the horizontal axis, the **x-axis**, of the graph. The valid percentages (remember we excluded missing cases from our graph) are displayed along the vertical axis, the **y-axis**, of the graph.

We interpret the bar chart in much the same way as a frequency distribution. We want to know what the general characteristics of the respondents for the variable are. In addition, charts help us answer the question "Does the distribu-

FIGURE 4.3
Bar chart for the variable *volchrty* in the GSS 2002 subset A file.

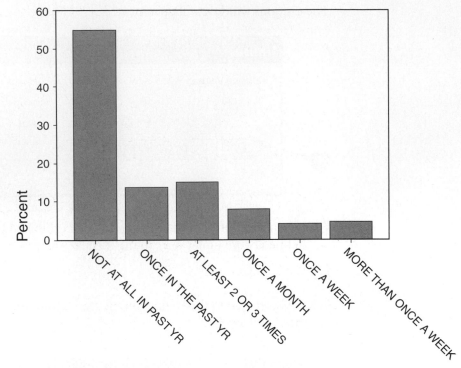

R done volunteer work for a charity

tion appear to be homogeneous or heterogeneous?" Bar charts in which the distribution of responses is more homogeneous will have large differences in the sizes of the bars, as in the bar chart for the variable *volchrty*. Bar charts in which the distribution of responses is more heterogeneous will have bars that are more equal in height. To see an example, let's look at the political party affiliations of GSS respondents using the variable *partyid*.

Skills Practice 4   Obtain a bar chart for the variable *partyid*. Use the command path Graphs ➡ Bar ➡ Define. When the Define Simple Bar: Summaries for Groups of Cases window opens, click on the Reset button to clear the window of all previous work. Then

- Select the variable *partyid*.
- Click on % of Cases.
- Click on Options.
- Turn off Display groups defined by missing values.
- Click on Continue.
- At the Define Simple Bar window, click on OK.

Does this distribution look more homogeneous or heterogeneous in comparison to the distribution of responses to the variable *volchrty*? Why do you think so?

Creating a histogram   Use the next SPSS Guide to create a histogram. Histograms assume that you are using numerical variables, so we will examine one of the demographic variables, *age,* which is numerical.

SPSS GUIDE: CREATING A HISTOGRAM

Look for the Graphs menu item—it appears at the top of the Output window. You can also return to the SPSS Data Editor to find it. (Use the GSS 2002 subset A button at the bottom of the screen to go back to the Data Editor.) When the list of options appears, click on Histogram.

At the Histogram window, scroll down to the variable *age* and click on it to highlight it. Click on the ▶pointing at the Variable box to select it; then click on OK.

FIGURE 4.4
Histogram for the variable *age* in the GSS 2002 subset A file.

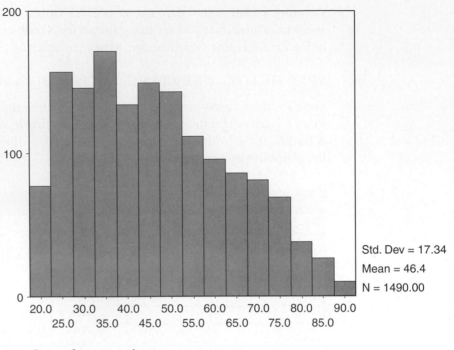

Age of respondent

A graph appears like the one in Figure 4.4.

Interpreting a histogram   Notice that, like in the bar chart, the *x*- (horizontal) axis is the variable axis, showing the categories of the variable *age*. On the *y*- (vertical) axis, you see the frequencies for the variable *age,* not the percentages. Only valid cases are counted.

SPSS automatically groups the respondents into age intervals, with each bar representing 5 years. How can you tell how many years are represented by each histogram bar? Simply subtract the midpoint of the first bar (20) from the midpoint of the second bar (25): 25 − 20 = 5. Each bar represents 5 years. Where do you find the midpoint for each bar? The midpoints are displayed along the horizontal (*x*-axis) of the histogram. The first bar shows how many respondents are in the age interval from 18 (the youngest person in the survey) to 22. SPSS displays the midpoint of the interval, age 20, under the first bar. The second bar shows how many respondents are in the interval 23 through 27. The midpoint of the interval is age 25.

Without percentages, histograms are a little more difficult to interpret. (There are some unique features of histograms that allow us to draw conclusions about distributions of numerical variables, which we will discuss in Chapter 5.) However, we can at least tell how homogeneous or heterogeneous a distribution is by looking at the relationships among the bars, just like for a bar chart. Does this distribution look more homogeneous or heterogeneous? The answer is that it is somewhat on the homogeneous side of the continuum, because most of the respondents seem to be clustered around age 40. The respondents could be characterized as mostly middle-aged or close to it.

Skills Practice 5 Obtain a histogram for the variable *educ*. Evaluate the distribution: Is it more homogeneous or heterogeneous?

Use the command path Graphs ➥ Histogram. When the Histogram window opens, click on the Reset button to clear any previous work. Then select the variable *educ* and click on OK.

Pie Charts

Pie charts are a very popular way to present data graphically. They can be used with variables measured at any level—categorical or numerical. As a practical matter, pie charts are harder to read the more categories a variable has. If a variable has many categories, you would be better off illustrating it with a bar chart or histogram. We'll use the variable *volchrty* to create a pie chart.

SPSS GUIDE: CREATING A PIE CHART

In the Output window or at the SPSS Data Editor window, click on the Graphs menu item. When the list of options appears, click on Pie.

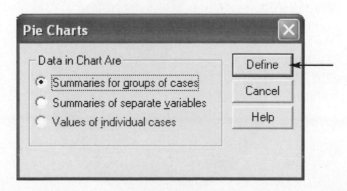

The Pie Charts window opens. There is no need to change the default setting, Summaries for Groups of Cases, in the Pie Charts window. Now click on Define.

The Define Pie: Summaries for Groups of Cases dialog box opens. It looks much like the Define Bar window and works the same way.

1 Select % of cases.

2 Select a variable (click on the variable *volchrty*, then click on the ▶ pointing at the Define Slices by box).

3 Click on Options. When the Options window opens, turn off Display groups defined by missing values. (Remove the ✔ from the box next to it.) Click on Continue. When you return to the Define Pie window, click on OK.

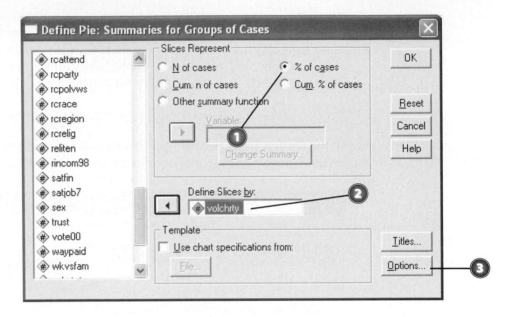

A pie chart like the one in Figure 4.5 appears in your Output window.

Interpreting a pie chart As with bar charts and histograms, we want to know the general characteristics of the respondents to the variable represented by the chart. We also want to know about the dispersion of responses across the

FIGURE 4.5
Pie chart for the variable *volchrty* in the GSS 2002 subset A file.

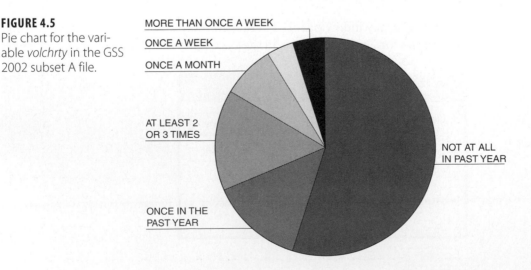

categories of the variable. Pie charts show us the distribution of meaningful responses by valid percentages (remember we excluded missing data). Unfortunately, the default settings in SPSS do not cause the percentages to be displayed. However, the sizes of the pie slices give a pretty good picture of the data. More heterogeneous distributions will have slices of roughly equal size, whereas more homogeneous distributions will have some slices that are much larger than others.

 Skills Practice 6   Produce a pie chart for the variable *givchrty*. Does it look more homogeneous or heterogeneous? Use the command path Graphs ➡ Pie ➡ Define. When the Define Pie window opens, click on the Reset button to clear your previous work. Remember to select % of cases and click on the Options button to turn off the Display groups defined by missing values.

Clustered Bar Charts

Clustered bar charts are an easy way to see visual representations of relationships between variables, as you were able to do statistically with the Split File command. They are particularly useful for variables measured at the nominal and categorical levels. I will use the variables *volchrty* and *sex* to illustrate the process of creating and interpreting clustered bar charts.

SPSS GUIDE: CREATING A CLUSTERED BAR CHART

In the Output window or at the SPSS Data Editor window, click Graphs ➡ Bar. Then from the list of options in the Bar Chart dialog box, click on Clustered. (Make sure that Summaries for Groups of Cases has also been selected.) Then click on Define. You should now be looking at the Define Clustered Bar: Summaries for Groups of Cases dialog box.

The Define Clustered Bar dialog box works much the same way as the dialog box for a simple Bar chart.

1 Select % of cases.

2 Select a variable for the category axis. Use *volchrty* for this exercise.

3 Select the variable for which you would like to see clusters. (This works the same way as the Split File variable. It allows you to see one variable grouped by the categories of a second variable. In this case, you will see the responses the *volchrty* variable broken down by the categories male and female.) Click on the *sex* variable and move it to the Define Clusters by box.

4 Click on Options. When the Options dialog box opens, turn off Display groups defined by missing values. (Remove the ✔ from the box next to it.) Click on Continue.

5 When you return to the Define Clustered Bar dialog box, click on OK.

A clustered bar chart like the one in Figure 4.6 appears in your Output window.

Interpreting a clustered bar chart   The clustered bar chart reinforces what we learned from splitting our GSS 2002 subset A file by the variable *sex* and then looking to see if males were more or less likely to have volunteered for a charity as compared to females. Notice that the key to the right of the bar chart shows you how males and females are represented (by different colors, if you are looking at a color monitor, or by different shades of gray in the text). Use the key to compare the height of the bars for males and females for each category of the variable *volchrty*. We can see from the clustered bar chart that males were more likely to say that they did not volunteer at all or only once in a year's time,

FIGURE 4.6
Clustered bar chart for the variables *volchrty* and *sex* in the GSS 2002 subset A file.

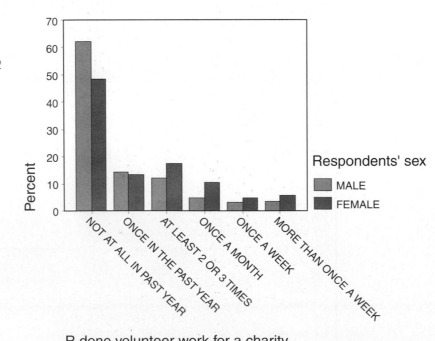

R done volunteer work for a charity

USING SPSS

whereas females were more likely than males to say that they volunteered at least two or three times a year, once a month, once a week, or more than once a week. In addition, you may notice the size of the differences between the bars. Even though males are more likely to say they volunteered very little or not at all as compared to females, the size of the differences between the bars is not very large. Consequently, the differences between the sexes on volunteering for charity are not very large ones. We will be making more of this analysis of the size of the differences between groups in Chapter 9.

Skills Practice 7   Produce a clustered bar chart for the variables *givchrty* and *sex.* Which group, males or females, tends to give more to charitable groups in a year's time? How large are the differences between the groups? What do you think might account for the differences between the groups?

In the next section you will learn how to take some of the General Social Survey variables and use SPSS to modify them through a process called recoding.

Recoding

WHAT IS RECODING?

Recoding is a technique for data analysis that allows us to change how the respondents to a variable are classified by recombining category values—grouping two or more categories of a variable together to simplify the process of analysis. For example, as one indicator of the extent to which American adults are involved in their communities, we might be interested in looking at the variable church attendance (*attend* in the GSS 2002 subset A file). If you produce a frequency distribution for this variable, you will notice that it has a lot of categories—nine to be exact. Generally speaking, the more values a variable has, the harder it is to see the patterns in the responses. The task becomes easier if we can recombine the values into variables with fewer categories. You will see how important this is as we analyze recoded variables in this section.

The process of recoding has six steps:

Step 1.   Preparing to recode a variable.

Step 2.   Using the SPSS Recode command to create a new variable.

Step 3.   Using the SPSS Define Variable command to label the new variable.

Step 4.   Checking the new variable to be sure the recoding is correct.

Step 5.   Saving the new variable in your data file (the GSS 2002 subset A, in this case).

Step 6.   Analyzing your recoded variable.

USING SPSS

The first step in the process of recoding a variable involves looking at a frequency distribution for an existing variable and deciding how to change it.

Step 1: Preparing to Recode

Use a frequency distribution to see current coding   If you want to recode a variable, you have to begin by looking at how the variable is currently coded. Produce a frequency distribution to see the original values and categories of the variable to be recoded, which we will call the **old variable**. Figure out which values and categories you want to combine to create a **new variable** with new categories.

 Skills Practice 8   Produce a frequency distribution for the variable *attend* using the GSS 2002 subset A file. Use the command path Analyze ➡ Descriptive Statistics ➡ Frequencies. (See the SPSS Guide, "Obtaining a Frequency Distribution," if you need help.)

Prepare a diagram of current and new values and categories   After you produce a frequency distribution, use it to list the values and value labels of the old variable on paper. Then decide how you want to change your variable. How you change it will depend on several considerations: the research question you are trying to answer, the statistics you want to apply to the variable, and how much sense it makes to combine specific categories of a variable. It would make sense to combine the categories indicating infrequent attendance, and it would make sense to combine the categories indicating frequent attendance. It wouldn't make sense to combine those who say they never attend with those who say they attend more than once a week.

For this exercise, assume we're interested in looking at the variable in four categories: never attend, attend once a year or less, attend at least once a month, and attend at least once a week. Having decided how we want to change our variable, *attend,* the next step is to complete the **recode diagram** you started on paper—like the one in Figure 4.7—showing how the variable is to be changed.

Name and label the new (recoded) variable   Decide on a name for the new variable you are creating. (Review the rules for naming variables in Chapter 3.) For consistency in the examples that follow, name the new variable *newattnd* and use the label Recoded church attendance. Write your new variable name and variable label on your recode diagram.

Identify the level of measurement of the new variable   Sometimes recoding a variable changes its level of measurement. Numerical variables may become categorical ones. Ordinal variables can become nominal ones. Sometimes we can even turn nominal variables into ordinal variables by changing the order of the categories. (See Chapter 2 if you need to review these concepts.) When you prepare to do a recode, take a look at the new categories you have created and ask yourself, "At what level is this variable being measured now that I have recoded it?" In this case, what is the level of measurement of the *newattnd* variable? Write it down on the recode diagram.

FIGURE 4.7
Recode diagram for the variable *attend*.

Old Values of *attend*	Old Labels of *attend*	New Labels	New Values
0	Never	Never	0
1	Less than once a year		
2	Once a year	Several times a year or less	1
3	Several times a year		
4	Once a month		
5	2–3 times a month	At least once a month	2
6	Nearly every week		
7	Every week	At least once a week	3
8	More than once a week		
9	DK/NA	DK/NA	9

The **old labels and values** come from the frequency distribution for the variable *attend*.

You make up the **new labels and values** based on how you want your new, recoded variable to look.

New variable name: *newattnd*
New variable label: RECODED CHURCH ATTENDANCE
Level of measurement: Ordinal

Step 2: Using the SPSS Recode Command to Create a New Variable

SPSS GUIDE: RECODING VARIABLES

Follow these steps to recode variables:

1 Click on the Transform menu item in the SPSS Data Editor window.

2 Then hold your cursor on Recode.

3 Two choices appear: Click on Into Different Variables, because choosing Into Same Variables will actually replace your original variable with a recoded new variable.

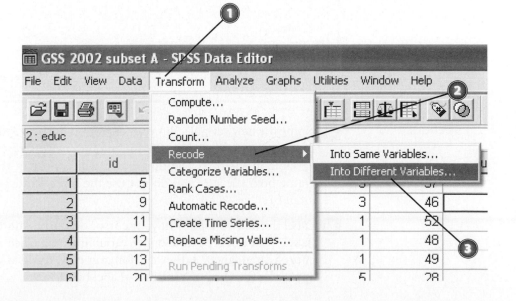

The Recode Into Different Variables dialog box opens. At this dialog box, there are five functions to perform. I will take you through the process step by step.

1 Select the variable to be recoded from the variable list (click on *attend,* then click on the ▶ pointing at the Input Variable → Output Variable box). The variable will appear in the Input Variable → Output Variable box.

2 Name the new variable. Put your cursor on the box under Output Variable— Name. Click and type in the mnemonic, *newattnd,* for your new, recoded variable in the box. The mnemonic will appear in the Output Variable— Name box. (Be sure you do not use the same name as the original variable *attend.*)

3 Label the new variable. Put your cursor on the box under Output Variable— Label. You can type in a longer variable name. Click and type in "Recoded church attendance" as the label for your new, recoded variable. The label will appear in the Output Variable—Label box.

④ Click on Change.

⑤ Click on Old and New Values.

When you click on Old and New Values, the Recode into Different Variables: Old and New Values dialog box opens. This dialog box lets us tell SPSS which old values of the variable *attend* are to be grouped into which new values of the new variable *newattnd*. An overview of the process follows, with step-by-step instructions. You will need to refer to the recode diagram (Figure 4.7) as you go through this process.

1. For *each category* of your new variable, enter the old value or range of old values to be combined to make the new category. Take these values directly from the recode diagram.

2. Enter the new value.

3. Click on Add or use your Alt–A keys.

4. After you have entered all of the old values and new values for your variable, click on Continue.

1 Start by giving SPSS the Old Value for the first set of values to be recoded, which involves making old value 0 (Never) into the new value 0 (Never). To do this, click on Value, then type in the first value, 0.

2 Move your cursor to New Value and type 0.

Recode into Different Variables: Old and New Values

Old Value
- ⦿ Value: 0
- ○ System-missing
- ○ System- or user-missing
- ○ Range:
  [ ] through [ ]
- ○ Range:
  Lowest through [ ]
- ○ Range:
  [ ] through highest
- ○ All other values

New Value
- ⦿ Value: 0   ○ System-missing
- ○ Copy old value(s)

Old --> New:
- Add
- Change
- Remove

[ ] Output variables are strings   Width: 8
[ ] Convert numeric strings to numbers ('5'->5)

Continue   Cancel   Help

3 Now click on Add. Your window will look like this:

Recode into Different Variables: Old and New Values

Old Value
- ⦿ Value: [ ]
- ○ System-missing
- ○ System- or user-missing
- ○ Range:
  [ ] through [ ]
- ○ Range:
  Lowest through [ ]
- ○ Range:
  [ ] through highest
- ○ All other values

New Value
- ⦿ Value: [ ]   ○ System-missing
- ○ Copy old value(s)

Old --> New:
0 --> 0
- Add
- Change
- Remove

[ ] Output variables are strings   Width: 8
[ ] Convert numeric strings to numbers ('5'->5)

Continue   Cancel   Help

If you make a mistake: Click on the error in the Old → New box. The values to be fixed will be highlighted. Go back to the Old Value or New Value boxes and make corrections. Then click on Change.

Repeat steps 1–3 for each category of your new variable   Give SPSS the next set of changes from your recode chart (Figure 4.7)—the Old Values 1 through 3, which will be recoded into the New Value 1. Because you are taking a range of values and transforming them into a single new value, use the Range feature under Old Value.

1 Click on Range. Enter the Old Value 1, and tab over to the next box. Type in the Old Value 3.

2 Put your cursor in the New Value box and type in 1.

3 Click on Add.

The Recode into Different Values window will look like this:

Move to the next set of values to be recoded:

> At Range, enter 4 through 6; at New Value, enter 2; then click on Add.
>
> At Range, enter 7 through 8; at New Value, enter 3; then click on Add.
>
> At Value, enter 9; at New Value, enter 9; then click on Add.

(For more information about when to use Value and when to use Range, see "Avoiding Common Pitfalls" on page 127.)

CHECKING YOUR WORK

All of your old and new values should appear in the Old → New box, and they should look like the ones that follow. If they don't, see the previous directions for making changes. When your changes are correct, click on Continue.

Complete the recode   When you return to the Recode into Different Variables window, your window should look like this:

Click on OK to execute the recode and return to the SPSS Data Editor window.

Find your new variable   At the SPSS Data Editor window, check to see whether your new variable is now part of your data set. Scroll (to the right, using the scroll arrow ▶ in the bottom right-hand corner of the screen) to go to the end of your variables. Your new variable, *newattnd,* should be the last variable on your list.

	rcrelig	rcage	rcparty	rcpolwws	rcattend	rcwrksta	rcvolchr	newattnd
1	5	1	3	3	1	1	2	1.00
2	1	2	3	0	3	1	0	3.00

GSS 2002 SUBSET A - SPSS Data Editor

File   Edit   View   Data   Transform   Analyze   Graphs   Utilities   Window   Help

1 : id   1

> ***Avoiding Common Pitfalls: The value and range options in the Recode dialog box***   When to use Value and when to use Range in the Recode into Different Variables: Old and New Values window is often a source of confusion. You have several options for specifying Old Values, depending on how many old values are being regrouped into a new value. When you are recoding a single value of an old variable into a single value of a new variable, use the Value button (as when value 0, Never, remains value 0, Never). When you are recoding several values of an old variable into a single value of a new variable, use the Range button (as when values 1 through 3, Less Than Once a Year through Several Times a Year, become value 1, Once a Year or Less).

Step 3: Labeling the New Variable and Its Values

The next step is to **define the recoded variable**—label the values of your variable (if your new variable is categorical—nominal or ordinal), label any missing values, and specify the level of measurement of your new variable. The skills involved are not new. They are the same ones you used in Chapter 3 to define new variables.

To define your new, recoded variable *newattnd,* switch to the Variable View window (using the tab in the lower left-hand corner of your screen). Find the name of your new variable in the list of variables in the Variable View window (it will be the last variable on your list because it is the newest variable). As you did when you were setting up your own data set, move across the Variable View window entering the information for your variable in the appropriate columns. You will notice that the variable has already been labeled using the label you created during the recode process. Everything else you need to set up your variable in Variable View is on your recode diagram (Figure 4.7). If you need help with the process, review the section in Chapter 3 entitled "SPSS Guide: Defining Variables in SPSS."

1. Specify the variable type (it should be set up as a numeric variable with no decimals).
2. Create values and value labels (using your recode diagram for the new values and labels you are going to enter).
3. Define any missing values (9 is the only missing value).
4. Specify the column format, if necessary (but default values should be acceptable).
5. Identify the level of measurement (ordinal).

Now you are ready to check your variable.

Step 4: Checking the Recoded Variable

To check your recoding, produce a frequency distribution for your new, recoded variable, *newattnd,* and compare it to a frequency distribution for the old variable, *attend.* Use the command path Analyze ➡ Descriptive Statistics ➡ Frequencies. Select the variables *attend* and *newattnd.* Click on OK. You should be looking at frequency distributions like the ones in Tables 4.12 and 4.13.

TABLE 4.12 Frequency Distribution for the Variable *attend* in the GSS subset A File

ATTEND How often R attends religious services

		Frequency	Percent	Valid Percent	Cumulative Percent
Valid	0 NEVER	282	18.8	19.0	19.0
	1 LT ONCE A YEAR	117	7.8	7.9	26.9
	2 ONCE A YEAR	212	14.1	14.3	41.1
	3 SEVRL TIMES A YR	192	12.8	12.9	54.1
	4 ONCE A MONTH	96	6.4	6.5	60.5
	5 2-3X A MONTH	127	8.5	8.6	69.1
	6 NRLY EVERY WEEK	105	7.0	7.1	76.2
	7 EVERY WEEK	238	15.9	16.0	92.2
	8 MORE THN ONCE WK	116	7.7	7.8	100.0
	Total	1485	99.0	100.0	
Missing	9 DK,NA	15	1.0		
Total		1500	100.0		

TABLE 4.13 Frequency Distribution for the Recoded *attend* Variable *newattnd*

NEWATTND Recoded church attendance

		Frequency	Percent	Valid Percent	Cumulative Percent
Valid	0 NEVER	282	18.8	19.0	19.0
	1 SEVERAL TIMES A YR OR LESS	521	34.7	35.1	54.1
	2 AT LEAST ONCE A MONTH	328	21.9	22.1	76.2
	3 AT LEAST ONCE A WEEK	354	23.6	23.8	100.0
	Total	1485	99.0	100.0	
Missing	9 DK/NA	15	1.0		
Total		1500	100.0		

USING SPSS

CHECKING YOUR WORK

How do you know whether your recoding is correct? Make sure that

- The variable name and label show up on the table exactly as you entered them.
- The values and their labels appear on the table.

If the variable name, label, or value labels are incorrect, go back to the Define Variable window to correct them.

Compare your frequency distribution for *newattnd* with the frequency distribution for *attend:*

- *N* for the recoded variable should be the same as *N* for the original variable.
- The number of valid cases and missing cases for the new variable should be the same as they were for the old variable.
- If you made a mistake, follow the command path Transform ➡ Recode ➡ Into Different Variables and correct your error(s).

Step 5: Saving the Variable

Ordinarily, when you are satisfied that a recoded variable is correct, you would save it by clicking on the Save File icon. However, you cannot save your *newattnd* variable, because the GSS 2002 subset A data file already contains the maximum number of variables that you can have (50 variables) in a single file. But don't worry. Your GSS 2002 subset A data file already contains a number of recoded variables that I created for you. They are all named with the prefix, "rc" for recode. So you will see a number of "rc" variables in your data set—including an *rcattend* variable—that we will be using as we go through the text. The *rcattend* variable should match your *newattnd* variable.

Step 6: Analyzing the Recoded Variable

Recoding a variable is an aid to the analysis of data, not an end in itself. What does recoding a variable help us to do? Let's use our recoded variable *newattnd* to, first of all, see if people tend to attend church regularly. You might want to start by thinking about what you consider to be regular church attendance. Is it once a week, a few times a month, or less frequent than that? You could also think about what the variable is trying to measure. In addition to simply finding out how often people attend church, researchers may also be interested in how religious American adults are. How often do you think someone you consider to be religious attends church? Are the respondents to the General Social Survey religious by those standards?

Look at frequency distributions for the variable *newattnd*.

- Follow the command path Analyze ➡ Descriptive Statistics ➡ Frequencies.
- Select the variable *newattnd,* and click on OK.

Skills Practice 9 What conclusions can you draw about church attendance? Do respondents to the GSS attend church regularly? What makes you think so? Do you consider the American adults represented by the GSS to be a religious group? Why or why not?

Skills Practice 10 Recode the variable *age*. Follow these steps:

• Produce a frequency distribution for the variable *age*.

• Create a recode diagram on a piece of paper showing how you will recode *age* into the following categories (you do not need to list every single category of the *age* variable in your recode diagram, just show how you are going to group the "old" categories of the *age* variable into the new categories of your recoded variable):

Group the respondents who are ages 18–25 into category 1 and label it 18–25.

Group the respondents who are ages 26–39 into category 2 and label it 26–39.

Group the respondents who are ages 40–64 into category 3 and label it 40–64.

Group the respondents who are ages 65–89 into category 4 and label it 65–89.

Category 99 (DK) will be new category 99, and it will be classified as a missing data value.

• Give your variable an 8-character name (call it *newage*) and a label, and decide at what level it is being measured.

• Create a new, recoded variable. Use the command path Transform ➡ Recode ➡ Into Different Variables.

If the work you did recoding the *attend* variable is still visible, click the Reset button in the Recode into Different Variables dialog box. Any work that you did previously will be erased. (Many of the SPSS dialog boxes have Reset buttons that you can use to clear prior work.)

• Define your new variable (using Variable View).
• Produce and check the frequency distribution for your new variable.

SUMMARY

The emphasis in this chapter has been on producing and analyzing frequency distributions. Frequency distributions summarize data for single variables, and they help us to see the patterns in the responses to variables so that we can describe or characterize the respondents.

Frequency distributions usually list the categories of a variable, the frequencies—or number of responses—for each category, and the percentage of the responses to each category. Frequency distributions in SPSS list percentages two ways: one percentage distribution for all cases and one for valid cases only. In addition, SPSS frequency distributions show cumulative percentages for the response categories of a variable.

You learned how to produce and analyze frequency distributions for 2002 General Social Survey variables using the command path Analyze ➡ Descriptive Statistics ➡ Frequencies in SPSS, and you learned how to produce frequency distributions by hand. Producing frequency distributions by hand is a six-step process of listing the categories of a variable, counting the frequencies of response to each category, summing the frequencies of response to find the total number of responses, calculating the percentages of response to each category, calculating the cumulative frequencies of response, and calculating the cumulative percentages of response.

More important is that you practiced writing about what you learned from frequency distributions—describing the general characteristics of the respondents to a variable using a headline or topic sentence and then elaborating on your general conclusions with details from the frequency distribution.

We went over the process of splitting a data file by one variable (using the Data ➡ Split File command path) and then comparing frequency distributions for a second variable. For example, we split the file by the variable *sex* to compare frequency distributions for the variable *volchrty* for male and female respondents. This procedure allows us to see whether there are differences between males and females in their responses to the variable on volunteering.

We supplemented our analysis of frequency distributions with various graphs—bar charts, histograms, pie charts, and clustered bar charts—that help us to analyze visually the distributions of responses to variables. Such graphs are particularly helpful aids for assessing the extent to which a distribution of responses to a variable is homogeneous or heterogeneous.

Finally, you learned to recode—combine categories of variables—to create new variables. The process of recoding involves preparing a diagram showing how we are going to combine categories of an existing variable to create a new one; using the SPSS Recode command to create a new variable; using the Define Variable window to label the new variable, its values, and its categories; and checking the new variable to be sure our recoding is correct. The goal of recoding is to help us analyze responses to variables. Consequently, the final step in the recoding process is to produce a frequency distribution for the variable we create through the recoding process and to analyze it.

In the next chapter you will learn to supplement the analysis of frequency distributions with a set of statistics called measures of central tendency.

KEY CONCEPTS

Univariate analysis	Cumulative frequencies	Clustered bar chart
Raw data	Cumulative Percent column	Percentage
Raw scores	Dispersion of response	Proportion
Frequency distribution	Heterogeneous distribution	Percentile
Valid cases	Homogeneous distribution	Recoding
Missing cases	Dialog box	Old variable
N	Bar chart	New variable
Frequency of response	Histogram	Recode diagram
Percent column	*x*-axis and *y*-axis	Define a recoded variable
Valid Percent column	Pie chart	

ANSWERS TO SKILLS PRACTICES

1. Your frequency distribution should look like this one:

Give money to charity in past year	Frequency	Percent	Cumulative Frequencies	Cumulative Percentages
Not at all in past year	4	20.0	4	20
Once in past year	2	10.0	6	30
2 or 3 times in past year	7	35.0	13	65
Once a month	2	10.0	15	75
Once a week	4	20.0	19	95
More than once a week	1	5.0	20	100
	N = 20	100.0		

Most respondents (80%) contributed at least once to a charity in a year's time. Only 20% did not contribute at all. Thirty-five percent of the respondents contributed at least once a month. More respondents are willing to give money to charity than volunteer their time.

2. *othshelp* Respondents to the 2002 General Social Survey generally agree that people should help others less fortunate. Nearly 88% agree or strongly agree that people should help. Ten percent are in the middle on this question, and only 2% disagree or strongly disagree that people should help others less fortunate than they are. This distribution of responses is fairly homogeneous, with most respondents agreeing that people should help others less fortunate.

givchrty Respondents to the 2002 General Social Survey tend to give money to charity. Over 78% of the respondents have given money at least once in a year's time. Over a third gave two or three times in a year. Over a quarter gave monthly or more often than that. Only 21.7% did not give at all in the span of a year. This distribution of responses is more heterogeneous, if you just focus on the differences in the percentages in the valid percent column of the frequency distribution. If you think about the variable in terms of giving money or not giving money, it is clear that most people have

contributed at least something in a year's time. Consequently, the respondents appear to be somewhat more homogeneous when viewed in that light.

grppol Respondents to the 2002 General Social Survey do not belong to political parties. Nearly three-quarters, 74.2%, say they do not belong to a political party. This leaves only slightly more than one-quarter of the respondents who say they do belong to a political party. Only 20% of the respondents actually participate in the activities of a political party. It is striking that about 80% of the respondents either do not belong to a political party or do not participate even if they do belong. This distribution of responses is very homogeneous.

3. As with volunteering time for charity, male respondents are a little more likely than female respondents to say that they did not make any monetary contribution to charity in a year's time. About 25% of male respondents said they didn't give anything compared to about 19% of female respondents. On the other hand, even though female respondents are a little more likely than male respondents to give one, two, or three times, or even once a month over the course of a year, male respondents are more likely to say they give weekly or more than once a week. Even so, the differences are fairly small.

4. Bar chart for the variable *partyid*. The distribution of responses to this variable is somewhat more heterogeneous, particularly in comparison to the responses to the *volchrty* variable. Although not perfectly even (the same height), they are somewhat more even.

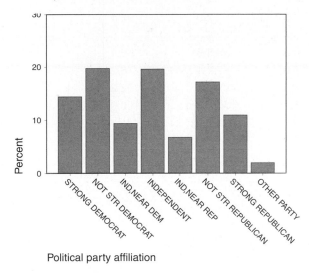

Political party affiliation

5. Histogram for the variable *educ*. Notice that each bar represents 2 years of education. (Subtract the midpoint of the first bar [0] from the midpoint of the second bar [2]: 2 − 0 = 2.) The histogram shows a relatively homogeneous distribution of responses to the variable, with most respondents having completed at least some high school or college training.

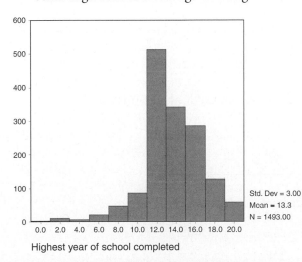

Highest year of school completed

6. Pie chart for *givchrty*. You may notice that some of the value labels on the pie chart have

been shortened. Nevertheless, it is fairly clear from the pie "slices" that the distribution of responses to this variable is more heterogeneous, because the slices of the pie are more similar than dissimilar in size.

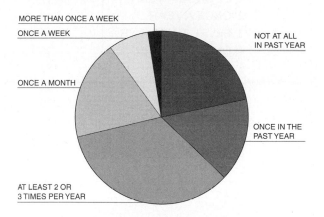

7. Clustered bar chart for the variables *givchrty* and *sex*. The clustered bar chart confirms our analysis using the Split File procedure. A larger percentage of males than females said they do not give at all in a year's time. In addition, larger percentages of females said they give once a year, two or three times a year, or monthly. On the other hand, higher percentages of males respondents give once a week or more often than once a week. The differences (as indicated by the height of the bars) are not very large ones, though.

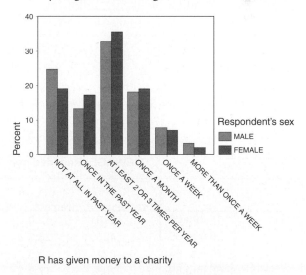

R has given money to a charity

8. Your frequency distribution for *attend* should look like this one:

ATTEND How often R attends religious services

		Frequency	Percent	Valid Percent	Cumulative Percent
Valid	0 NEVER	282	18.8	19.0	19.0
	1 LT ONCE A YEAR	117	7.8	7.9	26.9
	2 ONCE A YEAR	212	14.1	14.3	41.1
	3 SEVRL TIMES A YR	192	12.8	12.9	54.1
	4 ONCE A MONTH	96	6.4	6.5	60.5
	5 2-3X A MONTH	127	8.5	8.6	69.1
	6 NRLY EVERY WEEK	105	7.0	7.1	76.2
	7 EVERY WEEK	238	15.9	16.0	92.2
	8 MORE THN ONCE WK	116	7.7	7.8	100.0
	Total	1485	99.0	100.0	
Missing	9 DK,NA	15	1.0		
Total		1500	100.0		

9. Respondents to the 2002 General Social Survey do not appear to be a church-going group. Over half (54%) of the respondents attend church infrequently if at all. Thirty-five percent go several times a year, once a year, or less than once a year. Nearly 20% never go. Forty-six percent go at least once a month, but less than one-quarter (23.8%) attend church on a weekly basis.

10. Your recode diagram for transforming *age* into *rcage* should look like the following:

Current Values	Labels[3]	New Labels	New Values
18–25		18–25	1
26–39		26–39	2
40–64		40–64	3
65–89		65–89	4
99	NA	99	NA

Variable name: *newage*
Variable label: RECODED AGE
Level of measurement (*newage*): Ordinal

---

[3] Age is numerical, so there are no value labels for the *age* variable.

Your frequency distribution for the recoded variable, *newage,* should look like this one:

NEWAGE Recoded age

		Frequency	Percent	Valid Percent	Cumulative Percent
Valid	1 18 thru 25	180	12.0	12.1	12.1
	2 26 thru 39	425	28.3	28.5	40.6
	3 40 thru 64	622	41.5	41.7	82.3
	4 65 thru 89	263	17.5	17.7	100.0
	Total	1490	99.3	100.0	
Missing	99 NA	10	.7		
Total		1500	100.0		

GENERAL EXERCISES

Construct and analyze frequency distributions for the responses to these variables using the following sets of data, randomly selected from the 2002 General Social Survey.

1. *news*

Case Summaries

	How often does the respondent read a newspaper
1	LESS THAN ONCE A WEEK
2	ONCE A WEEK
3	EVERY DAY
4	EVERY DAY
5	EVERY DAY
6	A FEW TIMES A WEEK
7	ONCE A WEEK
8	ONCE A WEEK
9	EVERY DAY
10	A FEW TIMES A WEEK
11	EVERY DAY
12	EVERY DAY
13	EVERY DAY
14	LESS THAN ONCE A WEEK
15	ONCE A WEEK

2. *grpchuh*

Case Summaries

	Has respondent participated in the activities of a church in the past 12 months?
1	I HAVE PARTICIPATED MORE THAN TWICE
2	I HAVE PARTICIPATED MORE THAN TWICE
3	I HAVE PARTICIPATED MORE THAN TWICE
4	I HAVE PARTICIPATED MORE THAN TWICE
5	I HAVE PARTICIPATED MORE THAN TWICE
6	I HAVE PARTICIPATED MORE THAN TWICE
7	I DO NOT BELONG TO SUCH A GROUP
8	I DO NOT BELONG TO SUCH A GROUP
9	I DO NOT BELONG TO SUCH A GROUP
10	I HAVE PARTICIPATED MORE THAN TWICE
11	I HAVE PARTICIPATED ONCE OR TWICE
12	I DO NOT BELONG TO SUCH A GROUP
13	I DO NOT BELONG TO SUCH A GROUP
14	I HAVE PARTICIPATED MORE THAN TWICE
15	I HAVE PARTICIPATED MORE THAN TWICE
16	I HAVE PARTICIPATED MORE THAN TWICE
17	I HAVE PARTICIPATED MORE THAN TWICE
18	I HAVE PARTICIPATED ONCE OR TWICE
19	I HAVE PARTICIPATED MORE THAN TWICE
20	I HAVE PARTICIPATED ONCE OR TWICE

3. *fund*

Case Summaries

	How fundamentalist is respondent currently
1	FUNDAMENTALIST
2	MODERATE
3	FUNDAMENTALIST
4	FUNDAMENTALIST
5	MODERATE
6	LIBERAL
7	MODERATE
8	FUNDAMENTALIST
9	MODERATE
10	MODERATE
11	MODERATE
12	MODERATE
13	FUNDAMENTALIST
14	LIBERAL
15	FUNDAMENTALIST
16	MODERATE
17	LIBERAL
18	MODERATE
19	LIBERAL
20	LIBERAL
21	FUNDAMENTALIST
22	MODERATE
23	MODERATE
24	MODERATE
25	FUNDAMENTALIST
26	MODERATE
27	MODERATE
28	FUNDAMENTALIST
29	MODERATE
30	LIBERAL
31	MODERATE
32	FUNDAMENTALIST
33	FUNDAMENTALIST
34	FUNDAMENTALIST
35	LIBERAL
36	FUNDAMENTALIST
37	LIBERAL
38	MODERATE
39	MODERATE
40	MODERATE
41	FUNDAMENTALIST
42	FUNDAMENTALIST
43	LIBERAL
44	MODERATE
45	FUNDAMENTALIST

4. *trust*

Case Summaries

	Can people be trusted?
1	CANNOT TRUST
2	CAN TRUST
3	CANNOT TRUST
4	CAN TRUST
5	CAN TRUST
6	CAN TRUST
7	CANNOT TRUST
8	DEPENDS
9	DEPENDS
10	CANNOT TRUST
11	CAN TRUST
12	CAN TRUST
13	CANNOT TRUST
14	CANNOT TRUST
15	CANNOT TRUST
16	CANNOT TRUST
17	CAN TRUST
18	CANNOT TRUST
19	CAN TRUST

SPSS EXERCISES

Often researchers use frequency distributions to describe the demographic characteristics of respondents to a survey (sex, race, age, education, and so on). Use SPSS and the GSS 2002 subset A file to produce a frequency distribution and then write an analysis of the following demographic variables in the 2002 General Social Survey.

1. *sex*
2. *rcrace*
3. *rcage*
4. *degree*
5. *class*
6. How civically engaged are the respondents to the 2002 General Social Survey? You have already analyzed the *volchrty, givchrty,* and *grppol* variables along with a recoded *attend* variable (*rcattend* in your GSS 2002 subset A file). In addition to those variables, analyze the *news, vote00, partthon, givchng, conoffcl,* and

protest variables. How would you describe the general level of civic involvement among 2002 General Social Survey respondents? Support your answer with evidence from the frequency distributions that you are using.

7. The "News to Use" articles in this chapter and in Chapter 3 discussed the issue of civic engagement among young adults. Split your data file using the *rcage* variable and analyze differences among age groups in their levels of participation in volunteering for charity with the *volchrty* variable. Do you see any differences in volunteering across age categories (ignoring that part of the table that includes no answer, not applicable, or don't know responses).

8. Examine whether participation in political groups (*grppol*) seems to be different for the various categories of the *rcage* variable. Split

your data file using *rcage* and analyze the frequency distributions for the variable *grppol* (ignoring that part of the table that includes no answer, not applicable, or don't know responses).

9. Are there differences across age categories for participation in protest activities? Split your data file with the *rcage* variable and analyze the frequency distributions for the variable *protest*. (Ignore the part of the table that includes the no answer, not applicable, or don't know responses.)

10. It has been argued that religious conservatives are more likely to be involved in civic activities as compared to those who are not religiously conservative. Let's see if the General Social Survey supports this claim. Are there differences among religiously fundamental, moderate, and liberal respondents in their levels of participation in volunteering for charity? If so, what are they? Split your GSS 2002 subset A file using the variable *fund*, then produce and analyze frequency distributions for *volchrty*. (Ignore the part of the table includes the no answer, not applicable, or don't know responses.)

For exercises 11–14, produce an appropriate graph (depending on the level of measurement) for the GSS variables listed. Is the distribution of responses more homogeneous or heterogeneous? Why do you think so?

11. *sex*
12. *rcrace*
13. *rcage*
14. *degree*

15. Use the clustered bar chart feature of SPSS to examine the association between the *rcage* and *volchrty* variables. (Hint: *volchrty* is your "category axis" variable and *rcage* is your "define clusters by" variable.)

16. Use the clustered bar chart feature of SPSS to examine the association between the *fund* and *volchrty* variables. (Hint: *volchrty* is your "category axis" variable and *fund* is your "define clusters by" variable.)

For exercises 17 and 18, do the recode. Then analyze your new variable. If you had to write a headline, what would it be? Use the frequency distribution for your new variable to characterize the respondents. Produce an appropriate graph. Does the distribution appear to be more homogeneous or heterogeneous?

17. Recode the GSS variable *partyid* as follows:
Strong Democrat and Not Strong Democrat into the category Democrat
Independent–Near Democrat, Independent, and Independent–Near Republican, into the category Independent
Strong Republican and Not Strong Republican into the category Republican
Other remains Other
Name your new variable *newparty*.

18. Recode the GSS variable *polviews* as follows:
Extremely Liberal, Liberal, and Slightly Liberal into the category Liberal
Moderate remains Moderate
Extremely Conservative, Conservative, and Slightly Conservative into the category Conservative
Name your new variable *newpolvw*.

## CHAPTER 5

Measures of Central Tendency

INTRODUCTION

Like all statistics, measures of central tendency—the mode, median, and mean—help us find patterns in data. Like frequency distributions, these measures are in use every day—in news reports about what is happening in our economy and how it is affecting the lives of American families, for example. In the "News to Use" section is an article illustrating how the median and the mean are often used. The article is about changes in household incomes.

N E W S *to* U S E
Statistics in the "Real" World

Poverty Rate Rises, Household Income Declines, Census Bureau Reports[1]

U.S. CENSUS BUREAU

PUBLIC INFORMATION OFFICE

After falling for four straight years, the nation's poverty rate rose from 11.3 percent in 2000 to 11.7 percent in 2001. Median household income declined 2.2 percent in real terms from its 2000 level to $42,228 in 2001, according to reports released today by the Commerce Department's Census Bureau.

"Like the last year-to-year increase in poverty in 1991–1992 and the last decrease in real household income in 1990–1991, these changes coincided with a recession," said Daniel Weinberg, chief of the Census Bureau's Housing and Household Economic Statistics Division.

The poverty rate and the number of poor increased among several population groups between 2000 and 2001, including all families, married-couple families, unrelated individuals, non-Hispanic Whites, people 18-to-64 years old and the native population. . . .

POVERTY

According to the poverty report, about 1.3 million more people were poor in 2001 than in 2000—32.9 million versus 31.6 million. The number of poor families increased from 6.4 million in 2000 (or 8.7 percent of all families, a record low rate) to 6.8 million (or 9.2 percent) in 2001.

For non-Hispanic Whites, the poverty rate rose from 7.4 percent in 2000 to 7.8 percent in 2001. But poverty remained at historic lows for African Americans (22.7 percent), Hispanics (21.4 percent) and Asians and Pacific Islanders (10.2 percent). Among these groups, only non-Hispanic Whites (up 905,000 to 15.3 million)

and Hispanics (up 250,000 to 8.0 million) saw an increase in the number of poor.

The three-year-average (1999–2001) poverty rate for American Indians and Alaska Natives was 24.5 percent, with an estimated 800,000 living in poverty. American Indians and Alaska Natives were the only group to show a decline in their poverty rate when the two-year 2000–2001 average was compared with the two-year 1999–2000 average. (The average was used because the American Indian and Alaska Native population is relatively small and multi-year averages provide more reliable estimates.)

The poverty rate for the population age 18 to 64 rose from 9.6 percent in 2000 to 10.1 percent in 2001. Children under 18 continued to have a higher poverty rate (16.3 percent) than people 18 to 64 or 65 and over; it was unchanged from 2000.

Increases in poverty were concentrated in metropolitan areas (particularly outside central cities) and in the South. The poverty rate for people living in the suburbs rose from 7.8 percent in 2000 to 8.2 percent in 2001, but did not change for those in central cities (16.5 percent) or in nonmetropolitan areas (14.2 percent).

The South was the only region to have an increase in its poverty rate from 2000 to 2001. Its rate of 13.5 percent was the highest among all regions. . . .

The average poverty threshold for a family of four in 2001 was $18,104 in annual income; compared with $14,128 for a family of three; $11,569 for a family of two; and $9,039 for unrelated individuals.

INCOME

"Like the increase in poverty, the decline in real median household income between 2000 and

[1] U. S. Census Bureau, 24 September 2002, <http://www.census.gov/Press-Release/www/2002/cb02-124.html>.

2001 coincided with the recession that started in March 2001," said Weinberg. "The decline was widespread. With the exception of the Northeast, where income was unchanged, all regions experienced a decline, as did each of the racial groups."

For non-Hispanic Whites, median household income declined 1.3 percent, in real terms, between 2000 and 2001 to $46,305. For African Americans and Asians and Pacific Islanders, the drops were 3.4 percent (a loss of $1,025) to $29,470 and 6.4 percent (a loss of $3,678) to $53,635, respectively. The percentage decline in median household income of African Americans did not differ from that of non-Hispanic Whites and Asian and Pacific Islanders. The real median income of Hispanics, however, remained unchanged at $33,565. This was the first annual decline for non-Hispanic Whites and Asians and Pacific Islanders since 1990–1991 and the first for African Americans since 1980–1981.

The three-year-average (1999–2001) median household income estimate for American Indians and Alaska Natives was $32,116. As with the poverty data, averages were used because the American Indian and Alaska Native population is relatively small and multiyear averages provide more reliable estimates. Based on comparisons of two-year-average medians (1999–2000 versus 2000–2001), the real median household income of American Indians and Alaska Natives did not change statistically.

The real median incomes of family households and of nonfamily households declined between 2000 and 2001. Family household income dropped 1.7 percent (from $53,155 to $52,275) and nonfamily household income declined 1.5 percent ($26,012 to $25,631). These percentage declines are not statistically different.

Real median household income did not change in the Northeast between 2000 and 2001, remaining at $45,716. It did, however, decline by 3.7 percent in the Midwest (to $43,834); 2.3 percent in the West (to $45,087); and 1.4 percent in the South (to $38,904). The South has the lowest median household income of all four regions. The percentage change in household income for the West was not statistically different from those for the South and the Midwest. The difference between the 2001 median household incomes for the Northeast and the West was not statistically significant.

Real median household income declined by 1.6 percent for households in metropolitan areas, falling to $45,219 between 2000 and 2001. Both those inside and outside the central cities of metropolitan areas experienced a decline. Households outside metropolitan areas did not experience a change between 2000 and 2001, remaining at $33,601.

Real per capita income was unchanged between 2000 and 2001 for the overall population ($22,851), each of the race groups and Hispanics. It was $26,134 for non-Hispanic Whites; $14,953 for African Americans; $24,277 for Asians and Pacific Islanders; and $13,003 for Hispanics. . . .

Measures of central tendency are univariate statistics, applied to one variable at a time. They help us find out, for example, whether the respondents to surveys—like the ones described in the "News to Use" sections—tend to be young or old, male or female, employed or unemployed, rich or poor, optimistic or pessimistic about their financial futures. In short, they tell us what the respondents to a survey are generally like.

Throughout this chapter and the next you'll be learning to describe survey respondents, first with measures of central tendency and then with measures of dispersion. The measures of central tendency we will be working with are the mode, the median, and the mean. I will show you what each measure means, how to compute it by hand, and how to find it using SPSS. More important, I will be showing you how each measure tells us something new and interesting about the respondents to a survey.

THE MODE

The **mode** tells us which category of a variable is the one most frequently chosen by respondents. Another way to describe the mode is that it is the category chosen by *the most* respondents. The mode is not the same as the category or categories that contain *most of* the respondents. We will look at this again in the next "Avoiding Common Pitfalls."

When to Use the Mode

The mode can be used with variables at any level of measurement, categorical or numerical; it is the *only* measure of central tendency for nominal variables.

Finding the Mode

Use a frequency distribution to find the mode. If you are trying to find the mode by hand, you must first put your data into that form. Then you simply read down the Frequency column and locate the highest number(s). The mode is the category or categories associated with the largest frequency (or frequencies, if there is a tie for the mode—more than one frequency with the same number).

It is important to remember that the mode is the *category* associated with the highest frequency and not the highest frequency itself. For example, if we want to know the mode—the most commonly occurring response—for the GSS respondents to the variable asking about their work status, we could produce a frequency distribution for *wrkstat*. Do that now; you will get a frequency distribution like the one in Table 5.1.

To find the mode, read down the Frequency column and find the largest number. In this case it is 781. Now look across the frequency distribution table to find the category of the *work status* variable associated with the largest frequency. It is Working Fulltime. We now know that the most commonly occurring response to the variable asking about work status is "working fulltime."

When there is more than one modal category, then the distribution of responses is called multimodal (bimodal, if there are two modes; trimodal, if there are three), and we report each of the modes we find.

TABLE 5.1   Frequency Distribution for the Variable *wrkstat* in the GSS 2002 subset A File

WRKSTAT Labor force status

		Frequency	Percent	Valid Percent	Cumulative Percent
Valid	1 WORKING FULLTIME	781	52.1	52.1	52.1
	2 WORKING PARTTIME	167	11.1	11.1	63.2
	3 TEMP NOT WORKING	31	2.1	2.1	65.3
	4 UNEMPL, LAID OFF	60	4.0	4.0	69.3
	5 RETIRED	224	14.9	14.9	84.2
	6 SCHOOL	41	2.7	2.7	86.9
	7 KEEPING HOUSE	148	9.9	9.9	96.8
	8 OTHER	48	3.2	3.2	100.0
	Total	1500	100.0	100.0	

Avoiding Common Pitfalls: Category values and category frequencies Students sometimes report the category value as the mode for categorical variables. Instead, you should be sure to use the category label when interpreting the mode. It doesn't make a lot of sense to say that the mode, or most frequently occurring response, for the variable *work status* is 1. No one knows what "1" means without its corresponding label, Working Fulltime.

Interpreting the Mode

Measures of central tendency—including the mode—can be used to back up or elaborate on the descriptions of GSS respondents we might come up with by analyzing a frequency distribution. For example, in discussing the frequency distribution for the variable *labor force status*, we might point out that

> respondents to the 2002 GSS tend to be employed. The most commonly occurring response to the question about labor force status is "working full-time," with a little over half of the respondents answering in that category.

Keep in mind that you may have more than one mode. If so, your interpretation will be along the lines of, "The most commonly occurring responses are . . ."

Avoiding Common Pitfalls: Using the word **most** The most frequently occurring response is not necessarily the same thing as the category or categories to which most respondents answered. When the word *most* is used to describe some characteristic of the respondents, it should refer to at least a majority of them. A little more than half of the respondents to the variable *labor force status* say that they are working full-time. In this case, we *can* say that a majority of the respondents—most of them—are working full-time (52.1%). When we use the mode, it is important to check the Percent column to see whether, in addition to being the most frequently chosen response category, it is also the one to which most respondents answered.

Let's practice the skills covered so far.

Skills Practice 1 It is a little surprising to me that only a little more than half of the GSS 2002 respondents are working full-time. What's going on? Could it be that there is more employment among some groups of respondents and less among others? What if we looked at the sample divided by the categories of the variable *sex*. Is a larger percentage of men working full-time as compared to women? Using Table 5.2, find the modes for males and females. Write a few sentences describing what you found—use the frequency distributions and the modes to compare the two groups. (Does the fact that the modes are the same mean that there are no differences between males and females on the *work status* variable? If not, what are the differences?)

TABLE 5.2 Frequency Distribution for the Variable *wrkstat* for Males and Females in the GSS 2002 subset A file

WRKSTAT Labor force status

SEX Respondents' sex				Frequency	Percent	Valid Percent	Cumulative Percent
1 MALE	Valid	1	WORKING FULLTIME	396	60.6	60.6	60.6
		2	WORKING PARTTIME	49	7.5	7.5	68.0
		3	TEMP NOT WORKING	13	2.0	2.0	70.0
		4	UNEMPL, LAID OFF	30	4.6	4.6	74.6
		5	RETIRED	117	17.9	17.9	92.5
		6	SCHOOL	21	3.2	3.2	95.7
		7	KEEPING HOUSE	7	1.1	1.1	96.8
		8	OTHER	21	3.2	3.2	100.0
			Total	654	100.0	100.0	
2 FEMALE	Valid	1	WORKING FULLTIME	385	45.5	45.5	45.5
		2	WORKING PARTTIME	118	13.9	13.9	59.5
		3	TEMP NOT WORKING	18	2.1	2.1	61.6
		4	UNEMPL, LAID OFF	30	3.5	3.5	65.1
		5	RETIRED	107	12.6	12.6	77.8
		6	SCHOOL	20	2.4	2.4	80.1
		7	KEEPING HOUSE	141	16.7	16.7	96.8
		8	OTHER	27	3.2	3.2	100.0
			Total	846	100.0	100.0	

THE MEDIAN

Whereas the mode is the value that occurs most often for a particular variable, the **median** tells us which value divides the respondents in half, such that half of the respondents to a variable fall at or below the median value and half of the respondents are at or above it. Probably the most common use of the median in the popular press is in reporting economic news. In the "News to Use" article at the beginning of the chapter, you see the median used to compare changes in household incomes between 2000 and 2001.

When to Use the Median

The median is used with variables that are ordinal or numerical. It cannot be used with variables that are nominal, because interpretation of the median assumes that variables have categories that can be ranked or ordered.

An advantage of the median is that, unlike the mean (the number commonly called *the average*), it is not affected by extreme scores in a set of data. I will illustrate how this works later on in this chapter.

Finding the Median by Hand

The process of finding the median involves three steps:

Step 1.   Arrange the respondents to a variable in order, low to high (or high to low), based on their categories of response.

Step 2.   Find the respondent in the middle (the **median case**).

FIGURE 5.1
Ages of nine students in a class.

Student: 1   2   3   4   5   6   7   8   9

Age: 19   20   20   20   21   22   22   23   24

Step 3. Find the category or value associated with the respondent in the middle (the **median value**).

To illustrate, suppose there is a college class of nine traditional-age students for which we want to know the median age. The first thing to do is arrange the students in order by age, youngest to oldest (or oldest to youngest, it doesn't matter). One way to do this is have the students line up by age, youngest on the left to the oldest on the right. Our line might look like the one in Figure 5.1.

Next, we have to find the student in the middle of the line. That's fairly easy—it's the fifth student from the beginning (or the end) of the line, student number 5. However, the number, 5, isn't the median; it is simply the rank assigned to the person in the middle of the line, or the number assigned to the person who is the median case.

To find the median value, we need to know the age of the person in the middle of the line. The age of the fifth student is 21, so we learn the median age of the students in the class is 21.

Half of the students are 21 or younger, and half are 21 or older.

What happens when there are 10 students instead of 9? We follow the same process. We line them up by age. With 10 traditional-age college students our line might look like Figure 5.2.

The question is, which student is in the middle: student #5 or student #6? The answer is neither. The student in the middle falls between student #5 and

FIGURE 5.2
Ages of ten students in a class.

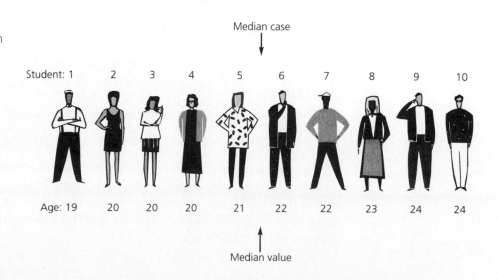

Median case
↓

Student: 1   2   3   4   5   6   7   8   9   10

Age: 19   20   20   20   21   22   22   23   24   24

↑
Median value

student #6. If we add 5 and 6 together (to get 11) and divide by 2, we regard the result, 5.5, as the middle student, or the middle case, in the line of respondents to the variable *age*.

What is the median value, the age associated with student 5.5? As you may have guessed, the median age is found by adding the ages associated with student #5 and student #6 together ($21 + 22 = 43$) and dividing by 2 to get 21.5, the median value.

Half of the students are younger than 21.5, and half are older.

When we are dealing with only a few cases in response to a particular variable, it is a fairly simple task to find the median by lining up the respondents, locating the one in the middle, and then identifying the value associated with that respondent. However, when we have a large number of cases—think about the 1,500 respondents to the GSS we are using in our 2002 GSS subset A file—we need shortcuts. We need a way to (1) arrange the respondents in order (without having to line them all up), (2) find the median case, and (3) find the median value.

Frequency distributions provide us with the shortcut. They can be used to arrange the respondents in order by response category or value, and formulas can be used to find the median case and locate the median value associated with it.

Follow this process with another example using a set of 25 raw scores for the variable *age* that were drawn at random from the 18-to-25-year-old respondents to the 2002 GSS. The data in the form of raw scores are displayed in Table 5.3.

Our first task is to arrange the respondents in order. We will follow the practice of listing variable values in order from low to high. With the categories of the variable arranged in this order, a frequency distribution for the data in Table 5.3, including the cumulative frequencies column, would look like Table 5.4.

Now we need to find the respondent in the middle of the distribution—the median case. A formula helps us do that. To find the median case, we add 1 to the total number of responses, *N*. Then we divide the result by 2. The formula for finding the median case can be expressed as follows.

Formula 5.1: Median case = $(N + 1) \times .50$

Note: Multiplying a value by $\frac{1}{2}$ (or .50) is the same mathematically as dividing it in half, by 2.

EXAMPLE:

The median case for the preceding distribution would be

median case = $(N + 1) \times .50 = (25 + 1) \times .50 = 26 \times .50 = 13$

The next step is to find the median value associated with the median case by reading down the Frequencies column. For example, if we look at the first category of the variable *age*, we see that the frequency for that category is 1. We already know that this number tells us that 1 respondent answered, "18," in response to the variable *age*.

TABLE 5.3   Ages of 25 Respondents between the Ages of 18 and 25 Selected at Random from the 2002 GSS subset A File

CASE	AGE Age of respondent
1	22
2	23
3	21
4	24
5	23
6	25
7	20
8	23
9	23
10	23
11	22
12	22
13	18
14	25
15	24
16	22
17	22
18	21
19	20
20	23
21	24
22	24
23	22
24	22
25	22

TABLE 5.4   Frequency Distribution for a Random Sample of Scores from the 2002 GSS for the Variable *age*

Reading the frequency distribution as an index to the cases.

respondent 1 ——————
respondents 2–3 ——————
respondents 4–5 ——————
respondents 6–13 ——————

Ages of randomly selected respondents

Age	Frequency	Percent	Valid Percent	Cumulative Frequencies	Cumulative Percent
18	1	4.0	4.0	1	4.0
20	2	8.0	8.0	3	12.0
21	2	8.0	8.0	5	20.0
22	8	32.0	32.0	13	52.0
23	6	24.0	24.0	19	76.0
24	4	16.0	16.0	23	92.0
25	2	8.0	8.0	25	100.0
	N = 25	100.0	100.0		

If we now understand that the frequency distribution has, in essence, lined up our respondents, low to high, according to their answers to the variable *age,* we can use the frequency distribution as an index to the order of the cases. Reading down the Frequencies column, we can see that respondent number 1 answered "18" to the variable *age;* respondents 2 and 3 answered "20"; respondents 4 and 5 answered "21"; and so on.

Where is respondent 13? He or she is in the frequency associated with the median value, 22.

Interpreting the Median

How do we interpret the median? Often, as in the "News to Use" article at the beginning of this chapter, you simply see the median reported. Those writing for popular consumption assume most people understand that the median divides a distribution of respondents in half. However, I will be writing about the median this way:

> Half of the respondents are 18 to 22 years old, and the other half are 22 to 25 years old.

Writing about the median this way includes information about the minimum and maximum values in the distribution. Anyone reading the interpretation gets a sense of the range of values in the distribution.

Finding the Median Using the Cumulative Percentage on a Frequency Distribution

An alternative to finding the median computationally is to use the Cumulative Percent column on a frequency distribution. Remember the median is the value that divides a set of data in half. This means that 50% of the respondents will fall at or below the median and 50% at or above it. Consequently, you can read down the Cumulative Percent column on a frequency distribution until you find the halfway point in the data, also known as the 50th percentile. Then read across the frequency distribution to find the value associated with the halfway point in the data.

EXAMPLE:

Look down the Cumulative Percent column for Table 5.4. Notice that 4% of the respondents are 18 years old, 12% are 18 to 20 years old, and so on. If you keep on reading down the Cumulative Percent column, you come to the cumulative percentage that includes the halfway point in the data (the 50th percentile) at 52%. Reading across the frequency distribution, you can find the value associated with the 50th percentile, 22.

Half of the respondents are 22 years old or younger (down to age 18), and half are 22 years old or older (up to age 25).

Note that when you are using the Cumulative Percent column to find the median, you will rarely find the data divided evenly at the median. This means that you will normally find the 50th percentile included in a range of per-

Median value between values 22 and 23 (value 22.5)

TABLE 5.5 Frequency Distribution for a Random Sample of 20 18-to-25-Year-Olds from the 2002 GSS subset A File for the Variable *age*

Ages of randomly selected respondents

Ages	Frequency	Percent	Valid Percent	Cumulative Frequencies	Cumulative Percent
18	1	5.0	5.0	1	5.0
19	1	5.0	5.0	2	10.0
20	1	5.0	5.0	3	15.0
21	5	25.0	25.0	8	40.0
22	2	10.0	10.0	10	50.0
23	5	25.0	25.0	15	75.0
24	2	10.0	10.0	17	85.0
25	3	15.0	5.0	20	100.0
	N = 20	100.0	100.0		

Median case between cases 10 and 11 (case 10.5)

centiles. In this example, the 50th percentile is included in the range of percentiles at age 22.

What to Do When the Median Falls between Two Values

What happens when the median case falls between two values? Sometimes this happens with a frequency distribution just like it did when we lined up our 10 students in the previous example. Calculate the median case for the frequency distribution in Table 5.5 to see how this might occur.

Follow the same process as you did in the example of the 10 college students. Find the median case using the formula

$$\text{median case} = (N + 1) \times .50 = (20 + 1) \times .50 = 21 \times .50 = 10.5.$$

Next, you would find the value associated with case 10.5. However, there is no case 10.5. What do you do? Use the cumulative frequencies column to locate the case immediately before the median case (case 10) and after the median case (case 11), then identify the values associated with each of those cases. The corresponding values are 22 and 23. Add the two values (22 and 23) to get 45, and divide by 2. The median value is 22.5.

Half of the respondents are 18 to 22 years old, and the other half are 23 to 25 years old.

Using the frequency distribution   Even if you locate the median using the Cumulative Percent column on a frequency distribution, you should be aware that sometimes the median can fall between two values. It would be tempting to look down the Cumulative Percent column of Table 5.5, find the 50th percentile, and identify the median as age 22. As we learned in the previous section, though, the median for the distribution of ages in Table 5.5 is 22.5, and not age 22. You need to be aware that when the number of valid cases in a distribution is even *and* one of the values in a frequency distribution is located exactly at the 50th percentile, the median has to be located between two values: the value at the 50th percentile and the value immediately above it.

EXAMPLE:

The frequency distribution in Table 5.5 illustrates this point. Notice that the number of valid cases in the distribution is even. The 50th percentile is at value 22 (22 years of age). Value 22 is the value associated with case 10. However, case 10 is not the median case. The median case is actually case 10.5. We determine this by using our formula for the median case: $(N + 1) \times .50$. Consequently, we have to locate the median value halfway between case 10 and case 11, or halfway between values 22 and 23. The median value, then, is 22.5.

Avoiding Common Pitfalls: The median case and the median value The most frequently occurring problem with finding the median value is that students often treat the median case as the median value. Consequently, they do the computation for the median case, using the formula $(N + 1) \times .50$, and then treat the result as the median value. Remember that finding the median value is a *two-step* process of (1) finding the median case and (2) using a frequency distribution to locate the median value.

CHECKING YOUR WORK

To make sure you have located the median value and have not stopped at finding the median case, ask yourself, "Does the number I am treating as the median value fall between the minimum and maximum values for the variable?" Usually (but not always), the median case doesn't make sense as a value of the variable. (This is especially true when you are finding the median for ordinal-level variables and when you are dealing with a large number of cases.) For example, when you found the median case 10.5 for the preceding frequency distribution, you couldn't assume it was the median value because there are no values of 10.5 among the categories of the variable *age*. It wouldn't make sense to say half the respondents are less than 10.5 years old and half the respondents are more than 10.5 years old.

Skills Practice 2   Use Table 5.6 to find the modes and medians for males and females for the variable *rincome98*. (You may need to add a cumulative frequencies column to the frequency distribution in order to find the medians.) Write an analysis comparing the two groups, males and females.

TABLE 5.6 Frequency Distributions for the Variable *rincom98* in the GSS 2002 subset A File for Males and Females (note that missing values and their frequencies are omitted from these tables)

RINCOM98 Respondents' income

SEX Respondents' sex			Frequency	Percent	Valid Percent	Cumulative Percent
1 MALE	Valid	1 UNDER $1 000	8	1.2	1.8	1.8
		2 $1 000 TO 2 999	10	1.5	2.2	4.0
		3 $3 000 TO 3 999	9	1.4	2.0	6.0
		4 $4 000 TO 4 999	4	.6	.9	6.9
		5 $5 000 TO 5 999	9	1.4	2.0	8.8
		6 $6 000 TO 6 999	5	.8	1.1	10.0
		7 $7 000 TO 7 999	2	.3	.4	10.4
		8 $8 000 TO 9 999	10	1.5	2.2	12.6
		9 $10000 TO 12499	8	1.2	1.8	14.4
		10 $12500 TO 14999	14	2.1	3.1	17.5
		11 $15000 TO 17499	14	2.1	3.1	20.6
		12 $17500 TO 19999	22	3.4	4.9	25.4
		13 $20000 TO 22499	22	3.4	4.9	30.3
		14 $22500 TO 24999	24	3.7	5.3	35.6
		15 $25000 TO 29999	25	3.8	5.5	41.2
		16 $30000 TO 34999	53	8.1	11.7	52.9
		17 $35000 TO 39999	37	5.7	8.2	61.1
		18 $40000 TO 49999	43	6.6	9.5	70.6
		19 $50000 TO 59999	44	6.7	9.7	80.3
		20 $60000 TO 74999	40	6.1	8.8	89.2
		21 $75000 - $89999	15	2.3	3.3	92.5
		22 $90000- $109999	9	1.4	2.0	94.5
		23 $110 000 OVER	25	3.8	5.5	100.0
		Total	452	69.1	100.0	
2 FEMALE	Valid	1 UNDER $1 000	12	1.4	2.4	2.4
		2 $1 000 TO 2 999	23	2.7	4.6	7.0
		3 $3 000 TO 3 999	10	1.2	2.0	9.0
		4 $4 000 TO 4 999	5	.6	1.0	10.0
		5 $5 000 TO 5 999	14	1.7	2.8	12.7
		6 $6 000 TO 6 999	8	.9	1.6	14.3
		7 $7 000 TO 7 999	15	1.8	3.0	17.3
		8 $8 000 TO 9 999	22	2.6	4.4	21.7
		9 $10000 TO 12499	32	3.8	6.4	28.1
		10 $12500 TO 14999	30	3.5	6.0	34.1
		11 $15000 TO 17499	18	2.1	3.6	37.6
		12 $17500 TO 19999	22	2.6	4.4	42.0
		13 $20000 TO 22499	32	3.8	6.4	48.4
		14 $22500 TO 24999	25	3.0	5.0	53.4
		15 $25000 TO 29999	51	6.0	10.2	63.5
		16 $30000 TO 34999	44	5.2	8.8	72.3
		17 $35000 TO 39999	32	3.8	6.4	78.7
		18 $40000 TO 49999	51	6.0	10.2	88.8
		19 $50000 TO 59999	26	3.1	5.2	94.0
		20 $60000 TO 74999	17	2.0	3.4	97.4
		21 $75000 - $89999	4	.5	.8	98.2
		22 $90000- $109999	3	.4	.6	98.8
		23 $110 000 OVER	6	.7	1.2	100.0
		Total	502	59.3	100.0	

THE MEAN

The **mean** is commonly referred to as the average. It is the measure with which you have probably had the most experience, as most students are interested in their grade point averages or their average grades for a course. You probably already know how to find the mean—add up all the grades you have and divide by how many grades there are.

Whereas the median is the value in a set of scores that is associated with the midpoint in a distribution of responses to a variable, the mean is the value that sits in the arithmetical middle of a set of values. To demonstrate this concept, find the average age of the students in Figure 5.3. You should obtain 21 as your average of the ages of the students. (Simply add up each of the ages in Figure 5.3 and divide by how many students there are in the illustration.)

Now subtract the mean from the ages of each of the students that are below the mean. Total your results. You should come up with –4.

$$19 - 21 = -2$$
$$20 - 21 = -1$$
$$20 - 21 = -1$$
$$\text{Total} = -4$$

Do the same thing for the ages of the students that are above the mean. You should get +4.

$$22 - 21 = 1$$
$$22 - 21 = 1$$
$$23 - 21 = 2$$
$$\text{Total} = +4$$

Notice that if you ignore the signs on the totals of the differences, the sums of the differences are the same, 4. The mean is in the arithmetical middle of the distribution of scores. It is, in effect, balancing the differences between the values below the mean and the mean itself with the values above the mean and the mean itself. If you add a higher value to the distribution (a 31-year-old student, for example), then the value of the mean increases in order to maintain the balance. Add the 31-year-old to the distribution of students in Figure 5.3 and see what happens to the mean.

FIGURE 5.3
Ages of nine students in a class.

Student:	1	2	3	4	5	6	7	8	9
Age:	19	20	20	21	21	21	22	22	23

In addition, notice that if you add the sum of the differences between the ages below the mean and the mean itself (−4) and the sum of the differences between the ages above the mean and the mean itself (+4), you get zero. This is always the case, and I will discuss this concept in more depth later on in this chapter.

Now let's look at how to apply the mean.

When to Use the Mean

The mean is typically used only with numerical variables. Although researchers sometimes use it with any type of continuous, ordinal variable, and you may also see it used with dichotomous variables, this text follows the practice of using the mean only with numerical variables.

Computing the Mean by Hand

Mean: Raw scores formula   The simplest way to find the mean is to add up a set of values and divide by the number of values you have. This process of finding the mean is called the *raw scores formula*. The scores are "raw" in that you haven't tried to condense them or process them in any way (by putting them into a frequency distribution, for example). The formula for the mean computed with raw scores is

Formula 5.2(a):   Mean (raw scores)

$$\overline{X} = \frac{\Sigma X}{N}$$

where $\overline{X}$ is the symbol for the mean; Σ means "add up the following"—in this formula, X, or scores; and N stands for the number of scores you have.

Thus, the equation can be read as follows:

Add up the scores you have, then divide by the number of scores.

EXAMPLE:

If you want to know the average of the ages of the students in a class, you would add up the ages of the students to get ΣX:

Student:	1	2	3	4	5	6	7	8	9	
Age:	19 +	20 +	20 +	20 +	21 +	22 +	22 +	23 +	24 =	191

Then divide the sum of their ages by the number of students (N):

$$\frac{191}{9} = 21.22$$

You could then say,

The average of the ages of the students is 21.22.

Skills Practice 3

1. Find the average of the ages of the students in Figure 5.2.
2. What is the average of the ages of the respondents to the General Social Survey in Table 5.3?

Mean: Ungrouped frequency distribution formula   Computing the mean scores for large numbers of cases becomes much easier if you first put them into a frequency distribution. The formula for the mean for an ungrouped frequency distribution is simply a variation on the formula for the mean—raw scores, with the exception that we must multiply each score (X) by its frequency of occurrence, f. When you multiply each score by its frequency, you are performing the same mathematical function as adding up the scores one by one.

Formula 5.2(b):   Mean (ungrouped frequency distribution)

$$\overline{X} = \frac{\Sigma\left(fX\right)}{N}$$

where Σ tells us to "add up the following"—in this formula, each frequency multiplied by each associated score or value, and N represents the number of cases (the sum of the Frequency column).

Order of operations   As formulas become more complex, it is important to understand the process for doing the computations within a formula. For any formula:

1. Do any computations within parentheses first, followed by computations within brackets (if any), working from left to right.
2. Within parentheses do the computations in this order:
   - Complete all of the computations in a numerator or denominator before dividing the numerator by the denominator.
   - Find any squares or square roots.
   - Next do the multiplication, followed by the division.
   - Then do the addition or subtraction.
3. Within brackets follow the same order of computations.
4. Follow the same order of computations for any computations outside of parentheses or brackets, working from left to right.

For this formula then:

1. Find each fX by multiplying each frequency by each of its associated scores or values.
2. Add up each of the results (each fX) to get the sum of fX.
3. Divide the sum of fX by N.

Understanding the order of operations allows us to read the formula as follows:

To find the mean, multiply each frequency by its associated score or value, and then add up the results. Divide the total, the sum of *fX*, by *N*.

EXAMPLE:

Let's apply this formula to the data in Figure 5.1, the ages of nine traditional-age college students. Begin by constructing a frequency distribution for the data.

Age (*X*)	*f*
19	1
20	3
21	1
22	2
23	1
24	1
	N = 9

Once you have constructed the frequency distribution, multiply each frequency by its corresponding value or score to get *fX*. Then add up the results (each *fX*) to get the sum of *fX* (Σ*fX*). Now your frequency distribution should look like this:

Age (*X*)	*f*	*f · X*
19	1	19
20	3	60
21	1	21
22	2	44
23	1	23
24	1	24
	N = 9	Σ*fX* = 191

With this table, you have everything you need to work the formula

$$\frac{\Sigma\left(fX\right)}{N} = \frac{191}{9} = 21.22$$

The average of the ages of the students is 21.22 years old.

Does the answer look familiar? It's the same one you got with the raw scores formula for the mean. Simply putting the data into a frequency distribution doesn't change the mean, but it does make the computation a little easier.

CHECKING YOUR WORK

The mean will always fall between the minimum and maximum values of the variable for which the mean is computed. For example, in the preceding set of data, the minimum value is age 19 and the maximum value is 24. You cannot have a mean less than 19 or greater than 24.

Interpreting the Mean

How do we write about the mean? Often you see the mean interpreted along the lines of "the average age of the respondents was 21.22 years old." Or you may see something like "on average, the respondents were 21.22 years old." Technically, the average is best understood as the average of a set of values. Interpretations of the mean, therefore, are best written like this:

The average of the ages of the students is 21.22 years old.

 Skills Practice 4   Find the mean using the formula for an ungrouped frequency distribution, first using the data in Figure 5.2 and then using the data in Table 5.3.

 Skills Practice 5   Use Table 5.7 to find the modes, medians, and means for male and female respondents between the ages of 18 and 25 to the variable *hrsrelax* (the number of hours per day the respondent has to relax) in the 2002 GSS subset A. Use the modes, medians, and means to compare male and female respondents.

TABLE 5.7   Frequency Distribution for the Variable *hrsrelax* for Male and Female Respondents between the Ages of 18 and 25 in the GSS 2002 subset A File (missing values and their frequencies are omitted from these tables)

HRSRELAX Hours per day R have to relax

SEX Respondents' sex			Frequency	Percent	Valid Percent	Cumulative Percent
1 MALE	Valid	2	8	10.7	16.3	16.3
		3	8	10.7	16.3	32.7
		4	13	17.3	26.5	59.2
		5	8	10.7	16.3	75.5
		6	6	8.0	12.2	87.8
		7	2	2.7	4.1	91.8
		8	3	4.0	6.1	98.0
		12	1	1.3	2.0	100.0
		Total	49	65.3	100.0	
2 FEMALE	Valid	0	8	7.6	11.9	11.9
		1	5	4.8	7.5	19.4
		2	12	11.4	17.9	37.3
		3	10	9.5	14.9	52.2
		4	7	6.7	10.4	62.7
		5	12	11.4	17.9	80.6
		6	8	7.6	11.9	92.5
		7	1	1.0	1.5	94.0
		8	2	1.9	3.0	97.0
		10	2	1.9	3.0	100.0
		Total	67	63.8	100.0	

CHARACTERISTICS OF THE MEAN, MEDIAN, AND MODE

Having an understanding of the characteristics of the mode, median, and mean is important for two reasons. First, it helps us interpret the measures of central tendency. Second, it helps us make sense of how we can make inferences or generalizations from samples, like the General Social Survey, to the populations (like the one the GSS is designed to represent) from which they're drawn.

Characteristics Affecting Interpretation: Susceptibility to Extreme Scores

The mode and the median are the measures of central tendency least changed or altered by unusually high or low (extreme) scores in a set of data. The mean, on the other hand, is the measure of central tendency most susceptible to (changed by) the presence of unusually high or low scores. For example, if we take the age data we used in Figure 5.1 and change the age of the ninth student from 24 to 42, we can see that the mode and median don't change, but the mean gets much larger. Compute the mode, median, and the mean for the following data:

Student:	1	2	3	4	5	6	7	8	9
Age:	19	20	20	20	21	22	22	23	42

The mode for this group of students remains 20 and the median is still 21, but the mean becomes 23.22. The age, 42, pulls the mean further from the center of the distribution of scores (the median). Consequently, when we report the mean for a distribution, we should look at the range of values to see whether the mean is being affected by extreme scores at either the low end or the high end of the distribution.

Characteristics Affecting Inferences

These characteristics of the mean, median, and mode are important because they form the foundation for statistics you will be learning later. When you get to Chapter 7 you will be introduced to inferential statistics—statistics for making generalizations about populations from samples. The concepts covered in this section help you understand the conceptual fundamentals of inferential statistics.

Stability in randomly drawn samples   The mean is the most stable measure of central tendency for randomly drawn samples. If you were to draw a series of samples from the same population, there would be less variability in the means than in either the medians or the modes.

Let's see how this works. I will use five randomly drawn samples from the 2002 General Social Survey to illustrate what is generally true of all possible samples that could be drawn from a specified population. (If you were to draw your own five samples, your results could differ from mine.) To illustrate the idea of stability of the mean in randomly drawn samples, I treated the 2,765 respondents to the 2002 General Social Survey as a population. From this population, I drew five random samples of respondents and I recorded the mean, median, and mode for each sample.

	Mean	*Median*	*Mode*
Sample 1	46.20	40	35
Sample 2	50.62	44	40
Sample 3	46.98	46	28
Sample 4	46.30	47	51
Sample 5	47.72	45	45

Notice the range of values you get for each of the three measures of central tendency. The means range from a low of 46.20 years to a high of 50.62 years—a difference of 4.42 years. The medians range from a low of 40 years to a high of 47 years—a difference of 7 years. The modes range from 28 years to 51 years, a difference of 23 years. The samples of the means show the least variation as measured by the range of values.

By making some simple calculations, you can see that the means obtained from the sample are close to the actual mean of the population. In fact, the sample means are closer to the population mean than the sample medians or modes in relation to the population median and mode. The average of the ages of the individuals in the population is 46.28. (This number comes from the mean for the variable *age* in the 2002 General Social Survey.) Now look at this number in relation to each of the sample means.

	Sample Mean	*Population Mean*	*Difference*
Sample 1	46.20	46.28	−.08
Sample 2	50.62	46.28	4.34
Sample 3	46.98	46.28	.70
Sample 4	46.30	46.28	.02
Sample 5	47.72	46.28	1.44

If we add up the differences between each of the sample means and the population mean, but ignore the signs (treating negative numbers as if they were positive), the sum of the differences is 6.58. If we divide the sum of the differences by 5 (the number of sample means we have), we can see that the average of the differences is 1.32 years; the average of the differences between our sample means and the population mean is a little over one year.

Now let's do the same sort of computation with our sample medians and our sample modes. Do we get similar results? If you add up the differences between each of the sample medians and the population median, you would get the following:

	Sample Median	*Population Median*	*Difference*
Sample 1	40.00	44	−4
Sample 2	44.00	44	0
Sample 3	46.00	44	2
Sample 4	47.00	44	3
Sample 5	45.00	44	1

TABLE 5.8   Ages of Nine Students, with an Average Age of 21, Illustrating How the Sum of the Deviations from the Mean Equals Zero

Age		Mean	Deviations From the Mean
19	−	21	= −2
20	−	21	= −1
20	−	21	= −1
21	−	21	= 0
21	−	21	= 0
21	−	21	= 0
22	−	21	= 1
22	−	21	= 1
23	−	21	= 2
Σ of the deviations from the mean =			0

Total the differences (ignoring the signs). The sum of the differences between the sample medians and the population median equals 10. Dividing this total by 5 (the number of samples) shows us that the average of the differences between the sample medians and the population median is 2 years.

You can do the same set of computations for the mode. The population mode is 33. If you add up the differences between each of the sample modes and the population mode (again ignoring the signs), you would get a difference of 44. If we divide 44 by the number of samples (5), we can see that the average of the differences between the sample modes and the population mode is 8.8 years.

In these examples, sample means were drawn from a population for which we know the population characteristics, like the mean, median, and mode. Later in the book, this characteristic of the mean—its stability across randomly drawn samples from populations—will be used to make estimates about populations, even when nothing is known about the population itself.

The sum of the deviations from the mean equals zero   Another property of the mean is that the sum of the deviations from the mean always equals zero. This means that if you subtract each score in a set of data from the average of all scores, you will always get zero. You may recall reading about this property of the mean on p. 153. Let's illustrate this property using the set of data in Table 5.8. The mean—the average of the ages of the students—is 21. Subtract the mean from each of the ages in the distribution. If you add up the results (don't ignore the signs!) you will get zero.

In the next chapter you will see how we can use the deviations from the mean to compute measures that assess the dispersion of distributions.

USING MEAN, MEDIAN, AND MODE TO ANALYZE DISTRIBUTIONS: ARE THEY NORMAL OR NOT?

Every graphic distribution of responses to a variable has a shape. If we produced a histogram for a variable and drew a line around the bars on the histogram, we

FIGURE 5.4
Histogram for the variable *age* in the GSS 2002 subset A file.

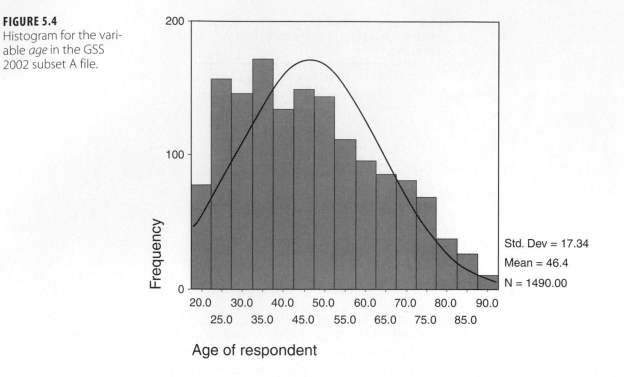

could look at the shape of the distribution. For example, if we produced a histogram for the variable *age* in the GSS 2002 subset A file, it would look like Figure 5.4.

When the shape of a distribution is perfectly bell-shaped (the curved line in Figure 5.4), the distribution is said to be **normal**. When we say a distribution is perfectly bell-shaped, we don't mean that it has to look exactly like the Liberty Bell, but it does have to be unimodal and symmetrical. A **unimodal** distribution has a single mode, and a **symmetrical distribution** has as many cases above the mean as below it (so the mean and median are equal). Moreover, if you draw a line through the middle of a symmetrical distribution, the shape of the distribution to the right of the line will mirror the shape of the distribution to the left.

A unimodal symmetrical distribution can have many possible shapes, from fairly flat-looking bells (like Figure 5.5) to bells that look like the Liberty Bell (Figure 5.6) to bells that are more peaked (Figure 5.7). In a unimodal symmetrical distribution, the mean, median, and mode have the same value. For each of the distributions in Figures 5.5 through 5.7, the mean, median, and mode have the same value.

We rarely encounter distributions that are perfectly normal. We are more likely to find distributions that are **skewed**—distributions in which there are more cases below the mean than above it (Figure 5.8), or distributions with more cases above the mean than below it (Figure 5.9). These distributions may look somewhat bell-shaped, but they are not symmetrical. Instead, the distributions of responses to the variables tend to be clustered to one side of the mean or the other.

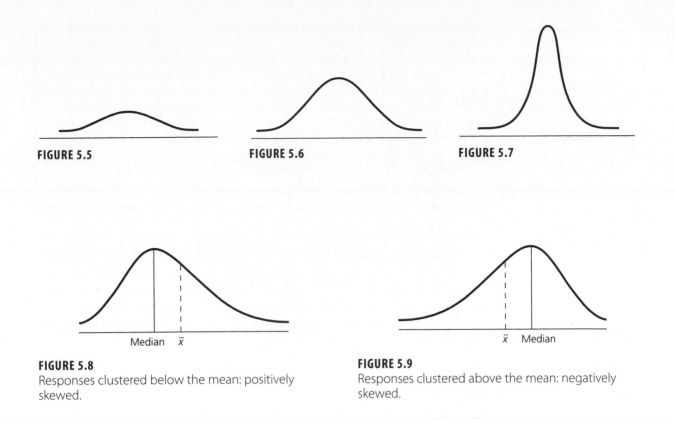

FIGURE 5.5   **FIGURE 5.6**   **FIGURE 5.7**

Median $\bar{x}$

FIGURE 5.8
Responses clustered below the mean: positively
skewed.

$\bar{x}$ Median

FIGURE 5.9
Responses clustered above the mean: negatively
skewed.

The mean in its relation to the median helps evaluate the shape of a distribution. When the mean and median are different, the distribution is skewed. (Keep in mind, however, that just because distributions have identical means and medians, they are not necessarily normal. In addition to having the same values for the mean, median, and mode, normal distributions must be unimodal and symmetrical.) When the mean is below the median, we know there are more cases clustered above the mean than below it. These distributions are described as **negatively skewed**. There are some unusually low values in a set of data pulling the mean down from the median. However, when the mean falls above the median, we know there are more cases clustered below the mean than above it. These distributions are described as **positively skewed**; there are some unusually high values in a set of data pulling the mean up from the median.

 Avoiding Common Pitfalls: Analyzing skew Students tend to treat the mean as the point of comparison, and they try to evaluate skew by looking at whether the median falls above or below the mean. Although skew can be looked at this way, it is more confusing. It is less confusing if you can remember that the median should be the statistic for comparison and always evaluate the mean in its relation to (whether it is above or below) the median. Even then, students have a hard time remembering how to evaluate skew—which is negative and which is positive? It is helpful to treat the median as the zero point on a number line. When the mean is below (less than) the median, it falls on the negative side of the median, and we label the distribution *negatively skewed;* when it is above (more than) the median, it falls on the positive side, and we label the distribution *positively skewed.* The following figure may help you to visualize this:

Evaluating Skew

–(Negative side) ————————Median———————— (Positive side)+
Mean less than median   Mean more than median

Why is it important to evaluate skew? First, the relationship between the mean, median, and mode helps us assess whether the mean is an accurate representation of the distribution of the responses to a variable. In some distributions, the mean can be affected by either extremely high or extremely low values in relation to other values in the distribution. By examining the mean in relation to the median we can tell if this is occurring. If so, then the median may be a better measure of central tendency than the mean.

The second reason it is important to evaluate skew is because the assumption that a set of responses to a variable is normally distributed underlies the computation of many statistics. Consequently, having the ability to evaluate this assumption is important for the correct applications of some of the statistics we will learn later on in this text and those you may learn about in advanced courses.

Skills Practice 6   Look at the measures of central tendency for the five samples I selected from the 2002 General Social Survey file for the variable *age* (see p. 158). Use the mean, median, and mode for each sample to answer these questions: Are the distributions skewed? If so, in which direction? How can you tell?

USING SPSS

Finding Measures of Central Tendency Using SPSS

Finding the measures of central tendency (mode, median, and mean) with SPSS is a fairly simple task, as described in the following SPSS Guide.

SPSS GUIDE: FINDING MEASURES OF CENTRAL TENDENCY

Open your SPSS program and the GSS 2002 subset A file. Use the command path Analyze ➥ Descriptive Statistics ➥ Frequencies to open the Frequencies dialog box (see the SPSS Guide, "Obtaining a Frequency Distribution," in Chapter 4 if you need help).

 Scroll down to a variable of interest. Let's try *wrktype.* Click on it to highlight it.

2 Click on the ▶ pointing at the Variable(s) box to put the variable in the box.

3 Then click on the Statistics button.

At the Frequencies: Statistics dialog box, find the box labeled Central Tendency.

1 Click on the measure(s) you want SPSS to compute. (You can select one or more than one.) *Wrktype* is a nominal variable, so we will only use the mode as our measure of central tendency.

2 Click on Continue to return to the Frequencies dialog box, and click on OK at the Frequencies dialog box.

TABLE 5.9   Statistics Table

Statistics

WRKTYPE Work arra

N	Valid	
	Missing	
Mode		

Valid	1 INDEPENDENT C	
	2 ON-CALL, WORK	
	3 PAID BY A TEMP	
	4 WORK FOR CON	
	5 REGULAR, PERM	
	Total	
Missing	0 NAP	
	8 DONT KNOW	
	9 NO ANSWER	
	Total	
Total		

Skills Practice 9   Write an analysis of the responses to the variable *hrs1*. It may help you in your analysis to keep in mind what you might think of as a full-time workweek. Do the GSS respondents tend to work full-time? What percentage of the respondents works full-time or more? What percentage of the respondents works full-time or less? What percentage seems to work excessively long hours to you? Use the mode, median, and mean in your analysis. Is this distribution skewed? If so, in which direction?

Using Measures of Central Tendency

Use the following chart as a guide to the correct application of the mode, median, and mean. The use of these statistics depends on the level of measurement of the variable to which the statistics are being applied. This chart should help you decide when and how to use each of the measures of central tendency.

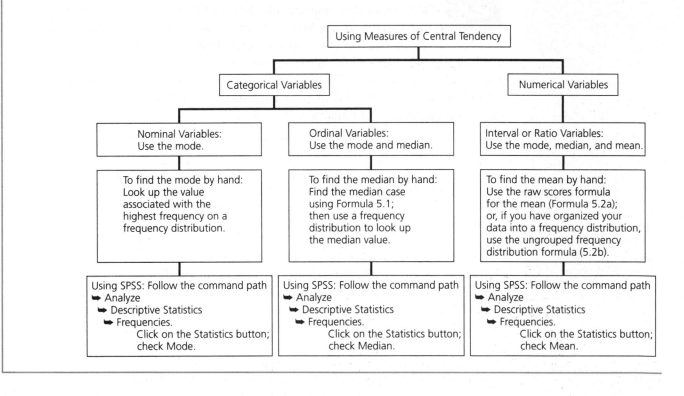

At this point you should understand the differences between the mode, median, and mean. The mode is the most frequently selected or chosen

value or category in a distribution of responses to a variable. The median is the category that divides a distribution of responses in half. The mean is the arithmetical average of a distribution of responses to a variable.

The mode is the only measure of central tendency appropriate for nominal variables, although it also can be used with ordinal and numerical variables. The median is used with ordinal and numerical variables, and the mean can be used only with numerical variables.

You should be able to calculate the mode, median, and mean by hand, and you should be able to use the SPSS command path Analyze ➡ Descriptive Statistics ➡ Frequencies to find them. More important, you should understand what they mean, and you should be able to interpret them. In addition, you should be able to use them together

to evaluate the extent to which a set of responses to a variable is skewed.

Finally, you should have an understanding of some of the properties of the mean, median, and mode. The mean is more susceptible to extreme scores in a distribution, unlike the mode and the median. The mean is more stable (it is subject to less variation than the mode or the median) in random samples drawn from a population. An important property of the mean is that the sum of the deviations from the mean equals zero.

In the next chapter we will be using these concepts, along with statistics that assess dispersion, to evaluate variability.

KEY CONCEPTS

Measures of central tendency
Mode
Median
Median case
Median value
Mean

Susceptibility of mean to
    extreme scores
Stability of mean in randomly
    drawn samples
Sum of deviations from the
    mean equals zero

Normal distribution
Unimodal distribution
Symmetrical distribution
Skew
Negative skew
Positive skew

ANSWERS TO SKILLS PRACTICES

1. Nearly 61% of the male respondents work full-time, and the most frequently occurring response is "working full-time." On the other hand, just under half of the female respondents work full-time (45.5%), the most commonly occurring response to the labor force status question. Nearly one-fifth, 16.7%, say they keep house. Although the mode for both groups is the same—working full-time—a larger percentage of males than females say they work full-time. In addition, a larger percentage of females say they keep house or work part-time as compared to male respondents.

2. For males: The mode is income category 16 ($30,000 to $34,999). The median is also income category 16. To find the median,

   a. Find the median case.
   Use the formula $(N + 1) \times .50$.
   $N = 452$ (valid cases only), and
   $N + 1 = 453$. $453 \times .50 = 226.5$.

   b. Use the median case to find the median value.
   Read down the frequency column, adding up the frequencies as you go, until you find the category that contains the median value. (Category 1, less than $1,000, contains cases 1–8; category 2, $1,000 to $2,999, contains cases 9–18, and so on.) The median case, 226.5, is in category 16 ($30,000–34,999). You can double-check your work by noticing that the 50th percentile is at category 16.

For females: There are two modes, category 15 ($25,000 to $29,999) and category 18 ($40,000 to $49,999), the categories associated with the largest numbers in the Frequency column of the Frequency Distribution. The median category is category 14 ($22,500 to $24, 999).

$N + 1 = 503$ (502, the number of valid responses, plus 1). $503 \times .50 = 251.5$.

Category 14 ($22,500–24,999) contains the median case, 256.5.

Comparing males and females: The income category most frequently reported by males is between the two modes for female respondents. However, the median income for male respondents is higher than the median income for female respondents. Half of the male respondents have incomes of $34,999 or less, whereas half of the female respondents have incomes of $24,999 or less. If you look at the high end of the income distribution, nearly 30% of male respondents report earning $50,000 or more, whereas only about 11% of female respondents report earning that much.

3. Use the formula for the mean—raw scores:

$$\overline{X} = \frac{\Sigma X}{N}$$

   a. Add up the ages ($\Sigma X = 215$). Divide by $N(10)$. $\overline{X} = 21.50$.
   b. Add up the ages ($\Sigma X = 560$). Divide by $N(25)$. $\overline{X} = 22.40$.

4. Use the formula for the mean—ungrouped frequency distribution:

$$\overline{X} = \frac{\Sigma\left(fX\right)}{N}$$

   a. Put the scores into a frequency distribution. Multiply each score by its frequency, then add them up to get $\Sigma fX = 215$. Divide by $N(10)$. $\overline{X} = 21.50$.
   b. Put the scores into a frequency distribution. Multiply each score by its frequency, then add them up to get $\Sigma fX = 560$. Divide by $N(25)$. $\overline{X} = 22.40$.

5. The mode for the male respondents is 4 hours. The median for males is also 4 hours. (The median case for males is found using Formula

5.1, $[N + 1] \times .50$, where $N = 49$. The median case is case 25.) The median value is the value associated with case 25 and the 50th percentile, 4 hours. The mean for males is found using Formula 5.2(b), the formula for an ungrouped frequency distribution.

$$\frac{\Sigma(fx)}{N} = \frac{218}{49} = 4.45$$

There are two modes for female respondents, 2 hours and 5 hours. The median for females is 3 hours. (The median case for females is found using Formula 5.1, $[N + 1] \times .50$, where $N = 67$. The median case is case 34.) The median value is the value associated with case 34 and the 50th percentile, 3 hours. The mean for females is found using Formula 5.2(b), the formula for an ungrouped frequency distribution.

$$\frac{\Sigma(fx)}{N} = \frac{238}{67} = 3.55$$

Males respondents ages 18 to 25 say they have a little more time to relax each day than do female respondents of the same age. The most commonly occurring response among males is 4 hours, but the most commonly occurring responses among females are 2 hours and 5 hours. The median response for males is 4 hours, but the median response for females is lower at 3 hours. Half of the male respondents say they have at least 4 hours to relax. For female respondents, though, half relax only up to 3 hours and half from 3 to 10 hours a day. The average of the responses for males is 4.45 hours, whereas for females the average of the responses is about an hour less, 3.55 hours.

6. The distribution of ages in samples 1, 2, 3, and 5 are positively skewed—the means is higher than the median in each one. The distribution of ages in sample 4 is negatively skewed—the mean falls below the median.

7. Among respondents who work, the most commonly occurring form of employment, as might be expected, is regular, permanent employment. Over 80% of all respondents answered in this category.

8. Your SPSS output should look like the output in Table 5.10. The most frequently occurring

TABLE 5.10 Statistics and Frequency Distribution for the Variable *income98* in the GSS 2002 subset A File

Statistics

INCOME98 Total family income

N	Valid	1333
	Missing	167
Median		17.00
Mode		23

INCOME98 Total family income

		Frequency	Percent	Valid Percent	Cumulative Percent
Valid	1 UNDER $1 000	29	1.9	2.2	2.2
	2 $1 000 TO 2 999	7	.5	.5	2.7
	3 $3 000 TO 3 999	19	1.3	1.4	4.1
	4 $4 000 TO 4 999	11	.7	.8	5.0
	5 $5 000 TO 5 999	14	.9	1.1	6.0
	6 $6 000 TO 6 999	19	1.3	1.4	7.4
	7 $7 000 TO 7 999	15	1.0	1.1	8.6
	8 $8 000 TO 9 999	37	2.5	2.8	11.3
	9 $10000 TO 12499	47	3.1	3.5	14.9
	10 $12500 TO 14999	38	2.5	2.9	17.7
	11 $15000 TO 17499	39	2.6	2.9	20.6
	12 $17500 TO 19999	42	2.8	3.2	23.8
	13 $20000 TO 22499	51	3.4	3.8	27.6
	14 $22500 TO 24999	46	3.1	3.5	31.1
	15 $25000 TO 29999	82	5.5	6.2	37.2
	16 $30000 TO 34999	96	6.4	7.2	44.4
	17 $35000 TO 39999	79	5.3	5.9	50.3
	18 $40000 TO 49999	123	8.2	9.2	59.6
	19 $50000 TO 59999	118	7.9	8.9	68.4
	20 $60000 TO 74999	125	8.3	9.4	77.8
	21 $75000 TO $89999	104	6.9	7.8	85.6
	22 $90000 - $109999	59	3.9	4.4	90.0
	23 $110000 OR OVER	133	8.9	10.0	100.0
	Total	1333	88.9	100.0	
Missing	24 REFUSED	108	7.2		
	98 DK	59	3.9		
	Total	167	11.1		
Total		1500	100.0		

response to the household income question in the 2002 GSS is $110,000 or over. However, only 10% of those who answered the question responded in this category. The median is category 17, $35,000 to $39,999. Half of the respondents have household incomes of $39,999 or less, and half have household incomes of $35,000 or more. If we use the poverty threshold for a family of four at $18,104 as an indicator of poverty, then we can see from the frequency distribution that at least 20.6% of the respondents (those in the $17,499 category and below) have household incomes less than that.

TABLE 5.11 Statistics Table for the Variable *hrs1* in the GSS 2002 subset A File

Statistics

HRS1 Number of hours worked last week

N	Valid	940
	Missing	560
Mean		41.86
Median		40.00
Mode		40

9. Your SPSS Statistics output should look like the output in Table 5.11. The frequency distribution is quite large, so I have not reproduced it here. Together, the statistics in the Statistics box and the frequency distribution indicate that the respondents to the 2002 GSS tend to work at least 40 hours a week. Nearly 73% of all respondents report working at least 40 hours a week. The most frequently occurring response is 40 hours, and the median is 40 hours. Half of the respondents work 40 hours or more, and half work 40 hours or less. The mean is slightly higher than the median. The average of the hours worked as reported by the respondents is 41.86 hours. The fact that the mean is higher than the median indicates that the distribution of responses is skewed in a positive direction and that there are some very high responses pulling the mean up from the median. Nearly 13% of the respondents report working at least 60 hours a week, and 2% report working 80 hours a week or more.

GENERAL EXERCISES

What are the characteristics of 2002 GSS respondents in the age group 18–25 years old? How are they doing financially? Next you will find a set of frequency distributions for variables you can use to answer these questions. Complete the following exercises for calculating measures of central tendency by hand. The tables below are SPSS frequency distributions. Use only valid cases when computing measures of central tendency. You may need to add a Cumulative Frequencies column in order to find the median.

1. Find and interpret the mode for the frequency distribution shown here.

WRKSTAT Labor force status

		Frequency	Percent	Valid Percent	Cumulative Percent
Valid	1 WORKING FULLTIME	91	50.6	50.6	50.6
	2 WORKING PARTTIME	26	14.4	14.4	65.0
	4 UNEMPL, LAID OFF	9	5.0	5.0	70.0
	6 SCHOOL	31	17.2	17.2	87.2
	7 KEEPING HOUSE	19	10.6	10.6	97.8
	8 OTHER	4	2.2	2.2	100.0
	Total	180	100.0	100.0	

2. Find and interpret the mode for the frequency distribution shown here.

WRKTYPE Work arrangement at main job

		Frequency	Percent	Valid Percent	Cumulative Percent
Valid	1 INDEPENDENT CONTRACTOR/CONSULTANT/FREELANCE WORKER	9	5.0	7.7	7.7
	2 ON-CALL, WORK ONLY WHEN CALLED TO WORK	4	2.2	3.4	11.1
	3 PAID BY A TEMPORARY AGENCY	1	.6	.9	12.0
	4 WORK FOR CONTRACTOR WHO PROVIDES WORKERS/SERVICES	4	2.2	3.4	15.4
	5 REGULAR, PERMANENT EMPLOYEE	99	55.0	84.6	100.0
	Total	117	65.0	100.0	
Missing	0 NAP	63	35.0		
Total		180	100.0		

3. Find and interpret the mode for the frequency distribution in General Exercise 5.

4. Find and interpret the mode for the frequency distribution in General Exercise 6.

5. Find and interpret the median for the frequency distribution shown here.

DEGREE RS highest degree

		Frequency	Percent	Valid Percent	Cumulative Percent
Valid	0 LT HIGH SCHOOL	29	16.1	16.1	16.1
	1 HIGH SCHOOL	118	65.6	65.6	81.7
	2 JUNIOR COLLEGE	8	4.4	4.4	86.1
	3 BACHELOR	23	12.8	12.8	98.9
	4 GRADUATE	2	1.1	1.1	100.0
	Total	180	100.0	100.0	

6. Find and interpret the median for the frequency distribution shown here.

RINCOM98 Respondents' income

		Frequency	Percent	Valid Percent	Cumulative Percent
Valid	1 UNDER $1 000	8	4.4	6.7	6.7
	2 $1 000 TO 2 999	13	7.2	10.9	17.6
	3 $3 000 TO 3 999	9	5.0	7.6	25.2
	4 $4 000 TO 4 999	2	1.1	1.7	26.9
	5 $5 000 TO 5 999	6	3.3	5.0	31.9
	6 $6 000 TO 6 999	4	2.2	3.4	35.3
	7 $7 000 TO 7 999	3	1.7	2.5	37.8
	8 $8 000 TO 9 999	6	3.3	5.0	42.9
	9 $10000 TO 12499	11	6.1	9.2	52.1
	10 $12500 TO 14999	7	3.9	5.9	58.0
	11 $15000 TO 17499	6	3.3	5.0	63.0
	12 $17500 TO 19999	2	1.1	1.7	64.7
	13 $20000 TO 22499	7	3.9	5.9	70.6
	14 $22500 TO 24999	7	3.9	5.9	76.5
	15 $25000 TO 29999	11	6.1	9.2	85.7
	16 $30000 TO 34999	6	3.3	5.0	90.8
	17 $35000 TO 39999	7	3.9	5.9	96.6
	18 $40000 TO 49999	1	.6	.8	97.5
	19 $50000 TO 59999	2	1.1	1.7	99.2
	20 $60000 TO 74999	1	.6	.8	100.0
	Total	119	66.1	100.0	
Missing	0 NAP	53	29.4		
	24 REFUSED	4	2.2		
	98 DK	2	1.1		
	99 NA	2	1.1		
	Total	61	33.9		
Total		180	100.0		

7. Find and interpret the median for the frequency distribution shown here.

SATJOB7 Job satisfaction in general

		Frequency	Percent	Valid Percent	Cumulative Percent
Valid	1 COMPLETELY DISSATISFIED	1	.6	1.5	1.5
	2 VERY DISSATISFIED	4	2.2	6.2	7.7
	3 FAIRLY DISSATISFIED	5	2.8	7.7	15.4
	4 NEITHER SAT NOR DISSAT	6	3.3	9.2	24.6
	5 FAIRLY SATISFIED	23	12.8	35.4	60.0
	6 VERY SATISFIED	14	7.8	21.5	81.5
	7 COMPLETELY SATISFIED	12	6.7	18.5	100.0
	Total	65	36.1	100.0	
Missing	0 NAP	113	62.8		
	8 Cannot choose	2	1.1		
	Total	115	63.9		
Total		180	100.0		

8. Find and interpret the median for the frequency distribution shown here.

LOTOFSAY R has lot of say in job

		Frequency	Percent	Valid Percent	Cumulative Percent
Valid	1 Strongly Agree	26	14.4	22.2	22.2
	2 Agree	56	31.1	47.9	70.1
	3 Disagree	31	17.2	26.5	96.6
	4 Strongly Disagree	4	2.2	3.4	100.0
	Total	117	65.0	100.0	
Missing	0 NAP	63	35.0		
Total		180	100.0		

9. Find and interpret the median for the frequency distribution in General Exercise 11.

10. Find and interpret the median for the frequency distribution in General Exercise 12.

11. Find and interpret the mean for the frequency distribution shown here.

EDUC Highest year of school completed

		Frequency	Percent	Valid Percent	Cumulative Percent
Valid	7	1	.6	.6	.6
	8	3	1.7	1.7	2.2
	9	5	2.8	2.8	5.0
	10	7	3.9	3.9	8.9
	11	20	11.1	11.1	20.0
	12	49	27.2	27.2	47.2
	13	21	11.7	11.7	58.9
	14	36	20.0	20.0	78.9
	15	7	3.9	3.9	82.8
	16	20	11.1	11.1	93.9
	17	9	5.0	5.0	98.9
	18	2	1.1	1.1	100.0
	Total	180	100.0	100.0	

12. Find and interpret the mean for the frequency distribution shown here.

HRSRELAX Hours per day R have to relax

		Frequency	Percent	Valid Percent	Cumulative Percent
Valid	0	8	4.4	6.9	6.9
	1	5	2.8	4.3	11.2
	2	20	11.1	17.2	28.4
	3	18	10.0	15.5	44.0
	4	20	11.1	17.2	61.2
	5	20	11.1	17.2	78.4
	6	14	7.8	12.1	90.5
	7	3	1.7	2.6	93.1
	8	5	2.8	4.3	97.4
	10	2	1.1	1.7	99.1
	12	1	.6	.9	100.0
	Total	116	64.4	100.0	
Missing	-1 NAP	63	35.0		
	98 DONT KNOW	1	.6		
	Total	64	35.6		
Total		180	100.0		

13. Find and interpret the mean for the frequency distribution shown here.

EARNRS How many in family earned money

		Frequency	Percent	Valid Percent	Cumulative Percent
Valid	0	5	2.8	2.8	2.8
	1	76	42.2	42.7	45.5
	2	53	29.4	29.8	75.3
	3	25	13.9	14.0	89.3
	4	14	7.8	7.9	97.2
	5	4	2.2	2.2	99.4
	7	1	.6	.6	100.0
	Total	178	98.9	100.0	
Missing	9 NA	2	1.1		
Total		180	100.0		

14. Find and interpret the mean for the frequency distribution shown here.

MOREDAYS Days per month respondent works extra hours

		Frequency	Percent	Valid Percent	Cumulative Percent
Valid	0	47	26.1	40.2	40.2
	1	2	1.1	1.7	41.9
	2	12	6.7	10.3	52.1
	3	5	2.8	4.3	56.4
	4	15	8.3	12.8	69.2
	5	8	4.4	6.8	76.1
	6	2	1.1	1.7	77.8
	8	4	2.2	3.4	81.2
	9	3	1.7	2.6	83.8
	10	2	1.1	1.7	85.5
	12	1	.6	.9	86.3
	15	4	2.2	3.4	89.7
	16	1	.6	.9	90.6
	20	6	3.3	5.1	95.7
	21	1	.6	.9	96.6
	30	4	2.2	3.4	100.0
	Total	117	65.0	100.0	
Missing	-1 NAP	63	35.0		
Total		180	100.0		

15. Is the distribution in General Exercise 11 skewed? Is it positively or negatively skewed? How do you know?

16. Is the distribution in General Exercise 12 skewed? Is it positively or negatively skewed? How do you know?

17. Is the distribution in General Exercise 13 skewed? Is it positively or negatively skewed? How do you know?

18. Is the distribution in General Exercise 14 skewed? Is it positively or negatively skewed? How do you know?

SPSS EXERCISES

Obtain and analyze frequency distributions along with the appropriate measures of central tendency to answer the following questions:

1. How many hours do GSS respondents say they have to relax each day? Use the variable *hrsrelax*.
2. How much do GSS respondents make? Use *rincome98*.

3. How long have GSS respondents been in their jobs? Use *yearsjob*.
4. How hard is it for respondents to get time off work if they need it to help their families? Use the *famwkoff* variable.
5. Are the GSS respondents satisfied with their financial situations and their work lives? Use

frequency distributions and appropriate measures of central tendency for the variables *satfin*, *satjob7*, and *wkvsfam* to answer this question.

6. Are there any differences in satisfaction with one's job *(satjob7)* by race? Split your GSS 2002 subset A file using the variable *rcrace* to find out.

7. Are there any differences in respondents' income *(rincome98)* by race? Split your GSS 2002 subset A file using the variable *race* to find out.

8. Are there any differences in satisfaction with one's job *(satjob7)* by sex? Split your GSS 2002 subset A file using the variable *sex* to find out.

9. Is it easier for men or women to get time off to deal with family issues? Split your GSS 2002 subset A file using variable *sex*, and then analyze frequency distributions for the *famwkoff* variable to find out.

CHAPTER **6**

Measures of Dispersion

INTRODUCTION

In Chapter 5 we analyzed a number of variables bearing on the work lives and incomes of those who responded to the General Social Survey. In this chapter we add a related question: How much are Americans working to secure their financial futures? From soccer moms to workaholic dads, there seems to be at least an article a week devoted to our stressed-out schedules. "How to work smarter instead of harder." "How to balance work and family." "How to simplify our lives." Thus I was struck when the article in the "News to Use" section of this chapter appeared, because it discusses issues of how hard Americans are working and what effect work schedules are having on families—issues that are related to some of the variables in the General Social Survey. For example, when you analyzed the GSS variable *hrs1* for an exercise at the end of Chapter 5, you learned that the average number of hours worked in a week by respondents to the 2002 General Social Survey is 41.86.

What does this mean? Do most of the respondents work 42 hours, or is the range of responses to the variable *hrs1* more spread out, with some respondents closer to 8 and others closer to 80? The answer tells us how accurate our measures of central tendency really are for describing the general characteristics of the respondents. Without knowing about the *dispersion* of responses, we may come away with an incomplete—or even misleading—picture of the patterns in our data.

Consequently, to form a more complete picture of the responses to a variable, we have to add measures of dispersion to the list of tools at our disposal. Whereas measures of central tendency reveal one set of patterns in data—the values around which distributions of responses tend to cluster—measures of dispersion reveal another—the extent to which distributions are dispersed or spread out. Measures of central tendency and dispersion work together. Measures of central tendency are statistics that give us an indication of the values around which respondents "gather." **Measures of dispersion** are statistics that show us show how tightly packed—or spread out—the respondents are in relation to one or more measures of central tendency.

Analysis of dispersion is closely connected to the analysis of frequency distributions. Frequency distributions help us evaluate the extent of homogeneity (similarity) and heterogeneity (difference) in the distribution of responses to variables. Measures of dispersion provide us with statistics for assessing how homogeneous or heterogeneous a distribution is.   ■

N E W S *to* U S E
Statistics in the "Real" World

More Americans Put Families Ahead of Work

STEPHANIE ARMOUR[1]

Family is important to Patrick Snow. It's so important that he'll stop working in the afternoon to coach his sons' basketball games. It's so important he's brought up family in job interviews, candidly telling managers he needs to limit work hours so he can be with his two boys.

He knows it means his job in high-tech sales could suffer, but that doesn't matter to him. Family is so important, he says, he'd leave any employer who didn't understand.

"If my company doesn't like it, I'll find another job," says Snow, 33, of Bainbridge Island, Wash. He is also a speaker, coach and author of *Creating Your Own Destiny.*

"Employees used to be willing to sacrifice because of things like stock options. Now, they're fed up. They realize that family is the only stabilizing force in this turbulent economy," he says.

Employees have long struggled to balance work and family, but the economic slowdown

is now tilting the scales in favor of home. Making time for family isn't just important for a few employees like Snow—it's a growing priority for many workers disillusioned by layoffs, corporate scandal and waning company loyalty.

It's also a challenge bedeviling employers. Companies facing profit pressures need to squeeze more work out of fewer employees, but they risk retention problems if they appear insensitive to their staffs' family needs.

That's because 70% of workers don't think there is a healthy balance between work and personal life, according to a poll of 1,626 respondents by online job board TrueCareers, based in Reston, Va. And more than half are considering looking for a new job because of problems coping with both.

"There's a real shift," says Debra Major, an associate professor of psychology at Old Dominion University in Norfolk, Va. "In this economy, working 70 hours a week no longer makes a difference in how much you get compensated or how fast you advance. Employees

[1]*USA Today,* 4 December 2002, <http://www.usatoday.com/news/nation/2002-12-04-family-work-usat_x.htm>.

want to prioritize their own values, not the values that the company says are important."

Consider other national studies:

- Finding time for family is a more pressing concern than layoffs. More than 30% of employees said balancing work and family demands was a top concern in a May survey of 567 full-time employees by staffing services firm OfficeTeam, based in Menlo Park, Calif. That eclipses the 22% who said job security was a top concern.
- Almost three times as many employees say family is their top priority as those who list work as a top priority, according to a survey of more than 1,000 employees by Atlanta-based staffing firm Randstad North America and market research firm RoperASW.
- Nearly twice as many employees took sick days for personal needs in 2002 as did so last year, according to a survey by human-resource and employment-law information provider CCH of 333 human resource professionals in 43 states and the District of Columbia.

TUGGED IN EVERY DIRECTION

It's not that work is no longer important. Job insecurity wrought by the down economy means some workers are clocking longer hours and sacrificing even more in a bid to avoid layoffs. Many feel less able to refuse bosses' requests that they relocate, travel or give up vacation to get work done.

People are like a puppet being pulled in every direction," says Stephen Covey, author of motivational books such as *The 7 Habits of Highly Effective People.* "People have reprioritized in their minds and hearts, but the economic struggles and all the uncertainty have people torn between what they'd like to do and what they have to do." Several factors are pushing family to the forefront and prompting many workers to prioritize home, even if that decision means paying a professional price.

Psychologists, researchers and other workplace experts credit the shift to the changing priorities of a younger generation, family burdens facing baby boomers, the aftereffects of the Sept. 11 attacks and a backlash against the profit-making fixation of the late 1990s.

Part of the shift is simply generational change. As Generation X and Y employees start families, they are increasingly likely to place importance on the home front, research shows.

More than 85% of Gen X women say having a loving family is extremely important, compared with 18% who put the priority on earning a great deal of money, according to a study by research group Catalyst, which is based in New York.

Also driving the emphasis on family are baby boomers, who are increasingly likely to be part of the so-called "sandwich generation" caring for both children and older relatives.

More than 25% of adults have provided care for a chronically ill, disabled or aged family member or friend during the past year, according to the National Family Caregivers Association. Based on current Census data, that translates into more than 50 million people.

For those employees, there's no choice but to put family first. And it's an issue employers are paying attention to—more than 20% of companies offer elder-care referral services, according to the Society for Human Resource Management. That's up from 15% in 1998.

NIPPING HOURS AT WORK

Mary Murphy-Hoye, 45, curtailed her work hours and changed job duties within Intel. That has allowed her more time to spend with her father, who is temporarily living with her family in Phoenix.

But the new focus she's put on family isn't just a result of elder-care needs. As it was for many Americans, the reprioritization was shaped by the events of Sept. 11. Workers' resolve to put family first hasn't faded with the passage of time.

In a report this year by New York-based *American Demographics* and Greenwich, Conn.-based marketing research firm NFO WorldGroup, nearly 80% of Americans say their family is more of a priority since Sept. 11, compared with 70% who said the same in October 2001. The poll of 2,500 adults found respondents with children were even more stalwart in their determination to prioritize family.

For Murphy-Hoye, a mother of two boys (Patrick, 8, and Thomas, 11), there have been big changes. The engineer used to work on site in Sacramento, and she traveled. But in June of 2001, she switched jobs to focus on research and work from home. She also trimmed her schedule and puts in fewer hours each day.

"We got a wake-up call," says Murphy-Hoye about Sept. 11. "Everything is about simplifying and getting back to what's really important. I don't feel quite as exhausted as I did before. I'm a lot more in touch with my kids."

EMPLOYEES ADJUST

The emphasis on family isn't lost on employers. Despite the recession, nearly all forms of work-life programs saw modest growth in the past year, according to a May survey of 945 major U.S. employers by Hewitt Associates, an outsourcing and consulting firm based in a Lincolnshire, Ill.

These benefits, such as flexible work schedules and job sharing, often cost little but provide a big return.

At New York Life Insurance, work-life benefits include on-site back-up childcare, adoption assistance, flexible schedules and an employee health department.

"We've been committed to work-life for many years now," says Angela Coleman, vice president of human resources at New York Life. "We want programs that meet the needs of our employees. It's about attracting and recruiting, but also about retaining employees."

At biotechnology company Genentech, programs include a subsidized child care center near the headquarters in South San Francisco, an on-site hair salon, domestic partner benefits and sabbatical programs that provide six weeks off at full pay after every six consecutive years of service.

"They're very important," says Stephanie Ashe, a spokeswoman at Genentech. "We ask a lot of our employees, but in return, we have many, many programs to help employees with work-life balance."

Kathy Eckert knows first-hand just how flexible some companies will be. After staying home with children Sarah, 10, and Jason, 7, she took a public relations job at software development company Benefitfocus. She was willing to accept the job in large part because the company catered to her family needs. Her bosses let her work 15 to 20 hours a week and give her leave as needed to attend her children's school events. Meetings are set around her schedule.

Just before Thanksgiving, her daughter's fourth-grade class staged a parade. On her way to work, Eckert took 45 minutes to drop in at the school and watch.

"No one was watching a clock," says Eckert, 42. "My family knows I work. My husband is appreciative of the extra income, yet my husband and children know they come first."

Shawn Jenkins, president and CEO of Benefitfocus in Mount Pleasant, S.C., says designing a position to be so flexible was a new endeavor for his company. "The result is an employee who is very focused when she is here, because when she wants to put family first, she can."

LOWERED EXPECTATIONS

Though the emphasis on family is shaped by demographics and events such as Sept. 11, the economy is also a major driver, experts say.

Expectations have changed. During the boom years of the dot-com era, pay raises were on the way up. More than 70% of college students polled said they expected to someday be millionaires, according to a 2000 Ernst & Young survey. There was money to be made in long hours on the job.

Now, advancement is blocked because fewer employees are changing jobs. Raises are paltry. And workers realize there's no guarantee their extra effort on the job will guarantee job security. Sacrifices don't seem as worth it.

Suddenly, family seems top priority.

It's what's most important to Luis Valdes, a vice president and consulting psychologist with management consulting firm Turknett Leadership Group, based in Atlanta.

He had been on the road three to four days a week, but after a spell at home with a mild illness, he realized he wanted more time to be with his three children, Timothy, 14, Jordan, 4, and Liana, 9 months. Now, he's focused on building a local consulting practice instead of being on the road.

"I wanted to be involved with my kids, and I was missing big parts of their lives," says Valdes, 47. "Now, my relationship with them is much better."

It's what's most important to Viveca Woods, 31, of New York, who six months ago left a secure job at a public relations agency to start a consultancy, VMW Public Relations. She can work from home and have a flexible schedule with daughter, Brittany, 4, and 1-year-old son, Logan.

"I love to work, but I want to be a very good mom," she says. "It was a risk, but my family is important."

Why is understanding the dispersion of responses important? There are several reasons. First, as mentioned already, we can make a more accurate characterization of the respondents—are they all alike on a certain variable, or are they different? Second, it helps us to understand the concept of variability. **Variability** refers to the degree of variation in the responses to a variable. The more homogeneous a distribution of responses, the less variability (or variation) there is in the responses to the variable. The more heterogeneous a distribution, the more variability (or variation) there is in the responses to the variable. As we will see later, the concept of variability plays an important role in our ability to use what we learn from random samples so we can generalize to the populations from which those samples are drawn.

In this chapter, we will be learning to calculate—by hand and with SPSS— several of the more common measures of dispersion: the index of qualitative variation, range, interquartile range, and standard deviation. Let's start with the index of qualitative variation to see whether General Social Survey respondents in the 18-to-25-year age bracket tend to be working full-time or not.

THE INDEX OF QUALITATIVE VARIATION

The **index of qualitative variation** (IQV) is a statistic that tells us how much variability there is in a variable with nominal categories. The IQV ranges in value from 0 to 1.0. The closer the IQV is to 0, the less variability there is in the distribution of responses to a variable; the closer to 1, the more variability. In other words, the closer to 0 the index is, the more homogeneous a set of responses; the closer to 1, the more heterogeneous. In a distribution in which the respondents are evenly divided among all of the categories of response, the IQV is 1, because the distribution is perfectly heterogeneous. In distributions like the ones on page 89 of Chapter 4, in which the respondents are all concentrated in a single category of the variable, the IQV is 0, because the distribution is perfectly homogeneous. The number line in Figure 6.1 will help in interpreting the index.

Calculations of the IQV assume that you have constructed a frequency distribution for a set of responses to a variable. Let's use the frequency distribution in Figure 6.1, responses to a recoded *wrkstat* (labor force status) variable for the male GSS respondents who are between 18 and 25 years old, as an illustration. Start by examining the frequency distribution in Table 6.1. What's

FIGURE 6.1
Interpreting the index
of qualitative variation.

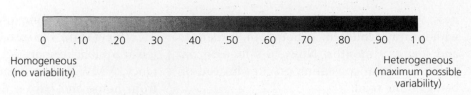

0   .10   .20   .30   .40   .50   .60   .70   .80   .90   1.0

Homogeneous
(no variability)

Heterogeneous
(maximum possible
variability)

your analysis? Does this appear to be a distribution with a lot of variability (more heterogeneous) or a little (more homogeneous)?

The IQV itself is a proportion—a statistical statement of the relationship between the *observed* differences among respondents to the categories of a variable and the maximum number of *possible* differences among respondents to the categories of a variable.

The idea of "differences among respondents" is a fairly abstract one. How do we figure out how many differences there are among the respondents? One way would be to ask ourselves: If one of the respondents is employed full-time, how many differences are there between that respondent and every other respondent? The answer resides in multiplying the full-time respondent by all of the other respondents who aren't working full-time. From the distribution in Table 6.1, we can see that there are 36 respondents who are working part-time, not working, or not in the labor force. Therefore, in relation to the respondent who is working full-time, there are 36 differences—36 other respondents different from the respondent working full-time.

However, there isn't only one respondent working full-time, there are 39 of them. As a result, to find the total number of differences that exist between all 39 respondents who are working full-time and the 36 respondents who aren't, we have to multiply 39 by 36. The product, 1,404, tells us there are 1,404 differences between the 39 respondents who are working full-time and all the 36 respondents who aren't.

If we multiply the number of those who are working part-time (11) by the total of those who are not working or who are not in the market (25), we can find out how many differences there are between those respondents. $11 \times 25 = 275$, so there are 275 differences between those who are working part-time and those who either are not working or are not in the market. (Remember that the differences between those who are working full-time and those who are working part-time are included in the 1,404 figure, which is the total number of differences between the full-timers and everyone else.)

TABLE 6.1   Frequency Distribution for Male Respondents Ages 18 to 25 to a Recoded *wrkstat* Variable in the GSS 2002 subset A File

	RCWRKSTA Recoded work status				
		Frequency	Percent	Valid Percent	Cumulative Percent
Valid	1 WORKING FULL TIME	39	52.0	52.0	52.0
	2 WORKING PART TIME	11	14.7	14.7	66.7
	3 NOT WORKING	4	5.3	5.3	72.0
	4 NOT IN THE MARKET	21	28.0	28.0	100.0
	Total	75	100.0	100.0	

The IQV expresses a relationship between the differences among the respondents and the number of *possible* differences among the respondents, or the number of differences there would be in a perfectly heterogeneous distribution of responses to a variable. What if the 75 respondents in the frequency distribution in Figure 6.1 were evenly divided among all four categories of the variable? How many differences between the respondents would there be then?

Fortunately, we don't have to answer that question by actually dividing the 75 respondents among the four categories and then multiplying to get an answer. The good news is that there is a formula to simplify this process of figuring out the total differences for us—the formula for the index of qualitative variation.

Formula 6.1: The index of qualitative variation (IQV)

$$IQV = \frac{\text{total observed differences}}{\text{maximum possible differences}}$$

There are separate formulas to help us with the numerator (the total number of observed differences in the frequency distribution) and the denominator (the number of maximum possible differences in a set of data).

Let's get started by finding the total number of observed differences, the numerator.

Formula 6.1(a): Total observed differences—the numerator of the IQV

Observed differences = $\Sigma f_i f_j$

where Σ means to add up or sum the following, and $f_i f_j$ means to multiply the frequency of a given category by the frequencies of the succeeding categories.

Taken as a whole, the equation asks you to sum the products you obtain when you multiply each frequency in a frequency distribution by the sum of the frequencies that follow it in the distribution. This isn't as complicated as it sounds.

EXAMPLE:

For Table 6.1,

Step 1. Multiply the first frequency, 39, by the sum of the succeeding frequencies:

$$\begin{aligned} f_i f_j &= (39)(11 + 4 + 21) \\ &= (39)(36) \\ &= 1,404 \end{aligned}$$

Step 2. Multiply the second frequency, 11, by the frequencies below it, like this:

$$\begin{aligned} f_i f_j &= (11)(4 + 21) \\ &= (11)(25) \\ &= 275 \end{aligned}$$

TABLE 6.2   RCWRKSTA Recoded work status

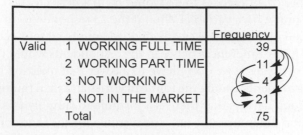

RCWRKSTA Recoded work status

		Frequency
Valid	1 WORKING FULL TIME	39
	2 WORKING PART TIME	11
	3 NOT WORKING	4
	4 NOT IN THE MARKET	21
	Total	75

Step 3.   Multiply the third frequency, 4, by the frequency just below it, 21:

$$f_i f_j = 4 \times 21$$
$$= 84$$

Step 4.   Add up all of the $f_i f_j$s to get their sum (Σ):

$$f_i f_j = 1{,}404 + 275 + 84$$
$$= 1{,}763$$

The process can be diagrammed as in Table 6.2.

Avoiding Common Pitfalls: Finding observed differences for the IQV   You have to find the $f_i f_j$ for as many categories as there are for a given variable. You may have four categories, as in the previous example, or you can have fewer or a lot more categories. The trick is to begin at the first category, multiplying the frequency for that category by the sum of the succeeding frequencies. Move to the second category and repeat the process. Continue until you reach the next-to-the-last category. Then add up the products of each $f_i f_j$.

Now let's find the denominator.

Formula 6.1(b): Maximum possible differences—the denominator of the IQV

$$\text{Possible differences} = \frac{K(K-1)}{2}\left(\frac{N}{K}\right)^2$$

where K is the number of (nonmissing data) categories for a variable, and N is the number of valid cases for a variable.

EXAMPLE:

If we apply this formula to the frequency distribution in Table 6.1, we would work the formula as follows:

$K = 4$, the number of categories for the variable (excluding missing value categories)

$N = 75$, the number of valid cases

$$\text{Possible differences} = \frac{K(K-1)}{2}\left(\frac{N}{K}\right)^2$$

$$= \frac{4(4-1)}{2}\left(\frac{75}{4}\right)^2 = \frac{4(3)}{2}(18.75)$$

$$= \frac{12}{2}(351.5625) = 6(351.5625)$$

$$\text{Possible differences} = 2,109.375$$

Finding the IQV

Remember that what we have so far are the numerator and the denominator for the formula for the IQV. Let's plug our values for the numerator and the denominator into the formula (6.1):

$$IQV = \frac{\text{total observed differences}}{\text{maximum possible differences}}$$

$$= \frac{1,763}{2,109.375}$$

$$IQV = .84$$

Interpreting the IQV

The IQV is much closer to 1.0 than to 0, indicating that the distribution is fairly heterogeneous. When we are working with statistics, we always have to ask ourselves whether our answers make sense. Are they supported by other ways of looking at a variable? In this case, does the frequency distribution support this claim? The answers are yes and no. Although the responses of males age 18 to 25 are somewhat dispersed across the categories of the labor force status variable, 52% of the respondents are concentrated in the working full-time category. Nearly 15% of the respondents said they are working part-time, and over one-quarter said they are not in the market. Responses to the labor force status variable are more homogeneous than the IQV indicates.

 Skills Practice 1   Find the IQV for the following frequency distribution for female respondents between the ages of 18 and 25 to a recoded *wrkstat* variable for the GSS 2002 subset A file. What does it tell you about the distribution of the responses to the variable? Is the IQV consistent with your analysis of the frequency distribution?

RCWRKSTA Recoded work status

		Frequency	Percent	Valid Percent	Cumulative Percent
Valid	1 WORKING FULL TIME	52	49.5	49.5	49.5
	2 WORKING PART TIME	15	14.3	14.3	63.8
	3 NOT WORKING	5	4.8	4.8	68.6
	4 NOT IN THE MARKET	33	31.4	31.4	100.0
	Total	105	100.0	100.0	

SPSS does not include a statistic like the index of qualitative variation for the analysis of variability in nominal-level variables.[2] There are several statistics for the analysis of variability among ordinal and numerical variables, like the range and the interquartile range.

THE RANGE AND THE INTERQUARTILE RANGE

Calculating the Range and the Interquartile Range by Hand

The range and interquartile range tell us about the distributions of responses to variables that are categorical and ordinal, or numerical.

The range　The **range** is one of the simplest statistics to compute. It is found by subtracting the lowest value in a set of data from the highest. Let's use the range to look at how many hours the GSS respondents between the ages of 18 and 25 worked in a week. Let's use the frequency distribution in Table 6.3. To find the range, subtract the lowest value—using only valid response categories—from the highest value. The lowest value is 5, and the highest value is 89. The range is simply 89 − 5 = 84.

Interpreting the range　What does the range tell us? Using the lowest value in the range (5) and the highest (89), we can say that

> the responses to the question about hours worked in a week ranged from 5 up to 89 hours per week.

In addition, the range gives us some idea of how much variation there is in the *categories* of a variable. Some variables have more response categories than others. Sometimes the number of response categories depends on the number of possible responses there are to a particular variable (like hours worked in a week), and sometimes it is determined by the researchers who collect the data (as with variables that measure attitudes in categories, like strongly agree, agree, neutral, disagree, strongly disagree). Generally, the higher the range, the more

---

[2]It is possible to write equations for SPSS so that it can do the computations for the IQV; however, these skills are beyond the scope of this text.

TABLE 6.3   Using the Frequency Distribution for the Variable *hrs1* for 18-to-25-Year-Old GSS 2002 Respondents to Find the Range, Quartile Values, and Interquartile Range

	Number of hours worked last week	Frequency	Cumulative Frequency	Percent	Cumulative Percent
case 1	5	1	1	.9	.9
cases 2–4	12	3	4	2.6	3.5
case 5	15	1	5	.9	4.4
cases 6–7	16	2	7	1.7	6.1
case 8	18	1	8	.9	7.0
cases 9–15	20	7	15	6.0	13.0
case 16	22	1	16	.9	13.9
cases 17–20	24	4	20	3.4	17.3
cases 21–22	25	2	22	1.7	19.0
case 23	26	1	23	.9	19.9
cases 24–25	27	2	25	1.7	21.6
cases 26–27	28	2	27	1.7	23.3
cases 28–31	30	4	31	3.4	26.7
case 32	32	1	32	.9	27.6
case 33	34	1	33	.9	28.5
cases 34–38	35	5	38	4.3	32.8
case 39	36	1	39	.9	33.7
cases 40–42	37	3	42	2.6	36.3
case 43	38	1	43	.9	37.2
case 44	39	1	44	.9	38.1
cases 45–79	40	35	79	29.9	68.0
case 80	41	1	80	.9	68.9
cases 81–82	43	2	82	1.7	70.6
cases 83–90	45	8	90	6.8	77.4
	47	1	91	.9	78.3
	48	2	93	1.7	80.0
	50	5	98	4.3	84.3
	51	1	99	.9	85.2
	52	1	100	.9	86.1
	53	2	102	1.7	87.8
	55	2	104	1.7	89.5
	60	5	109	4.3	93.8
	61	1	110	.9	94.7
	65	2	112	1.7	96.4
	66	2	114	1.7	98.1
	70	1	115	.9	99.0
	80	1	116	.9	99.9
	89	1	117	.9	100.8
		N = 117		100.8	

variation in the categories of response; the smaller the range, the less variation in the categories of response.

In addition to its inherent meaning, the range provides us with a context in which to interpret other measures of dispersion, like the interquartile range and standard deviation. These statistics help us evaluate the dispersion of responses to a variable (as opposed to the variability in response categories). These dispersions may be homogeneous or heterogeneous in relation to the number of response categories for a variable. We will discuss this further in the next section.

Interquartile range   The **interquartile range** (IQR) is a measure of dispersion that tells us about the distribution of responses to a variable in relation to the median. It is used with variables that are ordinal or numerical, and it tells us the range of values that encompass the middle 50% of the respondents to a variable. Conceptually, it is a lot like the median. Whereas the median divides a set of data into two parts by splitting the data in half, the IQR is computed by dividing the responses to a variable into four parts, or quarters, with each part having the same number of cases.

Each quarter has a value associated with it, called a **quartile**. The value at the first quartile, Q_1, is the value at or below which the first 25% of the respondents to a variable fall. The value at the second quartile, Q_2, is the value at or below which 50% of the respondents fall—the median. The value at the third quartile, Q_3, is the value at or below which 75% of the respondents fall. The formula for the IQR is

Formula 6.2: The interquartile range (IQR)

$$IQR = Q_3 - Q_1$$

where Q_3 is the value at the third quartile, and Q_1 is the value at the first quartile.

Let's illustrate the concept of the interquartile range by going back to our example of lining up students by some characteristic or variable. This time, we'll line up the students according to how many hours they work in a week.

Student	1	2	3	4	5	6	7	8
Hours	9	9	10	10	10	10	11	11

Given that we have only eight cases (students), it's easy to see that if we divide the respondents into four equal parts (quarters), there will be two students in each part.

Student	1	2	3	4	5	6	7	8
Hours	9	9	10	10	10	10	11	11
			Q_1		Q_2		Q_3	

Simply dividing the students into four parts doesn't tell us much. We need to know the values associated with each of the quarters so we can describe the distribution of responses. In this example, we can see that the first one-quarter of the students includes those who worked 9 hours. The second quarter includes those who worked 10 hours. The third quarter includes those who work 10 hours, and the last quarter of the students includes those who worked 11 hours.

Is this distribution homogeneous or heterogeneous? Let's look at it in the context of the range of response categories. For this set of responses to the variable *hrs1* there are three response categories—9, 10, and 11. We can see from the preceding diagram that half of the respondents, the respondents between Q_1 and Q_3, are clustered into only one of the response categories (10 hours). Thus, half of the respondents are grouped into one-third of the response categories. Consequently, this distribution is fairly homogeneous—respondents are more alike than different. Half of the respondents worked 10 hours, while the other half are split between 9 and 11 hours.

As with the median, it is rarely practical to find quartile values by lining up respondents. Instead, we put our data into a frequency distribution first. Having done that, it is fairly easy to find the quartile values for a group of respondents using the cumulative percent column on a frequency distribution. If you understand that the first quartile is the value associated with the first quarter of the distribution—the first 25% of your respondents—then you can look down the cumulative percent column on the frequency distribution until you locate the 25th percentile. The 25th percentile in Table 6.3 is associated with value 30. If you read across the frequency distribution you will see that the cumulative frequency for 30 hours of work in a week is 26.7%. The cumulative percent, 26.7, includes the 25th percentile. At least one-quarter of the respondents worked 5 to 30 hours in a week.

Likewise, we can find the 75th percentile by reading down the cumulative percent column of Table 6.3 until we find the value associated with the 75th percentile. Do you see it? It is value 45—77.4% of all respondents worked from 5 to 45 hours in a week. Value 45 includes the 75th percentile. At least 75% of all respondents worked 5 to 45 hours in a week.

A more accurate way of locating the values at the first and third quartiles and computing the interquartile range is by putting our data into a frequency distribution and using formulas to find the *case*—or respondent—at each quartile and the corresponding *value* at each quartile. This is the method that the SPSS program uses for finding quartile values and for computing the interquartile range. The process of finding the interquartile range is like the one for finding the median but it involves a few more steps.

Step 1. Find the case at the first quartile, using Formula 6.2(a).

Formula 6.2(a): Case at the first quartile $= (N + 1) \times .25$

Note: Notice the similarity to the formula for the case at the median. To find the median case, we multiplied $N + 1$ by .50 to divide the data in half. To find the case at the first quartile, we multiply $N + 1$ by .25 to divide the data into quarters. Multiplying $N + 1$ by .25 is the same mathematically as dividing $N + 1$ by 4.

Step 2. Find the value at the first quartile. Look up the case on a frequency distribution using the cumulative frequency column, as you did to find the median value. Then identify the value associated with the case at the first quartile.

Step 3. Find the case at the third quartile, using Formula 6.2(b).

Formula 6.2(b): Case at the third quartile $= (N + 1) \times .75$

Step 4. Find the value at the third quartile. Look up the case at the third quartile using a frequency distribution, and then find the value associated with the case at the third quartile.

Step 5.   Insert the values for Q_3 and Q_1 in the formula for the IQR (Formula 6.2).

EXAMPLE:

Let's follow this process using the frequency distribution for the wage earners variable, *hrs1*, in Table 6.3.

Step 1.   The case at the first quartile is $(N + 1) \times .25$, where N is the number of valid cases only.

$118 \times .25 = 29.50$

Step 2.   The value at the first quartile is the category (number of wage earners) associated with case 29.50. How do we find it? By reading down the frequency column, as we did for the median. At value 5, we have case 1. At value 12, we have cases 2 through 4.[3] If you keep reading down the cumulative frequencies column, then, you can see that case 5 is at value 15, cases 6 and 7 are at value 16, and so on. Keep going until you locate the range of cases in the cumulative frequency column that includes case 29.50. You should see that case 29.50 is in the range of cases between 28 and 31, so the value associated with the case at the first quartile is 30. At least one-quarter of the 18-to-25-year-old respondents to the 2002 General Social Survey work 30 hours or less in a week.

Step 3.   The case at the third quartile is:

$(N + 1) \times .75 = 118 \times .75 = 88.50$

Step 4.   The value of the case at the third quartile is the value associated with case 88.50. Read down the frequencies column until you come to the category that includes case 88.50. You should find the case at the third quartile, case 88.50, in the range of cases from 83 through 90, so the value at the third quartile is 45.

CHECKING YOUR WORK

It is easy to confuse the case at quartile 1 or 3 with the value at each quartile, as it's easy to confuse the median case with the median value. To check your work,

(1) Make sure that the number you are calling the quartile value falls within the range of values for the variable you are analyzing. You won't have a quartile value lower than the lowest value or higher than the highest value for your variable.

---

[3]Find the upper limit of the range of cases at the second value (12) by adding the frequency at the second value, 3, to the frequency at the first value, 1. Find the upper limit of the range of cases at the third value, 15, by adding the frequency at the third value, 1, to the combined frequencies for the first and second values, 1 and 3.

(2) Use the Cumulative Percent column on your frequency distribution to make sure that the quartile values you find are associated with the 25th percentile (for the value at quartile 30) and the 75th percentile (for the value at quartile 45). Notice that the 25th percentile is contained within the range of percentiles at value 30. Value 30 is at percentile 26.7. This means that at least 26.7% of the respondents work 30 hours or less. However, we can also say that value 30 encompasses percentiles 23.4 through 26.7. This range of percentiles includes the 25th percentile. Likewise, the 75th percentile is in the range of percentiles associated with value 45. Using the Cumulative Percent column we can see that 77.4% of the respondents work 45 hours or less. Value 45 encompasses percentiles 70.7 through 77.4, a range that includes the 75th percentile.

Step 5. The IQR (interquartile range) is found by subtracting the value at Q_1 from the value at Q_3. Use formula 6.2. IQR $= Q_3 - Q_1$. In this case, the IQR $= 45 - 30 = 15$.

Interpreting the interquartile range   As in the preceding example, the IQR, in the context of the range for this variable, 84, tells us we have a very homogeneous distribution. A diagram of the dispersion of responses to the variable might help us see this.

Range   5 10 15 20 25 30 35 40 45 50 55 60 65 70 75 80 85 89

IQR Q_1 ·············· Q_3

Notice the relationship of the interquartile range (Q_1 and Q_3) to the full range of values in the variable. Fifty percent of the cases (the cases between Q_1 and Q_3) are concentrated in the interquartile range, and this 50% of the cases is distributed among only 16 values of the variable. Generally, the smaller the IQR is in relation to the range, the more homogeneous is a distribution of responses to a variable (and the less variability there is in the distribution). The larger the IQR is in relation to the range, the more heterogeneous is a distribution of responses (and the more variability there is).

We can say that the distribution of responses to the variable *hrs1* among respondents to the 2002 GSS who are 18 to 25 years old is fairly homogeneous. At least half of the respondents worked from 30 to 45 hours in a week. Only about a quarter worked 45 hours or more in a week, and only about a quarter worked 30 hours or less in a week.

 Skills Practice 2   Let's compare our analysis of the variable *hrs1* for 18-to-25-year-old respondents with another distribution. Use the frequency distribution below, the hours worked in a week among 2002 GSS respondents ages 65 and up, to find and interpret the range, the values at the first and third quartiles, and the interquartile range.

Number of hours worked last week	Frequency	Cumulative Frequency	Percent	Cumulative Percent
3	3	3	7.3	7.3
7	1	4	2.4	9.7
9	1	5	2.4	12.1
12	1	6	2.4	14.5
14	1	7	2.4	16.9
15	1	8	2.4	19.3
16	3	11	7.3	26.6
20	2	13	4.9	31.5
24	2	15	4.9	36.4
25	4	19	9.8	46.2
30	1	20	2.4	48.6
32	1	21	2.4	51.0
35	2	23	4.9	55.9
36	1	24	2.4	58.3
37	1	25	2.4	60.7
38	1	26	2.4	63.1
40	8	34	19.5	82.6
45	1	35	2.4	85.0
48	1	36	2.4	87.4
50	2	38	4.9	92.3
60	1	39	2.4	94.7
70	1	40	2.4	97.1
72	1	41	2.4	99.5
	N = 41		99.5	

What happens when the cases at the first or third quartiles fall between two values? As with the median, the cases for quartiles 1 and 3 can fall between two values. Let's look at an example to see how this is possible. Find the cases at the first and third quartiles for the frequency distribution in Table 6.4 (created by taking a random sample of 10 cases from the 2002 GSS).

Let's do the computations to find the interquartile range.

First, find the case at Q_1.

$$(N + 1) \times .25 = (10 + 1) \times .25 = 11 \times .25 = 2.75$$

Next, look up case 2.75 in the frequency distribution in Table 6.4.

You will notice that it doesn't fall at one of the values, because case 2.75 is between value 27, which contains case 2, and value 31, which has case 3. Thus case 2.75 ($2\frac{3}{4}$) falls between values 27 and 31—but where, exactly, does it fall? The answer is three-quarters of the way between value 27 and value 31.

We know this by once again thinking of the case as an index to the value. If you think of the case at quartile 1 as case 2 and 3/4—three-quarters of the way between case 2 and 3—then the value has to correspond and be three-quarters of

TABLE 6.4 Frequency Distribution for a Randomly Selected Sample of Cases from the GSS 2002 subset A File for the Variable *hrs1*

Number of hours worked last week	Frequency	Cumulative Frequency	Percent	Cumulative Percent
20	1	1	10.0	10.0
27	1	2	10.0	20.0
31	1	3	10.0	30.0
32	1	4	10.0	40.0
40	3	7	30.0	70.0
44	1	8	10.0	80.0
60	1	9	10.0	90.0
70	1	10	10.0	100.0
	N = 10		100.0	

the distance between the values 27 and 31. This would make the value at quartile 1 equal to 30, three-quarters of the way between 27 and 31.

Now find the case and value at quartile 3.

The case at $Q_3 = (N + 1) \times .75 = 11 \times .75 = 8.25$

The value at $Q_3 = 48$ (one-quarter of the distance between cases 8 and 9)

Finally, compute the IQR and interpret it. The IQR $= 48 - 30 = 18$. The range for this distribution is 50 (70 − 20). The distribution is fairly homogeneous because the IQR, 18, is small in relation to the range, 50.

Skills Practice 3 Find and interpret the range and the IQR for the following frequency distribution.

Number of hours worked last week	Frequency	Cumulative Percent	Valid Percent	Cumulative Percent
3	1	1	5.0	5.0
10	1	2	5.0	10.0
25	1	3	5.0	15.0
32	1	4	5.0	20.0
35	1	5	5.0	25.0
40	6	11	30.0	55.0
42	1	12	5.0	60.0
43	1	13	5.0	65.0
45	2	15	10.0	75.0
50	2	17	10.0	85.0
55	2	19	10.0	95.0
60	1	20	5.0	100.0
	N = 20		100.0	

MEAN DEVIATION, VARIANCE, AND STANDARD DEVIATION

Mean deviation, variance, and standard deviation are conceptually similar to the interquartile range in that they provide us with measures of how similar or dissimilar, homogeneous or heterogeneous, respondents are to a particular variable. Because the mean is part of the formulas for these measures, they are used only with numerical variables.

Mean Deviation

Deviations can be computed in relation to any of the measures of central tendency. To find a deviation simply means to figure out how much a set of scores deviates from one of the measures of central tendency—the mode, the median, or the mean.

The **mean deviation** is the average of the deviations from the mean. It is a fairly simple but little-used measure of dispersion. SPSS doesn't compute it, but I am presenting it here because understanding it helps us make sense of measures like variance and standard deviation. The mean deviation draws on the property of the mean discussed in Chapter 5—the sum of the deviations from the mean equals 0. However, instead of adding up the differences, we will average them.

The process involves the following:

Step 1. Subtract the mean for a set of data from each score in the set to find its deviation from the mean.

Step 2. Find the absolute value of each of the deviations from the mean.[4]

Step 3. Add up the results to get the sum of the deviations from the mean.

Step 4. Divide the sum of the deviations from the mean by *N*, to get the average of the deviations from the mean.

The following illustrates the process.

Age		Mean		Deviations from the Mean	Absolute Values of the Deviations from the Mean
19	–	21	=	−2	2
20	–	21	=	−1	1
20	–	21	=	−1	1
21	–	21	=	0	0
21	–	21	=	0	0
21	–	21	=	0	0
22	–	21	=	1	1
22	–	21	=	1	1
23	–	21	=	2	2

Σ of the deviations from the mean = 0 Σ of absolute values = 8

---

[4]Taking an absolute value means to remove the positive or negative sign from a number. In essence, when we use absolute values we are treating all numbers as positive values.

The mean deviation is computed by dividing the sum of the absolute values of the deviations from the mean by N: $8 \div 9 = .89$. The average of the deviations from the mean is .89 year.

As a very broad guideline, smaller mean deviations indicate dispersions with less variability than larger mean deviations, but the mean deviation has to be interpreted in the context of the range of values for a variable. Mean deviation can also be used to compare distributions of a variable across different samples or subsets of data. For example, we can use the mean deviation to compare the variability of ages in the GSS for 2002 with the variability of ages in another set of data. We can also use mean deviation to compare groups. For example, we can analyze the variable *age* for males and females. We can use mean deviation to see whether the distribution of male respondents to *age* is more homogeneous or heterogeneous than the distribution of female respondents.

Variance

Variance is a measure computed somewhat like the mean deviation. The difference is that instead of taking the absolute values of each of the deviations from the mean, we square each one. The squares of the deviations from the mean are totaled. Then the squares of the deviations are averaged by dividing the sum of the squares by $N - 1$:

Age		Mean		Deviations from the Mean	Squaring the Deviations from the Mean
19	–	21	=	–2	4
20	–	21	=	–1	1
20	–	21	=	–1	1
21	–	21	=	0	0
21	–	21	=	0	0
21	–	21	=	0	0
22	–	21	=	1	1
22	–	21	=	1	1
23	–	21	=	2	4

Σ of the deviations from the mean $= 0$ $\quad$ Σ of the squares $= 12$

The variance is computed by dividing the sum of the squares of the deviations from the mean by $N - 1$: $12 \div 8 = 1.50$. Thus the variance equals 1.50.[5]

---

[5]You may be guessing that, although the computation of the variance seems relatively straightforward for small sets of data, it is more complicated for larger sets. As there is for the mean, there is a raw scores method (the process in the preceding illustration) and a method for use with ungrouped frequency distributions. Because variance and standard deviation are so closely related, I will show you how to find both in the next section.

As with mean deviation, the variance can be used to compare the distribution of responses to a variable in one set of data with the distribution of responses in another. In addition, it can be used to compare groups, like males and females. What is the advantage of the variance over the mean deviation? The variance has a property that mean deviation doesn't have—it can be used to find the standard deviation, which is simply the square root of the variance. Standard deviation also has some unique characteristics that make it a very powerful tool for analyzing distributions.

Standard Deviation

Standard deviation is a measure of dispersion that uses a measure of central tendency—the mean—as a point of comparison and, like variance, gives us an indication of the dispersion of responses to a variable. The standard deviation helps us to assess variability by using what is "standard" about standard deviation.

What *is* "standard" about standard deviation? To answer this question, I need to explain one of the properties of a normal distribution. (Remember the normal distribution from the previous chapter? It is a symmetrical and unimodal distribution of responses to a variable in which the mean, median, and mode are the same.) You may recall from previous math experience that we can compute the area of any object, whether it's a square, a rectangle, a circle, or even a curve. A normal distribution is a curve, and we can picture the area under a curve as follows:

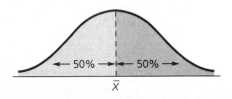

When a distribution is normal, the area under a curve is divided into two equal portions at the mean (which has the same value as the median in a normal distribution). In effect, the mean divides the area under the curve in half. Half of the area under the curve falls below the mean and half falls above it.

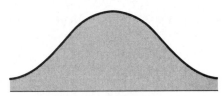

Even more important is that we can use the area under the curve of a normal distribution to make more precise measurements of the dispersion of responses in relation to the mean. The "standard" in the standard deviation is the mathematical "given" that 34.13% of the area under a normal curve always falls between the mean and one standard deviation above the mean, while another 34.13% of the area falls between the mean and one standard deviation below it. Because the area under a normal curve represents the responses to a variable, this "given" allows us to assume that in a normal distribution 34.13% of all respondents to a variable will fall between the mean and one standard deviation above the mean. By the same token, 34.13% of all respondents will fall between the mean and one standard deviation below the mean. If you add these percentages together, then we can see that 68.26% (34.13 + 34.13) of all respondents will fall between one standard deviation below the mean and one standard deviation above it. The following shows this distribution.

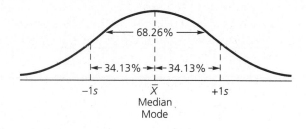

How do we find the standard deviation? Two of the methods, the raw scores method and the ungrouped frequencies distribution method, are demonstrated in the next two sections.

Raw scores method   The raw scores method of finding the standard deviation is used whenever we have a set of scores that have not been organized into a frequency distribution and every score or category for a variable is listed for each one of the respondents, like the set of raw scores in Table 6.5. Conceptually, the raw scores formula finds the standard deviation (symbolized by the letter s) by taking the square root of the variance. The variance is computed by summing the squared deviations from the mean and dividing them by $N - 1$. This method is expressed in the following formula, often called the conceptual formula:

$$s = \sqrt{\frac{\Sigma(X - \overline{X})^2}{N - 1}}$$

However, this formula can be cumbersome to compute, even for small sets of data. Therefore, we will use Formula 6.3(a) for finding the standard deviation from raw scores, sometimes called the computational formula.[6]

Formula 6.3 (a): Standard deviation—raw scores

$$s = \sqrt{\left(\frac{\Sigma X^2}{N - 1}\right) - \left[\left(\frac{N}{N - 1}\right)(\overline{X})^2\right]}$$

where s stands for standard deviation, ΣX^2 means to sum (add up) each of the scores in a distribution after they have each been squared,[7] $N - 1$ is equal to the number of scores you have minus 1, and $\overline{X}^2$ means to square the mean.

---

[6]Standard deviation can be computed in a number of ways using a variety of formulas. For the sake of consistency with SPSS, the formulas in the text follow the SPSS methods of computation.
[7]To "square" a score or value means to multiply the score or value against itself. For example, to square the score or value 2 means to multiply 2 × 2. The score or value 2 squared equals 4.

TABLE 6.5 A Random Sample of GSS 2002 Respondents for the Variable *hrs1*

Cases	Number of hours worked last week
1	45
2	25
3	60
4	3
5	42
6	50
7	32
8	40
9	40
10	40
11	43
12	55
13	45
14	40
15	35
16	10
17	40
18	40
19	50
20	55

A look at the formula tells us we need to do a few computations before we can begin finding the standard deviation. First, we need to know the mean. Second, we need to have the sum of the scores squared (we need to square each score and then add up the results). Once we have this information, we can find the standard deviation by filling in the information required by the formula.

EXAMPLE:

Find the standard deviation for the set of scores in Table 6.5 for the variable *number of hours worked last week* (drawn from a random sample of GSS respondents).

Step 1. Find the mean for the distribution. Use the raw scores formula to find the mean.

$$\overline{X} = \frac{\Sigma X}{N} = \frac{790}{20} = 39.50$$

Step 2. Square the mean ($39.50 \times 39.50 = 1,560.25$).

Step 3. Square each of the scores in the distribution. You can create a table like Table 6.6 to keep track of each of the scores and the result.

Step 4. Add up each of the *squared* scores. The sum of the squared scores is 34,896.

Step 5. Now, plug the results into the formula for standard deviation, as illustrated in Box 6.1.

TABLE 6.6 Squaring Raw Scores for a Random Sample of GSS 2002 Respondents for the Variable *hrs1*

Cases	Number of hours worked last week	X^2
1	45	2025
2	25	625
3	60	3600
4	3	9
5	42	1764
6	50	2500
7	32	1024
8	40	1600
9	40	1600
10	40	1600
11	43	1849
12	55	3025
13	45	2025
14	40	1600
15	35	1225
16	10	100
17	40	1600
18	40	1600
19	50	2500
20	55	3025
		$\Sigma X^2 = 34{,}896$

BOX 6.1

Computing Standard Deviation Using the Raw Scores Formula

Step 1. Write down the formula.

$$s = \sqrt{\left(\frac{\Sigma X^2}{N-1}\right) - \left[\left(\frac{N}{N-1}\right)(\bar{X})^2\right]}$$

Step 2. Fill in the values from the table:
$\Sigma X^2 = 34{,}896$
$N = 20$
$\bar{X} = 39.50$

$$= \sqrt{\left(\frac{34{,}896}{20-1}\right) - \left[\left(\frac{20}{20-1}\right)(39.50)^2\right]}$$

Step 3. Do the computations required by the formula. Subtract within the denominators of the formula and square the mean.
Divide (convert fractions to decimals).
Multiply.
Subtract.
Find the square root of the result.

$$= \sqrt{\left(\frac{34{,}896}{19}\right) - \left[\left(\frac{20}{19}\right)\right](1{,}560.25)}$$

$$= \sqrt{(1{,}836.6316) - [(1.0526)(1{,}560.25)]}$$

$$= \sqrt{(1{,}836.6316) - (1{,}642.3192)}$$

$$= \sqrt{194.3124} \quad (194.3124 \text{ is the variance})$$

$$s = 13.94$$

Interpreting Variance and Standard Deviation

What do we learn from computing the standard deviation? First, notice the variance, which we computed on our way to finding the standard deviation. The variance for the random sample of cases in Table 6.6 for the variable *hrs1* is 194.3124, the number we find before taking its square root to get standard deviation. We can use the variance to compare distributions.

For example, a distribution of responses with a variance smaller than 194.3124 is more homogeneous than the distribution in Table 6.5. A distribution with a variance larger than 194.3124 is more heterogeneous.

Second, knowledge of the standard deviation, combined with the assumptions we are allowed to make about normal distributions, allows us to estimate the dispersion of values in relation to the mean. In this case we know the mean is 39.50. One standard deviation from the mean is 13.94. If we add one standard deviation to the mean (39.50 + 13.94), the score at +1*s* (one standard deviation) from the mean is 53.44. If we subtract one standard deviation from the mean (39.50 − 13.94), we find the score at −1*s* from the mean, 25.56. We can diagram this relationship as follows:

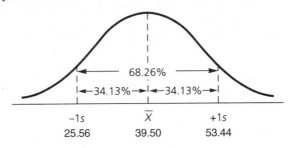

We can assume that, in a normally distributed set of responses to a variable, about 68.26% of the responses will fall within one standard deviation of the mean. 34.13% of the responses will fall between the mean and one standard deviation above it (the score at +1*s*, or 53.44 in this example). 34.13% of the responses will fall between the mean and one standard deviation below it (the score at −1*s*, or 25.56 in this example).

Finally, note that the standard deviation is expressed in units of the original variable. A standard deviation of 13.94 for number of hours worked tells us that 34.13% of the respondents lie no more than 13.94 hours above the mean of 39.50 and another 34.13% lie no more than 13.94 hours below the mean, if the distribution of responses is approximately normal.

When we say that a given score is one standard deviation above the mean, we are saying that about 34.13% of the respondents work between 39.50 (the mean) and 53.44 hours in a week (the mean plus one standard deviation). Similarly, a score that is one standard deviation below the mean tells us that 34.13% of the respondents work between 25.56 and 39.50 hours.

Consequently, we can claim that, in a normally distributed set of responses to the variable *hours worked in a week*, with a mean of 39.50 and a variance of 194.3124, about 68% of the responses will fall between 25.56 hours and 53.44 hours.

Is this a homogeneous distribution (one with little variability) or a heterogeneous distribution (one with a lot of variability)? To answer this question we have to look at the standard deviation *in relation to the range*. Like the interquartile range, the standard deviation has no absolute interpretation. The same standard deviation in two different distributions could have entirely different meanings.

Let's assume we have two different sets of responses to an hours worked variable. In one set, the range of hours in a sample of the adult population in the United States is 2–80. In another distribution, the range of hours in a sample of students at a college is 2–30. Both distributions have standard deviations of 7. Which distribution is more homogeneous than the other: the one with the larger range or the one with the smaller range? I hope you answered the one with the larger range. Why? Because in the distribution with hours ranging from 2 to 80, about 68% of the respondents are clustered into relatively few values of the variable (a total of 14 years, 7 years—or standard deviations—below the mean and 7 above it). The range of values is 78, and 68% of the respondents are "crammed" into only 14 of them. However, with the smaller range, the distribution of hours from 2 to 30 has a range of 28, and 68% of the respondents are spread across 14 of the 29 categories of the variable, a more heterogeneous distribution.

In Table 6.5, with which we've been working, a distribution of responses to the hours worked variable, the range of scores is 57 (60 − 3). One standard deviation above the mean plus one standard deviation below the mean is 27.88 (13.94 + 13.94). Approximately 68%—over two-thirds—of the responses fall within an interval that encompasses less than half of the range of nearly 57 categories. More than half of the responses are within an interval of less than half the response categories. The data are more concentrated (homogeneous) than spread out (heterogeneous).

Skills Practice 4   Find and interpret the standard deviation for the following set of data for the variable *hrs1* (number of hours worked last week).

Case Summaries

	HRS1 *NUMBER OF HOURS WORKED LAST WEEK*
1	46
2	40
3	40
4	50
5	20
6	40
7	15
8	40
9	35
10	50
11	40
12	40
13	40
Total N	13

Ungrouped frequency distribution method   As with the mean, we can use a variation on the raw scores technique to compute standard deviation from an ungrouped frequency distribution.

Formula 6.3(b): Standard deviation—ungrouped frequency distribution

$$s = \sqrt{\left(\frac{\Sigma fX^2}{N-1}\right) - \left[\left(\frac{N}{N-1}\right)(\overline{X})^2\right]}$$

where ΣfX^2 means to square each score, multiply the squared score by its associated frequency, and then add up all of the fX^2; $N-1$ is the number of valid responses minus one; and $\overline{X}^2$ is the mean squared.

Like the raw scores formula for standard deviation, the formula for computing standard deviation from an ungrouped frequency distribution tells us we need to do a few computations before we can begin finding the standard deviation. Unlike the raw scores method, the first task is to put our data into a frequency distribution. Let's do this, using the data in Table 6.5 as an example. You should have a frequency distribution like this one to work with.

Hours worked (X)	f	fX
3	1	3
10	1	10
25	1	25
32	1	32
35	1	35
40	6	240
42	1	42
43	1	43
45	2	90
50	2	100
55	2	110
60	1	60
	N = 20	$\Sigma(fX) = 790$

The next step is to find the mean. Because we are working with an ungrouped frequency distribution, we need to use the ungrouped frequency distribution formula for finding the mean:

$$\overline{X} = \frac{\Sigma(fX)}{N} = \frac{790}{20}$$

You should come up with the same answer as for the raw scores mean, 39.50.

Now we need to square each score and multiply it against its corresponding frequency. As with standard deviation for raw scores, the easiest way to keep track of the steps in the process is by simply adding the relevant computations to our frequency distribution. We can add a column for each of the scores squared. Then we can add a column that shows each squared score multiplied by its associated frequency.

Hours worked (X)	f	Square each score to get X^2	Multiply each squared score by its frequency to get fX^2
3	1	9	9
10	1	100	100
25	1	625	625
32	1	1024	1024
35	1	1225	1225
40	6	1600	9600
42	1	1764	1764
43	1	1849	1849
45	2	2025	4050
50	2	2500	5000
55	2	3025	6050
60	1	3600	3600

Finally, we can add up the results to get ΣfX^2: $\Sigma fX^2 = 34,896$

By filling in the information required by the formula for standard deviation from an ungrouped frequency distribution, you should be able to set up the problem this way:

$$\bar{X} = 39.50 \qquad \Sigma fX^2 = 34,896 \quad N = 20$$

$$s = \sqrt{\left(\frac{\Sigma fX^2}{N-1}\right) - \left[\left(\frac{N}{N-1}\right)(\bar{X})^2\right]}$$

$$= \sqrt{\left(\frac{34,896}{20-1}\right) - \left[\left(\frac{20}{20-1}\right)(39.50)^2\right]}$$

As you do the computations required by the formula, remember to follow the rules for order of operations.

Step 1. Work within the brackets and square the mean first.

Step 2. Do the subtraction within the denominators of each portion of the formula in parentheses.

Step 3. Do the division for each portion of the formula in parentheses.

Step 4. Do the multiplication required by the portion of the formula in the brackets.

Step 5. Do the subtraction.

Step 6. Find the square root of the result.

Your answer should be identical to the one you obtained using the raw scores method, $s = 13.94$.

Skills Practice 5 Put the data in Skills Practice 4 into an ungrouped frequency distribution and calculate standard deviation using the formula for an ungrouped frequency distribution. Identify the variance in your computations.

USING SPSS

Finding and Interpreting Measures of Dispersion

In this section, you will learn how to find and interpret the range, interquartile range, and standard deviation using SPSS. SPSS does not compute the Index of Qualitative Variation.

Finding the Range and Interquartile Range Using SPSS

With our analysis of range and interquartile range, you have been learning about the dispersion of responses to the GSS variable about the number of earners in a household. Now let's look at household earnings. How much are these earners bringing in? In the examples that follow, we will use SPSS and the GSS 2002 subset A file to find the range and interquartile range for the variable *income98*.

Like the measures of central tendency, the measures of dispersion are found at the Frequencies dialog box.

SPSS GUIDE: FINDING THE RANGE AND INTERQUARTILE RANGE

Start by opening your GSS 2002 subset A file. At the SPSS Data Editor window, follow the command path Analyze ➡ Descriptive Statistics ➡ Frequencies. At the Frequencies dialog box, select the variable *income98*. Then click on Statistics.

At the Frequencies: Statistics window, do the following:

① Select your measures of dispersion: Click on Quartiles, then click on Range.

② Select your measures of central tendency.

③ Click on Continue.

When you return to the Frequencies dialog box, click on OK. Your statistics and your frequency distribution appear in the Output window. They should look like the ones in Table 6.7.

Interpreting the interquartile range using SPSS

In Chapter 5 (Skills Practice 8), by using measures of central tendency appropriate for the *income98* variable—the mode and the median—you found that the most commonly occurring income category is category 23, $110,000 and up. The median category is 17 ($35,000–$39,999). Half of the respondents have family incomes in the $35,000 to $39,999 range or less, and half have family incomes in the $35,000 to $39,999 range or more.

What do measures of dispersion add to our analysis? Notice the value at the first quartile (Percentile 25 on the table of Statistics) is 13, while the value at the third quartile (Percentile 75 on the table of Statistics) is 20. By locating the value labels associated with these values, we can see that

at least half of the respondents have family incomes from $20,000 up to $74,999.

The range of values is 22, whereas the interquartile range is 7. (Note that SPSS doesn't actually compute the IQR from the Frequencies dialog box, but it is easy to calculate from the values at percentiles 25 and 75. The IQR = 20 – 13.)

The interquartile range is fairly small in relation to the range, suggesting a more homogeneous than heterogeneous distribution of responses to the variable.

TABLE 6.7 Statistics and Frequency Distribution for the Variable *income98*

Statistics

INCOME98 Total family income

N	Valid	1333	
	Missing	167	
Median		17.00	
Mode		23	
Range		22	
Percentiles	25	13.00	—— Value at Quartile 1
	50	17.00	—— Value at Quartile 2 (the median)
	75	20.00	—— Value at Quartile 3

INCOME98 Total family income

		Frequency	Percent	Valid Percent	Cumulative Percent
Valid	1 UNDER $1 000	29	1.9	2.2	2.2
	2 $1 000 TO 2 999	7	.5	.5	2.7
	3 $3 000 TO 3 999	19	1.3	1.4	4.1
	4 $4 000 TO 4 999	11	.7	.8	5.0
	5 $5 000 TO 5 999	14	.9	1.1	6.0
	6 $6 000 TO 6 999	19	1.3	1.4	7.4
	7 $7 000 TO 7 999	15	1.0	1.1	8.6
	8 $8 000 TO 9 999	37	2.5	2.8	11.3
	9 $10000 TO 12499	47	3.1	3.5	14.9
	10 $12500 TO 14999	38	2.5	2.9	17.7
	11 $15000 TO 17499	39	2.6	2.9	20.6
	12 $17500 TO 19999	42	2.8	3.2	23.8
	13 $20000 TO 22499	51	3.4	3.8	27.6
	14 $22500 TO 24999	46	3.1	3.5	31.1
	15 $25000 TO 29999	82	5.5	6.2	37.2
	16 $30000 TO 34999	96	6.4	7.2	44.4
	17 $35000 TO 39999	79	5.3	5.9	50.3
	18 $40000 TO 49999	123	8.2	9.2	59.6
	19 $50000 TO 59999	118	7.9	8.9	68.4
	20 $60000 TO 74999	125	8.3	9.4	77.8
	21 $75000 TO $89999	104	6.9	7.8	85.6
	22 $90000 - $109999	59	3.9	4.4	90.0
	23 $110000 OR OVER	133	8.9	10.0	100.0
	Total	1333	88.9	100.0	
Missing	24 REFUSED	108	7.2		
	98 DK	59	3.9		
	Total	167	11.1		
Total		1500	100.0		

If you picture the distribution on a graph, it is easier to see how the distribution of responses to the variable is concentrated.

Income Categories   1 2 3 4 5 6 7 8 9 10 11 12 13 14 15 16 17 18 19 20 21
                               Q_1 -------------- Q_2 --------- Q_3

Although there is some concentration of responses in the higher income categories, it is not a highly concentrated distribution. Thus the distribution, while more homogeneous than heterogeneous, is not a very homogeneous one.

Skills Practice 6 Analyze the incomes of the individual respondents to the 2002 GSS using *rincom98*. Use appropriate measures of central tendency and dispersion.

Graphing the Interquartile Range

SPSS has a feature called boxplot that allows us to see the interquartile range pictorially. A **boxplot** is a graphic representation of the distribution of responses to a variable focusing on the responses in the interquartile range. Let's use the command path Graphs ➥ Boxplot to obtain a boxplot.

SPSS GUIDE: CREATING BOXPLOTS FOR THE INTERQUARTILE RANGE

Start at the SPSS Data Editor window. With a data file open, click on the Graphs menu item and then on Boxplot.

When the Boxplot window opens, click on Summaries of separate variables, then on Define.

At the Define Simple Boxplot dialog box, scroll down to the variable *income98*.

(1) Click on your variable to highlight it.

(2) Click on the ▶ to move your variable into the Boxes Represent area.

(3) Click on OK.

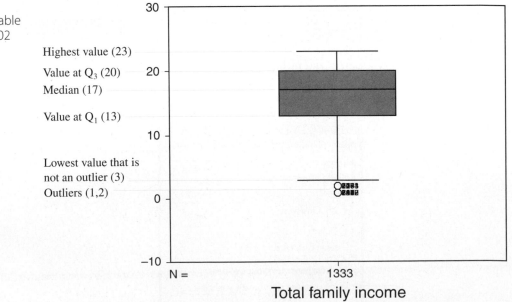

In your Output window, you will get a boxplot like the one in Figure 6.2.

To interpret the diagram, notice that the boxplot is constructed so that the values of the variable are on the *y*- (vertical) axis. The box itself represents the cases in the interquartile range—the cases between Q_1 and Q_3. The heavy black

FIGURE 6.2
Boxplot for the variable *income98* in the 2002 GSS subset A file.

line across the box is the median value. The lines that extend beyond the box are called *whiskers* (and boxplots are sometimes referred to as *box and whiskers* diagrams.) Boxplots may also show you which values are **outliers**, unusually high or low values of a variable, and **extreme values**, exceptionally high or low values, in relation to the interquartile range. SPSS uses specific formulas for assessing whether a particular value is an outlier or an extreme value.

The whisker at the bottom of the boxplot represents either the smallest value in the range of category values or the smallest value that is not an *outlier*. An **outlier in the bottom range** of a variable's values is a value that is equal to or less than the value at Q_1 minus the interquartile range (IQR) times 1.5, as indicated by the formula $Q_1 - (IQR \times 1.5)$.

The whisker at the top represents either the highest value in the range of category values or the largest value that is not an outlier. An **outlier in the upper range** of a variable's values is a value that is equal to or greater than the value at Q_3 plus the interquartile range times 1.5, as indicated by the formula $Q_3 + (IQR \times 1.5)$.

For the preceding example, the bottom whisker represents the lowest value in the range that is not an outlier (category 3, for this variable) and the top whisker represents the highest value in the range.

Interpretation   The larger the box is in relation to the range of values in the diagram, the more heterogeneous is the distribution (the more variability in the responses). The smaller the box is in relation to the range of values, the more homogeneous is the distribution (the less variability in the responses).

For the variable *income98,* the distribution appears to be somewhat homogeneous, because the interquartile range appears relatively small in relation to the range of values for the variable.

You may also encounter an asterisk at the bottom of a boxplot that represents a value that is not only an outlier but an extreme value. Extreme values of a variable are values that are equal to or less than the value at the first quartile minus the IQR times 3, or equal to or greater than the value at the third quartile plus the IQR times 3.

Finding Variance and Standard Deviation Using SPSS

Finding the variance and standard deviation with SPSS follows the same process as finding the interquartile range. Let's look at the variable *hrs1*, number of hours worked in the last week. Follow the procedures in the next SPSS Guide to find the standard deviation for *hrs1*.

SPSS GUIDE: FINDING THE STANDARD DEVIATION

Start by opening your GSS 2002 subset A file. Then open the Frequencies dialog box using the command path Analyze ➡ Descriptive Statistics ➡ Frequencies. At the Frequencies dialog box, select your variable, *hrs1*.

Next click on the Statistics button at the bottom of the dialog box to open the Frequencies: Statistics window.

① Select your measures of dispersion: Click on Std. deviation, Variance, and Range.

② Select your measures of central tendency.

③ Click on Continue. When the Frequencies dialog box returns, click on OK.

A set of statistics like the one in Table 6.8, along with the frequency distribution for *hrs1*, appears in the Output window.

What do measures of dispersion add to what you learned about *hrs1* using measures of central tendency? We already know that the average number of hours worked is 41.86—a full-time work week. Half of the respondents worked 40 hours a week or less, and half worked 40 hours a week or more, and the most commonly occurring work schedule is 40 hours. The distribution is nearly normal, but the mean is higher than the median, so we know the distribution is positively skewed. When a distribution is positively skewed, there are values at the high end of the distribution pulling the mean away from the median. Some people worked a lot of hours and skewed the distribution—pulled it away from normal.

Now let's add measures of dispersion to the analysis. Are the respondents grouped fairly closely around the mean, or are they spread out around it? The standard deviation tells the story. The range of values is 87—quite a large range. One standard deviation from the mean is 14.24. In a normal distribution with a mean of 41.86 (and, by extension, a mode and median of 41.86) and a variance of 202.824, we could assume about 34% of the respondents worked between 27.62 hours per week (the mean minus one standard deviation, or 41.86 minus 14.24) and 41.86 hours (the mean), whereas another 34% worked between 41.86 hours per week (the mean) and 56.10 hours per week (the mean plus one stan-

TABLE 6.8   Statistics for the Variable *hrs1* in the GSS
2002 subset A File

Statistics

HRS1 Number of hours worked last week

N	Valid	940
	Missing	560
Mean		41.86
Median		40.00
Mode		40
Std. Deviation		14.242
Variance		202.824
Range		87

dard deviation, or 41.86 plus 14.24). Sixty-eight percent of the respondents are dispersed across about 28 (two standard deviations) of the 87 intervals in the range. Over two-thirds of the respondents are spread across about one-third of the intervals in the range of values, suggesting a more homogeneous than heterogeneous distribution. Assuming a normal distribution of responses, over two thirds of the respondents to the GSS worked nearly 28 hours up to about 56 hours.

Although the standard deviation helps us analyze dispersions for single variables, it can also be used, along with variance, as a basis of comparison between two groups of respondents for the same variable. For example, we can use variance and standard deviation to compare males and females. Which group is more homogeneous (has less variability) than the other in their responses to a particular variable? The answer is: the group with the lower of the two standard deviations for that variable.

 Skills Practice 7   Split the GSS 2002 subsct A file by *sex*. Analyze the dispersion of *hrs1* for each of the two groups—using the mean, median, mode, range, variance, and standard deviation. Then answer these questions: Which group worked the most hours? Which group is the most homogeneous?

Now let's look at another use of standard deviation—to evaluate the dispersion of responses in two groups with similar means. Ordinarily, we might be tempted to believe that in two groups with similar means, the dispersion of responses is also similar. However, this is not always the case, and analyzing the dispersion of responses allows us to test our assumption that groups with similar means have similar distributions of responses to a variable.

Take, for example, the means for hours worked in a week for those respondents to the 2002 GSS who are ages 26 through 40 as compared to those who are ages 41 through 60. If you were to compare the means for these two groups, as

TABLE 6.9 Statistics for Respondents Ages 26 through 40 and Ages 41 through 60 for the *hrs1* Variable in the GSS 2002 subset A File

Statistics[a]			Statistics[a]		
HRS1 Number of hours worked last week			HRS1 Number of hours worked last week		
N	Valid	353	N	Valid	386
	Missing	98		Missing	128
Mean		43.03	Mean		43.09
Median		40.00	Median		40.00
Mode		40	Mode		40
Std. Deviation		12.919	Std. Deviation		14.203
Variance		166.911	Variance		201.730
Range		85	Range		87

[a] RCAGE Recoded age variable = 2 26 THRU 40   [a] RCAGE Recoded age variable = 2 26 THRU 40

illustrated in the statistics in Table 6.9, you would assume that they are alike. The means for the two groups are only six one-hundredths (.06) apart. However, if you compare the variances and the standard deviations for the two groups, a different picture emerges. You should see that the distribution of responses to the variable *hrs1* is a little more homogeneous for those ages 26 through 40 than it is for those who are ages 41 through 60. How can you tell? The standard deviation is lower (12.92) for the distribution of responses of those in the younger age group as compared to the distribution of responses of those in the older age group (14.20).

Graphing the Normal Distribution: Creating Histograms with the Normal Curve

To assist us with our evaluation of the dispersion of numerical variables, we can obtain a **histogram with a normal curve**—a histogram that has a normal curve superimposed on it. From the shape of the curve and the relationship between the distribution of responses and the normal curve, we can assess the degree of variability and the skew.

SPSS GUIDE: HISTOGRAMS WITH THE NORMAL CURVE

At the SPSS Data Editor window, use Split File with the variable *sex* to divide your GSS 2002 subset A file into two groups, males and females. Next, click on Graphs, then Histogram.

1 When the Histogram dialog box opens, scroll down to the variable *educ.* Click on it to highlight it, and click on the arrow to move it into the Variable box.

2 Click on Display normal curve.

3 Click on OK.

You should get two charts—one for males and one for females—like the ones in Figure 6.3.

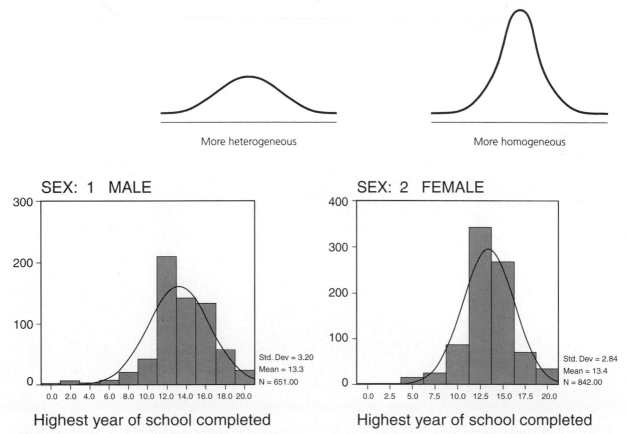

Notice the shape of the normal curve in the charts you created. The normal curve shows you what a distribution would look like for a set of data having the same mean and variance as the data you see in the histogram but having a unimodal and symmetrical distribution of values in relation to the mean. The more peaked is the normal curve, the more homogeneous is the distribution; the less peaked, or the flatter, is the normal curve, the more heterogeneous is the distribution. See the following illustrations, which show you how to compare the shapes of normal distributions.

FIGURE 6.3
Histograms for the variable *educ* with the GSS 2002 subset A file split by *sex*.

Compare the normal curves of the years of education for males and females and notice that the curve for male respondents looks a little less pointed than the curve for female respondents. This tells us that the distribution of scores for years of education is more heterogeneous for males than females. This conclusion is borne out by the standard deviations—notice that the standard deviation for the distribution of male respondents is higher than the standard deviation for the female respondents, indicating more heterogeneity or variability in the dispersion of years of education. You may also notice that males report having, on average, more years of education than females.

Using Measures of Dispersion

Use the following chart as a guide to the correct applications of measures of dispersion. Different statistics are appropriate depending on the level of measurement of the variable being evaluated. This chart will help you decide when and how to apply these statistics.

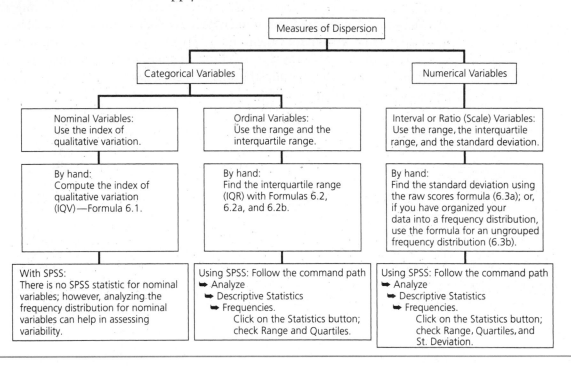

SUMMARY

After finishing this chapter you should be able to apply measures of dispersion appropriately. They include the index of qualitative variation, range, interquartile range, variance, and standard deviation, and they help us to determine how homogeneous or heterogeneous a distribution is, or how much variation there is in the responses to a variable. The index of qualitative variation is used with nominal variables, whereas the range and interquartile range can be applied to ordinal or numerical variables. The standard deviation (interpreted in the context of the range) is used only with numerical variables.

You should be able to compute the index of qualitative variation, range, interquartile range, and standard deviation by hand, and you should know how to obtain the range, interquartile range, variance, and standard deviation, along with either a boxplot or a histogram with a normal curve, using SPSS. The range, interquartile range, and standard deviation can all be found using the Statistics button in the Frequencies dialog box.

As in previous chapters, emphasis has been placed on the interpretation of the measures, starting with the index of qualitative variation (the IQV). The IQV is a guide to the dispersion of responses across the categories of a variable based on a scale of 0 (more homogeneous) to 1.00 (more heterogeneous).

The range assesses the degree of variability in response categories (but not necessarily the dispersion of responses across those categories), and it provides the context for the interpretation of the interquartile range and standard deviation. The interquartile range (IQR) allows us to focus on the middle 50% of the responses to a variable. Analyzing the IQR in relation to the range lets us assess the homogeneity or heterogeneity of these responses without the influence of outliers or extreme values. The standard deviation, on the other hand, allows us to focus on the middle 68% of the responses. Like the IQR, it has to be interpreted in relation to the range. Unlike the IQR, the interpretation of the standard deviation assumes a normal distribution of responses to a variable.

In the next chapter you will be introduced to making inferences—generalizing from samples to populations—for single variables. We will begin by using what we have learned about the standard deviation to understand Z scores and their application to inferential statistics.

KEY CONCEPTS

Measures of dispersion	Quartile	Outlier
Variability	Standard deviation	Extreme value
Index of qualitative variation	Mean deviation	Outlier in the bottom range
Range	Variance	Outlier in the upper range
Interquartile range	Boxplot	Histogram with a normal curve

ANSWERS TO SKILLS PRACTICES

1. The formula for the IQV is

$$IQV = \frac{\text{total observed differences}}{\text{maximum possible differences}}$$

Begin by finding the numerator, using Formula 6.1(a):

observed differences $= \Sigma f_i f_j$

1. Multiply the first frequency, 52, by the sum of the succeeding frequencies:

$f_i f_j = (52)(15 + 5 + 33) = (52)(53) = 2{,}756$

2. Multiply the second frequency, 15, by the frequencies below it, like this:

$f_i f_j = (15)(5 + 33) = (15)(38) = 570$

3. Multiply the third frequency, 5, by the frequency below it, 33:

$f_i f_j = (5)(33) = 165$

4. Add up all of the $f_i f_j$s to get their sum (Σ):

$\Sigma f_i f_j = 2{,}756 + 570 + 165 = 3{,}491$

Find the denominator, using Formula 6.1(b):

$$\text{possible differences} = \frac{K(K-1)}{2}\left(\frac{N}{K}\right)^2$$

$$= \frac{4(4-1)}{2}\left(\frac{105}{4}\right)^2$$

$$= \frac{4(3)}{4}(26.25)$$

$$= \frac{12}{2}(689.0625)$$

$$= 6(689.0625)$$

$$\text{possible differences} = 4{,}134.375$$

Finally, insert the values for the total differences (the numerator) and the maximum differences (the denominator) into the formula for the IQV:

$$IQV = \frac{\text{total observed differences}}{\text{maximum possible differences}}$$

$$= \frac{3{,}491}{4{,}134.375}$$

$$IQV = .84$$

Interpretation: The distribution of responses among GSS female respondents in the 18-to-25 age bracket appears more heterogeneous. At .84, the IQV is closer to 1.0 than to 0. Although the female respondents ages 18 to 25 are fairly well distributed across the categories of the variable, nearly half the respondents (49.5%) are concentrated in the working full-time category. Nearly one-third said they are not in the market, and a little over 14% said they are working part-time. Only about 5% of the respondents said they are not working. The distribution appears to be a little more homogeneous than the IQV by itself would lead us to believe.

2. If you locate the quartile values using the cumulative percent column, you would locate quartile 1 at value 16 (because at least 25% of the respondents to the 2002 GSS who are 65 or older have worked 16 hours in a week). Quartile 3 is located at value 40. At least 75% of the respondents 65 and older have worked 40 hours in a week.

To find the quartile values using computations, start by finding the cases at quartile 1 and quartile 3.

Step 1. The case at quartile $1 = (N + 1) \times .25 = 42 \times .25 = 10.50$.

Step 2. The value at quartile 1 is the value associated with case 10.50. Reading down the Cumulative Frequency column, we see that value 16 consists of cases 9 through 11. Case 10.50 is included in that range of cases, so the value of quartile 1 is 16 hours.

Step 3. The case at quartile $3 = (N + 1) \times .75 = 42 \times .75 = 31.50$.

Step 4. The value at quartile 3 is the value associated with case 31.50. Reading down the Cumulative Frequency column, we find case 31.50 in the range of cases, 27–34, associated with the value 40.

Step 5. Find the interquartile range IQR $= Q_3 - Q_1 = 40 - 16 = 24$.

If we plot these values on a graph, it helps us to analyze the distribution of responses to the variable.

Range   3 8 13 18 23 28 33 38 43 48 53 58 63 68 72
Quartiles Q_1 ------------- Q_3

The range is equal to $72 - 3 = 69$, and the interquartile range is equal to $40 - 16 = 24$. In this case, the dispersion of responses is also homogeneous, but not as homogeneous as the distribution for 18-to-25-year-olds.

3. The case at $Q_1 = (N + 1) \times .25 = 21 \times .25 = 5.25$.
The value at $Q_1 = 36.25$ (the value that is one-quarter of the distance between values 35 and 40).
The case at $Q_3 = (N + 1) \times .75 = 21 \times .75 = 15.75$.
The value at $Q_3 = 48.75$ (three-quarters of the distance between value 45 and value 50, because case 15.75 is three-quarters of the distance between cases 15 and 16).

The IQR = 48.75 − 36.25 = 12.50. The range = 60 − 3 = 57. The distribution of responses is fairly homogeneous because the IQR (12.50) is small in relation to the range (57).

4. The formula requires that we have the mean for the distribution. Using the formula for the mean for raw scores, the mean is computed as follows:

$$\overline{X} = \frac{\Sigma X}{N} = \frac{496}{13} = 38.1538$$

The next step is to find the sum of the scores squared. We can add a column to our set of data for the squared scores, square each score, and add up the results as follows:

	HRS1	X^2
1	46	2,116
2	40	1,600
3	40	1,600
4	50	2,500
5	20	400
6	40	1,600
7	15	225
8	40	1,600
9	35	1,225
10	50	2,500
11	40	1,600
12	40	1,600
13	40	1,600
		$\Sigma X^2 = 20,166$

Finally, we can plug the relevant computations into our formula for standard deviation from raw scores as follows:

$$\overline{X} = 38.1538 \quad \Sigma X^2 = 20,166 \quad N = 13$$

$$s = \sqrt{\left(\frac{\Sigma X^2}{N-1}\right) - \left[\left(\frac{N}{N-1}\right)(\overline{X})^2\right]}$$

$$= \sqrt{\left(\frac{20,166}{13-1}\right) - \left[\left(\frac{13}{13-1}\right)(38.1538)^2\right]}$$

$$= \sqrt{\left(\frac{20,166}{12}\right) - \left[\left(\frac{13}{12}\right)(1,455.7125)\right]}$$

$$= \sqrt{(1,680.5) - (1.0833)(1,455.7125)} = 10.17$$

Now we can interpret our results. Assuming a normal distribution, about 34% of the respondents to the number of hours worked fall between the mean (38.15) and one standard deviation above the mean (38.15 + 10.17 = 48.32), while another 34% of the responses fall between the mean and one standard deviation below the mean (38.15 − 10.17 = 27.98). In a normally distributed set of responses, about 68% of the responses would fall between 27.98 and 48.32, suggesting a more homogeneous set of responses. Sixty-eight percent of the responses fall across an interval of about 20 hours out of the range of 35 hours (range = 50 − 15 = 35). Nearly two-thirds of the responses fall within a range encompassing a little over half of the values of the variable. In plainer English, nearly two-thirds of the respondents work a little less than a full (40-hour) workweek up to a little more than a full workweek. It is a fairly homogeneous distribution.

5. Your frequency distribution for the data should look like this:

Hours Worked (X)	Frequency
15	1
20	1
35	1
40	7
46	1
50	2
Total	$N = 13$

Once the frequency distribution is complete, you can find the mean (using the formula for an ungrouped frequency distribution).

$$\overline{X} = \frac{\Sigma fX}{N} = \frac{496}{13} = 38.1538$$

Now, complete the frequency distribution for the squared scores. Multiply each squared score by its frequency (to get fX^2) and then sum the results (to get ΣfX^2).

Hours Worked

(X)	Frequency	X²	fX²
15	1	225	225
20	1	400	400
35	1	1,225	1,225
40	7	1,600	11,200
46	1	2,116	2,116
50	2	2,500	5,000
Total	N = 13		ΣfX² = 20,166

Plug the results into your formula for standard deviation using an ungrouped frequency distribution.

$$\overline{X} = 38.1538 \quad \Sigma fX^2 = 20,166 \quad N = 13$$

$$s = \sqrt{\left(\frac{\Sigma fX^2}{N-1}\right) - \left[\left(\frac{N}{N-1}\right)(\overline{X})^2\right]}$$

$$= \sqrt{\left(\frac{20,166}{13-1}\right) - \left[\left(\frac{13}{13-1}\right)(38.1538)^2\right]}$$

Follow the order of operations for solving the formula for standard deviation. You should get the same result, $s = 10.17$, as you did for the raw scores computation. The variance is 103.5266 (the standard deviation squared).

6. You should get the following statistics using SPSS.

Statistics

RINCOM98 Respondents' income

N	Valid		954
	Missing		546
Median			15.00
Mode			16
Range			22
Percentiles	25		10.00
	50		15.00
	75		18.00

Interpretation: The median income for 2002 GSS respondents is in the $25,000–$29,999 category, with half of the GSS respondents having incomes in that range or less. Relatively few, 6.5%, have incomes of $75,000 or more. The most frequently occurring response to the

income question is $30,000 to $34,999, although only about 10% of the respondents answered to that category. Two-thirds of the respondents have incomes in the $30,000 to $34,999 range or less. Half of the respondents have earnings in the $12,500 to $49,999 range. The distribution of responses seems fairly homogeneous, with a range of 22 and an IQR of 8.

You can picture the relationship between the categories of the variable and the interquartile range like this:

Income Categories

1 2 3 4 5 6 7 8 9 10 11 12 13 14 15 16 17 18 19 20 21 22 23

Quartiles Q_1------------Q_2--------Q_3

7. Here are the Statistics boxes you should get for the variable *hrs1*, split by categories of the variable *sex*.

Statistics

HRS1 Number of hours worked last week

1 MALE	N	Valid	442
		Missing	212
	Mean		45.37
	Median		43.00
	Mode		40
	Std. Deviation		15.015
	Variance		225.458
	Range		87
2 FEMALE	N	Valid	498
		Missing	348
	Mean		38.74
	Median		40.00
	Mode		40
	Std. Deviation		12.746
	Variance		162.465
	Range		86

The 40-hour workweek seems to be alive and well for both men and women. Sixty-five percent of the female respondents and about 81% of the male respondents report working 40 hours or more per week. The most commonly occurring response to the question about the number of hours worked last week is 40, with over one-quarter (28%) of the male respondents and over one-third (33.9%) of the female respondents answering in that category. Women are more likely than men to work 40 hours, but men are more likely than women to work more than 40 hours. Men worked a few more hours on average (45.37 hours per week) than women (38.74 hours per week). Half of the male respondents worked 43 hours or less per week, and half worked 43 hours or more. Half of the female respondents reported working 40 hours or more in one week, and half reported working 40 hours or less.

The distribution of responses for males is more heterogeneous than the distribution for females, based on both the variance (larger for males than females) and standard deviation (also larger for males than females).

Assuming normal distributions for both sets of data, we can estimate that 68% of male respondents worked between 30.35 hours per week (the mean minus one standard deviation) and 60.39 hours per week (the mean plus one standard deviation). Sixty-eight percent of the female respondents worked between 25.99 and 51.49 hours per week.

GENERAL EXERCISES

1. Compute and interpret the index of qualitative variation for the table in General Exercise 1 in Chapter 5.
2. Compute and interpret the index of qualitative variation for the table in General Exercise 2 in Chapter 5.
3. Compute and interpret an appropriate measure of central tendency and the index of qualitative variation for the following frequency distribution (for 2002 GSS respondents ages 18 to 25).

RCRACE Recoded race first mention

		Frequency	Percent	Valid Percent	Cumulative Percent
Valid	1 WHITE	137	76.1	76.1	76.1
	2 BLACK OR AFRICAN AMERICAN	25	13.9	13.9	90.0
	3 AMERICAN INDIAN OR ALASKA NATIVE	3	1.7	1.7	91.7
	4 HISPANIC	8	4.4	4.4	96.1
	5 OTHER	7	3.9	3.9	100.0
	Total	180	100.0	100.0	

4. Compute and interpret an appropriate measure of central tendency and the index of qualitative variation for the frequency distribution below (for 2002 GSS respondents ages 18 to 25).

RCRELIG Recoded RS religious preference

		Frequency	Percent	Valid Percent	Cumulative Percent
Valid	1 PROTESTANT	81	45.0	45.0	45.0
	2 CATHOLIC	42	23.3	23.3	68.3
	3 JEWISH	1	.6	.6	68.9
	4 NONE	40	22.2	22.2	91.1
	5 OTHER	16	8.9	8.9	100.0
	Total	180	100.0	100.0	

For the tables in exercises 5 through 8, compute and interpret appropriate measures of central tendency and the interquartile range. The tables are SPSS frequency distributions for GSS 2002 respondents ages 18 through 25. You may need to add a cumulative frequency column to the table in order to find the interquartile range. Remember to use valid cases only in your computations.

5. Respondents' income

RINCOM98 Respondents' income

		Frequency	Percent	Valid Percent	Cumulative Percent
Valid	1 UNDER $1 000	8	4.4	6.7	6.7
	2 $1 000 TO 2 999	13	7.2	10.9	17.6
	3 $3 000 TO 3 999	9	5.0	7.6	25.2
	4 $4 000 TO 4 999	2	1.1	1.7	26.9
	5 $5 000 TO 5 999	6	3.3	5.0	31.9
	6 $6 000 TO 6 999	4	2.2	3.4	35.3
	7 $7 000 TO 7 999	3	1.7	2.5	37.8
	8 $8 000 TO 9 999	6	3.3	5.0	42.9
	9 $10000 TO 12499	11	6.1	9.2	52.1
	10 $12500 TO 14999	7	3.9	5.9	58.0
	11 $15000 TO 17499	6	3.3	5.0	63.0
	12 $17500 TO 19999	2	1.1	1.7	64.7
	13 $20000 TO 22499	7	3.9	5.9	70.6
	14 $22500 TO 24999	7	3.9	5.9	76.5
	15 $25000 TO 29999	11	6.1	9.2	85.7
	16 $30000 TO 34999	6	3.3	5.0	90.8
	17 $35000 TO 39999	7	3.9	5.9	96.6
	18 $40000 TO 49999	1	.6	.8	97.5
	19 $50000 TO 59999	2	1.1	1.7	99.2
	20 $60000 TO 74999	1	.6	.8	100.0
	Total	119	66.1	100.0	
Missing	0 NAP	53	29.4		
	24 REFUSED	4	2.2		
	98 DK	2	1.1		
	99 NA	2	1.1		
	Total	61	33.9		
Total		180	100.0		

6. Job satisfaction

SATJOB7 Job satisfaction in general

		Frequency	Percent	Valid Percent	Cumulative Percent
Valid	1 COMPLETELY DISSATISFIED	1	.6	1.5	1.5
	2 VERY DISSATISFIED	4	2.2	6.2	7.7
	3 FAIRLY DISSATISFIED	5	2.8	7.7	15.4
	4 NEITHER SAT NOR DISSAT	6	3.3	9.2	24.6
	5 FAIRLY SATISFIED	23	12.8	35.4	60.0
	6 VERY SATISFIED	14	7.8	21.5	81.5
	7 COMPLETELY SATISFIED	12	6.7	18.5	100.0
	Total	65	36.1	100.0	
Missing	0 NAP	113	62.8		
	8 Cannot choose	2	1.1		
	Total	115	63.9		
Total		180	100.0		

7. How hard it is to take time off from work for family matters

FAMWKOFF How hard to take time off

		Frequency	Percent	Valid Percent	Cumulative Percent
Valid	1 Not at all hard	51	28.3	44.0	44.0
	2 Not too hard	33	18.3	28.4	72.4
	3 Somewhat hard	22	12.2	19.0	91.4
	4 Very hard	10	5.6	8.6	100.0
	Total	116	64.4	100.0	
Missing	0 NAP	63	35.0		
	8 DONT KNOW	1	.6		
	Total	64	35.6		
Total		180	100.0		

8. Satisfaction with financial situation

SATFIN Satisfaction with financial situation

		Frequency	Percent	Valid Percent	Cumulative Percent
Valid	1 NOT AT ALL SATIS	22	12.2	25.9	25.9
	2 MORE OR LESS	39	21.7	45.9	71.8
	3 SATISFIED	24	13.3	28.2	100.0
	Total	85	47.2	100.0	
Missing	0 NAP	95	52.8		
Total		180	100.0		

For exercises 9 and 10, use the data in the tables below and compute and interpret standard deviation. You can use the raw scores formula, or you can put your data into a frequency distribution and use the formula for finding standard deviation from an ungrouped frequency distribution.

9. Hours respondent worked in a week

Cases	Number of hours worked last week
1	45
2	51
3	66
4	40
5	40
6	48
7	35
8	15
9	40
10	30
11	40
12	50
13	40
14	45
15	45
16	60
17	16

10. Hours respondent has to relax each day

Cases	Hours per day respondents have to relax
1	2
2	4
3	2
4	3
5	4
6	4
7	6
8	6
9	6
10	5
11	2
12	4
13	5
14	1
15	0
16	3
17	2

In Exercises 11 through 14, for the given tables in Chapter 5, pages 173–175, compute and interpret the standard deviation.

11. The table in General Exercise 11.
12. The table in General Exercise 12.
13. The table in General Exercise 13.
14. The table in General Exercise 14.
15. Compute and interpret appropriate measures of central tendency and the standard deviation for the following frequency distribution (for 2002 male GSS respondents ages 18 through 25).

EDUC Highest year of school completed[a]

		Frequency	Percent	Valid Percent	Cumulative Percent
Valid	7	1	1.3	1.3	1.3
	8	1	1.3	1.3	2.7
	9	3	4.0	4.0	6.7
	10	3	4.0	4.0	10.7
	11	8	10.7	10.7	21.3
	12	23	30.7	30.7	52.0
	13	8	10.7	10.7	62.7
	14	14	18.7	18.7	81.3
	15	3	4.0	4.0	85.3
	16	7	9.3	9.3	94.7
	17	3	4.0	4.0	98.7
	18	1	1.3	1.3	100.0
	Total	75	100.0	100.0	

[a] SEX Respondents' sex = 1 MALE

16. Compute and interpret appropriate measures of central tendency and the standard deviation for the following frequency distribution (for 2002 female GSS respondents ages 18 through 25).

EDUC Highest year of school completed[a]

		Frequency	Percent	Valid Percent	Cumulative Percent
Valid	8	2	1.9	1.9	1.9
	9	2	1.9	1.9	3.8
	10	4	3.8	3.8	7.6
	11	12	11.4	11.4	19.0
	12	26	24.8	24.8	43.8
	13	13	12.4	12.4	56.2
	14	22	21.0	21.0	77.1
	15	4	3.8	3.8	81.0
	16	13	12.4	12.4	93.3
	17	6	5.7	5.7	99.0
	18	1	1.0	1.0	100.0
	Total	105	100.0	100.0	

[a] SEX Respondents' sex = 2 FEMALE

SPSS EXERCISES

Use appropriate measures of dispersion to analyze responses of the respondents in the GSS 2002 subset A file to the following variables.

1. *satjob7*
2. *satfin*
3. *wkvsfam*
4. *lotofsay*

Split your GSS 2002 subset A file using the variable *sex*. Analyze the frequency distributions and appropriate measures of dispersion to describe the differences, if any, between male and female respondents on the following variables.

5. *rincom98*
6. *wkvsfam*

Use appropriate measures of dispersion to analyze responses in the GSS 2002 subset A file to the following variables. (If you have been using the Split File command, remember that you need to click on Data ➥ Split File ➥ OK to "unsplit" your file.)

7. *educ*
8. *hrsrelax*

Split your GSS 2002 subset A file using the variable *rcrace*. Use appropriate measures of central tendency and dispersion to see if there are differences among the respondents in the GSS 2002 subset A file on the following variables.

9. *hrs1*
10. *hrsrelax*

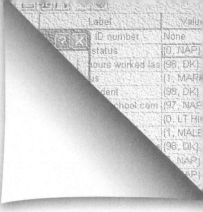

CHAPTER  7

An Introduction to Making Inferences

INTRODUCTION

In this chapter we will use some of our measures of central tendency from Chapter 5 and the characteristics of the normal distribution that were introduced in Chapter 6 to begin understanding the process of making inferences—generalizations from samples to the populations from which samples are drawn. Inferential statistics are in action just about anywhere you look in a newspaper or magazine, and they are prominent in scholarly research. The president of the United States can rarely do anything without surveys being conducted to determine whether the public supports a particular plan of action. Samples are drawn and polls are taken. You may have been on the receiving end of one of these surveys. Researchers who take the polls are hardly ever satisfied to simply describe the characteristics of their samples. They want to be able to say if (or, more accurately, the likelihood that) what they are observing in samples is characteristic of entire populations. And this is where inferential statistics come into play.

You have already encountered some examples of inferential statistics in action in this text. For instance in the "News to Use" article in Chapter 2, you learned about the results of a survey, "Short-Term Impacts, Long-Term Opportunities: The Political and Civic Engagement of Young Adults in America," designed to assess the extent to which the youth of America are civically engaged. The surveys were based on samples drawn from the population of young Americans ages 15 through 25. In the footnote to the article (see Chapter 2, p. 36), you may have noticed a description of how the poll participants were selected and the results analyzed. Please review that description now and pay particular attention to the explanation of how to use the results of the sample to generalize, or draw conclusions about, the views of all American young people. These are inferential statistics in action.

You will also notice similar, albeit much shorter, explanations almost any time you see poll results reported in a newspaper. For example, the "News to Use" article in this chapter reports on a Washington Post–ABC News poll regarding support for the president of the United States, and the article briefly describes how the results are to be used to generalize from the sample of people interviewed to the entire population represented by the sample. In this chapter you will learn how to understand these kinds of statements so that you will know what they mean when you run across them in the popular press or in scholarly research.

First, let's review what we mean by inferential statistics. **Inferential statistics** are numbers that help us assess the likelihood that patterns we observe in randomly drawn samples will be found in the populations from which those samples were drawn. A very important part of this definition is that inferential statistics should be used only with randomly drawn samples.[1] In the footnote to the "News to Use" article in Chapter 2, there is an unusually detailed description of an application of inferential statistics. The authors of the article wrote,

> In interpreting survey results, all sample surveys are subject to possible sampling error; that is, the results of a survey may differ from those which would be obtained if the entire population were interviewed. The size of the sampling error depends upon both the total number of respondents in the survey and the percentage distribution of responses to a particular question. For example, in Question 13, which all respondents answered, 53% said that generally speaking, you can't be too careful in dealing with people; we can therefore be 95% confident that the true percentage will fall within 2.5% of this percentage, or between 55.5% and 50.5%.[2]

In statistical terminology, the authors of the analysis of the civic engagement survey are discussing confidence limits (the reference being 95% confident) and confidence intervals (the reference to the 2.5% percentage range within which the "true" population percentages fall).

In the Washington Post article in the "News to Use" section of this chapter, "Support for Bush Declines As Casualties Mount in Iraq," you see a more typical reference to confidence intervals (in the last line of the article), "The margin of sampling error for the overall results is plus or minus 3 percentage points." There is no reference to a confidence limit. Generally, we can assume the same 95% confidence limit as in the civic engagement survey.

Where do these numbers come from and what do they mean? To begin, I will lay the groundwork for understanding inferential statistics by introducing the

---

[1]Some would argue, however, that inferential statistics can be used with any sample that is at least representative of the population from which it was drawn, regardless of the randomness of the process by which the sample itself was drawn.

[2]From "Short-Term Impacts, Long-Term Opportunities: The Political and Civic Engagement of Young Adults in America," p. 2, Lake Snell Perry & Associates, with the Tarrance Group, March 2002, <http://www.civicyouth.org/research/products/National_Youth_Survey_outside.htm.>.

assumptions on which inferential statistics are based, beginning with the difference between a sample and a population. Then I will cover the properties of randomly drawn samples that allow us to make inferences from samples to populations. In the next chapter you will learn how to apply these principles to the computation of confidence intervals at specified confidence levels, like the one in the "News to Use" articles in this chapter and in Chapter 2.

Samples and Populations

As you may recall from Chapter 1, **samples** are subsets of populations. **Populations** are sets of elements that researchers are interested in knowing something about. Populations can be sets of individuals, organizations, states, or even nations. In the "News to Use" article in this chapter, the population of interest is the set of American adults. Samples are those subsets of populations about which researchers gather data, usually to make generalizations about the populations from which the samples are drawn. To make generalizations from samples to populations, researchers must draw their samples at random from frames (lists—as complete as researchers can make them—of all elements in a population). The sample in the Washington Post–ABC News Poll consists of the 1,000 adults who were interviewed by telephone. Was the sample drawn randomly? The article indicates in the last line that the sample was randomly drawn, but it does not specify how the sample was drawn.

Sample Statistics

The question then becomes, How likely is it that the sample selected by the pollsters is representative of the population? You will probably argue that if the sample has been drawn randomly, it's logical to assume it will be representative, and you may be right—most of the time. However, if you have had any experience drawing random samples, you have seen that sometimes you can draw a sample not at all representative of the population from which the sample was drawn.

To illustrate this point, look at Table 7.1 on p. 234. You will see the means for the variable *age* in five different randomly drawn samples from the 2002 General Social Survey. How close are these sample means to the actual average age (46.28 years old) of the respondents? In a couple of cases they are extremely close, but in one case, not very close at all—over four years off.

How can researchers know whether their sample is one of the representative ones or one of the samples that doesn't represent the population? The frustrating answer is, they can't. They can never know with 100% certainty whether their sample is representative or not. All they can do is assess the likelihood—the probability—that their sample *is* representative. They can never guarantee that it is.

It's somewhat like buying a new car. You do a lot of research on the different makes and models. You find one you like—it looks nice, drives well, and has an excellent repair record. The odds are that you've got a good car. However, you won't know for sure until you own it whether you've got a car that acts like most cars or is a "lemon." The proof is in the outcome—and so it is with social science research. We can never know for sure. Sometimes pollsters see the proof in the outcome. Who wins the election? The candidate the pollsters said would win or the opponent? Often, researchers don't know for sure how accurate their samples are as representations of populations. Look at some of the General Social Survey questions. We can never know for certain whether the percentage of respondents who are satisfied with their jobs, or say they attend church regularly, or graduate from high school, is identical (or even close) to the percentage of people in the population who share those characteristics.

How then can we know the likelihood that our sample represents the population? We can use inferential statistics—statistics that assess the probability or likelihood. To begin understanding how these statistics work, we need to revisit the normal distribution and get a handle on the related concept of Z scores. ∎

NEWS *to* USE
Statistics in the "Real" World

Support for Bush Declines As Casualties Mount in Iraq[3]
BY RICHARD MORIN AND CLAUDIA DEANE

Public support for President Bush has dropped sharply amid growing concerns about U.S. military casualties and doubts whether the war with Iraq was worth fighting, according to a new Washington Post-ABC News poll.

Bush's overall job approval rating dropped to 59 percent, down nine points in the past 18 days. That decline exactly mirrored the slide in public support for Bush's handling of the situation in Iraq, which now stands at 58 percent.

And for the first time, slightly more than half the country—52 percent—believes there has been an "unacceptable" level of U.S. casualties in Iraq, up eight points in less than three weeks.

Still, only 26 percent said there had been more casualties than they had expected. Three in four say they expect "significantly more" American dead and wounded.

The poll found that seven in 10 Americans believe the United States should continue to keep troops in Iraq, even if it means additional casualties. That view was shared by majorities of Republicans, Democrats and political independents.

[3]Washingtonpost.com, 12 July 2003, <http://www.washingtonpost.com/wp-dyn/articles/A45480-2003Jul11.html>.

A majority of the country—57 percent—still consider the war with Iraq to have been worth the sacrifice. That's down 7 percentage points from a Post-ABC News poll in late June, and 13 points since the war ended 10 weeks ago.

Taken together, the latest survey findings suggest that the mix of euphoria and relief that followed the quick U.S. victory in Iraq continues to dissipate, creating an uncertain and volatile political environment. The risks are perhaps most obvious for Bush, whose continued high standing with the American people has been fueled largely by his handling of the war on terrorism and, more recently, the war in Iraq.

On the domestic front, meanwhile, fewer than half the nation approves of Bush's handling of the economy.

The poll found that the failure to locate weapons of mass destruction in Iraq has sharply divided the country. Fifty percent said Bush intentionally exaggerated evidence suggesting Iraq had such weapons, while nearly as many—46 percent—disagreed.

"If we have the capability of finding out that Joe Blow No-Name has dodged his taxes for the past 10 years, why don't we have the capability of . . . finding a foolproof method of finding out whether the intelligence we gather is accurate and making it rock-solid before we jump into another situation?" said James Pike, 41, an auto mechanic from Ogdensburg, N.Y.

Earlier this week, Bush administration officials acknowledged that the president should not have claimed in the State of the Union speech that Iraq had tried to buy uranium from African countries in a bid to build nuclear weapons.

The survey also found that Americans are divided over whether the United States should send troops to Liberia to help enforce a cease-fire in that West African nation's civil war, a move the Bush administration is considering. Fifty-one percent opposed sending troops to Liberia as part of a broader peacekeeping operation, while 41 percent favored the idea.

"I don't really know that we have any business there," said Penny Tarbert, 50, who is disabled and lives in Bucyrus, Ohio. "They've been fighting this [civil war] for a long time. I think we've got ourselves in enough right now that we don't need to be spreading ourselves any thinner."

An overwhelming majority of Americans—80 percent—said they fear the United States will become bogged down in a long and costly peacekeeping mission in Iraq, up eight points in less than three weeks.

"I'm worried about how long we're going to be there," said Betty Stillwell, 71, a writer from central California. "We were supposed to be in there and out. By now I thought they would have set up a government, and they haven't done that yet. . . . I think the whole thing was poorly planned, no thought to the aftermath."

Despite broad doubts and growing concerns, few Americans say it's time for the troops to come home. Three in four support the current U.S. presence in Iraq—a view shared by large majorities of Republicans (89 percent), Democrats (60 percent) and political independents (75 percent).

The number of U.S. casualties, while troubling to many, has not outstripped most people's expectations. One in four said there had

been more casualties than they had anticipated, while 36 percent said there had been fewer and 37 percent said it was about what they had expected.

"I don't think any [casualties] are acceptable, but they're necessary," said Chris Eldridge, 29, an electronics technician from Louisville. "They're a lot lower than I expected. I expected there would be more during the initial fighting. I expected a lot more killed. Fortunately there hasn't been."

Danny Buckner, 53, a Navy retiree who lives in Brownwood, Tex., had a somewhat different view. "Considering we are having a cease-fire we sure are losing a lot of lives," he said. "They're killing us right and left. I don't know what the deal is."

The poll suggests growing public belief that the United States must kill or capture Saddam Hussein for the war to be successful. A 61 percent majority now believe Hussein must be found, up 11 points since April. That view was shared by roughly similar majorities of Republicans, Democrats and political independents.

"It would be nice if we could find Saddam Hussein and get it over with," said Susan Leidich, 39, a homemaker from Birch Run, Mich. "It seems like if the military leaves, it could be like Desert Storm [the 1991 Persian Gulf War], and then Saddam Hussein would take right back over."

The survey suggests that most Americans believe the recent war produced mixed results. Six in 10 said it damaged the image of the United States abroad, and half said the conflict caused permanent damage to U.S. relations with France, Germany and other allies who opposed the war. The public was equally divided whether the war contributed to long-term peace and stability in the Middle East.

But seven in 10 said the war helped improve the lives of the Iraqi people. And six in 10 said it contributed to the long-term security of the United States.

A total of 1,006 randomly selected adults were interviewed July 9 and 10. The margin of sampling error for the overall results is plus or minus 3 percentage points.

THE NORMAL DISTRIBUTION REVISITED: *Z* SCORES

Do you recall the discussion of the normal distribution, commonly known as the bell-shaped curve, from Chapter 6? The normal distribution is a symmetrically distributed set of scores for which there is only one mode and the mean, median, and mode are identical. If you were to graph the distribution, it would look somewhat like a bell. In Chapter 6 you learned how to use the properties of the normal distribution to evaluate the distribution or dispersion of responses to a variable in relation to the mean. As a rule, the smaller a standard deviation is in relation to the range of responses to a variable, the more homogeneous are the responses. The larger the standard deviation is in relation to the range, the more heterogeneous are the responses. Moreover, we can assume that, in a normally distributed set of responses to a variable, about 68% of the responses will fall within a range of values 1 standard deviation below the mean to 1 standard deviation above the mean. About 95% of the responses will fall within a range of values 2 standard deviations below the mean to 2 standard deviations above it.

Skills Practice 1 Compare the means, medians, and standard deviations for the educational levels of male and female respondents to the 2002 General Social Survey (see the tables below).

A. Which distribution is the most homogeneous?
B. Use the standard deviation for males to find out the range of values 1 standard deviation below the mean and 1 standard deviation above the mean, and the range of values 2 standard deviations below the mean to 2 standard deviations above it.

Statistics[a]

EDUC Highest year of school completed

N	Valid	651
	Missing	3
Mean		13.30
Median		13.00
Mode		12
Std. Deviation		3.202
Range		20

[a] SEX Respondents' sex = 1 MALE

Statistics[a]

EDUC Highest year of school completed

N	Valid	842
	Missing	4
Mean		13.38
Median		13.00
Mode		12
Std. Deviation		2.843
Range		19

[a] SEX Respondents' sex = 2 FEMALE

As this exercise demonstrates, you can use the properties of the normal distribution to find out the value of 1 or more standard deviations from the mean (by adding 1 or more standard deviations to the mean, or subtracting 1 or more standard deviations from the mean).

Besides using the characteristics of the normal distribution to describe the dispersion of responses to a variable, we can use it to tell where in the distribution a particular value might fall. For example, if we want to describe the educational achievements of the male respondents to the General Social Survey, we can find the value of 1 standard deviation below the mean by subtracting 1 standard deviation from the mean, and we can find 1 standard deviation above the mean by adding 1 standard deviation to the mean. Then we can make the statement that about 68% of the male respondents have between 10.10 and 16.50 years of education. If we subtract 2 standard deviations from the mean and then add 2 standard deviations to the mean, we can say that about 95% of the male respondents have between 6.90 and 19.70 years of education.

We can also use the properties of the normal distribution to find out how many standard deviations from the mean a particular respondent or group of respondents might fall. Suppose we want to know where in the distribution we would find respondents with 10 years of education. We can find the answer by finding the *Z* score for that value.

A **Z score** expresses the relationship between a particular value in a distribution and the mean in units of the standard deviation. Using the example in Skills Practice 1, you found that for males the value 10.10 is 1 standard deviation below the mean. Another way of expressing this same idea is to say that the value 10.10 has a *Z* score of −1. In other words, the value 10.10 is 1 standard deviation below the mean. On the other hand, the value 16.50 has a *Z* score of +1. It is 1 standard deviation above the mean.

Suppose we want to work the relationship the other way. Instead of finding out what the value is at a certain *Z* score 1 or 2 units above or below the mean, we want to know, given a certain value, what its *Z* score is. How far is it from the mean? The solution is fairly simple: We can use a formula for finding a *Z* score.

Formula 7.1: *Z* scores for samples

$$Z = \frac{X_i - \overline{X}}{s}$$

where X_i is a given score within the range of values for a variable, $\overline{X}$ is the mean for the distribution of scores, and s is the standard deviation.

EXAMPLE:

Where in the distribution of scores does a male respondent with 10 years of education fall? Use the formula for *Z* scores:

$$Z = \frac{X_i - \overline{X}}{s}$$

$$= \frac{10 - 13.30}{3.20} = -\frac{3.30}{3.20}$$

$$Z = -1.03$$

Interpretation

What does the Z score tell us? Fundamentally, a Z score is nothing more than a deviation from the mean divided by a standard deviation. Remember that the formula for finding a deviation from the mean is $X - \overline{X}$, the numerator of the formula for the Z score. In essence then, the Z score is a proportion, and a Z score of -1.03 for a respondent with 10 years of education tells us that a respondent with 10 years of education falls 1.03 standard deviations *below* the mean. We know the respondent is below the mean and not above it because the sign on the Z score is negative.

 Skills Practice 2 What is the Z score for a male respondent with 14 years of education? What does the Z score tell us about where that respondent falls in relation to the mean?

Besides learning that a respondent with 10 years of education falls 1.03 standard deviations below the mean, we can find out where the other respondents fall in relation to those who have 10 years of education. We can use the Z score to answer the question, What percentage of the respondents fall between someone who has 10 years of education and the mean of 13.30 years of education? We answer this question by looking up the Z score on a table of scores, called "Area under the Normal Curve" (Appendix A), which tells us the area that falls between a given Z score and the mean.

Go to Appendix A now and find the Z score 1.03, in the (a) column labeled Z. Look to the (b) column immediately to the right, and you will see the number .3485. You can read this number as a percentage. It tells us that about 35% of the male respondents have between 10 and 13.30 (the mean) years of education. You can also read it as a probability—there are 35 chances out of 100 that a male respondent has between 10 and about 13 years of education.

Finally, you can find out what percentage of the respondents have less than 10 years of education by reading across to column (c) on the right, where you find the number .1515. The number tells us that about 15% of the respondents have less than 10 years of education. See Figure 7.1 for an illustration of the relationship between Z scores and the area under the normal curve.

 Skills Practice 3 Use the Z score you computed for Skills Practice 2 and Appendix A to answer these questions:

A. What percentage of male respondents have between 13.30 and 14 years of education?

B. What percentage have more than 14 years of education?

FIGURE 7.1
Relationship of $Z =$ -1.03 to the mean of 13.30 for the male respondents to the variable *educ* in the GSS 2002 subset A file.

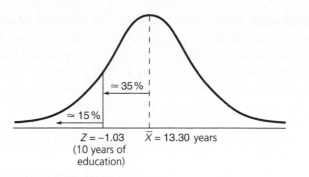

$\simeq 35\%$

$\simeq 15\%$

$Z = -1.03$ $\bar{X} = 13.30$ years
(10 years of
education)

Soon you will see the importance of Z scores for making generalizations about populations from samples. However, before I can get to that, I need to introduce a few more of the concepts central to understanding inferential statistics, beginning with the concept of sample statistics.

SAMPLE STATISTICS

Z scores are a type of sample statistic. A **sample statistic** is any statistic that describes the distribution of values for a variable, or relationships between variables, in a sample. Sample statistics apply only to the samples they are designed to describe. Examples of sample statistics, besides Z scores, include measures of central tendency, such as the mean, median, and mode; measures of dispersion, like the interquartile range and the standard deviation; and measures of association, including lambda and gamma.

You have already seen how useful sample statistics are for describing the characteristics of respondents. Sample statistics serve another important function—they can be used to estimate **population parameters**. Population parameters are the characteristics of a population estimated from sample statistics.

The concept of population parameters is an abstract idea. The true characteristics of a population are usually not knowable. For example, it would be impossible to know for sure the average age of American adults, because there are too many adults to account for. We can only estimate the average age of all adults based on the average age of the adults we might include in a random sample designed to represent everyone. This estimate of the age of a population based on what we learn from a sample is an example of a population parameter.

How can estimates of populations be made with any degree of accuracy from samples alone? To find out, let's explore the characteristics of sampling distributions.

The Sampling Distribution

For any particular population, we can draw any one of a number of possible samples of a given sample size. The General Social Survey for 2002 is one possible sample of nearly 3,000 individuals drawn to represent all English-speaking, noninstitutionalized American adults (18 years old or older). In actuality, there are a tremendous number of different samples that could *possibly* be drawn. It's hard to imagine how many there could be—so many that it would be impossible to draw them all. Even among a small group of people, there are many possible samples of a given size that could be drawn. Look around your classroom. Suppose you wanted to draw a random sample of only 10 people to represent your class. Think about how many possible configurations there are of 10 people in your class. In a class of only 20 people there are 184,756 possible combinations of 10!

For each of the samples we might draw, we can compute sample statistics—a mean, a median, a mode, a standard deviation for specific variables in the sample. We have already done this for many of the GSS variables. The key to understanding inferential statistics is this next point—these sample statistics themselves have a distribution. Think about this for a second.

- For any population, we can draw a large number of different samples of a certain sample size. From a population of 20 students, we can draw 184,756 different samples of 10.
- For each of the samples we might draw, we can compute one or more sample statistics. Let's say we find the average age of the students in each of our samples.
- For these means of ages, we can construct a distribution, and this distribution will have its own mean, median, standard deviation, and so on.

This distribution of sample statistics from all possible samples of a given size drawn from the same population is called the **sampling distribution**. Unfortunately, this distribution is hypothetical—imaginary. We couldn't ever draw all possible samples of a given size from a particular population, especially if the population is a large one. However, understanding the idea is key to understanding inferential statistics.

Let's make this more concrete by going back to an example I used in Chapter 5, p. 158 when I discussed the stability of the mean. For this example, let's treat our respondents to the 2002 GSS as a population—a population of respondents. In Chapter 5 I showed you five samples drawn at random from the 2002 GSS. For each of these samples, I computed a mean, median, and mode for the variable *age*. I came up with the set of figures you see in Table 7.1.

Although these five samples are far from every conceivable sample I could draw, they can be used to illustrate the concept of the sampling distribution.

TABLE 7.1   Measures of Central Tendency for the Variable *age* in Five Randomly Drawn Samples from the 2002 General Social Survey

	Mean	Median	Mode
Sample 1	46.20	40	35
Sample 2	50.62	44	40
Sample 3	46.98	46	28
Sample 4	46.30	47	51
Sample 5	47.72	45	45

First, think about how each of the measures of central tendency—the mean, median, and mode—could be treated as separate variables. For each of them, I could compute descriptive statistics, like an average of the means and an average of the medians, and I could compute the standard deviation of the means and the standard deviation of the medians.

Now picture what would happen if I had hundreds of samples from the General Social Survey for 2002 and, therefore, hundreds of sample statistics—means, medians, and modes. Figure 7.2 illustrates this process. For each of these sets of sample statistics, I could come up with a sampling distribution. Let's explore just one of the possibilities—coming up with a distribution for all of the means in a sampling distribution, also called the sampling distribution of sample means.

The Sampling Distribution of Sample Means

The **sampling distribution of sample means** is the hypothetical distribution of all possible sample means of a given sample size from a particular population. Whereas the term *sampling distribution* refers generally to the distribution of all sample statistics for a particular set of samples drawn from a population, the sampling distribution of sample means refers specifically to the distribution of just one sample statistic, the mean. For the five samples in Table 7.1, the sampling distribution of sample means could be displayed as a frequency distribution of the means.

As I mentioned earlier, it is not only possible to construct a frequency distribution for all of the sample means in a sampling distribution, I can also compute descriptive statistics for the sample means. To find the average of all of the sample means in Table 7.1, I would sum the means from each of the five samples and divide the total by the number of samples I have. The result is called the mean of the sampling distribution of sample means. It is the average of the sample means. The mean of the sampling distribution of sample means is expressed with the symbol $\mu_{\bar{X}}$, where the Greek symbol μ (mu, pronounced "mew") with its subscript $\bar{X}$ (X-bar) is read as "the mean of the sampling distribution of sample means."

FIGURE 7.2
The hypothetical sampling distribution of sample means for all possible samples of size $N = 2{,}751$ that could be drawn from the population of American adults, 18 years of age or older, noninstitutionalized, English-speaking.

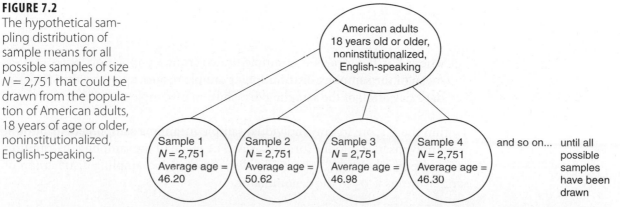

In addition to finding the mean for a sampling distribution, we can compute any other statistic that might help us characterize the distribution of the samples. For example, we could find the standard deviation of the sample means. The standard deviation of the means of the samples would tell us how homogeneous or heterogeneous the distribution is or how much variation we would expect to find in the sample means. The standard deviation of the sampling distribution of sample means is represented by the symbol $\sigma_{\overline{X}}$, where the Greek symbol σ (sigma) represents the standard deviation, and the subscript $\overline{X}$ represents the mean. The symbol is read as the standard deviation of the sampling distribution of sample means.

You may be wondering where the statistics $\mu_{\overline{X}}$ and $\sigma_{\overline{X}}$ come from—are they computed from something that I just said is theoretical and doesn't really exist? In actuality, these statistics cannot be computed but they can be estimated. In Chapter 8 you will be introduced to the idea of point estimates—sample statistics that stand in the place of statistics like the mean of the sampling distribution of sample means. In the next section, I will discuss how to estimate the standard deviation of the sampling distribution of sample means, which is also known as the standard error of the mean.

Bringing It All Back Home

Let us tie these two ideas together—the mean of the sampling distribution of sample means and the standard deviation of the sampling distribution of sample means—with our concept of Z scores introduced at the beginning of this chapter. In addition to learning about the average of the means and their distribution (using standard deviation), we can use Z scores to find out where each of the individual sample means falls in relation to the rest of the distribution of sample means. Remember the Z score formula applied to a sample:

$$Z = \frac{X_i - \overline{X}}{s}$$

When applied the theoretical sampling distribution of all possible sample means, the Z score formula changes somewhat.

Formula 7.2: Computing Z scores for a sampling distribution of sample means

$$Z = \frac{\overline{X} - \mu_{\overline{X}}}{\sigma_{\overline{X}}}$$

where $\overline{X}$ is the mean for a sample drawn from a population, $\mu_{\overline{X}}$ is the mean of the sampling distribution of sample means, and $\sigma_{\overline{X}}$ is the standard deviation of the sampling distribution of sample means.

To find the Z score for any individual sample mean in a sampling distribution, we simply insert it into the formula as $\overline{X}$. The mean of the sampling distribution of sample means is $\mu_{\overline{X}}$. The standard deviation for the sampling distribution of sample means is $\sigma_{\overline{X}}$ in the denominator.

The Standard Error of the Mean

The standard deviation of the sampling distribution of sample means is also called the **standard error of the mean**. As I pointed out earlier in this chapter, the sampling distribution is a theoretical idea. It doesn't actually exist, because the sampling distribution is the distribution of all possible samples of a certain size that could be drawn from a particular population.

However, we can *estimate* the standard deviation of the sampling distribution of sample means from sample statistics using Formula 7.3:

Formula 7.3: The standard error of the mean

$$\sigma_{\bar{X}} = \frac{\sigma}{\sqrt{N}}$$

where $\sigma_{\bar{X}}$ is the standard deviation of the sampling distribution of sample means; σ, the standard deviation of a set of scores, is the standard deviation of the distribution of a set of scores from a population for a particular variable; and N is the sample size.

To use the formula, though, we have to know the standard deviation of a distribution of scores in a population. As you may be guessing already, that statistic is not and cannot be known. So what do we do? We use the standard deviation for the distribution of scores in a sample to stand in its place.

EXAMPLE:

Let's find the standard error of the mean for the variable *age* in the GSS 2002 subset A file. The standard deviation for the variable *age* in the sample is 17.34, and we know N (the sample size) is 1,490. Insert these values into the formula for the standard error of the mean.

$$\sigma_{\bar{X}} = \frac{\sigma}{\sqrt{N}}$$

$$= \frac{17.34}{\sqrt{1490}} = \frac{17.34}{38.6005}$$

$$\sigma_{\bar{X}} = .45$$

Interpretation   What does this tell us? Think about the meaning of the standard deviation in any normal distribution. The smaller the standard deviation is in relation to the range of values, the more homogeneous is the distribution. In this case, the distribution of values is the dispersion of sample means in a set of randomly drawn samples from a population. More specifically, the standard error of .45 is our estimate of the standard deviation of the sampling distribution of sample means for all possible samples of 1,490 respondents from the 2002 population of U.S. adults. It tells us that about 68% of the sample means could be expected to fall within a range of only a little less than one year (extending slightly less than one-half year below the mean of the sampling distribution of sample means to slightly less than one-half year above the mean of the sampling distribution of sample means), a very narrow range indicating a very homogeneous distribution of means. Another way to put it is that the standard error of the mean indicates little variation in the means of the sampling distribution of sample means.

Avoiding Common Pitfalls: Symbols for sample characteristics and population parameters   The terminology at this point is probably getting confusing: population parameters, sample statistics, sample means, the sampling distribution of sample means, and the mean of the sampling distribution of sample means. To help sort all of this out, notice that population parameters (estimates of population characteristics based on sample statistics) are designated by Greek letters (like μ and σ), whereas sample statistics (the characteristics of samples) are represented by phonetic symbols (like $\bar{X}$ and s).

You're probably wondering why this concept of the standard error of the mean is important. The reason is that when there is little variation in the sampling distribution of sample means, we can have more confidence that our predictions about populations will be accurate. The more homogeneous the characteristics of the sampling distribution (the mean, for example) are, the more likely it is that any single sample we draw from a population will be representative of the population as a whole. We can't guarantee that the sample is an accurate reflection of the population, but the likelihood of the sample reflecting the population is improved.

Skills Practice 4   In the 2002 GSS subset A file there are 1,493 responses to the education variable. The standard deviation for the distribution of responses is 3.00. Find the standard error of the mean. Write a sentence explaining what the standard error tells you.

The Central Limit Theorem

The **Central Limit Theorem** is a theory about the characteristics of the sampling distribution. It tells us that the larger the size of a sample from a population is, the more likely it is that the mean of a single sample will be close to (or approximate) the mean of the population from which the sample was drawn. If you are a researcher interested in learning about the characteristics of a population, the more people you include in your sample, the more likely it is that any mean you compute for the sample will be close to the actual mean in the population as a whole.

Think about this for a second and you will see how intuitively simple this is. Suppose you have a bag of 100 balls of different colors. Someone asks you to draw one out and guess the characteristics of all of the balls in the bag. If you draw out one red ball, you would have to guess that all of the balls are red. Then you get to draw out another ball. It's green. Now you know there are some green balls and some red balls. You would probably guess that half the balls in the bag are red and the other half are green. You may not be right, but by doubling the size of the sample (from one ball to two balls) your accuracy at guessing the characteristics of all the balls has improved. The more balls you draw out, the more accurate you can be at predicting what all of the balls look like.

Let's apply this to the General Social Survey. The more individuals the researchers include in their sample, the more likely it is that any average computed for any particular numerical variable (like *age, years of education, number of people in a household*) will be representative of the average for that variable in the population of American adults. In addition, the larger the size of the samples in a sampling distribution, the more likely it is that the sampling distribution of sample means will itself be normal. This means that

- The mean and the median for the sampling distribution of sample means should be identical (one of the properties of a normal distribution) or pretty close to it.
- There should be only one mode in the sampling distribution.
- The distribution of means in the sampling distribution should be symmetrical.
- A frequency distribution of the means in the sampling distribution would look like the normal curve.

This is important because if this is so, then you can find out how likely it is that a particular range of values constructed in relation to a sample mean contains the "true" population mean. How can you do this? Isn't the population mean a theoretical number, a number we can't ever really know? How can we figure out, for example, if a range of values constructed around the mean for the *age* variable in the General Social Survey contains the average of the ages of all U.S. adults in 2002? We can do this by using some of the concepts we have discussed to construct *confidence intervals* at specified *confidence levels* around *point estimates* to approximate the parameters of a population, skills you will learn in the next chapter.

USING SPSS

Finding Z Scores and the Standard Error of the Mean

Now, let's see how SPSS can help us find some of the statistics we have been working with in this chapter.

SPSS GUIDE: FINDING *Z* SCORES

Finding *Z* scores is a fairly simple process. Open the SPSS program and your GSS 2002 subset A file. Follow the command path Analyze ➡ Descriptive Statistics ➡ Descriptives to open the Descriptives window.

① Select the variable for which you want *Z* scores. Scroll down to *educ* and click on it. Place it in the Variable selection box.

② Click on Save standardized values as variables.

③ Click on OK.

In the Output window, you will see a set of descriptive statistics like the one in Table 7.2. For the variable *educ,* you will see the total number of valid responses, the minimum and maximum values of the variable, the mean, and the standard deviation.

TABLE 7.2   Descriptive Statistics for the Variable *educ* in the GSS 2002 subset A File

Descriptive Statistics

	N	Minimum	Maximum	Mean	Std. Deviation
EDUC Highest year of school completed	1493	0	20	13.35	3.004
Valid N (listwise)	1493				

Where are the *Z* scores? They show up in your Data Editor (Data View) window as a new variable. Switch back to the Data Editor window, and scroll to the end of the variables list on the screen.

You will see a new variable, *zeduc*. (SPSS automatically assigns this variable name—the name of your original variable preceded by the letter Z.) The values of *zeduc* are the Z scores for each of the values of the *educ* variable. You can read these values (find their associated value for *educ*) by scrolling back across the screen until you find the corresponding *educ* value for a particular Z score.

 Skills Practice 5 Use SPSS to obtain the mean and standard deviation for the variable *age*. Find the Z scores for the values 25, 38, and 50.

SPSS GUIDE: FINDING THE STANDARD ERROR OF THE MEAN

Follow the command path Analyze ➡ Descriptive Statistics ➡ Frequencies. Select the variable you want to analyze. Let's use *age*. In the Frequencies dialog box, click on the Statistics button. In the lower left-hand corner of the dialog box, in the list of statistics under "Dispersion," you will find "S.E. Mean." In addition to the other statistics that are appropriate for a variable (standard deviation, range, mean, median, and mode), click on the box next to S.E. Mean to select this statistic. Then click on Continue.

At the Frequencies dialog box click on OK. The output that you see should look like the table of statistics in Table 7.3 below.

In addition to the statistics that you are used to seeing, notice that the standard error of the mean is included in the table. The result should look familiar. It is the same statistic, .45 (rounded to the second decimal), that you computed by hand earlier in this chapter.

Skills Practice 6 Use the variable *educ* in the GSS 2002 subset A file to find the standard error of the mean.

TABLE 7.3 Statistics for the Variable *age* in the GSS 2002 subset A File, Including the Standard Error of the Mean

Statistics

AGE Age of respondent

N	Valid	1490
	Missing	10
Mean		46.40
Std. Error of Mean		.449
Median		45.00
Mode		33
Std. Deviation		17.343
Range		71

SUMMARY

This chapter introduced you to some of the fundamental concepts of inferential statistics. You should understand the relation of Z scores to a normal distribution, and you should be able to calculate a Z score by hand and use SPSS to find Z scores. More important, you should be able to interpret a Z score.

It is also important to be able to distinguish between sample statistics (the characteristics of samples) and population parameters (the estimated characteristics of populations).

The concepts you should understand at this point include the sampling distribution, a hypo-thetical distribution of the characteristics of all possible samples of a certain size drawn from the same population. The distribution of sample means is the distribution of means in the sampling distribution, and the mean of the sampling distribution of sample means is the average of the sample means in the sampling distribution. The standard error of the mean is the standard deviation of the sampling distribution of sample means. These concepts will be used more extensively in the next chapter as we compute confidence limits and levels for point estimates in samples.

KEY CONCEPTS

Inferential statistics
Sample
Population
Sample statistics

Z score
Population parameter
Sampling distribution

Sampling distribution of
  sample means
Standard error of the mean
Central Limit Theorem

ANSWERS TO SKILLS PRACTICES

1. A. The distribution for females is the most homogeneous, because the standard deviation is smaller for females than for males.

   B. The answer to part B follows the Skills Practice.

2. To compute Z scores for the male respondents to the variable *educ*, use the formula for the Z score.

   X_i (the given) = 14 years of education
   $\overline{X}$ (the mean for *educ*) = 13.30
   s (the standard deviation for the variable *educ*) = 3.20

   $$Z = \frac{X_i - \overline{X}}{s}$$

   $$= \frac{14 - 13.30}{3.20} = \frac{.70}{3.20}$$

   $$Z = .22$$

   A respondent with 14 years of education falls more than two-tenths of a standard deviation (or .22 standard deviations) above the mean.

3. Use the table in Appendix A to show that
   A. About 9% of the male respondents have between 13.30 and 14 years of education.
   B. About 41% of the male respondents have more than 14 years of education.

4. To find the standard error of the mean, use formula 7.3.

   $$\sigma_{\overline{X}} = \frac{\sigma}{\sqrt{N}}$$

   $$= \frac{3.00}{\sqrt{1493}} = \frac{3.00}{38.6394}$$

   $$\sigma_{\overline{X}} = .08$$

   The standard deviation of the sampling distribution of sample means for the variable *educ* is .08. About 68% of the means would fall within a range of a little more than one-tenth of a year. Given the range of values for this variable, this is a very homogeneous distribution of sample means.

5. You can use SPSS to find Z scores as follows. First, get the Z scores for the variable *age* using SPSS. Then find the specific age for which you want a Z score under the *age* variable and scroll across the screen to match it with its corresponding Z score. For example, locate a respondent who is 25 years old under the *age* variable. Then, scroll across the screen until you get to the *age* variable, where you can see the Z score associated with 25 years of age, −1.23410.

6. The standard error of the mean is .078 (or .08 rounded to the second decimal). This should look familiar—it is the same statistic that you computed by hand for Skills Practice 4.

GENERAL EXERCISES

Use the statistics for female respondents to the *educ* variable (in Skills Practice 1) to answer questions 1–4:

1. Find and interpret the Z scores for respondents with 12 years of education. What percentage of the female respondents have between 13.38 (the mean) and 12 years of education? What percentage of the female respondents have less than 12 years of education?

2. Find and interpret the Z scores for respondents with 14 years of education. What percentage of the female respondents have between 13.38 (the mean) and 14 years of education? What percentage of the female respondents have more than 14 years of education?

3. Find and interpret the Z scores for respondents with 16 years of education. What percentage of the female respondents have between 13.38 (the mean) and 16 years of education? What percentage of the female respondents have more than 16 years of education?

4. Find and interpret the Z scores for respondents with 18 years of education. What percentage of the female respondents have between 13.38 (the mean) and 18 years of education? What percentage of the female respondents have more than 18 years of education?

For the exercises below, I am using variables that you can find in the GSS 2002 subset B file that comes with this textbook. The subset B file consists largely of numerical variables. You can do the computations below by hand and then check your work by finding the standard error of the mean for the corresponding variable in the GSS 2002 subset B file.

5. Find the standard error of the mean for the variable *rhhwork,* how many hours a week the respondent spends on household work. The mean for the variable is 11.02, and the standard deviation for the distribution of the 365 responses to the variable is 10.622.

6. Find the standard error of the mean for the variable, *sphhwork,* how many hours a week the respondent's spouse spends on household work. The mean for the variable is 9.13, and the standard deviation for the distribution of the 363 responses to the variable is 9.817.

7. Find the standard error of the mean for the male respondents to the variable *rhhwork* (how many hours a week the respondent spends on household work). The mean for the variable is 8.32, and the standard deviation for the distribution of the 155 responses to the variable is 8.556.

8. Find the standard error of the mean for the female respondents to the variable *rhhwork* (how many hours a week the respondent spends on household work). The mean for the variable is 13.01, and the standard deviation for the distribution of the 210 responses to the variable is 11.539.

9. Find the standard error of the mean for the variable *emailhr,* the number of hours respondents spend on email each week. The mean for the variable is 4.02, and the standard deviation for the distribution of the 1026 responses to the variable is 7.058.

10. Find the standard error of the mean for the variable *chathr,* the number of hours respondents spend in Internet chat rooms each week. The mean for the variable is 1.84, and the standard deviation for the distribution of the 165 responses to the variable is 4.702.

11. Why is it that the standard error of the mean is smaller for the variable *emailhr* as compared to the variable *chathr,* even though the standard deviation for the *chathr* variable is smaller than the standard deviation for the *emailhr* variable?

SPSS EXERCISES

For the following exercises, use the GSS 2002 subset B file—a file of mostly numerical variables from the 2002 General Social Survey.

1. Use SPSS to compute the Z scores for the variable *rhhwork* (how many hours a week the respondent spends on household work). Then answer these questions:
   A. What is the Z score for a respondent who does 4 hours of housework?
   B. What is the Z score for a respondent who does 8 hours of housework?
   C. What is the Z score for a respondent who does 14 hours of housework?
   D. What is the Z score for a respondent who does 20 hours of housework?

2. Use SPSS to compute the Z scores for the variable *emailhr* (the number of hours respondents spend on email each week). Then answer these questions:
   A. What is the Z score for a respondent who uses email 2 hours a week?
   B. What is the Z score for a respondent who uses email 3 hours a week?

C. What is the Z score for a respondent who uses email 6 hours a week?

D. What is the Z score for a respondent who uses email 10 hours a week?

3. Use SPSS to find the standard error of the mean for the variable *emhrw*, the number of hours per week respondents use email at work. What does the standard error of the mean tell us about the likely distribution of sample means for this variable?

4. Use SPSS to find the standard error of the mean for the variable *wwwhrw*, the number of hours per week respondents use the World Wide Web at work. What does the standard error of the mean tell us about the likely distribution of sample means for this variable?

Making Inferences for Single Variables

INTRODUCTION

The "News to Use" article in the previous chapter tried to estimate how all American adults felt about the president of the United States based on the responses of a relatively small sample of 1,006 adults. The researchers can't guarantee that what they are learning from their sample is true of all American adults. However, they can tell us there is a 95% chance that what they learned from their sample—the percentage of respondents who feel one way or another about the race—would differ from the population by no more than 6% (3% more or 3% less). How did they determine that? In this chapter you will learn the skills to construct confidence intervals at specified confidence levels in relation to point estimates such as sampling means and percentages, just like the pollsters who conducted the "News to Use" survey you read in Chapter 7.

A **point estimate** is simply a characteristic of a sample that we are using as an estimate of a population parameter.[1] For example, when we use the average age of the respondents in the General Social Survey (46.40) to estimate or represent the age of all American adults, the average age of GSS respondents is being used as a point estimate. In the Chapter 7 "News to Use" article, there are many examples of point estimates. When the authors say that the president's job approval rating dropped to 59%, they are using a point estimate in the sample to represent a characteristic of the population (the percentage of people in the population who believe the president is doing a good job).

---

[1] Recall that a population parameter is a statistical characteristic of a population, like the mean, median, mode, or a percentage.

A **confidence interval** is the range of values within which a given population parameter or characteristic (like the mean or a proportion) is likely to fall, and a **confidence level** specifies how likely or probable it is that a population parameter or characteristic will fall within that range. Confidence intervals with their associated levels are constructed around or in relation to point estimates. Confidence intervals and confidence levels are often used in newspapers and magazines, most commonly when poll results are reported. For example, in the "News to Use" article at the beginning of Chapter 7, you read the statement, "A total of 1,006 randomly selected adults were interviewed July 9 and 10. The margin of sampling error for the overall results is plus or minus 3 percentage points."[2]

We can translate this into plain English by looking at the confidence interval and level in relation to one of the point estimates. According to the Washington Post-ABC News poll, 59% of the respondents in the *sample* approved of the way that the president was handing his job. Now, let's apply the confidence interval and the confidence level to this point estimate. The confidence *level* (not specified in the article, but assumed to be at 95%) tells us that 95 out of 100 confidence intervals that are constructed from samples of a specified size ($N = 1,006$, in this case) would contain the population percentage of those who approve of the way that the president is handling his job. Coupled with the confidence *interval*, 59% plus or minus 3%, the confidence level tells us that there are 95 chances out of 100 that the confidence interval, 56% to 62%, contains the percentage of people in the population who approved of the way that the president was handling his job.

Confidence intervals and confidence levels can be constructed around many different estimates of population parameters, including means and proportions. This chapter focuses on confidence intervals and levels for means and proportions, beginning with confidence intervals and levels for means. ■

POINT ESTIMATES, CONFIDENCE INTERVALS, AND CONFIDENCE LEVELS FOR MEANS

We come up with these intervals and levels by (1) applying many of the concepts we learned in Chapter 7 about the characteristics of a sampling distribution and (2) employing the assumptions of the Central Limit Theorem, which tells us that the sampling distribution of sample means is normal.

Finding the Standard Error of the Mean

To begin, let's understand how we can apply the concept of the sampling distribution of sample means by revisiting the standard error of the mean. Remember that the **standard error of the mean** is the standard deviation of the sampling distribution of sample means for a particular population. We calculate this standard error of the mean with the formula you learned in Chapter 7:

$$\sigma_{\bar{X}} = \frac{\sigma}{\sqrt{N}}$$

---

[2] Richard Morin and Claudia Deane, "Support for Bush Declines as Casualties Mount in Iraq," 12 July 2003, <http:www.washingtonpost.com/wp-dyn/articles/A45480-2003Jul11.html>.

How do we compute the standard error of the mean for a variable when its standard deviation in a population is not known? We substitute the standard deviation of a sample to estimate or represent the standard deviation of the population. By dividing the standard deviation of a sample by the square root of the number of respondents in the sample, we can come up with a valid estimate of the standard deviation of the sampling distribution of sample means (the standard error of the mean).

To illustrate, let's find the standard error of the mean for the variable *age* in the 2002 GSS subset A file. The standard deviation for the distribution of responses to the variable is 17.343, and the size of the sample is $N = 1,490$. Use these values in your formula for the standard error of the mean.

$$\sigma_{\bar{X}} = \frac{\sigma}{\sqrt{N}}$$

$$= \frac{17.343}{\sqrt{1490}} = \frac{17.343}{38.6005}$$

$$\sigma_{\bar{X}} = .45$$

Interpretation   The standard deviation of the sampling distribution of sample means is .45, and it tells us that the sampling means are fairly homogeneously distributed. Ninety-five percent of all sample means (calculated for the set of all possible random samples of 1,490 respondents from the population of American adults) would fall within a range of only a relatively few values.

 Skills Practice 1   Use the standard deviation (14.242) for the sample of respondents ($N = 940$) to the variable *hrs1* in the GSS 2002 subset A file to calculate the standard error of the mean.

Using the Standard Error of the Mean to Specify Confidence Intervals and Levels

As applied to the sampling distribution of sample means, 68% of all sample means will fall in the range of values that is one standard error of the mean,[3] symbolized by $\sigma_{\bar{X}}$, above the mean of the sampling distribution of sample means ($\mu_{\bar{X}}$) and one standard error of the mean below the mean of the sampling distribution of sample means. Ninety-five percent of all sample means will fall in the range of values that is about two standard errors (1.96 standard errors, to be exact) above the mean of the sampling distribution of sample means and two standard errors below the mean of the sampling distribution of sample means. (See Figure 8.1 for an illustration of the sampling distribution of sample means.)

Therefore, the likelihood that any single sample mean falls within one standard error of the mean above or below the mean of the sampling distribution of

---

[3] Remember that the standard error of the mean, $\sigma_{\bar{X}}$, is the standard deviation of the sampling distribution of sample means.

FIGURE 8.1
The estimated distribution of sample means in the relation to the mean of the sampling distribution of sample means ($\mu_{\bar{X}}$).

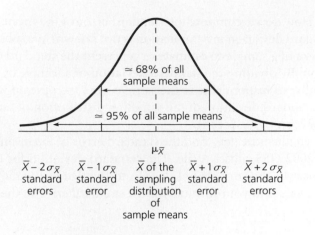

≈ 68% of all sample means

≈ 95% of all sample means

$\mu_{\bar{X}}$

| $\bar{X} - 2\sigma_{\bar{X}}$ standard errors | $\bar{X} - 1\sigma_{\bar{X}}$ standard error | $\bar{X}$ of the sampling distribution of sample means | $\bar{X} + 1\sigma_{\bar{X}}$ standard error | $\bar{X} + 2\sigma_{\bar{X}}$ standard errors |

sample means is 68 in 100, and the likelihood that any single sample mean falls within approximately two standard errors of the mean above or below the mean of the sampling distribution of sample means is 95 in 100. See Figure 8.2 for an illustration of this idea.

The likelihood that a single sample mean—the mean for the variable *age* in the GSS 2002 subset A file, for example—falls within one standard error of the mean above or below the mean of the sampling distribution of sample means is 68 in 100, and the likelihood that the mean for the variable *age* falls within two standard errors of the mean above or below the mean of the sampling distribution of sample means is 95 in 100.

Before I explain how these ideas are related to the construction of confidence intervals, we need to understand one more characteristic of the sampling distribution of sample means:

> The mean of the sampling distribution of sample means for a variable will be equal to the mean in the population for the same variable.

If we were to compute the mean of the sampling distribution of sample means for the variable *age,* for example, the value that we would obtain would be equal to the population mean itself. If we replace the mean of the sampling distribution of sample means—$\mu_{\bar{X}}$, in Figure 8.2 with the population mean, symbolized by

FIGURE 8.2
The estimated distribution of sample means with the likelihood of any single sample mean lying ±1 $\sigma_{\bar{X}}$ from $\mu_{\bar{X}}$ and ± 2 $\sigma_{\bar{X}}$ from $\mu_{\bar{X}}$).

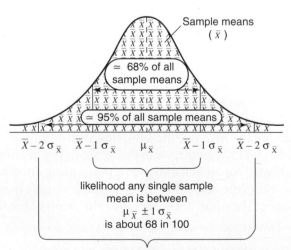

Sample means ($\bar{x}$)

≈ 68% of all sample means

≈ 95% of all sample means

| $\bar{X} - 2\sigma_{\bar{x}}$ | $\bar{X} - 1\sigma_{\bar{x}}$ | $\mu_{\bar{x}}$ | $\bar{X} - 1\sigma_{\bar{x}}$ | $\bar{X} - 2\sigma_{\bar{x}}$ |

likelihood any single sample mean is between
$\mu_{\bar{x}} \pm 1\sigma_{\bar{x}}$
is about 68 in 100

likelihood any single sample mean is between
$\mu_{\bar{x}} \pm 2\sigma_{\bar{x}}$
is about 95 in 100

μ—then we can see that the likelihood of any single sample mean falling within one standard error of the mean above or below the population mean, μ, is 68 in 100, and the likelihood of any single sample mean falling within two standard errors of the mean above or below the population mean is about 95 in 100.

The problem is that we still don't know the value of the population mean. However, we can find out how likely it is (confidence level) that a specific range of values (confidence interval) is a range of values that includes the mean. We do this by constructing confidence intervals at specified levels, using (1) our sample mean as a point estimate around which we can build a normal distribution and (2) the one characteristic of the sampling distribution of sample means that we *can* estimate, its standard deviation (the standard error of the mean).[4]

This process is best explained using an example, the variable *age* in the GSS 2002 subset A file. Our point estimate for the variable is the mean of the sample for the variable *age*, 46.40. We can use this point estimate to construct a distribution of sample means that would have the same standard error of the mean as the sampling distribution of sample means, .45 (from our computation of the standard error of the mean for the variable *age* earlier in this chapter). By taking the point estimate, 46.40, and adding one standard error of the mean (.45) to get 46.85 and subtracting one standard error of the mean to get 45.95, we could conclude that 68% of all sample means would fall within a range of values from 45.95 to 46.85. Furthermore, if we took approximately two standard errors of the mean (1.96 standard errors of the mean, to be exact) and added them to the mean, 46.40, we would get the value 47.28 (the sample mean plus .45 × 1.96). If we subtracted two standard errors of the mean from 46.40, then we would get the value 45.52 (the mean minus .45 × 1.96). Since we have gone nearly two standard errors of the mean above our sample mean and two standard errors below it, how much of the normal distribution of sample means have we encompassed? The answer is 95%. Ninety-five percent of all sample means would fall between 45.52 and 47.28. See Figure 8.3 for an illustration.

The question is, do either of these ranges of values—the smaller one that goes from 45.95 to 46.85 or the larger one that goes from 45.52 to 47.28—encompass the population mean? We can almost never know. But which range of values has the greater likelihood of encompassing the population mean? The larger one does, because it would encompass 95% of all sample means. There are

FIGURE 8.3

Normal distribution of sample means constructed around the mean for the variable *age* in the 2002 GSS subset A file using $\sigma_{\bar{x}} = .45$.

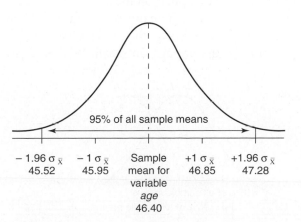

95% of all sample means

$-1.96\,\sigma_{\bar{x}}$	$-1\,\sigma_{\bar{x}}$	Sample	$+1\,\sigma_{\bar{x}}$	$+1.96\,\sigma_{\bar{x}}$
45.52	45.95	mean for	46.85	47.28
		variable		
		age		
		46.40		

---

[4] Keep in mind that the sampling distribution is the *theoretical* set of all possible means for samples of a given sample size drawn from the same population.

95 chances out of 100 that the range of values between 45.52 and 47.28 includes the population mean.

Why is this so? The answer is tied to the idea that 95% of all sample means lie within about two standard errors of the mean above and below the population mean. If 95% of all sample means can be encompassed in the range of values that is about two standard errors of the mean above the population mean and two standard errors of the mean below it, then 95% of all of the normal distributions that can be constructed around those sample means with the same standard error of the mean that we estimate for the population will include the population mean.

Let's see how this can be so by superimposing the distribution we created with our point estimate on the theoretical sampling distribution of sample means. As we do so, keep two things in mind. First, remember that the population mean sits in the middle of the theoretical sampling distribution of sample means. Second, we don't know (and cannot know) the value of the sample mean *in relation to* the population mean (because the population mean is unknown). For the sake of illustrating the concept, let's guess that the sample mean is higher than the mean. Would 95% of the normal distribution of sample means that we constructed around our point estimate (the mean for the variable *age*) capture the population mean? If the sample mean lies within that range of means that is about two standard errors of the mean above and two standard errors below the population mean, then the normal distribution that we constructed around the sample mean would encompass the population mean. Figure 8.4 illustrates this idea by showing you how the range of values between 45.52 and 47.28 that we computed in relation to our point estimate, 46.40, using approximately two standard errors of the mean could include the population mean.

It is important to note that this will be true ONLY IF the sample mean is within about two standard errors of the mean above or two standard errors below the population mean. We can never be sure where the sample mean is in relation to the population mean. If it is *more than* two standard errors of the mean above or below the population mean, then a normal distribution constructed around a sample mean will not include the population mean. Figure 8.5 illustrates how this can happen. The diagram assumes that our sample mean falls outside the range of values that is about two standard errors above or two standard errors below the population mean.

We can never know where our sample mean lies in relation to the population mean. We can only deal in the probabilities and likelihoods of proximity of a sample mean to the population mean. What we *can* say is that there are 95

FIGURE 8.4
Normal distribution constructed around a sample mean for the variable *age* in the GSS 2002 subset A file superimposed on the sampling distribution of sample means for the variabe *age*.

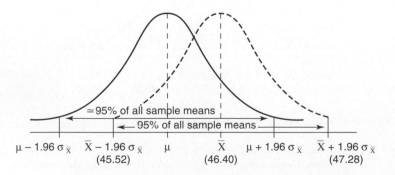

≈95% of all sample means

95% of all sample means

$\mu - 1.96\,\sigma_{\bar{x}}$ $\bar{X} - 1.96\,\sigma_{\bar{x}}$ μ $\bar{X}$ $\mu + 1.96\,\sigma_{\bar{x}}$ $\bar{X} + 1.96\,\sigma_{\bar{x}}$
(45.52)   (46.40)   (47.28)

FIGURE 8.5
Normal distribution constructed around a sample mean for the variable *age* in the GSS 2002 subset A file superimposed on the sampling distribution of sample means for the variable *age*.

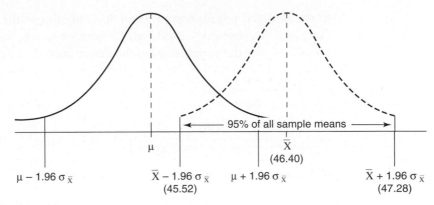

chances out of a hundred that the range of ages from 45.52 and 47.28 contains the population mean. This is a confidence *interval* at the 95% *level*.

Let's summarize what we have done so far.

- We used a point estimate, 46.40, the mean for a variable in a sample (the GSS 2002 subset A file for the variable *age*) to construct a confidence interval.
- A confidence interval at the 95% level was constructed by (1) multiplying 1.96 by the standard error of the mean (.45) for the variable *age* and (2) adding the result to the point estimate $(46.40 + (1.96)(.45) = 47.28)$ and subtracting the result from the point estimate $(46.40 - (1.96)(.45) = 45.52)$.
- We interpreted the result—there are 95 chances out of 100 that the range of ages between 45.52 and 47.28 contains the population mean.

Skills Practice 2   Use the mean for the variable *hrs1*, 41.86, in the GSS 2002 subset A file and the standard error of the mean computed from the *hrs1* variable, .46 (rounded to the second decimal), to construct and interpret a confidence interval at the 95% level.

What If We Want to Be More or Less Confident? The Return of the *Z* Score

From understanding how we can use the standard error of the mean to develop confidence intervals around sampling means, it's a fairly small step to understanding how we can specify confidence intervals of almost any size. Taking this step brings us full circle to the concept of the *Z* score. Let's see how *Z* scores tie in to the concept of confidence intervals.

Remember that the *Z score* tells us the distance from the mean, expressed in standard deviations, of a particular value in a set of data. Let's assume just for the moment that our mean from our GSS 2002 subset A file for the variable *age*, 46.40, matches the mean of the sampling distribution of sample means for the variable *age*. (We cannot ever know if it does, but for this example let's assume we were lucky.) Using *Z* scores and the population mean, we could find out how far from that mean every other mean in a sampling distribution of sample means might be. For instance, where would a sample mean of 45.52 be found in relation to the assumed population mean of 46.40? Let's use the Z scores formula for a sampling distribution to find out. Remember to use the standard error of the mean (.45) for the variable *age* in the denominator.

$$Z = \frac{\overline{X} - \mu_{\overline{X}}}{\sigma_{\overline{X}}}$$

$$= \frac{45.52 - 46.40}{.45} = -\frac{.88}{.45}$$

$$Z = -1.96$$

The mean of 45.52 is 1.96 standard deviations below the mean of the sampling distribution of sample means of 46.40. What do you think might be the Z score for a mean that is above the mean of the sampling distribution of sample means? Find the Z score for a sample mean of 47.28. You may have guessed, even before you did the math, that it is +1.96. If you look up the Z score in the table in Appendix A, you will see that about 47.5% of all values fall within the range of values 1.96 standard deviations below or above the mean in a normal distribution—equal to 95%, the confidence level.

We can work this process in reverse to produce confidence levels of any size. For example, suppose we create a confidence interval for which there are 99 chances out of 100 that the interval includes the population mean rather than just 95 chances—a confidence interval with a level of 99%. Let's find out what the Z score for such an interval would be.

First, realize that for a confidence level of 99% we have to construct a distribution around a point estimate within which 99% of the sample means in a sampling distribution are likely to fall. Half of this range will fall below the mean of the sampling distribution of the sample means, and half will fall above it. Thus, we divide 99 by 2 to find the Z score, or the distance in standard deviation units from the mean, for the half of the means that will fall below the mean of the sampling distribution and the half that will fall above it. The result of 99 ÷ 2 is 49.5. Figure 8.6 shows the distribution of the area under a normal curve for a 99% confidence interval.

Turn the percentage, 49.5, into a proportion by dividing it by 100, and look up the result, .495, on the table in Appendix A. To look up a proportion, use the *second* column (b) of the table (the area between the mean and Z). The first proportion you come to that is closest to .495 is .4949. The Z score associated with .4949 is 2.57. This tells us that the portion of the normal distribution that contains about 49.5% of the values or scores falls about 2½ standard deviations below the mean to 2½ standard deviations above the mean (Figure 8.7).

FIGURE 8.6
Area under normal curve for a 99% confidence level.

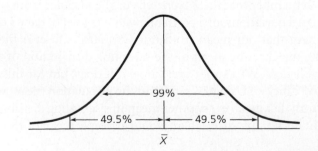

FIGURE 8.7
Z scores associated
with a 99% confidence
level.

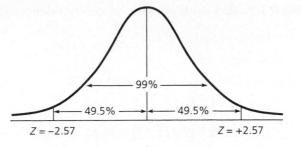

Now let's find the value that is 2.57 standard deviations *above* the sample mean we are using as our point estimate. This value will form the upper limit of our confidence interval. To locate the upper limit of our confidence interval, solve the *Z* score formula for the value that falls at the upper limit.

$$Z = \frac{\overline{X} - \mu_{\overline{X}}}{\sigma_{\overline{X}}}$$

$$2.57 = \frac{? - 46.40}{.45}$$

Another expression of this same formula, one that makes clearer how to solve for the missing sample mean, is the following set of formulas for finding confidence intervals:

Formula 8.1: The confidence interval formulas

$$CI_u = \overline{X} + \left(Z\right)\left(\sigma_{\overline{X}}\right)$$
$$CI_l = \overline{X} - \left(Z\right)\left(\sigma_{\overline{X}}\right)$$

where *CI* is the upper (*CI_u*) or lower (*CI_l*) limit of the confidence interval, $\overline{X}$ is the sample mean, *Z* represents the *Z* score at the lower or upper limit, and $\sigma_{\overline{X}}$ represents the standard error of the mean.

EXAMPLE:

Let's find the upper limit of the interval with a confidence level of .99 for the variable *age*. We know it has a *Z* score of 2.57. We know because we divided .99 by 2 to get .495, and we looked up .495 in column (b) of the table for the area under the normal curve (Appendix A). Then we matched .495 with its associated *Z* score of 2.57 in column (a). We also know the standard error of the mean for *age* is .45 (computed earlier by hand).

$\overline{X}$ (sample mean) = 46.40

Z (*Z* score) = 2.57

$\sigma_{\overline{X}}$ (standard error of the mean) = .45

$$CI_u = \overline{X} + \left(Z\right)\left(\sigma_{\overline{X}}\right)$$
$$= 46.40 + \left(2.57\right)\left(.45\right) = 46.40 + 1.1565$$

$$CI_u = 47.56$$

Now, let's find the lower limit of the confidence interval.

$\overline{X}$ (sample mean) = 46.40

Z (Z score) = 2.57

$\sigma_{\overline{X}}$ (standard error of the mean) = .45

$$CI_l = \overline{X} - \left(Z\right)\left(\sigma_{\overline{X}}\right)$$
$$= 46.40 - \left(2.57\right)\left(.45\right) = 46.40 - 1.1565$$
$$CI_l = 45.24$$

Interpretation   What do these confidence limits at the 99% confidence level tell us? There are 99 chances out of 100 that the age interval between 45.24 and 47.56 years contains the population mean.

> **Skills Practice 3**   Find the confidence interval with a confidence level of 99% for the variable *hrs1*. (You will probably figure out right away that the Z score is identical to that for *age*, but what changes is the mean for the sample and the standard error of the mean for *hrs1*—$\overline{X}$ = 41.86, $\sigma_{\overline{X}}$ = .46.)

So far, we have concentrated on how to establish confidence intervals for means. However, you may have noticed that the article about President Bush's popularity in the "News to Use" at the beginning of Chapter 7 doesn't use means, it uses percentages. What do we do when we want to know how likely it is that a sample percentage represents the population? You'll be happy to know that the process is substantially the same.

CONFIDENCE INTERVALS AND LEVELS FOR PERCENTAGES

Let's look at a few of the variables in the General Social Survey that explore participation in various aspects of the political process. Lots of people want to criticize the president and other politicians, but are they doing anything about the policies of which they disapprove? The General Social Survey contains a series of variables—some of which we explored in Chapters 2 and 3—that ask about political involvement. One of them is the *vote00* variable in the GSS 2002 subset A file asking respondents to the GSS if they voted in the 2000 general election—the one that resulted in the electoral college victory of George W. Bush. Table 8.1 is a frequency distribution for the variable.

What percentage of the respondents said they voted in the 2000 election? A little less than two-thirds of the respondents to the GSS said they voted. What percentage of those in the population of American adults, 18 years of age or older, English-speaking, and noninstitutionalized, voted? We can never know, but we can construct a confidence interval, with our sample *percentage* as a point estimate, that has 95 chances out of 100 of containing the population percentage of people who voted.

TABLE 8.1   Frequency Distribution for the Variable *vote00* in the GSS 2002 subset A File

VOTE00 Did R vote in 2000 election

		Frequency	Percent	Valid Percent	Cumulative Percent
Valid	1 VOTED	961	64.1	64.8	64.8
	2 DID NOT VOTE	443	29.5	29.9	94.7
	3 INELIGIBLE	79	5.3	5.3	100.0
	Total	1483	98.9	100.0	
Missing	4 REFUSED TO ANSWER	8	.5		
	8 DONT KNOW/REMEMBER	9	.6		
	Total	17	1.1		
Total		1500	100.0		

The first step is to find the standard error of proportions.

Standard Error of Proportions

Just as there are sampling distributions of sample means, there are sampling distributions of sample proportions. We can assume that for a sample of a given size, the sampling distribution of sample proportions will be normal. Moreover, we can calculate descriptive statistics for the sampling distribution of sample proportions, just as we can for the sampling distribution of sample means. We can find the standard deviation of the sampling distribution of sample proportions, for example, called the **standard error of proportions.** We can compute it using the following formula.

$$\sigma_P = \sqrt{\frac{(\pi)(1-\pi)}{N}}$$

where σ_P is the standard error of proportions (the standard deviation of the sample proportions in the sampling distribution), π (called pi) is the population proportion of the category of a particular variable, and N is the size of the population.

Of course, we don't know the population proportion. If we did, we would not need a random sample to try to estimate it. We can, however, come up with a valid estimate of the standard error of proportions by substituting our sample proportion for pi in the formula, which then can be expressed as follows.

Formula 8.2: The standard error of proportions

$$\sigma_P = \sqrt{\frac{(P)(1-P)}{N}}$$

where σ_P is the standard error of proportions, P is the sample proportion, and N is the number of valid cases in a sample.

EXAMPLE:

To find the standard error of the proportion for the variable *vote00*, we need to know the proportion of respondents who said they voted, and we need to know how many respondents there are for this variable. Both of these numbers can be found in the frequency distribution. Use the number of valid cases, 1,483, for N. For the proportion, divide the percentage who answered "Voted" by 100 to get .648. Then use these values in Formula 8.2.

P (proportion of respondents to the GSS for 2002 who voted) = .648 N (number of valid responses to the variable *vote00*) = 1,483

$$\sigma_P = \sqrt{\frac{(P)(1-P)}{N}}$$

$$= \sqrt{\frac{(.648)(1-.648)}{1,483}} = \sqrt{\frac{(.648)(.352)}{1,483}}$$

$$= \sqrt{\frac{.2881}{1,483}} = \sqrt{.0005381}$$

$$\sigma_P = .01$$

Interpretation   The standard error of proportions is .01, which tells us that the standard deviation among the sample proportions in the sampling distribution is very small. It isn't likely that there is much variance among the proportions in the sampling distribution of sample proportions.

Once we find the standard error of proportions we can find confidence intervals for a proportion.

Constructing Confidence Intervals at Specified Levels for Proportions

Remember the formula for finding confidence intervals for means? With a slight modification, we can also use it to find confidence intervals for proportions.

Formula 8.3: Confidence intervals for proportions

$$CI_u = P + (Z)(\sigma_P)$$
$$CI_l = P - (Z)(\sigma_P)$$

where CI is the confidence interval at the upper (CI_u) or lower (CI_l) limit of the confidence interval, P is the sample proportion, Z is the Z score associated with the confidence level for which you are trying to find the interval, and σ_P is the estimated standard error of proportions.

EXAMPLE:

Let's find the confidence interval associated with a confidence level of 95%. We already know that the sample proportion, or point estimate, around which we want to construct an interval is .648. We know that the Z score associated with a 95% level of confidence is 1.96. (Why? Because the range of scores 1.96 standard deviations below the mean to 1.96 standard deviations above the mean encompasses 95% of all scores in a normal distribution of scores.) We also found that the standard error of proportions is .01. With these values we can find our confidence interval, starting with the upper limit—the value of the interval that falls above the sample proportion.

P (sample proportion) $= .648$

Z (Z score) $= 1.96$

σ_P (standard error of proportions) $= .01$

$$CI_u = P + \left(Z\right)\left(\sigma_P\right)$$
$$= .648 + \left(1.96\right)\left(.01\right) = .648 + .0196$$
$$CI_u = .668$$

Next, find the confidence interval for the lower limit of the interval.

P (sample proportion) $= .648$

Z (Z score) $= 1.96$

σ_P (standard error of proportions) $= .01$

$$CI_l = P - \left(Z\right)\left(\sigma_P\right)$$
$$= .648 - \left(1.96\right)\left(.01\right) = .648 - .0196$$
$$CI_l = .628$$

Interpretation   There are 95 chances out of 100 that the range of proportions between .628 and .668 contains the population proportion for people who voted in the 2000 election.

 Skills Practice 4   Use the frequency distribution for the variable about participation in the activities of a political party, *grppol*, in Table 8.2 to do the following:

A. Find the standard error of proportions for those who do not belong to a political party.
B. Find and interpret the confidence interval with a level of 95% for those who do not belong to a political party.

Constructing Confidence Intervals for Any Category

Although I picked the proportion Voted in the frequency distribution in Table 8.1 for the variable *vote00* as my point estimate for constructing a confidence interval at the 95% level, you can construct a confidence interval around any of the

TABLE 8.2 Frequency Distribution for the Variable *grppol* in the GSS 2002 subset A File

GRPPOL Participated in activity of political party

		Frequency	Percent	Valid Percent	Cumulative Percent
Valid	1 I DO NOT BELONG TO SUCH A GRP	446	29.7	74.2	74.2
	2 I BELONG TO SUCH A GRP BUT DON'T PARTICIPATE	35	2.3	5.8	80.0
	3 I HAVE PARTICIPATED ONCE OR TWICE	57	3.8	9.5	89.5
	4 I HAVE PARTICIPATED MORE THAN TWICE	63	4.2	10.5	100.0
	Total	601	40.1	100.0	
Missing	0 NAP	893	59.5		
	8 DONT KNOW	1	.1		
	9 NO ANSWER	5	.3		
	Total	899	59.9		
Total		1500	100.0		

proportions in the distribution. For example, you can use the category Voted as your point estimate, as I did. You can also use any of the other proportions in the frequency distribution.

Skills Practice 5   Try constructing a confidence interval at the 95% level using the category of Did Not Vote for the *vote00* variable in Table 8.1 as your point estimate. Begin by finding the standard error of proportions for the category Did Not Vote, and then use the result in the formula for finding confidence intervals. What do you come up with?

You are not limited to a confidence level of 95%. You can construct confidence intervals for any level of confidence.

Skills Practice 6   Having found the confidence interval for a 95% level of confidence for the category I Do Not Belong (to a political party) in Table 8.2, now construct a confidence interval at the 99% level of confidence. You will not have to recompute the standard error of proportions, but you will have to find the *Z* score for the 99% confidence level.

Although it's fairly simple to construct confidence intervals for specified confidence levels by hand using means or proportions as point estimates, SPSS will find confidence intervals, too, as you can see in the following SPSS Guides.

USING SPSS

Finding Confidence Intervals

SPSS GUIDE: FINDING CONFIDENCE INTERVALS FOR
MEANS

Open SPSS and your GSS 2002 subset A file. Click on Analyze, then Descriptive
Statistics, and look on the menu list for Explore. Click on Explore to open that
dialog box.

1 Select the variable for which you want confidence intervals. Try *age*. Click on
the arrow (▶) pointing to the Dependent List box.

2 Click on Statistics in the Display box.

3 Click on the Statistics button to open the Explore: Statistics window.

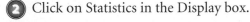

At the Explore: Statistics window,

1 Make sure there is a check (✔) in the Descriptives box.

2 Click on Continue to return to the Explore window. At the Explore dialog
box, click on OK.

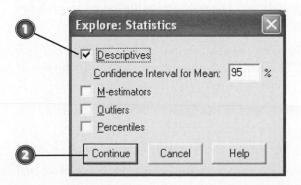

TABLE 8.3 Descriptive Statistics for the Variable *age* Using the Explore Command with the GSS 2002 subset A File

Descriptives

			Statistic	Std. Error
AGE Age of respondent	Mean		46.40	.449
	95% Confidence Interval for Mean	Lower Bound	45.52	
		Upper Bound	47.28	
	5% Trimmed Mean		45.81	
	Median		45.00	
	Variance		300.787	
	Std. Deviation		17.343	
	Minimum		18	
	Maximum		89	
	Range		71	
	Interquartile Range		27.00	
	Skewness		.424	.063
	Kurtosis		-.741	.127

You will get a set of Descriptive statistics in the Output window like those in Table 8.3. In addition to the mean and the confidence interval, you will see many other statistics you recognize: the median, the variance, standard deviation, the minimum and maximum values of the variable, the range, and the interquartile range.

To interpret the confidence interval, focus on the first three statistics in the Statistics column and the standard error of the mean (.449) in the Std. Error column. The first of the statistics in the Statistics column is the mean for the variable *age*. The second statistic is the lower limit of the confidence interval (the mean minus 1.96 standard errors of the mean). The third statistic, the upper limit of the confidence interval, is equal to the mean plus 1.96 standard errors of the mean.

The confidence level is given in the table at 95%. (Even if it weren't specified, we could tell what it was because the lower limit is 1.96 standard errors below the mean, whereas the upper limit is 1.96 standard errors above the mean. Remember that a standard error of the mean is the standard deviation of the sampling distribution of sample means, and we know that, in a normally distributed set of values, approximately 95% of the values will fall within the range of values that are within 1.96 standard deviations of the mean—1.96 above and 1.96 below.)

Interpretation What do the confidence intervals and the confidence level tell us? Very simply put:

There are 95 chances out of 100 that the range of ages between 45.52 and 47.28 contains the population mean for the age of American adults.

You can specify different confidence levels using SPSS simply by changing the confidence level in the Explore: Statistics window.

SPSS GUIDE: SPECIFYING CONFIDENCE LEVELS

Follow the command path Analyze ➡ Descriptive Statistics ➡ Explore.

①　Scroll down the variable list to find your variable. Let's use *age*. Click on the variable to highlight it, then click on the ▶ pointing at the Dependent List box to select it.

②　Under Display, click on Statistics.

③　Click on the Statistics button to open the Explore: Statistics window.

When the Explore: Statistics window opens,

①　Place your cursor in the box next to Confidence Interval for Mean, and backspace over 95 to remove it. Then type in the confidence level you want to specify. Let's try 99.

②　Click on Continue to return to the Explore dialog box.

At the Explore dialog box, click on OK. You will get a report in your Output window like the one you see in Table 8.4.

TABLE 8.4　Descriptive Statistics for the Variable *age* in the GSS 2002 subset A File, Using a 99% Confidence Level

Descriptives

			Statistic	Std. Error
AGE Age of respondent	Mean		46.40	.449
	99% Confidence Interval for Mean	Lower Bound	45.24	
		Upper Bound	47.56	
	5% Trimmed Mean		45.81	
	Median		45.00	
	Variance		300.787	
	Std. Deviation		17.343	
	Minimum		18	
	Maximum		89	
	Range		71	
	Interquartile Range		27.00	
	Skewness		.424	.063
	Kurtosis		-.741	.127

What does this table tell us? There are 99 chances out of 100 that the range of ages from 45.24 to 47.56 contains the population mean for the age of American adults.

Skills Practice 7   Use SPSS and your GSS 2002 subset A file to find the confidence interval at the 99% level for the *hrs1* variable.

How can we find these sorts of confidence intervals for proportions using SPSS? Unfortunately, SPSS doesn't have the capability to find confidence intervals for the various categories of ordinal and nominal variables. However, if we dichotomize a variable, we can use the Explore command to find the confidence intervals for a specified level.

Finding Confidence Intervals and Levels for Proportions

SPSS can be used to find confidence intervals and levels for proportions with dichotomized variables. As you learned in Chapter 2, a dichotomy is any variable with only two categories. However, for the purpose of using SPSS to find confidence intervals, we will employ a specific type of dichotomy called a dummy variable. A **dummy variable** is any variable for which the categories indicate either the presence or the absence of a characteristic. For example, we can think of the variable *sex* as a dichotomy—males and females—or we can think of it as two categories, one that is the absence of the characteristic of maleness and the other that is the presence of the characteristic. When we create dichotomies to reflect the presence or absence of a characteristic, a dichotomy is coded to reflect this definition. Rather than coding the categories 1 for Male and 2 for Female, we code them 0 for Not Male and 1 for Male. We could also code them 0 for Not Female and 1 for Female. It doesn't really matter for our purposes.

Almost any variable can be dichotomized. We could turn the religion variable into Not Christian and Christian, or the race variable into Not White and White. To see how we can specify confidence levels and intervals using SPSS, let's turn the variable *vote00* into Voted and Did Not Vote.

To dichotomize the *vote00* variable, use the Recode command. Start the process by looking at the frequency distribution for the variable and deciding how to recode it. Create a recode diagram on paper.

1. Take the category Voted and make it category 1 (the presence of the characteristic *voted*).
2. Take the next two categories, Did Not Vote and Ineligible, and group them together to make the new category, Did Not Vote with a code of 0 (the absence of the characteristic *voted*).
3. Make categories 4 (Refused to Answer) and 8 (Don't Know/Remember) your missing value categories.

FIGURE 8.8
Recode diagram for the
variable *vote00* in the
GSS 2002 subset A file.

Old Values of *vote00*	Old labels of *vote00*	New Labels	New Values
1	Voted	Voted	1
2	Did Not Vote	Did Not Vote	0
3	Ineligible		
4	Refused to Answer	Refused to Answer	4
8	Don't Know/Remember	Don't Know/Remember	8

New variable name: *divote00*
New variable label: Dichotomized Vote in 2000 Variable
Level of measurement: Ordinal

4. Call the new variable *divote00* and label it Dichotomized vote in 2000 variable.

Use Figure 8.8 to check your recode diagram for the variable *vote00*.

In the SPSS Data Editor window, use the command path Data ➡ Recode ➡ Into Different Variables to enter your old and new values. After you create your new variable, don't forget to give your variable new values and new value labels, define the missing values, and specify the level of measurement. (If you need help with recoding or defining your values and labels, see the SPSS Guide, "Recoding Variables," in Chapter 4.) Finally, check your new, recoded variable against the frequency distribution in Table 8.5.

Now you can use the Analyze ➡ Descriptive Statistics ➡ Explore command path to find the confidence interval at the 95% level for the variable *divote00*. Notice that the confidence interval is expressed as the interval around the proportion with the value of 1, or Voted in this case. You will get a Descriptives report like the one in Table 8.6.

The Descriptives report shows us that there are 95 chances out of 100 that the range of proportions between .62 and .67 contains the proportion of American adults who voted.

TABLE 8.5   Recoded *vote00* Variable *divote00*

DIVOTE00 Dichotomized Vote in 2000 Variable

		Frequency	Percent	Valid Percent	Cumulative Percent
Valid	0 DID NOT VOTE	522	34.8	35.2	35.2
	1 VOTED	961	64.1	64.8	100.0
	Total	1483	98.9	100.0	
Missing	4 REFUSED	8	.5		
	8 DON'T KNOW/REMEMBER	9	.6		
	Total	17	1.1		
Total		1500	100.0		

Skills Practice 8 Produce a frequency distribution for the variable *grppol*. Use it to create a recode diagram for recoding the variable *grppol* into two categories—those who have participated in a political party at least once and those who have not participated at all (because they don't belong to a party or because they haven't participated in political party activities even if they do belong). When you recode your missing values, be sure to set your NAP value to a value other than 0 (I used 7). Then find the confidence interval at the 99% level for the proportion of respondents who said they have participated in political party activities at least once.

TABLE 8.6 Statistics for the Variable *divote00* (a Recoded Vote in 2000 Variable) Created from the *vote00* Variable in the GSS 2002 subset A File

Descriptives

			Statistic	Std. Error
DIVOTE00 Dichotomized Vote in 2000 Variable	Mean		.65	.012
	95% Confidence Interval for Mean	Lower Bound	.62	
		Upper Bound	.67	
	5% Trimmed Mean		.66	
	Median		1.00	
	Variance		.228	
	Std. Deviation		.478	
	Minimum		0	
	Maximum		1	
	Range		1	
	Interquartile Range		1.00	
	Skewness		-.620	.064
	Kurtosis		-1.617	.127

In the next three chapters we will turn our attention to analyzing associations between at least two variables, measuring associations between at least two variables, and testing hypotheses about associations between two variables.

SUMMARY

With this chapter we began our application of the principles of making inferences from samples to populations. Our first application involved drawing inferences from sampling characteristics involving single variables, such as the mean for a distribution of responses to a variable and the proportion of responses to a category of a variable.

The sampling characteristic about which we want to make an inference is called a point estimate. A point estimate can be a mean or a proportion. Using the point estimate, we can construct a confidence interval for a specified confidence level. For example, we can determine the likelihood that a particular range of means contains the population mean. We can never be sure that the population mean falls within the specified range, but we can assess the probability that it is contained within

a range of values. We can also construct confidence limits at specified levels for proportions.

You should be able to perform these functions—finding confidence limits at specified levels—by hand and using SPSS. In the next chapter we'll begin to apply the principles of inferential statistics to associations between variables.

Point estimate
Confidence interval

Confidence level
Standard error of the mean

Standard error of proportions
Dummy variable

ANSWERS TO SKILLS PRACTICES

1. The standard deviation for the variable *hrs1* is 14.242, and *N* is equal to 940. Use these values in the formula for the standard error of the mean.

$$\sigma_{\bar{X}} = \frac{\sigma}{\sqrt{N}}$$
$$= \frac{14.242}{\sqrt{940}} = \frac{14.242}{30.6594}$$
$$\sigma_{\bar{X}} = .46$$

2. To construct a confidence interval at the 95% level, add 1.96 standard errors of the mean to the sample mean (41.86). The standard error of the mean, .46, times 1.96 equals .90. 41.86 plus .90 equals 42.76. 41.86 minus .90 equals 40.96. There are 95 changes out of one hundred that the range of hours worked in a week between 40.96 and 42.76 includes the population mean for hours worked in a week by American adults.

3. To construct a confidence interval with a level of 99%, begin by finding the upper limit of the interval, using Formula 8.1. The *Z* score at the upper limit for an interval that will include 99% of the means in the sampling distribution of sample means is 2.57.

For the variable *hrs1*, the mean is 41.86 and the standard error of the mean is .46. Use these values in the formula for the confidence interval to find the lower and upper limits of the interval.

$$CI_u = \bar{X} + (Z)(\sigma_{\bar{X}})$$
$$= 41.86 + (2.57)(.46) = 41.86 + 1.1822$$
$$CI_u = 43.04$$
$$CI_l = \bar{X} - (Z)(\sigma_{\bar{X}})$$
$$= 41.86 - (2.57)(.46) = 41.86 - 1.1822$$
$$CI_l = 40.68$$

Interpretation: There are 99 chances out of 100 that the range of hours between 40.68 and 43.04 contains the population mean for the number of hours worked in a week.

4. A. To find the standard error of proportions, use Formula 8.2. Notice the formula asks for a proportion and the *N* for the variable from Table 8.2. The proportion of those who do not belong to political party is .742, and the *N* (number of valid cases) is 601. Use these values to work the formula for the standard error of proportions.

$$\sigma_P = \sqrt{\frac{(P)(1-P)}{N}}$$

$$= \sqrt{\frac{(.742)(1-.742)}{601}} = \sqrt{\frac{(.742)(.258)}{601}}$$

$$= \sqrt{\frac{.1914}{601}} = \sqrt{.0003185}$$

$$\sigma_P = .02$$

B. To find the confidence interval with a confidence level of 95%, use Formula 8.3. Start by finding the value at the upper limit of the confidence interval.

$$CI_u = P + (Z)(\sigma_P)$$

$$= .742 + (1.96)(.02) = .742 + .04$$

$$CI_u = .78$$

Then find the value of the lower limit of the confidence interval.

$$CI_l = P - (Z)(\sigma_P)$$

$$= .742 - (1.96)(.02) = .742 - .04$$

$$CI_l = .70$$

There are 95 chances out of 100 that the interval between .70 and .78 contains the proportion of Americans who do not belong to a political party.

5. First, find the standard error of proportions. For the proportion of responses to the category Did Not Vote, the proportion in Table 8.1 is .299 (29.9 ÷ 100), and N is 1,483, the number of valid responses to the variable *vote00*.

$$\sigma_P = \sqrt{\frac{(P)(1-P)}{N}}$$

$$= \sqrt{\frac{(.299)(1-.299)}{1,483}} = \sqrt{\frac{(.299)(.701)}{1,483}}$$

$$= \sqrt{\frac{.2096}{1,483}} = \sqrt{.00001413}$$

$$\sigma_P = .01$$

Second, use the standard error of proportions in the formula for the confidence interval. The Z score at the 95% confidence level is 1.96.

Lower Limit

$$CI_l = P - (Z)(\sigma_P)$$

$$= .299 - (1.96)(.01)$$

$$= .299 - (.02)$$

$$CI_l = .28$$

Upper Limit

$$CI_u = P + (Z)(\sigma_P)$$

$$= .299 + (1.96)(.01)$$

$$= .299 + (.02)$$

$$CI_u = .32$$

There are 95 chances out of 100 that the interval from .28 to .32 contains the proportion of American adults who did not vote in 2002.

6. To find the confidence interval at the 99% level, it is only necessary to change the Z score. The Z score at the 99% level is 2.57. Use this Z score, the standard error of proportions (.02), and the proportion .742 in the formula for the confidence interval.

Upper Limit

$$CI_u = P + (Z)(\sigma_P)$$

$$= .742 + (2.57)(.02)$$

$$= .742 + (.0514)$$

$$CI_u = .79$$

Lower Limit

$$CI_l = P - (Z)(\sigma_P)$$

$$= .742 - (2.57)(.02)$$

$$= .742 - (.0514)$$

$$CI_l = .69$$

There are 99 chances out of 100 that the interval from .69 to .79 contains the proportion of American adults who do not belong to a political party.

7. Using the Explore command from the Descriptives menu, you should get a table of statistics like the one below.

Interpretation: There are 99 chances out of 100 that the range of hours worked in a week from 40.66 to 43.06 contains the population mean for the number of hours worked in a week.

Descriptives

			Statistic	Std. Error
HRS1 Number of hours worked last week	Mean		41.86	.465
	99% Confidence Interval for Mean	Lower Bound	40.66	
		Upper Bound	43.06	
	5% Trimmed Mean		41.66	
	Median		40.00	
	Variance		202.824	
	Std. Deviation		14.242	
	Minimum		2	
	Maximum		89	
	Range		87	
	Interquartile Range		13.00	
	Skewness		.239	.080
	Kurtosis		1.196	.159

8. You should get a frequency distribution for the dichotomized *grppol* variable like the one below.

DIGRPPOL Dichotomized Participation in Politcal Party Variable

		Frequency	Percent	Valid Percent	Cumulative Percent
Valid	0 DOES NOT PARTICIPATE	481	32.1	80.0	80.0
	1 PARTICIPATES IN POLITCAL ACTIVITIES	120	8.0	20.0	100.0
	Total	601	40.1	100.0	
Missing	7 NAP	893	59.5		
	8 DON'T KNOW	1	.1		
	9 NO ANSWER	5	.3		
	Total	899	59.9		
Total		1500	100.0		

Using the Explore feature from the Descriptives menu, you should get a set of statistics like the ones below for your recoded *grppol* variable.

Descriptives

			Statistic	Std. Error
DIGRPPOL Dichotomized Participation in Politcal Party Variable	Mean		.20	.016
	99% Confidence Interval for Mean	Lower Bound	.16	
		Upper Bound	.24	
	5% Trimmed Mean		.17	
	Median		.00	
	Variance		.160	
	Std. Deviation		.400	
	Minimum		0	
	Maximum		1	
	Range		1	
	Interquartile Range		.00	
	Skewness		1.506	.100
	Kurtosis		.270	.199

Interpretation: There are 99 chances out of 100 that the range of proportions between .16 and .24 contains the proportion of adults in the population who participate in political activities to at least some extent.

GENERAL EXERCISES

Use the standard deviation and N for the following variables in the **GSS 2002 subset B** file to compute the standard error of the mean for each variable. Be sure to show your work.

1. Variable   Standard Deviation N
   hrsrelax   2.859   958
2. Variable   Standard Deviation N
   chathr   4.702   165
3. Variable   Standard Deviation N
   emailhr   7.058   1,026
4. Variable   Standard Deviation N
   wwwhr   8.659   863

For General Exercises 5 and 6, construct a confidence interval at the 95% level for the group of respondents ages 18 through 25 who responded to these variables in the GSS 2002 subset B file.

5. *hrs1* (the number of hours the respondents worked in a week). The mean for the sample is 39.28, the standard deviation for the distribution of responses in the sample is 14.313, and $N = 117$.

6. *educ* (the highest year of education completed by the respondents). The mean for the sample is 13.03, the standard deviation for the distribution of responses in the sample is 2.141, and $N = 180$.

For General Exercises 7 and 8, construct a confidence interval at the 99% level for these variables in the GSS 2002 subset B file.

7. *hrsrelax* (the number of hours the respondents have to relax each day). The mean for the sample is 3.93, the standard deviation for the distribution of responses in the sample is 2.264, and $N = 116$.

8. *tvhrs* (the number of hours the respondents spend watching TV in a day). The mean for the sample is 2.73, the standard deviation for the distribution of responses in the sample is 2.939, and $N = 60$.

Use the frequency distribution in the following table to answer General Exercises 9 through 14.

CONOFFCL Have ever contacted an elected official

		Frequency	Percent	Valid Percent	Cumulative Percent
Valid	1 NO	537	35.8	70.8	70.8
	2 YES	222	14.8	29.2	100.0
	Total	759	50.6	100.0	
Missing	0 NAP	734	48.9		
	8 DONT KNOW	2	.1		
	9 NO ANSWER	5	.3		
	Total	741	49.4		
Total		1500	100.0		

9. Compute the standard error of proportions for those who have not contacted an elected official.

10. Compute the standard error of proportions for those who have contacted an elected official.

11. Compute and interpret the confidence interval at the 95% level for those who have not contacted an elected official.

12. Compute and interpret the confidence interval at the 95% level for those who have contacted an elected official.

13. Compute and interpret a confidence interval at the 99% level for those who have not contacted an elected official.

14. Compute and interpret a confidence interval at the 99% level for those who have contacted an elected official.

SPSS EXERCISES

Use the **GSS 2002 subset B** file to find and interpret confidence intervals at the 95% level for these variables.

1. *hrsrelax* (the number of hours the respondents have to relax each day)
2. *chathr* (the number of hours the respondents spend in a chat room each week)

Use the **GSS 2002 subset B** file to find and interpret confidence intervals at the 99% level for these variables.

3. *emailhr* (the number of hours the respondents spend on email each week)
4. *wwwhr* (the number of hours the respondents spend on the World Wide Web each week)

Use the **GSS 2002 subset A** file to do the following:

5. Dichotomize the variable *news* (how often respondents read a newspaper). Put those who never read a newspaper in category 0 and those who read a newspaper at least once in a while in category 1. Be sure to change the

missing value NAP to a value other than 0. Then use SPSS to find the confidence interval at the 95% level for the category proportion of those who read a newspaper at least once in a while.

6. Dichotomize the variable *givchrty* (have respondents given to charity in the past year). Put those who have never given to charity in category 0 and those who have given at least once in category 1. Be sure to change the missing value NAP to a value other than 0. Then use SPSS to find the confidence interval at the 95% level for the category proportion of those who have given at least once in the last year.

CHAPTER 9

Analyzing Contingency Tables

INTRODUCTION

In this chapter, you will begin learning techniques for analyzing two variables together, **bivariate** (two variable) analysis. Bivariate analysis allows us to examine relationships between variables to answer questions such as What is the effect of one variable on another? and Which characteristics of one variable are generally associated with which characteristics of a second variable? We have already started thinking about relationships among variables while working with the General Social Survey data. In the previous chapters we used the Split File command to separate the data into groups to answer questions like the following:

- Who is more likely to volunteer for a charity—males or females?
- Who is more likely to give money to a charity—males or females?
- Are religiously involved people more likely to also give to charities or volunteer for charities than others?
- Are older people more likely to volunteer for charities as compared to younger people?

As with the statistical techniques we have used so far, we can see applications of bivariate analysis around us every day. *Newsweek* magazine and its online counterpart at MSNBC.com recently carried the headline "We're Not in the Mood," over an article about the state of sex in American marriages. The authors of the article claimed that married couples are having sex less frequently. Among the causes of this decline, the authors argue, are stress, antidepressant pills, children, and two-income families. In effect, the authors are hypothesizing a relationship between a number of independent variables (like stress, children, and so on) that are having an influence on a dependent variable (frequency of sex). You can read the authors' arguments for yourself in the "News to Use" article in this chapter.

Bivariate analysis can help us see if, in fact, frequency of sexual activity is related to any of the causes hypothesized by the authors of "We're Not in the Mood." To begin, we will learn to construct contingency tables, very simple yet very powerful tools for examining the associations between the values or categories of variables. We can use contingency tables to examine one of the underlying questions in the "News to Use" article: Are married people having sex less frequently than others? To see an example of what a contingency table looks like, see Table 9.1 below, which is a contingency table drawn from the 2002 General Social Survey showing the relationship between frequency of sex and marital status.

As a general rule, we can do contingency table analysis with any combination of nominal, ordinal, or numerical variables. As a practical matter, however, contingency tables are more difficult to interpret when you work with variables that have large numbers of categories. To begin with, we will keep our tables simple by working with variables that have only a few categories each. ■

 Skills Practice 1 Write three questions that you could answer using General Social Survey variables. Identify the independent and dependent variables in each of your questions.

TABLE 9.1   Contingency Table for the Recoded *frequency of sexual activity* and *marital* Variables in the GSS 2002 subset C File

RCSXFREQ Recoded sex frequency variable * MARITAL Marital status Crosstabulation

			MARITAL Marital status					
			1 MARRIED	2 WIDOWED	3 DIVORCED	4 SEPARATED	5 NEVER MARRIED	Total
RCSXFREQ Recoded sex frequency variable	0 NOT AT ALL	Count	37	86	69	10	64	266
		% within MARITAL Marital status	7.1%	90.5%	33.0%	23.8%	21.8%	22.9%
	1 ONCE A MONTH OR LESS	Count	95	5	44	13	63	220
		% within MARITAL Marital status	18.1%	5.3%	21.1%	31.0%	21.4%	18.9%
	2 ABOUT ONCE A WEEK	Count	230	4	53	7	90	384
		% within MARITAL Marital status	43.9%	4.2%	25.4%	16.7%	30.6%	33.0%
	3 2-3 TIMES A WEEK OR MORE	Count	162		43	12	77	294
		% within MARITAL Marital status	30.9%		20.6%	28.6%	26.2%	25.3%
Total		Count	524	95	209	42	294	1164
		% within MARITAL Marital status	100.0%	100.0%	100.0%	100.0%	100.0%	100.0%

NEWS *to* USE
Statistics in the "Real" World

We're Not in the Mood[1]

BY KATHLEEN DEVENY, WITH HOLLY PETERSON, PAT WINGERT, KAREN SPRINGEN, JULIE SCELFO, MELISSA BREWSTER, TARA WEINGARTEN AND JOAN RAYMOND

Lately, it seems, we're just not in the mood. We're overworked, anxious about the economy—and we have to drive our kids to way too many T-Ball games. Or maybe it's all those libido-dimming antidepressants we're taking. We resent spouses who never pick up the groceries or their dirty socks. And if we actually find we have 20 minutes at the end of the day—after bath time and story time and juice-box time and e-mail time—who wouldn't rather zone out to Leno than have sex? Sure, passion ebbs and flows in even the healthiest of relationships, but judging from the conversation of the young moms at the next table at Starbucks, it sounds like we're in the midst of a long dry spell.

It's difficult to say exactly how many of the 113 million married Americans are too exhausted or too grumpy to get it on, but some psychologists estimate that 15 to 20 percent of couples have sex no more than 10 times a year, which is how the experts define sexless marriage. And even couples who don't meet that definition still feel like they're not having sex as often as they used to. Despite the stereotype that women are more likely to dodge sex, it's often the men who decline. The number of sexless marriages is "a grossly underreported statistic," says therapist Michele Weiner Davis, author of "The Sex-Starved Marriage." . . .

Marriage counselors can't tell you how much sex you should be having, but most agree that you should be having some. Sex is only a small part of a good union, but happy marriages usually include it. Frequency of sex may be a measure of a marriage's long-term health;

if it suddenly starts to decline, it can be a leading indicator of deeper problems, just like "those delicate green frogs that let us know when we're destroying the environment," says psychologist John Gottman, who runs the Family Research Lab (dubbed the Love Lab) at the University of Washington. Marriage pros say intimacy is often the glue that holds a couple together over time. If either member of a couple is miserable with the amount of sex in a marriage, it can cause devastating problems—and, in some cases, divorce. It can affect moods and spill over into all aspects of life—relationships with other family members, even performance in the office. . . .

The statistical evidence would seem to show everything is fine. Married couples say they have sex 68.5 times a year, or slightly more than once a week, according to a 2002 study by the highly respected National Opinion Research Center at the University of Chicago, and the NORC numbers haven't changed much over the past 10 years. At least according to what people tell researchers, DINS [dual income no sex couples] are most likely an urban myth: working women appear to have sex just as often as their stay-at-home counterparts. And for what it's worth, married people have 6.9 more sexual encounters a year than people who have never been married. After all, you can't underestimate the value of having an (occasionally) willing partner conveniently located in bed next to you.

But any efforts to quantify our love lives must be taken with a shaker of salt. The problem, not surprisingly, is that people aren't very candid about how often they have sex. Who wants to sound like a loser when he's trying to

[1]*MSNCB News*, 30 June 2003, <http://www.msnbc.com/news/928868.asp>.

make a contribution to social science? When pressed, nearly everyone defaults to a respectable "once or twice a week," a benchmark that probably seeped into our collective consciousness with the 1953 Kinsey Report, a study that's considered flawed because of its unrepresentative, volunteer sample.

"As a result, we have no idea what's 'normal'," says Pepper Schwartz, a sociologist and author of "Everything You Know About Love and Sex Is Wrong." Her best guess: three times a week during the first year of marriage, much less over time. When people believe they have permission to complain, she says, they often admit to having sex less than once a month: "And these are couples who like each other!" . . .

Marriage experts say there's no single reason we're suddenly so unhappy with our sex lives. Many of us are depressed; last year Americans filled more than 200 million prescriptions for antidepressants. The sexual landscape may have been transformed in the last 40 years by birth control, legalized abortion and a better understanding of women's sexuality. But women have changed, too. Since they surged into the workplace in the 1970s, their economic power has grown steadily. Women now make up 47 percent of the work force; they're awarded 57 percent of all bachelor's degrees. About 30 percent of working women now earn more than their husbands. . . .

Meanwhile, families have changed. The year after the first child is born has always been a hazardous time for marriages—more divorces happen during those sleepless months than at any other time in a marriage, except for the very first year. But some researchers say parents are now obsessed with their children in a way that can be unhealthy. Kids used to go to dance class or take piano lessons once a week; now parents organize an array of activities—French classes, cello lessons and three different sports—that would make an air-traffic controller dizzy. And do you remember being a child at a restaurant with your parents and having every adult at the table focus on your happiness? No? That's probably because you weren't taken along. . . .

UNDERSTANDING A CONTINGENCY TABLE

Contingency tables, or crosstabs (short for crosstabulations) in SPSS lingo, display data in such a way that we can look at whether one variable (referred to as the **independent variable**) *seems to be* having an effect or influence on a second variable (the **dependent variable**). Does one's marital status (an independent variable) have any effect on one's frequency of sexual activity (the dependent variable)? The difference between saying that one variable *seems to be having an effect* on another and saying that one variable *causes* changes in another was discussed in the first chapter. It bears repeating, because it is important to understand that we are not usually able to conclude from single contingency tables whether one variable is causing changes in a second variable. We can only tell whether there is an association or relationship between the two variables. More precisely, we can tell whether the differences in response to the categories (or values) of one variable are associated with or related to differences of response to the categories (or values) of a second variable.

In Chapter 4, we learned to approach questions like these using the Split File feature in SPSS and then finding frequency distributions. For example, in Chapter 4 you may remember splitting your data file by the variable *sex* and then producing frequency distributions for the variable *volchrty* to answer the question, are there any differences between males and females in the extent to which they volunteer for charitable work? You analyzed two tables—one for males and one for females—like the ones in Table 9.2. By focusing on differences in the valid percentages between males and females for the categories of the variable *volchrty*, you noticed that a larger percentage of men than women said they did not volunteer at all in a year's time (62% compared to 48.4%), and a larger percentage of men as compared to women said they volunteered once in a year's time (14.2% for men and 13.3% for women). However, a larger percentage of women as compared to men volunteered two or three times or more in a year's time (38.3% of women and 23.8% of men).

Another, more efficient, way to explore the same relationship is by using a single table, like the one in Table 9.3, that shows us the categories of the variable *volchrty* broken down by the variable *sex* in one chart.

Notice the similarities between Table 9.3 and the frequency distributions in Table 9.2. The contingency table for the variables *sex* and *volchrty* is simply a combined display of information from the frequency distributions in Table 9.2. For the variable *sex*, the information in the first column of Table 9.3, Male, is identical to the information in the frequency distribution (Frequency and Valid Percent columns) for males; the information in the second column, Female, is identical to the information in the Frequency and Valid Percent columns for females.

Let's look at Table 9.3 in a little more detail. In each of the squares, or **cells**, under the column headings Male and Female, you see a **cell frequency**. In the first cell, the number 214 is the number of respondents who are both male and did not volunteer at all. In addition, there is a column percentage. The percentage, 62%, in the first cell, is identical to the valid percent for the category Did Not Volunteer At All, in the frequency distribution for males in Table 9.2. Now let's turn our attention to the format of the contingency table.

The Independent and Dependent Variables

Notice how the two variables, *sex* and *volchrty*, are displayed. The independent variable, *sex*, is displayed across the top of the table, and its categories—male and female—form the columns of the table. The categories of the dependent variable, *volchrty*, are displayed down the left side of the table, and its categories—Not at all in Past Year, Once in the Past Year, and so on—form the rows of the table. Generally, contingency tables are set up in this fashion (although you will undoubtedly see many exceptions in newspapers, magazines, and other publications).[2] Deciding how one variable stands in relation to another (as an independent or dependent variable) was discussed in Chapter 1. You may want to review that material now.

Cell Frequencies and Column Percentages

Look at the numbers in each of the table's squares (or cells). There are two of them in each cell, a cell frequency and a column percentage.

---

[2]It is possible to set up a contingency table with the categories of the dependent variable across the top of the table and the categories of the independent variable down the side. When a table is set up this way, the cell percentages have to be calculated differently than when the table is set up with the categories of the independent variable in the columns.

TABLE 9.2 Frequency Distributions for the Variable *volchrty* with the GSS 2002 subset A File Split by *sex*

VOLCHRTY R done volunteer work for a charity

SEX Respondents' sex			Frequency	Percent	Valid Percent	Cumulative Percent
1 MALE	Valid	1 NOT AT ALL IN PAST YR	214	32.7	62.0	62.0
		2 ONCE IN THE PAST YR	49	7.5	14.2	76.2
		3 AT LEAST 2 OR 3 TIMES IN PAST YR	42	6.4	12.2	88.4
		4 ONCE A MONTH	17	2.6	4.9	93.3
		5 ONCE A WEEK	11	1.7	3.2	96.5
		6 MORE THAN ONCE A WEEK	12	1.8	3.5	100.0
		Total	345	52.8	100.0	
	Missing	0 NAP	308	47.1		
		8 DONT KNOW	1	.2		
		Total	309	47.2		
	Total		654	100.0		
2 FEMALE	Valid	1 NOT AT ALL IN PAST YR	186	22.0	48.4	48.4
		2 ONCE IN THE PAST YR	51	6.0	13.3	61.7
		3 AT LEAST 2 OR 3 TIMES IN PAST YR	67	7.9	17.4	79.2
		4 ONCE A MONTH	40	4.7	10.4	89.6
		5 ONCE A WEEK	18	2.1	4.7	94.3
		6 MORE THAN ONCE A WEEK	22	2.6	5.7	100.0
		Total	384	45.4	100.0	
	Missing	0 NAP	458	54.1		
		8 DONT KNOW	2	.2		
		Total	462	54.6		
		9 NO ANSWER	2	.2		
	Total		846	100.0		

TABLE 9.3 Contingency Tables for the Variables *volchrty* and *sex* in the GSS 2002 subset A file

VOLCHRTY R done volunteer work for a charity * SEX Respondents' sex Crosstabulation

			SEX Respondents' sex		Total
			1 MALE	2 FEMALE	
VOLCHRTY R done volunteer work for a charity	1 NOT AT ALL IN PAST YR	Count	214	186	400
		% within SEX Respondents' sex	62.0%	48.4%	54.9%
	2 ONCE IN THE PAST YR	Count	49	51	100
		% within SEX Respondents' sex	14.2%	13.3%	13.7%
	3 AT LEAST 2 OR 3 TIMES IN PAST YR	Count	42	67	109
		% within SEX Respondents' sex	12.2%	17.4%	15.0%
	4 ONCE A MONTH	Count	17	40	57
		% within SEX Respondents' sex	4.9%	10.4%	7.8%
	5 ONCE A WEEK	Count	11	18	29
		% within SEX Respondents' sex	3.2%	4.7%	4.0%
	6 MORE THAN ONCE A WEEK	Count	12	22	34
		% within SEX Respondents' sex	3.5%	5.7%	4.7%
Total		Count	345	384	729
		% within SEX Respondents' sex	100.0%	100.0%	100.0%

Frequencies A cell frequency (called the cell count) is simply the number of respondents who belong in each cell. When we look at the first cell, the cell frequency tells us there are 214 males who did not volunteer at all in a year's time.

Column percentages The percentage you see in each cell is called a **column percentage**. (You may also see these percentages referred to as "percentages on the independent variable" or "percentages down.") They are computed by dividing the cell frequency by the number of responses in the column (the column total) and multiplying by 100. The column percentage (214 divided by the column total, 345, and multiplied by 100) is 62%. This means that 62% of the male respondents did not volunteer in a year's time.

Reading down the column labeled Male is like reading a frequency distribution. We can see that a larger percentage of males said they did not volunteer for a charity in the past year, 62%, as compared to volunteering once in the past year, two or three times, once a month, and so on. Men are more likely to have not volunteered at all than to have volunteered even one time in a year. Unlike males, females are more likely to have volunteered at least once in a year's time than not to have volunteered at all. Even though 48.4% of all female respondents said they did not volunteer at all, 51.6%—the rest—volunteered at least one time.

So far we have emphasized reading contingency tables down the columns like frequency distributions. It is even more important for assessing associations between variables to read across the rows of a contingency table. Reading across the rows allows us to look for variations in responses to a dependent variable by categories of the independent variable. What we are looking for are differences in percentages across the rows. For example, reading across the top row of the table for the association between sex and volunteering for a charity, we learn that larger percentages of men do not volunteer at all as compared to women. Consequently, we learn there is a relationship between the independent and dependent variables: Men are more likely than women to say they do not volunteer at all to work for charities. We will be working on reading across the rows of contingency tables throughout this chapter.

Column Marginals and Column Marginal Percentages

The summary statistics labeled Total at the bottom of each column tell us how many of the respondents are male (345) and female (384). These totals of the number of respondents in each column are called **column marginals**. In addition, there is a column marginal percentage, 100% for each column. If you add up the column percentages in each cell, you should get at or close to 100%. (You may not get exactly 100% due to the rounding that occurs in each cell.)

Row Marginals and Row Marginal Percentages

The totals at the end of each horizontal row tell us how many (and what percentage) of the respondents fall into each of the categories of the dependent variable. In essence, these row totals—called **row marginals**—are a frequency distribution of the dependent variable *volchrty*. We can tell how many respondents (ignoring whether they are male or female) say they did not volunteer at all (400), volunteered only once (100), volunteered at least two or three times (109) and so on. We can also tell what percentage of all respondents say they did not volunteer at all (54.9%), volunteered once (13.7%), or volunteered at least two or three times (15%).

The Table Total (*N*)

The number in the bottom right corner of the table, 729, tells us that there were 729 respondents who answered both the sex question *and* the volunteering for a charity question. This number can be found by adding up the row marginals *or* the column marginals (but not both together), and it constitutes *N* for a contingency table (total number of respondents).

 Skills Practice 2   Test your ability to read and interpret a contingency table by using Table 9.1 to answer the following questions about the relationship between *marital status* and *frequency of sexual activity*.

A.   How many of the respondents who are married say they do not have sex at all?
B.   What percentage of the respondents who are married say they do not have sex at all?
C.   What percentage of all the respondents say they do not have sex at all?
D.   What is the total number of respondents (*N*) for the table?
E.   How many of the respondents are married?

SETTING UP A CONTINGENCY TABLE BY HAND

To understand better how contingency tables work, I will show you how to set them up by hand. To practice setting up a contingency table by hand, let's assume you have gathered data from 25 people. You have asked them their sex and you have asked them how often they have sex. These data have been gathered in a table like the one in Table 9.4 that lists each of your respondents by identification number and gives their responses to your questions.

Before you begin constructing a table, notice the total number of cases you will be dealing with. This number, *N* for the contingency table, allows us to check our work when we are finished and make sure we have counted all of our respondents. There are 25 cases listed in Table 9.4.

To set up a contingency table, assign the categories of one of the two variables to the columns of the table, and assign the categories of the other to the rows, depending on which variable is to be regarded as independent and which variable is to be regarded as dependent. In this example, *sex* is the independent variable and *sex frequency* is the dependent variable. Your table should be set up as the one following, with *sex* as the column variable and *sex frequency* as the row variable.

Sex Frequency	Sex	
	Male	*Female*
Not at all		
Once a month or less		
About once a week		
2–3 times a week or more		

Then fill in each of the cells (squares) of the table with the number of respondents who meet the criteria for each cell. For example, in the first cell (the cell in the upper left corner), we would enter the number of respondents who are both male and have sex not at all. If we count down our table of data in Table 9.4, we see that there are none in this category. Moving over one cell to the right, we count the number of respondents who are female and have sex not at all There are 3. Going on to the next row, we count the number of respondents who are male and have

TABLE 9.4   Table of 25 Responses to the Variables *sex* and *frequency of sex*

Case Summaries

	Respondents sex	Recoded sex frequency variable
1	FEMALE	ABOUT ONCE A WEEK
2	MALE	ABOUT ONCE A WEEK
3	FEMALE	ONCE A MONTH OR LESS
4	MALE	ABOUT ONCE A WEEK
5	FEMALE	NOT AT ALL
6	MALE	2-3 TIMES A WEEK OR MORE
7	FEMALE	2-3 TIMES A WEEK OR MORE
8	FEMALE	2-3 TIMES A WEEK OR MORE
9	MALE	ONCE A MONTH OR LESS
10	FEMALE	NOT AT ALL
11	MALE	2-3 TIMES A WEEK OR MORE
12	FEMALE	NOT AT ALL
13	FEMALE	ABOUT ONCE A WEEK
14	MALE	2-3 TIMES A WEEK OR MORE
15	MALE	2-3 TIMES A WEEK OR MORE
16	FEMALE	ABOUT ONCE A WEEK
17	MALE	ABOUT ONCE A WEEK
18	FEMALE	ONCE A MONTH OR LESS
19	FEMALE	2-3 TIMES A WEEK OR MORE
20	MALE	ABOUT ONCE A WEEK
21	MALE	ONCE A MONTH OR LESS
22	MALE	2-3 TIMES A WEEK OR MORE
23	FEMALE	ABOUT ONCE A WEEK
24	FEMALE	ONCE A MONTH OR LESS
25	FEMALE	ABOUT ONCE A WEEK

sex once a month or less (2). We continue with this process until all of the cells of the table are filled in. Now your table should look like the one here.

	Sex	
Sex Frequency	*Male*	*Female*
Not at all	0	3
Once a month or less	2	3
About once a week	4	5
2–3 times a week or more	5	3

The last step in the process of completing the table involves finding the column and row marginals, computing the table total, figuring the column percentages, and computing the row marginal percentages. The steps for completing the table are compiled in the following list:

To find the	*Do the following*	*Use the formula*
Column marginals	Add up the number of respondents in each column.	
Row marginals	Add up the number of respondents in each row.	
Table total	Add up the row marginals; check your answer by adding up the column marginals (you should get the same answer either way).	
Row marginal percentages	Divide the total number of respondents in each row by N (the table total) and multiply by 100.	$(\text{Row } f/N) \times 100$, where f is the row marginal frequency
Column percentages	Divide each cell frequency (the number of respondents in each cell) by its column total, then multiply by 100.	$(\text{Cell } f/\text{column total}) \times 100$, where cell f is the cell frequency
Column marginal percentages	Add up the column percentages for each column.	

Now your table should look like the following:

| | Sex | | |
Sex Frequency	Male	Female	Row Marginals
Not at all	0 (0%)	3 (21%)	3 (12%)
Once a Month or Less	2 (18%)	3 (21%)	5 (20%)
About Once a Week	4 (36%)	5 (36%)	9 (36%)
2–3 Times a Week or More	5 (45%)	3 (21%)	8 (32%)
Totals	11 (99%)	14 (99%)	25 (100%)

Skills Practice 3 Use the set of data in the following table to construct a contingency table for the variables *sex* and *number of sexual partners in the last year*.

Case Summaries

	Respondents' sex	Number of sex partners in last year
1	MALE	2-4 PARTNERS
2	FEMALE	1 PARTNER
3	FEMALE	NO PARTNERS
4	FEMALE	2-4 PARTNERS
5	FEMALE	1 PARTNER
6	FEMALE	1 PARTNER
7	MALE	NO PARTNERS
8	FEMALE	2-4 PARTNERS
9	MALE	1 PARTNER
10	FEMALE	1 PARTNER
11	FEMALE	1 PARTNER
12	FEMALE	1 PARTNER
13	FEMALE	1 PARTNER
14	FEMALE	1 PARTNER
15	MALE	5 OR MORE PARTNERS
16	FEMALE	NO PARTNERS
17	FEMALE	NO PARTNERS
18	FEMALE	1 PARTNER
19	MALE	1 PARTNER
20	MALE	2-4 PARTNERS

CHECKING YOUR WORK

How can you make sure the table you've created is correct? There are several ways to check your work.

• Make sure the *N* for the table matches the number of cases you have in your list of raw scores. If it doesn't, check your cell frequencies and your row and column totals.
• Your column marginal percentages should be at or near 100%. If they aren't, check the work you did to calculate your column percentages.
• Your row marginal percentages should add up to or be near 100%. If not, check your computations.

INTERPRETING CONTINGENCY TABLES

As we have already seen, contingency tables help us find the patterns of association between variables in sets of data. They are a very commonly used and powerful tool. Academic researchers are not the only ones who use them; you will undoubtedly find examples in nearly every daily newspaper or weekly magazine.

Skills Practice 4 Find an article in a newspaper or magazine that displays and interprets a contingency table. Is it being displayed according to the techniques previously described? If not, how is it different? How do the differences affect the way the table is interpreted? Write down the sentences in the article that draw conclusions from the contingency table.

Finding the Patterns in a Contingency Table

The most important part of interpreting a contingency table is understanding what it is telling us about the association between two variables. Interpreting a table can be divided into two parts: understanding the nature of an association and assessing its strength.

Understanding the nature of the association When researchers construct contingency tables, it is usually with some question in mind, like the one we have been working with: Do married people have sex less often than others? You may already have a sense of the answer from looking over Table 9.1 to answer the questions in Skills Practice 3. What do you think Table 9.1 is telling us? Overall, it seems to be contradicting what the authors of the "News to Use" article were claiming. It appears that married respondents to the 2002 General Social Survey were more likely to say they have sex about once a week or two to three times a week or more as compared to widowed, divorced, separated, and even never married respondents. How can we come to this conclusion?

If you read across the rows of the table, starting with the first category, Not at All, you can see that a larger percentage of respondents who are widowed (90.5%) say they have no sex at all as compared to the respondents in any other category of the independent variable (married, divorced, separated, or never married). This comes as no surprise. Reading across the next category of the dependent variable, Once a Month or Less, we see that respondents who are separated are more likely than respondents who are married, widowed, divorced, or never married to say they have sex once a month or less. Thirty-one percent of separated respondents say they have sex once a month or less. Again, this is probably no surprise. In the category of the dependent variable About Once a Week, you may be surprised to learn (especially after reading the "News to Use" article) that married respondents are more likely to have sex about once a week (43.9%) than are respondents who are widowed, divorced, separated, or never married. (Those who are never married are not too far behind, though, at 30.6%). Finally, in the category Two to Three Times a Week or More, a higher percentage of married respondents (30.9%) answered that they have sex two to three times a week or more as compared to respondents who are widowed (0%), divorced (20.6%), separated (28.6%), or never married (26.2%). Notice in this row (Two to Three Times a Week or More) there is an empty cell. SPSS contingency tables with no respondents in them are left empty, so the cell frequency is zero and the cell percentage is zero.

Moreover, reading down the column Married, you can see that 43.9% of all married respondents say they have sex about once a week and 30.9% say they have sex two to three times a week or more. Nearly 75% of all married respondents say they have sex about once a week or more often than that.

What accounts for the difference between what we are seeing in the GSS 2002 data and what the authors of the "News to Use" article are telling us? The "News to Use" article itself actually provides a couple of clues. First, sex may be more available to married people than it is to those who are not married—if you are married, you don't have to hunt for a partner. Second, there may be some overstatement of sexual frequency in the responses to the variable. As the "News to Use" article says, who wants to look like a loser in front of an interviewer? Nevertheless, the data available to us are suggesting that the picture is not as bleak as the "News to Use" article portrays it to be.

You may be noticing that the contingency tables are generally interpreted in sentences that describe relationships between variables. Generally, one interprets contingency tables in statements that link the independent and dependent variables, much like a hypothesis statement, as illustrated in Box 9.1.

Understanding the strength of the association A question that remains is, How sizable is the difference between married respondents and others in the frequency of sexual activity? Is it a small difference or a large one? How *much more* likely is it that married people will say they have sex more often than other respondents—those who are widowed, divorced, separated, or never married? The answer resides in the size of the differences in the percentages when you read across the rows of the contingency table. If the size of the difference is large, then the association is strong. If the size of the difference is small, then the association

---

BOX 9.1

Models for Interpreting Contingency Tables

Respondents who <exhibit a particular characteristic of the independent variable> are also more likely to <exhibit a particular characteristic of the dependent variable> than are respondents who <exhibit another characteristic of the independent variable>.

Example: Respondents who <are married> are also more likely to <have sex more frequently> than are respondents who <are widowed, divorced, separated or never married>.

---

is weak. The differences in the percentages across the rows in Table 9.1 are somewhat sizable, so we would describe the relationship between the two variables as perhaps moderate to fairly strong.

To get at the implications of this statement, we can make an analogy to gambling. If there was a way to maximize our likelihood of winning a bet, we would use it, wouldn't we? In one sense, that is exactly what a contingency table can help us do. Contingency tables help us determine how likely it is that, if we know something about one variable (*marital status,* in this example), we can correctly guess a second variable (i.e., *frequency of sex*). The larger are the differences in the percentages across the rows, the better are the odds of predicting the dependent variable if one knows the independent variable.

Suppose I show you the numbers in Table 9.1, and then I select at random one married respondent and one never married respondent from the General Social Survey. Next I ask you to bet $100 on the person most likely to be having sex not at all. Knowing what you know now, you would probably (and correctly) bet on the never married respondent. There are 21.8 chances in 100 that the never married respondent is, in fact, not having sex at all. (How do we know? Because 21.8% of the never married respondents said they are not having sex.) Likewise, there are 7.1 chances in 100 that a married respondent is not having sex at all. If you bet on the never married respondent the odds of winning are better, but far from perfect. How much better are the odds, in your opinion? If they aren't much better, then we can conclude that the size of the difference between married and never married respondents, although it exists, is small. If the odds are a lot better, then we can conclude that the size of the difference is large.

Is this an important difference? That depends on the context in which one is interpreting the data. In the context of the article, "We're Not in the Mood," the data seem to refute the argument that married people are not having sex as frequently as others. Even when you look at the category Two to Three Times a Week or More, the data are saying that married people have sex a little more often than people who are not married. Even though the difference is not a very large one in that category (30.9% of married respondents say they have sex two to three times a week compared to 26.2% of never married respondents), it is easy to see that married respondents are having sex no less frequently than never married respondents.

TABLE 9.5 Contingency Table for the recoded *frequency of sexual activity* and *sex* Variables in the GSS 2002 subset C File

RCSXFREQ Recoded sex frequency variable * SEX Respondents' sex Crosstabulation

			SEX Respondents' sex		
			1 MALE	2 FEMALE	Total
RCSXFREQ Recoded sex frequency variable	0 NOT AT ALL	Count	78	188	266
		% within SEX Respondents' sex	15.1%	29.0%	22.9%
	1 ONCE A MONTH OR LESS	Count	108	112	220
		% within SEX Respondents' sex	20.9%	17.3%	18.9%
	2 ABOUT ONCE A WEEK	Count	182	202	384
		% within SEX Respondents' sex	35.3%	31.2%	33.0%
	3 2-3 TIMES A WEEK OR MORE	Count	148	146	294
		% within SEX Respondents' sex	28.7%	22.5%	25.3%
Total		Count	516	648	1164
		% within SEX Respondents' sex	100.0%	100.0%	100.0%

 Skills Practice 5 Analyze the contingency table in Table 9.5. Describe the nature and strength of the association between the *sex* and recoded *frequency of sexual activity* variables in the GSS 2002 subset C file.

Interpreting Tables with Ordinal or Numerical Variables

Contingency tables in which you are examining the relationships between ordinal variables, numerical variables, or some combination of the two can be interpreted a little differently than tables in which one or both variables are nominal. In these cases, we can look for the **direction of an association**—whether an increase (or decrease) in the value of one variable is associated with an increase (or decrease) in the value of a second variable. These kinds of **linear** (straight line) **associations** between variables can be interpreted along the lines of the models in Box 9.2.

Generally, a linear association can be detected by circling the highest percentage in each row of a contingency table. If the values line up diagonally—top

---

BOX 9.2

Model for Interpreting Contingency Tables (Ordinal or Numerical Variables)

The more (or less) of <a given characteristic respondents exhibit>, the more (or less) likely the respondents are to <exhibit a second characteristic>.

Example: The more <sex partners respondents have>, the more likely they are to <report having sex more often>.

FIGURE 9.1
Positive association.

FIGURE 9.1
Positive association.

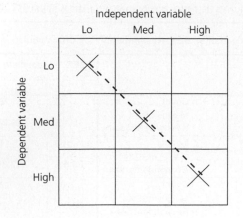

left to bottom right or bottom left to top right—then you have a linear association. In linear associations, increases in the values of one variable are associated with increases or decreases in the values of a second variable. Two illustrations follow that use hypothetical variables, which I have simply labeled as an Independent Variable and a Dependent Variable. In each row, I have marked with an X the cell with the highest percentage.

Positive associations   Figure 9.1 shows you what a linear association might look like in which the diagonal runs top left to bottom right—a **positive association** between the variables. Positive associations are ones in which increases in the values of one variable are associated with increases in the values of a second variable, like the association between education and income. One of the reasons you may be in college is because you believe that the more education you have, the more money you are likely to earn. Conversely, the less education you have, the less money you are likely to earn.

Negative associations   Figure 9.2 shows you what a linear association might look like in which the diagonal runs bottom left to top right—a **negative association**. Negative associations are ones in which increases in the values of one variable are associated with decreases in the values of a second variable, or vice versa. A neg-

FIGURE 9.2
Negative association.

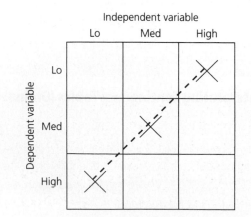

TABLE 9.6   Contingency Table for the Recoded *number of sex partners in the last year* and *frequency of sex* variables in the GSS 2002 subset C File

RCSXFREQ Recoded sex frequency variable * RCPRTNRS Recoded number of sex partners in last year Crosstabulation

			0 NO PARTNERS	1 1 PARTNER	2 2-4 PARTNERS	3 5 OR MORE PARTNERS	Total
			RCPRTNRS Recoded number of sex partners in last year				
RCSXFREQ Recoded sex frequency variable	0 NOT AT ALL	Count	250	14			264
		% within RCPRTNRS Recoded number of sex partners in last year	87.1%	2.0%			22.8%
	1 ONCE A MONTH OR LESS	Count	18	153	47	2	220
		% within RCPRTNRS Recoded number of sex partners in last year	6.3%	21.7%	31.5%	10.5%	19.0%
	2 ABOUT ONCE A WEEK	Count	13	303	60	7	383
		% within RCPRTNRS Recoded number of sex partners in last year	4.5%	43.0%	40.3%	36.8%	33.0%
	3 2-3 TIMES A WEEK OR MORE	Count	6	234	42	10	292
		% within RCPRTNRS Recoded number of sex partners in last year	2.1%	33.2%	28.2%	52.6%	25.2%
Total		Count	287	704	149	19	1159
		% within RCPRTNRS Recoded number of sex partners in last year	100.0%	100.0%	100.0%	100.0%	100.0%

ative association would be interpreted as follows: The more education respondents have, the fewer the children they are likely to have. Conversely, the less education respondents have, the more children they are likely to have.

To illustrate what a linear (and in this case, positive) association might look like, examine the contingency table for the recoded *number of sex partners in the last year* and *frequency of sex* variables to answer the question: Does the number of sexual partners affect the frequency of sexual activity? (See Table 9.6.) Notice that by circling the highest percentage in each row (excluding the row marginal percentage), a diagonal line can be drawn through the circled boxes, running from the upper left corner to the lower right corner. The diagonal line tells us we have a positive association that can be interpreted as follows:

> The more sexual partners respondents say they have, the more frequently they have sex. (Conversely, the fewer partners they say they have, the less frequently they say they have sex.)

Skills Practice 6   Look at the relationships between the respondents' ages and their frequency of sexual activity in Table 9.7. Is the association you find positive or negative? How can you tell? Write a short paragraph to describe the association.

TABLE 9.7   Contingency Table for the Recoded *age* and *frequency of sex* Variables in the GSS 2002 subset C File

RCSXFREQ Recoded sex frequency variable * RCAGE Recoded age variable Crosstabulation

| | | | RCAGE Recoded age variable | | | | |
			1 18 THRU 25	2 26 THRU 40	3 41 THRU 60	4 61 THRU 89	Total
RCSXFREQ Recoded sex frequency variable	0 NOT AT ALL	Count	18	33	87	128	266
		% within RCAGE Recoded age variable	11.5%	9.0%	22.1%	52.5%	23.0%
	1 ONCE A MONTH OR LESS	Count	34	61	72	53	220
		% within RCAGE Recoded age variable	21.7%	16.7%	18.3%	21.7%	19.0%
	2 ABOUT ONCE A WEEK	Count	50	144	137	50	381
		% within RCAGE Recoded age variable	31.8%	39.5%	34.9%	20.5%	32.9%
	3 2-3 TIMES A WEEK OR MORE	Count	55	127	97	13	292
		% within RCAGE Recoded age variable	35.0%	34.8%	24.7%	5.3%	25.2%
Total		Count	157	365	393	244	1159
		% within RCAGE Recoded age variable	100.0%	100.0%	100.0%	100.0%	100.0%

Interpreting tables with nonlinear associations   Not all associations involving ordinal or numerical variables will be linear. In fact, most won't be. You will find any number of other patterns in data, and you have to be open to the possibility of nonlinear associations, too. It is important to interpret a set of data as it presents itself, not as you would like it to be, expect it to be, or wish it were. For example, you may have tables that show associations in any of a number of patterns or different combinations. (When you are working with real data, the possibilities are limitless.) Figures 9.3–9.6 illustrate some of the possible "shapes" that associations can take. You may have a table showing little or no association at all between two variables.

As an illustration of a nonlinear association, let's look at a contingency table for the variables *sex of one's sex partner in the last year* and *frequency of sex* (Table 9.8). Note that if you circle the highest column percentage in each row (along with the second highest percentage in that row, excluding the row marginal percentage), the line that best fits the data is a curved one—a **curvilinear** relationship or **association**, the solid line in Table 9.8. Woody Allen's quip seems to be right, being bisexual improves your chances of getting a date on a Saturday night. Respondents with partners of both sexes had sex more often than respondents whose sex partners were either exclusively male or exclusively female.

Next, look at how consistent the general pattern seems to be and how large the differences are in the percentages across the rows of the contingency table. The consistency of the pattern and the size of the differences in the percentages tell us how strong the association is: The more consistent is the pattern and the larger are the differences in the percentages, the stronger is the association; the

FIGURE 9.3

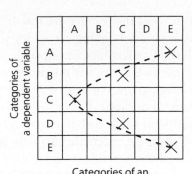

A B C D E
A B C D E
Categories of a dependent variable
Categories of an independent variable

FIGURE 9.4

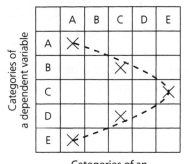

A B C D E
A B C D E
Categories of a dependent variable
Categories of an independent variable

FIGURE 9.5

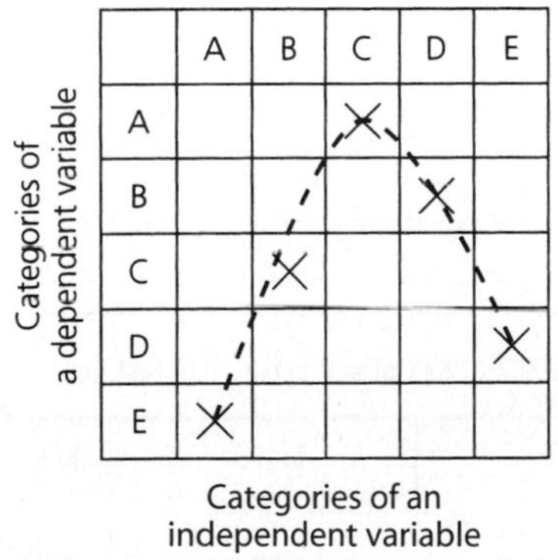

A B C D E
A B C D E
Categories of a dependent variable
Categories of an independent variable

FIGURE 9.6

A B C D E
A B C D E
Categories of a dependent variable
Categories of an independent variable

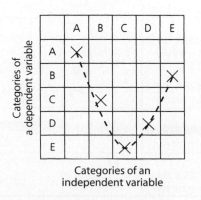

less consistent is the pattern and the smaller are the differences in the percentages, the weaker is the association. Looking across the row of the first category, Not at All, you can see that the percentage of respondents with exclusively male or exclusively female partners who have sex not at all is almost the same. There are no respondents who have partners of both sexes who have had sex not at all. This pattern is consistent with our overall conclusion, but the size of the differences in the percentages (0% for those with partners of both sexes, and less than 2% for those with exclusively male or female partners) is pretty small.

In the second category of the dependent variable Once a Month or Less, the pattern is consistent with our overall description of the association between the variables in the table. In this row, however, the differences in the percentages—between those who have partners of both sexes and those who have partners of exclusively one sex—is much larger (the difference between 0% and about 23%).

In the third and fourth rows of the contingency table, the pattern continues to hold. We see that respondents with partners of both sexes are more likely to say they have had sex About Once a Week or Two to Three Times a Week or More as compared to respondents with partners of exclusively one sex. The sizes of the differences are larger in the category Two to Three Times a Week or More than they are in the category About Once a Week.

What conclusion can we now draw about the strength of the association? Overall, it appears to be at least a moderate one, perhaps even somewhat strong. Having partners of both sexes increases the likelihood that respondents have sex frequently.

I need to add a note of caution. You may have noticed that the column of the independent variable for respondents with same sex partners has only a few respondents—six to be exact. Although Table 9.8 illustrates the point I was trying

TABLE 9.8 Contingency Table for the Recoded *frequency of sex* and *sex of one's partners in the last year* Variables in the GSS 2002 subset C File

RCSXFREQ Recoded sex frequency variable * SEXSEX Sex of sex partners in last year Crosstabulation

| | | | SEXSEX Sex of sex partners in last year | | | |
			1 EXCLUSIVELY MALE	2 BOTH MALE AND FEMALE	3 EXCLUSIVELY FEMALE	Total
RCSXFREQ Recoded sex frequency variable	0 NOT AT ALL	Count	8		6	14
		% within SEXSEX Sex of sex partners in last year	1.8%		1.5%	1.6%
	1 ONCE A MONTH OR LESS	Count	108		94	202
		% within SEXSEX Sex of sex partners in last year	23.6%		22.9%	23.1%
	2 ABOUT ONCE A WEEK	Count	201	3	167	371
		% within SEXSEX Sex of sex partners in last year	44.0%	50.0%	40.6%	42.4%
	3 2-3 TIMES A WEEK OR MORE	Count	140	3	144	287
		% within SEXSEX Sex of sex partners in last year	30.6%	50.0%	35.0%	32.8%
Total		Count	457	6	411	874
		% within SEXSEX Sex of sex partners in last year	100.0%	100.0%	100.0%	100.0%

to make about being open to different types of associations between variables, the sample of respondents in the table may not accurately represent the population from which the sample was drawn. In Chapter 11 we will learn how to assess the likelihood that a pattern of response found in a sample will be found in the population from which the sample was drawn. But first, let's turn our attention to learning how to create and interpret contingency tables using SPSS.

USING SPSS

Producing Contingency Tables

To create your own contingency table using SPSS, use the Crosstabs command, which can be found by using the command path Analyze ➡ Descriptive Statistics. To illustrate the process, let's see whether there is a relationship between frequency of sex and the health of the respondents.

SPSS GUIDE: PRODUCING A CONTINGENCY TABLE

Open the GSS 2002 subset C data file. Then click on Analyze and Descriptive Statistics. From the list of options that appears, click on Crosstabs.

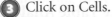

The Crosstabs dialog box opens.

① Select your dependent variable (*rcsxfreq*): scroll down to *rcsxfreq*, highlight it with your mouse, and click on the arrow key, ▶, which points at the box labeled Row.

② Select your independent variable (*health1*): scroll down to *health1*, highlight it with your mouse, and click on the arrow key, ▶, which points at the box labeled Column.

③ Click on Cells.

④ In the Crosstabs: Cell Display window, look under Percentages and click on Column.

⑤ Click on Continue to return to the Crosstabs dialog box.

⑥ At the Crosstabs dialog box, click on OK.

ample, in the second row of Table 9.9, it is apparent that those respondents in excellent health are the ones most likely to say they are having sex once a month or less. You might expect the respondents whose health is not quite so good to have the highest percentages of response to this category of the dependent variable.

To lend credence to your conclusions and to describe the *strength* of the association, support your conclusions with relevant statistics from your table. In addition to saying that the better the health of the respondents, the more active their sex lives, mention that

> The association seems at least moderate. The association is fairly consistent in the first and fourth rows of the table (the better the respondents' health, the more often they say they have sex). However, it is less consistent in the third row of the table. The differences in the percentages across the rows are not very large ones, though, except in the first row. Overall, the association seems to be at least a moderate one.

A complete analysis for the association between the respondents' health and their frequency of sexual activity would look like the following:

> Data from the General Social Survey for 2002 indicate that there is a positive association between having good health and an active sex life. Whereas the respondents were fairly evenly divided among four general categories of sexual activity, respondents in very good or excellent health were more likely to have active sex lives than respondents whose health was poor or fair. Nearly 49% of the respondents whose health is poor do not have sex at all compared to only about 14% of those whose health is excellent. On the other hand, over 38% of those whose health is excellent have sex about once a week and about 27% have sex two to three times a week compared to 25.6% and 12.8%, respectively, for those whose health is poor. The association is not as strong as one might expect, though, and it appears to be a moderate one at best.

Skills Practice 7   Use SPSS and the GSS 2002 subset C file to examine the association between the respondents' health and the number of sexual partners they have. Use the *health1* and *rcprtnrs* variables to produce a contingency table. Remember to obtain column percentages. Write an analysis of the association that describes the nature of the association and its direction and strength.

At this point, you should be able to use a number of tools for data analysis: frequency distributions, measures of central tendency, measures of dispersion, and now contingency table analysis. The goal of learning all of these skills is to combine them in different ways to analyze data. In the next chapter we will be building on these skills by learning to add measures of association to our analysis of contingency tables and by learning how to control for third variables.

This chapter has introduced you to the process of bivariate, or two-variable, analysis using contingency tables. A contingency table is a display of the categories of one variable by the categories of a second variable. Generally, they are set up in such a way that the independent variable forms the columns of the table and the dependent variable forms the rows. Consequently, it is important to be able to tell which variable in an association ought to be treated as the independent variable and which variable ought to be treated as the dependent variable.

Two techniques for producing contingency tables were described: producing contingency tables using SPSS and the Analyze ➡ Descriptive Statistics ➡ Crosstabs command path and producing contingency tables by hand.

The process of analyzing a contingency table is much like the process of examining frequency distributions when a data file has been split by some other variable. Contingency tables are more efficient means to the same end—understanding associations between variables. To analyze an association between two variables, you have to first obtain the column percentages—the percentages

of response in each category of the independent variable. Then these percentages are analyzed by reading across each row or category of the dependent variable and looking for variations in the percentages across the rows.

Interpreting contingency tables involves using the column percentages, but analyzing them across the rows to describe the nature of an association—what the association is, exactly, between an independent and dependent variable. In addition, the strength of the association should be assessed. Finally, when you are dealing with two ordinal variables or higher, the direction of the association has to be evaluated.

A great deal of attention is given to the interpretation of contingency tables in this chapter. There are models of interpretation throughout the chapter, and you should come away with a fairly good idea of how you can write about bivariate relationships.

In the next chapter we will extend our analysis of bivariate associations with statistics for measuring associations, beginning with statistics based on contingency tables.

KEY CONCEPTS

Bivariate analysis
Contingency table
Independent variable
Dependent variable
Cell
Cell frequency

Column percentage
Column marginals
Row marginals
Nature of an association
Strength of an association
Direction of an association

Linear association
Positive association
Negative association
Curvilinear association

ANSWERS TO SKILLS PRACTICES

2. A. 37 of the respondents who are married don't have sex at all.
   B. 7.1% of the respondents who are married don't have sex at all.

   C. 22.9% of all respondents don't have sex at all.
   D. N for the table is 1,164.
   E. 524 of the respondents are married.

3. Your contingency table should look like this one:

| | Sex | | |
Number of partners	Male	Female	Row Marginals
No partners	1 (17%)	3 (21%)	4 (20%)
1 partner	2 (33%)	9 (64%)	11 (55%)
2–4 partners	2 (33%)	2 (14%)	4 (20%)
5 or more partners	1 (17%)	0 (0%)	1 (5%)
Totals	6 (100%)	14 (99%)	20 (100%)

5. As one might expect, male respondents report having sex more often than do female respondents. Twenty-nine percent of female respondents say they do not have sex at all as compared to 15% of male respondents. Nearly 29% of male respondents say they have sex two to three times a week or more as compared to 22.5% of female respondents. Male respondents are also more likely to say they have sex once a month or less (20.9%) and about once a week (35.3%) as compared to female respondents (17.3% and 31.2%, respectively). The association appears to be weak to moderate. The pattern of the association is consistent, but the differences in the percentages across the rows are not very large ones—only a few percentage points in all categories of the dependent variable except the first one.

6. The association between respondents' ages and their frequency of sexual activity is a positive one—the older the respondent the less sexual activity they report. Over half (52.5%) of those respondents in the 61 through 89 age category report having sex not at all as compared to only 11.5% of those who are in the 18 through 25 age category. Conversely, 35% of those in the age 18 through 25 age category say they have sex two to three times a week or more as compared to only 5.3% of those respondents who are ages 61 through 85. The association seems to be a fairly strong one. It is consistent across most of the categories of the dependent variable, and the differences in the percentages are fairly sizable.

7. You should get a contingency table for *health1* and *rcprtnrs* like the one below.

RCPRTNRS Recoded number of sex partners in last year * HEALTH1 Rs health in general Crosstabulation

| | | | HEALTH1 Rs health in general | | | | | |
			1 POOR	2 FAIR	3 GOOD	4 VERY GOOD	5 EXCELLENT	Total
RCPRTNRS Recoded number of sex partners in last year	0 NO PARTNERS	Count	18	46	61	55	43	223
		% within HEALTH1 Rs health in general	46.2%	34.6%	19.9%	20.1%	16.4%	22.0%
	1 1 PARTNER	Count	16	70	197	175	183	641
		% within HEALTH1 Rs health in general	41.0%	52.6%	64.2%	64.1%	69.8%	63.2%
	2 2-4 PARTNERS	Count	4	15	45	36	32	132
		% within HEALTH1 Rs health in general	10.3%	11.3%	14.7%	13.2%	12.2%	13.0%
	3 5 OR MORE PARTNERS	Count	1	2	4	7	4	18
		% within HEALTH1 Rs health in general	2.6%	1.5%	1.3%	2.6%	1.5%	1.8%
Total		Count	39	133	307	273	262	1014
		% within HEALTH1 Rs health in general	100.0%	100.0%	100.0%	100.0%	100.0%	100.0%

Generally speaking, the relationship between the respondents' health and their number of sexual partners is a positive one. The better the respondents' health, the more sexual partners they have had. However, it should be noted that most respondents (63%) had only one partner in the prior year. Nevertheless, the better the respondents' health, the more likely they were to have even one partner. Forty-six percent of those respondents in poor health had no partners, whereas only 16.4% of those in excellent health had no partners. Nearly 84% of those in excellent health had a least one partner compared to 53.8%—slightly more than half—of those in poor health. The association seems to be moderate at best. The pattern is most consistent in the first and second categories of the dependent variable (no partners and 1 partner) and is less consistent in the second and third categories of the dependent variable (2–4 partners and 5 or more partners).

GENERAL EXERCISES

For Exercises 1 through 4, construct and analyze a contingency table for the given set of data (a set of randomly selected cases from the 2002 General Social Survey).

1.

Case Summaries

	Respondents' sex	Sex of sex partners in last year
1	MALE	EXCLUSIVELY FEMALE
2	FEMALE	EXCLUSIVELY MALE
3	FEMALE	EXCLUSIVELY MALE
4	MALE	EXCLUSIVELY FEMALE
5	FEMALE	EXCLUSIVELY MALE
6	FEMALE	EXCLUSIVELY MALE
7	MALE	EXCLUSIVELY FEMALE
8	MALE	EXCLUSIVELY FEMALE
9	FEMALE	EXCLUSIVELY MALE
10	MALE	EXCLUSIVELY FEMALE
11	FEMALE	EXCLUSIVELY FEMALE
12	FEMALE	EXCLUSIVELY MALE
13	MALE	EXCLUSIVELY FEMALE
14	FEMALE	EXCLUSIVELY MALE
15	FEMALE	EXCLUSIVELY MALE
16	MALE	EXCLUSIVELY FEMALE
17	FEMALE	EXCLUSIVELY MALE
18	FEMALE	EXCLUSIVELY MALE
19	MALE	EXCLUSIVELY FEMALE
20	FEMALE	EXCLUSIVELY MALE
21	MALE	EXCLUSIVELY FEMALE
22	MALE	EXCLUSIVELY FEMALE
23	FEMALE	EXCLUSIVELY MALE
24	FEMALE	EXCLUSIVELY MALE
25	FEMALE	EXCLUSIVELY MALE
26	MALE	EXCLUSIVELY FEMALE
27	FEMALE	EXCLUSIVELY MALE
28	FEMALE	EXCLUSIVELY MALE
29	MALE	EXCLUSIVELY FEMALE
30	MALE	EXCLUSIVELY FEMALE
31	MALE	EXCLUSIVELY FEMALE
32	MALE	EXCLUSIVELY FEMALE
33	FEMALE	BOTH MALE AND FEMALE
34	FEMALE	EXCLUSIVELY MALE
35	FEMALE	EXCLUSIVELY MALE
36	MALE	EXCLUSIVELY FEMALE
37	MALE	EXCLUSIVELY FEMALE
38	MALE	EXCLUSIVELY FEMALE

2.

Case Summaries

	Respondents' sex	Ever have sex with someone other than spouse while married?
1	FEMALE	NO
2	MALE	NO
3	FEMALE	YES
4	MALE	YES
5	MALE	NO
6	MALE	NO
7	FEMALE	NO
8	FEMALE	NO
9	FEMALE	NO
10	FEMALE	NO
11	MALE	NO
12	FEMALE	NO
13	MALE	NO
14	FEMALE	NO
15	FEMALE	NO
16	MALE	NO
17	FEMALE	NO
18	FEMALE	NO
19	FEMALE	NO
20	FEMALE	YES
21	MALE	NO
22	FEMALE	NO
23	MALE	NO
24	MALE	NO
25	MALE	NO
26	MALE	NO
27	MALE	NO
28	FEMALE	NO
29	FEMALE	NO
30	MALE	YES
31	MALE	NO

3.

Case Summaries

	Frequency of sexual activity	Is life exciting, routine, or dull?
1	NOT AT ALL	ROUTINE
2	ABOUT ONCE A WEEK	EXCITING
3	ONCE A MONTH OR LESS	ROUTINE
4	2-3 TIMES A WEEK OR MORE	ROUTINE
5	ONCE A MONTH OR LESS	ROUTINE
6	2-3 TIMES A WEEK OR MORE	EXCITING
7	ABOUT ONCE A WEEK	EXCITING
8	NOT AT ALL	EXCITING
9	2-3 TIMES A WEEK OR MORE	EXCITING
10	ABOUT ONCE A WEEK	EXCITING
11	ABOUT ONCE A WEEK	EXCITING
12	ONCE A MONTH OR LESS	EXCITING
13	ABOUT ONCE A WEEK	EXCITING
14	2-3 TIMES A WEEK OR MORE	EXCITING
15	ABOUT ONCE A WEEK	ROUTINE
16	2-3 TIMES A WEEK OR MORE	EXCITING
17	ONCE A MONTH OR LESS	EXCITING
18	ABOUT ONCE A WEEK	EXCITING
19	ABOUT ONCE A WEEK	EXCITING
20	2-3 TIMES A WEEK OR MORE	ROUTINE

4.

Case Summaries

	Age in categories	Ever have sex with someone other than spouse while married?
1	26 THRU 40	NO
2	61 THRU 89	NO
3	26 THRU 40	YES
4	41 THRU 60	YES
5	26 THRU 40	NO
6	26 THRU 40	NO
7	41 THRU 60	NO
8	18 THRU 25	NO
9	61 THRU 89	NO
10	61 THRU 89	NO
11	41 THRU 60	NO
12	41 THRU 60	NO
13	26 THRU 40	NO
14	41 THRU 60	NO
15	41 THRU 60	NO
16	26 THRU 40	NO
17	41 THRU 60	NO
18	26 THRU 40	NO
19	26 THRU 40	NO
20	41 THRU 60	YES
21	26 THRU 40	NO
22	26 THRU 40	NO
23	41 THRU 60	NO
24	61 THRU 89	NO
25	26 THRU 40	NO
26	26 THRU 40	NO
27	41 THRU 60	NO
28	41 THRU 60	NO
29	61 THRU 89	NO
30	61 THRU 89	YES
31	26 THRU 40	NO

SPSS EXERCISES

For the following exercises use your **GSS 2002 subset C file.**

1. Produce a contingency table for the association between *sex* and *homosex* (the attitude toward homosexuality variable). Make sure that the independent variable is the column variable and the dependent variable is the row variable in your table. Check to see that you have obtained column percentages for the table.
   A. Which group, males or females, had the highest number of respondents who said homosexuality is not wrong at all? Which group had the highest number who said homosexuality is always wrong?
   B. Which group, males or females, had the highest percentage of respondents who said homosexuality is not wrong at all? Which group had the highest percentage who said homosexuality is always wrong?
   C. What percentage of all respondents said homosexuality is not wrong at all? What percentage said homosexuality is always wrong?
   D. How many respondents answered both questions—sex of respondent and attitude toward homosexuality?

2. Produce a contingency table for the association between *sex* and *evstray*. Make sure that the independent variable is the column variable and the dependent variable is the row variable in your table. Check to see that you have obtained column percentages for the table.
   A. Which group, males or females, had the highest number of respondents who have had sex with someone other than their spouses while married? Which group had the highest number who did not stray from their marriages?

B. Which group, males or females, had the highest percentage of respondents who had sex with someone other than their spouses while married? Which group had the highest percentage of respondents who did not stray from their marriages?
   C. What percentage of all respondents strayed from their marriages?
   D. How many respondents answered both questions—sex of respondent and did you ever have sex with someone other than your spouse while married?

3. Write a few sentences analyzing the nature and the strength of the association between *sex* and *homosex*.

4. Write a few sentences analyzing the nature and the strength of the association between *sex* and *evstray*.

5. Interpret the association between watching television and frequency of sexual activity using the *rctvhrs* and *rcsxfreq* variables (analyze the nature, strength, and direction, if appropriate).

6. Interpret the association between strength of religious convictions and frequency of sexual activity using the *reliten* and *rcsxfreq* variables (analyze the nature, strength, and direction, if appropriate).

7. Interpret the association between sexual activity and the GSS respondents' perceptions of life as dull to exciting using the *life* and *rcsxfreq* variables (analyze the nature, strength, and direction, if appropriate).

8. Interpret the association between sexual activity and the GSS respondents' general level of happiness using the *happy* and *rcsxfreq* variables (analyze the nature, strength, and direction, if appropriate).

CHAPTER 10

Measures of Association for Contingency Tables

INTRODUCTION

In the last chapter, you learned how to analyze contingency tables and evaluate the nature and strength of associations between variables. In this chapter and the next, you will be introduced to **measures of association**—statistics that help us evaluate these relationships. It may help to begin with a brief review of what we mean by "association." When two variables are associated, variations in the responses to the values or categories of one variable are related to or coupled with variations in the responses to the values or categories of a second variable. For example, if we say that the variables *marital status* and *frequency of sexual activity* are associated, we are saying that variations in the responses to the categories of the variable *marital status* are related to or coupled with variations in the responses to the categories of the variable *frequency of sexual activity*. Measures of association allow us to assess the degree to which variations in the responses to the categories of one variable are related to or consistent with the variations in the responses to the categories of a second variable.

Measures of association function as indexes, somewhat like the index of qualitative variation you learned to calculate in Chapter 6. Whereas the index of qualitative variation provided you with an indication of the degree of variability in a frequency distribution, measures of association act as a guide to the degree of association between two variables. The measure or statistic itself ranges in value between –1 and +1, and it gives us information about the strength of an association. The closer to +1 or –1 the value is, the stronger is the association between two variables, and the closer to 0 the value is, the weaker is the association

303

FIGURE 10.1

−1	0	+1
Strong negative association	No association	Strong positive association

between two variables. The sign on the value—positive or negative—gives us information about the nature of an association (Figure 10.1).

To demonstrate how a measure of association works, let's go back to the example with which we began the last chapter, the association between *marital status* and *frequency of sexual activity* (Table 10.1). We found that married respondents were more likely to report higher levels of sexual activity than were nonmarried respondents. The association appeared to be at least moderate, because the differences in the percentages across the rows (the categories of the dependent variable—Not at All, Once a Month or Less, and so on) are fairly substantial in most of the rows.

Other than just "eyeballing" a contingency table, is there another way to assess the strength of an association? The answer is yes, with measures of association. Let's take one measure, called lambda. It is a measure appropriate for the variables *marital status* and *sex frequency,* and for Table 10.1, it has a value of .133.

The advantage of a measure like lambda is that it can be read as an index to the strength of an association, with 0 indicating no association and 1.0 indicating a perfect association. When there is no association between two variables, variations in the responses to the categories of one variable have no relationship to variations in responses to the categories of the second. Whether a respondent is married, widowed, separated, divorced, or never married would have nothing to do with, or no relationship to, how respondents answered the question about frequency of sexual activity. On the other hand, in perfect associations, the variations in the responses to the categories of one variable are tied to variations in the responses to the categories of a second variable. In a perfect association, every married respondent would have sex two to three times a week or more,

TABLE 10.1 Contingency Table for the *marital* and Recoded *sexual frequency* Variables in the GSS 2002 subset C File

RCSXFREQ Recoded sex frequency variable * MARITAL Marital status Crosstabulation

			MARITAL Marital status					
			1 MARRIED	2 WIDOWED	3 DIVORCED	4 SEPARATED	5 NEVER MARRIED	Total
RCSXFREQ Recoded sex frequency variable	0 NOT AT ALL	Count	37	86	69	10	64	266
		% within MARITAL Marital status	7.1%	90.5%	33.0%	23.8%	21.8%	22.9%
	1 ONCE A MONTH OR LESS	Count	95	5	44	13	63	220
		% within MARITAL Marital status	18.1%	5.3%	21.1%	31.0%	21.4%	18.9%
	2 ABOUT ONCE A WEEK	Count	230	4	53	7	90	384
		% within MARITAL Marital status	43.9%	4.2%	25.4%	16.7%	30.6%	33.0%
	3 2-3 TIMES A WEEK OR MORE	Count	162		43	12	77	294
		% within MARITAL Marital status	30.9%		20.6%	28.6%	26.2%	25.3%
Total		Count	524	95	209	42	294	1164
		% within MARITAL Marital status	100.0%	100.0%	100.0%	100.0%	100.0%	100.0%

and those respondents who are not married would not have sex at all. Whether one is married would guarantee one's response to a variable measuring frequency of sexual activity.

Very few measures of association will produce values indicating no association whatsoever or a perfect association. Most will fall somewhere in between. A value of .113, because it's much closer to 0 (no association) than 1 (perfect association), suggests that the association between the variables *marital status* and *sex frequency* is a fairly weak one. We will explore exactly what this means in this chapter.

In addition, you will learn how to apply measures of association: which measures can be used with which levels of measurement, how some of the measures are computed, and how they can be interpreted. We will start with interpretation, because many of these measures have common characteristics: They give us information about the strength and, in some cases, the nature of an association. Some of them tell us even more, because they have a proportional reduction in error interpretation that allows us to be more precise in our assessment of how much an independent variable is associated with a dependent variable. I will be illustrating the use of measures of association by returning to many of the variables we analyzed in Chapter 9. In this way, I can show you how the analysis of contingency tables is supplemented with (but not replaced by) measures of association.

Measures of Association and the Number Line

For interpreting measures of association it is helpful to have an understanding of the relationship between the numbers on a number line, because we rarely get measures of association that are at 0 or close to +1 or −1. It is more likely that we will get measures that are somewhere in between, and you have to know how to describe them. For example, in the association between marital status and frequency of sexual activity, a measure of association we might use equals .113. Where on the number line does that fall—closer to 0 or closer to 1? Let's break down the number line to find out (Figure 10.2).

The value .113 falls between .10 and .20, suggesting a fairly weak association between marital status and frequency of sexual activity.

Proportional Reduction in Error Interpretation

What does "weak association" mean exactly? In addition to their interpretation in the context of the number line, some measures of association have an interpretation called **proportional reduction in error** (or PRE). To understand this

FIGURE 10.2

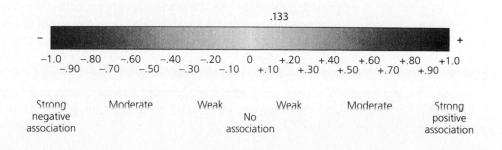

concept, let's remember back to when we were trying to assess the strength of the association between marital status and frequency of sexual activity. I asked you to think of the situation in terms of gambling. Imagine that I pick a married respondent and a widowed respondent at random from the respondents to the General Social Survey. Then I ask you to bet on the one most likely to be sexually active. If you know something about the association between the variables *marital status* and *sex frequency,* you can make a better guess than if you don't know anything about the association. The extent to which you can make a better guess is what proportional reduction in error assesses.

How much does knowing the nature of an independent–dependent variable relationship improve our ability to guess (or, more precisely, to reduce our errors in guessing) the dependent variable? In this case, the PRE statistic tells us the proportion (.113) by which errors at guessing someone's party affiliation would be reduced if we knew the association between marital status and frequency of sexual activity. By multiplying the PRE statistic times 100, we can compute the percentage of the reduction in errors, or 13%. Knowing that married respondents are likely to be having sex more frequently than widowed, separated, divorced, or never married respondents reduces our errors at predicting or guessing the respondents' level of sexual activity by 13%. This is a small reduction, suggesting a somewhat weak association between the variables *marital status* and *sex frequency.*

Nature of an Association

Measures of association for ordinal and numerical variables have signs, positive and negative. A negative association is indicated by the minus sign (–) attached to the measure. A positive association is indicated by the absence of any sign at all.

What does the sign tell us? If you remember the discussion in Chapter 9 about positive and negative associations (see "Interpreting Tables with Ordinal or Numerical Variables" on page 287), you may guess that a positive association means that as the value of one variable increases, the value of the second variable increases as well. The larger is the value of an independent variable, the larger is the value of a dependent variable. If you looked at the association between education and income, you would get a measure of association with a positive value, suggesting that the more education a respondent has, the higher the person's earnings are likely to be.

A negative sign on an association indicates that as the value of one variable goes up, the value of the other variable goes down. As the value of an independent variable rises, for example, the value of a dependent variable may fall (or as the value on an independent variable falls, the value of a dependent variable goes up). For example, the sign on an appropriate measure of association for the relationship between education and the number of children a respondent has would be negative, suggesting that the more education respondents have, the fewer children they are likely to have (or, conversely, the less education respondents have, the more children they are likely to have).

These concepts may become clearer as we turn our attention to some of the specific measures we can use, their applications, and their interpretations. ■

MEASURES OF ASSOCIATION FOR NOMINAL VARIABLES

Measures of association, like all other statistics, have to be applied correctly. Each measure of association is more (or less) appropriate depending on the level at which variables are being measured. In addition, they each make certain assumptions about relationships between variables, such as whether a chart of the relationship between the variables reveals a linear association. They also make certain assumptions about the variables involved in an association, such as whether they are continuous or discrete and, in the case of numerical level variables, if the distribution of responses to the variable is normal.

Measures of association for nominal variables are used whenever one or both variables in a bivariate association are nominal. For example, in the association between marital status and frequency of sexual activity, we are working with one nominal variable and one ordinal variable, but in the association between sex and marital status we are working with two nominal variables. In either case, measures of association for nominal variables are applied.

There are several measures of association we can use with nominal variables. Of these measures, we will look at one, lambda, in detail. You will be introduced to a few more later on.

Lambda

Lambda is a measure of association for use with nominal variables, which means that it is used whenever both of the variables in a pair are nominal, or when one of the variables is nominal and the other is ordinal.

Interpreting lambda   Lambda can range in value from 0 to 1.0. The closer the value of lambda is to 0, the weaker is the association; the closer it is to 1, the stronger is the association. Associations involving nominal variables have no direction. Consequently, lambda has no direction; it can never be a negative number, but the fact that it is positive doesn't tell us anything about the nature of an association.

Lambda has a proportional reduction in error interpretation, however. To get a better handle on this concept, let's go through the logic of the computation of lambda. Suppose you had to place a bet on how often someone picked at random from the respondents to the General Social Survey has sex, knowing only that people in general are more likely to have sex about once a week than not at all, once a month or less, or two to three times a week or more. You would have to guess that the person has sex about once a week. Now imagine you do this for each and every respondent to the General Social Survey. Assume they are having sex about once a week. How many mistakes or errors would you make in trying to guess their level of sexual activity?

To find out, you have to compare the number of respondents who really have sex about once a week to the number that you guessed might be having sex about once a week (all of them). How can you do that? Just look back at the contingency table for the variables *marital* and *sex frequency* in Table 10.1. You guessed that all 1,164 respondents are having sex about once a week, but it turns out that only 384 of them are having sex about once a week. (How do you know?

Look at the row marginal total for the category About Once a Week.) Thus, 384 of your guesses were right, but 780 of your guesses (1,164 minus 384) were wrong. If you divide the number of wrong guesses, 780 by the total number of guesses you made, 1,164, you will find your proportion of error, .67. If you multiply your proportion of error by 100 you will obtain your percentage of error, 67%. This means that 67% of your guesses were wrong.

Now, assume you know something about the association between the independent and dependent variables—that married respondents are more likely to have sex frequently than are widowed, divorced, separated, or never married respondents. What happens to your ability to guess? If you are presented with a respondent to the GSS, told that the respondent is married, then asked to place a bet on his or her frequency of sexual activity, you will bet that he or she has sex about once a week. On the other hand, if you are presented with a widowed respondent, you will bet that he or she does not have sex at all. You will bet that divorced respondents do not have sex at all, that separated respondents have sex once a month or less, and that never married respondents have sex about once a week.

How many respondents will be correctly classified if you do this for each person in the GSS? Again, the answer can be found in the contingency table. You can see that 230 married respondents have sex about once a week. This mean that you will get 230 of your guesses right for married respondents, but you will get 294 wrong (524, the total number of married respondents, minus 230). For widowed respondents, you will get 86 guesses right (the number of widowed respondents who do not have sex at all), but you will get 9 wrong (95, the number of widowed respondents, minus 86).

 Skills Practice 1 Find out how many correct guesses you will make for the divorced, separated, and never married respondents. How many errors will you make for each of those categories?

If you add up all of your correct guesses for all categories of the variable *marital*, you will make a total of 488 correct guesses (230 + 86 + 69 + 13 + 90). You will make a total of 676 mistakes (294 + 9 + 140 + 29 + 204). By dividing your mistakes, 676, by 1,164 (the total number of respondents), you can figure your proportion of error, .58. If you multiply the proportion of error by 100, you can compute the percentage of error, 58%.

Are your guesses better if you know something about the association between the independent and dependent variables? Yes, but not much. If you try to guess frequency of sexual activity without knowing anything about the association between the variables *marital status* and *sex frequency*, you will guess correctly 384 times, and if you know the association between the variables, you will guess correctly 488 times, for a total of 104 *more* correct guesses (488 minus 384).

The *proportion* of the reduction in error is found by dividing this difference, 104, by the number of mistakes you would make if you knew nothing about the association between the variables, 780. The PRE = 104 ÷ 780 = .13. If you multiply this result by 100, you have the PRE as a percentage, 13%. How is this interpreted?

First, very roughly, this tells us that knowing the nature of the association between the variables (married respondents have sex more often than widowed, divorced, separated, or never married respondents) improves our ability to guess the dependent variable (frequency of sexual activity) by 13%. More specifically, what this number tells us is that we make 13% fewer errors at guessing the dependent variable if we know the association between the independent and dependent variables than if we don't know what it is.

We can look at this number another way using the proportions of error we computed. We found that

> the proportion of errors you would make if you try to guess the dependent variable not knowing anything about the association between the independent and dependent variables is .67, and

> the proportion of errors you would make if you do know the association is .58.

We can subtract .58 from .67 to find the *difference* between the proportions of errors we would make based on whether we know what the association is between the independent and dependent variables. To find the proportional *reduction* in error, we divide the amount of the difference, .09, by the proportion of errors we would make if we don't know what the association is between the independent and dependent variables: .09 ÷ .67 = .13. Hence, the proportional reduction in error is .13, or 13%.

Computing lambda   Fortunately, the process described at length in the preceding section can be reduced to a fairly simple formula:

Formula 10.1: Lambda

$$\lambda = \frac{E_1 - E_2}{E_1}$$

where E_1 is the number of errors you would make guessing the dependent variable if you did not know the independent variable, and E_2 is the number of errors you would make guessing the dependent variable if you knew the categories of the independent variable.

To find E_1, simply subtract the largest row marginal total from N. To find E_2, add up the highest frequencies of each category of the independent variable and subtract the sum from N.

EXAMPLE:

Let's find lambda for the association between the recoded region variable (*rcregion*) and frequency of sexual activity (*rcsxfreq*). Table 10.2 is a contingency table for the association between *rcregion* and *rcsxfreq*.

TABLE 10.2   Contingency Table for the Association between the Recoded *region* and *sex frequency* Variables in the GSS 2002 subset C File

RCSXFREQ Recoded sex frequency variable * RCREGION Recoded region of interview Crosstabulation

| | | | RCREGION Recoded region of interview | | | | |
			1 NORTHEAST	2 MIDWEST	3 SOUTHEAST	4 WEST	Total
RCSXFREQ Recoded sex frequency variable	0 NOT AT ALL	Count	73	65	69	59	266
		% within RCREGION Recoded region of interview	29.7%	22.0%	19.4%	22.1%	22.9%
	1 ONCE A MONTH OR LESS	Count	46	59	66	49	220
		% within RCREGION Recoded region of interview	18.7%	19.9%	18.6%	18.4%	18.9%
	2 ABOUT ONCE A WEEK	Count	80	101	106	97	384
		% within RCREGION Recoded region of interview	32.5%	34.1%	29.9%	36.3%	33.0%
	3 2-3 TIMES A WEEK OR MORE	Count	47	71	114	62	294
		% within RCREGION Recoded region of interview	19.1%	24.0%	32.1%	23.2%	25.3%
Total		Count	246	296	355	267	1164
		% within RCREGION Recoded region of interview	100.0%	100.0%	100.0%	100.0%	100.0%

Skills Practice 2   Analyze the association between *rcregion* and *rcsxfreq* in Table 10.2. Describe the nature and the strength of the association.

Let's see whether lambda confirms our analysis of the strength of the association. Start the process of computing lambda by finding E_1.

Step 1.   Look down the row marginal totals until you find the highest frequency of the dependent variable *rcsxfreq*. The highest frequency is associated with the category About Once a Week, so circle the frequency for that category, 384. Find E_1 by subtracting 384 from N. $E_1 = 1,164 - 384 = 780$.

Step 2.   Find E_2 by looking down each column of the independent variable and circling the highest frequency in each column (excluding the column marginal totals). In the column Northeast, the highest frequency is 80. Circle it. In the next column, Midwest, the highest frequency is 101, so circle it. Circle 114 in the Southeast column and 97 in the West column. Now add the circled frequencies. $80 + 101 + 114 + 97 = 392$. Subtract 392 from N to get E_2. $E_2 = 1,164 - 392 = 772$.

Step 3.   Apply Formula 10.1.

$$E_1 = 780 \qquad E_2 = 772$$

$$\lambda = \frac{E_1 - E_2}{E_1} = \frac{780 - 772}{780} = \frac{8}{780} = .010$$

Interpretation   Read the value .010 as a guide to the strength of the association between one's region of residence and party affiliation.

Our conclusion that the relationship is very weak is confirmed. Knowing the nature of the association between the independent and dependent variables improves our ability to predict the dependent variable very little. In relation to the errors we might make in predicting sexual activity *without* knowing the independent variable, we can reduce our mistakes (or improve our guesses) only by about 1% (.010 × 100).

CHECKING YOUR WORK

Lambda will always result in a positive number with a value between 0 and 1.0. If you get a negative number, or a number greater than 1.0, you have done something wrong. Make sure you have

- Subtracted the *single* highest row marginal total from *N*.
- Circled and added up each of the highest frequencies for *each* of the categories of the independent variable (you will have as many frequencies as there are categories) and subtracted the result from *N*.

Skills Practice 3   Analyze the nature and strength of the association between the *work status* and *sex frequency* variables in Table 10.3. Then compute and interpret lambda.

A limitation of lambda   All statistics have their limits—patterns they are good at finding and not so good at finding. For lambda, one limitation is that it treats as "no association" (with a value of 0) those patterns in which all of the highest frequencies for each category of the independent variable line up in the same row. To see how this can happen, find lambda for Table 10.4.

Your computations should look like these:

$$\lambda = \frac{E_1 - E_2}{E_1} = \frac{780 - 780}{780} = \frac{0}{780} = 0$$

When you get a lambda equal to zero, does that necessarily mean there is no association between these two variables? No. If you read across the rows—the categories of the dependent variable—it is clear that there is an association. Males have sex more frequently than do females. The association is not particularly strong, but there is a clear pattern of association nevertheless.

For a contingency table like this one, lambda is misleading. Even though lambda is zero, it doesn't mean that there is no association between the variables. The table shows us that there is an association. The fact that we get a computation of zero is simply a limitation of the statistic. Later on in this chapter you will be introduced to some additional measures of association for nominal variables that do not have this limitation.

TABLE 10.3 Contingency Table for the Recoded *work status* and *sex frequency* Variables in the GSS 2002 subset C File

RCSXFREQ Recoded sex frequency variable * RCWKSTAT Recoded labor force status Crosstabulation

			RCWKSTAT Recoded labor force status			
			1 WORKING	2 NOT WORKING	3 NOT IN THE MARKET	Total
RCSXFREQ Recoded sex frequency variable	0 NOT AT ALL	Count	122	14	130	266
		% within RCWKSTAT Recoded labor force status	16.4%	17.9%	37.9%	22.9%
	1 ONCE A MONTH OR LESS	Count	131	17	72	220
		% within RCWKSTAT Recoded labor force status	17.6%	21.8%	21.0%	18.9%
	2 ABOUT ONCE A WEEK	Count	279	29	76	384
		% within RCWKSTAT Recoded labor force status	37.6%	37.2%	22.2%	33.0%
	3 2-3 TIMES A WEEK OR MORE	Count	211	18	65	294
		% within RCWKSTAT Recoded labor force status	28.4%	23.1%	19.0%	25.3%
Total		Count	743	78	343	1164
		% within RCWKSTAT Recoded labor force status	100.0%	100.0%	100.0%	100.0%

TABLE 10.4 Contingency Table for the *sex* and Recoded *sex frequency* Variables in the GSS 2002 subset C File

RCSXFREQ Recoded sex frequency variable * SEX Respondents' sex Crosstabulation

			SEX Respondents' sex		Total
			1 MALE	2 FEMALE	
RCSXFREQ Recoded sex frequency variable	0 NOT AT ALL	Count	78	188	266
		% within SEX Respondents' sex	15.1%	29.0%	22.9%
	1 ONCE A MONTH OR LESS	Count	108	112	220
		% within SEX Respondents' sex	20.9%	17.3%	18.9%
	2 ABOUT ONCE A WEEK	Count	182	202	384
		% within SEX Respondents' sex	35.3%	31.2%	33.0%
	3 2-3 TIMES A WEEK OR MORE	Count	148	146	294
		% within SEX Respondents' sex	28.7%	22.5%	25.3%
Total		Count	516	648	1164
		% within SEX Respondents' sex	100.0%	100.0%	100.0%

MEASURES OF ASSOCIATION FOR ORDINAL VARIABLES

In addition to measures of association for nominal variables, there are separate measures for pairs of variables in which *both* variables are ordinal. The most meaningful difference between measures for nominal variables and measures for ordinal variables is that the sign—positive or negative—of the measures is important. As with nominal variables, there are a variety of measures of association that can be used with pairs of ordinal variables. Let's start by learning about one of them, gamma.

Gamma

Gamma is a measure of association that, like lambda, has a proportional reduction in error interpretation. Conceptually, though, gamma is a little different. To explain it, let's assume we are interested in the relationship between a respondent's frequency of sexual activity and the person's perception of his or her life as exciting, routine, or dull. You may recall from the SPSS exercise in the previous chapter that the general pattern among the 2002 GSS respondents is that the higher the level of sexual activity, the more likely respondents were to say that life is exciting. How can we assess the strength of the association? The answer is relatively simple—by comparing each of the respondents on their answers to each of the variables.

It will help to follow this example if you recall that the values of the variable, is life exciting or dull, are scored form 1 (dull) to 3 (exciting). The *higher* the value of the variable, the more exciting the respondent says life is. The values of the variable, frequency of sexual activity, run from 1 (not at all) to 4 (two to three times a week or more). The higher the value is, the greater the frequency of sexual activity.

To illustrate the process of comparing respondents on their answers to pairs of variables, let's take the answers given by four respondents to the two variables *is life exciting or dull* and *sex frequency.*

	sex frequency	*is life exciting or dull*
Respondent A	About once a week (value 3)	Routine (value 2)
Respondent B	2–3 times a week or more (value 4)	Exciting (value 3)
Respondent C	2–3 times a week or more (value 4)	Dull (value 1)
Respondent D	About once a week (value 3)	Exciting (value 3)

If we start by comparing the answers of respondent A to those given by respondent B, we see that respondent B has sex more frequently and thinks life is more exciting than respondent A. Respondent B scores higher (when looking at the values) on both categories of each variable. Based on just these two respondents, this suggests a positive association between the two variables. The more sex one has, the more exciting life is likely to be; the less sex, the less exciting. We call these relationships between cases **concordant pairs**. One respondent is lower (or higher) than the other on both categories of the variables being compared.

Now let's compare respondent A to respondent C. In this case, we see that respondent C has sex more often than respondent A, but also says life is less exciting than respondent A. Based on the comparison between these two cases—A and C—we can assume a negative association between these two variables. Respondent C scores *higher* on the sex frequency scale than respondent A, but *lower* on the life excitement variable (based on the values of the categories). This is called a **discordant pair**—one respondent scores higher (or lower) than the other on one category of the variable being compared, but lower (or higher) on the second category.

Finally, let's compare respondent A to respondent D. Respondent D is tied with respondent A on the sex frequency variable (they each have the same value), but respondent D is higher than respondent A on the life excitment variable. This is called a **tied pair**. Pairs for which the respondents are the same on either or both values of the categories being compared are called tied pairs.

Skills Practice 4   Test your knowledge of these concepts of concordant, discordant, and tied pairs by comparing respondent A in the following chart below with respondents B, C, D, and E. Are A's responses concordant, discordant, or tied in comparison to those of the others?

	sex frequency	*is life exciting or dull*
Respondent A	About once a week (value 3)	Routine (value 2)
Respondent B	Once a month or less (value 2)	Dull (value 1)
Respondent C	Once a month or less (value 2)	Routine (value 2)
Respondent D	About once a week (value 3)	Dull (value 1)
Respondent E	Once a month or less (value 2)	Exciting (value 3)

Although you have compared only a few cases to get a handle on the concept of concordant, discordant, and tied pairs, the computation of gamma, in essence, involves comparing every case (every respondent) in a set of data against every other respondent in the data. Can you imagine doing this for 1,500 cases? Luckily for us, it isn't necessary to do these one by one to compute gamma.

The gamma statistic is figured by dividing the difference between the number of concordant and discordant pairs by the sum of all concordant and discordant pairs. The formula for gamma is

Formula 10.2: Gamma

$$\text{Gamma} = \frac{C - D}{C + D}$$

where C stands for the number of concordant pairs, and D represents the number of discordant pairs.[1]

To find gamma, subtract the number of discordant pairs from the number of concordant pairs, then divide the result by the sum of concordant and discordant pairs. As you can probably tell, if there are more concordant than discordant pairs, the gamma value will be positive. If there are more discordant

---

[1]Note that tied pairs are excluded from the computation of gamma. Excluding tied pairs has consequences for the interpretation of gamma that will be discussed later in this chapter.

TABLE 10.5 Contingency Table for the Recoded *sex frequency* and *life* Variables for a Randomly Selected Sample of 47 Respondents from the GSS 2002

LIFE Is life exciting or dull? * RCSXFREQ Recoded sex frequency variable Crosstabulation

| | | | RCSXFREQ Recoded sex frequency variable | | | | |
			0 NOT AT ALL	1 ONCE A MONTH OR LESS	2 ABOUT ONCE A WEEK	3 2-3 TIMES A WEEK OR MORE	Total
LIFE Is life exciting or dull?	1 DULL	Count	1		1		2
		% within RCSXFREQ Recoded sex frequency variable	11.1%		5.0%		4.3%
	2 ROUTINE	Count	4	3	8	3	18
		% within RCSXFREQ Recoded sex frequency variable	44.4%	37.5%	40.0%	30.0%	38.3%
	3 EXCITING	Count	4	5	11	7	27
		% within RCSXFREQ Recoded sex frequency variable	44.4%	62.5%	55.0%	70.0%	57.4%
Total		Count	9	8	20	10	47
		% within RCSXFREQ Recoded sex frequency variable	100.0%	100.0%	100.0%	100.0%	100.0%

than concordant pairs, the gamma value will be negative. The larger the difference is between the number of concordant and discordant pairs, the larger the gamma value will be. Because gamma can be positive or negative, the possible values of gamma range from −1.0 to +1.0. The closer gamma is to either −1 or +1, the stronger is the association; the closer to 0, the weaker the association.

To show you how to find the number of concordant and discordant pairs, let's use a table constructed from a random sample of 47 respondents to the 2002 GSS for the variables *sex frequency* and *is life exciting or dull* (Table 10.5).

As with all measures of association, begin your analysis with an understanding of the association in the contingency table. The general pattern in this subsample of 2002 GSS respondents is like the one we saw among all respondents. It appears that the more sex respondents have, the more exciting they think life is. The relationship appears to be somewhat strong.

Finding concordant pairs   How can we assess the strength and nature of the association with gamma? First, we find the number of concordant pairs in the table. To do so we start with the cell in the top left corner of the table as our point of comparison—equivalent to our respondent A in the previous illustration. Let's call this cell A. In cell A there is one respondent who has sex not at all and says his life is dull—scoring a 1 on the sex frequency variable as well as on the life excitement variable. Where do we find the respondents who scored higher on both variables in relation to the respondent in cell A? They are below and to the right of cell A, in cells F, G, H, J, K, and L. (Figure 10.3 illustrates the relationship.) Why? Think about it a second. The respondents in cell F all said they have sex once a month or less (value 2 on the sex frequency variable) *and* they think that life is routine (value 2 on life excitement)—higher on both categories of the

Cell A 1	Cell B 0	Cell C 1	Cell D 0
Cell E 4	Cell F 3	Cell G 8	Cell H 3
Cell I 4	Cell J 5	Cell K 11	Cell L 7

FIGURE 10.3
Concordant pairs in relation to Cell A.

Cell A 1	Cell B 0	Cell C 1	Cell D 0
Cell E 4	Cell F 3	Cell G 8	Cell H 3
Cell I 4	Cell J 5	Cell K 11	Cell L 7

FIGURE 10.4
Concordant pairs for Cell B.

variables being compared to the respondent in cell A. The respondents in cell G have sex about once a week (value 3) and think life is routine (value 2)—also higher on both categories in comparison to the respondent in cell A.

To find the number of concordant pairs in relation to cell A, we add the number of respondents in all of the cells below and to the right of cell A together, and we multiply the result by the number of respondents in cell A. We call the number of respondents in a cell the cell frequency, so we can find the number of concordant pairs in relation to cell A by multiplying the frequency for cell A by the sum of the cell frequencies for cells F, G, H, J, K, and L. The concordant pairs in relation to cell A are $1(3 + 8 + 3 + 5 + 11 + 7) = 1(37) = 37$.

This isn't the end of the process, because we have to find the number of concordant pairs for all of the cells in the table. Having found the number of concordant pairs in relation to cell A, we move to the right across the table to cell B. This is a little tricky, because there are no respondents in cell B (Figure 10.4). Consequently, there are no concordant pairs in relation to that cell. When you encounter empty cells (cells with no respondents in them), the value of the concordant or discordant pairs in relation to the empty cell is zero.

Let's move another cell to the right, to cell C. What are the concordant pairs in relation to cell C? They are found in cells H and L—the only two cells below and to the right of cell C. The number of concordant pairs in relation to cell C is 10. Multiply the cell frequency in cell C, 1, by the frequencies in cells H and L: $1(3 + 7) = 1(10) = 10$ (see Figure 10.5).

Let's move one more cell to the right, to cell D. What are the concordant pairs in relation to cell D? This is a trick question, because there aren't any. There are no cells below and to the right (except for the row and column marginals, which don't count for the purpose of finding concordant pairs).

We do have to move down to the next row, though, starting on the left side, at cell E. Are there any concordant pairs for cell E? Yes, cells J, K, and L (see Figure 10.6). Can you calculate the total of concordant pairs in relation to cell E? The answer is $4(5 + 11 + 7) = 4(23) = 92$.

Move one cell to the right to cell F. Are there concordant pairs in relation to cell F? Yes, there are, but in cells K and L. Thus, the number of concordant pairs in relation to cell F is: $3(11 + 7) = 3(18) = 54$. See Figure 10.7.

Cell A 1	Cell B 0	Cell C 1	Cell D 0
Cell E 4	Cell F 3	Cell G 8	Cell H 3
Cell I 4	Cell J 5	Cell K 11	Cell L 7

FIGURE 10.5
Concordant pairs in relation to Cell C.

Cell A 1	Cell B 0	Cell C 1	Cell D 0
Cell E 4	Cell F 3	Cell G 8	Cell H 3
Cell I 4	Cell J 5	Cell K 11	Cell L 7

FIGURE 10.6
Concordant pairs for Cell E.

Cell A 1	Cell B 0	Cell C 1	Cell D 0
Cell E 4	Cell F 3	Cell G 8	Cell H 3
Cell I 4	Cell J 5	Cell K 11	Cell L 7

FIGURE 10.7
Concordant pairs for Cell F.

Cell A 1	Cell B 0	Cell C 1	Cell D 0
Cell E 4	Cell F 3	Cell G 8	Cell H 3
Cell I 4	Cell J 5	Cell K 11	Cell L 7

FIGURE 10.8
Concordant pairs for Cell G.

Move one more cell to the right to cell G. There is only one cell, cell H, that is concordant (below and to the right) in relation to cell G (see Figure 10.8). The number of concordant cells in relation to cell G is $8 \times 7 = 56$.

Note that there are no concordant cells for cells I, J, K, or L, because there are no cells below and to the right of those cells.

To get the total number of concordant pairs for all cells, we have to add up the number of concordant pairs we found in relation to cells A, B, C, E, F, and G.

Concordant pairs in relation to cell A = 37
Concordant pairs in relation to cell B =   0
Concordant pairs in relation to cell C = 10
Concordant pairs in relation to cell E = 92
Concordant pairs in relation to cell F = 54
Concordant pairs in relation to cell G = 56
Total number of concordant pairs   = 249

Cell A 1	Cell B 0	Cell C 1	Cell D 0
Cell E 4	Cell F 3	Cell G 8	Cell H 3
Cell I 4	Cell J 5	Cell K 11	Cell L 7

Cell A 1	Cell B 0	Cell C 1	Cell D 0
Cell E 4	Cell F 3	Cell G 8	Cell H 3
Cell I 4	Cell J 5	Cell K 11	Cell L 7

FIGURE 10.9
Discordant pairs for Cell D.

FIGURE 10.10
Discordant pairs for Cell C.

Finding discordant pairs   The next step is to find the discordant pairs—the pairs that would be higher on the values of one variable but lower on the values of the other. Start the process of finding discordant pairs in the upper right corner of the contingency table, with cell D. This is a little tricky, because there are no respondents in cell D. Remember that when you encounter empty cells, the value of the concordant or discordant pairs in relation to the empty cell is zero.

Had there been respondents in cell D, which cells would have been discordant in relation to cell D? The answer is all cells below and to the left of cell D. Respondents in cell D would have had sex two to three times a week or more (at value 4 of the sex frequency variable) and they would think life is dull (at value 1 of the life excitement variable). Respondents below and to the left are all lower on the values of the independent variable but higher on the values of the dependent variable. Take for example the respondents in cell G, who have less sex (value 2, lower than any respondents who might have been in cell D) and think life is routine (value 2, higher than any respondents who might have been in cell D). See Figure 10.9.

Now we move one cell to the left, to cell C. The cells that are discordant in relation to cell C are below and to the left: cells E, F, I, and J. To find the number of discordant pairs in relation to cell C, multiply the cell frequency of cell C by the sum of the cell frequencies of cells E, F, I, and J: $1(4 + 3 + 4 + 5) = 1(16) = 16$. See Figure 10.10.

Move another cell to the left, to cell B. Cell B has no respondents, so there are no discordant pairs in relation to cell B (see Figure 10.11). There are also no discordant pairs in relation to cell A (because there are no cells below and to the left), so we move down one row and all the way to the right to cell H.

The cells that are discordant in relation to cell H are cells I, J, and K. The number of pairs that are discordant in relation to cell H are $3(4 + 5 + 11) = 3(20) = 60$. See Figure 10.12.

Now move to cell G. There are two discordant cells in relation to cell G, cells I and J. The number of pairs discordant in relation to cells I and J are $8(4 + 5) = 72$.

Finally, find the number of discordant pairs in relation to cell F. There is only one cell below and to the left of cell F, cell I, so the number of discordant pairs is just $3(4) = 12$.

To find the total number of discordant pairs, total the discordant pairs we found in relation to cells D, C, B, H, G, and F:

Cell A 1	Cell B 0	Cell C 1	Cell D 0
Cell E 4	Cell F 3	Cell G 8	Cell H 3
Cell I 4	Cell J 5	Cell K 11	Cell L 7

FIGURE 10.11
Discordant pairs for Cell B.

Cell A 1	Cell B 0	Cell C 1	Cell D 0
Cell E 4	Cell F 3	Cell G 8	Cell H 3
Cell I 4	Cell J 5	Cell K 11	Cell L 7

FIGURE 10.12
Discordant pairs for Cell H.

Discordant pairs in relation to cell D =   0
Discordant pairs in relation to cell C =   16
Discordant pairs in relation to cell B =   0
Discordant pairs in relation to cell H =   60
Discordant pairs in relation to cell G =   72
Discordant pairs in relation to cell F =   12
Total number of discordant pairs   = 160

Finding gamma   We have all the information we need to work our formula for gamma. C is the number of concordant pairs (249) and D is the number of discordant pairs (160).

$$\text{Gamma} = \frac{C - D}{C + D}$$

$$= \frac{249 - 160}{249 + 160} = \frac{89}{409}$$

$$\text{Gamma} = .22$$

CHECKING YOUR WORK

The result of your computation of gamma will always be a number between −1 and +1. You should not get a value of gamma less than −1 or greater than +1. If you do, you have made a mistake and you need to go back and check your work.

In reading gamma as a guide to the strength of the association, it is clear that the association in our table of 47 GSS respondents is weak. The sign on gamma is important. In this case it is positive, which tells us that a high value on the independent variable is associated with a high value on the dependent variable. The more sex respondents have, the more exciting they find life to be. Conversely, the less sex they have, the less exciting they find life to be. Finally, the PRE interpretation of gamma suggests that knowing the association between the independent and dependent variables improves our ability to predict the dependent variable by about 22%.

Avoiding Common Pitfalls: Computing gamma by hand

There are two aspects of computing gamma that students find a little tricky. First, it's easy to include row and column totals in the computations, especially when you are working with SPSS tables to practice your skills. Be sure you are clear about the difference between cell frequencies and the row and column marginals so that you only work with cell frequencies in your computations.

Second, the number of computations you have to do expands and contracts depending on the size of the table you are working with. The more cells a table has, the more computations you have to do; the fewer cells, the fewer computations. The number of computations is determined by how many concordant pairs (the cells below and to the right) and the number of discordant pairs (the cells below and to the left). Be sure when you do your computations that you are picking up all possible concordant and discordant pairs (without including row totals and column totals).

Another example of gamma   Let's try another example. This time, use the contingency table in Table 10.6.

Skills Practice 5   Write an analysis of the contingency table in Table 10.6. For this random sample of GSS respondents, what's the nature of the association between the respondents' ages and their frequency of sexual activity? Is it positive or negative; strong or weak?

TABLE 10.6   Contingency Table for the Recoded *age* and *sex frequency* Variables in the GSS 2002 for a Random Sample of 102 Respondents

RCSXFREQ Recoded sex frequency variable * RCAGE Recoded age variable Crosstabulation

			RCAGE Recoded age variable				
			1 18 THRU 25	2 26 THRU 40	3 41 THRU 60	4 61 THRU 89	Total
RCSXFREQ Recoded sex frequency variable	0 NOT AT ALL	Count	1	3	7	11	22
		% within RCAGE Recoded age variable	6.3%	8.6%	21.9%	57.9%	21.6%
	1 ONCE A MONTH OR LESS	Count	3	8	7	2	20
		% within RCAGE Recoded age variable	18.8%	22.9%	21.9%	10.5%	19.6%
	2 ABOUT ONCE A WEEK	Count	7	12	12	3	34
		% within RCAGE Recoded age variable	43.8%	34.3%	37.5%	15.8%	33.3%
	3 2-3 TIMES A WEEK OR MORE	Count	5	12	6	3	26
		% within RCAGE Recoded age variable	31.3%	34.3%	18.8%	15.8%	25.5%
Total		Count	16	35	32	19	102
		% within RCAGE Recoded age variable	100.0%	100.0%	100.0%	100.0%	100.0%

Now let's find gamma, using Formula 10.2.

$$\text{Gamma} = \frac{C - D}{C + D}$$

Find the concordant pairs   As you did in the preceding example, begin in the upper left corner of the table with cell A to find the number of pairs concordant in relation to cell A. Multiply the frequency in cell A by the sum of the frequencies in all cells below and to the right of cell A. You probably notice that you are working with more cells in this example than in the previous example, because the table is bigger. Remember that the number of computations you have to do depends on the size of (the number of cells in) the table. The concordant pairs in relation to cell A are $1(8 + 7 + 2 + 12 + 12 + 3 + 12 + 6 + 3) = 1(65) = 65$. See Figure 10.13.

 Skills Practice 6   Find the rest of the *concordant* pairs in Table 10.6. (Hint: Move to the right, to cell B. Find the concordant pairs in relation to cell B. Then move to the right again, to cell C, and find the concordant pairs in relation to cell C. When you have found all of the concordant pairs for the first row, move down to the second row. Begin on the far left with cell E. Find all of the concordant pairs for the cells on the second row. Move down to the third row and find the concordant pairs in relation to the cells in the third row.) When you have finished, add up all of the concordant pairs to get the total number of concordant pairs for the table.

Find the discordant pairs   Starting with the cell in the upper right corner of the table, cell D, find the discordant pairs. The discordant pairs in relation to cell D are those below and to the left of cell D. Multiply the cell frequency for cell D by the sum of the frequencies of the cells that are discordant in relation to cell D. The discordant pairs in relation to cell D are $11(3 + 8 + 7 + 7 + 12 + 12 + 5 + 12 + 6) = 11(72) = 792$. See Figure 10.14.

Cell A 1	Cell B 3	Cell C 7	Cell D 11
Cell E 3	Cell F 8	Cell G 7	Cell H 2
Cell I 7	Cell J 12	Cell K 12	Cell L 3
Cell M 5	Cell N 12	Cell O 6	Cell P 3

FIGURE 10.13
Concordant pairs for Cell A.

Cell A 1	Cell B 3	Cell C 7	Cell D 11
Cell E 3	Cell F 8	Cell G 7	Cell H 2
Cell I 7	Cell J 12	Cell K 12	Cell L 3
Cell M 5	Cell N 12	Cell O 6	Cell P 3

FIGURE 10.14
Discordant pairs for Cell D.

Skills Practice 7   Find the rest of the discordant pairs in Table 10.6. (Hint: Move to the left, to cell C. Find the discordant pairs in relation to cell C. Then move to the left again, to cell B, and find the discordant pairs in relation to cell B. When you have found all of the discordant pairs for the first row, move down to the second row. Begin on the far right with cell H. Find all of the discordant pairs for the cells on the second row. Follow the same process for the cells in the third row.) When you have finished, add up all of the discordant pairs to get the total number of discordant pairs for the table.

Finding gamma   Plug the total numbers of concordant pairs and discordant pairs into your formula for gamma.

$$\text{Gamma} = \frac{C - D}{C + D}$$
$$= \frac{889 - 1955}{889 + 1955} = \frac{-1066}{2844}$$
$$\text{Gamma} = -.37$$

Interpreting Gamma

The gamma statistic confirms the negative association we observed in the contingency table. The older the respondents are, the higher the values on the *age* variable, and the less sex the respondents have, the lower the values on the sex frequency variable. The younger the respondents are, the more sex they have. The association is fairly consistent across most categories of the sexual frequency variable. The gamma statistic is closer to 0 than to –1, indicating an association that is on the weaker side. Nevertheless, the PRE interpretation tells us that knowing the independent–dependent variable relationship improves our ability to predict the dependent variable by about 37%, and that's relatively good.

Limitations of Gamma

Like lambda, gamma is better at picking up on some kinds of patterns than others. First, gamma is a measure of association most appropriately used with symmetric associations—relationships between variables in which there is no clear independent–dependent association or causal relationship. Nevertheless, you often see gamma used as a measure of association, even when there is a clear logical causal connection between two variables.

Second, gamma is best at finding linear relationships between variables—associations in which the highest percentages across the rows of the table line up on the diagonal (as in Table 9.6 in Chapter 9). In Chapter 9 you learned that patterns of association could take other forms besides straight lines through the data in a table. Some examples of these patterns were illustrated in Figures 9.3 through 9.6 on p. 291. When patterns of association look more like those in Fig-

Skills Practice 8 Use the contingency table shown here to analyze the association between a respondent's television watching and his or her frequency of sexual activity. The table consists of a randomly selected sample of 72 respondents from the 2002 GSS.

A. What is the nature of the association between the variables? How strong is it? What is its direction?
B. Calculate and interpret gamma. Does gamma support your analysis of the table?

RCSXFREQ Recoded sex frequency variable * RCTVHRS Recoded hours per day watching TV Crosstabulation

| | | | RCTVHRS Recoded hours per day watching TV | | | | |
			0 NONE	1 ONE OR TWO HOURS	2 THREE OR FOUR HOURS	3 FIVE OR MORE HOURS	Total
RCSXFREQ Recoded sex frequency variable	0 NOT AT ALL	Count	1	2	5	5	13
		% within RCTVHRS Recoded hours per day watching TV	25.0%	6.7%	22.7%	31.3%	18.1%
	1 ONCE A MONTH OR LESS	Count		4	9	4	17
		% within RCTVHRS Recoded hours per day watching TV		13.3%	40.9%	25.0%	23.6%
	2 ABOUT ONCE A WEEK	Count	3	12	3	6	24
		% within RCTVHRS Recoded hours per day watching TV	75.0%	40.0%	13.6%	37.5%	33.3%
	3 2-3 TIMES A WEEK OR MORE	Count		12	5	1	18
		% within RCTVHRS Recoded hours per day watching TV		40.0%	22.7%	6.3%	25.0%
Total		Count	4	30	22	16	72
		% within RCTVHRS Recoded hours per day watching TV	100.0%	100.0%	100.0%	100.0%	100.0%

ures 9.3 through 9.6, taking gamma at face value, without complementing its interpretation with an analysis of the contingency table, would be misleading. To supplement (or replace) gamma in certain situations, you could use one or more of the measures described later on in this chapter.

Next, let's learn how to find and interpret measures of association using SPSS. In this section, you will learn how to find and interpret lambda and gamma, how to find and interpret some additional measures of association for nominal and ordinal variables, and how to use SPSS to introduce third variables into your analysis.

USING SPSS

Finding and Interpreting Measures of Association

SPSS GUIDE: MEASURES OF ASSOCIATION

To see the various measures of association available for use with contingency tables in SPSS, open the SPSS program, the GSS 2002 subset C file, and the Crosstabs dialog box. (Use the command path Analyze ➡ Descriptive Statistics ➡ Crosstabs.)

1 Click on the Statistics button to open the Crosstabs: Statistics window.

2 Notice the list of measures for nominal variables and the list for ordinal variables. Put the cursor on any of the measures and click with the right-most key on your mouse to see a description of it. Try it. Click again to close the description.

3 Click on Cancel to return to the Crosstabs dialog box.

Finding Lambda using SPSS

All of the measures of association for contingency tables, including lambda, are found using the Crosstabs command. At the Crosstabs dialog box, let's find lambda for the association between religion and attitudes toward premarital sex using the variables *rcrelig* and *premarsx*.

1 Enter the dependent variable, *premarsx,* as the row variable.

2 Enter the independent variable, *rcrelig,* as the column variable.

3 Click on Cells. At the Crosstabs: Cell Display window, look under Percentages and click on Column. Then click on Continue.

4 Click on Statistics.

The Crosstabs: Statistics window opens. Look for the measure of association you would like SPSS to compute. There are two sets of statistics, one labeled Nominal and one labeled Ordinal. Lambda is under the heading Nominal.

- Click on the box next to the measure you want to use, Lambda in this case, to make the ✔ appear in it.

If you want to see a description of the statistic, put your cursor on the word Lambda. Use the right-most click key on your mouse, and click. A description like this one will appear:

> A measure of association which reflects the proportional reduction in error when values of the independent variable are used to predict values of the dependent variable. A value of 1 means that the independent variable perfectly predicts the dependent variable. A value of 0 means that the independent variable is no help in predicting the dependent variable.

To close the description, click again with the right-most key.

■ Then click on Continue to return to the Crosstabs dialog box. At the Crosstabs dialog box, click on OK.

In addition to the contingency table for *rcrelig* and *premarsx*, you will get a set of statistics like the ones in Table 10.7.

There is quite a bit of output, but we will focus on just a few of the statistics, the lambda statistics. (If you do advanced work in this area, more of these results will make sense.) Lambda is the first set of statistics you come to in the table labeled Directional Measures, and there are three values of lambda in the column labeled Value.

The first value is a **symmetric value** of lambda, followed by two asymmetric measures. The symmetric computation of lambda is useful for pairs of variables in which there is no clear independent–dependent variable relationship. When lambda is figured this way, neither variable is treated as independent in relation to the other. Instead, it is assumed that the variables are *associated*, without one variable necessarily *causing* an effect on the other. (See the section in Chapter 1 on deciding which variable is independent in relation to the other if you need to review this concept.)

TABLE 10.7 Lamda Statistics for the Association between the Recoded *religion* and *attitudes toward premarital sex* Variables in the GSS 2002 subset C File

① Symmetric lambda

② Asymmetric lambda as you set up the table (consistent with the manual computation of lambda)

Directional Measures

			Value	Asymp. Std. Error[a]	Approx. T[b]	Approx. Sig.
Nominal by Nominal	Lambda	Symmetric	.025	.026	.927	.354
		PREMARSX Sex before marriage Dependent	.047	.050	.927	.354
		RCRELIG Recoded RS religious preference Dependent	.000	.000	.[c]	.[c]
	Goodman and Kruskal tau	PREMARSX Sex before marriage Dependent	.064	.014		.000[d]
		RCRELIG Recoded RS religious preference Dependent	.050	.013		.000[d]

a. Not assuming the null hypothesis.
b. Using the asymptotic standard error assuming the null hypothesis.
c. Cannot be computed because the asymptotic standard error equals zero.
d. Based on chi-square approximation.

③ Asymmetric lambda, looking at the independent–dependent relationship opposite from the way the table is set up, treating the column variable as dependent.

The next values are **asymmetric values** of lambda. These computations treat one of the variables in the pair as independent in relation to the other. The first asymmetric value treats the row variable in the contingency table as the dependent variable, as you did when you set up the table in SPSS. It is the value for which you learned the manual computation. The second value treats the column variable as the dependent variable, and it allows you to look at the relationship differently from the way you set it up in SPSS.

Even though these values make different assumptions about which variable is independent and which is dependent, most arrive at about the same number. In using lambda as an index, the values of lambda do not indicate a very strong association. Focusing on the asymmetric value of lambda that treats *premarsx* as the dependent variable (the second of the three computations of lambda), lambda indicates a weak association between the respondents' religious affiliation and their attitude toward premarital sex. Knowing the association between a respondent's religion and their attitude toward premarital sex only improves our ability to predict their attitude toward premarital sex by 5%.

Other Measures for Nominal Variables

Goodman and Kruskal's tau   When lambda doesn't help us out, what can we use instead? Look at the output chart in Table 10.7. There is another statistic that accompanies lambda—Goodman and Kruskal's tau. It has a similar (although not identical) PRE interpretation. It is an index to the strength of an association as well as an indicator of how much knowing the independent–dependent variable relationship improves our ability to predict the dependent variable. Moreover, tau doesn't have the limitation that lambda does; it won't show you a zero when there is an association between two variables.

As with lambda, you get more than one computation of tau, but both are asymmetric computations. The first one is for the association between *rcrelig* and *premarsx* with *premarsx* as the dependent variable. The second one treats *religion* as the dependent variable. What does it mean? First, like lambda, tau indicates that the association between religion and attitudes toward premarital sex is pretty weak. Second, it tells us that knowing the association between the independent and dependent variables reduces the proportion of errors we might make in predicting the dependent variable by about 6%.

Phi and Cramer's V   There is another set of measures in SPSS for nominal variables that you may find helpful—phi and Cramer's V. Phi can be used with contingency tables with no more than four cells (which means that each variable can have only two categories). Like lambda, the value of phi ranges from 0 to 1, and the value allows us to estimate the strength of an association. Unlike lambda, it does *not* have a proportional reduction in error interpretation.

Cramer's V is for contingency tables with more than four cells. Like phi, the value of Cramer's V ranges from 0 to 1, and it measures the strength of an association. Like phi, it does *not* have a proportional reduction in error interpretation.

Both of these measures can be found in the Crosstabs: Statistics window under the list of Nominal measures (follow the command path Analyze ➥ Descriptive Statistics ➥ Crosstabs, and at Crosstabs click on Statistics).

Skills Practice 9 Produce a contingency table, and find and interpret lambda for the following variables. (Before trying to interpret lambda, be sure you have a handle on what the contingency table reveals about the nature and strength of the association between the variables.)

A. Region of the country in which the respondents reside and attitudes toward premarital sex using *rcregion* and *premarsx*.
B. Martial status and life excitement using *marital* and *life*.
C. Sex of the respondents and attitudes toward premarital sex using *sex* and *premarsx*.

You have to decide which variables are the independent and dependent ones in each set. Depending on how you set up your table, be sure to select the correct version of lambda for interpretation. *For extra practice at computing lambda*, obtain the contingency tables by themselves first. Compute lambda by hand. Then get lambda using SPSS and check your answer.

Finding Gamma Using SPSS

Finding gamma is just like finding lambda. Follow the command path Analyze ➥ Descriptive Statistics ➥ Crosstabs. At the Crosstabs dialog box, click on the Statistics button. Look for gamma in the Crosstabs: Statistics window in the column labeled Ordinal. (See the SPSS Guide "Measures of Association" if you need help with this.)

Let's try finding gamma using the variables *reliten* (strength of respondents' religious affiliations) and *rcsxfreq* (frequency of sexual activity over the past year).

- Use the command path Analyze ➥ Descriptive Statistics ➥ Crosstabs to open the Crosstabs dialog box.
- At the Crosstabs window, scroll down the variable list to select your independent and dependent variables.
- Click on the Cells button to select Percentages for the Column. Then click on Continue.
- Click on the Statistics button to select Gamma from the list of Ordinal measures. Click on Continue.
- At the Crosstabs dialog box, click on OK.

Your output should include a contingency table and a set of statistics like the ones in Table 10.8.

TABLE 10.8   Contingency Table for the *reliten* and *rcsexfreq* Variables in the GSS 2002 subset C File

RCSXFREQ Recoded sex frequency variable * RELITEN Strength of affiliation Crosstabulation

| | | | RELITEN Strength of affiliation | | | | |
			1 NO RELIGION	2 NOT VERY STRONG	3 SOMEWHAT STRONG	4 STRONG	Total
RCSXFREQ Recoded sex frequency variable	0 NOT AT ALL	Count	33	88	33	110	264
		% within RELITEN Strength of affiliation	20.0%	19.1%	25.4%	27.3%	22.8%
	1 ONCE A MONTH OR LESS	Count	31	90	31	67	219
		% within RELITEN Strength of affiliation	18.8%	19.6%	23.8%	16.6%	18.9%
	2 ABOUT ONCE A WEEK	Count	56	163	38	125	382
		% within RELITEN Strength of affiliation	33.9%	35.4%	29.2%	31.0%	33.0%
	3 2-3 TIMES A WEEK OR MORE	Count	45	119	28	101	293
		% within RELITEN Strength of affiliation	27.3%	25.9%	21.5%	25.1%	25.3%
Total		Count	165	460	130	403	1158
		% within RELITEN Strength of affiliation	100.0%	100.0%	100.0%	100.0%	100.0%

Symmetric Measures

		Value	Asymp. Std. Error[a]	Approx. T[b]	Approx. Sig.
Ordinal by Ordinal	Gamma	-.070	.035	-1.980	.048
N of Valid Cases		1158			

[a.] Not assuming the null hypothesis.
[b.] Using the asymptotic standard error assuming the null hypothesis.

Interpretation

First, remember that you should begin your analysis with the contingency table. What does it tell us about the nature of the association, its strength and direction? Second, what does gamma add to the analysis?

> The association between strength of religious affiliation and frequency of sexual activity is a negative one. The stronger the respondents' religious affiliation, the lower the frequency of sexual activity reported. The relationship does not appear to be a very strong one. The differences in the percentages across the categories of the dependent variable are fairly small. Moreover, the pattern is not a consistent one across the categories of the dependent variable. For example, 27.3% of the respondents with no religious affiliation report having sex two to three times a week or more, but respondents with strong religious affiliations are close behind. 25.1% of those respondents report having sex two to three times a week or more.
>
> What does gamma add? The gamma statistic, −.070, is found in the column headed Value. It confirms our analysis of the association from the contingency table. The association is negative, meaning that the stronger the respondents' religious affiliation, the less frequently they have sex.
>
> The relationship is a weak one, with gamma much closer to 0 than to 1. Knowing the association between the respondents' strength of religious

affiliation and their frequency of sexual activity improves our ability to predict the respondents' level of sexual activity by about 7%.

Skills Practice 10 In a previous Skills Practice, you looked at the association between age, *rcage*, and frequency of sexual activity, *rcsxfreq*, for a random sample of GSS respondents. Now look at the association for all respondents. Produce a contingency table for the association between *rcage* and *rcsxfreq*, and use SPSS to find and interpret gamma.

Additional Measures of Association for Ordinal Variables

In addition to gamma, SPSS will compute several other statistics for measuring associations between ordinal variables. You can find these statistics by using the Analyze ➡ Descriptive Statistics ➡ Crosstabs command path. In the Crosstabs dialog box, click on the Statistics button. Under the heading, "Ordinal," you will see gamma, Somer's d, Kendall's tau-*b*, and Kendall's tau-*c*.

Somer's *d*

Unlike gamma (and like lambda), Somer's *d* has both a symmetric and an asymmetric computation. It doesn't ignore tied pairs, as does gamma. Consequently, it usually indicates weaker associations than does gamma. Somer's *d* is normally used instead of gamma when the association between two variables is clearly asymmetric.

Kendall's tau-*b* and Kendall's tau-*c*

Kendall's tau-*b* and tau-*c* are symmetric measures of association. They are similar in interpretation to gamma in that they function as indexes of association to help assess the strength of an association. The values of tau-*b* and tau-*c* range from −1 to +1. Tau-*b* can be used only with square contingency tables (tables in which the independent variable has the same number of categories as the dependent variable). Tau-*c* can be used with tables of any size. Tau-*b* and tau-*c* are different from gamma in that they do not ignore tied pairs. As a result, they normally indicate weaker associations than does gamma.

In the next section we will apply our measures of association to the analysis of third variables.

Controlling for a Third Variable

What Does "Control for a Third Variable" Mean?

Sometimes it is useful to examine relationships between two variables in the light of a **control (third) variable** through a process of analysis called **elabora-**

tion. For example, in addition to looking at the association between marital status and frequency of sexual activity, we may want to know whether the association is likely to be affected by the sex of the respondent. Is the association—that married respondents have sex more frequently than respondents who are widowed, separated, divorced, or never married—as true for males as for females? To explore this question, we can separate our sample into the categories of this third, or control, variable, *sex*.

To get an idea of what is happening to the data set when we control for a third variable, let's recall that the variable *sex* is divided into two categories—male and female. When we control for a variable like sex, we are, in effect, dividing our data set by the categories of the control variable, creating as many subsets of our data as there are categories of the control variable. In this case, using sex, we are creating two subsets of data: one for Male and one for Female. Dividing the data this way allows us to examine the association between marital status and frequency of sexual activity for each of our subsets, males and females. We can now see whether the association between marital status and sex frequency is as true for males as it is for females. Let's use SPSS and the GSS 2002 subset C file to perform this function and produce the partial tables and associated statistics.

Creating Contingency Tables Using a Control Variable

To control for third variables (subdivide our data set by the categories of a variable), we return to the Crosstabs command in SPSS.

SPSS GUIDE: PRODUCING CONTINGENCY TABLES USING A CONTROL VARIABLE

At the SPSS Data Editor window, follow the command path Analyze ➡ Descriptive Statistics ➡ Crosstabs. At the Crosstabs dialog box, follow these steps:

1 Select your dependent variable, *rcsxfreq*, from the variables list. Put it in the Row box.

2 Select your independent variable, *marital*, and put it in the Column box.

3 Select your control variable, *sex*: Scroll down to it with your mouse, click on it, and then click on the arrow pointing at the Layer 1 of 1 box.

4 Click on Cells. When the Crosstabs: Cell Display window opens, look under Percentages and click on Column. Then, click on Continue to return to the Crosstabs dialog box.

5 Click on the Statistics button and select an appropriate measure of association. The levels of measurement of your independent and dependent variables, not the control variable, govern the measure of association that you use. For the variables *marital* and *rcsxfreq*, lambda is appropriate.

6 Click on OK.

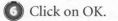

You should now be looking at a set of two tables—one contingency table for each category of the control variable. (The output looks like one large table, but note that it is really made up of several smaller tables—one for each of the categories of the control variable.) These smaller tables are also known as **partial tables** or simply "partials." In addition to the partial tables, you should see a set of statistics that contains measures of association for the relationship between *marital* and *rcsxfreq* in two groups—one for males and one for females. The partial tables and the statistics should look like the ones in Table 10.9.

Interpreting contingency tables using a control variable

How do we make sense of all this information? What are we looking for? There are several general patterns we should explore. First, we should look to see whether any association we saw between our variables of interest (without the influence of the control variable) is changed in any way across the categories of the control variable. Second, we should look to see in what way the association changes.

If the association weakens considerably, to the point where there is almost no association at all between the variables of interest across the categories of a third variable, we can conclude that something else accounts for the dependent and independent variables. When there is a third variable that operates as a logical causal explanation for an independent *and* a dependent variable, then the association that we observe between an independent and dependent variable is a **spurious association**. In order to conclude that an association between an independent and a dependent variable is a spurious one, the association that we observe between an independent and a dependent variable in a contingency table would have to weaken considerably in the partial tables when a third variable is

TABLE 10.9 Partial Tables for the Variables *marital* and *rcsxfreq* with the Control Variable *sex* in the GSS 2002 subset C File

RCSXFREQ Recoded sex frequency variable * MARITAL Marital status * SEX Respondents' sex Crosstabulation

SEX Respondents' sex					MARITAL Marital status					
				1 MARRIED	2 WIDOWED	3 DIVORCED	4 SEPARATED	5 NEVER MARRIED	Total
1 MALE	RCSXFREQ Recoded sex frequency variable	0 NOT AT ALL	Count	19	14	17	5	23	78
			% within MARITAL Marital status	7.7%	77.8%	19.8%	27.8%	15.5%	15.1%
		1 ONCE A MONTH OR LESS	Count	49	2	17	6	34	108
			% within MARITAL Marital status	19.9%	11.1%	19.8%	33.3%	23.0%	20.9%
		2 ABOUT ONCE A WEEK	Count	99	2	29	3	49	182
			% within MARITAL Marital status	40.2%	11.1%	33.7%	16.7%	33.1%	35.3%
		3 2-3 TIMES A WEEK OR MORE	Count	79		23	4	42	148
			% within MARITAL Marital status	32.1%		26.7%	22.2%	28.4%	28.7%
	Total		Count	246	18	86	18	148	516
			% within MARITAL Marital status	100.0%	100.0%	100.0%	100.0%	100.0%	100.0%
2 FEMALE	RCSXFREQ Recoded sex frequency variable	0 NOT AT ALL	Count	18	72	52	5	41	188
			% within MARITAL Marital status	6.5%	93.5%	42.3%	20.8%	28.1%	29.0%
		1 ONCE A MONTH OR LESS	Count	46	3	27	7	29	112
			% within MARITAL Marital status	16.5%	3.9%	22.0%	29.2%	19.9%	17.3%
		2 ABOUT ONCE A WEEK	Count	131	2	24	4	41	202
			% within MARITAL Marital status	47.1%	2.6%	19.5%	16.7%	28.1%	31.2%
		3 2-3 TIMES A WEEK OR MORE	Count	83		20	8	35	146
			% within MARITAL Marital status	29.9%		16.3%	33.3%	24.0%	22.5%
	Total		Count	278	77	123	24	146	648
			% within MARITAL Marital status	100.0%	100.0%	100.0%	100.0%	100.0%	100.0%

Directional Measures

SEX Respondents' sex				Value	Asymp. Std. Error[a]	Approx. T[b]	Approx. Sig.
1 MALE	Nominal by Nominal	Lambda	Symmetric	.031	.013	2.333	.020
			RCSXFREQ Recoded sex frequency variable Dependent	.045	.015	3.027	.002
			MARITAL Marital status Dependent	.015	.024	.617	.537
		Goodman and Kruskal tau	RCSXFREQ Recoded sex frequency variable Dependent	.037	.009		.000[c]
			MARITAL Marital status Dependent	.024	.008		.000[c]
2 FEMALE	Nominal by Nominal	Lambda	Symmetric	.191	.024	7.433	.000
			RCSXFREQ Recoded sex frequency variable Dependent	.229	.031	6.756	.000
			MARITAL Marital status Dependent	.146	.024	5.840	.000
		Goodman and Kruskal tau	RCSXFREQ Recoded sex frequency variable Dependent	.152	.012		.000[c]
			MARITAL Marital status Dependent	.120	.014		.000[c]

[a.] Not assuming the null hypothesis.
[b.] Using the asymptotic standard error assuming the null hypothesis.
[c.] Based on chi-square approximation.

introduced. To illustrate this concept, think about the research project I described in Chapter 1 that examined the effects of service-learning on student learning outcomes. My independent variable was whether students had participated in a service-learning course. My dependent variables were various student learning outcomes. Before I could conclude that service-learning accounted for higher achievement among service-learning students as compared to non-service-learning students, I had to take into account other variables that may have rendered the relationship spurious. Can you think of any variables that may have accounted for both the independent and dependent variables—involvement in a service-learning course and learning outcomes? One such variable that came to my mind was student motivation. Perhaps highly motivated students were more attracted to service-learning courses than less motivated students and highly motivated students tended to do better in their courses. If so, then student motivation could account for both participation in service-learning courses and higher achievement. In order to explore this idea, I looked at partial tables for the relationship between service-learning and various learning outcomes, controlling for variables such as student grade point averages to see if the independent–dependent variable relationship would hold even among students of similar academic achievement levels.

Associations between variables don't have to disappear in order to establish that a third variable has an effect on a relationship between and independent and dependent variable. After introducing a third variable, we may see that an association between the two variables still exists, but the nature and/or strength of the association changes across the categories of the control variable. Situations in which the strength or nature of an association between two variables changes across the categories of the control variable are called **conditional associations**. The strength of an association is conditional upon the category of the third variable. We can expect to find many associations that are at least conditional.

To begin the process of elaboration, we can analyze the association between marital status and sex frequency for *each category* of the control variable, males and females. Circle the highest percentage in each row of each table (not including the row marginal percentages or column marginal percentages). Commenting on the nature and the strength of the association in each table, we can make statements like the following:

Among males, it appears that the association between marital status and frequency of sexual activity is one in which married respondents have sex more frequently than do widowed, divorced, separated, or never married respondents. Widowed respondents are the respondents most likely to report having sex not at all, and separated respondents are the ones most likely to report having sex once a month or less.

Among females, the association between martial status and frequency of sexual activity is similar to that of male respondents. There are some important differences, though. Married female respondents are the ones most likely to report having sex about once a week, but separated respondents are the ones most likely to report having sex two to three times a week or more. Widowed respondents are the ones most likely to report having sex not at all, and separated respondents are the ones most likely to report having sex once a month or less.

Now we can compare the nature of the association and its strength for the two categories of the control variable with the association that we observed at the beginning of this chapter for all respondents. You may recall that the nature of the association among all respondents is just like the association we saw among the male respondents. Married respondents report having sex more frequently than do widowed, divorced, separated, or never married respondents. Widowed respondents are the ones most likely to report having sex not at all. Separated respondents are the ones who are most likely to say they have sex once a month or less. Lambda for the association among all respondents is .13. Does the nature or strength of the association between marital status and frequency of sexual activity change for males or females as measured by lambda?

It appears that, when the control variable is introduced, the nature of the association remains the same for males but changes a little among females. In addition, the association weakens for males (lambda = .045) but is stronger for females (lambda = .229). Consequently, the association is conditional. For males, the nature of the association between martial status and frequency of sexual activity is the same as it is among all respondents, but it is a weaker association. For females, the nature of the association changes a little. Separated (rather than married) respondents are the ones most likely to report having sex two to three times a week or more. However, the association among females is much stronger than it is for males and it is stronger among females than among respondents as a whole.

Skills Practice 11   Use the variables *marital* and *rcsxfreq* to look at the association between marital status and sex frequency, and control for the variable age using the *rcage* variable. Answer the following questions:

A. Is the nature of the association the same across the categories of the age variable?
B. For which category of the control variable is the association the strongest? For which is it the weakest? Use lambda to help you answer this question.
C. What general conclusions can you draw about the effect of the control variable, *rcage*, on the association between marital status and sex frequency?

Another Example

Let's try another example, this time using two ordinal variables: sex frequency *(rcsxfreq)* and life excitment *(life)*, controlling for *sex*. When we looked at the association between these variables earlier in this chapter, we found that the more frequently the respondents have sex, the more exciting they say their lives are. The association is positive, but gamma (.219) seems somewhat weak.

Produce a set of contingency tables for the association between *rcsxfreq* and *life*, controlling for *sex*. Don't forget to ask for percentages on the columns and for the gamma statistic. Your tables should look like the ones in Tables 10.10.

TABLE 10.10 Partial Tables for the Variables *rcsxfreq* and *life* with the Control Variable *sex* in the GSS 2002 subset C File

LIFE Is life exciting or dull? * RCSXFREQ Recoded sex frequency variable * SEX Respondents' sex Crosstabulation

				RCSXFREQ Recoded sex frequency variable				
				0 NOT AT ALL	1 ONCE A MONTH OR LESS	2 ABOUT ONCE A WEEK	3 2-3 TIMES A WEEK OR MORE	Total
SEX Respondents' sex								
1 MALE	LIFE Is life exciting or dull?	1 DULL	Count	3	2	2	1	8
			% within RCSXFREQ Recoded sex frequency variable	13.6%	4.4%	2.9%	1.8%	4.2%
		2 ROUTINE	Count	12	20	21	20	73
			% within RCSXFREQ Recoded sex frequency variable	54.5%	44.4%	30.4%	36.4%	38.2%
		3 EXCITING	Count	7	23	46	34	110
			% within RCSXFREQ Recoded sex frequency variable	31.8%	51.1%	66.7%	61.8%	57.6%
	Total		Count	22	45	69	55	191
			% within RCSXFREQ Recoded sex frequency variable	100.0%	100.0%	100.0%	100.0%	100.0%
2 FEMALE	LIFE Is life exciting or dull?	1 DULL	Count	3		2	1	6
			% within RCSXFREQ Recoded sex frequency variable	5.1%		3.8%	4.2%	3.8%
		2 ROUTINE	Count	31	15	25	11	82
			% within RCSXFREQ Recoded sex frequency variable	52.5%	60.0%	48.1%	45.8%	51.3%
		3 EXCITING	Count	25	10	25	12	72
			% within RCSXFREQ Recoded sex frequency variable	42.4%	40.0%	48.1%	50.0%	45.0%
	Total		Count	59	25	52	24	160
			% within RCSXFREQ Recoded sex frequency variable	100.0%	100.0%	100.0%	100.0%	100.0%

Symmetric Measures

SEX Respondents' sex			Value	Asymp. Std. Error[a]	Approx. T[b]	Approx. Sig.
1 MALE	Ordinal by Ordinal	Gamma	.260	.103	2.438	.015
	N of Valid Cases		191			
2 FEMALE	Ordinal by Ordinal	Gamma	.092	.118	.781	.435
	N of Valid Cases		160			

[a.] Not assuming the null hypothesis.
[b.] Using the asymptotic standard error assuming the null hypothesis.

Interpretation

For males and females, the general pattern remains—there is a positive association between frequency of sex and how exciting respondents say life is. The more frequently the respondents have sex, the more exciting they say life is. The association is somewhat stronger for males than for females, though. Across the categories of the dependent variable, the percentage differences are larger for males than for females, particularly in the Dull and Exciting categories.

Gamma is consistent with our analysis—stronger for males and weaker for females. It is positive for both groups. In sum, frequency of sexual activity has more of an effect on whether life is perceived as dull or exciting for males than for females. Knowing the association between frequency of sexual activity and life excitement helps us reduce our errors in predicting male respondents' views on how dull or exciting life is by 26%, but it only helps in reducing our errors in predicting female respondents' outlook on life excitement by 9%.

Skills Practice 12 Examine the association between sexual frequency *(rcsxfreq)* and life excitement *(life)*, controlling for age (using *rcage*).

Avoiding Common Pitfalls: Using measures of association with control variables   Problems students have with measures of association for control variables largely stem from questions about how to assess the level of measurement of the variables in order to apply the correct measure of association. This problem is easy to solve, because the level of measurement of the control variable has no bearing on the measure of association used. The measure of association is selected based solely on the level of measurement of the independent and dependent variables. Thus, if the independent and dependent variables are nominal, lambda can be used, even if the control variable is ordinal or numerical. Similarly, if the independent and dependent variables are ordinal, gamma can be applied, even if the control variable is nominal or numerical.

SUMMARY

In this chapter you were introduced to measures of association, statistics that allow us to assess the extent of an association between two variables. We focused on two primary measures: lambda for nominal variables and gamma for ordinal variables. You learned to compute both measures by hand and to find them using SPSS. See the chart on p. 417 for a guide to the correct application of these statistics.

Measures of association are evaluated on a scale of 1 or −1 to 0. The closer to zero a measure is, the weaker is the association between an independent and dependent variable. The closer to either 1 or −1, the stronger is the association.

In addition to telling us about the strength of a relationship, many of the measures introduced in this chapter have a proportional reduction in error (PRE) interpretation. By multiplying the association statistic by 100, you can read the statistic as a percentage. Doing so tells you how much your ability to predict the dependent variable is improved if you know the nature of the association between an independent and dependent variable.

Finally, you learned to control for third variables and apply measures of association to partial tables in order to assess changes in an independent–dependent variable relationship when a third, control, variable is introduced.

In the next chapter you will learn some techniques for assessing the extent of an association between two numerical variables.

KEY CONCEPTS

Measures of association
Proportional reduction in error (PRE)
Lambda
Gamma

Concordant pair
Discordant pair
Tied pair
Symmetric value
Asymmetric value

Control (third) variable
Elaboration
Partial table
Spurious association
Conditional association

ANSWERS TO SKILLS PRACTICES

1. For Divorced responses, you will guess Not at All (because that is the highest percentage in the Divorced column), and you will be right 69 times but wrong 140 times. For Separated respondents, you will guess Once a Month or Less and you will be right 13 times and wrong 29 times. For Never Married respondents, you will guess About Once a Week and you will be right 90 times and wrong 204 times.

2. The nature of the association is that respondents in the Northeast have sex less frequently than respondents in other regions. Over 29% of the respondents in the Northeast answered that they have sex Not at All, compared to about 22% of the respondents in the Midwest, 19.4% of the respondents in the Southeast, and 22.1% of the respondents in the West. Respondents in the Southeast say they have sex more frequently than respondents in other regions. Nearly one-third of respondents in the Southeast say they have sex two to three times a week or more compared to 19.1% of the respondents in the Northeast, 24% of the respondents in the Midwest, and 23.2% of the respondents in the West. Respondents in the West are the ones most likely to say they have sex about once a week, and respondents in the Midwest are the ones most likely to say they have sex about once a month or less. The association does not appear to be particularly strong, because the differences in the percentages across the categories of the dependent variable are not very large ones.

3. Respondents who are working have sex more frequently than respondents who are either not working or who are not in the labor market. 37.6% of working respondents say they have sex about once a week (compared to 37.2% of respondents who are not working and 22.2% of respondents who are not in the market). 28.4% of the respondents who are working say they have sex two to three times a week or more (compared to 23.1% of respondents who are not working and 19% of the respondents who are not in the market). On the other hand, 37.9% of the respondents who are not in the market say they have sex not at all (compared to 16.4% of the working and 17.9% of the not working respondents). The respondents who are not working are the ones most likely to say they have sex once a month or less. The association does not appear to be a particularly strong one, because the differences in the percentages across most categories of the dependent variable are not large ones (with the exception of the first category, Not at All).

Follow Formula 10.1 to find lambda.

Step 1. Look down the row marginal totals until you find the highest frequency of the dependent variable *rcwkstat*. The highest frequency is associated with the category About Once a Week, so circle the frequency for that category, 384. Find E_1 by subtracting 384 from N. $E_1 = 1,164 - 384 = 780$.

Step 2. Find E_2 by looking down each column of the independent variable and circling the highest frequency in each column (excluding the column marginal totals): Working, 279; Not Working, 29, and Not in the Market, 130. Now add the circled frequencies: 279 + 29 + 130 = 438. Subtract 130 from N to get E_2. $E_2 = 1,164 - 438 = 726$.

Step 3. Apply Formula 10.1.

$$E_1 = 780 \qquad E_2 = 726$$
$$\lambda = \frac{E_1 - E_2}{E_1} = \frac{780 - 726}{780} = \frac{54}{780} = .069$$

What does lambda tell us? As we thought, the relationship isn't very strong. Knowing the association between the independent and dependent variables, *work status* and *sex frequency*, doesn't help us very much at guessing the dependent variable, *sex frequency*. Our ability to predict the dependent variable is improved only by about 7%.

4. A compared to B is concordant. A compared to C is tied. A compared to D is tied. A compared to E is discordant.

5. In general, the association is that the older the respondents, the less frequently they have sex. The association is a negative one, and it appears to be a moderate to fairly strong association.

6. Concordant pairs for Table 10.6:

Concordant pairs in relation to—
cell A = 1(8 + 7 + 2 + 12 + 12 + 3 + 12 + 6 + 3) = 65
cell B = 3(7 + 2 + 12 + 3 + 6 + 3) = 99
cell C = 7(2 + 3 + 3) = 56
cell E = 3(12 + 12 + 3 + 12 + 6 + 3) = 144
cell F = 8(12 + 3 + 6 + 3) = 192
cell G = 7(3 + 3) = 42
cell I = 7(12 + 6 + 3) = 147
cell J = 12(6 + 3) = 108
cell K = 12(3) = 36
Total concordant pairs = 889

7. Discordant pairs for Table 10.6:

Discordant pairs in relation to—
cell D = 11(3 + 8 + 7 + 7 + 12 + 12 + 5 + 12 + 6) = 792
cell C = 7(3 + 8 + 7 + 12 + 5 + 12) = 329
cell B = 3(3 + 7 + 5) = 45

cell H = 2(7 + 12 + 12 + 5 + 12 + 6) = 108
cell G = 7(7 + 12 + 5 + 12) = 252
cell F = 8(7 + 5) = 96
cell L = 3(5 + 12 + 6) = 69
cell K = 12(12 + 5) = 204
cell J = 12(5) = 60
Total number of discordant pairs = 1,955

8. Analyzing and computing gamma for the contingency table:

A. As you probably expected, the association is a negative one in which the more TV the respondents say they watch, the less sex they say they have. Nearly one-third (31.3%) of those who watch television five hours or more a day have sex not at all. Only 6.7% of those who watch television one or two hours a day do not have sex at all. However, among those who watch television one or two hours day, 40% have sex two to three times a week or more compared to 6.3% of those who watch TV five hours or more a day. The association appears to be a moderate to fairly strong one, given the differences in the percentages across the rows. On the other hand, the pattern is not as consistent as it could be across the categories of the dependent variable. For example, 25% of those who do not watch TV at all say they do not have sex at all, and none of those who watch no television have sex two to three times a week or more.

B. Computation of gamma:

Concordant pairs for—
cell A = 1(4 + 9 + 4 + 12 + 3 + 6 + 12 + 5 + 1) = 56
cell B = 2(9 + 4 + 3 + 6 + 5 + 1) = 56
cell C = 5(4 + 6 + 1) = 55
cell E = 0(12 + 3 + 6 + 12 + 5 + 1) = 0
cell F = 4(3 + 6 + 5 + 1) = 60
cell G = 9(6 + 1) = 63
cell I = 3(12 + 5 + 1) = 54
cell J = 12(5 + 1) = 72
cell K = 3(1) = 3
Total concordant pairs = 419

discordant pairs for—
cell D = 5(0 + 4 + 9 + 3 + 12 + 3 + 0 + 12 + 5) = 240
cell C = 5(0 + 4 + 3 + 12 + 0 + 12) = 155

cell B = 2(0 + 3 + 0) =   6

cell H = 4(3 + 12 + 3 + 0 + 12 + 5) =   140

cell G = 9 (3 + 12 + 0 + 12) =   243

cell F = 4(3 + 0) =   12

cell L = 6(0 + 12 + 5) =   102

cell K= 3(0 + 12) =   36

cell J = 12(0) =   0
                                                        ———
Total discordant pairs =   934

Apply the formula for gamma:

$$\text{Gamma} = \frac{C - D}{C + D} = \frac{419 - 934}{419 + 934} = -\frac{515}{1353} = -.38$$

Interpretation: Gamma confirms our impression that the association is negative. The more television the respondents watch, the less sex they say they have. Gamma is fairly weak (closer to 0 than to –1). However, knowing the association between hours spent watching television and frequency of sexual activity improves our ability to predict sex frequency by 38%, and that is a fairly sizable improvement.

9. A. Asymmetric lambda (.067), with premarital sex as the dependent variable, indicates a fairly weak relationship between region of the country and attitudes toward premarital sex. Knowing the relationship between region of the country and attitudes toward premarital sex improves our ability to predict attitudes toward premarital sex by only 6.7%.

B. Asymmetric lambda (.068), with life excitement as the dependent variable, shows a weak relationship between marital status and how exciting life is. Knowing the relationship between these variables only improves our ability to predict how exciting respondents think life is by 6.8%.

C. On its face, asymmetric lambda (.00) with premarital sex as the dependent variable would appear to indicate a nonexistent association between the sex of the respondents and attitudes toward premarital sex. However, lambda is misleading in this case. The contingency table reveals a clear association in which males are more likely to think that premarital sex is not wrong at all or only sometimes wrong as compared to females who are more likely to believe that it is almost always wrong or always wrong. Goodman and Kruskal's *tau* at .011 (with premarital sex dependent) indicates a weak association between sex and attitudes toward premarital sex. Knowing the relationship between sex and attitudes toward premarital sex only improves our ability to predict attitudes toward premarital sex by 1%.

10. Gamma at –.405 indicates a negative association between the variables age and sex frequency. The older the respondent, the less frequent the sex. Gamma is fairly week (somewhat closer to 0 than –1). However, knowing the association between age and sex frequency improves our ability to predict sex frequency by 41%, and that's a sizable increase in the ability to predict sex frequency.

11. In general, the pattern among all respondents—that married respondents report having sex more frequently than widowed, divorced, separated, or never married respondents—hold true for all age groups of respondents except for those in the 61 through 89 age category. Although married respondents in the 61 through 89 age category are the ones most likely to report having sex about once a week, it is the separated respondents who are the ones most likely to report having sex two or three times a week or more.

Among all respondents, the association between marital status and sex frequency is fairly weak (lambda = .133). It is interesting, though, that as the age group goes up, the strength of the association (as measured by lambda and by *tau*) increases as well. The association is strongest among those who are in the age group 61 and up.

In sum, age clearly has an impact on the association between marital status and frequency of sexual activity. The nature of the association changes by age group, particularly among the 61-to-89-year-old respondents. The strength of the association changes, too, growing stronger as age increases.

12. In general, the pattern of association between sex frequency and life excitement found among all respondents—the more frequently

respondents have sex, the more exciting they say life is—is true across each of the categories of the recoded age variable. Among all respondents, gamma at .219 indicates a positive but somewhat weak association. When controlling for age, though, gamma is weaker among those who are in the 26 through 40 age category, but somewhat stronger for those in the 61 through 89 age category (gamma = .452). Age is clearly affecting the strength of the association between sex frequency and life excitement. The association is a little weaker among those who are 26 through 40, a little stronger among those who are 18 through 25 and 41 through 60, and a lot stronger among those who are 61 through 89.

GENERAL EXERCISES

For Exercises 1–4, evaluate the nature and strength of the association in the given contingency table. Then compute and interpret lambda for the table, which is drawn from the 2002 GSS for respondents ages 18 through 25.

1.

RCPRTNRS Recoded number of sex partners in last year * SEX Respondents' sex Crosstabulation

| | | | SEX Respondents' sex | | |
			1 MALE	2 FEMALE	Total
RCPRTNRS Recoded number of sex partners in last year	0 NO PARTNERS	Count	5	13	18
		% within SEX Respondents' sex	7.5%	13.8%	11.2%
	1 1 PARTNER	Count	28	54	82
		% within SEX Respondents' sex	41.8%	57.4%	50.9%
	2 2-4 PARTNERS	Count	29	26	55
		% within SEX Respondents' sex	43.3%	27.7%	34.2%
	3 5 OR MORE PARTNERS	Count	5	1	6
		% within SEX Respondents' sex	7.5%	1.1%	3.7%
Total		Count	67	94	161
		% within SEX Respondents' sex	100.0%	100.0%	100.0%

2.

RCSXFREQ Recoded sex frequency variable * RCREGION Recoded region of interview Crosstabulation

| | | | RCREGION Recoded region of interview | | | | |
			1 NORTHEAST	2 MIDWEST	3 SOUTHEAST	4 WEST	Total
RCSXFREQ Recoded sex frequency variable	0 NOT AT ALL	Count	4	2	4	8	18
		% within RCREGION Recoded region of interview	15.4%	4.3%	9.1%	20.0%	11.5%
	1 ONCE A MONTH OR LESS	Count	4	10	10	10	34
		% within RCREGION Recoded region of interview	15.4%	21.3%	22.7%	25.0%	21.7%
	2 ABOUT ONCE A WEEK	Count	11	19	10	10	50
		% within RCREGION Recoded region of interview	42.3%	40.4%	22.7%	25.0%	31.8%
	3 2-3 TIMES A WEEK OR MORE	Count	7	16	20	12	55
		% within RCREGION Recoded region of interview	26.9%	34.0%	45.5%	30.0%	35.0%
Total		Count	26	47	44	40	157
		% within RCREGION Recoded region of interview	100.0%	100.0%	100.0%	100.0%	100.0%

3.

PREMARSX Sex before marriage * RCRELIG Recoded RS religious preference Crosstabulation

| | | | RCRELIG Recoded RS religious preference | | | | |
			1 PROTESTANT	2 CATHOLIC	4 NONE	5 OTHER	Total
PREMARSX Sex before marriage	1 NOT WRONG AT ALL	Count	10	7	12	6	35
		% within RCRELIG Recoded RS religious preference	33.3%	87.5%	92.3%	66.7%	58.3%
	2 SOMETIMES WRONG	Count	3	1		1	5
		% within RCRELIG Recoded RS religious preference	10.0%	12.5%		11.1%	8.3%
	3 ALMOST ALWAYS WRONG	Count	4				4
		% within RCRELIG Recoded RS religious preference	13.3%				6.7%
	4 ALWAYS WRONG	Count	13		1	2	16
		% within RCRELIG Recoded RS religious preference	43.3%		7.7%	22.2%	26.7%
Total		Count	30	8	13	9	60
		% within RCRELIG Recoded RS religious preference	100.0%	100.0%	100.0%	100.0%	100.0%

4.

HOMOSEX Homosexual sex relations * RCRELIG Recoded RS religious preference Crosstabulation

			RCRELIG Recoded RS religious preference				
			1 PROTESTANT	2 CATHOLIC	4 NONE	5 OTHER	Total
HOMOSEX Homosexual sex relations	1 NOT WRONG AT ALL	Count	4	7	7	2	20
		% within RCRELIG Recoded RS religious preference	13.8%	53.8%	70.0%	25.0%	33.3%
	2 SOMETIMES WRONG	Count	3	1		1	5
		% within RCRELIG Recoded RS religious preference	10.3%	7.7%		12.5%	8.3%
	3 ALMOST ALWAYS WRONG	Count	1	1		2	4
		% within RCRELIG Recoded RS religious preference	3.4%	7.7%		25.0%	6.7%
	4 ALWAYS WRONG	Count	21	4	3	3	31
		% within RCRELIG Recoded RS religious preference	72.4%	30.8%	30.0%	37.5%	51.7%
Total		Count	29	13	10	8	60
		% within RCRELIG Recoded RS religious preference	100.0%	100.0%	100.0%	100.0%	100.0%

For Exercises 5–8, evaluate the nature and strength of the associations in the given contingency table. Then compute and interpret gamma for the table, which is drawn from the 2002 GSS for respondents ages 18 through 25.

5.

LIFE Is life exciting or dull? * RCSXFREQ Recoded sex frequency variable Crosstabulation

			RCSXFREQ Recoded sex frequency variable				
			0 NOT AT ALL	1 ONCE A MONTH OR LESS	2 ABOUT ONCE A WEEK	3 2-3 TIMES A WEEK OR MORE	Total
LIFE Is life exciting or dull?	1 DULL	Count				1	1
		% within RCSXFREQ Recoded sex frequency variable				5.6%	2.0%
	2 ROUTINE	Count	3	7	7	4	21
		% within RCSXFREQ Recoded sex frequency variable	42.9%	63.6%	46.7%	22.2%	41.2%
	3 EXCITING	Count	4	4	8	13	29
		% within RCSXFREQ Recoded sex frequency variable	57.1%	36.4%	53.3%	72.2%	56.9%
Total		Count	7	11	15	18	51
		% within RCSXFREQ Recoded sex frequency variable	100.0%	100.0%	100.0%	100.0%	100.0%

6.

RCPRTNRS Recoded number of sex partners in last year * DEGREE RS highest degree Crosstabulation

| | | | DEGREE RS highest degree | | | | |
			0 LT HIGH SCHOOL	1 HIGH SCHOOL	2 JUNIOR COLLEGE	3 BACHELOR	Total
RCPRTNRS Recoded number of sex partners in last year	0 NO PARTNERS	Count	1	14	1	2	18
		% within DEGREE RS highest degree	3.7%	13.2%	14.3%	9.5%	11.2%
	1 1 PARTNER	Count	15	51	4	12	82
		% within DEGREE RS highest degree	55.6%	48.1%	57.1%	57.1%	50.9%
	2 2-4 PARTNERS	Count	8	39	2	6	55
		% within DEGREE RS highest degree	29.6%	36.8%	28.6%	28.6%	34.2%
	3 5 OR MORE PARTNERS	Count	3	2		1	6
		% within DEGREE RS highest degree	11.1%	1.9%		4.8%	3.7%
Total		Count	27	106	7	21	161
		% within DEGREE RS highest degree	100.0%	100.0%	100.0%	100.0%	100.0%

7.

RCSXFREQ Recoded sex frequency variable * DEGREE RS highest degree Crosstabulation

| | | | DEGREE RS highest degree | | | | |
			0 LT HIGH SCHOOL	1 HIGH SCHOOL	2 JUNIOR COLLEGE	3 BACHELOR	Total
RCSXFREQ Recoded sex frequency variable	0 NOT AT ALL	Count	1	14	1	2	18
		% within DEGREE RS highest degree	3.7%	13.7%	14.3%	9.5%	11.5%
	1 ONCE A MONTH OR LESS	Count	7	23	2	2	34
		% within DEGREE RS highest degree	25.9%	22.5%	28.6%	9.5%	21.7%
	2 ABOUT ONCE A WEEK	Count	11	27	3	9	50
		% within DEGREE RS highest degree	40.7%	26.5%	42.9%	42.9%	31.8%
	3 2-3 TIMES A WEEK OR MORE	Count	8	38	1	8	55
		% within DEGREE RS highest degree	29.6%	37.3%	14.3%	38.1%	35.0%
Total		Count	27	102	7	21	157
		% within DEGREE RS highest degree	100.0%	100.0%	100.0%	100.0%	100.0%

8.

RCPRTNRS Recoded number of sex partners in last year * CLASS Subjective class identification Crosstabulation

			CLASS Subjective class identification				
			1 LOWER CLASS	2 WORKING CLASS	3 MIDDLE CLASS	4 UPPER CLASS	Total
RCPRTNRS Recoded number of sex partners in last year	0 NO PARTNERS	Count	1	6	10	1	18
		% within CLASS Subjective class identification	5.9%	8.0%	16.4%	14.3%	11.3%
	1 1 PARTNER	Count	9	48	23	1	81
		% within CLASS Subjective class identification	52.9%	64.0%	37.7%	14.3%	50.6%
	2 2-4 PARTNERS	Count	7	19	25	4	55
		% within CLASS Subjective class identification	41.2%	25.3%	41.0%	57.1%	34.4%
	3 5 OR MORE PARTNERS	Count		2	3	1	6
		% within CLASS Subjective class identification		2.7%	4.9%	14.3%	3.8%
Total		Count	17	75	61	7	160
		% within CLASS Subjective class identification	100.0%	100.0%	100.0%	100.0%	100.0%

SPSS EXERCISES

Use the GSS 2002 subset C file to analyze the associations between the following pairs of variables. Describe the nature and the strength of the association between the variables. Supplement your analysis by obtaining and interpreting lambda and Goodman and Kruskal's tau.

1. Race (using the recoded race, *rcrace,* variable) and attitudes toward premarital sex (using *premarsx*).

2. Marital status (using the *marital* variable) and attitudes toward premarital sex (using the *premarsx* variable).

3. Marital status (using the *marital* variable) and strength of religious affiliation (using the *reliten* variable).

4. Sex and strength of religious affiliation (using the *reliten* variable).

Use the GSS 2002 subset C file to analyze the associations between the following pairs of variables.

Describe the nature, strength, and direction of the association between the variables. Supplement your analysis by obtaining and interpreting gamma.

5. Age (using the recoded age, *rcage,* variable) and attitudes toward premarital sex (using *premarsx*).

6. Age (using the recoded age, *rcage,* variable) and strength of religious affiliation (using the *reliten* variable).

7. The recoded frequency of sex variable, *rcsxfreq,* and general happiness (using the *happy* variable).

8. The recoded frequency of sex variable, *rcsxfreq,* and marital happiness (using the *hapmar* variable).

Use the GSS 2002 subset C file to analyze the associations between the following pairs of variables with a control variable. Describe changes in the nature, strength, and, if appropriate, the direction of the association between the variables after introducing the control variable. Supplement your analysis by obtaining and interpreting lambda or gamma, as appropriate.

9. Marital status (using the *marital* variable and strength of religious affiliation (using the *reliten* variable), controlling for age, using the *rcage* variable.

10. Marital status (using the *marital* variable) and attitudes toward premarital sex (using the *pre-* *marsx* variable), controlling for age, using the *rcage* variable.

11. The recoded frequency of sex variable, *rc-* *sxfreq*, and general happiness (using the *happy* variable), controlling for *sex*.

12. The recoded frequency of sex variable, *rc-* *sxfreq*, and age, using the *rcage* variable, controlling for *health*.

## CHAPTER 11

Making Inferences for Associations between Categorical Variables: Chi-Square

INTRODUCTION

Like the inferential statistics for single variables that you learned about in Chapters 7 and 8, inferential statistics for measures of association allow us to answer the question, How likely is it that what we are learning from a sample is true of the population from which the sample was drawn? Finding out whether we can generalize about an association from a sample to a population involves a process of analysis called *hypothesis testing*.

The process of hypothesis testing, which occurs in the next-to-last step of the research process (described in Chapter 1), is outlined as follows:

STEP 1. Specify a research hypothesis and the null hypothesis.

STEP 2. Compute the value of a test statistic for the relationship.

STEP 3. Calculate the degrees of freedom for the variables involved.

STEP 4. Look up the distribution of the test statistic to find its critical value at a specified level of probability (to determine the likelihood that a test statistic of a particular value could have occurred by chance alone).

STEP 5. Decide whether to reject the null hypothesis.

TABLE 11.1 Contingency Table for the Association between the Variables *degree* and *volchrty* in the GSS 2002 subset A File

VOLCHRTY R done volunteer work for a charity * DEGREE RS highest degree Crosstabulation

			DEGREE RS highest degree					
			0 LT HIGH SCHOOL	1 HIGH SCHOOL	2 JUNIOR COLLEGE	3 BACHELOR	4 GRADUATE	Total
VOLCHRTY R done volunteer work for a charity	1 NOT AT ALL IN PAST YR	Count	83	224	20	50	23	400
		% within DEGREE RS highest degree	72.2%	57.4%	46.5%	39.7%	41.8%	54.9%
	2 ONCE IN THE PAST YR	Count	9	55	9	21	6	100
		% within DEGREE RS highest degree	7.8%	14.1%	20.9%	16.7%	10.9%	13.7%
	3 AT LEAST 2 OR 3 TIMES IN PAST YR	Count	12	56	10	21	10	109
		% within DEGREE RS highest degree	10.4%	14.4%	23.3%	16.7%	18.2%	15.0%
	4 ONCE A MONTH	Count	6	24	1	20	6	57
		% within DEGREE RS highest degree	5.2%	6.2%	2.3%	15.9%	10.9%	7.8%
	5 ONCE A WEEK	Count		16	1	7	5	29
		% within DEGREE RS highest degree		4.1%	2.3%	5.6%	9.1%	4.0%
	6 MORE THAN ONCE A WEEK	Count	5	15	2	7	5	34
		% within DEGREE RS highest degree	4.3%	3.8%	4.7%	5.6%	9.1%	4.7%
Total		Count	115	390	43	126	55	729
		% within DEGREE RS highest degree	100.0%	100.0%	100.0%	100.0%	100.0%	100.0%

In this chapter and the next, you will be learning to do hypothesis testing for associations involving two variables. We will begin with hypothesis testing for categorical variables using chi-square. In the next chapter you will learn about hypothesis testing for associations involving numerical variables. To get started we'll review what a hypothesis is, and then I will introduce some of the concepts important to hypothesis testing.

As defined in Chapter 1, a hypothesis is simply a statement that describes a relationship between at least two variables. So far, we have analyzed all sorts of relationships, including that between marital status and frequency of sexual activity. The "News to Use" excerpts in this chapter address two issues—the effects of social connectedness on individuals and the effect of education on volunteering (which itself is an aspect of social connectedness). The hypothesis suggested by the first excerpt is that the more socially connected one is, the happier he or she is likely to be. The hypothesis suggested by the second excerpt is that education is associated with volunteering.

 Skills Practice 1 Let's examine the association between education and volunteering. Table 11.1 is a SPSS contingency table for the association between level of education and volunteering for a charity. Describe the nature, strength, and direction of the association.

How can we tell if it is likely that the association we found in our sample of GSS respondents—the more education respondents have, the more they are likely to volunteer for charity—is true of all American adults, 18 years old or older, noninstitutionalized, and English-speaking? The answer is, by engaging in hypothesis testing. Before we can do that, we have to develop an understanding of a set of core concepts related to making inferences, or generalizations, from samples to populations. ■

N E W S *to* **U S E**
Statistics in the "Real" World

Community Connectedness Linked to Happiness and Vibrant Communities[1]

Social capital and social trust matter a lot for both the quality of life in our communities and our personal happiness.

Social connectedness is a much stronger predictor of the perceived quality of life in a community than the community's income *or* educational level. In the five communities surveyed having the highest social trust, 52% of residents rated their community as an *excellent* place to live, the highest possible grade. In the five communities with the lowest levels of social trust, only 31% felt that good about their quality of life.

Similarly, personal happiness is also much more closely tied to the level of community so-cial connectedness and trust than to income or educational levels. This is true, even controlling for individual characteristics, such as income, education, and so on. That is, even comparing two persons of identical income, education, race, age, and so on, the one living in a high social capital community typically reports greater personal happiness than his/her "twin" living in a low social capital community. The same thing is *not* true of the overall level of *community* income or education. In other words, your personal happiness is *not* directly affected by the affluence of your community, but it *is* quite directly affected by the social connectedness of your community.

Education is the Best Predictor of Civic Involvement[2]

EFFECTS OF EDUCATION ON FUTURE COMMUNITY ENGAGEMENT

Individuals with a college education are more likely to:
- Register to vote
- Vote
- Sign a petition
- Work on community service projects

- Volunteer more often
- Participate in church activities outside of attending services
- Participate in charity or social welfare organization
- Contribute money to church or religious cause
- Contribute money to non-religious charities

---

[1] Excerpt from, The Saguaro Seminar: Civic Engagement in America, "Social Capital Community Benchmark Survey: Executive Summary," <http://www.ksg.harvard.edu/saguaro/communitysurvey/docs/exec_summ.pdf>, 19 August 2003.
[2] Campus Cares, < http://www.campuscares.org/resources/Effects_of_Education.pdf>, 19 August 2003. Data drawn from the U.S. Census Bureau, Current Population Survey, November 2000, and the John F. Kennedy School of Government, Harvard University, "Social Capital Benchmark Survey, 2000."

CORE CONCEPTS FOR HYPOTHESIS TESTING

The Research Hypothesis and the Null Hypothesis

The first concept to understand involves the difference between a research hypothesis and the null hypothesis. A **research hypothesis**, symbolized by H_1, involves specifying the nature of the relationship between two variables. We have been exploring research hypotheses throughout this text. For example, a research hypothesis might state one of the following:

H_1: Men have sex more often than do women.

H_1: The healthier GSS respondents are, the more frequently they have sex.

H_1: The more education people have, the more likely they are to volunteer for charity.

The **null hypothesis**, on the other hand, speculates that there is no association between two variables. Null hypotheses are symbolized with H_0. The following are some examples of null hypotheses:

H_0: Men are no different from women in their frequency of sexual activity.

H_0: There is no relationship between a respondent's health and his or her frequency of sexual activity.

H_0: Well-educated people are no more likely to volunteer than less educated people.

The null hypothesis has a specific purpose in hypothesis testing; it is the only hypothesis that can be tested. We often assume that if we reject the null hypothesis, the research hypothesis is confirmed. Technically, however, we can only reject or fail to reject the null hypothesis—nothing more.

Let's illustrate this with an example. The null hypothesis related to education and volunteering for charity says that

H_0: There is no association between education and volunteering among American adults.

To test this hypothesis—to see whether it is true—we draw a random sample from the population. When we examine the association between the two variables in our sample, we find that there is an association between them. In fact, you learned from the contingency table you analyzed for the first Skills Practice in this chapter (Table 11.1 on p. 348) that the more educated the respondents, the more likely they are to say they volunteer for charity.

However, there's a problem. You may recall from our work in Chapters 7 and 8 that randomly drawn samples are *likely* to represent the populations from which they are drawn, but they don't always. The question we have to ask ourselves now is, How likely is it that the association we are seeing in our sample reflects real differences in volunteering based on education in the population? Is what we are seeing merely a chance occurrence, the result of the sample we were unlucky enough to draw? More to the point, what is the likelihood that we could have drawn a sample at random for which there appears to be an association *even when* there is no association in the population as a whole?

If it is likely that the association we find is *not* a chance occurrence, then the null hypothesis can be rejected. In other words, we would be on fairly firm ground in rejecting the idea that we have drawn a sample showing an association between education and volunteering from a population in which there is no such association. Where does that leave us? Generally, most researchers argue for the relationship observed in the sample. If we reject the null hypothesis, then it is assumed there is a relationship in the population like the one in the sample—the more education people have, the more often they volunteer for charity.

On the other hand, what happens if we find that there is a good chance that the association between education and volunteering *is* an accident, and we simply happened to have selected a sample for which education is related to volunteering? Then we cannot reject the null hypothesis. We conclude, at least for the time being, that there is not enough evidence to reject the idea that there is no association between the variables. In failing to reject the null hypothesis, we are not saying for certain that there is no association. All we are saying is that we don't have enough evidence to reject that idea.

In the absence of rejecting the null hypothesis, researchers often say that they are "accepting" the null hypothesis. I don't think it's because they don't know better. Saying that they are "failing to reject" the null hypothesis is too convoluted for the lay person to understand. I will sometimes discuss hypothesis testing in these terms—rejecting the null hypothesis or accepting the null hypothesis. I hope you will keep in mind that using the term "accepting" the null hypothesis is a substitute for the more accurate phrase, "failing to reject" the null hypothesis.

Statistical Independence

The concept of statistical independence provides us with another way to look at the difference between a research hypothesis and the null hypothesis. When two variables are **statistically independent**, changes in one variable *(education of respondents)* have nothing to do with changes in a second *(volunteering)*. They vary *independently* of one another. Conversely, when two variables are statistically dependent on one another, changes in one variable are associated with changes in a second variable. For example, changes in education (more education) are associated with changes in levels of volunteering (more volunteering).

We can use this concept of statistical independence in framing a null hypothesis. For instance, we can hypothesize that education is statistically independent of volunteering. We are saying that differences among respondents on the variable *degree* are unrelated to any differences we may see in their levels of reported volunteering. With hypothesis testing, we can assess the likelihood that the degree of statistical independence we see in a sample is due to chance. If we find that the degree of statistical independence found in the sample is not likely to be due to chance, the null hypothesis is rejected. If we find that it is likely to be due to chance, the null hypothesis is accepted. Either way, we always run the risk of making mistakes.

Type I and Type II Errors

The mistakes we can make are of two types. Both arise from the fact that any given sample may or may not be representative of a population. We can only assess the likelihood that it is, never the certainty.

Type I errors We can reject a null hypothesis, even when there really is no association between two variables. Based on what we learn from a sample, it is possible to reject the idea that there is no association between age and happiness *even though* the null hypothesis is correct—there is no association between age and happiness in the population. This type of mistake or error, rejecting a null hypothesis when there really is no association between two variables, is called a **Type I error.**

Type II errors We can do the opposite; that is, we can accept the null hypothesis—the idea that there is no association between two variables—even though there is one. We could, for example, accept the idea that there is no association between education and volunteering even though, in reality, there is an association between these variables in the population at large. This kind of mistake—accepting the null hypothesis when there really is an association between two variables—is called a **Type II error.**

As you will see later on in this chapter, we can take steps statistically to avoid Type I errors. The problem is that taking steps to limit Type I errors increases the likelihood of Type II errors. In this chapter, we will focus on how to avoid Type I errors. If you move on to higher level courses in research methods, you will learn about techniques for reducing Type II errors.

To assess whether we can reject a null hypothesis, we must first compute an appropriate test statistic (given the levels of measurement of the variables involved in our association and other assumptions that I will go into as the various test statistics are introduced). One such test statistic, chi-square, can be computed from contingency tables.

CALCULATING AND INTERPRETING THE TEST STATISTIC FOR CONTINGENCY TABLES: CHI-SQUARE (χ^2)

A measure of inference appropriate for use with contingency tables (and therefore any pair of variables for which contingency table analysis is appropriate) is called **chi** (pronounced "ki" with a long i)-**square** and indicated by the symbol χ^2. Like many measures of inference, chi-square has two components: a test statistic, called the **obtained value** of chi-square, and a **critical value** of the statistic, which is the value the test statistic must reach to reject the null hypothesis. We will examine this later.

The Test Statistic for Chi-Square

The first component of chi-square is a test statistic. Most measures of inference start off with the computation of a statistic called a **test statistic**. The value of the test statistic varies (can be larger or smaller) based on the degree of statistical independence, or the extent to which two variables change together (are dependent) or are acting independently of one another. Chi-square is not a measure of association, but the value of chi-square is affected by the degree to which two variables are dependent on one another. For example, chi-square will be larger if levels of volunteering are dependent on levels of education. Chi-square will be smaller if volunteering varies independently—without regard to the level of education of the respondents. The formula for the obtained value of chi-square is fairly straightforward.

Formula 11.1: Obtained chi-square

$$\chi^2 = \sum \left[\frac{\left(f_o - f_e \right)^2}{f_e} \right]$$

where f_o represents the observed frequencies in a contingency table, and f_e represents the expected frequencies in a contingency table.

To understand how to work this formula, we have to learn the difference between observed and expected frequencies.

Expected and observed frequencies The concept of chi-square is based on the difference between expected and observed frequencies in a distribution involving two variables (a contingency table). Let's evaluate another claim in the "News to Use" article about the association between education and voting. (We will return to the question of whether the association we see in our sample between education and volunteering is likely to be true of all American adults, 18 years of age or older, non-institutionalized, and English speaking, later on in this chapter.) Examine the association between education and voting in the 2000 elections in Table 11.2. What is the nature and the strength of the association? It seems clear that the more education respondents have, the more likely they are to have voted in 2000. The less education, the less likely they are to have voted. Those with graduate degrees were the respondents most likely to say they were ineligible to vote, though. The association looks like a fairly strong one, because it is consistent across the first two categories of the dependent variable and the differences in the percentages across the rows of the table are sizable.

The frequencies that we see in each cell on Table 11.2—the ones on which the column percentages are based—are called the **observed frequencies.**

The **expected frequencies** for a contingency table are the cell frequencies that we would expect to see in a contingency table in which there is no association between two variables.

Let's assume there is no association between *degree* and *vote00*. What would the cell frequencies look like? To answer this question you have to understand that a table with no association between two variables would show no differences in percentages across the categories (rows) of the dependent variable. They would be identical all the way across. To reconstruct our contingency table so that it shows no association between the variables, we have to recalculate the cell frequencies. How can we do this?

TABLE 11.2 Contingency Table for the Association between *degree* and *vote00* in the GSS 2002 subset A File

The observed frequency

VOTE00 Did R vote in 2000 election * DEGREE RS highest degree Crosstabulation

			DEGREE RS highest degree					
			0 LT HIGH SCHOOL	1 HIGH SCHOOL	2 JUNIOR COLLEGE	3 BACHELOR	4 GRADUATE	Total
VOTE00 Did R vote in 2000 election	1 VOTED	Count	93	476	82	206	103	960
		% within DEGREE RS highest degree	42.9%	60.6%	75.9%	83.4%	82.4%	64.8%
	2 DID NOT VOTE	Count	105	272	24	33	9	443
		% within DEGREE RS highest degree	48.4%	34.6%	22.2%	13.4%	7.2%	29.9%
	3 INELIGIBLE	Count	19	37	2	8	13	79
		% within DEGREE RS highest degree	8.8%	4.7%	1.9%	3.2%	10.4%	5.3%
Total		Count	217	785	108	247	125	1482
		% within DEGREE RS highest degree	100.0%	100.0%	100.0%	100.0%	100.0%	100.0%

Start by imagining the contingency table with the cells empty, as in Table 11.3.

To find the expected frequencies, we work with the column *marginal totals* for each category of the independent variable and the row *marginal percentages* for each category of the dependent variable. To find the expected cell frequency for those who have less than high school and voted, multiply the column marginal total for less than high school (217) by the row marginal proportion[3] for those who voted (.648). Round to the first decimal.

TABLE 11.3 Contingency Table for the Variables *degree* and *vote00* in the GSS 2002 subset A File with the Cells Empty

Row marginal percentage
(row proportion = row marginal % ÷ 100)

VOTE00 Did R vote in 2000 election * DEGREE RS highest degree Crosstabulation

			DEGREE RS highest degree					
			0 LT HIGH SCHOOL	1 HIGH SCHOOL	2 JUNIOR COLLEGE	3 BACHELOR	4 GRADUATE	Total
VOTE00 Did R vote in 2000 election	1 VOTED	Count						960
		% within DEGREE RS highest degree						64.8%
	2 DID NOT VOTE	Count						443
		% within DEGREE RS highest degree						29.9%
	3 INELIGIBLE	Count						79
		% within DEGREE RS highest degree						5.3%
Total		Count	217	785	108	247	125	1482
		% within DEGREE RS highest degree	100.0%	100.0%	100.0%	100.0%	100.0%	100.0%

Column marginal total

---

[3] To find the row marginal proportion, divide the row marginal percentage (64.8%) by 100 to get .648.

217 × .648 = 140.6, so the expected cell frequency for the categories less than high school and voted is 140.6. Record the expected cell frequency in the contingency table in Table 11.3.

Move down to the next cell, those with less than high school who did not vote. To find the expected cell frequency, multiply the column marginal (217) by the row marginal proportion for those who did not vote. The row marginal proportion = 29.9% ÷ 100, or .299. We see that 217 × .299 = 64.9, so the expected cell frequency for those who have less than high school and did not vote is 64.9.

Skills Practice 2   Fill in the rest of the expected cell frequencies for the contingency table. The answers are in Table 11.4.

What do we do with the expected frequencies? First, we can recalculate the cell column percentages to demonstrate that there is no association between the independent *(degree)* and dependent *(vote00)* variables.

Start by using your expected frequency to calculate the column percentage for those respondents who have less than high school educations but who voted in the 2000 election. (Divide 140.6 by 217 and multiply the result by 100. Round your percentage to the first decimal.) You should get 64.8%. Does this look familiar? It is the same as the row marginal percentage for the dependent variable category *Voted*.

Skills Practice 3   Use the expected cell frequencies to recalculate the rest of the column percentages in Table 11.4. Round to the second decimal. Your table should look like Table 11.5.

What's the association between education and voting? If you read across the first row of the dependent variable *Voted*, you will see there is no association at all—the percentages are identical. The same is true of the second and third rows.

You should now be able to see how the computation of expected frequencies produces a contingency table in which there is no association between two variables. The next step is to use the differences between these expected frequencies and the observed frequencies to assess the degree of statistical independence between two variables. Remember that the observed cell frequencies are those we obtained for the variables *degree* and *vote00* in our sample of 2002 GSS respondents (see Table 11.2). We need to know how much difference there is between the expected frequencies and the observed ones. The *smaller* the difference between observed and expected frequencies, the *greater* the statistical independence.

How is this so? Remember that in a table of *expected* frequencies, there is no association between two variables. How much education one has has no effect on voting. There is no change in voting behavior across the categories of the variable *degree*. The variable *vote00* has nothing to do with the variable *degree;* they

TABLE 11.4 Table with Expected Frequencies for the Variables *degree* and *vote00* in the GSS 2002 subset A File

VOTE00 Did R vote in 2000 election * DEGREE RS highest degree Crosstabulation

			DEGREE RS highest degree					
			0 LT HIGH SCHOOL	1 HIGH SCHOOL	2 JUNIOR COLLEGE	3 BACHELOR	4 GRADUATE	Total
VOTE00 Did R vote in 2000 election	1 VOTED	Expected Count	140.6	508.7	70.0	160.0	81.0	960.0
								64.8%
	2 DID NOT VOTE	Expected Count	64.9	234.7	32.3	73.9	37.4	443.0
								29.9%
	3 INELIGIBLE	Expected Count	11.5	41.6	5.7	13.1	6.6	79.0
								5.3%
Total		Expected Count	217.0	785.0	108.0	247.0	125.0	1482.0
			100.0%	100.0%	100.0%	100.0%	100.0%	100.0%

vary independently of one another. If the frequencies we obtain through observation of a sample (the 2002 GSS respondents, in this case) are substantially the same as the expected ones, then there is no association between the two variables. If the expected and observed frequencies are different, there is more statistical dependence—more effect of one variable on the other.

We rarely see either no association whatsoever between two variables or only perfect associations between two variables. Instead, we see something in between, and in the social sciences we tend to see smaller associations rather than larger ones. Consequently, what we have to measure is not the presence or absence of statistical independence, but the extent. We do that with the obtained chi-square formula, Formula 11.1.

$$\chi^2 = \Sigma \left[\frac{\left(f_o - f_e \right)^2}{f_e} \right]$$

The chi-square formula requires us to go through the contingency table cell by cell, as follows:

Step 1. Find the observed (f_o) and expected (f_e) frequency.

Step 2. Subtract the expected from the observed frequency ($f_o - f_e$).

Step 3. Square the result: $(f_o - f_e)^2$.

Step 4. Divide the result by the expected frequency (f_e).

Step 5. Add up the computations for each of the cells.

EXAMPLE:

To find chi-square for Table 11.5, go through the cells in the table one by one. Start with the first cell, the respondents who have less than high school and who voted.

Step 1. Find the observed frequency in Table 11.2 ($f_o = 93$) and the expected frequency in Table 11.5, rounded to the nearest first decimal ($f_e = 140.6$).

TABLE 11.5   Table with Expected Frequencies and Recalculated Column Percentages for the Variables *degree* and *vote00* in the GSS 2002 subset A File

VOTE00 Did R vote in 2000 election * DEGREE RS highest degree Crosstabulation

| | | | | DEGREE RS highest degree | | | | | |
			0 LT HIGH SCHOOL	1 HIGH SCHOOL	2 JUNIOR COLLEGE	3 BACHELOR	4 GRADUATE	Total
VOTE00 Did R vote in 2000 election	1 VOTED	Expected Count	140.6	508.7	70.0	160.0	81.0	960.0
		Recalculated column percentages	64.8%	64.8%	64.8%	64.8%	64.8%	64.8%
	2 DID NOT VOTE	Expected Count	64.9	234.7	32.3	73.9	37.4	443.0
		Recalculated column percentages	29.9%	29.9%	29.9%	29.9%	29.9%	29.9%
	3 INELIGIBLE	Expected Count	11.5	41.6	5.7	13.1	6.6	79.0
		Recalculated column percentages	5.3%	5.3%	5.3%	5.3%	5.3%	5.3%
Total		Expected Count	217.0	785.0	108.0	247.0	125.0	1482.0
		Recalculated column percentages	100.0%	100.0%	100.0%	100.0%	100.0%	100.0%

Step 2.   Subtract the expected from the observed frequencies: $93 - 140.6 = -47.6$.

Step 3.   Square the result: $-47.6^2 = 2265.76$.

Step 4.   Divide by the expected frequency ($f_e = 140.6$): $2265 \div 140.6 = 16.115$ (rounded to the nearest thousandth).

Move down to the next cell in the column less than high school, the respondents who did not vote, and repeat the process:

Step 1.   Find the observed frequency in Table 11.2 ($f_o = 105$) and the expected frequency in Table 11.5 ($f_e = 64.9$).

Step 2.   Subtract the expected from the observed frequencies: $105 - 64.9 = 40.1$.

Step 3.   Square the result: $40.1^2 = 1608.01$.

Step 4.   Divide by the expected frequency ($f_e = 64.9$): $1608.01 \div 64.9 = 24.777$ (rounded to the nearest thousandth).

Skills Practice 4   Complete the process for each cell in the table:

Step 1.   Record the observed frequency and expected frequency.

Step 2.   Find the difference between the observed and expected frequencies.

Step 3.   Square the difference.

Step 4.   Divide the result by the expected frequency.

Check your answers against Table 11.6.

TABLE 11.6   Table for the Variables *degree* and *vote00* in the GSS 2002 subset A File with Chi-Square Computations: $(f_o - f_e)^2 / f_e$

VOTE00 Did R vote in 2000 election * DEGREE RS highest degree Crosstabulation

		DEGREE RS highest degree				
		0 LT HIGH SCHOOL	1 HIGH SCHOOL	2 JUNIOR COLLEGE	3 BACHELOR	4 GRADUATE
VOTE00 Did R vote in 2000 election	1 VOTED	16.115	2.102	2.057	13.225	5.975
	2 DID NOT VOTE	24.777	5.928	2.133	22.636	21.566
	3 INELIGIBLE	4.891	.509	2.402	1.985	6.206

Finally, the formula for chi-square calls for us to sum the proportion computed for each cell:

$$\chi^2 = \sum \left[\frac{\left(f_o - f_e \right)^2}{f_e} \right]$$

$$= 16.115 + 24.777 + 4.891 + 2.102 + 5.928 + .509 + 2.057 +$$
$$2.402 + 13.225 + 22.636 + 1.985 + 5.975 + 21.566 + 6.206$$
$$= 132.507$$

The result is an obtained chi-square of 132.507. Generally, the larger the chi-square, the more statistical dependence between two variables. However, the value of chi-square is not a measure of association and it has no absolute meaning by itself. We have to interpret it in the context of its associated degrees of freedom and the likelihood of obtaining it by chance.

Degrees of freedom   Having found the test statistic for chi-square, the next question to ask is, What is the likelihood that we could obtain a chi-square of this magnitude in a contingency table of this size strictly by chance? Put another way, What is the probability that we could find this much statistical dependence in a sample drawn from a population in which the two variables are statistically independent?

To find the answer, we have to consider the size of the contingency table. The size of the table is measured in degrees of freedom. The concept of degrees of freedom derives from the idea that once you know the values of a certain number of cells, the values in the rest of the cells are determined. Let's illustrate this point with a simple example. Suppose we construct a contingency table with only four cells, like the one in Table 11.7, to examine the association between education and voting. We have 25 respondents and we classify them according to how much education they have and whether they voted in 2000. Of the 25 respondents, we notice right away that 15 have no more than high school and 10 have gone beyond high school. We enter those values in our contingency table as the column marginal totals for the two categories of the independent variable. Then we discover that 22 voted and 3 did not vote. We enter those numbers as the row marginal totals for the two categories of the dependent variable. Next we start to fill in the cells of the table. We begin by finding out how many belong in the first cell, no more than high school and voted. We learn that 13 belong in the first cell, so we enter the number 13.

TABLE 11.7   Understanding Degrees of Freedom Using a Hypothetical Set of Data

	Degree	No more than high school	Beyond high school	Row Totals
Voting	Voted	13		22
	Did Not Vote			3
	Column Totals	15	10	$N = 25$

Once we have done that, notice that all of the values in the rest of the cells are determined by the row and column marginal totals—we don't even have to count the respondents cell by cell. We know that there are 2 respondents in the no more than high school and did not vote cell. (How? Because 13 + 2 = the column marginal total, 15.) We know there are 9 respondents in the beyond high school and voted cell (because 13 + 9 = the row marginal frequency, 22). There is one respondent who went beyond high school and did not vote.

When we know the row and column marginal totals, we only have to know the contents of one of the cells in the table to complete the whole contingency table. Only one cell, therefore, is free to vary. Consequently, this table is one in which there is only one degree of freedom. The concept **degrees of freedom** tells us how many cells in a table are free to vary, once the row and column marginal totals are known.

 Skills Practice 5   See whether you can figure out how many degrees of freedom there are in Table 11.8. How many cell frequencies do you have to fill in before the values in the rest of the cells are determined? You will see the answer when you get to Example 2 in the next section. (Hint: Try filling in the cells with hypothetical frequencies to see how many you have to fill in before the rest are determined.)

Although it's important to understand how degrees of freedom are determined, the degrees of freedom in a table can be found more easily using a formula.

Formula 11.2: Degrees of freedom for chi-square

$$df = (r - 1)(c - 1)$$

where r represents the number of rows in a contingency table, and c represents the number of columns.

EXAMPLE 1:

For Table 11.7, we can compute the degrees of freedom with the formula by counting the number of rows and number of columns and entering them in the formula.

$$df = (r - 1)(c - 1) = (2 - 1)(2 - 1) = (1)(1) = 1$$

There is only one degree of freedom in Table 11.7. The frequency for only one cell is free to vary. Once that frequency has been determined, the row and column marginal totals dictate the contents of the rest of the cells.

EXAMPLE 2:

For Table 11.8, we can compute the degrees of freedom as follows:

$$df = (r - 1)(c - 1) = (3 - 1)(4 - 1) = (2)(3) = 6$$

 Skills Practice 6   How many degrees of freedom are there in Table 11.4? (See whether you can figure it without applying the formula. Then check yourself by using the formula for degrees of freedom.)

Interpreting Chi-Square Values

We use chi-square to decide whether to accept or reject the null hypothesis by using chi-square along with its associated degrees of freedom in conjunction with a statistic called a probability or *p* value. You see these often in scholarly articles. Researchers may write something like, "We learned that the more education respondents have, the more likely they are to vote ($p < .05$)."

To understand how chi-square works with probability values, you have to look at chi-square as a sample statistic—a characteristic of the observed relationship between two variables in a sample. Just like other sample statistics (the sample mean, for example), chi-square has its own distribution for tables of different sizes. I will not go into the mechanics of the construction of chi-square distributions. Suffice it to say that the likelihood of chi-square values of a specific magnitude occurring by chance in tables of different sizes has been computed and made available to us in statistical charts of critical values of chi-square and their associated *p* values.

Probability values and alpha values   Generally, the *p* **or probability value** indicates the likelihood that a test statistic of a particular magnitude computed from a sample is simply a chance or random occurrence rather than a consequence of real associations between the variables in a population. For chi-square, it tells us the likelihood that the degree of statistical dependence observed in a sample is simply due to the luck of the random draw.

TABLE 11.8   Estimating Degrees of Freedom Using a Hypothetical Set of Data

	Degree	Less than high school	At least some high school	At least some college	Beyond college	Row Totals
Voting:	Voted					28
	Did not vote					19
	Ineligible to vote					3
	Column Totals	7	15	15	13	N = 50

The lower the p value is, the *less* likely it is that the statistical dependence observed in a sample is due to chance. A p value of .05, for instance, tells us that there are no more than 5 chances in 100 that the statistical dependence observed in a sample is due to chance. There are, therefore, 95 chances in 100 that the statistical dependence found in the sample is *not* due to chance. We can conclude, therefore, that we have enough evidence to reject the null hypothesis, the hypothesis of no association between two variables. However, it is often assumed to be highly likely that the specific association we find in the sample is present in the population.

If the likelihood is not high that the degree of statistical dependence found in a sample is a chance occurrence, the null hypothesis—that there is no association between two variables—is rejected. On the other hand, if we find that the likelihood is high, the null hypothesis cannot be rejected. We have to accept the fact that we cannot rule out the possibility of no association between two variables.

Setting alpha levels at .05 (or even lower) is not entirely arbitrary. By setting the alpha level at .05, we are taking steps to minimize the chances that we will make Type I errors. That is, we are reducing the likelihood that we are going to reject the null hypothesis even when there is no association between two variables in a population. At an alpha level of .05, the odds have to be very high that the association we see in a sample is not merely a chance occurrence. Alpha levels of .05 (or even lower) do not rule out that possibility altogether, though. On the other hand, at extremely low values of p we are more likely to make Type II errors. That is, we will accept the null hypothesis even when there is an association between two variables in the population from which a sample was drawn. For example, we could accept the null hypothesis for a p value even as low as .02 or .03, but we could very well be accepting the null hypothesis even when an association between two variables is present in a population.

Nevertheless, setting p values at .05 (and sometimes even lower at .01) has emerged as standard practice in the social sciences.

The concept of the alpha value (indicated by the symbol α) is closely related to the probability value. The **alpha value** is the level at or below which we would expect a particular probability value to fall before we decide to reject the null hypothesis. The alpha value is not computed so much as it is set. I think of the alpha value as a bar the probability has to jump over before we can reject the null hypothesis.

Perhaps Figure 11.1 will help you to understand this concept. Probability values range from .00 to 1.00. The lower the probability value, the less likely you are to find that an association in a sample is a chance occurrence. By extension, the higher the probability value, the more likely it is that an association in a sample is due only to the specific elements you happened to draw into the sample. If you have a sample of individuals, a low p value tells you it is highly unlikely that the degree of statistical dependence found in the sample is an accident. A high p value tells you the opposite—that the degree of statistical dependence you observe is probably due to chance.

Anything with a p value of .50 or more indicates the likelihood that an association in a sample will not be found in the population. At .50, the p value is telling us that the likelihood is 50–50 that an association we see in a sample is due to nothing more than chance. But at p values higher than .50—let's pick .70 as

FIGURE 11.1
Relationship between
probability values and
alpha levels.

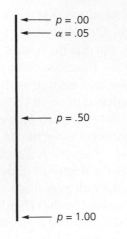

an example—the odds are greater that associations we find in samples are due to dumb luck and are not real associations between variables in populations. We can't base decisions on dumb luck so we don't draw conclusions from associations in samples that are far more likely than not due to chance.

However, what happens when p values fall below .50? Are we willing to conclude that the more education one has, the more likely he or she is to vote if the odds of an association being due to chance are only 1 in 4 ($p = .25$)? (By extension, can we say the odds are 3 in 4 that the association is reflective of a real association in the population?) Some would say yes—go ahead and reject the null hypothesis. However, in the social sciences, alpha levels—hurdles that p values have to jump over before the null hypothesis can be rejected—have been set fairly low, usually at .05 or less. Consequently, as a rule (and there is considerable debate about this) alpha levels of .05 have been established as the "bar" that p values have to clear. Before we can reject the null hypothesis that the associations we see in samples are due to chance and are not real associations between variables in populations, we must have p values at .05 or less. I will follow this practice in this chapter and in Chapter 13 as we test various null hypotheses.

Testing the null hypothesis   Table 11.2 has a chi-square value of 132.507 (which we computed earlier) and 8 degrees of freedom. What is the likelihood of obtaining a chi-square of 132.507 in a table with 8 degrees of freedom constructed for a sample drawn from a population in which there is no association between the variables *degree* and *vote00*? Is it probable that we would get a chi-square this large in a table with 8 degrees of freedom simply by chance? We can use a statistical table of critical chi-square values to find out. There is an excerpt from such a statistical table in Table 11.9. (A more complete table is found in Appendix B.)

Tables of critical chi-square values are formatted like the segment in Table 11.9. The degrees of freedom are listed down the side (the rows) of the table. Alpha values are listed across the top (the columns of the table). The critical values of chi-square make up the body of the table.

For a chi-square value of 132.507 in a table with 8 degrees of freedom, the likelihood is low that the association we see in our table is simply due to chance. How do we know? Note first that the higher the chi-square value, the less likely it is that the value obtained is due to chance. Look at the last column in the table.

TABLE 11.9   Section of a Statistical Table of Values of Chi-Square for Contingency Tables with 8 Degrees of Freedom

				p Values				
df	.50	.30	.20	.10	.05	.02	.01	.001
8	7.344	9.524	11.030	13.362	15.507	18.168	20.090	26.125

It tells us that for a chi-square value of 26.125 or more in a table with 8 degrees of freedom, there is no more than 1 chance in 1,000 that the result is due to chance. On the other hand, look at the first column in the table. It tells us that for a chi-square value of 7.344 or less, there are at least 50 chances in 100 that the association is due to mere chance. Our chi-square value is 132.507, much more than the critical value of 26.125, so there is no more than 1 chance in 1,000 that our association is due to chance.

As a rule of thumb, to reject the null hypothesis we have to reach the critical value of chi-square associated with the .05 alpha level. Why? Because with an alpha level of .05 we can say that there are only 5 chances in 100 that the statistical dependence we find in the sample is due to chance. For a table with 8 degrees of freedom, the critical chi-square for the .05 level is 15.507. Our value is a lot more. We can reject the null hypothesis and make the assumption that education and voting are much more likely than not statistically dependent in the population from which we drew our sample.

Interpretation   How do you put all of this together to write about your analysis of chi-square? Here's an example:

> For the association between education and voting in the 2002 GSS, we can reject the null hypothesis. We have enough evidence to rule out the idea that the association we observed in our sample is due to chance. As a result, we can conclude that the association between education and voting in the sample is very likely to reflect a connection between these variables in the population of American adults from which the sample was drawn.

In the next example, the following Skills Practice, we'll see what happens when we get a different value of chi-square.

Skills Practice 7   Let's explore the research hypothesis that the more education a person has, the more likely he or she is to have contacted an elected official. State the null hypothesis for this association. Then describe the association between education and contacting elected officials in the contingency table in Table 11.10. Analyze the table first. Next compute chi-square for the table. How many degrees of freedom does the table have? What is the likelihood that any association you observe between these variables is due to chance? (Use Appendix B to find out.)

TABLE 11.10 Contingency Table for the Variables *degree* and *conoffcl* in the GSS 2002 subset A File

CONOFFCL Have ever contacted an elected official * DEGREE RS highest degree Crosstabulation

| | | | DEGREE RS highest degree | | | | | |
			0 LT HIGH SCHOOL	1 HIGH SCHOOL	2 JUNIOR COLLEGE	3 BACHELOR	4 GRADUATE	Total
CONOFFCL Have ever contacted an elected official	1 NO	Count	98	303	43	58	34	536
		% within DEGREE RS highest degree	91.6%	76.7%	67.2%	47.5%	48.6%	70.7%
	2 YES	Count	9	92	21	64	36	222
		% within DEGREE RS highest degree	8.4%	23.3%	32.8%	52.5%	51.4%	29.3%
Total		Count	107	395	64	122	70	758
		% within DEGREE RS highest degree	100.0%	100.0%	100.0%	100.0%	100.0%	100.0%

When we find that a chi-square value (or any measure of inference) is more than likely a consequence of real associations between variables (and not merely chance), then we say that the association is "statistically significant." Often, you will see something like, "The association between self-identified social class and happiness is significant at the .001 level." This means simply that there is no more than 1 chance in 1,000 that the association found in the sample is due to the luck of the draw. We infer that it is far more likely than not due to real associations between the variables in the population from which the sample was drawn.

Statistical significance refers to the likelihood of any pattern in a sample being no more than a chance occurrence. It is distinct from the concept of strength or the concept of practical significance. Whether a pattern we observe in a sample is important or not, or whether an association between two variables is strong or weak, is another matter, independent of statistical significance. We'll explore this point further in the last section of this chapter.

Limitations of Chi-Square

Chi-square, like measures of association, has its limits or conditions under which the chi-square value may be misleading in its assessment of statistical independence.

First, chi-square assumes that you are working with samples drawn using a probability design. It is not appropriate to use chi-square, or any other measure of inference, for samples that are not selected using probability techniques.

Second, chi-square shouldn't be used with contingency tables for which the expected frequency for one or more cells is less than 5. When expected frequencies are less than 5, it is possible for the difference between expected and observed frequencies in a single cell to have an inordinate impact on the chi-square value. There are situations in which the difference in a single cell can result in a chi-square value high enough to reject the null hypothesis. Consequently, when we see expected values less than 5, we should be cautious in our use of the chi-square statistic.

This is the case when we compute chi-square for the association between education and volunteering for a charity (using the variables *degree* and *volchrty* in the GSS 2002 subset A file). There are several cells with expected frequencies that are less than 5. Consequently, chi-square may be inflated and we could end up rejecting the null hypothesis even though there may be no association between the education and volunteering for charity variables in the population.

What can you do to overcome these limitations? Sometimes it is possible to collapse some of the categories of one or both variables in the contingency table to create larger observed and expected frequencies within the cells. You can use the recoding procedure to accomplish this. However, you can only combine categories of variables when the categories are logically related to one another. In general, you can only combine adjacent categories of ordinal variables. For example, you can take a variable like *volchrty* and combine the respondents who have volunteered once in a year with those who have volunteered two or three times a year, but it wouldn't make any sense to combine those who volunteer once a year and those who volunteer once a week merely to get larger observed and expected frequencies. You will work with a recoded volunteering for charity variable in the next section of this chapter.

For small contingency tables, those with only two categories of the independent and dependent variables (also called 2-by-2 tables) and only 1 degree of freedom, you cannot use chi-square if any of the expected cell frequencies fall below 5. If cell frequencies are 5 or more, but less than 10, you must use a slight variation on the chi-square formula, called **Yates' correction**.

Formula 11.3: Yates' correction for chi-square

$$\chi^2 = \sum \left\{ \frac{\left[\left(f_o - f_e \right) - .5 \right]^2}{f_e} \right\}$$

Note that you are simply subtracting .5 from the difference between the observed and expected cell frequencies before squaring the result. The effect of this adjustment is to reduce the impact on the chi-square value of the difference between observed and expected frequencies in a single cell.

The third limitation is that chi-square can be affected by large sample sizes. When you compute chi-square in a contingency table showing a weak association between two variables in a small sample, chi-square will probably indicate that the association you are observing is due to chance. However, when an association of the same strength is observed in a larger sample, chi-square gets much larger. Consequently, for an association observed in a small sample, you may be more likely to accept the null hypothesis. In an association observed in a larger sample, you will be more likely to reject the null hypothesis, even though the strength of the association is the same.

Some researchers believe that this limitation of chi-square causes us to reject null hypotheses for fairly minor associations. As a result, you will see reports of "statistically significant" associations that are very weak. Even though the association is weak, we find that it is not likely due to mere chance.

Other researchers believe that this is not a limitation of chi-square at all. As sample sizes grow larger, we *should* be more confident that associations we find in samples are representative of the populations from which the samples are drawn.

These researchers separate the issues of practical significance from the issue of statistical significance, which is a skill you will work on later in this chapter.

In the next section you will practice finding and interpreting chi-square using SPSS.

USING SPSS

Finding and Interpreting Chi-Square Statistics

SPSS GUIDE: FINDING CHI-SQUARE

Finding chi-square is fairly simple. At the SPSS Data Editor window, open the GSS 2002 subset A file and the Crosstabs dialog box by following the command path Analyze ➡ Descriptive Statistics ➡ Crosstabs.

1 At the Crosstabs window, select the variables for your contingency table. (Let's use *degree* and *rcvolchr*.)

2 Click on Cells, look under Percentages, and click on Column. Then click on Continue to go to back to the Crosstabs dialog box.

3 Click on Statistics to open the Statistics window. Look for Chi-Square in the upper left corner and click on it.

4 Click on Continue to go back to the Crosstabs dialog box. Then click on OK. You will get a contingency table for the variables *degree* and *rcvolchr* along with a set of chi-square statistics like the ones in Table 11.11. The chi-square you learned to calculate by hand is the Pearson chi-square.

Interpretation The *p* value, .000, tells us that there are less than 5 chances in 10,000 that the association we see in our contingency table is a chance occur-

TABLE 11.11   Chi-Square Values for the Variables *degree* and *rcvolchr* in the GSS 2002 subset A File

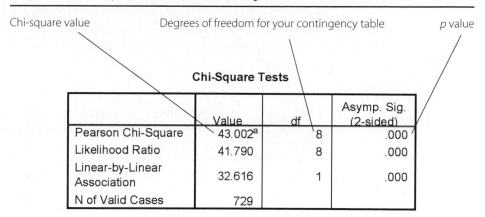

Chi-square value   Degrees of freedom for your contingency table   *p* value

Chi-Square Tests

	Value	df	Asymp. Sig. (2-sided)
Pearson Chi-Square	43.002[a]	8	.000
Likelihood Ratio	41.790	8	.000
Linear-by-Linear Association	32.616	1	.000
N of Valid Cases	729		

[a.] 0 cells (.0%) have expected count less than 5. The minimum expected count is 7.08.

rence and does not reflect real associations between education and volunteering for charity in the population. We know we can assign the value $p < .0005$, because if the fourth digit of the p value were 5 or greater, then SPSS would round it up to the nearest thousand ($p = .001$). SPSS provides a more precise reading of the probability value than you get in the tables of critical values of chi-square, but the bottom line is the same—we reject the null hypothesis that there is no association between education and volunteering for charity.

Skills Practice 8   Let's test the research hypothesis that there is a relationship between education and church attendance. State the null hypothesis for this association. Then use SPSS to produce a contingency table with column percentages for the association between *degree* and *rcattend*. Describe the association between these two variables (nature, direction, and strength). Use chi-square to assess the likelihood that a table showing this degree of statistical independence between the two variables could have been produced by chance.

Using Chi-Square with Measures of Association

Earlier in this chapter I said that the issues of statistical and practical significance are distinct. Chi-square is a measure of statistical significance, not a measure of practical significance. It can't tell you how strong an association is or (in the case of ordinal variables) anything about its direction. You may notice that chi-square does tend to be higher in tables with strong associations between variables, and smaller in tables with weaker associations. This is not always the case. Chi-square has to be used in conjunction with some other, appropriate (given the level of measurement of variables in the table) measure of association.

For the example for the association between *degree* and *rcvolchr,* the appropriate measure of association is gamma or Somer's d. As you should recall from Chapters 9 and 10, measures of association allow us to evaluate the nature (including direction for ordinal and numerical variables) and strength of an association.

Skills Practice 9 Use SPSS to find gamma for *degree* and *rcvolchr.* What do you learn about the association (its nature, direction, and strength)? You will find the answer next.

Let's combine what you just learned about the relationship between *degree* and *rcvolchr* using an appropriate measure of association with what you learned about the likelihood that the association is not simply due to chance.

There appears to be an association between level of education and volunteering for charity. The more education respondents have, the more they tend to volunteer. The relationship is somewhat weak. With a gamma of .304 we can confirm that the association is positive. Knowing the association between education level and volunteering improves our ability to predict how often respondents volunteer by 30%. It is not likely that a chi-square value of 43.002 in a table with 8 degrees of freedom is a chance occurrence ($p < .0005$). The null hypothesis, that there is no association between education and volunteering for charity in the population from which this sample was drawn, is rejected.

Skills Practice 10 Use SPSS to find an appropriate measure of association to examine the relationship between *degree* and *rcattend.* Write an analysis of the contingency table for these variables. Describe the nature, direction, and strength of the association. Add your chi-square statistics to your analysis.

In the next two chapters you will learn about measures of association and inference for associations involving numerical variables.

SUMMARY

This chapter introduced you to measures of inference for variables in contingency tables. Measures of inference allow us to decide whether to reject the null hypothesis, the hypothesis that there is no association between two variables in the population from which a random sample is drawn. Testing a null hypothesis involves computing a test statistic, chi-square in this case, and then seeing whether the test statistic reaches the values of the statistic that are critical for rejecting the null hypothesis.

For computing chi-square, it is necessary to understand the difference between expected frequencies in a frequency table (those frequencies we would expect to see in a table in which there is no association between two variables), and the observed frequencies in a table (those frequencies we find when we do some sort of observation of a sample drawn using probability techniques). The chi-square statistic is based on the extent of difference between the expected and observed frequencies. The difference between the two allows us to assess the degree of statistical independence—the extent to which the values (or responses to the values) of one variable change independently of the values (or responses to the values) of a second variable.

Once we compute a test statistic, we can compare it to a table of critical values of the test statistic. This comparison allows us to see whether our test value is likely to have occurred by chance or whether it represents associations in samples that are likely to be representative of the populations from which the samples were drawn. If it is likely that the test value of chi-square is simply due to a chance occurrence, then we cannot reject the null hypothesis. We cannot give up the idea that the sample does not represent real associations between variables in a population. If the value of chi-square isn't likely to be due merely to chance, then we can reject the null hypothesis.

KEY CONCEPTS

Research hypothesis

Null hypothesis

Statistical independence

Type I error

Type II error

Chi-square (χ^2)

Obtained value of a test statistic

Critical value of a test statistic

Test statistic

Observed frequencies

Expected frequencies

Degrees of freedom

Probability value (p value)

Alpha value, alpha level

Statistical significance

Yates' correction

ANSWERS TO SKILLS PRACTICES

1. Like the association in the "News to Use" excerpt, there is a relationship between education and volunteering for charity among the respondents to the 2002 General Social Survey. The more education respondents have, the more likely they are to volunteer. The association is positive, and it appears to be at best a moderate one. The association is not entirely consistent across the categories of the dependent variable, and the differences in the percentages in most rows are not very large.

6. Table 11.4 has 8 degrees of freedom.

7. The null hypothesis is that there is no association between education and contacting elected officials, or that education and contacting elected officials are statistically independent. The association between education and contacting elected officials in Table 11.10 is one in which the higher the respondents' education, the more likely they are to have contacted an elected official. It is a positive association. To find out whether it is likely that the statistical dependence found in the sample could come from a population in which there is no association between the two variables, we compute chi-square.

The following table gives the observed (count) and expected cell frequencies (expected count) for Table 11.10.

Observed frequency   Expected frequency

CONOFFCL Have ever contacted an elected official * DEGREE RS highest degree Crosstabulation

| | | | DEGREE RS highest degree | | | | | |
			0 LT HIGH SCHOOL	1 HIGH SCHOOL	2 JUNIOR COLLEGE	3 BACHELOR	4 GRADUATE	Total
CONOFFCL Have ever contacted an elected official	1 NO	Count	98	303	43	58	34	536
		Expected Count	75.6	279.3	45.2	86.3	49.5	536.0
	2 YES	Count	9	92	21	64	36	222
		Expected Count	31.4	115.7	18.8	35.7	20.5	222.0
Total		Count	107	395	64	122	70	758
		Expected Count	107.0	395.0	64.0	122.0	70.0	758.0

Next are given the computations for each cell for the chi-square formula

$$\frac{\left(f_o - f_e\right)^2}{f_e}$$

For the first cell (Less than High School and NO), the computations are as follows:

$$\frac{\left(f_o - f_e\right)^2}{f_e} = \frac{\left(98 - 75.6\right)^2}{75.6} = \frac{\left(22.4\right)^2}{75.6} = \frac{501.76}{75.6} = 6.637$$

See the following table for the rest of the computations. (Note: The computations assume expected cell frequencies are rounded to the first decimal.)

CONOFFCL Have ever contacted an elected official * DEGREE RS highest degree Crosstabulation

| | | DEGREE RS highest degree | | | | |
		0 LT HIGH SCHOOL	1 HIGH SCHOOL	2 JUNIOR COLLEGE	3 BACHELOR	4 GRADUATE
CONOFFCL Have ever contacted an elected official	1 NO	6.637	2.011	.107	9.280	4.854
	2 YES	15.980	4.855	.257	22.434	11.720

Add up the contents of each cell to get the chi-square statistic:

6.637 + 15.980 + 2.011 + 4.855 + .107 + .257 + 9.280 + 22.434 + 4.854 + 11.720 = 78.135

Interpretation   The likelihood of obtaining a chi-square value of 78.135 by chance in a contingency table with four degrees of freedom is less than 1 in 1,000 ($p < .001$). The null hypothesis—that education and contacting elected officials are statistically independent—is rejected. By extension, then, we accept the premise that there is an association between education and contacting elected officials in the population—the more education the respondents' have, the more likely they are to contact elected officials.

8. The null hypothesis is that there is no association between education and church attendance (or that education and church attendance are statistically independent).

Your contingency table should look like the one that follows.

RCATTEND Recoded how often R attends religious services * DEGREE RS highest degree Crosstabulation

			DEGREE RS highest degree					
			0 LT HIGH SCHOOL	1 HIGH SCHOOL	2 JUNIOR COLLEGE	3 BACHELOR	4 GRADUATE	Total
RCATTEND Recoded how often R attends religious services	0 NEVER	Count	53	158	13	32	26	282
		% within DEGREE RS highest degree	23.9%	20.1%	12.0%	13.1%	21.0%	19.0%
	1 SEVERAL TIMES A YR OR LESS	Count	64	282	41	97	36	520
		% within DEGREE RS highest degree	28.8%	35.9%	38.0%	39.6%	29.0%	35.0%
	2 AT LEAST MONTHLY	Count	59	157	26	52	34	328
		% within DEGREE RS highest degree	26.6%	20.0%	24.1%	21.2%	27.4%	22.1%
	3 AT LEAST WEEKLY	Count	46	188	28	64	28	354
		% within DEGREE RS highest degree	20.7%	23.9%	25.9%	26.1%	22.6%	23.9%
Total		Count	222	785	108	245	124	1484
		% within DEGREE RS highest degree	100.0%	100.0%	100.0%	100.0%	100.0%	100.0%

What's the association? The more education respondents have, the more likely they are to attend church. The association is positive, and it isn't very strong because the highest percentages in each row are not lined up on a diagonal, the differences between the percentages are not very large, and the pattern of association across the categories of the dependent variable is not consistent.

Your chi-square statistics should look like the ones in the following table.

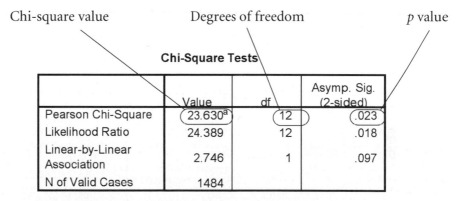

Chi-square value   Degrees of freedom   *p* value

Chi-Square Tests

	Value	df	Asymp. Sig. (2-sided)
Pearson Chi-Square	23.630[a]	12	.023
Likelihood Ratio	24.389	12	.018
Linear-by-Linear Association	2.746	1	.097
N of Valid Cases	1484		

[a]. 0 cells (.0%) have expected count less than 5. The minimum expected count is 20.52.

There are only 2.3 chances in 100 that the association we see in the table is a chance occurrence. As a result, the null hypothesis is rejected. More likely than not, the association between education and church attendance is the result of a real relationship between these variables in the population from which the sample was drawn.

10. Using gamma, we see that the association is weak (.058) and positive. The more education respondents have, the more likely they are to attend church. Knowing the association between the independent and dependent variables improves our ability to predict the dependent variable by only 6%.

The likelihood of obtaining a chi-square of 23.630 in a table with 12 degrees of freedom by chance is about 2 in 100. Consequently, we can reject the null hypothesis that there is no association between one's level of education and how often one attends church in the population the sample represents.

For the contingency tables in Exercises 1–4, find the obtained chi-square for the 2002 GSS respondents. Calculate degrees of freedom. Compare your obtained chi-square values with the critical values of chi-square in Appendix B. Interpret what you find.

1.

VOTE00 Did R vote in 2000 election * RCAGE Recoded age variable Crosstabulation

			RCAGE Recoded age variable				
			1 18 THRU 25	2 26 THRU 40	3 41 THRU 60	4 61 THRU 89	Total
VOTE00 Did R vote in 2000 election	1 VOTED	Count	61	261	363	270	955
		% within RCAGE Recoded age variable	34.5%	58.4%	71.0%	79.2%	64.7%
	2 DID NOT VOTE	Count	90	155	132	65	442
		% within RCAGE Recoded age variable	50.8%	34.7%	25.8%	19.1%	29.9%
	3 INELIGIBLE	Count	26	31	16	6	79
		% within RCAGE Recoded age variable	14.7%	6.9%	3.1%	1.8%	5.4%
Total		Count	177	447	511	341	1476
		% within RCAGE Recoded age variable	100.0%	100.0%	100.0%	100.0%	100.0%

2.

RCATTEND Recoded how often R attends religious services * RCAGE Recoded age variable Crosstabulation

			RCAGE Recoded age variable				
			1 18 THRU 25	2 26 THRU 40	3 41 THRU 60	4 61 THRU 89	Total
RCATTEND Recoded how often R attends religious services	0 NEVER	Count	41	75	105	60	281
		% within RCAGE Recoded age variable	22.9%	16.9%	20.6%	17.4%	19.0%
	1 SEVERAL TIMES A YR OR LESS	Count	65	173	177	103	518
		% within RCAGE Recoded age variable	36.3%	38.9%	34.7%	29.9%	35.0%
	2 AT LEAST MONTHLY	Count	41	105	108	74	328
		% within RCAGE Recoded age variable	22.9%	23.6%	21.2%	21.4%	22.2%
	3 AT LEAST WEEKLY	Count	32	92	120	108	352
		% within RCAGE Recoded age variable	17.9%	20.7%	23.5%	31.3%	23.8%
Total		Count	179	445	510	345	1479
		% within RCAGE Recoded age variable	100.0%	100.0%	100.0%	100.0%	100.0%

3.

RCVOLCHR Recoded has R done volunteer work for charity * SEX Respondents' sex Crosstabulation

			SEX Respondents' sex		Total
			1 MALE	2 FEMALE	
RCVOLCHR Recoded has R done volunteer work for charity	1 NOT AT ALL IN PAST YR	Count	214	186	400
		% within SEX Respondents' sex	62.0%	48.4%	54.9%
	2 AT LEAST ONCE IN PAST YR	Count	91	118	209
		% within SEX Respondents' sex	26.4%	30.7%	28.7%
	3 AT LEAST ONCE A MONTH IN PAST YR	Count	40	80	120
		% within SEX Respondents' sex	11.6%	20.8%	16.5%
Total		Count	345	384	729
		% within SEX Respondents' sex	100.0%	100.0%	100.0%

4.

HAPPY General happiness * RCVOLCHR Recoded has R done volunteer work for charity Crosstabulation

			RCVOLCHR Recoded has R done volunteer work for charity			Total
			1 NOT AT ALL IN PAST YR	2 AT LEAST ONCE IN PAST YR	3 AT LEAST ONCE A MONTH IN PAST YR	
HAPPY General happiness	1 NOT TOO HAPPY	Count	55	22	8	85
		% within RCVOLCHR Recoded has R done volunteer work for charity	13.8%	10.5%	6.7%	11.7%
	2 PRETTY HAPPY	Count	233	119	67	419
		% within RCVOLCHR Recoded has R done volunteer work for charity	58.4%	56.9%	55.8%	57.6%
	3 VERY HAPPY	Count	111	68	45	224
		% within RCVOLCHR Recoded has R done volunteer work for charity	27.8%	32.5%	37.5%	30.8%
Total		Count	399	209	120	728
		% within RCVOLCHR Recoded has R done volunteer work for charity	100.0%	100.0%	100.0%	100.0%

SPSS EXERCISES

For the variables in Exercises 1–4, write an appropriate null hypothesis, then use SPSS to test it. Produce a contingency table. Analyze it and find and interpret an appropriate measure of association and chi-square.

1. *sex* and *othshelp*
2. *sex* and *rcattend*
3. *rcattend* and *grppol*
4. *rcattend* and *rcvolchr*

CHAPTER 12

Evaluating Associations between Numerical Variables

INTRODUCTION

By now you should have a sense of how measures of association work to help us make predictions. These numbers can help us make more accurate guesses about important characteristics of individuals. For example, we learned that if you know a person's education, you can make a better guess about his or her involvement in civic activities like volunteering and voting. You may not always guess correctly, but your chances of making an accurate prediction are improved.

In this chapter we will look at some measures of association for numerical variables—statistics that will do for numerical variables what lambda, phi, Cramer's V, and gamma can do for categorical variables. You will be learning about two techniques in this chapter. The first technique, comparison of means, is a simple way to look at the relationship between categorical variables and numerical variables. The second technique is called regression analysis and it is used with pairs of numerical variables.

We will use these techniques to answer questions such as, Are there differences in educational achievement among the respondents to the General Social Survey? Does educational achievement vary by sex, race, age, or region of residence? To what extent do fathers' or mothers' educational achievements account for their offsprings' achievements? Do people tend to have spouses with educational backgrounds similar to their own?

In the "News to Use" section there is a report from the U.S. Bureau of the Census that addresses a number of these questions. You will notice as you read the article that a variety of techniques are employed to address these issues, including the analysis of frequency distributions, contingency tables, and the comparison of means. (See Table 12.1 at the end of the article.) ■

NEWS to USE
Statistics in the "Real" World

The Big Payoff: Educational Attainment and Synthetic Estimates[1] of Life Earnings[2]

BY JENNIFER CHEESEMAN DAY AND ERIC C. NEWBURGER

Does going to school pay off? Most people think so. Currently, almost 90 percent of young adults graduate from high school and about 60 percent of high school seniors continue on to college the following year. People decide to go to college for many reasons. One of the most compelling is the expectation of future economic success based on educational attainment.

This report illustrates the economic value of an education, that is, the added value of a high school diploma or college degree. It explores the relationship between educational attainment and earnings and demonstrates how the relationship has changed over the last 25 years. Additionally, it provides, by level of education, synthetic estimates of the average total earnings adults are likely to accumulate over the course of their working lives.

These synthetic estimates of work-life earnings, which are based on data from the Current Population Survey (CPS), are illustrative and do not predict actual future earnings. The synthetic work-life earnings are "expected average amounts" based on cross-sectional earnings data for the preceding calendar year by age, sex, full- or part-time work experience, race, Hispanic origin, and educational attainment groupings, as collected in the March 1998, 1999, and 2000 Current Population Surveys (CPS).[3] The synthetic work-life estimates are thus based on 1997–1999 earnings data and are shown in terms of "present value" (constant 1999 dollars).[4] These synthetic estimates are shown in detail in three tables at the end of this report.

EDUCATION AND EARNINGS

We are more educated than ever.

In 2000, 84 percent of American adults ages 25 and over had at least completed high school; 26 percent had a bachelor's degree or higher . . .

---

[1] "Synthetic" estimates of work-life earnings are created by using the working population's 1-year annual earnings and summing their age-specific average earnings for people ages 25 to 64 years. The resulting totals represent what individuals with the same educational level could expect to earn, on average, in today's dollars, during a hypothetical 40-year working life. A typical worklife is defined as the period from age 25 through age 64. While many people stop working at an age other than 65, or start before age 25, this range of 40 years provides a practical benchmark for many people.

[2] U.S. Bureau of the Census *Current Population Report Special Studies.* July 2002, <http://www.census.gov/prod/2002pubs/pdf23-210.pdf>.

[3] This report refers to "work-life earnings" rather than "life-time earnings." The latter would account for the probability of life events, which might alter the average number of years people work, such as early death or accidents leading to disability.

[4] See the Methodology section of this report [available on the Internet at the Web site listed in footnote 2 above] for a detailed explanation of the limitations of these estimates. The estimates in this report are based on responses from a sample of the population. As with all surveys, estimates may vary from the actual values for the entire population because of sampling variation, or other factors. All statements made in this report have undergone statistical testing and meet Census Bureau standards for statistical accuracy.

Both figures were all-time highs. In 1975, 63 percent of adults had a high school diploma, and 14 percent had obtained a bachelor's degree . . . Much of the increase in educational attainment levels of the adult population is due to a more educated younger population replacing an older, less educated population. As more and more people continue their schooling, this more highly educated population pursues opportunities to enter into occupations yielding higher returns in earnings.

Earnings increase with educational level.

Adults ages 25 to 64 who worked at any time during the study period[5] earned an average of $34,700 per year.[6] Average earnings ranged from $18,900 for high school dropouts to $25,900 for high school graduates, $45,400 for college graduates, and $99,300 for workers with professional degrees (M.D., J.D., D.D.S., or D.V.M.) . . . [W]ith the exception of workers with professional degrees who have the highest average earnings, each successively higher education level is associated with an increase in earnings.

Work experience also influences earnings. Average earnings for people who worked full-time, year-round were somewhat higher than average earnings for all workers (which include people who work part-time or for part of the year). Most workers worked full-time and year-round (74 percent). However, the commitment to work full-time, year-round varies with demographic factors, such as educational attainment, sex, and age. For instance, high school dropouts (65 percent) are less likely than people with bachelor's degrees (77 percent) to work full-time and year-round. Historically, women's attachment to the labor force has been more irregular than men's due mostly to competing family responsibilities . . .

[5] The study period covers 3 years—1997, 1998, and 1999. Earnings are represented in 1999 dollars.
[6] Though medians provide a measure of central tendency less sensitive to outliers, and so are often used in describing earnings data, means present fewer computational difficulties, both in modeling the synthetic work-life estimates and in creating statistical procedures to test these estimates.

Earnings estimates based on all workers (which includes part-time workers) include some of this variability. Yet, regardless of work experience, the education advantage remains. . . .

Historically, education has paid off

Over the past 25 years, earnings differences have grown among workers with different levels of educational attainment . . . [I]n 1975, full-time, year-round workers with a bachelor's degree had 1.5 times the annual earnings of workers with only a high school diploma . . . By 1999, this ratio had risen to 1.8. Workers with an advanced degree, who earned 1.8 times the earnings of high school graduates in 1975, averaged 2.6 times the earnings of workers with a high school diploma in 1999. During the same period, the relative earnings of the least educated workers fell. While in 1975, full-time, year-round workers without a high school diploma earned 0.9 times the earnings of workers with a high school diploma; by 1999, they were earning only 0.7 times the average earnings of high school graduates. . . .

SEX, EDUCATION, AND EARNINGS

The educational gap between men and women is narrowing.

Among people ages 25 and older, the percentage of men and women with a bachelor's degree has increased sharply over the past 25 years, with women markedly narrowing the gap. In 1975, 18 percent of men and 11 percent of women had attained a bachelor's degree. By 2000, 28 percent of men and 24 percent of women had a bachelor's degree. In fact, in each year since 1982, more American women than men have received bachelor's degrees . . . Additionally, 84 percent of both men and women had completed high school in 2000, up from 63 percent for men and 62 percent for women in 1975.

Men earn more than women at each education level

Men had higher average earnings than women with similar educational attainment. Among full-time, year-round workers ages 25 to 64, the female-to-male earnings ratio was 0.67 during the study period . . . This wage gap occurred with very little variation at every level of educational attainment.

Across the ages, however, the female-to-male earnings ratio was higher among younger full-time, year-round workers (0.84) than among older workers (0.56). Clearly, younger women begin their work-life with earnings much closer to those realized by men.[7] This pattern of male and female younger workers starting with closer earnings than those of older workers is not new. In 1975, the earnings ratio was 0.69 for younger workers compared with 0.56 for older workers. The age differences remain, although the earnings gap between younger men and women is closing . . . At both the high school and bachelor's attainment level, the earnings of younger women and men are relatively close with women earning about four-fifths of men's earnings. However, for workers with a bachelor's attainment, the earnings difference between men and women becomes more pronounced as workers age (from 0.81 for ages 25 to 29 years compared with 0.60 for ages 60 to 64), compared with a relatively flat earnings difference for workers at the high school level.[8]

Numerous events over one's worklife may account for the expanding wage gap with age, such as continuous participation in the labor force, commitment to career goals, competing events, discrimination, and promotions. These and other factors may lower the earnings of women relative to men, and these differences play out dramatically with total work-life earnings. . . .

[7] Some of the persistent, though shrinking, differences in earnings may be related to field of study. Women have historically tended to major in fields with lower economic rewards than have men. While this remains the case, a growing proportion of female college graduates now receive bachelor's degrees in more highly paid fields, such as business or computers (National Center for Education Statistics, "1999 Digest of Education Statistics," U.S. Department of Education, NCES 2000-031).

[8] The female-to-male earnings ratio for workers ages 60–64 with a high school diploma does not differ significantly from the ratio for younger workers, ages 25–29.

RACE AND HISPANIC ORIGIN, EDUCATION, AND EARNINGS

Educational attainment and work-life earnings vary by race and Hispanic origin.

Educational attainment differs significantly by race and Hispanic origin. Among adults 25 years old and over in 2000, 88 percent of White non-Hispanics, 86 percent of Asians and Pacific Islanders, and 79 percent of Blacks had attained at least a high school diploma.[9] Similarly, 28 percent of White non-Hispanics, 44 percent of Asians and Pacific Islanders, and 17 percent of Blacks had received a Bachelor's degree. For Hispanics (who may be of any race), only 57 percent had a high school diploma and 11 percent a bachelor's degree. Even accounting for these large differences in educational attainment by looking at earnings within each education category, earnings differences persist and can accumulate dramatically over a 40-year work-life . . .

White non-Hispanics earn more than Blacks or Hispanics at almost every level of educational attainment.[10] For example, among full-time, year-round workers with a high school education, White non-Hispanics will earn an average of $1.3 million during their working life, compared with about $1.1 million earned by Blacks and Hispanics . . . At the bachelor's level, White non-Hispanics can expect total earnings of about $2.2 million, compared with $1.7 million for Blacks or Hispanics.

[9] Because Hispanics may be of any race, data in this report for Hispanics overlap slightly with data for the Black population and for the Asian and Pacific Islander population. Based on the March 1998, 1999, and 2000 Current Population Survey samples, 3 percent of Black adults 25 to 64 years old and 2 percent of Asian and Pacific Islanders 25 to 64 years old are also of Hispanic origin. Data for the American Indian and Alaska Native population are not shown in this report because of their small sample size in the March 1998, 1999, and 2000 Current Population Surveys.

[10] With the exception of workers with an associates degree where the work-life earnings estimates for Hispanics do not differ significantly than those for White non-Hispanics.

TABLE 12.1   Average Annual Earnings by Educational Attainment, Sex, and Race Based on 1997–1999 Work Experience (in 1999 Dollars)

Characteristic	Not a High School Graduate	High School Graduate	Some College	Associate's Degree	Bachelor's Degree	Master's Degree	Professional Degree	Doctoral Degree
Total	18,894	25,909	31,192	33,020	45,294	54,537	99,253	81,430
Male	22,636	32,024	39,031	40,608	56,779	67,202	115,931	91,982
Female	13,217	19,156	23,015	26,104	32,816	41,270	63,904	56,807
							Advanced Degree	
White	19,490	26,721	32,170	33,685	46,673			67,590
Black	15,987	21,692	26,362	28,146	36,311			47,699
Hispanic	16,792	22,572	26,507	29,367	36,172			58,299

Source: U.S. Bureau of the Census, *Current Population Reports Special Studies,* "The Big Payoff: Educational Attainment and Synthetic Estimates of Work-Life Earnings," Tables 1–3, July 2002.

COMPARING MEANS

Some of the questions we want to answer require us to examine a numerical variable (like educational achievement—*educ* in the General Social Survey) in concert with one or more categorical variables *(sex, race, age, region of residence,* and *labor force status).* Trying to produce a contingency table with a numerical variable can create an enormous table that runs over several pages. The larger the contingency table, the more difficult it is to see the patterns in the data. **Comparing means** is an easy way to see patterns in numerical variables when they are paired with categorical variables.

The "News to Use" article in this chapter makes extensive use of the comparison of means as it examines differences in average annual earnings by levels of education, sex, and race. For example, using the statistics in the first row of Table 12.1 you can describe the nature of the association between the variables *level of education* and *annual earnings.* Average annual earnings go up as education levels rise. In addition, you can get an indication of the strength of the association by looking at the sizes of the differences in the means across the first row of the table and the consistency of the pattern. (Do incomes rise consistently across all categories of the education level variable or are there exceptions to the general pattern?) Finally, if both variables involved in the analysis are ordinal or higher, then you can also describe the direction of the association. In the case of the association between annual earnings and education level, the association appears to be fairly strong because the differences in the averages across the first row are fairly substantial and the pattern is generally consistent. It is a positive association (as education level rises, annual earnings go up).

Researchers create tables like Table 12.1 by dividing a set of data by a characteristic (such as education level) and then computing the average of the responses to a second variable for each group. In Table 12.1 you see average annual earnings for those who are not high school graduates, those who did complete high school, and so on. By comparing average of annual earnings for each cate-

TABLE 12.2 A Comparison of Means for the Variables *sex* and *educ* in the GSS 2002 subset B File

Report

Mean

SEX Respondents sex	EDUC Highest year of school completed
1 MALE	13.30
2 FEMALE	13.38
Total	13.35

gory of the education level variable, you can see if there are differences in the averages (the means) across the categories of the education level variable.

Similarly, you can see if this pattern holds for both males and for females in the second and third rows of Table 12.1. And it does. The more education respondents have, the higher their average annual earnings. In essence, the second and third rows of Table 12.1 control for the variable *sex*. Besides allowing us to tell if the general pattern for all respondents still holds for a particular group, the second and third rows enable us to compare males and females and see if there are differences between the two. What can you tell about differences between male and female respondents? Although education seems to lead to higher earnings for both groups, it is clear that the average of the annual earnings for males is higher than it is for females in every category of educational level. Moreover, the gap generally widens as educational level goes up.

You can do the same kind of analysis with the last three rows of Table 12.1. What happens to average annual earnings when you look at White, Black, and Hispanic respondents to the U. S. Bureau of the Census survey separately? Does the pattern you see among all respondents hold for each category of race? What are the differences between White, Black, and Hispanic respondents?

Later on in this chapter you will learn how to produce a table to compare means using SPSS.

Skills Practice 1 Practice your skills for comparing means by using Table 12.2 to evaluate differences in educational levels *(educ)* by the variable, *sex*. What is the nature of the association? Is the association a very strong one?

Now let's turn our attention to techniques for examining the association between two numerical variables—regression analysis.

REGRESSION ANALYSIS

Regression analysis involves the application of a set of statistics to evaluate the association between two numerical variables. Just as the analysis of associations between nominal or ordinal variables begins by using contingency tables to assess a relationship, regression analysis begins with a visual display of data called a scatterplot. To the visual display, we can add a line, called the regression line, which provides additional information about the association. Finally, we can supplement what we learn visually with a set of statistics—Pearson's *r* (a measure of association), the coefficient of determination (or *r*-squared), and statistics about the characteristics of the line through the data—that allow us to make predictions about the relationship.

The Scatterplot

The visual display of the association between two numerical variables is called a scatterplot. A **scatterplot** is simply the graphic representation of the responses to two variables plotted along a horizontal *x*-axis (for the independent variable) and a vertical *y*-axis (for the dependent variable). The scatterplot shows us how changes in the values of one variable are related to changes in the values of a second.

Let's start by seeing whether the respondents' educational achievements influence their earning power. For this example, I am using some made-up data—for an association between years of education and annual income—so you can see how a scatterplot illustrates associations (Figure 12.1). Notice that the points on the scatterplot rise from the lower left to the upper right corners of the diagram. This pattern suggests that changes (increases) in the values of the first variable, *years of education,* are associated with or related to changes (increases) in the values of the second variable, *annual income.* Responses to the two variables change together.

FIGURE 12.1
Scatterplot for the association between years of education and annual income for a set of hypothetical data.

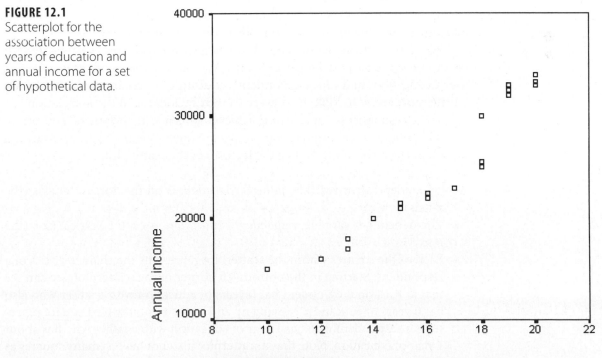

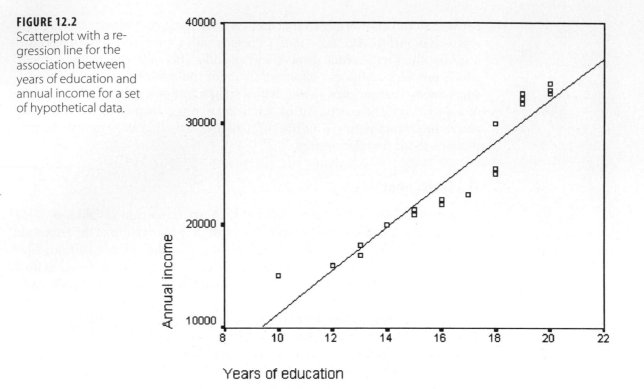

The association between the variables is very clear in Figure 12.1. If we drew a line through the middle of the points on the scatterplot (Figure 12.2), it would be a fairly steep line, and most of the points in the scatterplot would fall very close to the line. Taken together, these features of the scatterplot suggest a very strong and positive association between these two variables. As the respondents' education rises, their level of income increases correspondingly.

We rarely see associations this clear when we are using real-world data, but we do see some fairly strong associations. We can use the variables *paeduc* (father's education) and *educ* (respondent's education) to see how scatterplots are a little more likely to look. If we were to start by looking at the association between the respondents' educational achievements and their fathers' education, we could obtain a scatterplot diagram like the one in Figure 12.3, which would represent the association. Notice the features of the scatterplot:

- The independent variable, *father's education,* is on the horizontal axis (the *x*-axis).
- The dependent variable, *respondent's education,* is on the vertical axis (the *y*-axis).
- Each of the squares within the scatterplot represents the characteristics of a respondent. Starting in the bottom left corner of the scatterplot, we can see that at least one respondent has 0 years of education with a father who also has 0 years of education. Moving up and to the right, the next square represents a respondent who has 1 year of education with a father who has about 1 year of education. Note that a scatterplot may not have as many squares as there are respondents, because there may be more than one respondent

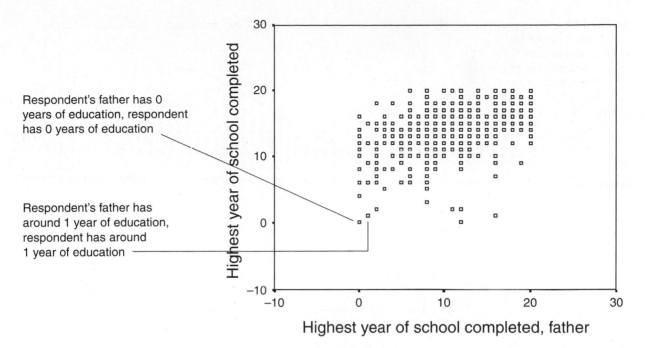

Respondent's father has 0 years of education, respondent has 0 years of education

Respondent's father has around 1 year of education, respondent has around 1 year of education

Highest year of school completed, father

FIGURE 12.3
Scatterplot for the variables *paeduc* and *educ* in the GSS 2002 subset B file.

sharing a particular set of characteristics. (Many respondents may have the same level of education, for example.)

What does the scatterplot tell us? First, we can see whether the general pattern of the association between two variables is positive or negative. How? By looking at the shape of the distribution. In Figure 12.3, we can see that the points tend to spread out across the graph starting in the lower left corner and moving upward toward the right corner. Low values of the independent variable, *father's education,* are associated with low values of the dependent variable, *respondent's education,* and vice versa. In short, there is a positive association between the two variables. The more education the respondents' fathers have, the more education the respondents are likely to have.

Second, we can assess the strength of the association by drawing a line around the points. Then

1. See whether the resulting shape looks more like a pencil (strong association), a cigar (weaker association), an oval (still weaker), or a circle (almost no association).
2. Look at the steepness of the slope of the shape we have drawn—as a rule, the steeper the slope the stronger the association. However, the steepness of the slope has to be interpreted in conjunction with the shape of the line drawn around the plot points.

Practice with Figure 12.3. Draw a line that encompasses most of the points (you can exclude for the time being those points that fall outside what appears to be the general pattern of the data). You should get a shape like the one in Figure 12.4.

FIGURE 12.4
Using a scatterplot to determine the direction of an association for the variables *paeduc* and *educ* in the GSS 2002 subset B file.

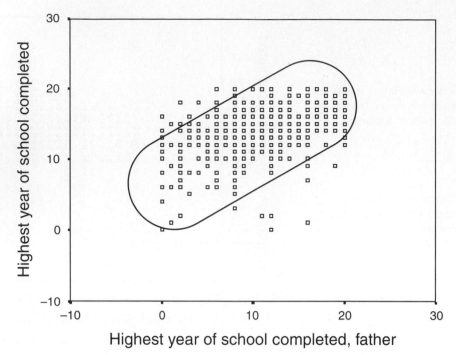

Highest year of school completed, father

Note that the shape extends from the lower left corner of the graph to the upper right corner, a positive association. It looks somewhat like an oval, but it is fairly steeply sloped. Taken together, the shape and slope indicate an association somewhere in the moderate range.

The Regression Line

Now, let's add one more feature to the graph—a straight line. Try drawing a straight line through the middle of the points to indicate the general direction and the slope of the association. Try to draw your line in such a way that the distance between the line and each of the points is minimized; the line should come as close to as many of the points as possible, while at the same time halving the distance between the points that aren't close to the line. I realize these instructions may be a little abstract, but do the best you can. You will probably come up with a line somewhat like the one in Figure 12.5.

The line you came up with is conceptually similar to a regression line. A **regression line,** like the one in Figure 12.5, is a mathematically derived line drawn through the points in a set of data so as to minimize the average of the squared distances between each point and the line itself—but more about that in a minute. Like the general shape of the distribution, the line itself can indicate the direction of an association. It's positive if the line slopes from the bottom left corner of the graph up toward the top right corner (Figure 12.6) and negative if the line slopes from the top left corner of the diagram toward the bottom right corner (Figure 12.7).

The strength of the regression line can be estimated by looking at the steepness of the slope and the relationship between the points and the line—the closer the points are to the line, the stronger the association is (Figure 12.8); the more spread out the points are in relation to the line, the weaker the association is (Figure 12.9).

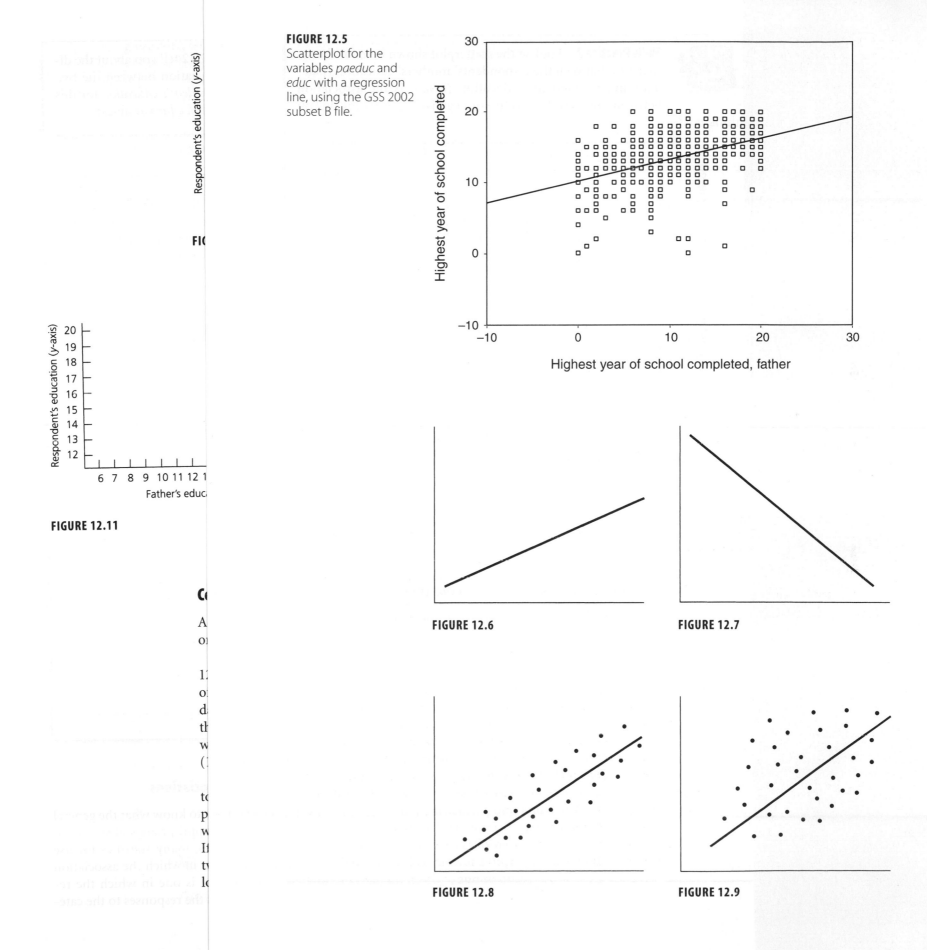

FIGURE 12.5
Scatterplot for the variables *paeduc* and *educ* with a regression line, using the GSS 2002 subset B file.

FIGURE 12.11

FIGURE 12.6

FIGURE 12.7

FIGURE 12.8

FIGURE 12.9

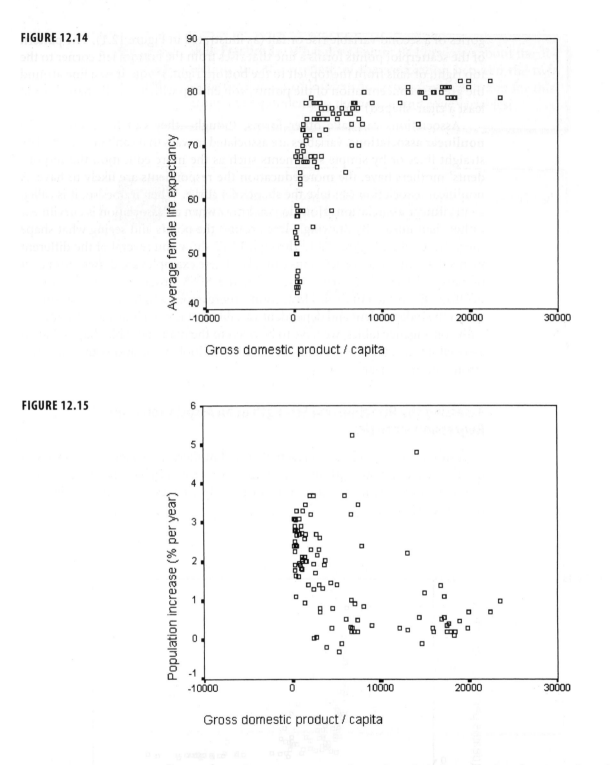

FIGURE 12.14

FIGURE 12.15

Pearson's *r* One very commonly used statistic for assessing the strength and direction of an association between two variables is called Pearson's *r* or Pearson's correlation. **Pearson's *r*** evaluates the extent to which the responses to two variables tend to vary together. For example, it answers the question, Do respondents whose fathers are highly educated tend to be more highly educated themselves (a positive association), or do respondents whose fathers have a lot of education tend to have less education (a negative association)?

Pearson's *r* ranges in value between –1 and +1. Like the measures for categorical variables, the closer the value is to –1 or +1, the stronger is the association. The closer Pearson's *r* is to 0, the weaker the association is. The sign on the variable—negative or positive (which is indicated by the absence of any sign at all)—tells us the direction of an association.

r-squared, the coefficient of determination   If you square Pearson's *r,* the result is a statistic called **r-squared** (represented symbolically as r^2) or the coefficient of determination. Unlike Pearson's *r,* the **coefficient of determination** doesn't indicate the direction of an association, but it does have a proportional reduction in error (PRE) interpretation.

The value of r^2 tells us how much of the variation in a dependent variable can be explained by the variation in the independent variable. It answers the question, *How much* of the variation in the respondents' educational achievements can be explained by the variation in their fathers' educational achievements? In the terms we used for describing the measures in Chapter 10, we can express *r*-squared as the degree of improvement in our ability to guess the dependent variable from knowledge of the general independent–dependent variable relationship.

The Computation of Pearson's *r* and *r*-squared

The computation of Pearson's *r* (and subsequently, *r*-squared) is similar to the computation of the deviations from the mean. The one twist is that you will have to find the mean, and the deviations from the mean, for two variables—the independent and the dependent variables. In addition, you will have to find the squares of the deviations (as you did to find the variance) for both variables as well as the products of the deviations. The formulas presented first are the conceptual formulas, which I am using largely to promote understanding of how the regression statistics work.

Formula 12.1(a): Conceptual formula for Pearson's *r*

$$\text{Pearson's } r = \frac{\Sigma\left(X - \overline{X}\right)\left(Y - \overline{Y}\right)}{\sqrt{\left[\Sigma\left(X - \overline{X}\right)^2\right]\left[\Sigma\left(Y - \overline{Y}\right)^2\right]}}$$

where *X* represents a value of the independent variable, *Y* represents a value of the dependent variable, $\overline{X}$ is the mean of the independent variable, and $\overline{Y}$ is the mean of the dependent variable.

This formula looks more difficult than it really is. The process of solving it involves the following steps:

Step 1.   Find the mean for each of your two variables—the independent, or *X,* variable and the dependent, or *Y,* variable.

Step 2.   Find the deviations from the mean for each value of your variables *X* and *Y.*

Step 3. Multiply the deviations from the mean—the deviation for X and the deviation for Y—by each other, and then add up the result (the numerator for Formula 12.1[a]).

Step 4. Square each of the deviations from the mean—first for X and then for Y, add them up, multiply the sum of the deviations squared for X and Y against each other, and take their square root (the denominator for Formula 12.1[a]).

Step 5. Divide the result you obtained in Step 3 by the result you obtained in Step 4.

TABLE 12.4 A Set of Hypothetical Data for the Association between a Father's Education and a Respondent's Education

Father's Education, X	Respondent's Education, Y
10	10
10	11
12	12
14	13
14	14

EXAMPLE:

Let's work with the small set of data in Table 12.4. The variables are *father's education* (the independent, or X, variable) and *respondent's education* (the dependent, or Y, variable).

Step 1. Begin by finding the means for each of these variables. (Use the raw scores formula for the mean, Formula 5.2[a]). You should obtain a mean for the independent variable (X) of 12, and a mean of the dependent variable (Y) of 12.

Step 2. Find the deviations from the mean for each of these variables (see the example on p. 194 of Chapter 6 for an illustration of the process). Start by subtracting the mean for the independent variable from each of the values of the independent variable. Then do the same for the dependent variable—subtract the mean for Y from each of the values of Y. You should get these answers:

Father's Education $X - \overline{X}$	*Respondent's Education,* $Y - \overline{Y}$
$10 - 12 = -2$	$10 - 12 = -2$
$10 - 12 = -2$	$11 - 12 = -1$
$12 - 12 = 0$	$12 - 12 = 0$
$14 - 12 = 2$	$13 - 12 = 1$
$14 - 12 = 2$	$14 - 12 = 2$

Step 3. Multiply each of the deviations from the means—the deviation for each value of X times the deviation for each value of Y.

Father's Education $X - \overline{X}$	Respondent's Education, $Y - \overline{Y}$	$(X - \overline{X})\,(Y - \overline{Y})$
$10 - 12 = -2$	$10 - 12 = -2$	$(-2)(-2) = 4$
$10 - 12 = -2$	$11 - 12 = -1$	$(-2)(-1) = 2$
$12 - 12 = 0$	$12 - 12 = 0$	$(0)(0) = 0$
$14 - 12 = 2$	$13 - 12 = 1$	$(2)(1) = 2$
$14 - 12 = 2$	$14 - 12 = 2$	$(2)(2) = \underline{4}$
		$\Sigma(X - \overline{X})(Y - \overline{Y}) = 12$

Then add up the results to get the sum of the deviations of the mean for X times the deviations from the mean for Y. The result is the numerator for the formula for Pearson's r.

Step 4.   Square each of the deviations from the mean, first for each value of the X variable and then for each value of the Y variable.

Father's Education $X - \overline{X}$	$(X - \overline{X})^2$	Respondent's Education $Y - \overline{Y}$	$(Y - \overline{Y})^2$
$10 - 12 = -2$	4	$10 - 12 = -2$	4
$10 - 12 = -2$	4	$11 - 12 = -1$	1
$12 - 12 = 0$	0	$12 - 12 = 0$	0
$14 - 12 = 2$	4	$13 - 12 = 1$	1
$14 - 12 = 2$	$\underline{4}$	$14 - 12 = 2$	$\underline{4}$
	$\Sigma(X - \overline{X})^2 = 16$		$\Sigma(Y - \overline{Y})^2 = 10$

Add up the squared deviations from the mean—first for the X variable, then for the Y variable. Multiply the sum of the squared deviations of X times the sum of the squared deviations of Y:

$$[\Sigma(X - \overline{X})^2][\Sigma(Y - \overline{Y})^2] = (16)(10) = 160$$

Take the square root of the product:

$$\sqrt{160} = 12.6491$$

The result is the denominator of the formula for Pearson's r.

Step 5.   Finally, plug these values into your formula for Pearson's r:

$$r = \frac{\Sigma\left(X - \overline{X}\right)\left(Y - \overline{Y}\right)}{\sqrt{\left[\Sigma\left(X - \overline{X}\right)^2\right]\left[\Sigma\left(Y - \overline{Y}\right)^2\right]}} = \frac{12}{12.6491} = .95$$

Computational formula for Pearson's r   As with the formula for standard deviation, there is a computational version of the formula for Pearson's r. The computational formula is easier to use because it avoids the process of subtraction, should you need to find Pearson's r by hand.

Formula 12.1(b): Computational formula for Pearson's r

$$r = \frac{\Sigma XY - \left(N\overline{X}\,\overline{Y}\right)}{\sqrt{\left(\Sigma X^2 - N\overline{X}^2\right)\left(\Sigma Y^2 - N\overline{Y}^2\right)}}$$

where X represents a value of the independent variable, Y represents a value of the dependent variable, $\overline{X}$ is the mean of the independent variable, and $\overline{Y}$ is the mean of the dependent variable.

To work this formula, follow these steps:

Step 1. Multiply each value of X by each value of Y, and add up the products (the result of each multiplication of X times Y) to get ΣXY.

Step 2. Find the mean for each of your two variables: the independent, or X, variable and the dependent, or Y, variable.

Step 3. Multiply N by the mean of X by the mean of Y to get $N\overline{X}\,\overline{Y}$.

Step 4. Square each value of X and add up the results to get ΣX^2, and square each value of Y and add up the results to get ΣY^2.

Step 5. Square the mean of X and multiply it by N to get $N\overline{X}^2$ and square the mean of Y and multiply it by N to get $N\overline{Y}^2$.

Step 6. Plug the results of these computations into your formula for Pearson's r (Formula 12.1[b]).

EXAMPLE:

Let's work with the data in Table 12.4.

Step 1. Begin by multiplying each value of X by each value of Y and adding up the products.

Father's Education, X	Respondent's Education, Y	XY
10	10	100
10	11	110
12	12	144
14	13	182
14	14	196
		$\Sigma XY = 732$

Step 2. Find the mean for each of the variables X and Y.

Father's Education, X	Respondent's Education, Y
10	10
10	11
12	12
14	13
14	14
$\Sigma X = 60$	$\Sigma Y = 60$

$$\overline{X} = \frac{\Sigma X}{N} = \frac{60}{5} = 12$$

$$\overline{X} = \frac{\Sigma Y}{N} = \frac{60}{5} = 12$$

Step 3. Multiply N by $\overline{X}$ by $\overline{Y}$ to get $N\overline{X}\overline{Y}$:

$$N\overline{X}\overline{Y} = 5 \times 12 \times 12 = 720$$

Step 4. Square each value of X and add up the results. Do the same for each value of Y.

Father's Education, X	Respondent's Education, Y	X^2	Y^2
10	10	100	100
10	11	100	121
12	12	144	144
14	13	196	169
14	14	196	196
		$\Sigma X^2 = 736$	$\Sigma Y^2 = 730$

Step 5. Square the mean of X and multiply by N to get $N\overline{X}^2$:

$$\overline{X}^2 = 12 \times 12 = 144$$

$$N\overline{X}^2 = 5 \times 144 = 720$$

Do the same for the mean of Y:

$$\overline{Y}^2 = 12 \times 12 = 144$$

$$N\overline{Y}^2 = 5 \times 144 = 720$$

Step 6. Plug the results into the computational formula for Pearson's r (Formula 12.1[b]):

$$\Sigma XY = 732 \qquad N\overline{X}\overline{Y} = 720 \qquad \Sigma X^2 = 736 \qquad \Sigma Y^2 = 730$$

$$N\overline{X}^2 = 720 \qquad N\overline{Y}^2 = 720$$

$$r = \frac{\Sigma XY - \left(N\overline{X}\overline{Y}\right)}{\sqrt{\left(\Sigma X^2 - N\overline{X}^2\right)\left(\Sigma Y^2 - N\overline{Y}^2\right)}}$$

$$= \frac{732 - 720}{\sqrt{\left(736 - 720\right)\left(730 - 720\right)}} = \frac{12}{\sqrt{16 \times 10}} = \frac{12}{12.6491}$$

$$r = .95$$

Note that the answer is the same as the one you obtained using the conceptual formula for Pearson's r (Formula 9.1[a]).

Interpreting Pearson's *r* and *r*-squared   Pearson's r, at .95, suggests a very strong association between the variables *father's education* and *respondent's education*, and it is a positive association. The more education respondents' fathers have, the more education the respondents are likely to have.

To find r-squared, simply square the value of Pearson's r (multiply .95 by .95). We get an r-squared of .90, suggesting that 90% of the variation in the respondents' years of education can be accounted for by variations in their fathers' years of education. In PRE terms, knowing the association between fathers' educational achievements and respondents' educational achievements improves our ability to predict respondents' educational levels by about 90% in this hypothetical case.

Skills Practice 5   Use the computational formula to calculate and interpret Pearson's r and r-squared for the following set of data:

Mother's Education, X	Respondent's Education, Y
13	12
13	14
14	15
15	16
15	13

Calculating the regression line   Once you have found Pearson's r, doing the computations for the regression line becomes easy. You may recall from algebra or geometry that a line can be represented by an equation, shown here as Formula 12.2.

Formula 12.2: The regression line

$$Y = a + (b)(X)$$

where Y is a value of the dependent variable; X is a value of the independent variable; a is the **y-intercept** or constant, the value of the dependent variable when the value of the independent variable is 0; and b is the **slope** of the line, or the amount by which the dependent variable changes for each unit change in the independent variable. (For example, the slope of the line for the association between *father's education* and *respondent's education* represents the increase in the number of years of education of the respondent for each year of education the father has.)

One of the most interesting aspects of this equation is that we can use it to make predictions. Suppose we want to know the predicted value of the dependent variable (Y) for any given value of the independent variable (X). We can figure it out if we also know a (the constant) and b (the slope of the line). How do we get a and b?

Step 1. Start by finding b, the slope of the line. The formula for the slope is:

Formula 12.2(a): Conceptual formula for the slope of a line

$$b = \frac{\Sigma(X - \overline{X})(Y - \overline{Y})}{\Sigma(X - \overline{X})^2}$$

You may recognize this formula. It has the same numerator as the central formula for Pearson's r. The denominator is different, but when you do the computations for Pearson's r, you have to find the denominator for the slope, which is the sum of the squared deviations from the mean for the independent variable.

EXAMPLE:

To find the slope of the regression line for the data in Table 12.4, plug in the numerator for Pearson's r and divide it by the sum of the squared deviations from the mean for the independent variable. For the previous example, we found the numerator for Pearson's r, 12, in Step 3. We found the sum of the squared deviations from the mean for the independent variable, 16, in Step 4 [see the column labeled $(X - \overline{X})^2$].

To find the slope of the regression line, divide 12 by 16.

$$b = \frac{\Sigma(X - \overline{X})(Y - \overline{Y})}{\Sigma(X - \overline{X})^2} = \frac{12}{16} = .75$$

As there is for Pearson's r, there is a computational formula for the slope of a regression line.

Formula 12.2(b): Computational formula for the slope of a line

$$b = \frac{\Sigma XY - (N\overline{X}\overline{Y})}{\Sigma X^2 - N\overline{X}^2}$$

Like the conceptual formula, the computational formula uses the numerator for Pearson's r. The computations for the denominator are similar, too. You find ΣX^2 and $N\overline{X}^2$ when you compute Pearson's r (in Steps 4 and 5).

EXAMPLE:

To find the slope of the regression line for the data in Table 12.4, plug the numerator for Pearson's r into the formula for the slope along with ΣX^2 and $N\overline{X}^2$.

$$\Sigma XY - N\overline{X}\overline{Y} = 12 \qquad \Sigma X^2 = 736 \qquad N\overline{X}^2 = 720$$

$$b = \frac{\Sigma XY - \left(N\overline{X}\overline{Y}\right)}{\Sigma X^2 - N\overline{X}^2}$$

$$= \frac{12}{736 - 720} = \frac{12}{16}$$

$$b = .75$$

Again, the answer is the same as the one you obtained with the conceptual formula.

Step 2.   Next find the value for a, the constant—the value of the dependent variable when the value of the independent variable is 0.

Formula 12.2(c): The constant for a regression line

$$a = \overline{Y} - (b)(\overline{X})$$

where $\overline{Y}$ is the mean of the dependent variable; $\overline{X}$ is the mean of the independent variable; and b is the slope of the regression line.

EXAMPLE:

For the data in Table 12.4, the mean of the independent variable is 12, and the mean of the independent variable is 12. (How do we know? We calculated the means as the first step toward finding Pearson's r.) We found that the slope of the regression line is .75. Insert these numbers into the formula.

$\overline{Y}$ (mean of the dependent variable) $= 12$

b (slope of the regression line) $= .75$

$\overline{X}$ (mean of the independent variable) $= 12$

$$a = \overline{Y} - (b)(\overline{X})$$

$$= 12 - (.75)(12) = 12 - 9$$

$$a = 3$$

Using the regression line   We can use the values for the slope and the constant in the formula for the regression line to predict the dependent variable. For example, we can use these values to ask, What would we predict a respondent's education to be if we know the father has 13 years of education? To answer this question, we solve the formula for the regression line, $Y = a + (b)(X)$, using the values for the slope (b) and the constant (a) along with the given, the value of the independent variable (13, in this case).

a (constant) $= 3$ b (slope) $= .75$ X
(given value of independent variable) $= 13$

$$Y = a + (b)(X)$$

$$= 3 + (.75)(13) = 3 + 9.75$$

$$Y = 12.75$$

This tells us that a respondent whose father has 13 years of education can be expected to have 12.75 years of education.

Does this answer make sense? Check it out. Construct a scatterplot for the values in Table 12.4. It should look like the scatterplot in Figure 12.16. How can you add the regression line? First, find the constant—the value of the dependent variable *(respondent's education)* when the independent variable *(father's education)* is 0. For the data in Table 12.4, the constant is 3. Draw a plot point in which the father's education is 0 and the respondent's education is 3. Now add a plot point for the predicted value of the respondent's education (12.75) when the father's education is 13. Finally, connect these two plot points with a line. Now your scatterplot should look like Figure 12.17.

Skills Practice 6   Find the slope, using the computational formula, and the constant for the set of data in Skills Practice 5. What is the predicted value of a respondent's education when the mother's education is 15? Draw the scatterplot and the regression line.

In the next section of this chapter you will learn how to evaluate associations between numerical variables using SPSS. I will begin with the comparison of means function, and then you will learn how to produce and interpret scatterplots, Pearson's *r,* and *r*-squared. You will also learn how to find the slope and the intercept of a regression line and use those statistics to predict the values of a dependent variable for given values of an independent variable. Finally, you will learn how to control for third variables using the comparison of means function and regression statistics.

FIGURE 12.16

Scatterplot of set of hypothetical data in Table 12.4 for the variables *father's education* and *respondent's education.*

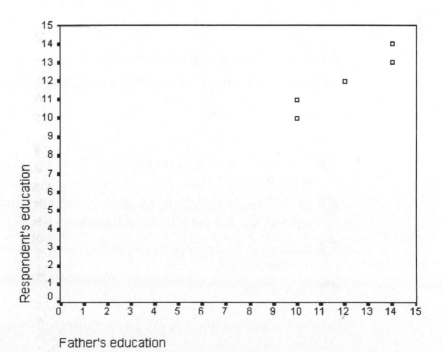

FIGURE 12.17
Scatterplot with regression line for set of hypothetical data for the variables *father's education* and *respondent's education.*

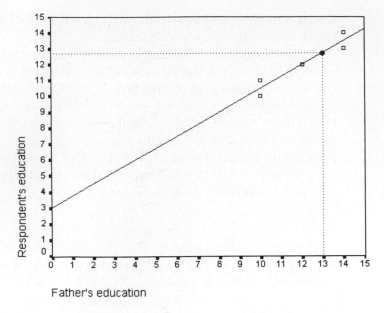

Respondent's education (y-axis)

Father's education (x-axis)

USING SPSS

Evaluating Associations between Variables

At the beginning of this chapter you read a "News to Use" article that used the comparison of means to examine the association between education and income. It also used a comparison of means to evaluate the association controlling for sex and race. In the first Skills Practice of this chapter you used a comparison of means to analyze the association between education and sex. In this section I will show you how to produce a comparison of means like the one you used in Table 12.1 for the first Skills Practice.

SPSS GUIDE: COMPARING MEANS

Open the SPSS program and your GSS 2002 subset B data file, then click on the Analyze menu item.

1 Click on Compare Means.

2 When the Compare Means menu opens, click on Means to open the Means dialog box.

3 At the Means dialog box, scroll down to your categorical (independent) variable, *sex,* and put it in the Independent List box.

4 Scroll up to your numerical (dependent) variable, *educ,* and put it in the Dependent List box.

5 Click on OK.

In your Output window, you will get a table labeled Report, like the one in Table 12.5.

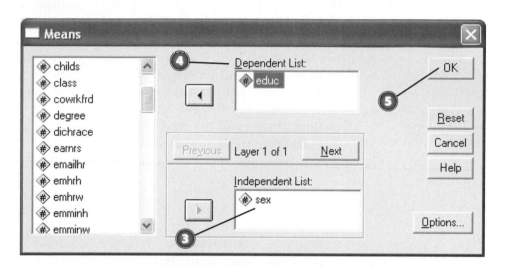

TABLE 12.5   Comparison of Means for the Variables *sex* and *educ* in the GSS 2002 subset B File

Report

EDUC Highest year of school completed

SEX Respondents sex	Mean	N	Std. Deviation
1 MALE	13.30	651	3.202
2 FEMALE	13.38	842	2.843
Total	13.35	1493	3.004

As with the Split File procedure, comparing the means allows us to see whether there is a difference, on average, in the educational achievements of male respondents compared to female respondents.

What do we look for in this table of information and how do we interpret it?

■ First, look at the differences in the means. Which group has the higher average years of education? The answer is females (an average of 13.38 years). Male respondents have an average of 13.30 years.

- Second, notice the size of the difference—is it a large one or a small one? The difference in this case is very, very small.
- Third, notice the size of the standard deviations and the differences in the standard deviations between the two groups. You may remember from Chapter 6 that, in general, the larger the standard deviation is in relation to the range, the more variability there is. In both of these groups, the standard deviation is relatively small in relation to the range. The distributions are more homogeneous than heterogeneous. The distribution of female responses is the most homogeneous, because it has a smaller standard deviation than the distribution of responses for males.

It is important to pay attention to the standard deviation because it can help us describe the two groups. Remember that we can subtract 1 standard deviation from the mean, and we can add 1 standard deviation to the mean to describe the middle 68% of the respondents. We can say something like, *assuming a normally distributed set of responses,* about 68% of the male respondents can be assumed to have between 10.10 years of education (the mean minus 1 standard deviation, or 13.30 − 3.20) and 16.50 years of education (the mean plus 1 standard deviation, or 13.30 + 3.20). About 68% of the female respondents have between 10.54 years of education (13.38 − 2.84) and 16.22 years of education (13.38 + 2.84). Looking at the range of values 1 standard deviation below the mean to 1 standard deviation above it reinforces our conclusion that the distribution for males is more heterogeneous than the distribution for females.

Skills Practice 7   Follow the command path Analyze ➥ Compare Means ➥ Means to open the Means dialog box. Analyze the association between race (using the variable *rcrace*) and educational achievement (using *educ*). Is race associated with educational achievement? What makes you think so?

The comparison of means procedure is useful when you want to evaluate an association between a numerical variable and a categorical variable. As you learned earlier in this chapter, a scatterplot and regression statistics are helpful if you want to evaluate an association between two numerical variables. In the next section of this chapter you will learn how to use SPSS to obtain and interpret scatterplots for numerical variables.

SPSS GUIDE: OBTAINING A SCATTERPLOT

Let's begin by learning how to produce a scatterplot for the respondents' fathers' education *(paeduc)* and respondents' education *(educ)* variables with SPSS.

1 Click on Graphs.

2 Click on Scatter to open the Scatterplot window.

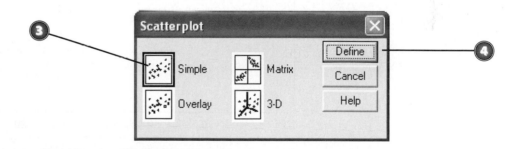

When the Scatterplot window opens:

3 Click on Simple.

4 Click on Define to open the Simple Scatterplot dialog box.

The Simple Scatterplot dialog box opens.

1 Select your dependent variable (let's use *educ*, respondent's education), and click on the ▶ to put it in the Y Axis (dependent variable) box.

2 Follow the same procedure to select your independent variable, *paeduc*, for the X Axis (independent variable) box.

3 Click on OK. A graph like the one in Figure 12.18 will appear in your Output window.

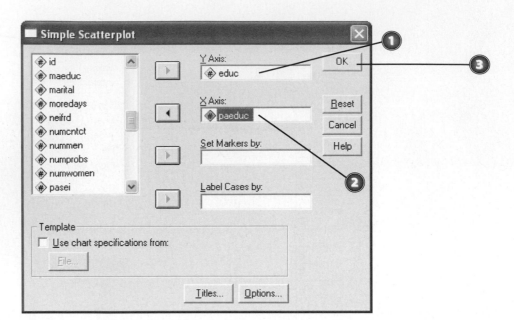

FIGURE 12.18
Scatterplot for the association between *paeduc* and *educ* in the GSS 2002 subset B file.

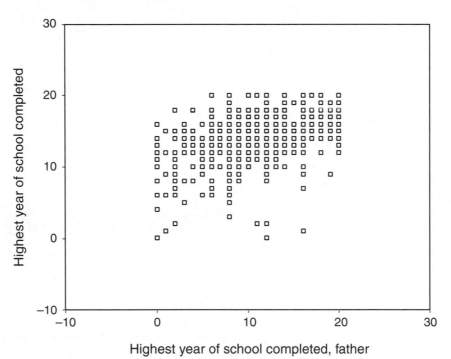

Now let's add sunflowers to our scatterplot (to show how many cases there are at each point on the scatterplot) and a regression line (to indicate the direction of an association and to help us evaluate its strength).

SPSS GUIDE: ADDING SUNFLOWERS AND A REGRESSION LINE TO A SCATTERPLOT

Place your cursor on your scatterplot in the SPSS Output window, and double-click. The SPSS Chart Editor window opens.

1 Click on Chart.

2 When the menu opens under Chart, click on Options. . . .

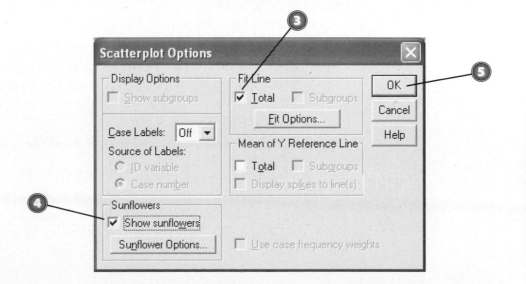

The Scatterplot Options window opens.

3 Under Fit Line, click on the box next to Total to make the $\sqrt{}$ appear.

4 Under Sunflowers, click on the box next to Show Sunflowers.

5 Click on OK. When you return to the Chart Editor window, click on the X (exit) button in the upper right corner of the window. Your scatterplot should now look like the one in Figure 12.19.

FIGURE 12.19
Scatterplot for the association between *paeduc* and *educ,* with sunflowers and a regression line, in the GSS 2002 subset B file.

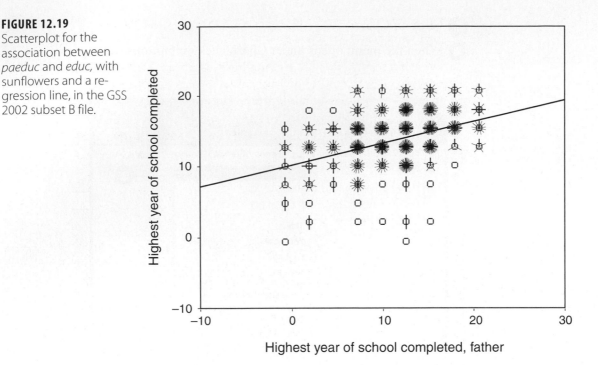

What can we tell about the association? First, notice the sunflowers. Some have very few petals, whereas others look more like dandelions. The more petals, the more cases there are at a particular point on the diagram. The density of the petals tells us where most of the cases are clustered. As might be expected, we can see that the respondents tend to be clustered around the 12 years of education category, for both the respondents themselves and their fathers. Second, we can tell that the association is positive by looking at the direction in which the line slopes (from lower left to upper right). The more education the respondents' fathers have, the more education the respondents have. Third, we can tell that the association seems to be in the moderate range—the slope of the line is fairly steep, and most cases fall close to the line.

Skills Practice 8 Produce a scatterplot with sunflowers and the regression line for the variables respondent's education *(educ)* and mother's education *(maeduc)*. What is its direction and strength?

In the next section of this chapter, you will learn how to produce and interpret Pearson's *r* and *r*-squared using SPSS. Once again we will use the variables *paeduc* and *educ* to illustrate the process of finding Pearson's *r* and *r*-squared with SPSS.

SPSS GUIDE: FINDING PEARSON'S *r* AND *r*-SQUARED FROM A SCATTERPLOT

There are several avenues to finding Pearson's *r* and *r*-squared. You will most often use these statistics in conjunction with a scatterplot, so it may be easiest to call them up while you are at the Output window looking at your scatterplot for the association between *paeduc* and *educ*.

With your cursor on the scatterplot for the relationship between the variables *paeduc* and *educ*, double-click to open the Chart Editor window.

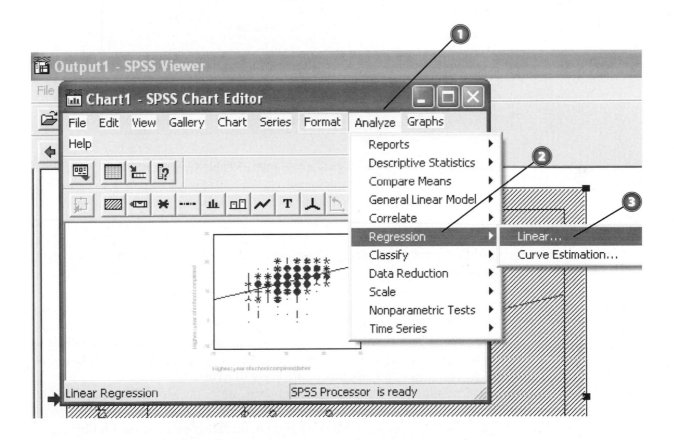

① Click on Analyze.

② Look under Analyze for Regression and click on it.

③ Then click on Linear.

The Linear Regression dialog box opens.

④ Select the dependent variable, *educ*, and put it in the Dependent box.

⑤ Select the independent variable, *paeduc*, and put it in the Independent(s) box.

⑥ Click on OK.

You will get a set of statistics like the ones in Table 12.6. Don't worry—we'll cut through the mass of information you get in your Output window to focus on a few of the most important statistics. (The rest will have to wait for an advanced course.)

Interpreting Pearson's *r* and *r*-squared   What do we focus on in the output from the regression command? First, notice Pearson's *r*. It appears in two places— under Model Summary *without* the sign as R, and then *with its sign* under Coefficients as the Standardized Coefficient.[11] Without the sign, Pearson's *r* at .421 confirms what we thought about the association—it is in the moderate range. With its sign (remember the absence of sign indicates a positive association) Pearson's *r* tells us that the more education the respondents' fathers have, the more education the respondents are likely to have.

The value for *r*-squared, which appears under the Model Summary, is .177. It tells us that 18% of the variation in a respondent's level of educational achievement can be accounted for by variations in the father's educational achievement. Using the PRE interpretation, we can also say that, knowing the association between fathers' educational achievements and respondents' educational achievements improves our ability to predict respondents' educational achievements by about 18%.

 Skills Practice 9   Find and interpret Pearson's *r* and *r*-squared for the association between *maeduc* and *educ*.

---

[11]The correlation statistic under the Model Summary agrees with the statistic under the Standardized Coefficient because we are doing regression involving only two variables. When you increase the number of variables in the regression model, these statistics will no longer be identical.

TABLE 12.6 Regression Statistics for *paeduc* and *educ* in the GSS 2002 subset B File

Variables Entered/Removed[b]

Model	Variables Entered	Variables Removed	Method
1	PAEDUC Highest year of school completed, father[a]	.	Enter

———— Independent variable

a. All requested variables entered.
b. Dependent Variable: EDUC Highest year of school completed.

Model Summary

———— Pearson's *r* reported without the sign

Model	R	R Square	Adjusted R Square	Std. Error of the Estimate
1	.421[a]	.177	.176	2.678

———— r-squared

a. Predictors: (Constant), PAEDUC Highest year of school completed, father

ANOVA[b]

Model		Sum of Squares	df	Mean Square	F	Sig.
1	Regression	1696.578	1	1696.578	236.505	.000[a]
	Residual	7883.734	1099	7.174		
	Total	9580.312	1100			

a. Predictors: (Constant), PAEDUC Highest year of school completed, father
b. Dependent Variable: EDUC Highest year of school completed.

Coefficients[a]

———— Pearson's *r* reported with the sign (the beta coefficient)

Model		Unstandardized Coefficients		Standardized Coefficients	t	Sig.
		B	Std. Error	Beta		
1	(Constant)	10.292	.239		43.083	.000
	PAEDUC Highest year of school completed, father	.304	.020	.421	15.379	.000

a. Dependent Variable: EDUC Highest year of school completed.

Predicting the Dependent Variable Using the Regression Line

Statistics that we get with the regression command in SPSS do more than allow us to assess the strength and direction of an association; they also enable us to make predictions about a dependent variable based on the value of an independent variable, as we did earlier using the data in Table 12.4 and Skills Practice 6. We can use regression statistics to predict a respondent's level of education if we know the father's level of education. Putting it another way, we can answer a question like, How much education can a respondent be expected to have whose father has 16 years of education?

We can make these kinds of predictions by using the slope and constant of the regression line for *paeduc* and *educ*—statistics produced whenever we perform the linear regression function in SPSS.

We find the *y*-intercept (the constant) and the slope among the regression statistics. They are in the box labeled Coefficients. See Table 12.7. How do we find out how many years of education a respondent has whose father has 16 years? We plug the statistics for the *y*-intercept and the slope into our formula:

a (the constant or *y*-intercept) = 10.292 b (the slope) = .304

X (the given value of the independent variable) = 16

$$Y = a + (b)(X)$$

$$= 10.292 + (.304)(16) = 10.292 + 4.864$$

$$Y = 15.156$$

CHECKING YOUR WORK

It's easy to see whether our answer is in the ballpark by looking at the scatterplot with the regression line for the variables *paeduc* and *educ* (Figure 12.20). Look up the value of the independent variable on the *x*-axis. Find where it intersects with the regression line, and then look across the scatterplot to see which value of the dependent variable on the *y*-axis is associated with the point at which the given value of the independent variable hits the regression line. The figure demonstrates the process.

TABLE 12.7   Coefficients from the Regression Output for the Relationship between *paeduc* and *educ* in the GSS 2002 subset B File

Constant or *y*-intercept (*a*)

Slope (*b*)

Coefficients[a]

Model		Unstandardized Coefficients		Standardized Coefficients		
		B	Std. Error	Beta	t	Sig.
1	(Constant)	10.292	.239		43.083	.000
	PAEDUC Highest year of school completed, father	.304	.020	.421	15.379	.000

[a.] Dependent Variable: EDUC Highest year of school completed.

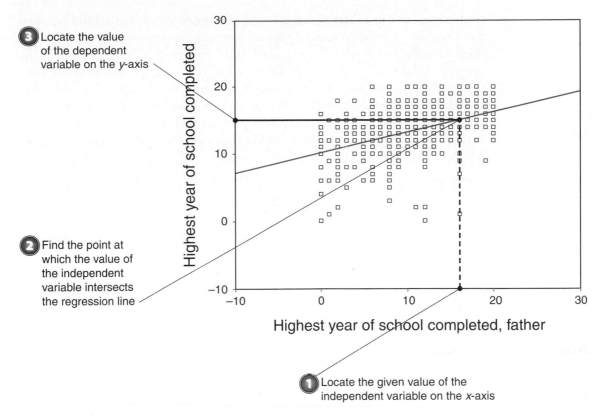

③ Locate the value of the dependent variable on the *y*-axis

② Find the point at which the value of the independent variable intersects the regression line

① Locate the given value of the independent variable on the *x*-axis

FIGURE 12.20
Process for estimating the value of a dependent variable from a value of an independent variable using the regression line for the variables *paeduc* and *educ* in the GSS 2002 subset B file.

Skills Practice 10

A. Use the statistics for the regression line in Table 12.7 to answer these questions: What is the predicted value of a respondent's years of education if the respondent's father has 12 years of education? What is the predicted value of a respondent's education if the father has 18 years of education?

B. Find the *y*-intercept (the constant) and the slope for the regression line for the association between *maeduc* and *educ*. What is the predicted value of a respondent's years of education if the respondent's mother has 16 years of education?

Controlling for Third Variables

Controlling for Third Variables Using the Compare Means Command

You may recall from your analysis of contingency tables with measures of association in Chapter 10 that we can add third variables to our analysis of an association between an independent and a dependent variable. We called this process controlling for third variables. It allowed us to examine an association between two variables to see if it changed (nature, strength, or direction) in the light of a third variable. For example, we learned in the first part of this chapter that the average of the years of education for male and female respondents to the 2002 GSS is about the same, but the average of the years of education for female respondents is slightly higher than that of male respondents. We might be interested in learning if this is a fairly recent phenomena or if this relative parity in average years of education is true across all age categories. We can use the Compare Means command and control for the age variable *rcage* to find out.

SPSS GUIDE: USING THE COMPARE MEANS COMMAND WITH A THIRD VARIABLE

Use the Analyze ➡ Means ➡ Compare Means command path to open the Means dialog box.

1 Enter your dependent and independent variables (*educ* and *sex,* respectively).

2 Click on the Next button.

3 Notice that the label on the Independent List box is now Layer 2 of 2. Enter the variable *rcage* as an independent variable. *rcage* shows up in the Layer 2 of 2: Independent List as a control variable.

4 Click on OK.

TABLE 12.8 A Comparison of Means for the Variables *sex* and *educ,* Controlling for *rcage,* in the GSS 2002 subset B File

Report

EDUC Highest year of school completed

SEX Respondents sex	RCAGE Recoded	Mean	N	Std. Deviation
1 MALE	1 18 THRU 25	12.83	75	2.177
	2 26 THRU 40	13.76	205	2.783
	3 41 THRU 60	13.40	218	3.397
	4 61 THRU 89	12.73	150	3.752
	Total	13.29	648	3.204
2 FEMALE	1 18 THRU 25	13.17	105	2.114
	2 26 THRU 40	13.75	244	2.515
	3 41 THRU 60	13.92	294	2.760
	4 61 THRU 89	12.21	194	3.336
	Total	13.38	837	2.846
Total	1 18 THRU 25	13.03	180	2.141
	2 26 THRU 40	13.76	449	2.638
	3 41 THRU 60	13.70	512	3.055
	4 61 THRU 89	12.44	344	3.528
	Total	13.34	1485	3.007

Average years of education for all male respondents

Average years of education for all female respondents

Included in your output will be a report like the one in Table 12.8. You will get a mean for the years of education broken down by sex, and within each of the categories of sex, the mean will be displayed by categories of the control variable.

Interpretation How do we read this? First, compare each of the means for males with the corresponding means for females for each category of age. Is the relationship between sex and education the same for each category of age as it is for all respondents together? Start with the first of the means for males. Notice that, unlike the respondents as a whole, males in the 18 through 25 age category have less education, on average, than females in the same age group.

Second, look at the size of the difference in the means: Is it larger or smaller for each age category than it is among respondents as a whole? You can see that, for all respondents, women had only .09 of a year more education than men. (You can find the means for males as a whole and females as a whole by looking at the Total mean for the category Male and the Total mean for the category Female.) You may notice that the mean for all males is slightly different than it was when you analyzed a comparison of means for the variables *sex* and *educ* without the control variable *rcage* (Table 12.4). The reason you are getting a different statistic when you add the control variable is that the comparison of means table is showing you only those respondents who answered all three variables—the *sex, years of education,* and *age* variables. Fewer respondents answered all three variables, so the number of respondents in the comparison of means table with the control variable is smaller. As a consequence, the means with the control variable are computed using fewer respondents than the means without the control variable. Among respondents in the 18-through-25 age category, the difference in average years of education is a little larger, with female respondents reporting .20 of a year more education, on average, than males.

As you make these comparisons for the rest of the age categories, you should see the following patterns.

Overall, the effect of age on the association between sex and education is slight. The nature of the association changes for two of the categories of the age variable, but the strength of the association remains fairly weak.

For two out of the four age categories (26 through 40 and 61 through 89), the average of the years of education for male respondents is higher than it is for female respondents. For the other two categories (18 through 25 and 41 through 60), the average of the years of education is higher for female respondents than it is for male respondents. The differences are all small ones, with no difference between males and females in any of the age categories greater than about six-tenths of a year. Even among the oldest respondents—those in the 61 through 89 age category—the difference between males and females is about half a year.

 Skills Practice 11 Analyze the association between sex and education, this time controlling for labor force status (using the *wrkstat* variable).

Using Regression Statistics with Third Variables

To examine an association between two numerical variables in light of a third variable, you can use the Selection box in the Linear Regression dialog box. For example, if you want to see whether the association between a father's education and a respondent's education is as strong for men as for women, use the command path Analyze ➡ Regression ➡ Linear to open the Linear Regression dialog box. Then follow these instructions.

SPSS GUIDE: USING LINEAR REGRESSION WITH CONTROL VARIABLES

1 Enter the variables *paeduc* (the independent variable) and *educ* (the dependent variable).

2 Click on the variable *sex* and put it in the Selection variable box. Note that the selection variable, *sex*, now has a question mark next to it; SPSS wants to know which category of the variable to use as the control category. Let's begin with Males or category 1.

3 Click on the Rule button to open the Linear Regression: Set Rule box.

4 Place your cursor under Value and enter 1 (for the category Male of the *sex* variable). Then click on Continue.

5 At the Linear Regression dialog box, click on OK.

You will get a set of regression statistics for the association between *paeduc* and *educ* for the male respondents. This is the first part of Table 12.9.

Now repeat the process, but this time when you enter your selection variable, *sex,* click on Rule and enter Value: 2 for the female respondents. You will get a table like the second part of Table 12.9. Remember that the goal of third-variable analysis is to examine the extent to which the nature (direction) and strength of an association changes when a third variable is introduced. For the respondents as a whole, the Pearson's *r* for the association between fathers' education and respondents' education is positive (indicating that the more education a father has, the more education a respondent has) and (at .421) moderate to moderately weak. The *r*-squared is .177. About 18% of the variation in respondents' educational levels can be explained by their fathers' educational achievements.

Does anything change when a third variable is introduced? To find out, look at the Model Summary for males and females. (They are reproduced in Table 12.9, but you won't see them this close together on your screen. You'll have to locate them among the many tables in your output.) Notice that for males, the direction of the association is unchanged, but it is slightly weaker (with Pearson's *r* = .372 and *r*-squared = .139). For females, however, the association is stronger than it is for males (with Pearson's *r* = .466 and *r*-squared = .217). For both groups, the strength of the association is moderate to moderately weak.

TABLE 12.9 Model Summaries for the Variables *paeduc* and *educ,* Controlling for the Variable *sex,* in the GSS 2002 subset B File

Model Summary

Model	R Respondents sex = 1 MALE (Selected)	R Square	Adjusted R Square	Std. Error of the Estimate
1	.372[a]	.139	.137	2.894

[a.] Predictors: (Constant), Highest years school completed, father

Model Summary

Model	R Respondents sex = 2 FEMALE (Selected)	R Square	Adjusted R Square	Std. Error of the Estimate
1	.466[a]	.217	.216	2.493

[a.] Predictors: (Constant), Highest years school completed, father

Interpretation Once again, be sure to note any changes in the direction or strength of an association. In this case, you could point out, for example, that

> for males, the association between fathers' educational achievements and respondents' educational achievements is slightly weaker than it is for respondents as a whole, but there is no change in direction. Among females, though, the association is stronger than it is for males, and it is a little stronger than for all respondents together. The direction is unchanged—the more education the respondents' fathers have, the more education the respondents are likely to have. The variable *sex* appears to have some influence on the association between a father's education and the respondent's education. The association is weaker for males than for females. Fathers' educational achievements explain more of the variations in respondents' educational achievements among females than among males.

 Skills Practice 12 Analyze the association between respondents' mothers' educational levels *(maeduc)* and the respondents' educational levels *(educ),* controlling for *sex.*

At this point, you should have a number of tools at your disposal for describing associations between variables in a set of data—lambda, gamma, and Pearson's *r,* to name a few. To review what you've learned so far, refer to the chart on the next page. It's a guide to the application of measures of association.

In the next chapter, I will introduce concepts for understanding inferential statistics—statistics that help us assess the likelihood that what we have been learning about the sample of GSS respondents is true of the larger population the sample is supposed to represent.

Using Measures of Association

Use the following chart as a guide to the correct application of measures of association. How you will use these statistics depends on the level of measurement of the variables you are analyzing. This guide will help you decide when and how to use each of the measures. For example, if you are wondering how to approach measuring associations involving categorical variables, look down the flow chart to the box Categorical Variables. Notice you have two choices—one for associations involving nominal variables and one for associations between ordinal variables. Under each of those boxes are the appropriate measures of associations, references to the formulas for the manual computations of the measure, and abbreviated SPSS instructions.

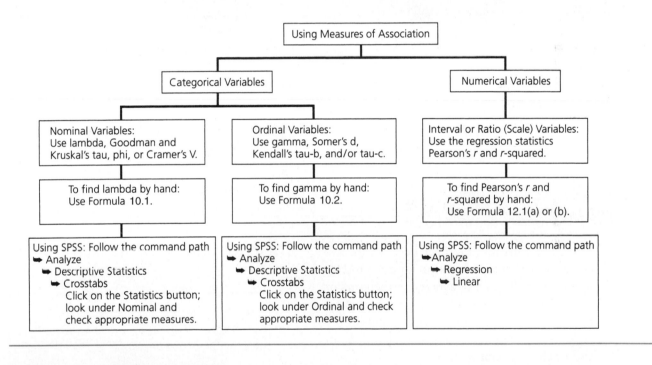

This chapter focused on two techniques for evaluating associations involving numerical variables: comparing means and linear regression. Comparing means is useful for associations between numerical variables and categorical variables. For example, you can see whether there are any differences in average years of education between men and women. Linear regression, on the other hand, is applied to associations involving two numerical variables, like the one between the respondents' educational levels and their parents' (mothers' or fathers') educational levels.

Although not explicitly covered in this chapter, the comparison of means can be calculated by hand simply by dividing a set of data by the values of a categorical variable (like males or females) and then computing means for each group. Pencil-and-paper computations for linear regression were covered, but largely for conceptual understanding. It is unlikely you would attempt computations of this sort without the help of a computer.

Consequently, greater attention was paid to using SPSS to obtain a comparison of means for a numerical variable and to interpret the statistical output. In addition, you learned to use SPSS to obtain and interpret a scatterplot with a regression line and sunflowers for two numerical variables,

Pearson's r (the correlation coefficient) and r^2 (r-squared, the coefficient of determination), and regression line statistics (the slope and the y-intercept or constant). Finally, you should be able to use regression line statistics to make predictions about the value of a dependent variable based on values of some independent variable.

In the concluding sections, you learned to use the Analyze ➡ Compare Means ➡ Means command path and the Selection Variable box of the Linear Regression dialog box to control for third variables.

KEY CONCEPTS

Comparison of means
Scatterplot
Regression line
Linear association
Nonlinear association

Curvilinear association
Pearson's r
r-squared (coefficient of
    determination)

y-intercept (constant)
Slope

ANSWERS TO SKILLS PRACTICES

1. There is almost no difference between the average of the years of education for male and female respondents. The average of the years of education for female respondents is slightly higher than it is for male respondents (only eight-tenths of a year). The association is an extremely weak one at best.

2. The scatterplot appears positive, much like the scatterplot for father's education and respondent's education. The association appears to be moderate.

3. The association appears to be positive, as the points flow generally from the lower left corner of the graph to the upper right corner. The association looks fairly weak, because the points are spread out rather than clustered near a single line.

4. A scatterplot would look like this:

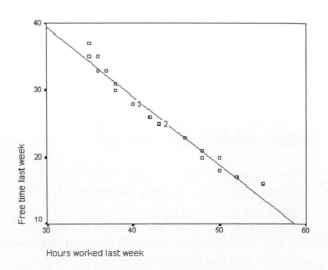

The association appears negative and strong. The more hours respondents work, the less free time they have.

5. The variables are *mother's education* (the independent, or *X*, variable) and *respondent's education* (the dependent, or *Y*, variable).

Step 1. Begin by multiplying each value of *X* by each value of *Y* and adding up the products.

Mother's Education, X	Respondent's Education, Y	XY
13	12	156
13	14	182
14	15	210
15	16	240
15	13	195
		$\Sigma XY = 983$

Step 2. Find the mean for each of the variables, *X* and *Y*.

Mother's Education, X	Respondent's Education, Y
13	12
13	14
14	15
15	16
15	13
$\Sigma X = 70$	$\Sigma Y = 70$

$$\bar{X} = \frac{\Sigma X}{N} = \frac{70}{5} = 14$$

$$\bar{Y} = \frac{\Sigma Y}{N} = \frac{70}{5} = 14$$

Step 3. Multiply *N* by *X* by *Y* to get $N\bar{X}\bar{Y}$.

$$N\bar{X}\bar{Y} = 5 \times 14 \times 14 = 980$$

Step 4. Square each value of *X* and add up the results. Do the same for each value of *Y*.

Mother's Education, X	Respondent's Education, Y	X²	Y²
13	12	169	144
13	14	169	196
14	15	196	225
15	16	225	256
15	13	225	169
		$\Sigma X^2 = 984$	$\Sigma Y^2 = 990$

Step 5. Square the mean of *X* and multiply by *N* to get $N\bar{X}^2$.

$$\bar{X}^2 = 14 \times 14 = 196$$

$$N\bar{X}^2 = 5 \times 196 = 980$$

Do the same for the mean of *Y*:

$$\bar{Y}^2 = 14 \times 14 = 196$$

$$N\bar{Y}^2 = 5 \times 196 = 980$$

Step 6. Plug the results into the computational formula for Pearson's *r* (Formula 12.1[b]):

$$\Sigma XY = 983 \quad N\bar{X}\bar{Y} = 980 \quad \Sigma X^2 = 984$$

$$\Sigma Y^2 = 990 \quad N\bar{X}^2 = 980 \quad N\bar{Y}^2 = 980$$

$$r = \frac{\Sigma XY - \left(N\bar{X}\bar{Y}\right)}{\sqrt{\left(\Sigma X^2 - N\bar{X}^2\right)\left(\Sigma Y^2 - N\bar{Y}^2\right)}}$$

$$= \frac{983 - 980}{\sqrt{(984 - 980)(990 - 980)}} = \frac{3}{\sqrt{4 \times 10}}$$

$$= \frac{3}{\sqrt{40}} = \frac{3}{6.3246}$$

$$r = .47$$

Interpreting Pearson's *r* and *r*-squared: Pearson's *r*, at .47, suggests a moderate association between the variables *mother's education* and *respondent's education*, and it is a positive association. The more education a respondent's mother has, the more education the respondent is likely to have.

To find *r*-squared, simply square the value of Pearson's *r* (multiply .47 by .47). The *r*-squared is .22, suggesting that 22% of the variation in the respondents' years of education can be accounted for by variations in their mothers' years of education. In PRE terms, knowing the association between mothers' educational achievements and respondents' educational achievements improves our ability to predict respondents' educational levels by about 22%.

6. To find the slope of the regression, use Formula 12.2(b):

numerator for Pearson's $r = 3$

(from Skills Practice 5)

sum of the squared values of X

minus $\overline{X}^2$ times $N = 4$

(from Skills Practice 5)

$$b = \frac{\Sigma XY - \left(N\overline{X}\,\overline{Y}\right)}{\Sigma X^2 - N\overline{X}^2}$$

$$= \frac{3}{4}$$

$$b = .75$$

The numerator, 3, was calculated in the process of finding Pearson's r for the previous exercise. The denominator, 4, is simply the sum of each of the squared values of the independent variable, *mother's education,* from which we subtracted the squared value of its mean times N. To work the formula, divide 3 by 4. To find the constant, use Formula 12.2(c):

$a = \overline{Y} - (b)(\overline{X})$

$= 14 - (.75)(14)$

$= 14 - 10.5$

$a = 3.5$

The predicted value of a respondent's education when the mother's education is 15 can be computed by plugging the relevant values into the formula for a line:

$Y = a + (b)(X)$

$\quad = 3.50 + (.75)(15) = 3.50 + 11.25$

$Y = 14.75$

A respondent whose mother has 15 years of education can be expected to have almost that much: 14.75 years of education.

Your scatterplot should look somewhat like the one that follows:

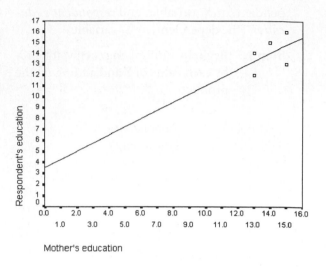

Mother's education

7. Respondents who are classified as Other have completed more years of education, on average, than any other group of respondents. White respondents have completed more years of education, on average, than Black, Native American, or Hispanic respondents. The differences in the averages are not large, though. The difference between those who say they are Other and White respondents is only one and one-half years, whereas the difference between Other and Black respondents is nearly two and one-half years. The difference between White and Black respondents is not quite a year.

8. A scatterplot with the regression line and sunflowers for *maeduc* and *educ* should look like the one you see on the next page.

Like the association with father's education, the association between a respondent's education and his or her mother's education is positive. The more education respondents' mothers have, the more education respondents are likely to have. The association looks to be at least moderate, given the steepness of the slope of the line along with the concentration of data near the line.

9. You should get regression statistics like the ones you see here:

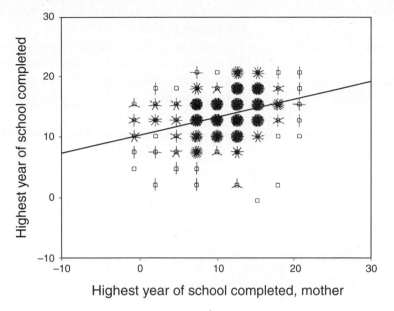

Model Summary

Model	R	R Square	Adjusted R Square	Std. Error of the Estimate
1	.355[a]	.126	.125	2.722

[a.] Predictors: (Constant), MAEDUC Highest year of school completed, mother

Constant
Slope

Coefficients[a]

Model		Unstandardized Coefficients		Standardized Coefficients	t	Sig.
		B	Std. Error	Beta		
1	(Constant)	10.154	.262		38.732	.000
	MAEDUC Highest year of school completed, mother	.301	.022	.355	13.699	.000

[a.] Dependent Variable: EDUC Highest year of school completed.

The association between mother's education and respondent's education is, at best, moderate with Pearson's r at .355. The absence of a sign on the Standardized Coefficient suggests that the association is positive. The more education respondents' mothers have, the more education the respondents have. The r-squared tells us that about 13% of the variation in the respondents' educational achievements can be explained by their mothers' educational achievements. The PRE interpretation suggests that knowing the relationship between mothers' educational levels and respondents' educational levels improves our ability to predict the respondents' educational levels by about 13%.

10. A. The predicted value of a respondent's educational level when the father has 12 years is:

$$Y = a + (b)(X)$$
$$= 10.292 + (.304)(12) = 10.292 + 3.648$$
$$Y = 13.94$$

The predicted value of a respondent's educational level when the father has 18 years is:

$$Y = a + (b)(X)$$
$$= 10.292 + (.304)(18)$$
$$= 10.292 + 5.472$$
$$Y = 15.764$$

B. Look for the constant and the slope of the regression line for the association between *maeduc* and *educ* in the coefficients table in the answer to Skills Practice 9.

The constant is 10.154 and the slope is .301. To predict a respondent's education when the mother's education is 16, use the following formula:

$$Y = a + (b)(X)$$
$$= 10.154 + (.301)(16)$$
$$= 10.154 + 4.816$$
$$Y = 14.97$$

11. You should get a table like the following:

Report

EDUC Highest year of school completed

SEX Respondents sex	WRKSTAT Labor force statuse	Mean	N	Std. Deviation
1 MALE	1 WORKING FULLTIME	13.68	394	2.882
	2 WORKING PARTTIME	13.43	49	3.942
	3 TEMP NOT WORKING	14.46	13	2.634
	4 UNEMPL, LAID OFF	12.31	29	3.733
	5 RETIRED	12.57	117	3.613
	6 SCHOOL	13.71	21	2.217
	7 KEEPING HOUSE	11.71	7	3.200
	8 OTHER	10.86	21	3.135
	Total	13.30	651	3.202
2 FEMALE	1 WORKING FULLTIME	13.90	383	2.572
	2 WORKING PARTTIME	13.71	118	2.632
	3 TEMP NOT WORKING	13.50	18	2.431
	4 UNEMPL, LAID OFF	12.83	30	2.705
	5 RETIRED	12.70	105	3.606
	6 SCHOOL	14.45	20	2.743
	7 KEEPING HOUSE	12.35	141	2.659
	8 OTHER	12.48	27	3.344
	Total	13.38	842	2.843
Total	1 WORKING FULLTIME	13.79	777	2.734
	2 WORKING PARTTIME	13.63	167	3.065
	3 TEMP NOT WORKING	13.90	31	2.521
	4 UNEMPL, LAID OFF	12.58	59	3.233
	5 RETIRED	12.63	222	3.602
	6 SCHOOL	14.07	41	2.484
	7 KEEPING HOUSE	12.32	148	2.678
	8 OTHER	11.77	48	3.321
	Total	13.35	1493	3.004

There doesn't seem to be much of an effect of work status on the nature of the association between sex and education. Across all work status groups except temporarily not working, women have more education than men. The size of the difference changes somewhat. For example, among respondents in the Other category, the difference is more than a year.

12. Here are the statistics you should focus on for the analysis (although they won't be this close together in your Output window):

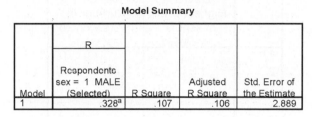

Model Summary

Model	R Respondents sex = 1 MALE (Selected)	R Square	Adjusted R Square	Std. Error of the Estimate
1	.328[a]	.107	.106	2.889

[a.] Predictors: (Constant), Highest year school completed, mother

Model Summary

Model	R Respondents sex = 2 FEMALE (Selected)	R Square	Adjusted R Square	Std. Error of the Estimate
1	.379[a]	.144	.143	2.591

[a.] Predictors: (Constant), Highest year school completed, mother

There does seem to be an effect of sex on the association between the respondents' education and their mothers' education. For men, the association is weaker ($r = .328$) than it is for women ($r = .379$). In addition, the association is weaker for men than among respondents as a whole, and it is stronger for women than it is among respondents as a whole. The r-squared tells us that about 11% of the variation in male respondents' educational achievements can be explained by their mothers' educational achievements. For women, their mothers' educational achievements account for 14% of the variation in the respondents' educational achievements—a little more than for men.

GENERAL EXERCISES

1. Use the table below to analyze the association between *sex* and *use of the World Wide Web*.

Report

Mean

SEX Respondents sex	WWWHR WWW hours per week (not counting email)
1 MALE	6.90
2 FEMALE	5.08
Total	5.88

2. Use the table below to analyze the association between *age* and *use of the World Wide Web*.

Report

Mean

RCAGE Recoded age variable	WWWHR WWW hours per week (not counting email)
1 18 THRU 25	6.84
2 26 THRU 40	6.65
3 41 THRU 60	5.25
4 61 THRU 89	3.88
Total	5.87

For Exercises 3 and 4, use the sets of data (drawn at random from the 2002 GSS) to construct and interpret (describing the nature, strength, and direction of the association) scatterplots. Think about how to set up each scatterplot—which variables should be independent and which should be dependent.

3.

Case Summaries

	EDUC Highest year of school completed	SPEDUC Highest year of school completed, spouse
1	13	13
2	13	16
3	18	18
4	18	16
5	12	14
6	12	12
7	12	12
8	12	12
9	14	12
10	12	14
11	18	14
12	16	14
13	12	11
14	16	20
15	12	12
16	12	14
17	15	16
18	14	12
19	16	20

4.

Case Summaries

	EDUC Highest year of school completed	HRS1 Number of hours worked last week
1	10	37
2	13	40
3	16	10
4	12	27
5	18	40
6	12	40
7	9	34
8	12	40
9	14	32
10	14	6
11	10	30
12	14	40
13	16	35
14	17	45
15	12	40
16	16	60
17	16	55
18	13	40
19	19	40
20	17	55
21	15	60
22	9	50
23	12	50
24	13	43

5. Use the following hypothetical data to compute and interpret Pearson's r and r-squared for the variables *years of education* and *spouse's education*.

Years of Education	Spouse's Education
10	11
11	12
13	14
15	15
16	18

6. Use the following hypothetical data to compute and interpret Pearson's r and r-squared for the variables *years of education* and *hours worked per week*.

Years of Education	Hours Worked per Week
10	40
11	50
13	40
15	45
16	50

7. Use the following hypothetical data to compute and interpret Pearson's *r* and *r*-squared for the variables *years of education* and *age*.

Years of Education	Age
10	45
11	50
13	35
15	40
16	55

8. Use the following hypothetical data to compute and interpret Pearson's *r* and *r*-squared for the variables *spouse's education* and *hours worked per week*.

Spouse's Education	Hours Worked per Week
11	40
12	50
14	40
15	45
18	50

9. Use the following hypothetical data to compute and interpret Pearson's *r* and *r*-squared for the variables *hours worked per week* and *age*.

Hours Worked per Week	Age
40	45
50	50
40	35
45	40
50	55

10. Use the following hypothetical data to compute and interpret Pearson's *r* and *r*-squared for the variables *spouse's education* and *age*.

Spouse's Education	Age
11	45
12	50
14	35
15	40
18	55

11. Use the data in General Exercise 5 to compute the slope and the constant for the regression line for the association between *years of education* and *spouse's education*.

12. Use the data in General Exercise 6 to compute the slope and the constant for the regression line for the association between *years of education* and *hours worked per week*.

13. Use the data in General Exercise 7 to compute the slope and the constant for the regression line for the association between *years of education* and *age*.

14. Use the data in General Exercise 8 to compute the slope and the constant for the regression line for the association between *spouse's education* and *hours worked per week*.

SPSS EXERCISES

Use the GSS 2002 subset B file to answer the following questions.

1. Is there any difference in educational achievement *(educ)* based on marital status *(marital)*?
2. Is there any difference in educational achievement *(educ)* based on religion *(rcrelig)*?
3. Is there any difference in educational achievement *(educ)* based on region of the country in which one resides *(rcregion)*?
4. Is there any difference in days respondents work extra hours *(moredays)* based on *(sex)*?

For Exercises 5–8, use SPSS and the GSS 2002 subset B file to obtain and interpret (describe the nature, strength, and direction of the association) scatterplots with sunflowers and the regression line for the association between the given variables. Think about how to set up each scatterplot—which variable should be independent, which should be dependent.

5. *speduc* (spouse's education) and *educ*.
6. *educ* and *age*.
7. *educ* and *earnrs*.
8. *childs* and *educ*.

Use the GSS 2002 subset B file for the following exercises

9. Find and interpret Pearson's *r* and *r*-squared for the association between *educ* and *speduc*. Use the slope and constant (*y*-intercept) to answer this question: How many years of education will a respondent's spouse have if the respondent has 16 years of education?
10. Find and interpret Pearson's *r* and *r*-squared for the association between *educ* and *age*. Use the slope and constant (*y*-intercept) to answer this question: How many years of education can we expect a respondent who is 21 years old to have?

11. Find and interpret Pearson's *r* and *r*-squared for the association between *educ* and *earnrs*. Use the slope and constant (*y*-intercept) to answer this question: How many wage earners would we expect to find in the household of a respondent with 14 years of education?
12. Find and interpret Pearson's *r* and *r*-squared for the association between *educ* and *childs*. Use the slope and constant (*y*-intercept) to answer this question: How many children would we predict a respondent with 18 years of education to have?
13. For Skills Practice 2, you looked at the association between education *(educ)* and race. Now see what happens to the nature and strength of the association when control variables are introduced. Use the Compare Means command to analyze the association between *educ* and *rcrace* and control for age *(rcage)*.
14. What happens to the association between *educ* and *rcrace* when you introduce the control variable *wrkstat*?
15. In Exercise 9, you used Pearson's *r* and *r*-squared to examine the association between a respondent's education and his or her spouse's education (using *educ* and *speduc*). Now control the association for the variable *sex*. Does the control variable affect the nature or strength of the association between *educ* and *speduc*?
16. Reexamine the association between *educ* and *speduc* using the control variable *race*. Does the control variable affect the nature or strength of the association between *educ* and *speduc*?

CHAPTER **13**

Making Inferences Involving Numerical Variables

INTRODUCTION

Do Americans watch a lot of television? Do they spend too much time on the Internet? How has the Internet affected TV viewing? These are all questions of interest to researchers for various reasons. Robert Putnam in his book, *Bowling Alone,* blames television, at least in part, for the decline of social capital in our society.[1] It has been hypothesized that the Internet is also to blame for the decline in social capital because it is another device that keeps us isolated from one another. Others argue that the Internet actually helps to sustain social capital because it is a means by which we can be more connected to one another (literally and figuratively) by participating in interaction that occurs in chat rooms and over email. In the "News to Use" article in this chapter you will find a summary of a report on the TV viewing and Internet habits of Americans.

In this chapter we will be exploring what the General Social Survey tells us about the TV viewing and Internet habits of American adults. As we do so, we will be learning how to make inferences about associations that involve numerical variables. To begin, let's review what we know about inferences involving numerical variables by finding and interpreting the confidence interval for the average number of hours GSS respondents watch television. You can do this with SPSS. You may recall from Chapter 8 that the process involves following the command path Analyze ➡ Descriptive Statistics ➡ Explore. The variable that we will be using is *tvhours* (in the GSS 2002 subset B file). You should produce a table like the one in Table 13.1.

---

[1] Social capital is defined in *Bowling Alone* as the extent to which we are connected with one another for the purpose of sustaining important social bonds as well as understanding others who may be different from us. See *Bowling Alone* by Robert Putnam (Simon and Schuster, 2000).

TABLE 13.1 Confidence Interval for the Variable *tvhours* in the GSS 2002 subset B File

Descriptives

			Statistic	Std. Error
TVHOURS Hours per day watching TV	Mean		3.03	.120
	95% Confidence Interval for Mean	Lower Bound	2.79	
		Upper Bound	3.26	
	5% Trimmed Mean		2.73	
	Median		2.00	
	Variance		6.870	
	Std. Deviation		2.621	
	Minimum		0	
	Maximum		24	
	Range		24	
	Interquartile Range		3.00	
	Skewness		3.344	.111
	Kurtosis		18.735	.222

Skills Practice 1 Interpret the confidence interval for the variable *tvhours* in Table 13.1.

Now let's look at some of the variables that may be associated with TV watching. Then we'll see whether any of these associations are likely to be found in the population of American adults that the General Social Survey represents. Like making inferences for associations involving categorical variables, making inferences for numerical variables involves the same hypothesis testing process introduced in Chapter 11 (p. 347). What is different when we are dealing with numerical variables is the test statistic. In addition, our assumptions about the null hypothesis change a little, and there are a few additional concepts related to hypothesis testing you need to have a handle on. I will introduce these concepts in the next section. ■

NEWS *to* USE
Statistics in the "Real" World

Stats from UCLA Internet Project Report[2]
DAWN ANFUSO

The third annual report of the UCLA Internet Project indicates that, despite a decreasing trust in all of the content online, Internet users are spending more time online primarily connecting with others, finding information, and shopping. The study also found that these people are buying that time away from viewing TV.

In 2000, the first report of the UCLA Internet Project created a baseline profile of behavior

[2]iMedia Connection.com, 3 February 2002, <http://www.imediaconnection.com/content/news/020303.asp>.

and attitudes about Internet use and non-use in five major subjects: who is online and who is not, media use and trust, consumer behavior, communication patterns, and social effects.

In 2001 and 2002, the UCLA Internet Project continued its year-to-year appraisal of more than 100 major issues, focusing on Internet users vs. non-users, as well as new users (less than one year of experience) compared to very experienced users (six or more years of experience).

Here are some highlights of the Year Three of the UCLA Internet Project:

WHO'S ONLINE & HOW OFTEN?

Internet access remained generally stable from 2001 to 2002, while online hours continued to increase, as did use of the Internet at home. The top five online activities in 2002 were email and instant messaging, Web surfing or browsing, reading news, shopping and buying online, and accessing entertainment information.

Each of the three studies by the UCLA Internet Project shows that Internet access spans every age range—and in some age ranges, access approaches 100%.

The average number of hours online per week continued to grow in 2002. Users reported an average of 11.1 hours online per week, up from 9.8 in 2001 and 9.4 in 2000. New Internet users in 2002 went online an average of 5.5 hours per week.

INTERNET VS. TV

The trend across the three years of the UCLA Internet Project shows that Internet users may be "buying" their time to go online from hours previously spent watching television. Overall, Internet users watched less television in 2002 than in 2001; 11.2 hours per week in 2002, compared to 12.3 hours in 2001. In 2002, Internet users watched about 5.4 hours of television less per week than non-users—this compared to 4.5 hours in 2001.

Almost one-third of children now watch less television than before they started using the Internet at home—up from 23% in 2001.

The decline in television viewing becomes even more pronounced as Internet experience increases; more than twice as many of the very experienced users than new users say that they spend less time watching television since using the Internet.

HOW THE NET IS USED

The Internet is viewed as an important source of information by the vast majority of people who go online; in 2002, 60.5% of all users considered the Internet to be a very important or extremely important source of information. However, the number of users who believe that information on the Internet is reliable and accurate continued to decline in 2002. In 2002, 52.8% of users believed that most or all of the information online is reliable and accurate—a decline from both 2001 and 2000. More than one-third of users (39.9%) in 2002 said that only about half of the information on the Internet is reliable and accurate.

Fewer adults bought online in 2002 than in 2001 or 2000. But while the overall number of buyers in 2002 declined, their average number of purchases increased substantially over 2001. The average dollars spent by online buyers in 2002 also increased substantially over 2001, but was still lower than in 2000.

A growing number of Internet purchasers in 2002 reported that their online buying is likely to increase; 71.2% of 2002 respondents agreed that they will probably make more purchases online, compared to 66.1% in 2001 and 54.5% in 2000.

Concerns about credit card security on the Internet remained as high as ever. Overall, 92.4% of all respondents age 18 or over expressed some concern about the security of their credit card information if they ever buy online.

More than half of users in 2002 said that since starting to use the Internet, they increased the number of people with whom they stay in contact. Large majorities of email users say that online communication: does not require too much time; makes them more likely to keep in contact with other people with email; and allows them to communicate with people they normally could not.

THE AT-WORK AUDIENCE

Internet users continue to report growing levels of online access at work for both personal and professional use. Of those who had Internet access at work in 2002, about 90% visit Web sites for business purposes; 60.5% visit Web sites for personal use while at work.

Overall, users of the Internet in 2002 were satisfied with online technology, rating satisfaction with the Internet at 4.0 on a scale of 1 (not satisfied) to 5 (completely satisfied). Users are most satisfied with the ability to communicate with other people on the Internet. Users continue to be least satisfied with the speed of their connection to the Internet.

CORE CONCEPTS FOR HYPOTHESIS TESTING WITH NUMERICAL VARIABLES

Directional and Nondirectional Hypotheses

To test hypotheses involving numerical variables, we have to understand the difference between two possible forms of the research hypothesis. Most commonly, research hypotheses specify the nature of an association. For example, we can hypothesize that men watch TV *more often* than do women. A hypothesis in this form is **directional**, because it tells us which category of the independent variable—males or females—is likely to score higher on the dependent variable, TV watching, than the other.

Another form of the research hypothesis states that there is a difference between groups of respondents in a sample, but we don't know the nature of the difference. For example, we can hypothesize that the average hours of television watching reported by men is different from the average hours reported by women. A research hypothesis in this form doesn't speculate about which group spends more time watching TV than the other. It is **nondirectional,** because it doesn't say anything about the nature of the association between the variables.

One- and Two-Tailed Tests of Significance

Whether a hypothesis is directional or nondirectional plays a role in how we determine if the null hypothesis can be rejected. Directional hypotheses require **one-tailed tests of significance**, whereas nondirectional hypotheses require **two-tailed tests of significance.**[3]

What do we mean by "tails"?   To understand the concept of one-tailed and two-tailed tests, we have to go back to the concept of the normal distribution. For some sampling distributions of sample statistics, like the sampling distribution of sample means, the distributions of sample statistics are normal or close to normal. You may recall that we can assume that the sampling distribution of sample means, a particular sample statistic, would look like the distribution pictured in Figure 13.1. The tails of the distribution are the regions under the normal curve that include extremely high or extremely low sample means (in

---

[3] Regardless of whether a hypothesis is directional, we test it using some sort of test statistic—a number, like chi-square, that is a sample characteristic (or a characteristic of differences between samples) and whose sampling distribution is known.

FIGURE 13.1
The tails of a normal
distribution.

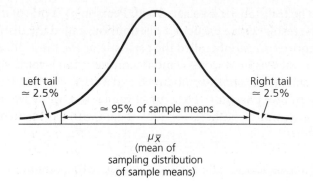

relation to those at the center of the distribution). The tails of the normal distribution are identified in Figure 13.1.

Not all distributions of test statistics are normal. Nevertheless, the distributions are *known*. That is, statisticians have calculated the distributions of various test statistics at their associated degrees of freedom. Using what is known about the distributions of test statistics and the likelihood of obtaining statistics of specified values by chance alone, we can assess the likelihood that a particular test statistic has occurred in a particular sample just due to chance. When we rule out the likelihood that a test statistic is nothing more than a chance occurrence, we assume that the pattern we observe in our sample is representative of the population from which the sample was drawn.

In a normal distribution of a test statistic, the closer a test statistic falls in relation to the "tails" of the distribution—the extreme values in the distribution at either the high end (above the midpoint for the distribution) or the low end (below the midpoint for the distribution), the less likely it is that the test statistic is an accident of sampling. With a research hypothesis that is directional—a hypothesis that specifies the nature of the association between two variables—we can establish that a test statistic is not very likely to be a chance occurrence if the test statistic falls in one of the tails of the distribution. With a hypothesis that is nondirectional—a hypothesis that says two variables are related but does not specify the nature of the relationship—we can establish that a test statistic is not very likely to be a chance occurrence if the test statistic falls in either of the two tails of the distribution.

This process will be made clearer as we encounter some examples. Let's begin with testing Pearson's *r* for statistical significance.

TESTING PEARSON'S *r* FOR SIGNIFICANCE

Calculating and Interpreting the *t* Statistic for Pearson's *r*

In Chapter 12 you learned to use Pearson's *r* as a measure of association for numerical variables. Like the measures of association for categorical variables, Pearson's *r* tells us about the strength and direction of an association. Like the other measures of association, it can be used in conjunction with an inferential statistic to tell us whether any association we observe in a sample is just a chance occurrence.

The test statistic associated with Pearson's *r* is one of a group of statistics that can be tested with a particular distribution, called the distribution of Student's *t*. It is more commonly called the *t* statistic or the *t* test. It can be positive or negative in value (like *Z* scores), and its computation is fairly simple. Like chi-square, the *t* statistic has both an obtained and a critical value. The obtained value is the value of *t* we compute. The critical value is the value we must obtain in order to reject the null hypothesis for a set of data with a particular number of degrees of freedom.

Formula 13.1(a): The *t* statistic for use with Pearson's *r*

$$t_o = r\sqrt{\frac{(N-2)}{1-r^2}}$$

where t_o is the obtained or computed value of the *t* statistic, *r* is Pearson's *r*, and *N* is the number of valid responses to the two variables being analyzed.

EXAMPLE:

Bearing in mind that Pearson's *r* is an assessment of the extent of the linear relationship between two variables, let's hypothesize that there is a linear relationship between age and the number of hours of television watched (a nondirectional hypothesis, because we aren't speculating about whether TV watching increases or decreases with age). The null hypothesis, the one we can test, is that there is no linear association between age and the number of hours spent watching television.

To evaluate our hypothesis, we can calculate the value of a test statistic, the obtained *t*, for the association between age and hours of television watched. To do so, we have to know the values of *r* and *N*. They are easy to find using SPSS. In Chapter 12 I showed you how to find Pearson's *r* from a scatterplot. Another way to find Pearson's *r* is by following the command path Analyze ➡ Correlate ➡ Bivariate. If you enter the variables *age* and *tvhours* (the order doesn't matter) in the Variables box and click on OK, you will get a set of statistics, called a correlation matrix, like the one in Table 13.2.

In a correlation matrix, each variable you enter will be correlated against every other variable you enter: *age* will be correlated with *tvhours*, and *tvhours* with *age*. In addition, the matrix correlates *age* with itself and *tvhours* with itself.

Take a second to analyze the association between hours spent watching TV and age. What do you find? Based on Pearson's *r*, we know the association is positive—the older the respondents, the more time they spend watching TV. However, the relationship is fairly weak, at *r* = .179. Is this association one that is more likely due to chance or to a real relationship between age and TV watching in the population from which the GSS respondents were selected? As the first step toward finding out, we compute the test statistic, the *t* statistic, for Pearson's *r*.

TABLE 13.2 Correlation Matrix (with Pearson's *r*) for *age* and *tvhours* in the GSS 2002 subset B File

Correlations

		AGE Age of respondent	TVHOURS Hours per day watching TV	
AGE Age of respondent	Pearson Correlation	1	.179**	Pearson's *r*
	Sig. (2-tailed)	.	.000	
	N	1490	474	*N*
TVHOURS Hours per day watching TV	Pearson Correlation	.179**	1	
	Sig. (2-tailed)	.000	.	
	N	474	480	

**. Correlation is significant at the 0.01 level (2-tailed).

Use Pearson's *r* and *N* in Formula 13.1(a):

$$N = 474 \qquad \text{Pearson's } r = .179$$

$$t_o = r\sqrt{\frac{(N-2)}{1-r^2}}$$

$$= .179\sqrt{\frac{(474-2)}{1-.179^2}} = .179\sqrt{\frac{472}{1-.0320}}$$

$$= .179\sqrt{\frac{472}{.968}} = .179\sqrt{487.6033}$$

$$= .179 \times 22.0817$$

$$t_o = 3.95$$

Degrees of freedom   Like chi-square, the test statistic has to be interpreted in the context of the degrees of freedom for the variables involved. Degrees of freedom for Pearson's *r* are computed using the following formula.

Formula 13.1(b): Degrees of freedom for Pearson's *r*

$$df = N - 2$$

EXAMPLE:

For the correlation matrix in Table 13.1, $df = N - 2 = 474 - 2 = 472$.

Interpretation   Generally, the *t* statistic for a specified number of degrees of freedom allows us to determine whether the association we see in a sample is more likely than not a chance occurrence. Keep in mind that, technically, we are always assessing the null hypothesis. In this case, the null hypothesis is that there is no linear association between *age* and *tvhours*. Expressed in terms of Pearson's *r*, the null hypothesis can be represented symbolically as:

$$H_0: r = 0$$

Alternatively, the research hypothesis is that age is associated with the self-reported number of hours spent watching television, or:

$$H_1: r \neq 0$$

We can answer the question, Is a t statistic as large as 3.95 for 472 degrees of freedom likely to have occurred by chance in a sample drawn from a population in which there is no association between these variables?

As with chi-square, an obtained value of the t statistic has to be compared with a critical value for a given alpha level. With an obtained value of 3.95, what is the critical value of t we need to reject the null hypothesis at an alpha level of .05 (a likelihood of only 5 chances in 100 that our association occurred by chance)? To find out, we have to use a table of the distribution of the critical values of t (like the table of critical values of chi-square). The table itself is huge; there is an abbreviated version of the t distribution table in Appendix C.

For 472 degrees of freedom, we have to obtain a t statistic of at least 1.960 (two-tailed) in order to reject the null hypothesis. (Notice that for all associations with more than 120 degrees of freedom the t statistics are substantially alike, so no breakdown is given for $df > 120$.) Our value of t is higher than 1.960, so we can reject the null hypothesis.

Let's explore the idea of two-tailed versus one-tailed tests a little more, beginning with the logic of the two-tailed test. To do so, we need to return to the normal distribution. The t statistic is a sample characteristic (like the sample mean), and as such, it has its own sampling distribution. For large samples (sample sizes larger than 120), it approximates the normal distribution. We can chart the distribution of t values on a normal curve, like the one in Figure 13.2.

The mean and median of the distribution of t values is 0. Approximately 95% of all t values fall in the range of values 2 standard deviations below the mean to 2 standard deviations above it. If our sample was drawn from a population in which there was *no* linear association between *age* and *tvhours,* then we would expect that obtained t would fall in the range of t values between −1.960 and +1.960. Our t value clearly falls outside this range.

Our t statistic, 3.95, is above +1.960, so it falls in one of the tails of the distribution, also called the **region of rejection**. If a test statistic falls within this area, we can reject the null hypothesis. Remember that the region of rejection for a two-tailed test can include positive or negative values of the t statistic, and when we do the computations for t you will see that you can get positive or negative t statistics. We can reject the null hypothesis if t exceeds the critical value in either tail of the distribution—the positive or the negative. (Negative values of t

FIGURE 13.2
Normal distribution of t values for $df > 120$ and $p = .05$.

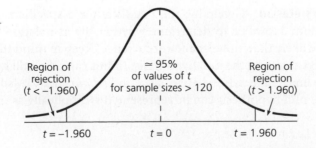

Region of rejection ($t < -1.960$)   ≈ 95% of values of t for sample sizes > 120   Region of rejection ($t > 1.960$)

$t = -1.960$ $t = 0$ $t = 1.960$

FIGURE 13.3
Distribution of the *t* statistic for a one-tailed test with *df* > 120 and *p* = .05.

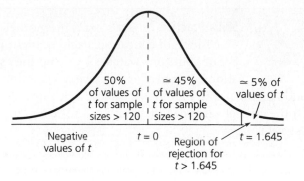

50% of values of *t* for sample sizes > 120

≈ 45% of values of *t* for sample sizes > 120

≈ 5% of values of *t*

Negative values of *t*

t = 0

Region of rejection for *t* > 1.645

t = 1.645

occur when an association between two variables is negative). When a test statistic falls within the region of rejection, there are less than 5 chances in 100 that our sample could have been drawn from a population in which there was no linear association between the variables of interest. It would therefore be highly likely that our sample was drawn from a population in which age was related to hours spent watching television.

For the one-tailed test, using a directional hypothesis, we make the same assumptions about the normal distribution. However, the region of rejection changes. Let's assume we hypothesized that older respondents watched more television than younger respondents, a positive association between the variables *age* and *tvhours*. To reject the null hypothesis, we would, first of all, have to come up with a positive value of *t*. Consequently, the region of rejection must exclude all negative values of the *t* statistic. (Why? Because we hypothesized a positive, not a negative association.) Remember that 50% of the area under the normal curve falls below the mean. For the distribution of the *t* statistic, the area below the mean includes all negative values of *t*. The area above the mean includes the positive values of *t*. Forty-five percent of the values of *t* will fall between the mean and the positive critical value of *t* of 1.645. Five percent will be in the positive tail of the distribution (more than 1.645). Consequently, to reject the null hypothesis, we would have to have a *t* statistic greater than 1.645 to conclude that there are less than 5 chances in 100 that our sample came from a population in which there is no association between age and TV watching. Figure 13.3 shows the distribution of *t* for a one-tailed test.

Like chi-square, the *t* statistic is a measure of inference rather than of strength or direction. When we use it, it has to be in conjunction with appropriate measures of association (Pearson's *r* and *r*-squared in this case). A more complete interpretation of the association between *age* and *tvhours* would be something along these lines:

A Pearson's *r* of .179 indicates a fairly weak association between a respondent's age and the number of hours he or she watches television. However, with a value of *t* equal to 3.95 and 472 degrees of freedom, we have enough evidence to reject the null hypothesis at the .05 level. Consequently, it is much more likely than not that the association we observed in our sample—the older the respondents are, the more hours they report watching television—will be found in the population of American adults represented by the General Social Survey.

Skills Practice 2 Let's explore another research hypothesis: One's level of educational achievement is related to the number of hours one watches TV. Find the *t* statistic for the association between *educ* and *tvhours*. Use the statistics for Pearson's *r* and *N* from Table 13.3 in Formula 13.1(a). Interpret the results. Assume that the critical value of *t* that you need to reject the null hypothesis at the .05 level is 1.960.

TABLE 13.3 Correlation Matrix (with Pearson's *r*) for *educ* and *tvhours* in the GSS 2002 subset B File

Correlations

		EDUC Highest year of school completed	TVHOURS Hours per day watching TV
EDUC Highest year of school completed	Pearson Correlation	1	-.231**
	Sig. (2-tailed)	.	.000
	N	1493	479
TVHOURS Hours per day watching TV	Pearson Correlation	-.231**	1
	Sig. (2-tailed)	.000	.
	N	479	480

** Correlation is significant at the 0.01 level (2-tailed).

Limitations of Pearson's *r*

Pearson's *r* can be used to analyze variables

1. for which we can assume a normal distribution of values for both variables in the population from which the sample was drawn.
2. that appear to have a linear association with one another (as observed in a scatterplot).
3. that are **homoscedastic** in relation to one another. This means that the values of the dependent variable need to be distributed evenly along a line drawn through the data, with about as many values of the dependent variable falling above the line as below it along the entire length of the line. Figure 13.4 shows how a homoscedastic association would look on a scatterplot.

When you are deciding whether Pearson's *r* is appropriate, you can look at a scatterplot for the association between two variables. If it looks more cigar-shaped than circular, then you can test Pearson's *r* with the *t* statistic.

In addition to testing the relationships between numerical variables to see whether patterns in samples are likely to be found in populations, we can test differences in means, like the differences between sample and population means and the differences between means for groups within a sample (like men and women). In the next section you will learn to apply inferential statistics to ex-

FIGURE 13.4
A homoscedastic association.

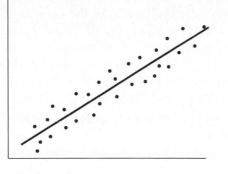

amine individual sample means (like the average number of hours spent watching TV) and associations between means (like the difference between the average of years of education for men as compared to women).

TESTING DIFFERENCES IN MEANS FOR STATISTICAL SIGNIFICANCE

The One-Sample *t* Test

In Chapters 7 and 8 you learned that one way to evaluate the representativeness of sample statistics was to compute confidence intervals around means and proportions. In addition, there are other ways to test for the representativeness of means. One of them uses a test statistic called the one-sample *t* test.

> ***Avoiding Common Pitfalls: The one-sample t test*** A word about terminology: The use of the word "sample" may be confusing. In the one-sample *t* test, we are making the assumption that the respondents to a single variable constitute one sample. Consequently, the one-sample *t* test refers to a test performed on the respondents to a single variable. It may make more sense for you think of the test as the "one-*variable t* test."

One question the **one-sample *t* test** allows us to answer is, How likely is it that any difference that we see between a sample mean and a specified population mean is just due to chance? Framed as a research hypothesis, we would speculate that the mean we find in a sample represents the population mean. Framed as a null hypothesis, we can test the proposition that our sample comes from a population with the mean that we specified.

As with other hypothesis testing that you have done (chi-square in Chapter 11, for example), the process involves constructing a null hypothesis and then using a test statistic along with its associated degrees of freedom to find out the likelihood of obtaining a test statistic of a particular magnitude by chance alone. The less likely it is that a test statistic is merely a chance occurrence, the more likely it is that a sample mean and a specified population mean are different. The more likely it is that a test statistic is merely a chance occurrence, the less likely it is that the mean for a sample and a specified population mean are different.

The one-sample t test is useful when you want to know if a sample characteristic (such as the mean) is likely to be the same as or different from the same specified characteristic of a population (the mean in this case). In *Bowling Alone,* Robert Putnam mentions that "[m]ost studies estimate that the average American now watches roughly 4 hours [of television] per day" (p. 222). We can use that mean, 4 hours per day, to speculate that Americans in 2002 watched an average of 4 hours of TV per day. Then we could use the one-sample t test to see if the mean for our sample was likely to come from a population with the specified mean or a different mean.

We start by framing the null hypothesis that our sample comes from a population with a mean of 4 hours of TV watching. Then we compute our test statistic, the t statistic. The t statistic for one sample is pretty easy to find. It is simply the difference between our sample mean and a specified population mean (4.00 in this case) divided by the standard error of the mean. (You may want to review the material on pp. 248–249 of Chapter 8 regarding the standard error of the mean). You may note that the larger the difference between a sample mean and the specified population mean, and the smaller the standard error of the mean, the larger the t statistic will be. As a rule, the larger the t statistic, the less likely it will be that the difference between the sample mean and the specified population mean is just a chance occurrence. If the difference between the sample mean and the specified population mean is not a chance occurrence, then we must reject the null hypothesis. On the other hand, if the difference we observe in our sample mean and a specified population mean *is* likely to be a chance occurrence, then we cannot reject the null hypothesis.

The computation of the t statistic is represented in the formula below.

Formula 13.2(a): t statistic for the one-sample t test

$$\text{one-sample } t \text{ statistic} = \frac{\overline{X} - \mu}{\sigma_{\overline{X}}}$$

where $\overline{X}$ is the sample mean, μ is a specified population mean, and $\sigma_{\overline{X}}$ is the standard error of the mean.

We know (from Chapter 7, Formula 7.3) that the standard error of the mean is

$$\sigma_{\overline{X}} = \frac{\sigma}{\sqrt{N}}$$

where σ is the standard deviation of a sample drawn from a population for which we are estimating the standard error of the mean, and N is the number of responses in our sample. For the purposes of computing the one sample t statistic, we can read Formula 13.2(a) as

$$\text{one-sample } t \text{ statistic} = \frac{\overline{X} - \mu}{\dfrac{s}{\sqrt{N}}}$$

where $\overline{X}$ is the sample mean; μ is a specified population mean; s is the standard deviation for a sample, and N is the number of respondents in the sample.

TABLE 13.4   Descriptive Statistics for the Variable *tvhours* in the GSS 2002 subset B File

Descriptive Statistics

	N	Minimum	Maximum	Mean	Std. Deviation
TVHOURS Hours per day watching TV	480	0	24	3.03	2.621
Valid N (listwise)	480				

EXAMPLE:

Let's find the t statistic for one sample—the GSS respondents to the variable *tvhours*—and compare it to the specified population mean of 4 hours. We can use SPSS to find the mean for our sample of respondents to the variable *tvhours* and the number of people who responded to the variable (in the GSS 2002 subset B file). If you follow the command path Analyze ➡ Descriptive Statistics ➡ Descriptives to find N, the mean, and the standard deviation for the variable *tvhours*, you will get a table of statistics like the one in Table 13.4. You can use values from the table in your formula for the one-sample t statistic.

$\overline{X}$ (sample mean for *tvhours*) = 3.03 s (sample standard deviation) = 2.621

μ (specified population mean) = 4.00 N = 480

$$one\text{-}sample\ t\ statistic = \frac{\overline{X} - \mu}{\dfrac{s}{\sqrt{N}}}$$

$$= \frac{3.03 - 4.00}{\dfrac{2.621}{\sqrt{480}}} = \frac{-.97}{\dfrac{2.621}{21.9089}}$$

$$= \frac{-.97}{.1196} = -8.11$$

Degrees of freedom   Like other test statistics, the one-sample t test has to be interpreted along with its associated degrees of freedom. The computation in this case is simple.

Formula 13.2(b): Degrees of freedom for the one-sample t test

$df = N - 1$

EXAMPLE

The degrees of freedom associated with the variable *tvhours* in the GSS sample is:

$df = N - 1 = 480 - 1 = 479$

Interpretation   What do we do with the one-sample *t* statistic and its degrees of freedom? Keep in mind that we are testing the null hypothesis that the sample mean is no different from the specified population mean.

In this case, our sample is the set of respondents to the variable *tvhours*. The mean is the average number of hours of television watched per day by these respondents, 3.03. What is the likelihood we would obtain a *t* statistic of −8.11 with 479 degrees of freedom by chance in a sample drawn from a population in which the specified population mean is *no different* from the sample mean? If it is more likely, then we cannot reject the null hypothesis that the sample and population means are no different. If it is less likely, then we must reject the null hypothesis that the sample and population means are no different.

How will we judge if our *t* statistic is more likely due to chance or less likely due to chance? As with hypothesis testing using chi-square, we have to arrive at a critical value of *t*—the value *t* must reach in order to establish that, at a given level of alpha, the null hypothesis can be rejected. As with other tests, we normally use .05 as our alpha value. At an alpha value of .05 or less, we can conclude that it is highly unlikely that our *t* value is just a chance occurrence. Said another way, it is highly unlikely that any differences we are observing between our sample mean and our specified population mean are just accidents of sampling. At alpha values of more than .05, we have to conclude that it is too likely that any difference we see between a sample mean and a specified population mean is merely an accident of sampling. Consequently, we cannot reject the null hypothesis and rule out the possibility that our sample does, in fact, come from a population with the specified population mean.

The next step is to determine if our critical value of *t* meets the standard we have set with our alpha value. How do we find out? We use the table of the distribution of the critical values of *t* (the same table we used to test the critical value of *t* associated with Pearson's *r*). If you turn to Appendix C at the back of this book, you will find that the critical value of the *t* statistic for 479 degrees of freedom at the .05 level (two-tailed) is ±1.960. Our *t* value falls below −1.960. Consequently, there are fewer than 5 chances in 100 that we would get a sample mean of 3.03 simply by chance in a sample drawn from a population with the specified population mean. The odds are too low that the difference we see between our sample mean and our specified population mean is just due to chance. Consequently, we can reject the null hypothesis that our sample comes from a population with a mean of 4 hours of TV watching.

> ***Avoiding Common Pitfalls: Once-tailed and two-tailed values of the t statistic***   You may be wondering when you would use the one-tailed values of the *t* statistic and when you would use the two-tailed values. Remember that the guiding principle here is how you framed your research hypothesis. If you framed the research hypothesis as a nondirectional hypothesis (the sample comes from a population with a different mean), then you use the two-tailed values. In a nondirectional hypothesis, you are simply saying that the sample comes from a population with a different mean, but you are not saying if you expect the sample mean to be less or more than the specified population mean. On the other hand, if you framed your research hypothesis as a directional hypothesis (the sample comes from a population with a mean that is more than—or less than—the specified population mean), then you have to use the one-tailed values of *t*.

Skills Practice 3 Let's test the null hypothesis that the GSS 2002 respondents come from a population with a mean of 12 years of education (the equivalent of a high school education). Use the descriptive statistics for the variable *educ* in Table 13.5 to calculate the one-sample *t* statistic. If the critical *t* for 1492 degrees of freedom at an alpha level of .05 is ±1.960, can we reject the null hypothesis that the sample comes from a population with a mean of 12 years of education?

Now let's turn our attention to testing hypotheses involving the differences in means between two different groups in a sample.

Differences in Means for Two Samples: The Independent Samples *t* Test

Suppose we are interested in finding out who is better educated—men or women. We can find the average for the number of years of education for males in a sample, and we can do the same for the females in a sample. Assuming we discover a difference, we may ask if the pattern in our sample is generalizable to the population from which the sample was drawn. One way to answer this question is by assessing the likelihood that any difference in averages that we see between our two groups, males and females, is accidental. A statistic that allows us to make this assessment is called the independent samples *t* test. If it is highly unlikely that the differences that we see between two groups in a sample is just an accident of sampling, then we can reject the null hypothesis that our sample was drawn from a population in which there is no difference in the average of the years of education that males have as compared to females.

The **independent samples *t* test** assesses the differences between the means—or averages—of one dependent, numerical variable, which we will call the **test variable**, when it is grouped by a second, independent variable that we will call the **grouping variable**. This idea of grouping should be familiar to you—it's what we did when we used the Split File command to divide the GSS into groups based on variables like *sex,* and it is what we did when we used the Compare Means command. When we group our GSS respondents by the categories of a variable like *sex,* we can look at differences in average years of education between males and females. Then we can assess the sampling distribution of the difference in the sample means for each group.

TABLE 13.5 Descriptive Statistics for the Variable *educ* in the GSS 2002 subset B File

Descriptive Statistics

	N	Minimum	Maximum	Mean	Std. Deviation
EDUC Highest year of school completed	1493	0	20	13.35	3.004
Valid N (listwise)	1493				

Avoiding Common Pitfalls: The independent samples t test
Another word about terminology: The independent samples *t* test treats the respondents to each of the categories of the independent or grouping variables involved in the test as separate samples. For example, if you are examining the test variable *educ* to see who has more education, males or females, you are treating the variable *sex* as an independent, grouping variable. You are, in effect, dividing the respondents into two groups—males and females—to see who has the higher average of years of education. For the independent samples *t* test, we make the assumption that each of these groups, males and females, is an independently selected sample of respondents. With the independent samples *t* test, you might want to think of the separate samples as categories of a variable.

Like other sampling statistics, the difference in two means has a sampling distribution. The sampling distribution of differences in means is assumed to be normal for sample sizes over 100. This means that there have to be at least 100 respondents, combined, to the categories of the variable for which we are finding means. In this case, we need at least 100 males and females to assume that the sampling distribution of the differences in means is normal.

With this in mind, let's begin by being clear about our research hypothesis. Suppose we speculate that men and women differ in how much education they have (a nondirectional hypothesis). Our null hypothesis is that there is no difference for men and women in the averages of their years of education. The *t* test allows us to assess the likelihood that any difference in average years of education in our sample is representative of real differences in our population (American adults).

The formulas for understanding the *t* test look a little more complicated than they really are. They begin with the assumption that the sampling distribution of differences in sample means can be tested with a *Z* score, like the one we used to analyze the distribution of means in Chapter 7.

Formula 13.3(a): *Z* scores for the sampling distribution of the differences in sample means

$$Z = \frac{\overline{X}_1 - \overline{X}_2}{\sigma_{\overline{X}_1} - \overline{X}_2}$$

where $\overline{X}_1$ is the mean of the first sample (or group), $\overline{X}_2$ is the mean of the second sample (or group), and $\sigma_{\overline{X}_1} - \overline{X}_2$ is the standard error of the sampling distribution of differences in sample means.

The problem is that we don't know the standard error of the sampling distribution of the differences in means. (Remember that the sampling distribution of anything is theoretical, consisting of the distribution of a statistic in all possible samples of a certain size that could conceivably be drawn from a single population.) We must estimate the standard deviation of the sampling distribution of the differences in sample means with one of two formulas. When we do so, we change the nature of the statistic. In essence, its distribution changes, from one that can be represented by the distribution of Z scores to one that is better represented by the distribution of Student's t.

If we can assume that the two samples (or groups) with which we are dealing have similar variances on the variable of interest (education, in this case), then we use a formula to estimate the standard error of the sampling distribution of the differences in means that assumes equality of variances. (You can look to see whether the variances in two groups are similar. I will show you how to do that later in this chapter.)

> **Formula 13.3(b):** Standard deviation of the sampling distribution of the differences in sample means for samples in which the variances are assumed to be equal

$$\sigma_{\overline{X}_1 - \overline{X}_2} = \sqrt{\frac{s_p^2}{N_1} + \frac{s_p^2}{N_2}}$$

> where s_p^2 is the weighted average of the variances in each sample or group, N_1 is the number of respondents in the first sample (or group), and N_2 is the number of respondents in the second sample (or group).

To find the weighted averages of the variances (s_p^2), we use the following formula:

> **Formula 13.3(c):** The weighted average of variances

$$s_p^2 = \frac{\left(N_1 - 1\right)s_1^2 + \left(N_2 - 1\right)s_2^2}{\left(N_1 + N_2\right) - 2}$$

> where N_1 is the number of cases in the first sample or group, s_1 is the standard deviation of the variable of interest in the first sample or group, N_2 is the number of cases in the second sample or group, and s_2 is the standard deviation of the variable of interest in the second sample or group.

Substitute Formula 13.3(b) for the denominator in the formula for the Z scores of the distribution of the differences in sample means (Formula 13.3[a]). With this modification, it becomes Formula 13.3(d), which we use to find the t statistic, assuming equality of variances between the two samples (or groups) being compared. Formula 13.3(d) (also called the **pooled variance t test**) is Formula 13.3(a) with Formula 13.3(b) replacing its denominator.

> **Formula 13.3(d):** Pooled variance t test for independent samples

$$\text{obtained pooled } t = \frac{\overline{X}_1 - \overline{X}_2}{\sqrt{\frac{s_p^2}{N_1} + \frac{s_p^2}{N_2}}}$$

EXAMPLE:

Your head may be swimming at this point, as you try to figure out where to begin to approach calculation of the t test statistic. Let's try to simplify the process. All you need to work the formula are the following pieces of information:

Two categories of a grouping variable for which the means on a dependent, test variable are known

The number of respondents in each category of the grouping variable

The standard deviations of the distributions of the test variable in each category of the grouping variable

If we want to know whether there is a difference between men and women on the education variable, we need to have the following:

The average number of years of education for men and women

The number of men and women in the sample

The standard deviations for the distributions of years of education for men and for women

These pieces of information are easily obtained using SPSS by following the command path Analyze ➡ Compare Means ➡ Means. Treat the variable *sex* as your independent variable and the variable *educ* as your dependent variable. You should obtain a set of statistics like those in Table 13.6.

Plug these numbers into the formula for the obtained t statistic. You will have to first find s_p^2. This isn't nearly as difficult as it appears. Use Formula 13.3(c):

N_1 (males) = 651 s_1 (standard deviation, males) = 3.202
N_2 (females) = 842 S_2 (standard deviation, females) = 2.843

$$s_p^2 = \frac{\left(N_1 - 1\right)s_1^2 + \left(N_2 - 1\right)s_2^2}{\left(N_1 + N_2\right) - 2}$$

$$= \frac{\left(651 - 1\right)3.202^2 + \left(842 - 1\right)2.843^2}{\left(651 + 842\right) - 2}$$

$$= \frac{\left(650\right)\left(10.2528\right) + \left(841\right)\left(8.0826\right)}{1493 - 2}$$

$$= \frac{6,664.3200 + 6,797.4666}{1491}$$

$$= \frac{13,461.7866}{1491}$$

$$s_p^2 = 9.03$$

Use s_p^2 in Formula 13.3(d) for the pooled t test, along with the means from Table 13.6.

TABLE 13.6 Comparison of Means Statistics for the Variables *sex* and *educ* in the GSS 2002 subset B File

Report

EDUC Highest year of school completed

SEX Respondents sex	Mean	N	Std. Deviation
1 MALE	13.30	651	3.202
2 FEMALE	13.38	842	2.843
Total	13.35	1493	3.004

$$\overline{X}_1 \text{ (males)} = 13.30 \qquad \overline{X}_2 \text{ (females)} = 13.38$$

$$s_p^2 \text{ from Formula 13.3(c)} = 9.03$$

$$N_1 \text{ (males)} = 651 \qquad \overline{X}_2 \text{ (females)} = 842$$

$$\text{obtained pooled } t = \frac{\overline{X}_1 - \overline{X}_2}{\sqrt{\dfrac{s_p^2}{N_1} + \dfrac{s_p^2}{N_2}}}$$

$$= \frac{13.30 - 13.38}{\sqrt{\dfrac{9.03}{651} + \dfrac{9.03}{842}}} = \frac{-.08}{\sqrt{.0139 + .0107}}$$

$$= \frac{-.08}{\sqrt{.0246}} = \frac{-.08}{.1568}$$

$$\text{obtained pooled } t = -.51$$

We cannot interpret the *t* statistic without the degrees of freedom that accompany it.

Degrees of freedom   Finding degrees of freedom for the independent samples *t* test is easy.

Formula 13.3(e): Degrees of freedom for the *t* statistic for independent samples

$$df = N_1 + N_2 - 2$$

EXAMPLE:

For the relationship between sex and TV watching,

$$df = 651 + 842 - 2 = 1{,}491$$

You may recognize the result from the denominator in Formula 13.3(c).

Interpretation   With the independent samples *t* test we can answer the question, How likely is it that we would obtain a *t* statistic of −.51 (with 491 degrees of freedom) in samples drawn from a population in which there is really no difference between the means for men and women on the variable *eudcation*? To answer the question, we need to decide the following:

1. Will we apply the one- or two-tailed test of significance?
2. What will our acceptable alpha level be?

Remember that our research hypothesis—there is a difference between men and women in average years of education—is nondirectional. Consequently, we use the two-tailed test of significance.

The most commonly used cut-off is an alpha level of .05. This means that we want there to be no more than 5 chances in 100 that a test statistic of this size could be found by chance in samples drawn from a population in which there are no differences in means. To reach an alpha level of .05, a two-tailed test of significance requires that we reach a critical t value of at least ±1.960. Our t statistic is somewhat less than −1.960. Consequently, there is insufficient evidence to reject the null hypothesis. We cannot assume that there is a difference between men and women on the variable *education*.

Remember that the t statistic is a measure of inference only. Even if we were able to reject the null hypothesis, we would have to ask ourselves whether the difference between men and women is of any practical significance. In this case, the differences between males and females of .08 years of education isn't an important difference.

 Skills Practice 4   Use the statistics in Table 13.7 to compare the means for the dependent variable *educ* by categories of the independent variable *dichrace* (a dichotomized race variable I created in the GSS 2002 subset B file). Compute the t statistic. Assume your research hypothesis is that there are differences in average years of education for White and non-White respondents. If the critical t statistic for the appropriate degrees of freedom is ±1.960 at alpha level .05 (for the two-tailed test), should we reject or accept the null hypothesis?

What if the variances aren't equal?   In the preceding computations, we have assumed that the variances are equal between men and women for years of education. What if they aren't? Then you use a different formula for the t statistic that assumes the variances are not equal, the *t* **test for unequal variances**.

TABLE 13.7   Comparison of Means Statistics for the Variables *dichotomized race* and *educ* in the GSS 2002 subset B File

Report

EDUC Highest year of school completed

DICHRACE Dichotomized race variable	Mean	N	Std. Deviation
1 WHITE	13.50	1190	2.998
2 NON-WHITE	12.76	303	2.960
Total	13.35	1493	3.004

How can we tell if variances are equal or not? One way is by looking at the differences in the standard deviations for the two groups being compared. In Table 13.7, you can use the standard deviation column to see if the variance in responses to the education variable for Whites and non-Whites is similar. You will notice that they are almost identical. We are fairly safe in assuming equality of variances. However, if you look at Table 13.6, there is a larger difference between the standard deviations of the two groups being compared (males and females) in their responses to the education variable. It may not be appropriate to assume equality of variances for males and females.

A more precise way to see if an assumption of equality of variances is justified is to use a test statistic to determine if any differences that you see in the *variances* between two groups are just a chance occurrence. If the differences in variances are not just a chance occurrence, then equality of variances cannot be assumed. You will be introduced to the test statistic for equality of variances in the SPSS section of this chapter.

When equality of variances cannot be assumed, you use a different formula for the *t* statistic that assumes the variances are not equal, the *t* test for unequal variances. In addition, you must use a different formula to compute the degrees of freedom associated with the *t* statistic than the formula you used for degrees of freedom assuming equality of variances.

Formula 13.3(f): *t* statistic assuming unequal variances

$$t \text{ (unequal variances)} = \frac{\overline{X}_1 - \overline{X}_2}{\sqrt{\dfrac{s_1^2}{N_1} + \dfrac{s_2^2}{N_2}}}$$

where $\overline{X}_1$ is the mean for the first sample, $\overline{X}_2$ is the mean for the second sample or group, s_1 is the standard deviation of the first sample (or group), N_1 is the number of respondents in the first sample (or group), s_2 is the standard deviation of a second sample (or group), and N_2 is the number of respondents in the second sample (or group).

EXAMPLE:

Let's use the statistics in Table 13.6 to find obtained *t* with Formula 13.3(f), the formula for samples with unequal variances.

$$\overline{X}_1 \text{ (males)} = 13.30 \qquad \overline{X}_2 \text{ (females)} = 13.38$$
$$s_1 \text{ (standard deviation, males)} = 3.202 \quad s_2 \text{ (standard deviation, females)} = 2.843$$
$$N_1 \text{ (males)} = 651 \qquad N_2 \text{ (females)} = 842$$

$$t \text{ (unequal variances)} = \frac{\overline{X}_1 - \overline{X}_2}{\sqrt{\dfrac{s_1^2}{N_1} + \dfrac{s_2^2}{N_2}}}$$

$$= \frac{13.30 - 13.38}{\sqrt{\dfrac{3.202^2}{651} + \dfrac{2.843^2}{842}}}$$

$$= \frac{-.08}{\sqrt{\dfrac{10.2528}{651} + \dfrac{8.0826}{842}}}$$

$$= \frac{-.08}{\sqrt{.0157 + .0096}}$$

$$= \frac{-.08}{\sqrt{.0253}}$$

$$= \frac{-.08}{.1591}$$

$$t \text{ (unequal variances)} = -.50$$

The t statistic for unequal variances is interpreted in the same way as the t statistic for equal variances. You cannot use the same degrees of freedom, though, if variances are unequal.

Formula 13.3(g): degrees of freedom for t statistic assuming unequal variances[4]

$$df \text{ (unequal variances)} = \frac{\left(\dfrac{s_1^2}{N_1} + \dfrac{s_2^2}{N_2}\right)^2}{\dfrac{\left(\dfrac{s_1^2}{N_1}\right)^2}{N_1 - 1} + \dfrac{\left(\dfrac{s_2^2}{N_2}\right)^2}{N_2 - 1}}$$

where s_1 is the standard deviation of the first sample (or group), s_2 is the standard deviation of the second sample (or group), N_1 is the number of respondents in the first sample (or group), and N_2 is the number of respondents in the second sample (or group).

This formula is very complicated to work because you cannot round very much at the intermediate steps and still get an accurate answer. I will show you where to look for the degrees of freedom in the SPSS output for the independent samples t test when you get to the SPSS portion of this chapter.

In the next section of this chapter you will learn how to make inferences for associations involving a numerical variable and a categorical variable that has more than two categories.

ANALYSIS OF VARIANCE

So far, you've learned how to use measures of inference with two numerical variables, with single numerical variables, and with numerical variables that are

---

[4] Source: Norman R. Kurtz, *Statistical Analysis for the Social Sciences*, Boston, MA: Allyn and Bacon, 1999, p. 181.

grouped by two categories of some other variable. What do you do when you want to analyze a variable by a categorical variable that has more than two categories? You use the **one-way analysis of variance** (sometimes called by its acronym, ANOVA).

Analysis of variance is based on assumptions similar to those of the *t* test for independent samples. It explores the likelihood that you could obtain a set of different means for a dependent (test) variable in a sample when there is no difference in those means in a population. For example, suppose we want to know whether TV watching is related to social class. We could conduct an analysis of variance to see whether the average hours of TV watched is different for those who identify themselves as members of the lower class, the working class, the middle class, and the upper class. If we found that, in fact, the means for the variable *tvhours* differed from one social class to another, we next want to know whether these differences are more likely due to chance or are the result of real differences in the average number of hours of TV watching among members of different social classes in the population. Analysis of variance helps us to find the answers.

How Analysis of Variance Works

Analysis of variance, like the *t* test, involves the computation of a test statistic that has a known distribution. The test statistic for analysis of variance is called an *F* ratio. It assesses the ratio of variance in a dependent, test variable *between* categories of a second grouping variable as compared to the variance *within* categories of the grouping variable. For example, in pursuing the issue of class differences in average hours spent watching TV, we would assess the variances in hours spent watching TV between categories of the variable *class* as compared to variances in hours spent watching TV within each category of the variable *class*. If there is greater variance between categories than there is within categories, we will get an *F* ratio greater than 1.00.

Formula 13.4: *F* ratio

$$F \text{ ratio} = \frac{\text{mean square estimates between categories}}{\text{mean square estimates within categories}}$$

Variations between and within categories are assessed using differences in mean squares. Differences in mean squares between categories are computed by squaring the differences between the mean for the categories of an independent variable and the mean for all categories of an independent variable taken together. The squared differences are weighted by the number of responses to each category of the independent variable. Differences in mean squares within categories are computed by squaring the variances for the distribution of responses to each category of an independent variable and weighting the squared variances by the number of responses in that category. Although some of the computations are fairly straightforward, some are very complex. I am presenting the formulas and examples in this section for conceptual understanding rather than computational simplicity. The computation of the F ratio begins with the differences in mean squares between categories.

Differences in mean squares between categories   The differences in mean squares between categories of a variable are assessed with the formula

$$\Sigma[N_k(\overline{X}_k - \overline{X})^2]$$

where N_k is the number of cases in a particular category (number of upper-class respondents, for example), $\overline{X}_k$ is the mean of the responses to a variable for a single category (average hours spent watching TV of upper-class respondents), and $\overline{X}$ is the mean across all categories of a given variable (mean for the variable *tvhours* for all respondents).

The formula requires that the difference between each category mean and the mean for all respondents be squared. Then each of the squared differences for each of the categories is multiplied by the number of respondents in the category. Finally, the results are added up to get the sum of the squares of the weighted differences in means between categories.

For example, to get the "between" category means for *tvhours* and *class,* you would need to know the number of respondents in each category, the mean for each category, and the mean for all respondents, regardless of class. You can find these easily with the Analyze ➡ Compare Means ➡ Means command path in SPSS, which produces a set of statistics like those in Table 13.8. To find the "between" category differences in means, start with the category Lower Class.

Step 1.   Subtract the mean for all categories from the mean for the lower-class respondents:

$$4.46 - 3.02 = 1.44$$

Step 2.   Square the result:

$$1.44 \times 1.44 = 2.0736$$

Step 3.   Multiply the result by the number of lower-class respondents:

$$2.0736 \times 28 = 58.0608$$

TABLE 13.8   Comparison of Means for the Variables *class* and *tvhours* in the GSS 2002 subset B File

Report

TVHOURS Hours per day watching TV

CLASS Subjective class identification	Mean	N	Std. Deviation
1 LOWER CLASS	4.46	28	3.203
2 WORKING CLASS	2.99	224	2.667
3 MIDDLE CLASS	2.91	211	2.492
4 UPPER CLASS	2.19	16	1.328
Total	3.02	479	2.614

Repeat the process for each of the categories, then add up the results for each of the categories. The result that you obtain is called the between-groups sums of squares. For Table 13.8, the between-groups sums of squares is 71.8379. As you see later on in this chapter, SPSS computes this number for you when it calculates the F ratio.

Differences in mean squares within categories   Differences in means within categories are computed using the formula

$$\Sigma\left(N_k - 1\right)s_k^2$$

where N_k is the number of respondents in a single category of the grouping variable and s_k^2 is the variance (the standard deviation squared) for the distribution of the dependent (test) variable in a single category of the grouping variable.

The formula requires us to find the variance (square the standard deviation) for a given category of the grouping variable and multiply the result by the number of respondents to the category minus 1. Repeat the process for each category of the grouping variable. Then add up the results.

Using the descriptive statistics in Table 13.8, start the process with the category Lower Class.

Step 1.   Find the variance for *tvhours* among the lower-class respondents:

$s^2 = 3.203^2 = 10.2592$

Step 2.   Find $N_k - 1$:

$28 - 1 = 27$

Step 3.   Multiply the variance times $N_k - 1$:

$10.2592 \times 27 = 276.9984$

Repeat the process for each category of the grouping variable, *class,* and add up the results. The result is called the within-groups sums of squares. For Table 13.8, the within-groups sums of squares is 3,193.7501. As you will see later on in this chapter, SPSS computes this value, too.

Degrees of Freedom

Like other test statistics, the F ratio has to be interpreted in light of the degrees of freedom involved. Unlike other test statistics, the F ratio uses two different computations of the degrees of freedom: one for the "between" category means and one for the "within" category means.

Degrees of freedom between categories   The degrees of freedom between categories is very simple to find. It is the number of categories (4, in this case) minus 1. The formula is degrees of freedom between categories = $k - 1$

where k is the number of categories.

Degrees of freedom within categories   The degrees of freedom within categories is found by subtracting the number of categories from N. The formula is

degrees of freedom within categories = $N - k$

where N is the number of respondents, and k is the number of categories. For the relationship between *tvhours* and *class*, the degrees of freedom within categories is $479 - 4 = 475$.

Computing the *F* Ratio from the Mean Square Estimates

To get the mean square estimates between categories and within categories, divide the sums of squares by their associated degrees of freedom. For example, to get the mean square estimates for the differences between categories, divide the between-categories sums of squares by the degrees of freedom for between category differences. The sums of squares for the association between *class* and *tvhours* is 71.8379 with 3 degrees of freedom, so the mean square estimate of between category differences (the numerator in the F ratio) is 23.9460 (71.8379 ÷ 3 = 23.9460). The *within* category sums of squares is 3,193.7501 with 475 degrees of freedom, so the mean square estimate of within category differences (the denominator in the F ratio formula) is 6.7237 (3,193.7501 ÷ 475 = 6.7237).

The mean square estimates are plugged into the F ratio formula to find the F ratio:

$$F \text{ ratio} = \frac{\text{mean square estimates between categories}}{\text{mean square estimates within categories}}$$

$$= 23.9460 \div 6.7237$$

$$= 3.5614$$

The F ratio is interpreted in relation to a critical value or p value of F. I will show you how to interpret the F ratio when I introduce the SPSS computations of the statistic.

A Limitation of One-Way Analysis of Variance

Unlike the t test, one-way analysis of variance assumes equality of variances. Consequently, the application of analysis of variance must include an evaluation of this assumption. Are we safe in assuming that the variances in the distribution of a variable among groups in a population are equal? In this case, can we assume that the variances in hours spent watching TV are the same among social classes, or do some groups show more (or less) heterogeneity than others? I will show you how to make this assessment when we examine the one-way analysis of variance statistics using SPSS.

USING SPSS

Inferential Statistics Involving Numerical Variables

SPSS GUIDE: FINDING THE *t* STATISTIC FOR PEARSON'S *r*

Getting the *t* statistic is easy. You don't have to do anything more than request a linear regression. With your GSS 2002 subset B file open, follow the command path Analyze ➡ Regression ➡ Linear. Select your dependent and independent variables. Let's use *age* and *tvhours.* Then click on OK.

You should get a set of output like the one in Table 13.9. (It will be familiar to you from your work in Chapter 12. There will be more output on your screen than is displayed in Table 13.9, so look for the charts that match the ones in the table). You should know how to find and interpret Pearson's *r* and *r*-squared. You should also know where to locate the slope and the *y*-intercept and how to use them to predict values of the dependent variable given values of the independent variable. What we will add is an understanding of the *t* statistic for Pearson's *r.*

The value of the *t* statistic (3.956) is listed next to the Standardized Coefficients—Beta (which we learned in Chapter 12 is the same as Pearson's *r*). Next to the value of the *t* statistic is the *p* value of .000 ($p < .0005$, two-tailed) associated with a statistic of that magnitude for the specified degrees of freedom. These numbers tell us that there are fewer than 5 chances in 10,000 that a *t* statistic of 3.956 with 472 degrees of freedom could have been obtained by chance in a sample drawn from a population in which there is no linear association between age and number of hours spent watching TV. We can reject the null hypothesis.

We can use the *p* value for the two-tailed test to make an assessment of the directional research hypothesis that the older respondents are, the more television they watch. All you have to do is divide the *p* value for the two-tailed test in half. Thus, the likelihood that we could have obtained a *t* statistic of 3.956 with

TABLE 13.9 Regression Statistics, the *t* Statistic, and Its *p* Value, for *age* and *tvhours* in the GSS 2002 subset B File

Model Summary

Model	R	R Square	Adjusted R Square	Std. Error of the Estimate
1	.179[a]	.032	.030	2.595

[a.] Predictors: (Constant), AGE Age of respondent

Coefficients[a]

Model		Unstandardized Coefficients		Standardized Coefficients		
		B	Std. Error	Beta	t	Sig.
1	(Constant)	1.787	.337		5.295	.000
	AGE Age of respondent	.027	.007	.179	3.956	.000

[a.] Dependent Variable: TVHOURS Hours per day watching TV

t statistic for Pearson's *r*   *p* value

472 degrees of freedom from a population with no linear association between *age* and *tvhours* is still very small (because the *p* of .0005 ÷ 2 = .00025). The null hypothesis is rejected.

Skills Practice 5   Use SPSS to find and interpret the *t* statistic and its *p* value for the association between *educ* and *tvhours*. Assume your research hypothesis is that there is an association between respondents' educational achievements and the number of hours they watch television.

SPSS GUIDE: THE ONE-SAMPLE *T* TEST

With your GSS 2002 subset B file open, follow the command path Analyze ➥ Compare Means ➥ One-Sample T Test to open the One-Sample T Test dialog box. Select the variable *tvhours*. Then set the Test Value at 4 (our hypothesized population mean drawn from Robert Putnam's book, *Bowling Alone*) and click on OK.

One-Sample T Test		
# age	Test Variable(s):	OK
# agekdbrn	# tvhours	
# byemprob		Reset
# chathr		
# childs		Cancel
# class		
# cowrkfrd		Help
# degree		
# earnrs	Test Value: 4	Options...

You will find a set of statistics like the ones in Table 13.10 in your Output window.

Interpretation   This table tells us that the *t* statistic is −8.132 (slightly higher than the one we computed by hand, because we rounded off the mean and standard deviation when we did our manual computations and SPSS doesn't round). We see the degrees of freedom are 479, as we thought. For a *t* statistic of this magnitude and these degrees of freedom, the likelihood that we would have drawn by chance a sample with a mean substantially different from the specified population mean of 4.00 is fewer than 5 chances in 10,000 (because *p* < .0005). These are pretty good odds, so we can reject *the null hypothesis* (that our sample comes from a population with the specified population mean). What can we assume in place of the null hypothesis, then? That our sample mean comes from a population that watches less television than the specified population mean of 4 hours per day.

TABLE 13.10   One-Sample *t* Test for *tvhours* in the GSS 2002 subset B File

One-Sample Statistics

	N	Mean	Std. Deviation	Std. Error Mean
TVHOURS Hours per day watching TV	480	3.03	2.621	.120

One-Sample Test

	Test Value = 4					
					95% Confidence Interval of the Difference	
	t	df	Sig. (2-tailed)	Mean Difference	Lower	Upper
TVHOURS Hours per day watching TV	-8.132	479	.000	-.97	-1.21	-.74

t statistic   Degrees of freedom   *p* value

Skills Practice 6   Perform the one-sample *t* test for the variable *educ*. Remember the hypothesized population mean is 12. How do the results compare with what you computed by hand?

SPSS GUIDE: CONDUCTING THE INDEPENDENT-SAMPLES *t* TEST

With your GSS 2002 subset B file open, follow the command path Analyze ➡ Compare Means ➡ Independent-Samples T Test.

Data Editor

Analyze Graphs Utilities Window Help

Reports
Descriptive Statistics
Compare Means   Means...
General Linear Model   One-Sample T Test...
Correlate   Independent-Samples T Test...
Regression   Paired-Samples T Test...
Classify   One-Way ANOVA...
Data Reduction
Scale
Nonparametric Tests
Time Series

The Independent-Samples T Test dialog box opens.

1 Select a test variable, the numerical variable *educ*.

2 Select a grouping variable (the independent samples, usually a categorical variable). Use *sex* in this example. Note that you get two question marks in the Grouping Variables box when you select your grouping variable. SPSS wants to know the values of the categories by which you want to group the variable *sex*.

3 Click on Define Groups and open the Define Groups window to enter the values.

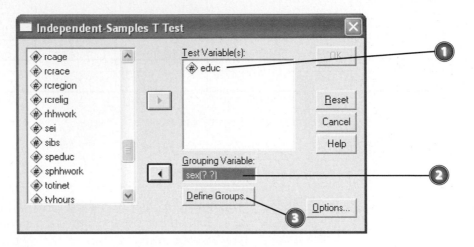

4 Type in 1 for the value of the category Male.

5 Type in 2 for the value of the category Female.

6 Click on Continue.

At the Independent-Samples T Test dialog box, click on OK.

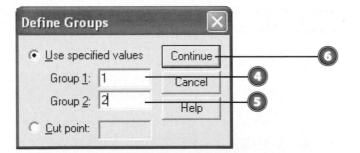

You will get a set of statistics like the ones in Table 13.11.

You get a great deal of information. In the first box, labeled Group Statistics, you get the means, the standard deviations, and the standard errors of the means for both groups or samples—one for males, one for females. You can see whether there is any difference between the means for the two groups on the variable of interest, *educ*, and how large the difference is.

In the second box, labeled Independent-Samples Test, you get the *t* statistic, degrees of freedom, and associated *p* values for the *t* statistics computed for pooled variances (top line) and unequal variances (bottom line).

TABLE 13.11   Independent Samples *t* test for Grouping Variable *sex* and Test Variable *educ* from the GSS 2002 subset B File

Group Statistics

	SEX_Respondents sex	N	Mean	Std. Deviation	Std. Error Mean
EDUC Highest year of school completed	1 MALE	651	13.30	3.202	.126
	2 FEMALE	842	13.38	2.843	.098

Independent Samples Test

		Levene's Test for Equality of Variances		t-test for Equality of Means						
									95% Confidence Interval of the Difference	
		F	Sig.	t	df	Sig. (2-tailed)	Mean Difference	Std. Error Difference	Lower	Upper
EDUC Highest year of school completed	Equal variances assumed	4.816	.028	-.524	1491	.600	-.08	.157	-.390	.225
	Equal variances not assumed			-.516	1308.016	.606	-.08	.159	-.395	.230

Test statistic for equality of variances (*F* statistic)

p value for the *F* statistic

t statistic assuming equality of variances

t statistic if equality of variances cannot be assumed

Degrees of freedom

p values for *t* statistics

Interpretation

What do we learn from all of this information? First, note the size of the difference between the average years of education for males as compared to females. We can say that, based on a comparison of means, females tend to have slightly more education than do males. The size of the difference is tiny, only eight one-hundredths of a year. Assuming equal variances in the years of education for males and females, a *t* statistic of −.524 with 1,491 degrees of freedom is likely to occur by chance 60 times in 100 ($p = .600$). Consequently, we have insufficient evidence to reject the null hypothesis that there are no differences in the average years of education for males and females in the population from which the sample was drawn.

Determining whether the variances are really equal

Based on what we observed in our sample, we assumed an equality of variances among male and female respondents to the variable of years of education. Moreover, we assumed that the equality of variances observed in the sample is representative of the population. Are we safe in making these assumptions? We can find out by using a statistic to test the null hypothesis that variances in years of education for men and women are equal. To test this null hypothesis, we need a test statistic (**Levene's test for equality of variances**), its degrees of freedom, and *p* value.

The first line of the Independent-Samples Test output shows us the test statistic, *F*. With Levene's test statistic and its associated probability value, we can answer the question, How likely is it that we would obtain a sample with unequal variances by chance from a population in which the variances are equal? The smaller the *p* value that is associated with the test statistic, the less likely it is that differences in variances found in a sample are due to chance. The larger the *p* value is, the more likely it is that differences in variances are due to chance. In this case, we have an *F* statistic of 4.816 with a *p* value of .028, suggesting that it is unlikely that chance alone could produce a sample of unequal variances from a population in which the variances are equal. Consequently, we are not allowed to assume that the variances in years of education are equal for males and females in the population of American adults. As a result, the *t* statistic in the second line of the Independent-Samples Test output, the *t* statistic for equal variances not assumed, is the most appropriate one to use for analyzing the association between *sex* and *educ*.

Had the *p* value been larger—more than an alpha level of .05—then equality of variances could be assumed. We would use the first line of the Independent-Samples Test output in our analysis of the association between *sex* and *educ*.

Skills Practice 7   Test the null hypothesis that there are no differences in average number of hours spent on household work each week for males as compared to females. Use *sex* and *rhhwork* to perform the independent samples *t* test using SPSS. Can we assume equality of variances?

SPSS GUIDE: ANALYSIS OF VARIANCE

Like other inferential statistics, analysis of variance begins with a research hypothesis and a null hypothesis. Let's explore the research hypothesis that there are differences among members of the lower, working, middle, and upper classes in the average number of hours of TV they watch. Our null hypothesis, by way of contrast, is that there are no differences among social classes in the mean hours of TV watched. Because the computations involved in the analysis of variance are complex, it is highly unlikely you would attempt them by hand. It is far more likely that you will turn to a computer for help, as we will do now.

Follow the command path Analyze ➨ Compare Means ➨ One-Way ANOVA.

The One-Way ANOVA dialog box opens.

① Select your dependent (numerical) variable, *tvhours*.

② Select your grouping variable, *class*.

③ Click on Options to open the One-Way ANOVA: Options window.

④ Click on Descriptive.

⑤ Click on Homogeneity of variance test.

⑥ Click on Continue to return to the One-Way ANOVA dialog box.

At the One-Way ANOVA dialog box, click on OK. You will see a set of output like that in Table 13.12.

Interpretation

What do we learn from all of this output? First, note the differences in the means for each category of the variable *class*. To see them, look in the chart labeled De-

TABLE 13.12 Analysis of Variances for *class* and *tvhours* in the GSS 2002 subset B File

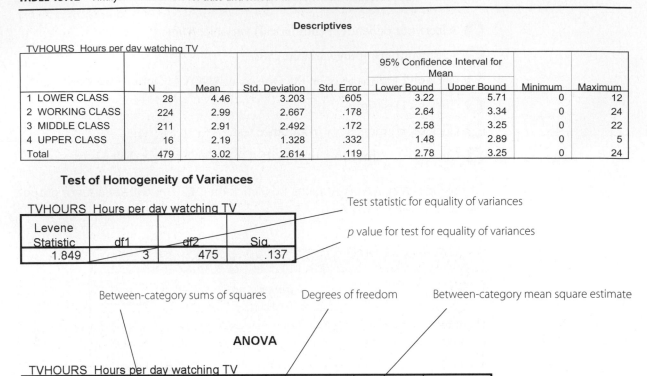

Descriptives

TVHOURS Hours per day watching TV

	N	Mean	Std. Deviation	Std. Error	95% Confidence Interval for Mean		Minimum	Maximum
					Lower Bound	Upper Bound		
1 LOWER CLASS	28	4.46	3.203	.605	3.22	5.71	0	12
2 WORKING CLASS	224	2.99	2.667	.178	2.64	3.34	0	24
3 MIDDLE CLASS	211	2.91	2.492	.172	2.58	3.25	0	22
4 UPPER CLASS	16	2.19	1.328	.332	1.48	2.89	0	5
Total	479	3.02	2.614	.119	2.78	3.25	0	24

Test of Homogeneity of Variances

Test statistic for equality of variances

p value for test for equality of variances

TVHOURS Hours per day watching TV

Levene Statistic	df1	df2	Sig.
1.849	3	475	.137

Between-category sums of squares   Degrees of freedom   Between-category mean square estimate

ANOVA

TVHOURS Hours per day watching TV

F statistic for ANOVA

	Sum of Squares	df	Mean Square	F	Sig.
Between Groups	72.018	3	24.006	3.570	.014
Within Groups	3193.848	475	6.724		
Total	3265.866	478			

p value for F statistic

Within-category sums of squares   Degrees of freedom   Within-category mean square estimate

scriptives and find the column for Mean. What do you see? The means vary from one class to another, generally decreasing. As social class increases, the average number of hours TV watched decreases. Respondents who identify themselves as lower class watch the most TV, with an average of 4.46 hours. Members of the upper class watch the least, at 2.19 hours. The difference is more than two hours. The differences by social class are fairly large ones.

Can we assume that the variances among the social classes in the number of hours TV is watched come from a population in which the variances are equal or unequal? To answer this question, we move down to the next chart, Test of Homogeneity of Variances. Using Levene's statistic and its associated *p* value (and interpreting them as we did for equality of variances in the independent samples *t* test), we can answer the question, How likely is it that we would obtain unequal variances by chance in a sample from a population in which the variances are equal? In this case, we see that the odds are fairly high that we could get unequal variances by chance alone. Therefore, we can assume that the sample we have drawn comes from a population in which the variances in the number of hours of TV watching are equal among the social classes.

Now let's see how likely it is that the differences in the means we are finding in our sample come from a population in which there is no difference in means. In terms of the null hypothesis, how likely is it that we could draw a sample by chance showing the differences in means we see here from a population in which there is no difference in mean hours of TV watched from one social class to another? The test statistic we use to assess the null hypothesis—the F ratio—is reported in the ANOVA chart, the third chart on your screen. In addition, you see the p value associated with the reported F ratio, .014. There are less than 14 chances in 1,000 that the differences we are finding in our sample could occur by chance. If we establish an alpha of .05 as our critical value, then we have more than met the standard for rejecting the null hypothesis. It is highly unlikely that we have by chance drawn a sample that shows differences in mean hours of TV watched, even when there are no differences in the population.

 Skills Practice 8   Test the research hypothesis that there are differences in the average number of hours spent watching TV by educational achievement. Specify the null hypothesis. Then test it using *tvhours* and *degree* with the one-way analysis of variance feature in SPSS. Can we assume equality of variances? Assuming you can make that assumption, what does the F ratio tell you?

SUMMARY

In this chapter you learned to compute, by hand and using SPSS, measures of inference for numerical variables. As with measures of inference for categorical variables, the process begins by computing a test statistic, Student's t (the t statistic), for most of the measures. Student's t has a distribution, like chi-square. We can compare the obtained or computed value of the t statistic against the critical values of the t statistic to assess the likelihood of obtaining a computed t strictly by chance.

We performed this procedure for single variables (using the one-sample t test) and for Pearson's r and the independent-samples t test. The one-way analysis of variance required us to use the F ratio as a test statistic.

KEY CONCEPTS

Directional research hypothesis
Nondirectional research
    hypothesis
One-tailed test of significance
Two-tailed test of significance
Region of rejection

Homoscedastic
One-sample t test
Independent samples t test
Test variable
Grouping variable
Pooled variance t test

t test for unequal variances
One-way analysis of variance
    (ANOVA)
Levene's test for equality of
    variances

ANSWERS TO SKILLS PRACTICES

1. Respondents to the 2002 GSS watch an average of about 3 hours of television a day. There are 95 chances in 100 that the confidence interval, 2.79 hours to 3.26 hours, contains the population mean.

2. Use the statistics from Table 13.3 in Formula 13.1(a):

$$t_o = r\sqrt{\frac{(N-2)}{1-r^2}}$$

$$= -.231\sqrt{\frac{(479-2)}{1-.231^2}} = .231\sqrt{\frac{477}{1-.0534}}$$

$$= -.231\sqrt{\frac{477}{.9466}} = -.231\sqrt{503.9087}$$

$$= -.231 \times 22.4479$$

$$t_o = -5.19$$

The more education a respondent has, the less TV the respondent watches. The association is weak to moderate (Pearson's $r = -.231$). With a t statistic of -5.19 and 477 degrees of freedom, the critical value of t, ±1.960, is exceeded. Consequently, the null hypothesis (that there is no linear association between education and hours spent watching television) is rejected. We can assume, therefore, that the association we see in the sample is likely to be present in the population of American adults.

3. Use the formula for the one-sample t statistic:

$$\text{one-sample } t \text{ statistic} = \frac{\overline{X} - \mu}{\dfrac{s}{\sqrt{N}}}$$

$$= \frac{13.35 - 12.00}{\dfrac{3.004}{\sqrt{1493}}}$$

$$= \frac{1.35}{\dfrac{3.004}{38.6394}}$$

$$= \frac{1.35}{.0777} = 17.37$$

The degrees of freedom $= N - 1 = 1493 - 1 = 1492$. Our value of t exceeds the critical value. The null hypothesis, that the sample comes from a population with a mean of 12 years of education, is rejected. We can be very confident that it is not likely we would obtain a t statistic of this magnitude at 1492 degrees of freedom by chance from a sample drawn from a population with a specified mean of 12.

4. To compute the t statistic, start with the formula (assuming equality of variances) for the t statistic for pooled variances:

$$\text{obtained pooled } t = \frac{\overline{X}_1 - \overline{X}_2}{\sqrt{\dfrac{s_p^2}{N_1} + \dfrac{s_p^2}{N_2}}}$$

The means and the N for each sample are in the set of statistics you obtained with the Compare Means procedure. You need to compute s_p^2 using the following formula:

$$s_p^2 = \frac{(N_1 - 1)s_1^2 + (N_2 - 1)s_2^2}{(N_1 + N_2) - 2}$$

$$= \frac{(1,190 - 1)2.998^2 + (303 - 1)2.960^2}{(1,190 + 303) - 2}$$

$$= \frac{(1,189)8.9880 + (302)8.7616}{(1,493 - 2)}$$

$$= \frac{10,686.732 + 2,646.0032}{1,491}$$

$$= \frac{13,332.7352}{1,491} = 8.94$$

Use s_p^2 in the formula for the pooled t test:

$$\text{obtained pooled } t = \frac{\overline{X}_1 - \overline{X}_2}{\sqrt{\dfrac{s_p^2}{N_1} + \dfrac{s_p^2}{N_2}}}$$

$$= \frac{13.50 - 12.76}{\sqrt{\dfrac{8.94}{1,190} + \dfrac{8.94}{303}}}$$

$$= \frac{.74}{\sqrt{.0075 + .0295}}$$

$$= \frac{.74}{\sqrt{.037}} = \frac{.74}{.1924}$$

obtained pooled $t = 3.85$

The degrees of freedom are computed as follows:

$$df = N_1 + N_2 - 2 = 1,190 + 303 - 2 = 1,491$$

Interpretation   First, we should note that the differences in the means is small. White respondents have a little more education(three quarters of a year more) than non-White repsondents. It is likely that this is not merely a chance difference. With a t value of 3.85 and 1,491 degrees of freedom, we exceed the critical t value of ± 1.960 (two-tailed) needed to reject the null hypothesis at the .05 level. There are no more than 5 chances in 100 that the difference in the means we see in our sample is an accident of sampling. In short, we have enough evidence to rule out the possibility that the differences in the means we find in our samples are simply a chance occurrence. It is more likely than not a result of real differences in average years of education between White and non-White adults in the population of American adults from which the sample was drawn.

5. You should get regression statistics for *educ* and *tvhours* like these:

Model Summary

Model	R	R Square	Adjusted R Square	Std. Error of the Estimate
1	.231[a]	.053	.051	2.555

[a.] Predictors: (Constant), EDUC Highest year of school completed

Coefficients[a]

Model		Unstandardized Coefficients		Standardized Coefficients		
		B	Std. Error	Beta	t	Sig.
1	(Constant)	5.656	.520		10.867	.000
	EDUC Highest year of school completed	-.199	.038	-.231	-5.179	.000

[a.] Dependent Variable: TVHOURS Hours per day watching TV

The t statistic of -5.179 (slightly lower than the one we computed by hand) with a p value of .000 tells us that the likelihood of finding the t statistic of -5.179 in a sample drawn from a population in which there is no linear association between education and TV watching is less than .0005 (5 chances in 10,000). Consequently, we have sufficient evidence to reject the null hypothesis.

6. You should get a set of statistics like these:

One-Sample Statistics

	N	Mean	Std. Deviation	Std. Error Mean
EDUC Highest year of school completed	1493	13.35	3.004	.078

One-Sample Test

	Test Value = 12					
					95% Confidence Interval of the Difference	
	t	df	Sig. (2-tailed)	Mean Difference	Lower	Upper
EDUC Highest year of school completed	17.352	1492	.000	1.35	1.20	1.50

The chances are less than 5 in 10,000 ($p < .0005$) that a t statistic of 17.352 with 1492 degrees of freedom could have been found by chance for a sample drawn from a population in which the specified population mean is 12 years of high school. The null hypothesis, that the sample comes from a population with the specified population mean of 12 years, is rejected. The computation of the t statistic by hand resulted in a t value of 17.37, about the same as the t statistic computed using SPSS.

7. Your output from the Independent Samples t Test should look like this:

Group Statistics

	SEX Respondents sex	N	Mean	Std. Deviation	Std. Error Mean
RHHWORK How many hours a week does R spend on housework	1 MALE	155	8.32	8.556	.687
	2 FEMALE	210	13.01	11.539	.796

Independent Samples Test

		Levene's Test for Equality of Variances		t-test for Equality of Means						
									95% Confidence Interval of the Difference	
		F	Sig.	t	df	Sig. (2-tailed)	Mean Difference	Std. Error Difference	Lower	Upper
RHHWORK How many hours a week does R spend on housework	Equal variances assumed	13.611	.000	-4.269	363	.000	-4.69	1.099	-6.853	-2.530
	Equal variances not assumed			-4.460	362.990	.000	-4.69	1.052	-6.760	-2.623

There is a difference between male and female respondents to the 2002 GSS in the average number of hours a week spent doing housework. The difference is fairly large, just a little less than 5 hours. Assuming equal variances in the hours of housework done by males and females, a t statistic of -4.269 with 363 degrees of freedom is likely to occur by chance less than 5 times in 10,000 ($p < .0005$) in samples drawn from populations in which there is no difference between males and females in the average number of hours spent doing housework. Consequently, we have sufficient evidence to reject the null hypothesis that there are no differences between males and females in the average number of hours spent doing housework in the population from which the sample was drawn.

Can we assume equality of variances? With an F statistic of 13.611 and a p value less than .0005, it is unlikely that chance alone could produce a sample of unequal variances from a population in which the variances are equal. Consequently, we are not allowed to assume that the variances in hours spent doing housework are equal for males and females in the population of American adults. As a result, the t statistic in the second line of the Independent-Samples Test output, the t statistic for equal variances not assumed, is the most appropriate one to use for analyzing the association between *sex* and *rhhwork*. The t value of -4.460 with 362.99 degrees of freedom is likely to occur less than 5 times in 10,000 in samples drawn from populations in which there is no difference in the average of the number of hours spent doing housework between males and females. Again, the null hypothesis is rejected.

8. Our null hypothesis is that there are no differences in average number of hours spent watching TV based on levels of education. Your output should include the following:

Descriptives

TVHOURS Hours per day watching TV

	N	Mean	Std. Deviation	Std. Error	95% Confidence Interval for Mean Lower Bound	Upper Bound	Minimum	Maximum
0 LT HIGH SCHOOL	69	4.48	4.097	.493	3.49	5.46	0	24
1 HIGH SCHOOL	276	3.11	2.419	.146	2.83	3.40	0	20
2 JUNIOR COLLEGE	26	1.73	1.282	.252	1.21	2.25	0	6
3 BACHELOR	78	2.27	1.345	.152	1.97	2.57	0	7
4 GRADUATE	31	2.03	1.760	.316	1.39	2.68	0	8
Total	480	3.03	2.621	.120	2.79	3.26	0	24

Test of Homogeneity of Variances

TVHOURS Hours per day watching TV

Levene Statistic	df1	df2	Sig.
7.425	4	475	.000

ANOVA

TVHOURS Hours per day watching TV

	Sum of Squares	df	Mean Square	F	Sig.
Between Groups	266.483	4	66.621	10.464	.000
Within Groups	3024.165	475	6.367		
Total	3290.648	479			

Interpretation   There seems to be a clear pattern among the differences in means. The more education respondents have, the fewer hours they spend watching television. The difference is fairly large between the respondents with the least and the most education, nearly two and a half hours per day. Can we assume equality of variances necessary to conduct an analysis of variance? No, we cannot, because the odds are low ($p < .0005$ for Levene's statistic) that we could have obtained unequal variances by chance from a population in which variances in the number of hours of TV watching are equal among those with different levels of education. Had we been able to assume equality of variances, the F ratio would tell us about the likelihood that we could have obtained differences in means in a sample by chance even though there are no differences in means in the population. The chances are less than 5 in 10,000 ($p < .0005$). The null hypothesis, that there are no differences in means by levels of education in the population, would have been rejected.

GENERAL EXERCISES

1. For the following correlation matrix, state the null hypothesis. Interpret Pearson's r. Then compute the t statistic and its associated degrees of freedom. Assume that the critical value of the t statistic at the .05 level is ±1.960, and interpret your results. Can the null hypothesis be rejected?

Correlations

		TVHOURS Hours per day watching TV	HRS1 Number of hours worked last week
TVHOURS Hours per day watching TV	Pearson Correlation	1	-.148**
	Sig. (2-tailed)	.	.009
	N	480	310
HRS1 Number of hours worked last week	Pearson Correlation	-.148**	1
	Sig. (2-tailed)	.009	.
	N	310	940

** Correlation is significant at the 0.01 level (two-tailed).

2. For the following correlation matrix, state the null hypothesis. Interpret Pearson's r. Then compute the t statistic and its associated degrees of freedom. Assume that the critical value of the t statistic at the .05 level is ±1.960, and interpret your results. Can the null hypothesis be rejected?

Correlations

		TVHOURS Hours per day watching TV	SEI Respondent socioeconomic index
TVHOURS Hours per day watching TV	Pearson Correlation	1	-.249**
	Sig. (2-tailed)	.	.000
	N	480	458
SEI Respondent socioeconomic index	Pearson Correlation	-.249**	1
	Sig. (2-tailed)	.000	.
	N	458	1426

** Correlation is significant at the 0.01 level (two-tailed).

3. Use the following table to compute the *t* statistic and its associated degrees of freedom for the one-sample *t* test. Use a specified population mean equal to 40.00. Assuming the critical value of *t* at the .05 level is ±1.960, interpret the *t* statistic. Can the null hypothesis be rejected?

Descriptive Statistics

	N	Minimum	Maximum	Mean	Std. Deviation
HRS1 Number of hours worked last week	940	2	89	41.86	14.242
Valid N (listwise)	940				

4. Use the following table to compute the *t* statistic and its associated degrees of freedom for the one-sample *t* test. Use a specified population mean equal to 12.00. Assuming the critical value of *t* at the .05 level is ±1.960, interpret the *t* statistic. Can the null hypothesis be rejected?

Descriptive Statistics

	N	Minimum	Maximum	Mean	Std. Deviation
PAEDUC Highest year school completed, father	1103	0	20	11.38	4.088
Valid N (listwise)	1103				

For the reports in Exercises 5 and 6, state the null hypothesis for the association between the variables. Use the statistics in the report to calculate the independent samples *t* statistic (assuming equality of variances) and its associated degrees of freedom. Next, assume that the critical value of *t* at the .05 level is ±1.960, and interpret the *t* statistics. Can you reject the null hypothesis?

5.

Report

HRSRELAX Hours per day R have to relax

SEX Respondents sex	Mean	N	Std. Deviation
1 MALE	4.20	451	2.768
2 FEMALE	3.48	507	2.898
Total	3.82	958	2.859

6.

Report

WEEKSWRK Weeks R. worked last year

SEX Respondents sex	Mean	N	Std. Deviation
1 MALE	36.24	650	21.549
2 FEMALE	31.37	841	23.042
Total	33.49	1491	22.526

SPSS EXERCISES

For the variables in Exercises 1 and 2, state the null hypothesis. Use the command path Analyze ➡ Regression ➡ Linear to find Pearson's *r* and the associated *t* statistics. Then interpret your results. Can the null hypothesis be rejected?

1. *tvhours* and *emailhr*
2. *tvhours* and *childs*

Use SPSS to conduct and interpret the one-sample *t* test for the variables in Exercises 3–4.

3. *childs* (use specified population mean equal to 2.00)
4. *earnrs* (use a specified population mean equal to 2.00)

5. Conduct and interpret the independent samples *t* test for the association between *dichrace* (a dichotomized race variable) and *tvhours*.

Can we assume equality of variances? Can the null hypothesis be rejected?
6. Conduct and interpret the independent samples *t* test for the association between *dichrace* and *hrs1*. Can we assume equality of variances? Can the null hypothesis be rejected?

For Exercises 7–10, use SPSS to perform a one-way analysis of variance for the given variables. Begin by stating the null hypothesis for each pair. Then use SPSS to obtain and interpret the relevant statistics (descriptives, test for equality of variance, and ANOVA).

7. *tvhours* and *rcrace*
8. *tvhours* and *wrkstat*
9. *tvhours* and *marital*
10. *tvhours* and *rcage*

Area under the Normal Curve

Column (a) lists Z scores from 0.00 to 4.00. Only positive scores are displayed, but, because the normal curve is symmetrical, the areas for negative scores will be exactly the same as areas for positive scores. Column (b) lists the proportion of the total area between the Z score and the mean. Figure A.1 displays areas of this type. Column (c) lists the proportion of the area beyond the Z score, and Figure A.2 displays this type of area.

FIGURE A.1
Area between mean and Z.

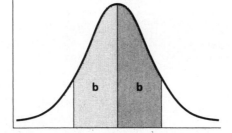

FIGURE A.2
Area beyond Z.

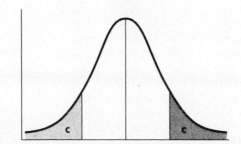

(a) Z	(b) Area between Mean and Z	(c) Area beyond Z	(a) Z	(b) Area between Mean and Z	(c) Area beyond Z
0.00	0.0000	0.5000	0.53	0.2019	0.2981
0.01	0.0040	0.4960	0.54	0.2054	0.2946
0.02	0.0080	0.4920	0.55	0.2088	0.2912
0.03	0.0120	0.4880	0.56	0.2123	0.2877
0.04	0.0160	0.4840	0.57	0.2157	0.2843
0.05	0.0199	0.4801	0.58	0.2190	0.2810
0.06	0.0239	0.4761	0.59	0.2224	0.2776
0.07	0.0279	0.4721	0.60	0.2257	0.2743
0.08	0.0319	0.4681	0.61	0.2291	0.2709
0.09	0.0359	0.4641	0.62	0.2324	0.2676
0.10	0.0398	0.4602	0.63	0.2357	0.2643
0.11	0.0438	0.4562	0.64	0.2389	0.2611
0.12	0.0478	0.4522	0.65	0.2422	0.2578
0.13	0.0517	0.4483	0.66	0.2454	0.2546
0.14	0.0557	0.4443	0.67	0.2486	0.2514
0.15	0.0596	0.4404	0.68	0.2517	0.2483
0.16	0.0636	0.4364	0.69	0.2549	0.2451
0.17	0.0675	0.4325	0.70	0.2580	0.2420
0.18	0.0714	0.4286	0.71	0.2611	0.2389
0.19	0.0753	0.4247	0.72	0.2642	0.2358
0.20	0.0793	0.4207	0.73	0.2673	0.2327
0.21	0.0832	0.4168	0.74	0.2703	0.2297
0.22	0.0871	0.4129	0.75	0.2734	0.2266
0.23	0.0910	0.4090	0.76	0.2764	0.2236
0.24	0.0948	0.4052	0.77	0.2794	0.2206
0.25	0.0987	0.4013	0.78	0.2823	0.2177
0.26	0.1026	0.3974	0.79	0.2852	0.2148
0.27	0.1064	0.3936	0.80	0.2881	0.2119
0.28	0.1103	0.3897	0.81	0.2910	0.2090
0.29	0.1141	0.3859	0.82	0.2939	0.2061
0.30	0.1179	0.3821	0.83	0.2967	0.2033
0.31	0.1217	0.3783	0.84	0.2995	0.2005
0.32	0.1255	0.3745	0.85	0.3023	0.1977
0.33	0.1293	0.3707	0.86	0.3051	0.1949
0.34	0.1331	0.3669	0.87	0.3078	0.1922
0.35	0.1368	0.3632	0.88	0.3106	0.1894
0.36	0.1406	0.3594	0.89	0.3133	0.1867
0.37	0.1443	0.3557	0.90	0.3159	0.1841
0.38	0.1480	0.3520	0.91	0.3186	0.1814
0.39	0.1517	0.3483	0.92	0.3212	0.1788
0.40	0.1554	0.3446	0.93	0.3238	0.1762
0.41	0.1591	0.3409	0.94	0.3264	0.1736
0.42	0.1628	0.3372	0.95	0.3289	0.1711
0.43	0.1664	0.3336	0.96	0.3315	0.1685
0.44	0.1700	0.3300	0.97	0.3340	0.1660
0.45	0.1736	0.3264	0.98	0.3365	0.1635
0.46	0.1772	0.3228	0.99	0.3389	0.1611
0.47	0.1808	0.3192	1.00	0.3413	0.1587
0.48	0.1844	0.3156	1.01	0.3438	0.1562
0.49	0.1879	0.3121	1.02	0.3461	0.1539
0.50	0.1915	0.3085	1.03	0.3485	0.1515
0.51	0.1950	0.3050	1.04	0.3508	0.1492
0.52	0.1985	0.3015	1.05	0.3531	0.1469

(a) Z	(b) Area between Mean and Z	(c) Area beyond Z	(a) Z	(b) Area between Mean and Z	(c) Area beyond Z
1.06	0.3554	0.1446	1.59	0.4441	0.0559
1.07	0.3577	0.1423	1.60	0.4452	0.0548
1.08	0.3599	0.1401	1.61	0.4463	0.0537
1.09	0.3621	0.1379	1.62	0.4474	0.0526
1.10	0.3643	0.1357	1.63	0.4484	0.0516
1.11	0.3665	0.1335	1.64	0.4495	0.0505
1.12	0.3686	0.1314	1.65	0.4505	0.0495
1.13	0.3708	0.1292	1.66	0.4515	0.0485
1.14	0.3729	0.1271	1.67	0.4525	0.0475
1.15	0.3749	0.1251	1.68	0.4535	0.0465
1.16	0.3770	0.1230	1.69	0.4545	0.0455
1.17	0.3790	0.1210	1.70	0.4554	0.0446
1.18	0.3810	0.1190	1.71	0.4564	0.0436
1.19	0.3830	0.1170	1.72	0.4573	0.0427
1.20	0.3849	0.1151	1.73	0.4582	0.0418
1.21	0.3869	0.1131	1.74	0.4591	0.0409
1.22	0.3888	0.1112	1.75	0.4599	0.0401
1.23	0.3907	0.1093	1.76	0.4608	0.0392
1.24	0.3925	0.1075	1.77	0.4616	0.0384
1.25	0.3944	0.1056	1.78	0.4625	0.0375
1.26	0.3962	0.1038	1.79	0.4633	0.0367
1.27	0.3980	0.1020	1.80	0.4641	0.0359
1.28	0.3997	0.1003	1.81	0.4649	0.0351
1.29	0.4015	0.0985	1.82	0.4656	0.0344
1.30	0.4032	0.0968	1.83	0.4664	0.0336
1.31	0.4049	0.0951	1.84	0.4671	0.0329
1.32	0.4066	0.0934	1.85	0.4678	0.0322
1.33	0.4082	0.0918	1.86	0.4686	0.0314
1.34	0.4099	0.0901	1.87	0.4693	0.0307
1.35	0.4115	0.0885	1.88	0.4699	0.0301
1.36	0.4131	0.0869	1.89	0.4706	0.0294
1.37	0.4147	0.0853	1.90	0.4713	0.0287
1.38	0.4162	0.0838	1.91	0.4719	0.0281
1.39	0.4177	0.0823	1.92	0.4726	0.0274
1.40	0.4192	0.0808	1.93	0.4732	0.0268
1.41	0.4207	0.0793	1.94	0.4738	0.0262
1.42	0.4222	0.0778	1.95	0.4744	0.0256
1.43	0.4236	0.0764	1.96	0.4750	0.0250
1.44	0.4251	0.0749	1.97	0.4756	0.0244
1.45	0.4265	0.0735	1.98	0.4761	0.0239
1.46	0.4279	0.0721	1.99	0.4767	0.0233
1.47	0.4292	0.0708	2.00	0.4772	0.0228
1.48	0.4306	0.0694	2.01	0.4778	0.0222
1.49	0.4319	0.0681	2.02	0.4783	0.0217
1.50	0.4332	0.0668	2.03	0.4788	0.0212
1.51	0.4345	0.0655	2.04	0.4793	0.0207
1.52	0.4357	0.0643	2.05	0.4798	0.0202
1.53	0.4370	0.0630	2.06	0.4803	0.0197
1.54	0.4382	0.0618	2.07	0.4808	0.0192
1.55	0.4394	0.0606	2.08	0.4812	0.0188
1.56	0.4406	0.0594	2.09	0.4817	0.0183
1.57	0.4418	0.0582	2.10	0.4821	0.0179
1.58	0.4429	0.0571	2.11	0.4826	0.0174

(a) Z	(b) Area between Mean and Z	(c) Area beyond Z	(a) Z	(b) Area between Mean and Z	(c) Area beyond Z
2.12	0.4830	0.0170	2.65	0.4960	0.0040
2.13	0.4834	0.0166	2.66	0.4961	0.0039
2.14	0.4838	0.0162	2.67	0.4962	0.0038
2.15	0.4842	0.0158	2.68	0.4963	0.0037
2.16	0.4846	0.0154	2.69	0.4964	0.0036
2.17	0.4850	0.0150	2.70	0.4965	0.0035
2.18	0.4854	0.0146	2.71	0.4966	0.0034
2.19	0.4857	0.0143	2.72	0.4967	0.0033
2.20	0.4861	0.0139	2.73	0.4968	0.0032
2.21	0.4864	0.0136	2.74	0.4969	0.0031
2.22	0.4868	0.0132	2.75	0.4970	0.0030
2.23	0.4871	0.0129	2.76	0.4971	0.0029
2.24	0.4875	0.0125	2.77	0.4972	0.0028
2.25	0.4878	0.0122	2.78	0.4973	0.0027
2.26	0.4881	0.0119	2.79	0.4974	0.0026
2.27	0.4884	0.0116	2.80	0.4974	0.0026
2.28	0.4887	0.0113	2.81	0.4975	0.0025
2.29	0.4890	0.0110	2.82	0.4976	0.0024
2.30	0.4893	0.0107	2.83	0.4977	0.0023
2.31	0.4896	0.0104	2.84	0.4977	0.0023
2.32	0.4898	0.0102	2.85	0.4978	0.0022
2.33	0.4901	0.0099	2.86	0.4979	0.0021
2.34	0.4904	0.0096	2.87	0.4979	0.0021
2.35	0.4906	0.0094	2.88	0.4980	0.0020
2.36	0.4909	0.0091	2.89	0.4981	0.0019
2.37	0.4911	0.0089	2.90	0.4981	0.0019
2.38	0.4913	0.0087	2.91	0.4982	0.0018
2.39	0.4916	0.0084	2.92	0.4982	0.0018
2.40	0.4918	0.0082	2.93	0.4983	0.0017
2.41	0.4920	0.0080	2.94	0.4984	0.0016
2.42	0.4922	0.0078	2.95	0.4984	0.0016
2.43	0.4925	0.0075	2.96	0.4985	0.0015
2.44	0.4927	0.0073	2.97	0.4985	0.0015
2.45	0.4929	0.0071	2.98	0.4986	0.0014
2.46	0.4931	0.0069	2.99	0.4986	0.0014
2.47	0.4932	0.0068	3.00	0.4986	0.0014
2.48	0.4934	0.0066	3.01	0.4987	0.0013
2.49	0.4936	0.0064	3.02	0.4987	0.0013
2.50	0.4938	0.0062	3.03	0.4988	0.0012
2.51	0.4940	0.0060	3.04	0.4988	0.0012
2.52	0.4941	0.0059	3.05	0.4989	0.0011
2.53	0.4943	0.0057	3.06	0.4989	0.0011
2.54	0.4945	0.0055	3.07	0.4989	0.0011
2.55	0.4946	0.0054	3.08	0.4990	0.0010
2.56	0.4948	0.0052	3.09	0.4990	0.0010
2.57	0.4949	0.0051	3.10	0.4990	0.0010
2.58	0.4951	0.0049	3.11	0.4991	0.0009
2.59	0.4952	0.0048	3.12	0.4991	0.0009
2.60	0.4953	0.0047	3.13	0.4991	0.0009
2.61	0.4955	0.0045	3.14	0.4992	0.0008
2.62	0.4956	0.0044	3.15	0.4992	0.0008
2.63	0.4957	0.0043	3.16	0.4992	0.0008
2.64	0.4959	0.0041	3.17	0.4992	0.0008

(a)	(b) Area between Mean and Z	(c) Area beyond Z	(a)	(b) Area between Mean and Z	(c) Area beyond Z
Z			Z		
3.18	0.4993	0.0007	3.37	0.4996	0.0004
3.19	0.4993	0.0007	3.38	0.4996	0.0004
3.20	0.4993	0.0007	3.39	0.4997	0.0003
3.21	0.4993	0.0007	3.40	0.4997	0.0003
3.22	0.4994	0.0006	3.41	0.4997	0.0003
3.23	0.4994	0.0006	3.42	0.4997	0.0003
3.24	0.4994	0.0006	3.43	0.4997	0.0003
3.25	0.4994	0.0006	3.44	0.4997	0.0003
3.26	0.4994	0.0006	3.45	0.4997	0.0003
3.27	0.4995	0.0005	3.46	0.4997	0.0003
3.28	0.4995	0.0005	3.47	0.4997	0.0003
3.29	0.4995	0.0005	3.48	0.4997	0.0003
3.30	0.4995	0.0005	3.49	0.4998	0.0002
3.31	0.4995	0.0005	3.50	0.4998	0.0002
3.32	0.4995	0.0005	3.60	0.4998	0.0002
3.33	0.4996	0.0004	3.70	0.4999	0.0001
3.34	0.4996	0.0004	3.80	0.4999	0.0001
3.35	0.4996	0.0004	3.90	0.4999	<0.0001
3.36	0.4996	0.0004	4.00	0.4999	<0.0001

Distribution of the Critical Values of Chi-Square

df	.99	.98	.95	.90	.80	.70	.50	.30	.20	.10	.05	.02	.01	.001
1	.0³157	.0³628	.00393	.0158	.0642	.148	.455	1.074	1.642	2.706	3.841	5.412	6.635	10.827
2	.0201	.0404	.103	.211	.446	.713	1.386	2.408	3.219	4.605	5.991	7.824	9.210	13.815
3	.115	.185	.352	.584	1.005	1.424	2.366	3.665	4.642	6.251	7.815	9.837	11.341	16.268
4	.297	.429	.711	1.064	1.649	2.195	3.357	4.878	5.989	7.779	9.488	11.668	13.277	18.465
5	.554	.752	1.145	1.610	2.343	3.000	4.351	6.064	7.289	9.236	11.070	13.388	15.086	20.517
6	.872	1.134	1.635	2.204	3.070	3.828	5.348	7.231	8.558	10.645	12.592	15.033	16.812	22.457
7	1.239	1.564	2.167	2.833	3.822	4.671	6.346	8.383	9.803	12.017	14.067	16.622	18.475	24.322
8	1.646	2.032	2.733	3.490	4.594	5.527	7.344	9.524	11.030	13.362	15.507	18.168	20.090	26.125
9	2.088	2.532	3.325	4.168	5.380	6.393	8.343	10.656	12.242	14.684	16.919	19.679	21.666	27.877
10	2.558	3.059	3.940	4.865	6.179	7.267	9.342	11.781	13.442	15.987	18.307	21.161	23.209	29.588
11	3.053	3.609	4.575	5.578	6.989	8.148	10.341	12.899	14.631	17.275	19.675	22.618	24.725	31.264
12	3.571	4.178	5.226	6.304	7.807	9.034	11.340	14.011	15.812	18.549	21.026	24.054	26.217	32.909
13	4.107	4.765	5.892	7.042	8.634	9.926	12.340	15.119	16.985	19.812	22.362	25.472	27.688	34.528
14	4.660	5.368	6.571	7.790	9.467	10.821	13.339	16.222	18.151	21.064	23.685	26.873	29.141	36.123
15	5.229	5.985	7.261	8.547	10.307	11.721	14.339	17.322	19.311	22.307	24.996	28.259	30.578	37.697
16	5.812	6.614	7.962	9.312	11.152	12.624	15.338	18.418	20.465	23.542	26.296	29.633	32.000	39.252
17	6.408	7.255	8.672	10.085	12.002	13.531	16.338	19.511	21.615	24.769	27.587	30.995	33.409	40.790
18	7.015	7.906	9.390	10.865	12.857	14.440	17.338	20.601	22.760	25.989	28.869	32.346	34.805	42.312
19	7.633	8.567	10.117	11.651	13.716	15.352	18.338	21.689	23.900	27.204	30.144	33.687	36.191	43.820
20	8.260	9.237	10.851	12.443	14.578	16.266	19.337	22.775	25.038	28.412	31.410	35.020	37.566	45.315
21	8.897	9.915	11.591	13.240	15.445	17.182	20.337	23.858	26.171	29.615	32.671	36.343	38.932	46.797
22	9.542	10.600	12.338	14.041	16.314	18.101	21.337	24.939	27.301	30.813	33.924	37.659	40.289	48.268
23	10.196	11.293	13.091	14.848	17.187	19.021	22.337	26.018	28.429	32.007	35.172	38.968	41.638	49.728
24	10.856	11.992	13.848	15.659	18.062	19.943	23.337	27.096	29.553	33.196	36.415	40.270	42.980	51.179
25	11.524	12.697	14.611	16.473	18.940	20.867	24.337	28.172	30.675	34.382	37.652	41.566	44.314	52.620

df	.99	.98	.95	.90	.80	.70	.50	.30	.20	.10	.05	.02	.01	.001
26	12.198	13.409	15.379	17.292	19.820	21.792	25.336	29.246	31.795	35.563	38.885	42.856	45.642	54.052
27	12.879	14.125	16.151	18.114	20.703	22.719	26.336	30.319	32.912	36.741	40.113	44.140	46.963	55.476
28	13.565	14.847	16.928	18.939	21.588	23.647	27.336	31.391	34.027	37.916	41.337	45.419	48.278	56.893
29	14.256	15.574	17.708	19.768	22.475	24.577	28.336	32.461	35.139	39.087	42.557	46.693	49.588	58.302
30	14.953	16.306	18.493	20.599	23.364	25.508	29.336	33.530	36.250	40.256	43.773	47.962	50.892	59.703

Source: Table IV from *Statistical Tables for Biological, Agricultural and Medical Research* (6th ed.), by Fisher and Yates, 1974, London: Longman Group Ltd. (previously published by Oliver & Boyd Ltd., Edinburgh). Reprinted by permission of Addison Wesley Longman Ltd.

Distribution of the Critical Values of Student's *t*

Degrees of Freedom (*df*)	Level of Significance for One-Tailed Test					
	.10	.05	.025	.01	.005	.0005
	Level of Significance for Two-Tailed Test					
	.20	.10	.05	.02	.01	.001
1	3.078	6.314	12.706	31.821	63.657	636.619
2	1.886	2.920	4.303	6.965	9.925	31.598
3	1.638	2.353	3.182	4.541	5.841	12.941
4	1.533	2.132	2.776	3.747	4.604	8.610
5	1.476	2.015	2.571	3.365	4.032	6.859
6	1.440	1.943	2.447	3.143	3.707	5.959
7	1.415	1.895	2.365	2.998	3.499	5.405
8	1.397	1.860	2.306	2.896	3.355	5.041
9	1.383	1.833	2.262	2.821	3.250	4.781
10	1.372	1.812	2.228	2.764	3.169	4.587
11	1.363	1.796	2.201	2.718	3.106	4.437
12	1.356	1.782	2.179	2.681	3.055	4.318
13	1.350	1.771	2.160	2.650	3.012	4.221
14	1.345	1.761	2.145	2.624	2.977	4.140
15	1.341	1.753	2.131	2.602	2.947	4.073
16	1.337	1.746	2.120	2.583	2.921	4.015
17	1.333	1.740	2.110	2.567	2.898	3.965
18	1.330	1.734	2.101	2.552	2.878	3.922
19	1.328	1.729	2.093	2.539	2.861	3.883
20	1.325	1.725	2.086	2.528	2.845	3.850

	Level of Significance for One-Tailed Test					
	.10	.05	.025	.01	.005	.0005
	Level of Significance for Two-Tailed Test					
Degrees of Freedom (*df*)	.20	.10	.05	.02	.01	.001
21	1.323	1.721	2.080	2.518	2.831	3.819
22	1.321	1.717	2.074	2.508	2.819	3.792
23	1.319	1.714	2.069	2.500	2.807	3.767
24	1.318	1.711	2.064	2.492	2.797	3.745
25	1.316	1.708	2.060	2.485	2.787	3.725
26	1.315	1.706	2.056	2.479	2.779	3.707
27	1.314	1.703	2.052	2.473	2.771	3.690
28	1.313	1.701	2.048	2.467	2.763	3.674
29	1.311	1.699	2.045	2.462	2.756	3.659
30	1.310	1.697	2.042	2.457	2.750	3.646
40	1.303	1.684	2.021	2.423	2.704	3.551
60	1.296	1.671	2.000	2.390	2.660	3.460
120	1.289	1.658	1.980	2.358	2.617	3.373
∞	1.282	1.645	1.960	2.326	2.576	3.291

Source: Table III from *Statistical Tables for Biological, Agricultural and Medical Research* (6th ed.), by Fisher and Yates, 1974, London: Longman Group Ltd. (previously published by Oliver & Boyd Ltd., Edinburgh).

Distribution of the Critical Values of F

$p = .05$

n_1 n_2	1	2	3	4	5	6	8	12	24	∞
1	161.4	199.5	215.7	224.6	230.2	234.0	238.9	243.9	249.0	254.3
2	18.51	19.00	19.16	19.25	19.30	19.33	19.37	19.41	19.45	19.50
3	10.13	9.55	9.28	9.12	9.01	8.94	8.84	8.74	8.64	8.53
4	7.71	6.94	6.59	6.39	6.26	6.16	6.04	5.91	5.77	5.63
5	6.61	5.79	5.41	5.19	5.05	4.95	4.82	4.68	4.53	4.36
6	5.99	5.14	4.76	4.53	4.39	4.28	4.15	4.00	3.84	3.67
7	5.59	4.74	4.35	4.12	3.97	3.87	3.73	3.57	3.41	3.23
8	5.32	4.46	4.07	3.84	3.69	3.58	3.44	3.28	3.12	2.93
9	5.12	4.26	3.86	3.63	3.48	3.37	3.23	3.07	2.90	2.71
10	4.96	4.10	3.71	3.48	3.33	3.22	3.07	2.91	2.74	2.54
11	4.84	3.98	3.59	3.36	3.20	3.09	2.95	2.79	2.61	2.40
12	4.75	3.88	3.49	3.26	3.11	3.00	2.85	2.69	2.50	2.30
13	4.67	3.80	3.41	3.18	3.02	2.92	2.77	2.60	2.42	2.21
14	4.60	3.74	3.34	3.11	2.96	2.85	2.70	2.53	2.35	2.13
15	4.54	3.68	3.29	3.06	2.90	2.79	2.64	2.48	2.29	2.07
16	4.49	3.63	3.24	3.01	2.85	2.74	2.59	2.42	2.24	2.01
17	4.45	3.59	3.20	2.96	2.81	2.70	2.55	2.38	2.19	1.96
18	4.41	3.55	3.16	2.93	2.77	2.66	2.51	2.34	2.15	1.92
19	4.38	3.52	3.13	2.90	2.74	2.63	2.48	2.31	2.11	1.88
20	4.35	3.49	3.10	2.87	2.71	2.60	2.45	2.28	2.08	1.84
21	4.32	3.47	3.07	2.84	2.68	2.57	2.42	2.25	2.05	1.81
22	4.30	3.44	3.05	2.82	2.66	2.55	2.40	2.23	2.03	1.78
23	4.28	3.42	3.03	2.80	2.64	2.53	2.38	2.20	2.00	1.76
24	4.26	3.40	3.01	2.78	2.62	2.51	2.36	2.18	1.98	1.73
25	4.24	3.38	2.99	2.76	2.60	2.49	2.34	2.16	1.96	1.71

n_1 / n_2	1	2	3	4	5	6	8	12	24	∞
26	4.22	3.37	2.98	2.74	2.59	2.47	2.32	2.15	1.95	1.69
27	4.21	3.35	2.96	2.73	2.57	2.46	2.30	2.13	1.93	1.67
28	4.20	3.34	2.95	2.71	2.56	2.44	2.29	2.12	1.91	1.65
29	4.18	3.33	2.93	2.70	2.54	2.43	2.28	2.10	1.90	1.64
30	4.17	3.32	2.92	2.69	2.53	2.42	2.27	2.09	1.89	1.62
40	4.08	3.23	2.84	2.61	2.45	2.34	2.18	2.00	1.79	1.51
60	4.00	3.15	2.76	2.52	2.37	2.25	2.10	1.92	1.70	1.39
120	3.92	3.07	2.68	2.45	2.29	2.17	2.02	1.83	1.61	1.25
∞	3.84	2.99	2.60	2.37	2.21	2.09	1.94	1.75	1.52	1.00

Values of n_1 and n_2 represent the degrees of freedom associated with the between and within estimates of variance, respectively.
Source: Table V from *Statistical Tables for Biological, Agricultural and Medical Research* (6th ed.), by Fisher and Yates, 1974, London: Longman Group Ltd. (previously published by Oliver and Boyd Ltd., Edinburgh). Reprinted by permission of Addison Wesley Longman Ltd.

$p = .01$

n_1 / n_2	1	2	3	4	5	6	8	12	24	∞
1	4052	4999	5403	5625	5764	5859	5981	6106	6234	6366
2	98.49	99.01	99.17	99.25	99.30	99.33	99.36	99.42	99.46	99.50
3	34.12	30.81	29.46	28.71	28.24	27.91	27.49	27.05	26.60	26.12
4	21.20	18.00	16.69	15.98	15.52	15.21	14.80	14.37	13.93	13.46
5	16.26	13.27	12.06	11.39	10.97	10.67	10.27	9.89	9.47	9.02
6	13.74	10.92	9.78	9.15	8.75	8.47	8.10	7.72	7.31	6.88
7	12.25	9.55	8.45	7.85	7.46	7.19	6.84	6.47	6.07	5.65
8	11.26	8.65	7.59	7.01	6.63	6.37	6.03	5.67	5.28	4.86
9	10.56	8.02	6.99	6.42	6.06	5.80	5.47	5.11	4.73	4.31
10	10.04	7.56	6.55	5.99	5.64	5.39	5.06	4.71	4.33	3.91
11	9.65	7.20	6.22	5.67	5.32	5.07	4.74	4.40	4.02	3.60
12	9.33	6.93	5.95	5.41	5.06	4.82	4.50	4.16	3.78	3.36
13	9.07	6.70	5.74	5.20	4.86	4.62	4.30	3.96	3.59	3.16
14	8.86	6.51	5.56	5.03	4.69	4.46	4.14	3.80	3.43	3.00
15	8.68	6.36	5.42	4.89	4.56	4.32	4.00	3.67	3.29	2.87
16	8.53	6.23	5.29	4.77	4.44	4.20	3.89	3.55	3.18	2.75
17	8.40	6.11	5.18	4.67	4.34	4.10	3.79	3.45	3.08	2.65
18	8.28	6.01	5.09	4.58	4.25	4.01	3.71	3.37	3.00	2.57
19	8.18	5.93	5.01	4.50	4.17	3.94	3.63	3.30	2.92	2.49
20	8.10	5.85	4.94	4.43	4.10	3.87	3.56	3.23	2.86	2.42
21	8.02	5.78	4.87	4.37	4.04	3.81	3.51	3.17	2.80	2.36
22	7.94	5.72	4.82	4.31	3.99	3.76	3.45	3.12	2.75	2.31
23	7.88	5.66	4.76	4.26	3.94	3.71	3.41	3.07	2.70	2.26
24	7.82	5.61	4.72	4.22	3.90	3.67	3.36	3.03	2.66	2.21
25	7.77	5.57	4.68	4.18	3.86	3.63	3.32	2.99	2.62	2.17
26	7.72	5.53	4.64	4.14	3.82	3.59	3.29	2.96	2.58	2.13
27	7.68	5.49	4.60	4.11	3.78	3.56	3.26	2.93	2.55	2.10
28	7.64	5.45	4.57	4.07	3.75	3.53	3.23	2.90	2.52	2.06
29	7.60	5.42	4.54	4.04	3.73	3.50	3.20	2.87	2.49	2.03
30	7.56	5.39	4.51	4.02	3.70	3.47	3.17	2.84	2.47	2.01
40	7.31	5.18	4.31	3.83	3.51	3.29	2.99	2.66	2.29	1.80
60	7.08	4.98	4.13	3.65	3.34	3.12	2.82	2.50	2.12	1.60
120	6.85	4.79	3.95	3.48	3.17	2.96	2.66	2.34	1.95	1.38
∞	6.64	4.60	3.78	3.32	3.02	2.80	2.51	2.18	1.79	1.00

Values of n_1 and n_2 represent the degrees of freedom associated with the between and within estimates of variance respectively.

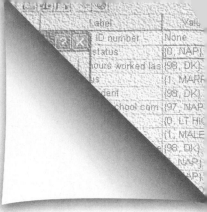

Codebook for the GSS 2002 subset A File

These questions correspond to each of the variables in the General Social Survey subset A file. Keep in mind that these questions are asked in face-to-face interviews with the respondents, with the interviewers recording the answers given by the respondents. The category (value) labels NA, NAP, and DK are used to record nonresponses. NA = no answer; NAP = question is not applicable to the respondent (and, therefore, not asked); DK = don't know. Responses in these categories are treated as missing data (you will see an "M" next to each of the values that is to be treated as missing data), and these categories, along with the category REFUSED, are not used to assess the level at which a variable is being measured.[1]

[1]Sources: *General Social Surveys, 1972-2002: Cumulative Codebook* by James Allan Davis and Tom W. Smith, 2002, Chicago: National Opinion Research Center, and the General Social Survey Data Information and Retrieval System Web site at <http://www.icpsr.umich.edu:800/GSS/homepage. html>. A number of variables have been recoded to change the order of the response categories. The codebook has been modified to include these changes.

1. **ID**   Respondent ID number
2. **WRKSTAT**   Labor force status

    Last week were you working full-time, part-time, going to school, keeping house, or what?

    Value Labels
    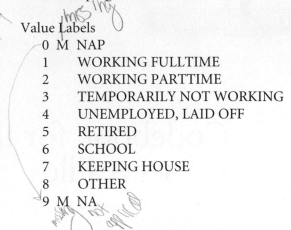
    0 M NAP
    1   WORKING FULLTIME
    2   WORKING PARTTIME
    3   TEMPORARILY NOT WORKING
    4   UNEMPLOYED, LAID OFF
    5   RETIRED
    6   SCHOOL
    7   KEEPING HOUSE
    8   OTHER
    9 M NA

3. **HRS1**   Number of hours worked last week

    How many hours did you work last week, at all jobs?

    Value Labels
    98 M DK
    99 M NA
    −1 M NAP

4. **MARITAL**   Marital status

    Are you currently married, widowed, divorced, separated, or have you never been married?

    Value Labels
    1   MARRIED
    2   WIDOWED
    3   DIVORCED
    4   SEPARATED
    5   NEVER MARRIED
    9 M NA

    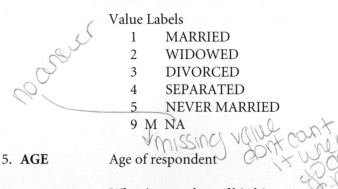

5. **AGE**   Age of respondent

    What is your date of birth?

    Value Labels
    98 M DK
    99 M NA

6. **EDUC**   Highest year of school completed

What is the highest grade in elementary school or high school that (you) finished and got credit for? _____ (A) Did (you) ever complete one or more years of college for credit—not including schooling such as business college, technical or vocational school? If yes, how many years did (you) complete? _____ (B) [Add (A) and (B) to get highest year of school completed:_____ *(educ)*]

Value Labels
   97 M NAP
   98 M DK
   99 M NA

7. **DEGREE**   RS highest degree

IF FINISHED NINTH–TWELFTH GRADE OR DK: Did you ever get a high school diploma or a GED certificate? Did you complete one or more years of college for credit—not including schooling such as business college, technical or vocational school? IF YES: How many years did you complete? Do you have any college degrees? (IF YES: What degree or degrees?) CODE HIGHEST DEGREE EARNED.

Value Labels
   0   LESS THAN HIGH SCHOOL
   1   HIGH SCHOOL
   2   JUNIOR COLLEGE
   3   BACHELOR
   4   GRADUATE
   7 M NAP
   8 M DK
   9 M NA

8. **SEX**   Respondent's sex

Value Labels
   1   MALE
   2   FEMALE

9. **HOMPOP**   Number of persons in household

Now I would like you to think about the people who live in this household. Please include any persons who usually live here but are away temporarily—on business, on vacation, or in a general hospital—and include all babies and small children. Do not include college students who are living away at college, persons stationed away from here in the armed forces, or persons away in institutions. Total Persons: _____

Value Labels
98 M DK
99 M NA

10. **INCOME98** Total family income

In which of these groups did your total family income from all sources fall, last year before taxes, that is? Just tell me the letter. [Note: The letter selected by the respondent was coded as one of the categories listed below.]

Value Labels
  0 M NAP
  1   UNDER $1, 000
  2    $1,000 TO 2,999
  3    $3,000 TO 3,999
  4    $4,000 TO 4,999
  5    $5,000 TO 5,999
  6    $6,000 TO 6,999
  7    $7,000 TO 7,999
  8    $8,000 TO 9,999
  9    $10,000 TO 12,499
10    $12,500 TO 14,999
11    $15,000 TO 17,499
12    $17,500 TO 19,999
13    $20,000 TO 22,499
14    $22,500 TO 24,999
15    $25,000 TO 29,999
16    $30,000 TO 34,999
17    $35,000 TO 39,999
18    $40,000 TO 49,999
19    $50,000 TO 59,999
20    $60,000 TO 74,999
21    $75,000 TO 89,999
22    $90,000-109,999
23    $110,000 OR OVER
24 M REFUSED
98 M DK
99 M NA

11. **RINCOM98**   Respondent's income

Did you earn any income from [your occupation] in [2001]? IF YES: in which of these groups did your earnings from [your occupation] for last year [2001] fall? That is, before taxes or other deductions. Just tell me the letter. [Note: The letter selected by the respondent was coded as one of the categories listed below.]

Value Labels

0	M	NAP
1		UNDER $1, 000
2		$1,000 TO 2,999
3		$3,000 TO 3,999
4		$4,000 TO 4,999
5		$5,000 TO 5,999
6		$6,000 TO 6,999
7		$7,000 TO 7,999
8		$8,000 TO 9,999
9		$10,000 TO 12,499
10		$12,500 TO 14,999
11		$15,000 TO 17,499
12		$17,500 TO 19,999
13		$20,000 TO 22,499
14		$22,500 TO 24,999
15		$25,000 TO 29,999
16		$30,000 TO 34,999
17		$35,000 TO 39,999
18		$40,000 TO 49,999
19		$50,000 TO 59,999
20		$60,000 TO 74,999
21		$75,000 TO 89,999
22		$90,000-109,999
23		$110,000 OR OVER
24	M	REFUSED
98	M	DK
99	M	NA

12. **PARTYID**   Political party affiliation

Generally speaking, do you usually think of yourself as a Republican, Democrat, Independent, or what?

Value Labels

0	STRONG DEMOCRAT
1	NOT STRONG DEMOCRAT
2	INDEPENDENT, NEAR DEMOCRAT
3	INDEPENDENT
4	INDEPENDENT, NEAR REPUBLICAN

5	NOT STRONG REPUBLICAN
6	STRONG REPUBLICAN
7	OTHER PARTY
8 M	DK
9 M	NA

13. **VOTE00**   Did R vote in 2000 election?

In 2000, you remember that Gore ran for President on the Democratic ticket against Bush for the Republican. Do you remember for sure whether you voted in that election?

Value Labels
0 M	NAP
1	VOTED
2	DID NOT VOTE
3	INELIGIBLE
4 M	REFUSED TO ANSWER
8 M	DON'T KNOW/REMEMBER
9 M	NA

14. **PRES00**   Vote for Gore, Bush, Nader

Did you vote for Gore or Bush?

Value Labels
0 M	NAP
1	GORE
2	BUSH
3	NADER
4	OTHER (SPECIFY)
6 M	DIDNT VOTE
8 M	DON'T KNOW
9 M	NA

15. **POLVIEWS**   Think of self as liberal or conservative

We hear a lot of talk these days about liberals and conservatives. I'm going to show you a seven-point scale on which the political views that people might hold are arranged from extremely liberal—point 1—to extremely conservative—point 7. Where would you place yourself on this scale?

Value Label
0 M	NAP
1	EXTREMELY LIBERAL
2	LIBERAL

    3   SLIGHTLY LIBERAL
    4   MODERATE
    5   SLGHTLY CONSERVATIVE
    6   CONSERVATIVE
    7   EXTREMELY CONSERVATIVE
    8 M DK
    9 M NA

16. **FUND**   How fundamentalist is R currently

Do you consider yourself Fundamentalist, Moderate, or Liberal?

Value Labels
    0 M NAP
    1   FUNDAMENTALIST
    2   MODERATE
    3   LIBERAL
    8 M DK
    9 M NA-EXCLUDED

17. **ATTEND**   How often R attends religious services

How often do you attend religious services?

Value Labels
    0   NEVER
    1   LESS THAN ONCE A YEAR
    2   ONCE A YEAR
    3   SEVERAL TIMES A YEAR
    4   ONCE A MONTH
    5   2-3 TIMES A MONTH
    6   NEARLY EVERY WEEK
    7   EVERY WEEK
    8   MORE THAN ONCE A WEEK
    9 M DK,NA

18. **RELITEN**   Strength of affiliation

Would you call yourself a strong [religious denomination specified in the religious preference question] or a not very strong [religious denomination]?

Value Labels
    0 M NAP
    1   NO RELIGION
    2   NOT VERY STRONG
    3   SOMEWHAT STRONG
    4   STRONG

```
                              8  M  DK
                              9  M  NA
```

19. **TRUST**   Can people be trusted

Generally speaking, would you say that most people can be trusted or that you can't be too careful in life?

Value Labels
```
    0  M  NAP
    1      CANNOT TRUST
    2      DEPENDS
    3      CAN TRUST
    8  M  DK
    9  M  NA
```

20. **CLASS**   Subjective class identification

If you were asked to use one of four names for your social class, which would you say you belong in: the lower class, the working class, the middle class, or the upper class?

Value Labels
```
    0  M  NAP
    1      LOWER CLASS
    2      WORKING CLASS
    3      MIDDLE CLASS
    4      UPPER CLASS
    8  M  DK
    9  M  NA
```

21. **SATFIN**   Satisfaction with financial situation

We are interested in how people are getting along financially these days. So far as you and your family are concerned, would you say that you are pretty well satisfied with your present financial situation, more or less satisfied, or not satisfied at all?

Value Labels
```
    0  M  NAP
    1      NOT AT ALL SATISFIED
    2      MORE OR LESS SATISFIED
    3      SATISFIED
    8  M  DK
    9  M  NA
```

22. **NEWS**   How often does R read newspaper

How often do you read the newspaper—every day, a few times a week, once a week, less than once a week, or never?

Value Labels
   0 M NAP
   1   NEVER
   2   LESS THAN ONCE A WEEK
   3   ONCE A WEEK
   4   FEW TIMES A WEEK
   5   EVERY DAY
   8 M DK
   9 M NA

23. **WRKTYPE**   Work arrangement at main job

How would you describe your work arrangement in your main job?

Value Labels
   0 M NAP
   1   INDEPENDENT CONTRACTOR/CONSULTANT/FREELANCE WORKER
   2   ON-CALL, WORK ONLY WHEN CALLED TO WORK
   3   PAID BY A TEMPORARY AGENCY
   4   WORK FOR CONTRACTOR WHO PROVIDES WORKERS/SERVICES
   5   REGULAR, PERMANENT EMPLOYEE
   8 M DON'T KNOW
   9 M NO ANSWER

24. **YEARSJOB**   Time at current job

How long have you worked in your present job for your current employer?

Value Labels
   98 M DON'T KNOW
   99 M NO ANSWER
   −1 M NAP

25. **WAYPAID**   How paid in main job

In your main job, are you salaried, paid by the hour, or what?

Value Labels
- 0 M NAP
- 1   SALARIED
- 2   PAID BY THE HOUR
- 3   OTHER
- 8 M DON'T KNOW
- 9 M NO ANSWER

26. **FAMWKOFF** How hard to take time off

How hard is it to take time off during your work to take care of personal or family matters?

Value Labels
- 0 M NAP
- 1   NOT AT ALL HARD
- 2   NOT TOO HARD
- 3   SOMEWHAT HARD
- 4   VERY HARD
- 8 M DON'T KNOW
- 9 M NO ANSWER

27. **WKVSFAM** How often job interferes with family life

How often do the demands of your job interfere with your family life?

Value Labels
- 0 M NAP
- 1   NEVER
- 2   RARELY
- 3   SOMETIMES
- 4   OFTEN
- 8 M DON'T KNOW
- 9 M NO ANSWER

28. **HRSRELAX** Hours per day R has to relax

After an average work day, about how many hours do you have to relax or pursue activities that you enjoy?

Value Labels
- 98 M DON'T KNOW
- 99 M NO ANSWER
- −1 M NAP

29. **LOTOFSAY**   R has lot of say in job

Please tell me whether you strongly agree, agree, disagree, or strongly disagree with . . . [this] statement. . . . , I have a lot of say about what happens on my job.

Value Labels
```
0 M  NAP
1    STRONGLY AGREE
2    AGREE
3    DISAGREE
4    STRONGLY DISAGREE
8 M  DON'T KNOW
9 M  NO ANSWER
```

30. **VOLCHRTY**   R done volunteer work for a charity

During the past 12 months, how often have you done volunteer work for a charity?

Value Labels
```
0 M  NAP
1    NOT AT ALL IN PAST YEAR
2    ONCE IN THE PAST YEAR
3    AT LEAST 2 OR 3 TIMES IN PAST YEAR
4    ONCE A MONTH
5    ONCE A WEEK
6    MORE THAN ONCE A WEEK
8 M  DON'T KNOW
9 M  NO ANSWER
```

31. **GIVCHRTY**   R has given money to a charity

During the past 12 months, how often have you given money to charity?

Value Labels
```
0 M  NAP
1    NOT AT ALL IN PAST YEAR
2    ONCE IN THE PAST YEAR
3    AT LEAST 2 OR 3 TIMES IN PAST YEAR
4    ONCE A MONTH
5    ONCE A WEEK
6    MORE THAN ONCE A WEEK
8 M  DON'T KNOW
9 M  NO ANSWER
```

32. **OTHSHELP**   People should help less fortunate others

Please tell me whether you strongly agree, agree, neither agree nor disagree, disagree, or strongly disagree with [this] statement . . . People should be willing to help others who are less fortunate.

Value Labels
   0 M NAP
   1   STRONGLY AGREE
   2   AGREE
   3   NEITHER AGREE NOR DISAGREE
   4   DISAGREE
   5   STRONGLY DISAGREE
   8 M DON'T KNOW
   9 M NO ANSWER

33. **PROTEST**   Have ever joined a protest rally past 5 years

Over the past 5 years have you joined a protest rally or march?

Value Labels
   0 M NAP
   1   NO
   2   YES
   8 M DON'T KNOW
   9 M NO ANSWER

34. **CONOFFCL**   Have ever contacted an elected official

Over the past 5 years have you contacted an elected official by phone, letter, or email?

Value Labels
   0 M NAP
   1   NO
   2   YES
   8 M DON'T KNOW
   9 M NO ANSWER

35. **GIVCHNG**   Have given money to group advocating social change

Over the past 5 years have you given money to a group advocating social change?

Value Labels
   0 M NAP
   1   NO

           2   YES
           8 M DON'T KNOW
           9 M NO ANSWER

36. **PARTTHON** Over the past 5 years have you participated in a walkathon
                   or marathon to raise money for a cause?

                   Value Labels
                        0 M NAP
                        1   NO
                        2   YES
                        8 M DON'T KNOW
                        9 M NO ANSWER

37. **GRPPOL**   Participated in activity of political party

                   People sometimes belong to different kinds of groups or
                   associations . . . For [a political party, club or association]
                   please select a response to say whether you have
                   participated in the activities of this group in the past 12
                   months.

                   Value Labels
                        0 M NAP
                        1   I DO NOT BELONG TO SUCH A GROUP
                        2   I BELONG TO SUCH A GROUP BUT DON'T
                              PARTICIPATE
                        3   I HAVE PARTICIPATED ONCE OR TWICE
                        4   I HAVE PARTICIPATED MORE THAN TWICE
                        8 M DON'T KNOW
                        9 M NO ANSWER

38. **GRPCHURH** Participated in activity of church past 12 months

                   People sometimes belong to different kinds of groups or
                   associations . . . For [a church or other religious
                   organization] please select a response to say whether you
                   have participated in the activities of this group in the past
                   12 months.

                   Value Labels
                        0 M NAP
                        1   I DO NOT BELONG TO SUCH A GROUP
                        2   I BELONG TO SUCH A GROUP BUT DON'T
                              PARTICIPATE
                        3   I HAVE PARTICIPATED ONCE OR TWICE
                        4   I HAVE PARTICIPATED MORE THAN TWICE
                        8 M DON'T KNOW
                        9 M NO ANSWER

39. **GRPCHRTY** Participated in a charitable org past 12 months

People sometimes belong to different kinds of groups or associations . . . For [a charitable organization or group] please select a response to say whether you have participated in the activities of this group in the past 12 months.

Value Labels
   0 M NAP
   1   I DO NOT BELONG TO SUCH A GROUP
   2   I BELONG TO SUCH A GROUP BUT DON'T PARTICIPATE
   3   I HAVE PARTICIPATED ONCE OR TWICE
   4   I HAVE PARTICIPATED MORE THAN TWICE
   8 M DON'T KNOW
   9 M NO ANSWER

40. **SATJOB7** Job satisfaction in general

All things considered, how satisfied are you with your (main) job?

Value Labels
   0 M NAP
   1   COMPLETELY DISSATISFIED
   2   VERY DISSATISFIED
   3   FAIRLY DISSATISFIED
   4   NEITHER SATISFIED NOR DISSATISFIED
   5   FAIRLY SATISFIED
   6   VERY SATISFIED
   7   COMPLETELY SATISFIED
   8 M CANNOT CHOOSE
   9 M NO ANSWER

41. **HAPPY** General happiness

Taken all together, how would you say things are these days—would you say that you are very happy, pretty happy, or not too happy?

Value Labels
   0 M NAP
   1   NOT TOO HAPPY
   2   PRETTY HAPPY
   3   VERY HAPPY
   8 M DK
   9 M NA

42. **RCRACE**   Recoded race first mention

What race do you consider yourself?

Value Labels
- 0 M NAP
- 1   WHITE
- 2   BLACK OR AFRICAN AMERICAN
- 3   AMERICAN INDIAN OR ALASKA NATIVE
- 4   HISPANIC
- 5   OTHER
- 98 M DK
- 99 M NA

43. **RCREGION**   Recoded region of interview

Value Labels
- 0 M NOT ASSIGNED
- 1   NORTHEAST
- 2   MIDWEST
- 3   SOUTHEAST
- 4   WEST

44. **RCRELIG**   Recoded RS religious preference

What is your religious preference? Is it Protestant, Catholic, Jewish, some other religion, or no religion?

Value Labels
- 0 M NAP
- 1   PROTESTANT
- 2   CATHOLIC
- 3   JEWISH
- 4   NONE
- 5   OTHER
- 98 M DK
- 99 M NA

45. **RCAGE**   Recoded age variable

Value Labels
- 1   18 THRU 25
- 2   26 THRU 40
- 3   41 THRU 60
- 4   61 THRU 89
- 99 M NA

46. **RCPARTY**   Recoded political party affiliation

Value Labels
    1   DEMOCRAT
    2   INDEPENDENT
    3   REPUBLICAN
    4   OTHER
    9 M NA

47. **RCPOLVWS**   Recoded think of self as liberal or conservative

Value Labels
    0 M NAP
    1   LIBERAL
    2   MODERATE
    3   CONSERVATIVE
    8 M DK
    9 M NA

48. **RCATTEND**   Recoded how often R attends religious services

Value Labels
    0   NEVER
    1   SEVERAL TIMES A YEAR OR LESS
    2   AT LEAST MONTHLY
    3   AT LEAST WEEKLY
    9 M DK, NA

49. **RCWRKSTA**   Recoded work status

Value Labels
    1   WORKING FULL TIME
    2   WORKING PART TIME
    3   NOT WORKING
    4   NOT IN THE MARKET

50. **RCVOLCHR**   Recoded has R done volunteer work for charity

Value Labels
    0 M NAP
    1   NOT AT ALL IN PAST YEAR
    2   AT LEAST ONCE IN PAST YEAR
    3   AT LEAST ONCE A MONTH IN PAST YEAR
    8 M DON'T KNOW
    9 M NO ANSWER

APPENDIX **F**

Bells and Whistles: Advanced Features of SPSS

THE EDIT-OPTIONS FEATURES OF SPSS

One of the SPSS menu items, Edit-Options, tells SPSS how to display variables, tables, and charts. You may need to access this feature at the beginning of each SPSS session so that your screens will look like the ones in the text. First, click on the Edit menu item. A list of options like these will appear:

🖻 Untitled - SPSS Data Editor

File	Edit	View	Data	Transform	Analyze	Graphs	Utilities	Window	Help

	Undo	Ctrl+Z						
	Redo	Ctrl+R			Width	Decimals		Labe
	Cut	Ctrl+X						
	Copy	Ctrl+C						
	Paste	Ctrl+V						
	Paste Variables...							
	Clear	Del						
	Find...	Ctrl+F						
	Options...							

Then click on Options. The Options window opens. It looks like a set of file folders. Each folder has its own tab, like General, Viewer, and so on.

Point to one of the items, like Display Labels, and click using the right-most click key on the mouse. A box will open up describing the item. To close the box, move your cursor off the item, and click again with the right-most key. Try this with a few of the other items on the screen.

Some of the options have circles next to them. The circles with the black dots in the center (called radio buttons) show you which options are active. Make sure the options selected under Variable Lists in the General folder are Display Names and Alphabetical. Those options should be the ones with the black dots in the radio buttons next to them, like on the following screen. (If they aren't, then point to the button next to the option and click with the left-most click key on the mouse.)

1 Under Variable Lists, click on Display Names.

2 Click on Alphabetical.

If you make a mistake and click on the wrong button, click again, and the black dot will disappear. When you're finished, put your cursor on the Output Labels tab and click. When you click on the Output Labels tab in the Options window, you will see a folder like the following:

Options

| General | Viewer | Draft Viewer | Output Labels | Charts | Interactive | Pivot Tables | Data | Currency |

Outline Labeling

Variables in item labels shown as:

    Labels

Variable values in item labels shown as:

    Labels

Pivot Table Labeling

Variables in labels shown as:

    Labels

Variable values in labels shown as:

    Labels

OK   Cancel   Apply   Help

Note that the choices are Outline Labeling and Pivot Table Labeling. Under each choice, look at the options. Point your cursor at each of the options, like Variables in item labels shown as, and click the right-most click key to see a description of it. A box will open showing a brief description of the option. To close the description box, move your cursor away from it and click again with the right-most click key.

Look at the choices under each of the Labeling options by clicking on the down arrows ▼ (in the box under each of the options). You will see choices like the ones following. To select one of the choices, place your cursor on it and click. Try it.

Use this feature to set the options under Outline Labeling and Pivot Table Labeling to look like the screen you see here:

Click on the Draft Viewer tab. Make sure the following items have been selected (that is, have a ✔ in the box next to them).

If the item isn't checked off (like it is in the preceding screen), click on the box next to the item. If it is checked off (but shouldn't be), click on the box next to the item and the ✔ will disappear. Click on OK to go back to the SPSS Data Editor. (If you get a Warning, like this one, click on OK.)

THE VIEW FEATURE

Another way to display the values of variables in the Data View screen is to use the menu item View. Open an SPSS file. Click on View. A dropdown menu appears. Click on Value Labels. A ✔ will appear next to it.

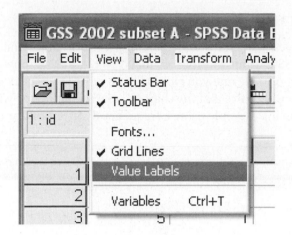

The SPSS Data Editor now shows you all of the value labels for each variable so you can see the data for each respondent in a way that makes more sense, but you may still need to use the Variables window to help interpret some of the variables.

	id	wrkstat	hrs1	marital	age	educ	degree	sex
1	1	WORKI	40	DIVORC	25	14	HIGH S	FEMAL
2	3	WORKI	40	SEPAR	30	13	HIGH S	FEMAL
3	5	WORKI	40	DIVORC	37	7	LT HIGH	MALE
4	7	RETIRE	NAP	MARRIE	57	16	BACHEL	FEMAL

If you want to see more of the variable label, place your cursor on the border between two variables. A bold black line with two arrows appears. Hold the left-click key down and scroll to the right to widen the variable labels display. An illustration follows. To turn off the Value Labels and return to showing all of your data as numbers, click on View and then click on Value Labels again.

	id	wrkstat
1	1	WORKING FULLTIME
2	3	WORKING FULLTIME
3	5	WORKING FULLTIME
4	7	RETIRED

PRINTING SPSS OUTPUT

Sometimes it's helpful to be able to print out tables and charts that appear in your SPSS Output window. At the SPSS Output window, place your cursor on the chart or table that you would like to print. Then click once with your mouse key. You will notice that the chart or table is highlighted with a black border, like the following example using a frequency distribution for the *degree* variable.

Frequencies

Statistics

DEGREE RS highest degree

N	Valid	1497
	Missing	3

DEGREE RS highest degree

		Frequency	Percent	Valid Percent	Cumulative Percent
Valid	0 LT HIGH SCHOOL	225	15.0	15.0	15.0
	1 HIGH SCHOOL	789	52.6	52.7	67.7
	2 JUNIOR COLLEGE	109	7.3	7.3	75.0
	3 BACHELOR	249	16.6	16.6	91.6
	4 GRADUATE	125	8.3	8.4	100.0
	Total	1497	99.8	100.0	
Missing	8 DK	3	.2		
Total		1500	100.0		

Now click on the printer icon (the "button" with the printer on it) to open the Print window. When the Print window opens, look under Print Range. Note that the option, Selection, is highlighted. This means that only the chart or table with the black border around it will be printed. (If you want to print everything in the Output window, you can change this option to All visible output. Be warned that *everything* in the Output window will be printed, so scroll up and down in the Output window before you choose this option to make sure you really want it all.) Once you have made your choice—either Selection or All visible output—

click on OK. The item(s) you requested should begin to print (provided the printer is turned on, there is paper in it, and so on).

USING CASE SUMMARIES TO CHECK DATA

When you are entering data, you can check it against its source using Case Summaries. The Case Summaries feature produces a list of each value of each variable for each case. This feature is most useful when you have your variable list in the dialog boxes in file order rather than alphabetical order (because file order is more likely to match the order of the survey documents against which you will be checking your data). To put your variable lists in file order, use the command path Edit ➡ Options. In the "General" folder, look under "Variable Lists" and make sure that the radio button, "File," is selected. Then click on OK. For the example that follows, I will use the "Civic Engagement Survey" file that you created in Chapter 3. Click on Analyze ➡ Reports ➡ Case Summaries.

At the Summarize Cases dialog box,

1 Select the variables for which you want to check the values. You should always include the respondent identification variable *(id)* as the first variable on your list.

2 If you have a large file of data, turn off the Limit cases to first feature.

3 Turn off the Show only valid cases option.

4 Click on OK.

You'll get a report like the one that follows. You can use this report to check your data against its original source to make sure you entered it correctly. Note that you have your *id* variable, the values of numerical values (like *age*), and the values and labels for categorical variables *(sex, marital,* and *partyid)*.

Case Summaries

	ID Respondent's identification	AGE Respondent's age	SEX Respondent's sex	MARITAL Marital status	PARTYID Party identification
1	1	48	2 Female	1 Married	3 Independent, close to Democrat
2	2	82	1 Male	1 Married	5 Independent, close to Republican
3	3	62	1 Male	4 Separated	5 Independent, close to Republican
4	4	71	2 Female	1 Married	4 Independent
5	5	21	1 Male	5 Never married	5 Independent, close to Republican
6	6	58	2 Female	3 Divorced	1 Strong Democrat
7	7	33	2 Female	5 Never married	9 No answer
8	8	70	2 Female	2 Widowed	9 No answer
9	9	72	1 Male	2 Widowed	3 Independent, close to Democrat
10	10	39	2 Female	5 Never married	1 Strong Democrat
11	11	60	2 Female	2 Widowed	3 Independent, close to Democrat
12	12	31	2 Female	5 Never married	3 Independent, close to Democrat
13	13	36	2 Female	5 Never married	5 Independent, close to Republican
14	14	55	1 Male	3 Divorced	6 Not very strong Republican
15	15	63	2 Female	2 Widowed	9 No answer
16	16	53	1 Male	2 Widowed	5 Independent, close to Republican
17	17	46	2 Female	3 Divorced	3 Independent, close to Democrat
18	18	46	1 Male	5 Never married	1 Strong Democrat
19	19	47	2 Female	3 Divorced	5 Independent, close to Republican
20	20	37	2 Female	3 Divorced	1 Strong Democrat
Total N	20	20	20	20	17

USING THE OUTLINE FEATURE IN THE OUTPUT WINDOW

When you create SPSS output by running one of the SPSS commands (a frequency distribution, for example), you create an outline of the work you are doing. For example, if you produce a frequency distribution for the variable *sex*, you will get

1 The frequency distribution.

2 An outline of the output on the left-hand side of the Output window.

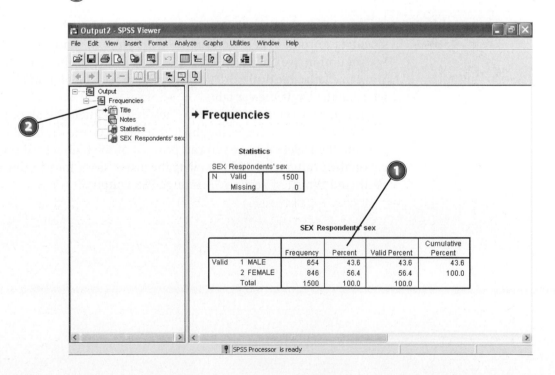

You can use the outline to move around in the Output window. For example, if you click on one of the items in the outline, the corresponding item in the Output window is highlighted with a black box.

1 Click on the outline item Statistics.

2 Note that the Statistics output is highlighted.

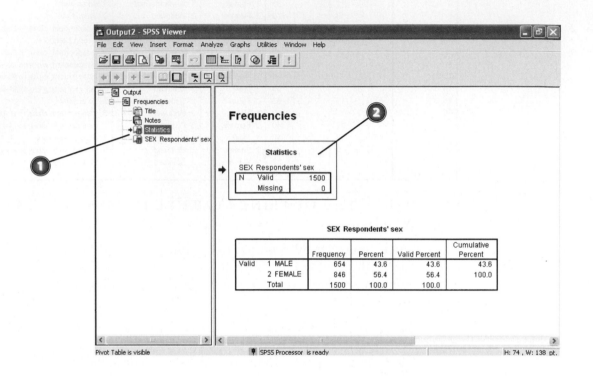

The Notes item in the outline is the only item that doesn't have corresponding output. When we used the Edit-Options feature to select the Draft Viewer option, we did not select the Notes feature, so the notes remain hidden. You can change the outline default settings by clicking on Edit then Options and selecting the Draft Viewer tab.

If you click on the main outline heading, Frequencies, all of the output associated with the heading is highlighted. You can delete the highlighted items by pressing the Delete key, or you can print all of the highlighted output by clicking on the printer icon and following the instructions for printing output in the "Bells and Whistles" section "Printing SPSS Output."

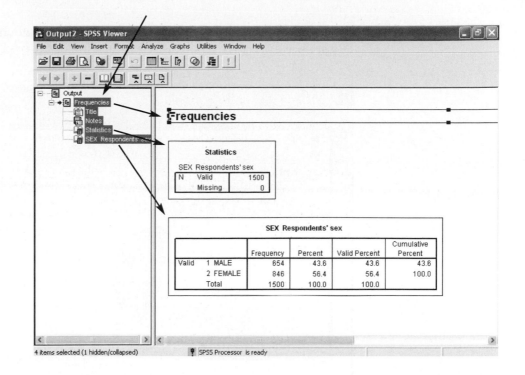

As you do more work in an SPSS session, the outline will become longer and longer. You can click on the Outline items to move back and forth in the Output window to select items to print or to delete output you no longer need.

USING THE CHART EDITOR TO CUSTOMIZE CHARTS

Whenever you create a chart with SPSS, it's a simple matter to customize it using the SPSS Chart Editor. To access the Chart Editor, just place your cursor on the chart in the SPSS Output window you want to customize. Let's illustrate this with a pie chart for the variable *sex* in the GSS 2002 subset Λ file. Use the SPSS Guide "Creating a Pie Chart" in Chapter 4 to obtain a pie chart like the following.

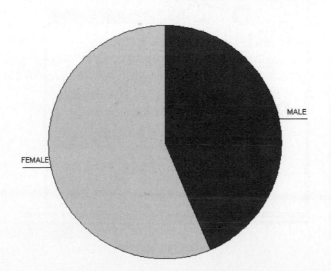

To customize the pie chart, put your cursor on it and double-click. The Chart Editor opens.

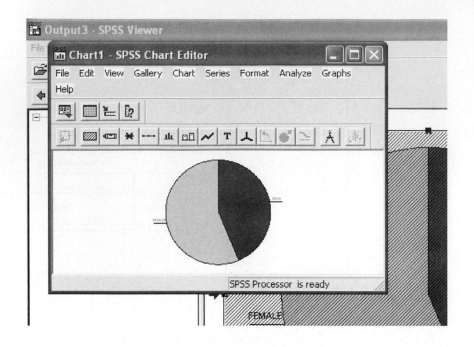

There are dozens of things you can do to a chart with the SPSS Chart Editor. (Don't be afraid to explore these features.) One of the features allows you to add percentages to a pie chart.

1 Click on Chart.

2 Click on Options.

3 When the Pie Options box opens, click on Percents.

4 Click on OK.

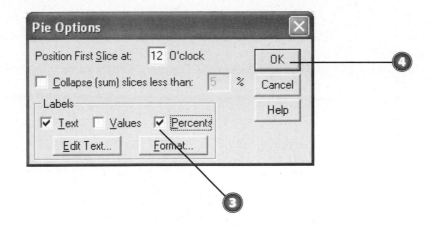

At the Chart Editor, click on the X in the upper right corner to exit from the editor. Your pie chart will look like the one here.

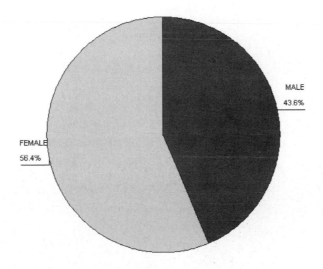

You can open the Chart Editor for any chart: bar charts, pie charts, histograms, and so on. Experiment with some of the features that allow you to customize your charts.

Answers to Odd-Numbered Exercises

CHAPTER 1

General Exercise 1:

a. Students at SUNY Cortland, or first-year students at SUNY Cortland.
b. Students.
c. Students.
d. Independent variable: type of Introduction to Sociology course (service learning or traditional). Dependent variable: student achievement (grades in the courses, attendance, and attitudes toward social justice, social responsibility, and ability to make change).
e. Age, sex, race, high school grade point average, SAT scores.

General Exercise 3:

Females are more likely than males to volunteer to work for a charitable organization. Control variables could include age (older females and older males may be more likely to volunteer to work for a charitable organization); class (individuals who are middle or upper class may be more likely to volunteer as compared to individuals in the lower or working classes); degree (individuals with more education are more likely to volunteer). Other possible control variables: race, religion, and religious fundamentalism.

General Exercise 5:

The older the respondents are, the more likely they are to participate in the activities of a political party. Control variables could include sex (with male respondents more likely to participate in the activities of a political party than are female respondents), religion, religious fundamentalism, political affiliation, race, class, and degree.

CHAPTER 2

General Exercise 1:

a. categorical and ordinal
b. categorical and nominal
c. categorical and ordinal
d. categorical and ordinal
e. numerical
f. categorical and ordinal
g. numerical
h. numerical
i. categorical and nominal
j. categorical and ordinal; dichotomous

General Exercise 3:

Variables A, C, and F are continuous. H is discrete.

SPSS Exercise 1:

Open your GSS 2002 subset A file. Click on the Variables icon (the one with the blue question mark on it). Check the level of measurement of each variable—nominal, ordinal, or scale (numerical)—against your own classification of the variables for General Exercise 4.

CHAPTER 3

General Exercise 1:

Suggested codes for the variables in General Exercise 1, Chapter 2. (The levels of measurement for each of the variables are in the answers to General Exercise 1 for Chapter 2.)

Respondent identification number variable name: **id**
Level of measurement: nominal

   a. Variable name: **attend** (or any name up to 8 characters that follows the SPSS rules for naming variables)
      1   More than once a week
      2   Once a week
      3   Once or twice a month

> 4   Several times a year
> 5   Almost never
> 9   Missing data

  b. Variable name: **marital**
> 1   Married
> 2   Unmarried with partner
> 3   Single
> 4   Separated or divorced
> 5   Widowed
> 9   Missing data

  c. Variable name: **degree**
> 1   11th grade or less
> 2   High school degree
> 3   Non-college post high school
> 4   Some college
> 5   Associate's degree
> 6   Bachelor's degree
> 7   Post-graduate degree
> 9   Missing data

  d. Variable name: **parvote**
> 1   Every election
> 2   Most elections
> 3   Only in important elections
> 4   Rarely
> 5   Not at all
> 9   Missing data

  e. Variable name: **age**
> 99   Missing data

  f. Variable name: **address**
> 1   Strongly agree
> 2   Not so strongly agree
> 3   Not so strongly disagree
> 4   Strongly disagree
> 9   Missing data

  g. Variable name: **pdjobs**
> 9   Missing data

  h. Variable name: **children**
> 99   Missing data

  i. Variable name: **party**
> 1   Republican
> 2   Independent
> 3   Democrat
> 4   Other
> 9   Missing data

  j. Variable name: **gotovote**
> 1   Yes
> 2   No
> 9   Missing data

SPSS Exercise 1:

Check your work by using the Variables icon to see each of the variables you created. Compare what you see for your variables with the variable names and labels and value names and labels you prepared for the variables. Make sure that

1. There is an identification code variable.
2. The variable names and labels appear as you entered them.
3. Each categorical variable has values and value labels, including values and labels for missing data.
4. Each numerical variable has at least one missing data value and label.
5. The level of measurement for each variable corresponds to the answers to General Exercise 1, Chapter 2.

CHAPTER 4

General Exercise 1:

Does respondent read newspaper (X)	Frequency (f)	Percent	Cumulative Frequencies	Cumulative Percentages
Less than once a week	2	13.3	2	13.3
Once a week	4	26.7	6	40.0
A few times a week	2	13.3	8	53.3
Every day	7	46.7	15	100.0
	N = 15	100		

Respondents to the GSS tend to read the paper at least a few times week. Sixty percent read the newspaper at least that often, and nearly half (46.7%) read the newspaper every day. The distribution of responses to the variable is fairly homogeneous.

General Exercise 3:

How fundamentalist is respondent (X)	Frequency (f)	Percent	Cumulative Frequencies	Cumulative Percentages
Fundamentalist	16	35.6	16	35.6
Moderate	20	44.4	36	80.0
Liberal	9	20.0	45	100.0
	N = 45	100.0		

Respondents to the GSS tend to be religiously moderate. Nearly half (44%) answered to this category. A little more than a third (35.6%) are fundamentalist, and 20% are liberal. The distribution of responses is fairly homogeneous.

SPSS Exercise 1:

The respondents to the 2002 General Social Survey are fairly evenly divided between males and females. Slightly more than half of the respondents (56.4%) are female, whereas a little less than half (43.6%) are male. The distribution of responses is fairly heterogeneous.

SPSS Exercise 3:

The respondents to the 2002 GSS tend to be fairly evenly divided among the four age categories. Nearly 65% of the respondents are in the age categories 26 through 60. About 12% are in their late teens or early twenties. Nearly one-quarter are over the age of 60. The distribution of responses is fairly heterogeneous.

SPSS Exercise 5:

Respondents to the 2002 GSS tend to be either working class or middle class. Over 90% of the respondents classify themselves as working class (45.2%) or middle class (44.9%). A little less than 7% of the respondents say they are lower class, whereas only a little over 3% say they are upper class. The distribution of responses to the social class variable is more homogeneous—most of the responses are clustered in just two categories of the class variable.

SPSS Exercise 7:

Among respondents to the 2002 GSS, the frequency of volunteering for charity appears to increase with age. Over 10% of the respondents who are in the 61 through 89 age category said they volunteered once a week or more, compared to slightly more than 8% of the respondents in the other age categories. Over 10% of the respondents in the age 61 through 89 category volunteered once a month, but only a little over 7% of the respondents in the 26 through 40 and 41 through 60 age categories volunteered that often. Less than 5% of the respondents ages 18 through 25 volunteered once a month. Respondents in the age category 61 through 89 are less likely than are respondents in other age categories to say they volunteered only once in a year's time or less. There are some exceptions to this general pattern. Respondents ages 18 through 25 are less likely than others to say they do not volunteer at all, and more likely to volunteer once a week.

SPSS Exercise 9:

The respondents to the 2002 GSS who are in the 26 through 40 and 41 through 60 age categories were those most likely to have been involved in protest activities. Over 10% of the respondents in the age category 26 through 40 and nearly 8% of the respondents in the age category 41 through 60 have been involved in protest activity. Less than 4% of those in the age category 61 through 89 and only a little over 5% of those in the age category 18 through 25 have been involved in such activities.

SPSS Exercise 11:

Either a pie chart or a bar chart could be used to examine the distribution of responses to the variable *sex*. The distribution of responses to the variable *sex* is fairly heterogeneous. In the pie chart, the pie "slices" for males and females are about the same size, and in the bar chart, the bars for males and females are about the same height.

SPSS Exercise 13:

Either a pie chart or a bar chart could be used to examine the distribution of responses to the variable *rcage*. The distribution of responses to the variable *rcage* is fairly heterogeneous. In the pie chart, the pie "slices" for those who are ages 18 to 25 to 40, 41 to 60, and 61 to 89 are about the same size, and in the bar chart, the bars are about the same height.

SPSS Exercise 15:

The clustered bar chart that you produce should look somewhat like the one below. (The absence of color in this reproduction may make the chart difficult to interpret, but you should be able to see if the features of the chart that you produced matches this one.)

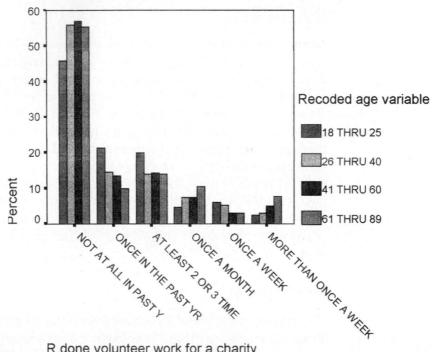

R done volunteer work for a charity

Your interpretation of the chart should be consistent with your answer to SPSS Exercise 7 above.

SPSS Exercise 17:

The frequency distribution for your new *newparty* variable should look like this one:

NEWPARTY Recoded political party affiliation

		Frequency	Percent	Valid Percent	Cumulative Percent
Valid	1 DEMOCRAT	507	33.8	34.2	34.2
	2 INDEPENDENT	531	35.4	35.8	70.0
	3 REPUBLICAN	417	27.8	28.1	98.1
	4 OTHER	28	1.9	1.9	100.0
	Total	1483	98.9	100.0	
Missing	9 NA	17	1.1		
Total		1500	100.0		

CHAPTER 5

General Exercise 1:

The mode is Working Full Time. The most frequently occurring response to the *labor force status* variable is Working Full Time. It is also the case that most respondents (50.6%) 18 to 25 years of age are working full-time.

General Exercise 3:

The mode is High School. The most commonly occurring response to the question about the respondents' highest degree obtained is High School. Slightly less than two-thirds of the respondents ages 18 to 25 have high school degrees.

General Exercise 5:

The median is High School. (The median case is 90.5. $N + 1 = 180 + 1 = 181$. $181 \times .50 = 90.5$. The value associated with case 90.5 is 1, High School; and the value at the 50th percentile is value 1, High School.) Half of the respondents ages 18 to 25 have at least finished high school, whereas half either have completed high school or have less than high school educations.

General Exercise 7:

The median is Fairly Satisfied. (The median case is 33. $N + 1 = 65 + 1 = 66$. $66 \times .50 = 33$. The value associated with case 33 is 5, Fairly Satisfied, and the value at the 50th percentile is 5, Fairly Satisfied.) Half of the respondents ages 18 to 25 are fairly satisfied to completely satisfied with their financial situations, whereas half are completely dissatisfied to only fairly satisfied.

General Exercise 9:

The median is 13 years of education. (The median case is 90.5. The value associated with case 90.5 is 13, and the value at the 50th percentile is 13.) Half of the respondents ages 18 to 25 have from 7 to 13 years of education, whereas half have 13 to 18 years of education.

General Exercise 11:

Use the formula for the mean of an ungrouped frequency distribution:

$$\overline{X} = \frac{\Sigma(fX)}{N} = \frac{2,345}{180} = 13.03$$

The average of the years of education for respondents ages 18 to 25 is 13.03.

General Exercise 13:

Use the formula for the mean of an ungrouped frequency distribution:

$$\overline{X} = \frac{\Sigma(fX)}{N} = \frac{340}{178} = 1.91$$

Respondents ages 18 to 25 have an average of 1.91 earners in their households.

General Exercise 15:

The distribution is positively skewed. The mean (13.03) is higher than the median (13) and the mode is 12.

General Exercise 17:

The distribution is negatively skewed. The mean (1.91) is below the median (2).

SPSS Exercise 1:

Respondents to the 2002 GSS tend to have at least a few hours each day to relax. About 64% have at least 3 hours each day to relax. Only about 6% say they no have time at all to relax, and about 30% say they relax for only 1 or 2 hours. The average of the responses is 3.82 hours. Half have 3 hours a day to relax or less and half have 3 hours to 24 hours each day to relax. The most commonly occurring response is 2 hours.

SPSS Exercise 3:

Respondents to the 2002 GSS don't seem to have been in their current jobs for very long. This conclusion may be somewhat misleading, though, because the variable appears to include respondents who are not holding jobs. About 18% of the respondents have been in their current jobs for ten years or more. Less than 7% have been in their current jobs for 20 years or more. Nearly 75% have been in their current jobs for 5 years or less. (This percentage includes those who appear to be unemployed or out of the workforce.) The average of the responses is 4.65 years. The most commonly occurring response is zero (most likely because the responses include those who are not currently employed). Half of the respondents report not being in a job, and half report not being in a job up to holding that job for 50 years.

SPSS Exercise 5:

Respondents to the 2002 GSS tend to at least be more or less satisfied with their financial situations. Most are at least fairly satisfied with their jobs, and they tend to believe that their jobs never or only rarely interfere with their family lives. About 73% of the respondents report being at least more or less satisfied with their financial situations. The most commonly occurring response to the question about satisfaction with one's financial situation is more or less satisfied. More or less satisfied is also the category that divides the respondents in half— half say they are not at all satisfied or more or less satisfied, and half say they are more or less satisfied or satisfied. Nearly 84% of the respondents say they are at least fairly satisfied with their jobs. Over half say they are very satisfied or completely satisfied. The most commonly occurring response to the job satisfaction question is Very Satisfied. Half of the respondents say they are very satisfied to completely satisfied, and half say they are completely dissatisfied to very satisfied. A relatively small percentage of respondents, 12%, say that their jobs interfere with their family lives. Most (61%) say their jobs rarely or never interfere. The most commonly occurring response is that jobs rarely interfere with family life. Half of the respondents say their jobs rarely or never interfere, and half say their jobs rarely, sometimes, or often interfere.

SPSS Exercise 7:

Incomes of White respondents are somewhat higher than those of other respondents. The median income of White respondents is $30,000 to $34,999. Half of White respondents earn in that category or less, and half earn in that range or more. The most commonly occurring response is $40,000 to $49,000. Just slightly less than one-third of White respondents have incomes within that range or higher. By way of contrast, the median income of Black respondents (the group closest in income to White respondents) is in the $22,500 to $24,999 range. Half of all African American respondents earn in that range or less, and half earn in that range or more. The most commonly occurring response among African American respondents is in the $30,000 to $34,999 range. A little over one-third earn in that range or higher. The median incomes for American Indian and Hispanic respondents, and respondents in the Other racial category, fall below the median for Black respondents. For example, half of Hispanic respondents earn only up to $12,499 and half earn $12,500 or more. The modes for Hispanic respondents are $8,000 to $9,999 and $10,000 to $12,499.

SPSS Exercise 9:

Male respondents to the 2002 GSS believe it's a little easier to take time off for family matters as compared to female respondents. The differences in the responses are not large, but they are noticeable. Over three-quarters of male respondents say that it is not at all hard or not too hard to take time off, but just a little over two-thirds of female respondents answered in those categories. On the other hand, less than a quarter of male respondents say that it is somewhat hard or very hard to take time off, but nearly 31% of female respondents say that it is somewhat hard or very hard to take time off. The most commonly occurring responses for both males and females are the same—not at all hard. However, the median response is higher for females (not too hard) than it is for males (not at all hard).

CHAPTER 6

General Exercise 1:

The formula for the IQV is:

$$\text{IQV} = \frac{\text{total observed differences}}{\text{maximum possible differences}}$$

To find the numerator, use the formula for observed differences:

$$\text{observed differences} = \Sigma f\, f_{i\ j}$$

$$
\begin{aligned}
91\left(26+9+31+19+4\right) = 91\left(89\right) &= 8{,}099 \\
26\left(9+31+19+4\right) = 26\left(63\right) &= 1{,}638 \\
9\left(31+19+4\right) = 9\left(54\right) &= 486 \\
31\left(19+4\right) = 31\left(23\right) &= 713 \\
19\left(4\right) = & \underline{76} \\
& 11{,}012
\end{aligned}
$$

To find the denominator, use the formula for maximum possible differences:

$$
\begin{aligned}
\text{Possible differences} &= \frac{K(K-1)}{2}\left(\frac{N}{K}\right)^2 \\[4pt]
&= \frac{6(6-1)}{2}\left(\frac{180}{6}\right)^2 \\[4pt]
&= \frac{6(5)}{2}\left(30\right)^2 \\[4pt]
&= \frac{30}{2}\left(900\right) = 15\left(900\right) \\[4pt]
&= 13{,}500
\end{aligned}
$$

Return to the formula for the IQV and insert the results for the total observed differences and the maximum number of possible differences:

$$
\begin{aligned}
\text{IQV} &= \frac{\text{total observed differences}}{\text{maximum possible differences}} \\[6pt]
&= \frac{11{,}012}{13{,}500} \\[6pt]
&= .82
\end{aligned}
$$

The distribution of responses is more heterogeneous than homogeneous (or you could say the distribution of responses is fairly heterogeneous). This interpretation of the IQV is only somewhat supported by an analysis of the frequency distribution. About half of the respondents (50.6%) are concentrated in one category of the variable, Working Full Time. The rest are somewhat evenly dispersed across the remaining categories of the variable.

General Exercise 3:

The mode is White. The formula for the IQV is:

$$IQV = \frac{\text{total observed differences}}{\text{maximum possible differences}}$$

To find the numerator, use the formula for observed differences:

$$\text{observed differences} = \Sigma f_i f_j$$

$$137\big(25 + 3 + 8 + 7\big) = 137\big(43\big) = 5{,}891$$

$$25\big(3 + 8 + 7\big) = 25\big(18\big) = 450$$

$$3\big(8 + 7\big) = 3\big(15\big) = 45$$

$$8\big(7\big) = \underline{56}$$

$$6{,}442$$

To find the denominator, use the formula for maximum possible differences:

$$\text{Possible differences} = \frac{K(K-1)}{2}\left(\frac{N}{K}\right)^2$$

$$= \frac{5\big(5-1\big)}{2}\left(\frac{180}{5}\right)^2 = \frac{5\big(4\big)}{2}\big(36\big)^2$$

$$= \frac{20}{2}\big(1{,}296\big) = 10\big(1{,}296\big)$$

$$= 12{,}960$$

Return to the formula for the IQV and insert the results for the total observed differences and the maximum number of possible differences:

$$IQV = \frac{\text{total observed differences}}{\text{maximum possible differences}}$$

$$= \frac{6{,}442}{12{,}960}$$

$$= .50$$

The distribution of responses is only somewhat homogeneous. This interpretation of the IQV is not supported by an analysis of the frequency distribution.

Most of the respondents (76.1%) are concentrated in one category of the variable, White, suggesting a very homogeneous distribution of responses.

General Exercise 5:

The mode is $1,000 to $2,999. The median is $10,000 to $12,499. The formula for the interquartile range is $Q_3 - Q_1$. First, find the value at Q_1:

One way to locate the value at the first quartile is by locating the value associated with the 25th percentile, value 3 ($3,000 to $3,999). You can also locate the case at Q_1 with the following formula $(N + 1)(.25) = (119 + 1)(.25) = (120)(.25) = 30$. Then locate the value at Q_1 that is associated with case 30, value 3 ($3,000 to $3,999).

Next locate the value at Q_3 using the 75th percentile. The value at the 75th percentile is value 14, $22,500 to $24,999. You can also locate the case at Q_3 with the following formula $(N + 1)(.75) = (119 + 1)(.75) = (120)(.75) = 90$. Then locate the value at Q_3 that is associated with case 90, value 14 ($22,500 to $24,999).

Find the interquartile range: $Q_3 - Q_1 = 14 - 3 = 11$. In relation to the range $(20 - 1 = 19)$, the distribution is somewhat heterogeneous. Half of the respondents ages 18 to 25 earn from $3,000 to $24,999 a year. One-quarter earn $3,999 a year or less, and one-quarter earn $22,500 a year or more.

General Exercise 7:

The mode is that it is not hard at all to take time off from work for family matters. The median is that it is not too hard to take time off from work. The formula for the interquartile range is $Q_3 - Q_1$. First, find the value at Q_1:

One way to locate the value at the first quartile is by locating the value associated with the 25th percentile, value 1 (not at all hard). You can also locate the case at Q_1 with the following formula $(N + 1)(.25) = (116 + 1)(.25) = (117)(.25) = 29.25$. Then locate the value at Q_1 that is associated with case 29.25, value 1 (not at all hard).

Next locate the value at Q_3 using the 75th percentile. The value at the 75th percentile is value 3 (somewhat hard). You can also locate the case at Q_3 with the following formula $(N + 1)(.75) = (116 + 1)(.75) = (117)(.75) = 87.75$. Then locate the value at Q_3 that is associated with case 87.75, value 3 (somewhat hard).

Find the interquartile range: $Q_3 - Q_1 = 3 - 1 = 2$. In relation to the range $(4 - 1 = 3)$, the distribution is somewhat heterogeneous. Half of the respondents ages 18 to 25 say that it is not at all hard to somewhat hard to take time off from work for family matters. One-quarter believe it is not at all hard, and one-quarter believe that it is somewhat hard or very hard.

General Exercise 9:

Apply the formula for the standard deviation from raw scores.

$$\overline{X} = 41.5294 \quad N = 17 \quad \Sigma X^2 = 32,042$$

$$s = \sqrt{\left(\frac{\Sigma X^2}{N-1}\right) - \left[\left(\frac{N}{N-1}\right)(\overline{X})^2\right]}$$

$$= \sqrt{\left(\frac{32{,}042}{17-1}\right) - \left[\left(\frac{17}{17-1}\right)(41.5294)^2\right]}$$

$$s = 13.04$$

Assuming a normal distribution of scores for the variable number of hours worked in a week, we can estimate that 68% of the respondents to the 2002 GSS who arc 18 to 25 years of age worked between 28.49 and 54.57 hours. The distribution is a little more homogeneous than heterogeneous. Sixty-eight percent of the respondents are clustered into around 26 of the 50 categories in the range (just slightly more than half of the categories in the range).

General Exercise 11:

The formula for a standard deviation from an ungrouped frequency distribution is:

$$\overline{X} = 13.0278 \qquad\qquad N = 180 \qquad\qquad \Sigma fX^2 = 31{,}371$$

$$s = \sqrt{\left(\frac{\Sigma fX^2}{N-1}\right) - \left[\left(\frac{N}{N-1}\right)(\overline{X})^2\right]}$$

$$= \sqrt{\left(\frac{31{,}371}{180-1}\right) - \left[\left(\frac{180}{180-1}\right)(13.0278)^2\right]}$$

$$s = 2.14$$

Assuming a normal distribution of responses to the question about years of education, about 68% of the responses fall in the range of 10.89 to 15.17, or from about 11 to 15 years of education. Given the range of responses to the variable $(18 - 7 = 11)$, this is a more homogeneous than heterogeneous distribution. Most respondents are concentrated in 4 of 11 categories.

General Exercise 13:

Apply the formula for the standard deviation from an ungrouped frequency distribution.

$$\overline{X} = 1.9101 \qquad\qquad N = 178 \qquad\qquad \Sigma fX^2 = 886$$

$$s = \sqrt{\left(\frac{\Sigma fX^2}{N-1}\right) - \left[\left(\frac{N}{N-1}\right)(\overline{X})^2\right]}$$

$$= \sqrt{\left(\frac{886}{178-1}\right) - \left[\left(\frac{178}{178-1}\right)(1.9101)^2\right]}$$

$$s = 1.16$$

Assuming a normal distribution of scores for the variable *number of earners in a family,* we can estimate that about 68% of the respondents to the 2002 GSS in the 18 to 25 age bracket have between .75 and 3.07 earners in their families. The distribution is fairly homogeneous. Sixty-eight percent of the respondents are concentrated in about two of the seven categories of the range.

General Exercise 15:

Appropriate measures of central tendency are the mode (12 years of education), the median (12 years of education), and the mean (12.8267 years of education). The most frequently occurring response to the question about how many years of school have been completed among male 2002 GSS respondents ages 18 to 25 is 12 years of education. Half have 7 to 12 years of education, and half have 12 to 18 years. Respondents completed an average of about 13 years of education. The formula for a standard deviation from an ungrouped frequency distribution is:

$$\overline{X} = 12.8267 \qquad\qquad N = 75 \;\; \Sigma fX^2 = 12{,}690$$

$$s = \sqrt{\left(\frac{\Sigma fX^2}{N-1}\right) - \left[\left(\frac{N}{N-1}\right)(\overline{X})^2\right]}$$

$$= \sqrt{\left(\frac{12{,}690}{75-1}\right) - \left[\left(\frac{75}{75-1}\right)(12.8267)^2\right]}$$

$$s = 2.18$$

Assuming a normal distribution of responses to the variable, about 68% of the responses fall in the range of 10.65 to 15.01, or about 11 years to about 15 years of education. Given the range of responses to the variable (18 − 7 = 11), this is a somewhat heterogeneous response, although there are concentrations of responses in the categories 12 Years of Education and 14 Years of Education, perhaps because these categories represent the completion of high school and two years of college.

SPSS Exercise 1:

Respondents to the 2002 GSS seem to be very satisfied with their jobs. The interquartile range runs from fairly satisfied to very satisfied, indicating that at least half of the respondents are in these categories. The IQR is 1 (6 − 5 = 1) and the range is 6, indicating a very homogeneous distribution of responses. Over half of the respondents are clustered into just two categories—fairly satisfied and very satisfied. Nearly 85% are in the fairly satisfied to completely satisfied categories.

SPSS Exercise 3:

Respondents to the 2002 GSS tend to think that their jobs never, rarely, or only sometimes interfere with family life. The interquartile range runs from never interferes to sometimes interferes. Nearly all of the respondents are in these categories (88%). The interquartile range is 2 (3 − 1 = 2), and the range is 3. Consequently, this distribution of responses is more heterogeneous than homogeneous. Respondents are fairly evenly divided among the never, rarely, and sometimes categories. A somewhat smaller percentage of respondents (12%) think that their jobs often interfere with family life.

SPSS Exercise 5:

Male respondents earn more than female respondents. The interquartile range for the income of male respondents runs from $17,500 to $59,999. At least half of the male respondents have incomes within that range. The interquartile range for female respondents runs from $10,000 to $39,999, somewhat lower than the interquartile range for males. At least 25% of the male respondents have incomes of $50,000 or more, but less than 12% of female respondents have incomes in that range. On the other end of the scale, at least 25% of the female respondents have incomes of $12,499 or less. Fourteen percent of male respondents have incomes that low. (You may also notice that the median income for males is in the $30,000 to $34,999 category, whereas median income for females is in the $22,500 to $24,999 category.) The IQR for males is 7 and for females it is 8. The distribution of responses for males is a little more homogeneous than it is for females. For both groups, males and females, the distributions of response are more homogeneous than heterogeneous.

SPSS Exercise 7:

Respondents to the 2002 GSS tend to have educations that extend beyond high school. At least half of the respondents have 12 to 16 years of education, and at least 25% of the respondents have 16 years or more. Less than one-quarter of the respondents have less than 12 years of education. If we assume a normal distribution of responses, 68% of the respondents have between 10.35 years of education and 16.35 years of education. The distribution of responses is fairly homogeneous. The IQR is 4 and the range of responses is 20, indicating a very homogeneous distribution. About 68% of the responses are clustered into about 6 categories of the range, another indication of a very homogeneous distribution of responses.

SPSS Exercise 9:

The differences are not large among 2002 GSS respondents in the number of hours worked in a week based on ethnicity. For all groups the median number of hours worked in a week is 40 and the mode is the same (40). The average of the number of hours worked in a week is highest for Hispanic respondents (42.26), but White respondents (at 42.03) and African American respondents (at 41.13) are close behind. The responses for African American respondents are the most homogeneous ($s = 12.33$). The responses for those of some other ethnicity ($s = 17.457$) and respondents who are American Indian or Alaska Native ($s = 15.052$) are the least homogeneous.

CHAPTER 7

General Exercise 1:

Use the formula for computation of a Z score.

$$X_i = 12 \qquad \overline{X} = 13.38 \qquad s = 2.84$$

$$Z = \frac{X_i - \overline{X}}{s}$$

$$= \frac{12 - 13.38}{2.84}$$

$$Z = -.49$$

The Z score of $-.49$ is almost one half of a standard deviation below the mean of 13.38. Assuming a normal distribution of scores, 19% of all respondents have between 12 and 13.38 years of education, whereas about 31% of the respondents have less than 12 years of education.

General Exercise 3:

Use the formula for computation of a Z score.

$$X_i = 16 \qquad \overline{X} = 13.38 \qquad s = 2.84$$

$$Z = \frac{X_i - \overline{X}}{s}$$

$$= \frac{16 - 13.38}{2.84}$$

$$Z = .92$$

The Z score of .92 is almost 1 standard deviation above the mean of 13.38. Assuming a normal distribution of scores, 32% of all respondents have between 13.38 and 16 years of education, whereas about 18% of the respondents have more than 16 years of education.

General Exercise 5:

The standard error of the mean for the variable *rhhwork* is simply the standard deviation for the responses to the variable (10.622) divided by the square root of N (365), so the standard error of the mean is .56.

General Exercise 7:

The standard error of the mean for male respondents to the variable *rhhwork* is the standard deviation for the responses to the variable (8.556) divided by the square root of N (155), so the standard error of the mean is .69.

General Exercise 9:

The standard error of the mean for the variable *emailhr* is the standard deviation for the responses to the variable (7.058) divided by the square root of N (1,026), so the standard error of the mean is .22.

General Exercise 11:

There are not as nearly as many respondents to the *chathr* variable ($N = 165$) as compared to the *emailhr* variable ($N = 1,026$).

SPSS Exercise 1:

    a. −.6610

    b. −.28451

    c. .28038

    d. .84527

SPSS Exercise 3:

The standard error of the mean for the variable *emhrw* is .346, indicating a fairly homogeneous distribution of sample means for this variable.

CHAPTER 8

General Exercise 1:

To find the standard error of the mean, use the following formula:

$$\sigma_{\bar{X}} = \frac{\sigma}{\sqrt{N}} = \frac{2.859}{\sqrt{958}} = .092$$

General Exercise 3:

$$\sigma_{\bar{X}} = \frac{\sigma}{\sqrt{N}} = \frac{7.058}{\sqrt{1,026}} = .220$$

General Exercise 5:

Use the confidence interval formulas:

$$CI_u = \bar{X} + (Z)(\sigma_{\bar{X}})$$
$$CI_l = \bar{X} - (Z)(\sigma_{\bar{X}})$$

To work the formulas we need the sample mean, the Z score for the confidence level specified, and the standard error of the mean.

$$\bar{X} = 39.28 \qquad\qquad Z = 1.96$$

$$\sigma_{\bar{X}} = 1.32$$

$$CI_u = 39.28 + (1.96)(1.32)$$

$$CI_u = 41.87$$

$$CI_l = 39.28 - (1.96)(1.32)$$

$$CI_l = 36.69$$

There are 95 chances out of 100 that the interval between 36.69 and 41.87 contains the population mean.

General Exercise 7:

To work the formulas we need the sample mean, the Z score for the confidence level specified, and the standard error of the mean.

$$\overline{X} = 3.93 \qquad\qquad Z = 2.57$$

$$\sigma_{\overline{X}} = .21$$

$$CI_u = 3.93 + (2.57)(.21)$$

$$CI_u = 4.47$$

$$CI_l = 3.93 - (2.57)(.21)$$

$$CI_l = 3.39$$

There are ninety-nine chances out of 100 that the population mean will fall within the interval of 3.39 hours to relax and 4.47 hours.

General Exercise 9:

Use the formula:

$$\sigma_P = \sqrt{\frac{(P)(1-P)}{N}}$$

$P = .708$ (from the frequency distribution on p. 271) $\qquad N = 734$

$$\sigma_P = \sqrt{\frac{(.708)(1 - .708)}{734}} = .02$$

General Exercise 11:

Use the formulas for confidence intervals for proportions:

$$CI_u = P + (Z)(\sigma_p)$$

$$CI_l = P - (Z)(\sigma_p)$$

$$P = .708 \qquad Z = 1.96 \qquad\qquad \sigma_p = .02$$

$$CI_u = .708 + (1.96)(.02)$$

$$CI_u = .75$$

$$CI_l = .708 - (1.96)(.02)$$

$$CI_l = .67$$

There are 95 chances out of 100 that the range of proportions from .67 to .75 contains the population proportion for people who have not had contact with an elected official.

General Exercise 13:

To construct a confidence interval at the 99% level, only the Z score changes (from 1.96 to 2.57).

$$CI_u = .708 + (2.57)(.02)$$

$$CI_u = .76$$

$$CI_l = .708 - (2.57)(.02)$$

$$CI_l = .66$$

There are 99 chances out of 100 that the range of proportions from .66 to .76 contains the proportion of people in the population who have not contacted an elected official. You may notice that, in this case, increasing the confidence level does not expand the confidence limits by very much.

SPSS Exercise 1:

There are 95 chances out of 100 that the interval from 3.64 hours to relax to 4.00 hours to relax in a day contains the population mean.

SPSS Exercise 3:

There are 99 chances out of 100 that the interval from 3.45 to 4.59 hours spent on email in a week to contains the population mean.

SPSS Exercise 5:

The frequency distribution for your dichotomized news variable should like the one in the table below.

Dichotomized news variable

		Frequency	Percent	Valid Percent	Cumulative Percent
Valid	0 Does not read a newspaper	41	2.7	8.5	8.5
	1 Reads a newspaper	442	29.5	91.5	100.0
	Total	483	32.2	100.0	
Missing	-1 NAP	1017	67.8		
Total		1500	100.0		

There are 95 chances out of 100 that the range of proportions from .89 to .94 contains the proportion of people in the population who read a newspaper at least once in a while.

CHAPTER 9

General Exercise 1:

Your contingency table should look like the one below.

Sex of sex partners in last year	Sex		Row Marginals
	Male	Female	
Exclusively female	18 (100%)	1 (5%)	19 (50.0%)
Both male and female	0 (0%)	1 (5%)	1 (2.6%)
Exclusively male	0 (0%)	18 (90%)	18 (47.4%)
Totals	18 (100%)	20 (100%)	38 (100.0%)

Males tend to have exclusively female partners whereas women tend to have exclusively male partners. One hundred percent of the male respondents have exclusively female partners, and 90% of the female respondents have exclusively male partners. Only 5% of the female respondents have female partners and 5% have both male and female partners. The association is a very strong one.

General Exercise 3:

Your contingency table should look like the one below.

Is life exciting, routine, or dull	Frequency of sexual activity				Row Marginals
	Not at all	Once a month or less	About once a week	2-3 times a week or more	
Routine	1 (50%)	2 (50%)	1 (12.5%)	2 (33.3%)	6 (30%)
Exciting	1 (50%)	2 (50%)	7 (87.5%)	4 (66.7%)	14 (70%)
Totals	2 (100%)	4 (100%)	8 (100%)	6 (100%)	20 (100%)

Respondents who have sex more frequently are more likely to say that life is exciting. Nearly 88% of those who have sex about once a week say life is exciting as do two-thirds of those who have sex two to three times a week or more. By way of contrast, 50% of those who have sex not at all or once a month or less say that life is exciting. The association appears to be moderate to strong.

SPSS Exercise 1:

a. Females; males
b. Females; males
c. 33.2%; 54.6%
d. 449

SPSS Exercise 3:

Male respondents to the 2002 GSS are more likely to think that homosexuality is wrong to at least some degree than are female respondents. Females respondents are more likely to say that homosexuality is not wrong at all. About 36% of female respondents believe that homosexuality is not wrong at all compared with about 31% of male respondents. Over two-thirds of male respondents believe that homosexuality is wrong to at least some degree compared with just less than two-thirds of female respondents. The association appears to be a weak one.

SPSS Exercise 5:

In general, it appears that the more television respondents to the 2002 GSS say they watch, the less frequently they have sex. A little more than 42% of those who watch TV five hours or more a day report having sex not at all, compared to about 20% of those who watch only one or two hours. However, nearly 43% of those who don't watch TV at all have no sex at all. On the other hand, 26.3% of those who watch TV one or two hours a day have sex two to three times a week or more as compared to only 12% of those who watch TV five or more hours a day. The pattern is not a consistent one, though. Although 12% of those who watch TV five or more hours a day report having sex two to three times a week, the percentage of those having sex two to three times a week is only a little higher for those who watch no TV (14.3%). While the general direction of the association is negative (the more respondents watch TV, the less sex they have), it appears to be a fairly weak association.

SPSS Exercise 7:

On the whole, respondents to the 2002 GSS who have sex frequently are more likely to say that life is exciting. Those who have sex less frequently are more likely to say that life is dull. The more sex the respondents have, the more exciting they say that life is. Nearly 59% of those who have sex about once a week and 58% of those who have sex two to three times a week or more say that life is exciting. About 40% of those who have sex not at all say that life is exciting. Seven percent of those who have no sex at all say life is dull, and 53% of them say that life is routine. Only 2.5% of those who have sex two to three times a week or more say that life is dull and about 39% of them say that life is routine. The association is a positive one. It appears to be weak to moderate, though. Clearly there are factors besides sexual activity that influence whether respondents see their lives as exciting or dull.

CHAPTER 10

General Exercise 1:

Among respondents to the 2002 GSS ages 18 through 25, male respondents have more sexual partners than do female respondents. Nearly 14% of female respondents have no partners compared to about 8% of male respondents. On the other hand, over half of the male respondents report 2 or more partners compared to about 29% of the female respondents. Females are more likely to have had only 1 partner (57.4%) as compared to male respondents (41.8%).

The association appears to be a moderate to weak one.

Lambda can be computed with the formula:

$$\lambda = \frac{E_1 - E_2}{E_1} = \frac{79 - 78}{79} = .01$$

Lambda is fairly weak, when interpreted on the number line between 0 and 1. Knowing the respondents' sex improves our ability to predict the number of their sexual partners by only 1%.

General Exercise 3:

Among respondents to the 2002 GSS ages 18 through 25, Catholics and those with no religion are the respondents most likely to believe that sex before marriage is not wrong at all. Protestant respondents are the respondents most likely to believe that sex before marriage is always wrong. A little over 92% of the respondents who practice no religion and nearly 88% of the Catholic respondents believe that sex before marriage is not wrong at all. Only about one-third of the Protestant respondents think that way, but over two-thirds of the respondents with some other religious preference believe that sex before marriage is not wrong at all. About 43% of the Protestant respondents believe that sex before marriage is always wrong. None of the Catholic respondents, 22.2% of those with some other religion, and about 8% of those with no religious preference think that sex before marriage is always wrong.

The association appears to be at least moderate.

Lambda can be computed with the formula:

$$\lambda = \frac{E_1 - E_2}{E_1} = \frac{25 - 22}{25} = .12$$

Lambda is fairly weak, when interpreted on the number line between 0 and 1 but knowing the respondents' religion improves our ability to predict their attitudes toward premarital sex by 12%.

General Exercise 5:

Among respondents to the 2002 GSS who are 18 to 25 years old, it seems clear that the more frequent the sex, the more likely are the respondents to say that life is exciting. Almost one-quarter (72.2%) of those who say they have sex two to three times a week or more say their lives are exciting. Fifty-seven percent of those who have sex not at all say their lives are exciting. About 64% of those who have sex once a month or less say their lives are routine as compared to 22.2% of those who have sex two to three times a week or more. Even so, the association is not a consistent one. None of those who have sex not at all say their lives are dull, but about 6% of those who have sex two to three times a week say their lives are dull.

The association appears to be somewhat weak to moderate.

Gamma can be computed using the formula:

$$G = \frac{C + D}{C - D} = \frac{313 - 181}{313 + 181} = \frac{132}{494} = .27$$

Gamma confirms the positive association between frequency of sex and life excitement. It is fairly weak at .27. However, knowing the respondents' frequency of sexual activity improves our ability to predict their perception of their lives as dull to exciting by 27%, and that's a fairly good level of improvement.

General Exercise 7:

Among respondents to the 2002 GSS ages 18 to 25, it seems that the more education the respondents have, the greater the frequency of sexual activity. For example, nearly 43% of those of junior college or bachelor's level educations have sex about once a week as compared to 26.5% of those with high school degrees. About 14% of those with high school degrees and 14% of those with junior college degrees have sex not at all compared to about 10% of those with bachelor's degrees. The association is not a consistent one, though. Whereas 38% of those with bachelor's degrees have sex two to three times a week or more, almost the same percentage of respondents with high school degrees have sex that often (37.3%).

The association appears to be fairly weak.

Gamma can be computed using the formula:

$$G = \frac{C + D}{C - D} = \frac{2,385 - 2,276}{2,385 + 2,276} = \frac{109}{4,661} = .02$$

Gamma confirms the positive association between education and frequency of sex, but it is very weak at .02. Knowing the respondents' level of education improves our ability to predict their frequency of sexual activity by only 2%.

SPSS Exercise 1:

Native American and Hispanic respondents to the 2002 GSS are the ones most likely to believe that premarital sex is not wrong at all. Black respondents and respondents of other ethnicities are the ones most likely to believe that sex before marriage is always wrong. Seventy percent of Native American and 62.5% of Hispanic respondents believe that sex before marriage is not wrong at all. Less than half of White respondents (47.8%) and about one-third of Black respondents (37.3%) believe that sex before marriage is not wrong at all. Only 10% of respondents of other ethnicities believe that sex before marriage is not wrong at all. On the other hand, nearly one-third of Black respondents and 40% of the respondents of other ethnicities believe that sex before marriage is always wrong. Only about one-quarter of White respondents, 20% of Native American respondents, and 12.5% of Hispanic respondents believe that sex before marriage is always wrong. The association appears to be fairly weak, though. In addition, the analysis depends on a fairly small number of responses, particularly in the Native American, Hispanic, and other categories of race.

Lambda, with premarital sex as the dependent variable, is weak at .012. Knowing the respondents' ethnic identification only improves our ability to predict their beliefs about premarital sex by 1.2%. Tau has about the same value as lambda at .013.

SPSS Exercise 3:

Divorced and never married respondents to the 2002 GSS are the ones most likely to have no religious affiliations, whereas respondents who are widowed are the ones most likely to have somewhat strong or strong religious affiliations. Divorced and married respondents are the respondents most likely to have not very strong religious ties. Nearly 25% of never married respondents and 14.4% of divorced respondents say that they have no religious affiliation. The percentage of those with no religious affiliation is somewhat less among married (9.6%) and widowed (6.3%) respondents. Widowed respondents are somewhat more likely to have strong religious ties (nearly half—48.4%) as compared to married, divorced, separated, or never married respondents. The differences in the percentages are not substantial, suggesting a fairly weak association between marital status and religious intensity. In addition, the fairly high percentages of widowed respondents with somewhat strong and strong religious ties suggest that strength of religious intensity might be a function of age rather than marital status.

Lambda at .030 (with religious intensity as the dependent variable) is weak. Knowing the respondents' marital status improves our ability to predict their strength of religious affiliation by only 3%. Tau is even weaker than lambda at .015.

SPSS Exercise 5:

Among respondents to the 2002 GSS, the older the respondents are, the more opposed they are to sex before marriage. A little over 42% of the respondents ages 61 through 89 believe that sex before marriage is always wrong, whereas about 27% of respondents ages 18 through 25 believe that premarital sex is always wrong. Nearly 60% of the respondents ages 18 through 25 believe that sex before marriage is not wrong at all, but less than one-third (27.9%) of respondents ages 61 through 89 believe that sex before marriage is not wrong at all.

The pattern of association is a clear one, and the differences in the percentages across the rows of the contingency table are fairly large. The association appears to be fairly strong.

Gamma is positive and somewhat weak at .231. However, knowing the respondents' ages improves our ability to predict their views on premarital sex by 23% and that's a sizable improvement.

SPSS Exercise 7:

The more frequently respondents to the 2002 GSS (say that they) have sex, the happier they say they are. Thirteen percent of those who have sex not at all say that they are not too happy, whereas 11.4% of those who have sex two to three times a week say they are not too happy. On the other hand, 37.4% of those who have sex two to three times a week are very happy compared to 21.6% of those who have sex not at all.

The pattern of association is clear, but it is not consistent in every category of the dependent variable. Even though 13.4% of those who have sex not at all are not very happy, those who have sex about once a week are close behind at 13.1%. Moreover, the differences in the percentages across the rows of the contingency table are not very large. Consequently, the association appears to be a fairly weak one.

Gamma is positive. At .168 it is fairly weak. Knowing how often respondents have sex improves our ability to predict their level of happiness by 16.8%.

SPSS Exercise 9:

Across most categories of age, the association between marital status and religious intensity seems fairly consistent—religious intensity is weakest among the respondents who are divorced or never married and strongest among those who are widowed. Among respondents ages 26 through 40 and 61 through 89, religious intensity is weakest among the divorced, separated, and never married respondents. In age category 18 through 25, religious intensity is strongest among divorced and separated respondents. Married respondents ages 41 through 60 express greater strength of religious affiliation than other respondents.

Lambda is very weak across all categories. It is only slightly stronger for those in the youngest age category. However, it is zero for those in the oldest age category, because nearly half of all of the respondents in that age category are strong in their religious affiliation. Overall, the weakening of the value of lambda suggests that religious intensity may, as we thought earlier, be more a function of age than of marital status. The association between marital status and religious intensity may be a spurious one.

SPSS Exercise 11:

The pattern of association—that there is a positive association between frequency of sexual activity and happiness—holds generally true for both male and female respondents. For both groups, the more sex respondents have, the happier they say they are. However, for male respondents the pattern is clearer and more consistent than it is for female respondents, suggesting a stronger association between frequency of sexual activity and happiness for males than for females. For example, 42% of males who have sex two to three times a week or more say they are very happy, whereas a smaller percentage of females who have sex that often say they are very happy (31.5%). In fact, female respondents who have sex less often are happier. About one-third of those who have sex about once a week say they are very happy.

Gamma confirms our analysis. It is positive for both groups, but stronger for males than for females (.198 for males; .105 for females). Knowing the frequency of sexual activity for male respondents improves our ability to predict their level of happiness by almost 20%, but knowing the frequency of sexual activity only improves our ability to predict happiness by about 11% for females.

CHAPTER 11

General Exercise 1:

The following table shows the observed frequencies, the expected frequencies, and the ratio between the differences squared divided by the expected cell frequency for each cell.

VOTE00 Did R vote in 2000 election * RCAGE Recoded age variable Crosstabulation

			RCAGE Recoded age variable			
			1 18 THRU 25	2 26 THRU 40	3 41 THRU 60	4 61 THRU 89
VOTE00 Did R vote in 2000 election	1 VOTED	Count	61	261	363	270
		Expected Count	114.5	289.2	330.6	220.6
		observed-expected frequencies squared/ expected frequencies	24.998	2.750	3.175	11.062
	2 DID NOT VOTE	Count	90	155	132	65
		Expected Count	52.9	133.7	152.8	102.0
		observed-expected frequencies squared/ expected frequencies	26.019	3.393	2.831	13.422
	3 INELIGIBLE	Count	26	31	16	6
		Expected Count	9.6	24.1	27.6	18.4
		observed-expected frequencies squared/ expected frequencies	28.017	1.976	4.875	8.357

The observed chi-square is 130.875. The table has 6 degrees of freedom. At 6 degrees of freedom, the observed value of chi-square exceeds the critical value (22.457) for $p = .001$. Consequently, the null hypothesis—that age and voting are statistically independent—is rejected. It is not likely we could obtain a chi-square of this size in a table with 6 degrees of freedom by accident. The older the respondents are, the more likely they are to have voted.

General Exercise 3:

The following table shows the observed frequencies, the expected frequencies, and the ratio between the differences squared divided by the expected cell frequency for each cell.

RCVOLCHR Recoded has R done volunteer work for charity * SEX Respondents' sex Crosstabulation

			SEX Respondents' sex	
			1 MALE	2 FEMALE
RCVOLCHR Recoded has R done volunteer work for charity	1 NOT AT ALL IN PAST YR	Count	214	186
		Expected Count	189.4	210.8
		observed - expected frequencies squared/ expected frequencies	3.195	2.918
	2 AT LEAST ONCE IN PAST YR	Count	91	118
		Expected Count	99.0	110.2
		observed - expected frequencies squared/ expected frequencies	.646	.552
	3 AT LEAST ONCE A MONTH IN PAST YR	Count	40	80
		Expected Count	56.9	63.4
		observed - expected frequencies squared/ expected frequencies	5.020	4.346

The observed chi-square is 16.677. The table has 2 degrees of freedom. At 2 degrees of freedom, the observed value of chi-square far exceeds the critical value (13.815) for $p = .001$. Consequently, the null hypothesis—that sex and volunteering for charity are statistically independent—is rejected. It is not likely we could obtain a chi-square of this size in a table with 2 degrees of freedom by accident. Males are less likely to have volunteered for charity as compared to females.

SPSS Exercise 1:

The null hypothesis (H_o) is that there is no association between the respondents' sex and their views on helping others less fortunate than themselves. Men and women are equally likely to say they agree or disagree that people should help others less fortunate than themselves. The contingency table for the variables *sex* and *othshelp* shows that there is very little difference between males and females in their views on helping others less fortunate, although a higher percentage of females agree that people should help others less fortunate (89%) as compared to males (86.6%). Conversely, a slightly higher percentage of males disagree that people should help others less fortunate (2.9%) as compared to females (1.3%). The association between sex and views on helping others less fortunate is a weak one.

Lamba is .026, indicating a weak association. Knowing the respondents' sex only improves our ability to predict their views on helping others less fortunate by 2.6%. A chi-square of 8.921 does not exceed the critical value needed to reject the null hypothesis at the .05 level. Consequently, we cannot rule out the possibility that the degree of statistical dependence we observe in our sample is due to chance instead of a real association between the variables in the population.

SPSS Exercise 3:

The null hypothesis (H_o) is that there is no association between the respondents' level of church attendance and their participation in a political party. Those who attend church regularly are no more likely to participate in political party activities than those who rarely or never attend church. The contingency table for the variables *rcattend* and *grppol* indicates a positive association between church attendance and participation in political party activities. Those who attend church regularly are more likely to say that they participate in political party activities. However, the association does not appear to be particularly strong. Over 12% of those who attend church at least monthly say they have participated more than once or twice in political party activities, and 11.5% of those who attend church at least weekly have participated more than once or twice. Only a slightly smaller percentage of those who never attend church have participated in political party activities (6.4%). On the other hand, 86.4% of those who never attend church do not belong or have not participated in political party activities as compared to 74.6% of those who attend church at least weekly.

Gamma at .177 indicates a positive but weak association between church attendance and participation in political party activities. Knowing the respondents' level of church attendance improves our ability to predict their participation in political party activities by 17.7%. Chi-square at 15.349 with 9 degrees of freedom does not exceed the critical value of chi-square needed to reject the null hypothesis. Therefore, we cannot rule out the possibility that the association we see in our contingency table is a chance occurrence rather than the result of a real association between church attendance and political party activity in the population.

CHAPTER 12

General Exercise 1:

Male respondents spend more time on the World Wide Web than do female respondents. Male respondents spend an average of 6.90 hours on the World Wide Web each week (not counting email), whereas female respondents spend almost two hours less on average, 5.08 hours. The difference is a noticeable one; males spend about one-third more time on the Web as compared to females.

General Exercise 3:

Your scatterplot should look like this one (with numbers instead of sunflower petals).

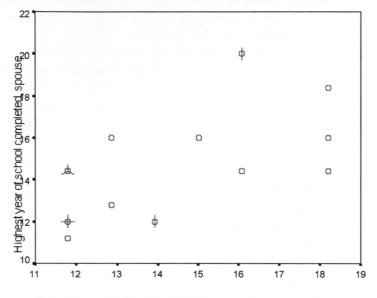

Highest year of school completed

The more education the respondents have, the more education their spouses are likely to have. The association is positive, and it appears to be fairly strong.

General Exercise 5:

The computational formula for Pearson's r is:

$$r = \frac{\Sigma XY - \left(N\overline{X}\,\overline{Y}\right)}{\sqrt{\left(\Sigma X^2 - N\overline{X}^2\right)\left(\Sigma Y^2 - N\overline{Y}^2\right)}}$$

$\Sigma XY = 937$ $\qquad N\overline{X}\,\overline{Y} = 910$ $\qquad \Sigma X^2 = 871$

$\Sigma Y^2 = 1,010$ $\qquad N\overline{X}^2 = 845$ $\qquad N\overline{Y}^2 = 980$

$$r = \frac{937 - 910}{\sqrt{\left(871 - 845\right)\left(1,010 - 980\right)}}$$

$r = .97$

Pearson's r indicates a very strong positive association between the respondents' years of education and their spouses' years of education. The more education the respondents have, the more education their spouses are likely to have. The r-squared (.94) tells us that 94% of the variation in the respondents' spouses' years of education can be accounted for by the respondents' years of education. Another way to express it is that knowing the respondents' years of education improves our ability to predict their spouses' years of education by 94% (assuming we know the general association between respondents' years of education and spouses' years of education).

General Exercise 7:

Use the computational formula for Pearson's r (see the formula in the answer to General Exercise 5).

$$\Sigma XY = 2,935 \quad N\overline{X}\overline{Y} = 2,925 \quad \Sigma X^2 = 10,375$$
$$\Sigma Y^2 = 871 \quad N\overline{X}^2 = 10,125 \quad N\overline{Y}^2 = 845$$

$$r = \frac{2,935 - 2,925}{\sqrt{\left(10,375 - 10,125\right)\left(871 - 845\right)}}$$

$$r = .12$$

Pearson's r indicates a fairly weak but positive association between the respondents' ages and their years of education. The older the respondents are, the more years of education they are likely to have. The r-squared (.01) tells us that 1% of the variation in the respondents' years of education can be accounted for by their ages. Another way to express it is that knowing the respondents' ages improves our ability to predict their years of education by 1% (assuming we know the general association between age and years of education).

General Exercise 9:

Use the formula for Pearson's r (see the formula in the answer to General Exercise 5).

$$\Sigma XY = 10,250 \quad N\overline{X}\overline{Y} = 10,125 \quad \Sigma X^2 = 10,375$$
$$\Sigma Y^2 = 10,225 \quad N\overline{X}^2 = 10,125 \quad N\overline{Y}^2 = 10,125$$

$$r = \frac{10,250 - 10,125}{\sqrt{\left(10,375 - 10,125\right)\left(10,225 - 10,125\right)}}$$

$$r = .79$$

Pearson's r indicates a strong positive association between the respondents' ages and the hours they work each week. The older the respondents are, the more hours they work each week. The r-squared (.62) tells us that 62% of the variation in the hours the respondents work each week can be accounted for by their ages. Another way to express it is that knowing the respondents' ages improves our ability to predict their hours worked by 62% (assuming we know the general association between age and hours worked per week).

General Exercise 11:

The computational formula for the slope of the regression line is:

$$r = \frac{\Sigma XY - \left(N\overline{X}\,\overline{Y}\right)}{\Sigma X^2 - N\overline{X}^2}$$

numerator for Pearson's $r = 27$ $\Sigma X^2 - N\overline{X}^2 = 26$

$$b = \frac{27}{26}$$

$$b = 1.0385$$

The constant for the regression line is equal to:

$$a = \overline{Y} - (b)(\overline{X}) = 14 - (1.0385)(13) = .50$$

General Exercise 13:

Use the computational formula for the slope of the regression line (see the formula in the answer to General Exercise 11).

numerator for Pearson's $r = 10$ $\Sigma X^2 - N\overline{X}^2 = 250$

$$b = \frac{10}{250} = .04$$

The constant for the regression line is equal to:

$$a = \overline{Y} - (b)(\overline{X}) = 13 - (.04)(45) = 11.2$$

SPSS Exercise 1:

There is a little difference in the years of school completed among 2002 GSS respondents when the sample is divided by marital status. The most notable difference is that respondents who are widowed have nearly 2 years less education (11.51 years) than the average for all respondents (13.35 years). Those who have never been married have the highest average years of education (13.71). The difference may have more to do with age than marital status.

SPSS Exercise 3:

There is not much difference in average years of education among 2002 GSS respondents based on region of the country. Those in the Southeast have the lowest average, 13.10, whereas those in the West have the highest average, 13.87. The difference between the lowest and highest averages is less than 1 year, not a very big difference.

SPSS Exercise 5:

With respondents' education (*educ*) on the *x*-axis (the independent variable) and spouses' education (*speduc*) on the *y*-axis (the dependent variable), the association is positive. The more education respondents have, the more education their spouses are likely to have. The association looks fairly strong—with the line sloping fairly steeply and the sunflowers being somewhat close to the line, although forming a shape more like an oval than a cigar.

SPSS Exercise 7:

With respondents' education *(educ)* on the *x*-axis (the independent variable) and number of wage earners *(earnrs)* on the *y*-axis (the dependent variable), the association is positive. The more education respondents have, the more earners there are likely to be in their households. The association appears to be fairly weak, however. The slope of the line is slight, and the sunflowers are spread out around the line more like a shapeless cloud than an oval or a cigar.

SPSS Exercise 9:

The more education respondents have, the more education their spouses tend to have. Among respondents to the 2002 GSS, the correlation between respondents' years of education and their spouses' years of education is more than moderate at .631 and it is positive. The *r*-squared of .398 indicates that about 40% of the variation in the respondents' spouses' years of education can be accounted for by variations in the respondents' years of education.

We can insert the constant (*a*) for the regression line (4.556) and its slope (*b*, or .654) into the formula for a line, $y = a + bx$, to find the predicted value of the dependent variable when the independent variable is 16. A respondent's spouse can be expected to have 15.02 years of education when the respondent has 16 years of education.

SPSS Exercise 11:

The more education respondents have, the more wage earners there are in their households. Among 2002 GSS respondents the association is a somewhat weak, positive one, with Pearson's *r* equal to .128. The *r*-squared, at .016, indicates that less than 2% of the variation in the number of wage earners respondents have in their households can be accounted for by differences in their years of education. A respondent with 14 years of education can be expected to have 1.43 wage earners in his or her household.

SPSS Exercise 13:

Among all respondents to the 2002 GSS, the average of the years of education are highest for respondents of some other ethnicity and for White respondents as compared to Black, Native American, or Hispanic respondents. The differences are noticeable but not substantial. The largest gap is between Native American respondents who have an average of 11.43 years of education and respondents of some other ethnicity who have an average of 14.97 years of education—a gap of about 3½ years.

The nature of the association remains generally the same among all age groups, with respondents of some other ethnicity and White respondents having the highest averages of years of education. The group whose average years of education are the lowest changes depending on the age category. For those who are ages 41 through 60, Native Americans have the lowest average years of education (10.11), but for those who are ages 18 through 25 and 61 through 89, Hispanic respondents have the smallest average years of education. For respondents who are 26 through 40, Black respondents have the lowest average.

The gap seems to be narrowing as the category of age decreases. Among respondents in the 61 through 89 age category, the gap is the largest. The average of the years of education for respondents of some other ethnicity is 16 years, and it is 9.75 for Native American respondents and 9 for Hispanic respondents, a difference of between 6.25 and 7 years. For respondents in the 18 through 25 age category, the gap between those of some other ethnicity and Hispanic respondents is less than 2 years, and, for respondents who are ages 26 through 40, the gap between respondents of some other ethnicity and Black respondents is 1.3 years.

Overall, the effect of age on the relationship between race and years of education is that the strength of the association weakens as the category of age declines. The association is weakest among respondents in the 18 through 25 and 26 through 40 age categories and strongest among those in the 41 through 60 and 61 through 89 age categories.

SPSS Exercise 15:

Sex has an effect on the strength of the association between respondents' years of education and their spouses' years of education, but it doesn't affect the nature of the association. When controlling for sex, the nature of the association between respondents' education and their spouses' education does not change. For both groups it is positive: The more education the respondents have, the more education their spouses are likely to have. The association is a little stronger for males than for females, however. Pearson's r for males is .702 as compared to .558 for females. The correlation for males is also a little stronger than it is for respondents as a whole, whereas the correlation for females is a little weaker than it is among respondents as a whole.

CHAPTER 13

General Exercise 1:

The null hypothesis is that for the association between the number of hours respondents said they worked in a week and the number of hours they said they watched TV, Pearson's r would be expected to equal zero. There is no association between the number of hours worked and the numbers of hours spent watching television.

Pearson's r at $-.148$ tells us the association is a fairly weak, negative one. As might be expected, the more hours the respondents said they worked in a week, the less the number of hours they reported watching television. An r-squared of .02 indicates that only about 2% of the variation in hours spent watching TV can be accounted for by differences in the number of hours worked in a week. Knowing how many hours respondents worked in a week doesn't help us very much in predicting the number of hours they say they watch television.

Use the formula for finding the observed value of the t statistic for Pearson's r:

$$t\text{ (obtained)} = r\sqrt{\frac{(N-2)}{1-r^2}} = -.148\sqrt{\frac{(310-2)}{1-.148^2}} = -2.63$$

Even though the relationship is weak, the t statistic of -2.63 at 308 degrees of freedom exceeds the critical value of t at the .05 level. Consequently, the null hypothesis can be rejected. It is not likely that we would obtain a t statistic of this magnitude at 308 degrees of freedom by chance. It is very likely that the association we find in our sample—the more hours respondents work in a week, the less they watch television—is true of the population.

General Exercise 3:

Use the formula for the one-sample t statistic:

$$\text{one-sample } t \text{ statistic} = \frac{\overline{X} - \mu}{\dfrac{s}{\sqrt{N}}} = \frac{41.86 - 40}{\dfrac{14.242}{\sqrt{940}}} = 4.00$$

The observed value of t at 939 degrees of freedom exceeds the critical value of t for $p = .05$. The likelihood is remote that a t of this magnitude with 939 degrees of freedom could be found by chance in a sample drawn from a population with a specified population mean of 40. Consequently, we reject the null hypothesis that the sample came from a population with the specified population mean.

General Exercise 5:

The null hypothesis is that the average number of self-reported hours spent watching TV will be the same for respondents who are male as it is for those respondents who are female.

To test the null hypothesis, start with the formula for the pooled t test:

$$\text{obtained pooled } t = \frac{\overline{X}_1 - \overline{X}_2}{\sqrt{\dfrac{s_p^2}{N_1} + \dfrac{s_p^2}{N_2}}}$$

From the table given in the exercise, you can find the following statistics you need to work the formula:

$$\overline{X}_1 \text{ (male)} = 4.20 \qquad \overline{X}_2 \text{ (female)} = 3.48$$
$$N_1 \text{ (male)} = 451 \qquad N_2 \text{ (female)} = 507$$

You will need to compute s_p^2 with the formula:

N_1 (male) = 451 s_1 (standard deviation, male) = 2.768
N_2 (female) = 507 s_2 (standard deviation, female) = 2.898

$$s_p^2 = \frac{\left(N_1 - 1\right)s_1^2 + \left(N_2 - 1\right)s_2^2}{\left(N_1 + N_2\right) - 2}$$

$$= \frac{\left(451 - 1\right)\left(2.768\right)^2 + \left(507 - 1\right)\left(2.898\right)^2}{\left(451 + 507\right) - 2}$$

$$s_p^2 = 8.0517$$

Returning to the formula for the pooled t test:

$$\text{obtained pool } t = \frac{\overline{X}_1 - \overline{X}_2}{\sqrt{\dfrac{s_p^2}{N_1} + \dfrac{s_p^2}{N_2}}} = \frac{4.20 - 3.48}{\sqrt{\dfrac{8.0517}{451} + \dfrac{8.0517}{507}}} = 3.92$$

The obtained t statistic of 3.92 with 956 degrees of freedom exceeds the critical value of t of ± 1.960. Consequently, it is not likely that the association between hours spent watching television and sex is due to chance. It is more likely the result of an actual association between the number of hours spent watching television and sex in the population. The null hypothesis, that there is no association between these two variables, is rejected.

SPSS Exercise 1:

The null hypothesis is that $r = 0$ for the association between the number of hours the respondents spend on email and the number of hours the respondents say they spent watching television. Another way to state the null hypothesis is that there is no association between the number of hours respondents spend on email and the number of hours the respondents say they watch television.

At $-.118$, Pearson's r is weak. The association between the number of hours the respondents spend on email and the number of hours the respondents say they spent watching television is minimal. However, at -2.122 the t statistic exceeds the critical value necessary for rejecting the null hypothesis at the .05 level. It is highly likely that, among American adults, the more one uses email, the less he or she watches television.

SPSS Exercise 3:

The t statistic for the variable *number of children* at -4.439 with 1,496 degrees of freedom exceeds the critical value of t at $p < .0005$. It is unlikely that a t statistic of this magnitude would be obtained by chance for a sample obtained from a population with a specified mean of 2. The null hypothesis, that the sample comes from a population with the specified population mean, is rejected.

SPSS Exercise 5:

White respondents to the 2002 GSS watch a little less television than do non-White respondents. The average of the hours watched by White respondents is 2.83, whereas the average of the hours watched by non-White respondents is about an hour more, 3.81 hours.

Assuming equality of variances, the *t*-statistic computed for the differences in the means between White and non-White respondents is –3.33. The value of *t* exceeds the critical value needed to reject the null hypothesis—that there are no differences between White and non-White respondents in the average of the number of hours that they watch television—at the $p = .001$ level. It is very likely, then, that the differences in the means that we see in our sample are indicative of real differences in the population in the number of hours of television watched by White people as compared to non-White people.

Can equality of variances be assumed? The answer is no, because the significance value associated with the *F*-statistic testing for equality of variances tells us that the likelihood is not high that the differences in the variances that we observe in our sample for television watching among White respondents as compared to non-White respondents are due to chance. Consequently, equality of variances cannot be assumed.

As a result, it is more appropriate to use the *t*-statistic labeled, "Equal variances not assumed." At –2.705 it still exceeds the critical value of *t* needed to reject the null hypothesis ($p = .008$).

SPSS Exercise 7:

Among respondents to the 2002 GSS, there are differences in the number of hours spent watching television based on the ethnic group with which the respondents identify. Respondents of other ethnicities and White respondents watch two to three hours of television a day on average. Respondents who are African American or Hispanic watch a little more than 4 hours per day on average. Native American respondents watch nearly 4 hours per day. The differences, although noticeable, are not particularly large ones. The biggest difference—between the average hours of television watched by members of other ethnic groups and Hispanic respondents is not quite 2 hours per day.

Can equality of variances be assumed? The answer is no. The significance attached to the value of Levene's statistic for testing homogeneity of variances tells us that it is not likely the differences in the variances in TV watching among ethnic groups that we observe in our sample are due to chance. Consequently, we must assume that there are real differences in the population in the variances in the number of hours spent watching television among ethnic groups.

Had we been able to assume equality of variances, could we reject the null the hypothesis that there are no differences in the hours spent watching TV among members of different ethnic groups? The answer is yes. The value of *F* is 3.925, and it exceeds the critical value need to reject the null hypothesis ($p = .004$). It is not likely that an *F* value of 3.925 could have been computed for samples drawn from a population in which there are no differences in the hours spent watching television among different ethnic groups.

SPSS Exercise 9:

Widowed respondents have the highest average of the hours spent watching TV (4.53 hours). Married respondents have the lowest average of the number of hours spent watching TV (2.62 hours). The difference between the two groups is nearly 2 hours a day. Divorced and never married respondents watch TV a little more than 3 hours a day as an average.

Levene's statistic for the test of homogeneity of variances suggests that equality of variances cannot be assumed. The significance statistic associated with the test of homogeneity of variances ($p = .014$) tells us that it is not likely the differences in the variances are just due to chance for married, widowed, divorced, never married, and separated respondents on the number of hours that they watch TV. Therefore, equality of variances cannot be assumed.

Had we been able to assume equality of variances, could we have rejected the null hypothesis that there is no difference in average number of hours of television watched based on marital status? Yes, because the value of F exceeds the critical value necessary to reject the null hypothesis ($p = .001$).

Glossary/Index

Page numbers in **boldface** type denote the primary use of key terms.

Credits

Chapter 1   Page 2, "Kids Teased Mostly for Physical Features," USA TODAY. Copyright ©
March 5, 2003. Reprinted with permission. Page 3, Barry Meier, "Disputed Statistics Fuel Politics
in Youth Smoking" from *The New York Times on the Web,* 20 May 1998. Copyright © 1998 by
the New York Times Co. Reprinted with permission. Page 4, "Condom Emphasis Works Over
Abstinence" from *USA Today Desktop News,* May 20, 1998. Copyright © 1998. Reprinted with
permission of The Associated Press. Page 32, "Amount of Schooling Affects Earning Potential,"
18 July 2002, Copyright © 2002. Reprinted with permission of The Associated Press.

Chapter 2   Page 36, excerpt from Lake Snell Perry and Associates and the Tarrance Group, Inc.,
"Short-Term Impacts, Long-Term Opportunities: The Political and Civic Engagement of Young
Adults in America," report for the Center for Information and Research in Civic Learning and
Engagement, March 2002. Reprinted by permission.

Chapter 4   Page 82, excerpt from John Della Volpe, "Campus Kids: The New Swing Voter,"
report for the Harvard University, John F. Kennedy School of Government, Institute of Politics,
21 May 2003. Reprinted with permission.

Chapter 5   Page 140, excerpt from U.S. Census Bureau, "Poverty Rate Rises, Household Income
Declines, Census Bureau Reports," 24 September 2002.

Chapter 6   Page 178, Stephanie Armour, "More Americans Put Families Ahead of Work," USA
TODAY. Copyright © December 4, 2002. Reprinted with permission.

Chapter 7   Page 228, Richard Morin and Claudia Deane, "Support for Bush Declines as Casualties Mount in Iraq," 12 July 2003. Copyright © 2003. *The Washington Post.* Reprinted with permission.

Chapter 9   Page 275, Kathleen Deveny, *et al.,* "We're Not in the Mood." From *Newsweek,* 30
June 2003. Copyright © 2003 Newsweek, Inc. All rights reserved. Reprinted by permission.

Chapter 11   Page 349, Campus Cares, "Education is the Best Predictor of Civic Involvement,"
19 August 2003. Reprinted with permission.

Chapter 12   Page 376, excerpt from U.S. Census Bureau, "The Big Payoff: Educational Attainment and Synthetic Estimates of Life Earnings," July 2002.

Chapter 13   Page 428, Dawn Anfuso, "Stats from UCLA Internet Project," 3 February 2002.
Reprinted with permission.

Appendix E   Page 481, General Social Survey data and codebook excerpts are distributed by
and used by permission of the Inter-university Consortium for Political and Social Research
(ICPSR).